ALSO IN SERIES OF Twenty Two (22) Sacred Maxims

*Lex Divina: Maxims of Divine Law*
*Lex Naturae: Maxims of Natural Law*
*Lex Cognitum: Maxims of Cognitive Law*
*Lex Virtus Naturae: Maxims of Bioethics Law*
*Lex Ecclesiasticum: Maxims of Ecclesiastical Law*
*Lex Positivum: Maxims of Positive Law*
*Lex Regia: Maxims of Sovereign Law*
*Lex Fidei: Maxims of Fiduciary Law*
*Lex Administratum: Maxims of Administrative Law*
*Lex Economica: Maxims of Economic Law*
*Lex Pecuniaria: Maxims of Monetary Law*
*Lex Civilis: Maxims of Civil Law*
*Lex Criminalis: Maxims of Criminal Law*
*Lex Educationis: Maxims of Education Law*
*Lex Nutrimens Et Medicina: Maxims of Food & Drugs Law*
*Lex Urbanus: Maxims of Urban Law*
*Lex Societatis: Maxims of Company Law*
*Lex Technologiae: Maxims of Technology Law*
*Lex Commercii: Maxims of Trade & Intellectual Property Law*
*Lex Securitas: Maxims of Security Law*
*Lex Militaris: Maxims of Military Law*
*Lex Gentium: Maxims of International Law*

*Pactum De Singularis Caelum*
**Covenant of One Heaven**

# Lex Ecclesiasticum

## Maxims of Ecclesiastical Law

**OFFICIAL ENGLISH FIRST EDITION**

**By**
**UCADIA**

Ucadia Books Company

**Lex Ecclesiasticum: Maxims of Ecclesiastical Law**. Official English First Edition. Copyright © 2002-2024 UCADIA. All Rights reserved in Trust.

No part of this book may be reproduced, or stored in a retrieval system, or transmitted in any form or by any means electronic, mechanical, photocopying, recording or otherwise, without the express and authentic written permission of the Publisher.

The Publisher disclaims any liability and shall be indemnified and held harmless from any demands, loss, liability, claims or expenses made by any party due or arising out of or in connection with any differences between previous non-official English drafts and this Official English First Edition.

A party that threatens, makes or enacts any demand or action, against this publication or the Publisher hereby acknowledge they have read this disclaimer and agree with this binding legal agreement and irrevocably consent to Ucadia and its competent forums as being the original and primary Jurisdiction for resolving any such issue of fact and law.

Published by Ucadia Books Company, a Delaware stock corporation (File Number 6779670).
8 The Green, STE B, Dover, Delaware, 19901 United States.
First edition.

UCADIA® is a US Registered Trademark in trust under Guardians and Trustees Company protected under international law and the laws of the United States.

ISBN 978-1-64419-027-2

# Lex Ecclesiasticum: Maxims of Ecclesiastical Law

By Right, Power and Authority of Article 135 (*Divine Collection of Maxims of Law*) of the most sacred Covenant *Pactum De Singularis Caelum*, also known as the *Covenant of One Heaven* these maxims of law known collectively as "**Lex Ecclesiasticum**" and "**Maxims of Ecclesiastical Law**" are hereby promulgated in the original form of Ucadian Language and official translations.

These Maxims of Ecclesiastical Law may be taken in official original document form and spoken form to represent one part of a complete set of the twenty-two (22) books known collectively as the Divine Collection of Maxims of Law.

The Maxims of Ecclesiastical Law represent the primary, one and only true first Maxims of Ecclesiastical Law. Excluding the most sacred Covenants *Pactum De Singularis Caelum*, *Pactum De Singularis Christus*, *Pactum De Singularis Islam* and *Pactum De Singularis Spiritus*, all other laws, claims and agreements claiming standards of Ecclesiastical Law shall be secondary and inferior to the Maxims of Ecclesiastical Law.

When referring to these Maxims of Ecclesiastical Law:-

(i) The entire book of Maxims of Ecclesiastical Law may be abbreviated in citation as "*Lex Ecclesiasticum*" or "*Lex Ecclesiasticum (Maxims of Ecclesiastical Law)*"; and

(ii) A Maxim within the book of Maxims of Ecclesiastical Law may be abbreviated in citation as (for example) "*Lex Ecclesiasticum max.1*" or "*Lex Ecclesiasticum (Ecclesiastical Law) max.1*".

In accordance with these Maxims of Ecclesiastical Law, Ucadia also known as the Unique Collective Awareness of all Meaning, also known as the Divine Creator reserves all rights to itself and its duly authorised organs, bodies and entities.

As all rights are reserved, no translation, copy, citation, duplication, registration in part or whole implies any transfer or conveyance of these rights.

When part or all of these laws is presented or spoken in any language other than the Official Ucadian Languages, it may be taken as a translation and not the primary language. Therefore, any secondary meaning implying deficiency, claimed abrogation of any right or any other defect of a word in a translated language shall be null and void ab initio (from the beginning).

Let no man, woman, spirit or officer place themselves in grave dishonour of Divine Law, Natural Law and the Living Law upon denying the validity of these maxims of law. As it is written, so be it.

# CONTENTS

### Title I: Introductory Provisions

#### 1.1 – Faith
Article 1 – Faith .................................................................................................. 23
Article 2 – Faith & Trust .................................................................................... 25
Article 3 – Faith & Hope .................................................................................... 26
Article 4 – Faith in Persons and Beings ............................................................ 26
Article 5 – Faith in Objects and Places ............................................................. 27
Article 6 – Faith in Models & Ideas ................................................................... 27

#### 1.2 – Spirituality
Article 7 – Spirituality ....................................................................................... 28
Article 8 – Spiritual Movement ......................................................................... 30

#### 1.3 – Religion
Article 9 – Religion ............................................................................................ 32
Article 10 – Religious Denomination ................................................................ 37
Article 11 – Religious Sect ................................................................................. 40
Article 12 – Religious Order .............................................................................. 40
Article 13 – Religious Movement ...................................................................... 41
Article 14 – Schism ............................................................................................ 44

#### 1.4 – Cult
Article 15 – Cult ................................................................................................. 44

#### 1.5 – False, Repugnant & Prohibited Spirituality, Religions & Cults
Article 16 – False & Prohibited Religions & Cults ............................................ 46
Article 17 – Commercial & Narcissistic Spirituality ......................................... 47
Article 18 – Parasitic & Fanatical Cults ............................................................. 48
Article 19 – Occult & Slavery Based Religions ................................................. 49

#### 1.6 – Ecclesia
Article 20 – Ecclesia ........................................................................................... 50
Article 21 – Ecclesiastical Law .......................................................................... 50
Article 22 – Ecclesiastical Law & Divine Law ................................................... 52
Article 23 – Ecclesiastical Law & Natural Law ................................................. 53
Article 24 – Ecclesiastical Law & Cognitive Law .............................................. 53
Article 25 – Ecclesiastical Law & Positive Law ................................................. 54

## Title II: Supernatural

### 2.1 – Supernatural
Article 26 – Supernatural ................................................................ 55

### 2.2 – Supernatural Dimension
Article 27 – Supernatural Dimension ........................................... 56
Article 28 – Afterlife ........................................................................ 62
Article 29 – Heaven ......................................................................... 63
Article 30 – Hell ............................................................................... 63
Article 31 – Purgatory ..................................................................... 64

### 2.3 – Supernatural Being
Article 32 – Supernatural Being ..................................................... 65
Article 33 – Supreme Being ............................................................ 66
Article 34 – Primary Being ............................................................. 67
Article 35 – Universal Being .......................................................... 67
Article 36 – Galactic Being ............................................................. 68
Article 37 – GAL .............................................................................. 69
Article 38 – Stellar Being ................................................................ 69
Article 39 – SOL ............................................................................... 70
Article 40 – Planetary Being .......................................................... 71
Article 41 – GAIA ............................................................................. 72
Article 42 – Cellular Being ............................................................. 72
Article 43 – CORPUS ...................................................................... 73
Article 44 – Animal Being .............................................................. 73
Article 45 – ANIMUS ...................................................................... 74
Article 46 – Sapient Singularity .................................................... 74
Article 47 – Saviour (Spirit) ........................................................... 78
Article 48 – Ordinary Spirit Being ................................................ 79
Article 49 – Exemplary Spirit (Saint) ........................................... 80
Article 50 – Penitent Spirit ............................................................ 81
Article 51 – Angel ............................................................................ 82
Article 52 – Demon .......................................................................... 83
Article 53 – Ethereal Being ............................................................ 83
Article 54 – Soul .............................................................................. 85

Article 55 – Lost Spirit (Ghost) .................................................................. 86
Article 56 – Wraith ..................................................................................... 89
Article 57 – Faerie ...................................................................................... 89
Article 58 – Elve ......................................................................................... 90
Article 59 – Elemental Being ...................................................................... 90
Article 60 – Imaginary Being ...................................................................... 91

## 2.4 – Supernatural Dominion
Article 61 – Supernatural Dominion .......................................................... 91
Article 62 – Kingdom of One Heaven ......................................................... 93
Article 63 – Universal Ecclesia of One Christ ............................................ 93
Article 64 – Holy Society of One Islam ...................................................... 94
Article 65 – Sacred Society of One Spirit ................................................... 95
Article 66 – Society of Light ....................................................................... 96
Article 67 – Society of Truth ....................................................................... 96

## 2.5 – Supernatural Objects
Article 68 – Supernatural Objects .............................................................. 97
Article 69 – Sacred & Venerated Supernatural Objects ............................. 98
Article 70 – Historic & Cultural Supernatural Objects .............................. 99
Article 71 – Cursed or Enchanted Supernatural Objects ........................... 101
Article 72 – Mythological & Legendary Supernatural Objects .................. 102

## 2.6 – Supernatural Ability
Article 73 – Supernatural Ability ................................................................ 103
Article 74 – Supernatural Sensual Ability .................................................. 104
Article 75 – Supernatural Remedial Ability ............................................... 105
Article 76 – Supernatural Informational Ability ........................................ 106
Article 77 – Supernatural Communicational Ability .................................. 106
Article 78 – Supernatural Physical Ability ................................................. 108
Article 79 – Supernatural Locational Ability ............................................. 109
Article 80 – Supernatural Mental Ability ................................................... 109
Article 81 – Supernatural Manifestational Ability ..................................... 110
Article 82 – Magic ....................................................................................... 110

## 2.7 – Supernatural Phenomena
Article 83 – Supernatural Phenomena ....................................................... 111

Article 84 – Miracle ............................................................................................ 112
Article 85 – Precognition .................................................................................. 113
Article 86 – Aura ............................................................................................... 114
Article 87 – Poltergeist ..................................................................................... 114
Article 88 – Conjuration ................................................................................... 115
Article 89 – Levitation ...................................................................................... 116
Article 90 – Possession ..................................................................................... 117
Article 91 – Voices ............................................................................................ 118
Article 92 – Haunting ....................................................................................... 118

**2.8 – Supernatural Evidence**

Article 93 – Supernatural Evidence ................................................................ 119

**2.9 – False and Prohibited Supernatural Notions**

Article 94 – False, Absurd and Prohibited Supernatural Notions ................ 120

## Title III: Sacred

**3.1 – Sacred**

Article 95 – Sacred ........................................................................................... 121

**3.2 – Sacred Space**

Article 96 – Sacred Circumscribed Space ...................................................... 121
Article 97 – Sacred Office ................................................................................ 124

**3.3 – Sacred Place**

Article 98 – Sacred Place .................................................................................. 134
Article 99 – Altar .............................................................................................. 135
Article 100 – Shrine .......................................................................................... 136
Article 101 – Sacred Buildings ......................................................................... 137
Article 102 – Sacred Ruins ............................................................................... 138
Article 103 – Ucadia Embassies, Consulates & Missions .............................. 139

**3.4 – Sacred Person**

Article 104 – Sacred Person ............................................................................. 140
Article 105 – Saint ............................................................................................ 142
Article 106 – Holly ........................................................................................... 142
Article 107 – Prophet ....................................................................................... 144
Article 108 – Saviour ........................................................................................ 144
Article 109 – Messiah ....................................................................................... 145

## 3.5 – Sacred Form

- Article 110 – Sacred Form ............................................................................... 147
- Article 111 – Sacred Numeracy ...................................................................... 149
- Article 112 – Sacred Geometry ...................................................................... 152
- Article 113 – Sacred Symbols ......................................................................... 153
- Article 114 – Sacred Art .................................................................................. 154
- Article 115 – Sacred Texts .............................................................................. 155
- Article 116 – Sacred Architecture .................................................................. 156
- Article 117 – Sacred Music ............................................................................. 157
- Article 118 – Sacred Language ....................................................................... 158
- Article 119 – Sacred Dance ............................................................................. 159
- Article 120 – Sacred Drugs ............................................................................. 160
- Article 121 – Sacred Clothes .......................................................................... 162

## 3.6 – Sacred Rites

- Article 122 – Sacred Rites .............................................................................. 163
- Article 123 – Sacred Mystery ......................................................................... 164
- Article 124 – Occult ........................................................................................ 164

## 3.7 – Profanity & Irreverence

- Article 125 – Profanity ................................................................................... 165
- Article 126 – Blasphemy ................................................................................ 167
- Article 127 – Sacrilege .................................................................................... 168
- Article 128 – Desecration ............................................................................... 169
- Article 129 – Impiety ...................................................................................... 169
- Article 130 – Spell .......................................................................................... 170

## 3.8 – False, Absurd and Prohibited Sacred Notions

- Article 131 – False, Absurd and Prohibited Sacred Notions ........................ 171
- Article 132 – Unholy ...................................................................................... 173
- Article 133 – Celibacy .................................................................................... 173
- Article 134 – Molestation .............................................................................. 175
- Article 135 – Blood Sacrifice ......................................................................... 175
- Article 136 – Holocaust ................................................................................. 176
- Article 137 – Cannibalism ............................................................................. 178
- Article 138 – Salvage & Claim of Souls ........................................................ 180

Article 139 – Universal Evil .................................................................................... 180

## Title IV: Revelation
### 4.1 – Revelation
Article 140 – Revelation ........................................................................................ 181

Article 141 – Classification of Revelation ............................................................ 181

Article 142 – Prophecy .......................................................................................... 185

Article 143 – Authentication of Revelation ......................................................... 187

Article 144 – Examples of Authentic Revelation ................................................ 191

### 4.2 – Scriptural Revelation
Article 145 – Scriptural Revelation ...................................................................... 195

Article 146 – Classification of Scriptural Revelation ......................................... 196

Article 147 – Authentication of Scriptural Revelation ...................................... 199

Article 148 – Interpretation of Scriptural Revelation ........................................ 200

## Title V: Theology
### 5.1 – Theology
Article 149 – Theology .......................................................................................... 203

Article 150 – Orthodoxy ........................................................................................ 209

Article 151 – Tradition .......................................................................................... 210

### 5.2 – Theology of Existence & Nature of the Divine
Article 152 – Diology (God & the Divine Creator) ............................................. 212

Article 153 – Daimology (Divine & Supernatural Beings) ................................ 212

Article 154 – Ouranology (Divine Dimension & Places) ................................... 213

Article 155 – Cosmology (Creation & Design) ................................................... 214

Article 156 – Physiology (Nature & the Physical World) ................................. 214

Article 157 – Pneumatology (Holy Spirit) .......................................................... 215

### 5.3 – Theology of Existence & Nature of Human Beings
Article 158 – Thymology (Soul and Spiritual Self) ............................................. 216

Article 159 – Psychology (Mind and Soul) .......................................................... 217

Article 160 – Protology (Species Singularity) ..................................................... 217

Article 161 – Ethology (Right Conduct & Morality) .......................................... 218

Article 162 – Anthropology (History of Humanity) ........................................... 218

Article 163 – Eschatology (End Times, Change & Renewal) ............................ 219

## 5.4 – Theology of Revelation, Faith, Hope & Trust — 220

Article 164 – Manteology (Revelation, Prophecy & Prophets) .......... 221

Article 165 – Graphology (Sacred Scripture) .......... 222

Article 166 – Christology (Messiahs) .......... 222

Article 167 – Hagiology (Holiness & Sanctification) .......... 223

Article 168 – Mysteriology (Sacraments, Rites & Ceremonies) .......... 224

Article 169 – Pistology (Faith, Hope & Trust) ..........

## 5.5 – Historic Eschatology Concepts — 224

Article 170 – Apocalypse .......... 225

Article 171 – Armageddon .......... 226

Article 172 – Antichrist .......... 227

Article 173 – Rapture .......... 228

Article 174 – Day & Year of Divine Agreement & Understanding .......... 233

Article 175 – Day & Year of Divine Protest & Dishonour .......... 238

Article 176 – Day & Year of Divine Judgement .......... 244

Article 177 – Day & Year of Divine Redemption .......... 247

Article 178 – New Covenant of Covenants ..........

## 5.6 – Theological Errors — 247

Article 179 – Doctrinology .......... 248

Article 180 – Eternal Damnation & Unforgiveness .......... 251

Article 181 – Divine Intervention for Some not Others .......... 253

Article 182 – Divine Favouritism & Exceptionalism .......... 255

Article 183 – Divinely Justified & Ordained War .......... 257

Article 184 – Suffering as Necessary Penance .......... 258

Article 185 – Contraception as Divine Sin & Offence .......... 260

Article 186 – Adult Same-Sex Relations as Divine Sin & Offence .......... 262

Article 187 – Suicide as Divine Sin & Offence .......... 264

Article 188 – Birth of Soul at Conception .......... 266

Article 189 – Divinely Ordained Clerical Misogyny .......... 267

Article 190 – Clerical Celibacy .......... 269

Article 191 – Papal Infallibility ..........

## 5.7 – False, Absurd and Prohibited Theological Notions — 271

Article 192 – False and Prohibited Theological Notions .......... 272

Article 193 – Divine Creator as Insecure Vindictive Sadist ................................. 272
Article 194 – God as Hidden Evil & Insane Deity .................................................. 273
Article 195 – Human Sacrifice as Necessary Divine Currency ............................ 276
Article 196 – Inheritance & Eternal Blemish of Sin .............................................. 276
Article 197 – Certain Persons as Incapable of Sin ................................................ 282
Article 198 – Mary as Mother of God ..................................................................... 283
Article 199 – Divine Birthright as the Sole Custodians of Earth ........................ 284
Article 200 – Divine Forfeit of Rights by Lesser Birth ......................................... 285
Article 201 – Baptism as Right of Salvage (Salvation) of Lesser Souls .............. 290
Article 202 – Gold as a Penitentiary Medium for Souls ....................................... 293
Article 203 – Office of Lesser God on Earth Incapable of Error ......................... 294
Article 204 – Divine Birthrights as Lesser Gods over Earth

## Title VI: Organisation

### 6.1 – Organisation

Article 205 – Organisation ...................................................................................... 297

### 6.2 – Organs

Article 206 – Organs ................................................................................................. 298
Article 207 – Universal Organs ............................................................................... 300
Article 208 – Union (Regional) Organs .................................................................. 301
Article 209 – University (National) Organs .......................................................... 303
Article 210 – Province (State) Organs .................................................................... 303
Article 211 – Campus (Local) Organs ..................................................................... 303

### 6.3 – Ecclesiastical Jurisdiction

Article 212 – Ecclesiastical Jurisdiction ................................................................. 303
Article 213 – Universal Ecclesiastical Jurisdiction ............................................... 304
Article 214 – Union (Regional) Ecclesiastical Jurisdiction .................................. 307
Article 215 – University (National) Ecclesiastical Jurisdictions ......................... 307
Article 216 – Provincial Ecclesiastical Jurisdiction .............................................. 310
Article 217 – Local Ecclesiastical Jurisdiction ...................................................... 310

### 6.4 – Ecclesiastical Institution

Article 218 – Ecclesiastical Institution ................................................................... 311
Article 219 – Consecrated Ecclesiastical Institution ............................................ 311
Article 220 – Secular Ecclesiastical Institution ..................................................... 312

## 6.5 – Ecclesiastical Corporation

Article 221 – Ecclesiastical Corporation ................................................................. 312

Article 222 – Ecclesiastical Religious Corporation ............................................... 313

Article 223 – Ecclesiastical Service Corporation .................................................. 313

## 6.6 – False and Prohibited Ecclesiastical Organisations

Article 224 – False and Prohibited Ecclesiastical Institutions ........................... 313

# Title VII: Systems

## 7.1 – Systems

Article 225 – Systems .................................................................................................. 315

Article 226 – Religious Associations, Institutes and Societies ........................... 319

Article 227 – Ecclesiastical Unions, Universities & Diplomacy ......................... 319

Article 228 – Ecclesiastical Province & Campus Systems .................................. 320

Article 229 – Vocational & Clerical Systems .......................................................... 320

Article 230 – Evangelical, Devotional & Veneration Systems ........................... 321

Article 231 – Doctrinal & Liturgical Systems ........................................................ 321

Article 232 – Sacred Rites & Tradition Systems ................................................... 322

Article 233 – Ecumenical & Collegial Systems ...................................................... 322

Article 234 – Families and Community Life Systems .......................................... 322

Article 235 – Member Assistance & Charitable Systems .................................... 323

Article 236 – Knowledge and Education Systems ................................................ 323

Article 237 – Justice and Jurisprudence Systems ................................................. 323

Article 238 – Health and Therapeutic Systems ..................................................... 324

Article 239 – Technology & Scientific Systems ..................................................... 324

Article 240 – Banking, Finance & Economic Systems ......................................... 324

Article 241 – Environmental Protection & Preservation Systems .................... 325

Article 242 – Ethical Agriculture, Food & Organic Systems .............................. 325

Article 243 – Military & Security Systems ............................................................. 326

Article 244 – Media & Communications Systems ................................................ 326

Article 245 – Facilities, Constructions & Preservation Systems........................ 326

Article 246 – Heritage, Arts & Cultural Systems .................................................. 327

Article 247 – Administrative & Logistical Systems .............................................. 327

# Title VIII: Ecclesiastical Rights

## 8.1 – Ecclesiastical Rights

Article 248 – Ecclesiastical Rights ........................................................................ 329

## 8.2 – Authoritative Ecclesiastical Rights

Article 249 – Authoritative Ecclesiastical Rights ............................................... 330

Article 250 – I. Ecclesiae (Ecclesiastical Rights) ................................................ 333

Article 251 – I. Ecc. Regnum (Sovereign Authority) ......................................... 334

Article 252 – I. Ecc. Consilium (Legislative Authority) .................................... 335

Article 253 – I. Ecc. Fraternitus (Religious Authority) ..................................... 336

Article 254 – I. Ecc. Collegium (Company or Charitable Body) ...................... 337

Article 255 – I. Ecc. Officium (Office, Duty and Service) ................................. 339

Article 256 – I. Ecc. Imperium (Command, Occupation and Enforcement) ...... 341

Article 257 – I. Ecc. Sacrum (Recognition, Devotion and Veneration) ........... 341

Article 258 – I. Ecc. Custoditum (Custody, Guardianship and Preservation) .... 342

Article 259 – I. Ecc. Alumentum (Sustenance, Maintenance and Alms) ........... 344

Article 260 – I. Ecc. Apostolicus (Divine Commission) .................................... 345

Article 261 – I. Ecc. Cancellarium (Chancery & Records) ................................ 346

Article 262 – I. Ecc. Oratorium (Forum of Law and Review) .......................... 347

Article 263 – I. Ecc. Templum (Treasury or Financial (Banking) Body) ........ 348

Article 264 – I. Ecc. Sacramentum (Grant and Impart Holy Sacraments) ...... 349

Article 265 – I. Ecc. Visum (Survey, Visit and Audit of Bodies) ..................... 349

Article 266 – I. Ecc. Commercium (Trade, Exchange and Communication) ...... 350

Article 267 – I. Ecc. Virtus (Strength, Honour, Excellence & Virtue) ............. 351

Article 268 – I. Ecc. Penitentiaria (Forced Confinement and Penitence) ........ 352

Article 269 – I. Ecc. Astrum (Association, Aggregate or Body) ....................... 352

Article 270 – I. Ecc. Magisterium (Sacred Texts & Divine Will) ..................... 353

Article 271 – I. Ecc. Decretum (Decree, Judgement and Edict) ....................... 354

## 8.3 – Instrumental Ecclesiastical Rights

Article 272 – Instrumental Ecclesiastical Rights ................................................ 355

Article 273 – I. Ecc. Iuris (Justice & Due Process) ............................................ 357

Article 274 – I. Ecc. Bona Fidei (Good Faith) .................................................... 358

Article 275 – I. Ecc. Aequum (Equality & Fairness) ......................................... 359

Article 276 – I. Ecc. Fidei (Trusts & Estates) ..................................................... 359

Article 277 – I. Ecc. Rationatio (Accounting, Credit & Funds) ........................ 360

Article 278 – I. Ecc. Concedere et Abrogare (Give or Grant Rights) ............... 361

Article 279 – I. Ecc. Delegare et Revocare (Assign or Delegate Rights) .............. 362

Article 280 – I. Ecc. Associatio et Conventio (Association) ............................... 363

Article 281 – I. Ecc. Consensum et Non (Consent) ............................................ 365

Article 282 – I. Ecc. Hereditatis (Inheritance) .................................................... 365

Article 283 – I. Ecc. Dominium (Absolute Ownership) ..................................... 366

Article 284 – I. Ecc. Possessionis (Possession) ................................................... 367

Article 285 – I. Ecc. Usus (Use) .......................................................................... 368

Article 286 – I. Ecc. Proprietatis (Ownership of Fruits) .................................... 368

Article 287 – I. Ecc. Vectigalis Proprietatis (Rent on Property) ........................ 369

Article 288 – I. Ecc. Moneta (Money) ................................................................ 370

Article 289 – I. Ecc. Vectigalis Moneta (Rent on Money) ................................. 371

Article 290 – I. Ecc. Registrum (Registers and Rolls) ....................................... 372

Article 291 – I. Ecc. Remedium (Remedy) ......................................................... 374

Article 292 – I. Ecc. Poena (Punishment) .......................................................... 375

Article 293 – I. Ecc. Clementia (Mercy & Forgiveness) ..................................... 376

Article 294 – I. Ecc. Actionum (Right of Action) ............................................... 377

## 8.4 – Sacramental Ecclesiastical Rights

Article 295 – Sacramental Ecclesiastical Rights ................................................ 378

Article 296 – I. Ecc. Sacr. Recognosco (Recognition) ........................................ 382

Article 297 – I. Ecc. Sacr. Purificatio (Purification) ........................................... 383

Article 298 – I. Ecc. Sacr. Invocatio (Invocation) .............................................. 383

Article 299 – I. Ecc. Sacr. Obligatio (Obligation) .............................................. 386

Article 300 – I. Ecc. Sacr. Delegatio (Delegation) ............................................. 386

Article 301 – I. Ecc. Sacr. Satisfactio (Satisfaction) ........................................... 387

Article 302 – I. Ecc. Sacr. Resolutio (Resolution) .............................................. 387

Article 303 – I. Ecc. Sacr. Sanctificatio (Sanctification) .................................... 387

Article 304 – I. Ecc. Sacr. Sustentatio (Sustentation) ....................................... 388

Article 305 – I. Ecc. Sacr. Unificatio (Unification (Matrimony)) ...................... 388

Article 306 – I. Ecc. Sacr. Amalgamatio (Amalgamation (Union)) ................... 389

Article 307 – I. Ecc. Sacr. Authentico (Authentication) .................................... 390

Article 308 – I. Ecc. Sacr. Absolutio (Absolution) ............................................. 391

Article 309 – I. Ecc. Sacr. Volitio (Volition) ....................................................... 392

Article 310 – I. Ecc. Sacr. Vocatio (Vocation) .................................................... 392

Article 311 – I. Ecc. Sacr. Testificatio (Testification) .......................... 393
Article 312 – I. Ecc. Sacr. Compassio (Compassion (Mercy)) .................. 393
Article 313 – I. Ecc. Sacr. Conscripto (Conscription (Binding)) .............. 394
Article 314 – I. Ecc. Sacr. Convocatio (Convocation) ............................ 394
Article 315 – I. Ecc. Sacr. Auctoriso (Authorisation) ............................ 395
Article 316 – I. Ecc. Sacr. Elucidato (Elucidation) ................................ 395
Article 317 – I. Ecc. Sacr. Inspiratio (Inspiration) ................................ 396
Article 318 – I. Ecc. Sacr. Resurrectio (Resurrection) ........................... 397
Article 319 – I. Ecc. Sacr. Incarnatio (Incarnation) .............................. 399
Article 320 – I. Ecc. Sacr. Confirmatio (Confirmation) ......................... 400
Article 321 – I. Ecc. Sacr. Illuminatio (Illumination) ............................ 401
Article 322 – I. Ecc. Sacr. Exultatio (Exultation) .................................. 402
Article 323 – I. Ecc. Sacr. Glorificatio (Glorification) ............................ 403
Article 324 – I. Ecc. Sacr. Divinatio (Divination) .................................. 403
Article 325 – I. Ecc. Sacr. Visitatio (Visitation) .................................... 404
Article 326 – I. Ecc. Sacr. Salvatio (Salvation) ..................................... 405
Article 327 – I. Ecc. Sacr. Emancipatio (Emancipation) ........................ 406
Article 328 – I. Ecc. Sacr. Veneratio (Veneration) ................................ 406

## 8.5 – Ecclesiastical Writs of Rights

Article 329 – Ecclesiastical Writs of Rights ......................................... 407
Article 330 – Recto Ecclesiae Originalis (Original Writ) ....................... 417
Article 331 – Recto Ecclesiae Apocalypsis (Revelation) ........................ 419
Article 332 – Recto Ecclesiae Investigationis (Inquiry or Review) ......... 420
Article 333 – Recto Ecclesiae Capimus (Arrest of Person) .................... 422
Article 334 – Recto Ecclesiae Custodiae (Seizure of Property) .............. 423
Article 335 – Recto Ecclesiae Corrigimus (Correction) ......................... 425
Article 336 – Recto Ecclesiae Expurgatio (Expurgation) ....................... 426
Article 337 – Recto Ecclesiae Abrogatio (Annulment) .......................... 428
Article 338 – Recto Ecclesiae Inhibitio (Prohibition or Restraint) ......... 430
Article 339 – Recto Ecclesiae Restitutio (Restitution) .......................... 431
Article 340 – Recto Ecclesiae Restoratio (Restoration) ........................ 432

## 8.6 – Ecclesiastical Bills of Exception & Agreement

Article 341 – Ecclesiastical Bills of Exception ..................................... 434

Article 342 – Rogatio Ecclesiae Recto (Bill of Rights) ......................................... 438
Article 343 – Rogatio Ecclesiae Apocalypsis (Revelation) ................................. 440
Article 344 – Rogatio Ecclesiae Capimus (Surrender or Arrest Person) ............ 440
Article 345 – Rogatio Ecclesiae Custodiae (Surrender or Seize Property) ......... 441
Article 346 – Rogatio Ecclesiae Corrigimus (Correct Records, Rulings, Laws) .. 442
Article 347 – Rogatio Ecclesiae Inhibitio (Prohibit or Impose Limits) ............... 443
Article 348 – Rogatio Ecclesiae Restitutio (Restitution or Compensation) ........ 444
Article 349 – Rogatio Ecclesiae Credito (Credit) ................................................ 445
Article 350 – Rogatio Ecclesiae Permutatio (Exchange) .................................... 445
Article 351 – Rogatio Ecclesiae Venditio (Sale) ................................................. 446
Article 352 – Rogatio Ecclesiae Traditio (Lading) .............................................. 446

**8.7 – Ecclesiastical Dogmata**

Article 353 – Ecclesiastical Dogmata ................................................................. 446
Article 354 – Dogma Ecclesiae Praeceptum (Proposed Dogma) ....................... 448
Article 355 – Dogma Ecclesiae Theologiae (Divine Science) ............................. 449
Article 356 – Dogma Ecclesiae Singularis Caelum (Dogma of One Heaven) ..... 449
Article 357 – Dogma Ecclesiae Ucadia (Dogma of Ucadia) ............................... 449
Article 358 – Dogma Ecclesiae Iuris (Dogma of Law) ....................................... 450
Article 359 – Dogma Ecclesiae Scientium (Dogma of Science) ......................... 450
Article 360 – Dogma Ecclesiae Revelatio (Dogma of Revelation) ..................... 450
Article 361 – Dogma Ecclesiae Sacramentum (Dogma of the Sacraments) ........ 450
Article 362 – Dogma Ecclesiae Singularis Christus (Dogma of One Christ) ....... 451
Article 363 – Dogma Ecclesiae Singularis Islam (Dogma of One Islam) ............ 451
Article 364 – Dogma Ecclesiae Singularis Spiritus (Dogma of One Spirit) ......... 451

**8.8 – Ecclesiastical Decrees**

Article 365 – Ecclesiastical Decrees ................................................................... 452
Article 366 – Decretum Ecclesiae Doctrinae (Doctrine) .................................... 454
Article 367 – Decretum Ecclesiae Absolutionis (Absolution) ............................ 454
Article 368 – Decretum Ecclesiae Damnationis (Damnation) ........................... 455
Article 369 – Decretum Ecclesiae Exemplificatio (Exemplification) .................. 455
Article 370 – Decretum Ecclesiae Testimonium (Proof) .................................... 455
Article 371 – Decretum Ecclesiae Instructionis (Instruction) ............................ 455
Article 372 – Decretum Ecclesiae Censurae (Censure) ...................................... 456

Article 373 – Decretum Ecclesiae Annullas (Annulment) .................................. 456

Article 374 – Decretum Ecclesiae Ratificationis (Ratification) ......................... 456

Article 375 – Decretum Ecclesiae Interdictum (Interdiction) .......................... 456

Article 376 – Decretum Ecclesiae Levationis (Relief and Restoration) ............. 457

### 8.9 – Ecclesiastical Notices

Article 377 – Ecclesiastical Notices ................................................................... 457

Article 378 – Notitiae Ecclesiae Eventus (Notice of Event) .............................. 461

Article 379 – Notitiae Ecclesiae Ius (Notice of Right) ....................................... 461

Article 380 – Notitiae Ecclesiae Actum (Notice of Action) ............................... 462

Article 381 – Notitiae Ecclesiae Decretum (Notice of Decree) ......................... 462

Article 382 – Notitiae Ecclesiae Iuris (Notice of Law) ...................................... 462

Article 383 – Notitiae Ecclesiae Citationis (Notice of Summons) .................... 463

Article 384 – Notitiae Ecclesiae Redemptio (Notice of Redemption) ............... 463

Article 385 – Notitiae Ecclesiae Rogatio (Notice of Exception) ....................... 463

Article 386 – Notitiae Ecclesiae Potentis (Notice of Authority) ....................... 463

Article 387 – Notitiae Ecclesiae Testamentum (Notice of Testament) ............. 464

Article 388 – Notitiae Ecclesiae Obligationis (Notice of Obligation) ............... 464

### 8.10 – False, Absurd and Prohibited Ecclesiastical Rights

Article 389 – False, Absurd and Prohibited Ecclesiastical Rights .................... 464

## Title IX: Ecclesiastical Registers

### 9.1 – Ecclesiastical Registers

Article 390 – Ecclesiastical Register ................................................................. 465

Article 391 – Ecclesiastical Roll ........................................................................ 470

Article 392 – Clerical Ministry Register ............................................................ 470

Article 393 – Sacramental Administration Register ......................................... 471

Article 394 – Congregational Member Register ............................................... 472

Article 395 – Liturgical Administration Register ............................................. 473

Article 396 – Parochial Property Register ........................................................ 473

Article 397 – Fiducial Administration Register ................................................ 474

Article 398 – Pastoral Transmittal Register ..................................................... 474

Article 399 – Canonical Judicial Register ......................................................... 475

### 9.2 – False, Absurd and Prohibited Ecclesiastical Registers

Article 400 – False, Absurd and Prohibited Ecclesiastical Register ................. 475

## Title X: Consecrated Life

### 10.1 – Consecrated Life

| | |
|---|---|
| Article 401 – Consecrated Life | 477 |
| Article 402 – Acolyte | 479 |
| Article 403 – Novice | 479 |
| Article 404 – Initiate | 480 |
| Article 405 – Minister | 480 |
| Article 406 – Cleric | 481 |
| Article 407 – Mendicant | 483 |

### 10.2 – False and Prohibited Notions of Consecrated Life

| | |
|---|---|
| Article 408 – False and Prohibited Notions of Consecrated Life | 483 |

## Title XI: Sacred Life

### 11.1 – Sacred Life

| | |
|---|---|
| Article 409 – Sacred Life | 485 |
| Article 410 – Seeker | 487 |
| Article 411 – Aspirant | 487 |
| Article 412 – Devotee | 487 |
| Article 413 – Practitioner | 487 |
| Article 414 – Adept | 487 |
| Article 415 – Mystic | 487 |

### 11.2 – Sacred Path

| | |
|---|---|
| Article 416 – Sacred Path | 488 |
| Article 417 – Sacred Matrimony (Marriage) | 489 |
| Article 418 – Sacred Union | 490 |
| Article 419 – Sacred Vacation | 491 |
| Article 420 – Sacred Pilgrimage | 492 |
| Article 421 – Sacred Course | 493 |
| Article 422 – Sacred Sponsor | 494 |
| Article 423 – Sacred Service | 495 |

### 11.3 – False and Prohibited Notions of Sacred Life

| | |
|---|---|
| Article 424 – False and Prohibited Notions of Sacred Life | 495 |

## Title XII: Ecclesiastical Offence

### 12.1 – Ecclesiastical Offence

Article 425 – Ecclesiastical Offence ........................................................................ 497
Article 426 – Offences against Stellar System ......................................................... 500
Article 427 – Offences against Planet ...................................................................... 502
Article 428 – Offences against Moon ....................................................................... 503
Article 429 – Offences against Humanity ................................................................ 505
Article 430 – Offences against Ecosystem ............................................................... 507
Article 431 – Offences against Human Life ............................................................. 508
Article 432 – Offences against Animal Life ............................................................. 510
Article 433 – Offences against Non-Carbon Higher Order Life ............................. 511
Article 434 – Offences against Congregation .......................................................... 512
Article 435 – Offences against Ecclesiastical Property ........................................... 513
Article 436 – Offences against Ecclesiastical Decency and Morals ....................... 514
Article 437 – Offences against Ecclesiastical Justice .............................................. 514
Article 438 – Offences against Ecclesiastical Security and Order ......................... 515
Article 439 – Offences against Ecclesiastical Sacraments ...................................... 515
Article 440 – Offences against Ecclesiastical Society ............................................. 516

## Title XIII: Ecclesiastical Process
### 13.1 – Ecclesiastical Process
Article 441 – Ecclesiastical Process ......................................................................... 517
Article 442 – Contentious Processes ........................................................................ 519
Article 443 – Special Processes ................................................................................ 521

## Title XIV: Ecclesiastical Remedy
### 14.1 – Ecclesiastical Remedy
Article 444 – Ecclesiastical Remedy ........................................................................ 523

# Title I - Introductory Definitions

## 1.1 – Faith

### Article 1 - Faith

1. ***Faith*** is the free and willing expression of loyalty and observance in ***Trust*** and ***Hope*** toward a particular spiritual or religious philosophy. <!-- margin: Faith -->

2. All Spiritual Movements, Religions and Cults fundamentally depend upon the existence of *Faith* among their adherents. In the absence of strong Faith among members, a Spiritual Movement, Religion or Cult declines and eventually may become extinct. <!-- margin: Faith & Organised Worship -->

3. Overwhelmingly, the vast majority of extinct Spiritual Movements, Religions and Cults throughout history ended not from disease, war or disaster but from a collapse of Faith among their former adherents:- <!-- margin: History of Organised Worship & Faith -->

    (i) There is scarce evidence of any Spiritual Movement, Religion or Cult in history ever becoming extinct purely from relentless persecution or prohibition. On the contrary, it appears that persecution is one of the formative forces that helps empower and transform cults and spiritual movements into broader religions, by strengthening the resolve and organisation of those who survive such persecutions; and

    (ii) History teaches that a precipitous collapse of Faith among adherents of a particular Spiritual Movement, Religion or Cult to be the primary catalyst for its extinction; and

    (iii) There appears to be two key factors in loss of Faith needed to cause the extinction of a Spiritual Movement, Religion or Cult being: (1) catastrophic loss of Faith in core beliefs; and (2) sustained loss of Trust and Faith in the clergy and religious organisation hierarchy; and

    (iv) A repeated trend across the history of human empires and civilisations appears to be that the more powerful and influential a Spiritual Movement, Religion or Cult becomes, the less its leadership focuses on the health and well being of the Faith of its adherents; and the greater the risk of its catastrophic collapse; and

    (v) Throughout history, there are examples of major religions surviving a catastrophic collapse of Trust and Faith in its fundamental beliefs. Two of the most famous examples are (1) the reconstitution of a new state religion under the "New Kingdom" by the Ramesses pharaohs that continued for another 1,000 years; and (2) the reconstitution of the Roman state religion in 71CE following the destruction of the Great Temple to Mithra in 69CE; and

(vi) There is no example in history of a major religion surviving a catastrophic and unresolved collapse of Trust and Faith among its adherents toward its clergy. Thus, it can be categorically concluded that a sustained and unresolved loss of faith in the clergy and hierarchy of a religion can contribute to the eventual loss of faith and trust in the core beliefs of a religion; and

(vii) Contrary to the false and deliberately ignorant notions of conservatism among religious hierarchies, no Spiritual Movement, Religion or Cult has ever survived an existential crisis of Faith by refusing to embrace reform; and

(viii) The entire history of human civilisation teaches that Faith is a living and constantly evolving relation between its adherents and a particular Spiritual Movement, Religion or Cult, that necessitates constant positive reform and growth, whilst paradoxically promoting consistency and immutability.

4. All authentic forms of Faith are founded on similar underlying assumptions and elements associated with a particular spiritual or religious philosophy:- *Elements of Faith*

(i) *Existence of the Unseen*: Faith assumes the existence of realities, beings, or forces beyond the scope of human perception or empirical evidence; and

(ii) *Existence of a Higher Power*: Faith assumes and trusts in the existence of a higher power or "Supreme Being" or supernatural force that influences the world and human lives; and

(iii) *Existence and Significance of Transcendence*: Faith assumes that there are aspects of existence that transcend the physical and material world; and

(iv) *Acceptance of Revelation*: Faith is most commonly based on the acceptance of certain divine revelations, scriptures, or sacred texts as authoritative sources of knowledge and guidance; and

(v) *Adherence to Interpretation and Formality*: Faith frequently involves the interpretation of revelation into some formalised methods of worship through religious teachings, doctrines, or dogmas, which may vary across different belief systems; and

(vi) *Significance of Ethics and Morality*: Faith frequently assumes that revelation, interpretation and formality brings forth a divine and superior moral and ethical framework of behavioural norms; and

(vii) *Personal Experience and Testimony:* Faith is often influenced by personal experiences, testimonials, and the accounts of others who claim to have encountered the divine or transcendent; and

(viii) *Hope and Meaning*: Faith commonly assumes that trust in something beyond the material realm provides hope, purpose, and meaning to life.

## Article 2 – Faith & Trust

5. **Trust** in terms of *Faith*, is confidence in the integrity and quality of the key elements of a particular spiritual or religious philosophy, including but not limited to one or more spiritual or religious persons, beings, objects, systems, models or ideas. Faith & Trust

6. *Faith* fundamentally depends upon the notion of Trust:- Faith and Trust

    (i) All authentic forms of Faith are founded on Trust in one or more persons, beings, objects, systems, models or ideas of a particular spiritual or religious philosophy being true; and

    (ii) The most significant forms of Trust associated with a Faith is trust relating to the higher beings and foundational elements of a particular Spiritual Philosophy or Religion. If a loss of Trust is experienced concerning any of these, then often there is a collapse of Faith; and

    (iii) The most common major form of loss of Trust associated with a Faith is usually a loss in trust in the portrayed existence, personality and intentions of a particular Supreme Being, often as a direct result of personal trauma and a lack of effective empathy and explanation on the Faith in question; and

    (iv) The lesser significant forms of Trust associated with Faith is trust relating to the organisation, function and behaviour of officials of a particular Spiritual Movement or Religion. If a loss of Trust is experienced concerning any of these, then there is usually a visible loss of participation, but not necessarily a complete loss of Faith; and

    (v) The most common lesser form of loss of Trust associated with a Faith is usually associated with repeated scandalous behaviour of clergy and the lack of integrity of a Religion in addressing such scandal and the plight of victims.

7. In the sustained loss, betrayal or absence of Trust, no true or authentic Faith can exist.  *Faith and loss of Trust*

## Article 3 – Faith & Hope

8. ***Hope*** is an emotional optimism and anticipation of positive future outcomes, even when faced with difficult or uncertain circumstances. Hope is having confidence that present circumstances can improve or a desired goal can be achieved, despite adversity.  *Hope*

9. *Faith* is historically seen within Civilised Societies as a primary source of *Hope*, given most Faiths have traditionally been founded on one or more concepts that express the possibility of positive outcomes through loyalty and observance to certain behaviours and concepts.  *Faith and Hope*

10. Hope is generally recognised as a primary source of motivation, resilience, and a sense of purpose during challenging times, helping individuals to persevere, overcome obstacles and maintain a positive outlook on life.  *Hope as Key Driver of Society*

11. In the loss or absence of Hope, a Faith may be severely damaged or even extinguished within the mind of an individual. However, a restoration of genuine Hope may assist in restoring a sense of Faith.  *Faith and loss of Hope*

## Article 4 – Faith in Persons and Beings

12. ***Faith in Persons and Beings*** is a fundamental concept of *Faith* whereby *Trust* in a particular spiritual or religious philosophy is underpinned and reinforced through understandings and details concerning supernatural beings and exemplary persons.  *Faith in Persons and Beings*

13. In reference to the general elements concerning Faith in Persons or Beings:-  *General Elements of Faith in Persons and Beings*

    (i) Most forms of Faith assume and trust in the existence of a higher power or "Supreme Being" or supernatural force of some kind that influences the world and human lives; and

    (ii) Generally, each spiritual or religious philosophy testifies to an account and succession of exemplary persons interacting and possessing personal relations with such supernatural beings from a point of origin to the present day; and

    (iii) The historical lives of such claimed exemplary persons then help to serve as both a moral standard and as a means of individuals forming their own relations and personal affinity with their lives, even if such persons are long since deceased.

14. Historically, the most powerful focus of Faith concerning Persons and Beings has always been the veneration and worship of human beings regarded as Divine Saviours, either as an anointed Messenger of the Divine, or as a personification of a Higher Supernatural Being.  *Divine Saviours*

## Article 5 – Faith in Objects and Places

15. ***Faith in Objects*** is a fundamental concept of *Faith* whereby *Trust* in a particular spiritual or religious philosophy is underpinned and reinforced through the witnessing or veneration of physical objects or places holding spiritual or religious significance.  *Faith in Objects and Places*

16. In reference to the general elements concerning *Faith in Objects*:-  *General Elements of Faith in Objects*

    (i) Objects or places considered especially significant to a particular spiritual or religious Faith are almost always considered sacred; and

    (ii) Some spiritual or religious philosophies may ascribe certain sacred objects as possessing supernatural properties, such as statues, the relics of exemplary persons and associated property and possessions; and

    (iii) Objects may also be considered especially significant and possessing special properties by virtue of rituals or ceremonies performed upon them.

17. Historically, the most significant sacred Objects or Places of the focus of Faith have been the ancient sites of Temples and collective worship. Even today, these sites mostly remain respected among different Religions and States.  *Sacred Temples and Sites*

## Article 6 – Faith in Models & Ideas

18. ***Faith in Models & Ideas*** is a key understanding of *Faith* whereby every spiritual and religious philosophies may be classified and described as a combination of various Ideas and Models even if such structural analysis by one or more particular faiths is rejected as being possible.  *Faith in Models & Ideas*

19. An *Idea* in its simplest terms is a conceptual archetype; or mental representation associated with some distinct Meaning. Every Faith rests upon multiple Ideas.  *Ideas and Faith*

20. A *Model* is an application of one or more Ideas, in a dimension of Reality, according to one or more rules and relations, representing a  *Models and Faith*

Cause as a *conceptual archetype*, or *axiom*, or *logical hypothesis*, or *scalable abstraction*, or *prototype*, or *physical production*. Every Faith exists upon at least one well formed Model.

# 1.2 – Spirituality

## Article 7 – Spirituality

21. ***Spirituality*** is a broad term describing the individual and personal pursuit of a deeper understanding, connection, and relationship with the sacred, the divine, or the universe. Whilst focused on the individual, *Spirituality* has a long history of connection to both western and eastern religions.  
    *Spirituality*

22. In modern terms, Spirituality has since come to mean and include a broad array of non-profit and commercial health and well-being practices and products.  
    *Modern Spirituality*

23. Key elements of Spirituality include (but are not limited to):-  
    *Key Elements of Spirituality*

    (i)    **Personal Growth**: A personal journey towards self-improvement, self-awareness and personal transformation. An inward exploration of one's values, beliefs and purpose in life; and

    (ii)   **Connection with the Transcendent**: Connecting with something greater than oneself, whether that be a higher power, the divine, the cosmos or the collective human spirit; and

    (iii)  **Experiential**: Personal experiences, feelings, and insights as the central focus of practical feedback, rather than primary focus on participation in organised formal rituals; and

    (iv)  **Holistic Approach**: A holistic view of life, integrating physical, emotional, mental and spiritual aspects of well-being; and

    (v)   **Mindfulness and Presence**: The importance of being present and mindful, including meditation, prayer, yoga and other practices that help individuals connect with their inner selves and the present moment; and

    (vi)  **Ethical and Moral Values**: The cultivation of virtues such as compassion, love, empathy and altruism. To encourage individuals to live in accordance with higher ethical and moral principles; and

    (vii) **Inner Peace and Contentment**: To achieve a sense of inner peace, contentment and fulfilment. This can be through understanding and accepting oneself and one's place in the world.

24. The growth in Spirituality to the point where more than one in ten people in the world do not affiliate with any formal Religion can be directly charted to the rise and dominance of Secularism as a quasi-global religion:- *(Secularisation and growth in Popularity of Spirituality)*

   (i) *US Declaration of Independence* (1776) promoted individual freedom and spirituality, while the *French Revolution* (1789) promoted secularism by challenging the authority of the Catholic Church and establishing a secular republic; and

   (ii) *Russian Revolution* (1917) led to the establishment of an atheist state in the Soviet Union, while in 1949 the Chinese Communists declared a new atheistic state in China as the Peoples Republic of China; and

   (iii) *Post World War Consumerism* (1945 to present) saw continued decline in religious observance and church attendance as growth in consumerism across Western Countries and globally has increased; and

   (iv) *Growth in Scientific Spirituality* (1960s to present) has presented new, detailed and highly advanced models of cosmology that support greater spirituality, whilst established Religions have been slow or refused to adapt to demands of their faithful for more coherence; and

   (v) *Rise in Accessible Spirituality Products* (1990s to present) whereby individuals can access more spiritual, holistic and well-being services in their own communities.

25. Whilst Religions have endured their own scandals, Spirituality and in particular products promoted by the spiritual, wellness and self-help industry have greatly damaged the global credibility of Spirituality as a viable and long term alternative:- *(Credibility Challenges within Spirituality)*

   (i) **Misleading Health Claims**: Many wellness products and practices have been criticised for making unverified or exaggerated health claims. This includes dietary supplements, detox regimens, and alternative therapies that lack scientific backing; and

   (ii) **Misuse of Indigenous Practices**: The wellness industry has been criticised for appropriating and commodifying indigenous and traditional spiritual practices without proper understanding or respect. This includes the misuse of practices like yoga, meditation and plant medicine; and

(iii) ***Expensive Programs and Products***: There have been numerous reports of spiritual and self-help gurus charging exorbitant fees for seminars, workshops and products, often without delivering promised results; and

(iv) ***Coercive Tactics***: Certain self-help groups and spiritual movements have been accused of using manipulative and coercive tactics to control members, including emotional abuse, isolation, and pressure to conform; and

(v) ***Abuse Allegations***: Several high-profile figures in the spiritual and wellness industry have faced allegations of sexual misconduct and abuse. This includes gurus and self-help leaders who have exploited their positions of power.

## Article 8 – Spiritual Movement

26. A *Spiritual Movement* is a group or collective alliance of individuals united by one or more common objectives that seek to use and promote certain spiritual beliefs, practices, and experiences with the express aim of achieving their underlying goals.

27. A *Spiritual Movement* may be distinguished from other Spiritual and Religious Bodies by one or more common characteristics including (but not limited to):-

    (i) ***Political***: Spiritual Movements are always political to some degree in that the promotion of any spiritual beliefs, practices and experiences is done with the aim of achieving one or more underlying goals. In contrast, if such a group or alliance did not have any goals, then they could not be classified as a Spiritual Movement; and

    (ii) ***Populist***: Spiritual Movements are commonly populist in their self promotion and in harnessing awareness to their cause; and

    (iii) ***Dramatic***: Spiritual Movements are frequently prone to promote their goals in terms of "romantic" and "altruistic" terms. Consequently, this may assist in the populist framing of such movements to accrue greater support; and

    (iv) ***Charismatic***: Spiritual Movements are almost always borne around the efforts and teachings of a single charismatic leader. Thus most Spiritual Movements evolve (or devolve) into Cults over time.

28. Major Spiritual Movements that have occurred over the past three hundred (300) years include (but are not limited to):-

(i) **Swedenborgianism**: ***Founder***: Emanuel Swedenborg; ***Origin***: Sweden, mid-18th century; ***Beliefs***: Based on the mystical and theological writings of Swedenborg, emphasizing the spiritual interpretation of the Bible and the existence of a complex spiritual world; and

past 300 years

(ii) **Spiritualism:** ***Founders***: The Fox Sisters; ***Origin***: United States, mid-19th century; ***Beliefs***: The belief in communication with the spirits of the dead through mediums. Focused on seances and spiritual communication; and

(iii) **Theosophy:** ***Founders***: Helena Blavatsky, Henry Steel Olcott; ***Origin***: United States, 1875; ***Beliefs***: Combined elements of Eastern religions, mysticism and occultism. Sought to explore the spiritual and mystical dimensions of human existence; and

(iv) **New Thought Movement:** ***Founders***: Phineas Quimby, Mary Baker Eddy (related to Christian Science); ***Origin***: United States, late 19th century; ***Beliefs***: Focuses on the power of positive thinking, the law of attraction, and the mental science of healing; and

(v) **Anthroposophy:** ***Founder***: Rudolf Steiner; ***Origin***: Germany, early 20th century; ***Beliefs***: A spiritual movement that emphasizes the importance of spiritual science and seeks to understand the spiritual world through rational thought and inner development; and

(vi) **Rosicrucianism:** ***Founders***: Various organizations, such as the Ancient Mystical Order Rosae Crucis (AMORC); ***Origin***: Claimed revival; ***Beliefs***: A mystical philosophical secret society believed to have been founded in late medieval Germany. Emphasizes esoteric truths, alchemy and spiritual enlightenment; and

(vii) **Scientology:** ***Founder***: L. Ron Hubbard; ***Origin***: United States, 1950s; ***Beliefs***: Combines elements of science fiction, psychology and Eastern religions. Focuses on spiritual rehabilitation through a process called auditing; and

(viii) **Human Potential Movement:** ***Founders***: Abraham Maslow, Carl Rogers; ***Origin***: United States, mid-20th century; ***Beliefs***: Focuses on the realization of human potential through self-improvement, psychological growth and spiritual development; and

(ix) **Transcendental Meditation (TM):** ***Founder***: Maharishi Mahesh Yogi; ***Origin***: India/United States, 1950s; ***Beliefs***: A meditation technique aimed at achieving inner peace and spiritual enlightenment through the repetition of mantras.; and

(x) **Esalen Institute and Humanistic Psychology:** *Founders*: Michael Murphy, Dick Price; *Origin*: United States, 1960s; *Beliefs*: Focuses on personal growth, human potential, and experiential learning. Integrates Eastern philosophies with Western psychology; and

(xi) **New Age Movement:** *Founders*: Various, such as Alice Bailey, David Spangler, Shirley MacLaine, Ken Wilber, Deepak Chopra; *Origin*: 1970s-1980s; *Beliefs*: Eclectic movement drawing from various spiritual and metaphysical traditions, emphasizing personal spirituality, holistic health, and universal consciousness; and

(xii) **Integral Theory:** *Founder*: Ken Wilber; *Origin*: Late 20th to early 21st century; *Beliefs*: Integrates insights from various fields of knowledge, including science, psychology, and spirituality, to create a comprehensive worldview; and

(xiii) **Mindfulness Movement:** *Founder*: Jon Kabat-Zinn; *Origin*: United States, late 20th to early 21st century; *Beliefs*: Emphasizes mindfulness practices derived from Buddhist meditation. Focuses on mental clarity, stress reduction and self-awareness.

## 1.3 – Religion

### Article 9 - Religion

29. A ***Religion*** in a formal sense is an ***Organised Faith*** of Beliefs, Practices and Systems first introduced by one (or more) proclaimed ***Divine Saviour*** associated with some claimed mandate and relation with at least one ***Higher Supernatural Being***. In an informal sense, *Religion* is a common term used to describe and distinguish the particular Creed or Beliefs of an individual, even if they be Non-Religious. — Religion

30. *Organised Faith* refers to the structured and institutionalised systems of belief and practice within a religious community. It involves the establishment of hierarchies, rituals, and doctrines that govern the behaviour and beliefs of followers. — Organised Faith (Faith & Systems)

31. A *System* is a type of Model being a Set of Objects or Concepts, capable of being uniquely defined by a Set of Rules as to their Properties, Relations and Behaviours. The most well formed and — Systems and Faith

mature Faiths exist upon at least one System.

32. A *Divine Saviour* is both an Ecclesiastical and Sovereign Claim or Mandate whereby a "flesh and blood" person is proclaimed through self-evident signs, attributes and qualifications that they are a Divine Saviour sent or appointed from Heaven to Earth. It is then their teachings that form the basis of the new Religion:-

    (i) The Claim of Divine Saviour is one of the oldest methods of claiming supreme sovereign authority and power from the beginning of Human Civilisation; and

    (ii) Almost every civilisation and culture has had a Divine Saviour such as the Akkadians who worshipped Adad, the Sumerians who worshipped Ishkur, the early Babylonians who worshipped Hadad, the ancient Egyptians who worshipped Horus, the early Greeks had Adonis, the Phrygians (Turkey and Syria) who worshipped Attis, the Persians and colonies who worshipped Mithra and the Celts who worshipped Esus (later listed as Jesus); and

    (iii) Within the faiths of Christianity, Islam, Judaism, Buddhism, Hinduism and many other faiths, the Rank and Title of *Divine Saviour* (or by some other specific cultural Title), is unquestionably accepted as the highest of all sovereign authority and power; and

    (iv) Many of these same cultures have recognised in the oldest forms of law the fact that the legitimate appearance of a Divine Saviour matching the specific cultural context requires all followers of a particular faith to acknowledge and obey the authority and direction of the Divine Saviour; and

    (v) The primary meaning and nature of "Saviour" is literally one who saves, as the architect of a new civilisation restoring the rule of law, as opposed to a tyrant or despot or impostor.

33. *Supernatural* is any Event or Form believed or perceived by the observer, to be above or beyond, what is understood to be natural or conforming to Natural Law of the observable physical universe, perceived through Mind.

34. A *Higher Supernatural Being* refers to an entity that is believed to possess power and existence beyond the natural world and ordinary human capabilities. Some of the common characteristics include (but are not limited to):-

    (i) **Transcendence**: Higher Supernatural Beings are typically seen as existing beyond the physical universe, not bound by natural laws or human limitations; and

(ii) ***Divine Attributes***: These beings often possess divine qualities such as omnipotence (all-powerful), omniscience (all-knowing), omnipresence (present everywhere), and perfect goodness; and

(iii) ***Creative Power***: Many traditions attribute the creation of the universe and life to a Higher Supernatural Being; and

(iv) ***Intervention***: These beings are believed to intervene in the world, influencing events, answering prayers, performing miracles, or providing guidance to followers; and

(v) ***Personification***: They are often personified, having personal attributes, intentions, and the ability to interact with humans, though some belief systems conceive them as abstract or impersonal forces.

35. By definition, for a belief system to be considered a Religion, it must assert six (6) fundamental presumptions:- Key elements of what constitutes a Religion

    (i) The existence of one (or more) Higher Supernatural Beings; and

    (ii) That the followers are less than these Higher Supernatural Beings; and

    (iii) Contact has been made between the Higher Supernatural Beings and one or more men or women considered unique from all other men and women; and

    (iv) This contact is "proven" by the existence of one or more sacred objects or texts or teachings that then also form a "mandate" of claimed authority; and

    (v) The administration and officials of the Religion represent the one, true and only successors to those Divine Saviours who first received divine instruction and founded the religion; and

    (vi) The leadership and officials of the Religion have the right to self administer the laws and forums of law of the Religion and decide what is pleasing, what is not and if anyone should be excluded or punished for failing certain rules.

36. Given Organised Faith has existed for as long as Human Civilisation itself, Religions may be generally classified according to six (6) different categories of structure being Sociological, Organisational, Theological, Doctrinal, Geographical and Historical:- Classification of Religions

    (i) ***Sociological Classification***: (a) *Official State-Based Religions* of Empires and Civilisations, evolving to World

Religions (e.g. Christianity, Islam, Hinduism, Buddhism, Chinese); and (b) *Indigenous and Cultural Religions* specific to a particular culture, ethnicity or geographic region (e.g. African Religions, Native American Religions, Australian Aboriginal Religions); and

(ii) **Organisational Classification**: (a) *Formal Institutional Structured Religions* with formal institutions, hierarchies and clergy (e.g. Roman Catholicism, Eastern Orthodoxy, Sunni Islam); and (b) *Semi-Autonomous Religions* with less rigid hierarchies and more informal structures (e.g. Evangelical and New Age Movements); and

(iii) **Theological Classification**: (a) *Monotheistic Religions* as belief in a single, all-powerful deity (e.g. Christianity, Islam, Hinduism (Brahman), Judaism); and (b) *Polytheistic Religions* as belief in multiple gods or deities (e.g. Hinduism (Deities), Ancient Greek Religion, Norse Mythology); and (c) *Pantheistic Religions* as belief that the divine is identical with the universe or nature (e.g. Hinduism, Taoism, and certain New Age beliefs); and (d) *Atheistic Religions* as lack of belief in deities; focus on philosophical and ethical teachings (e.g. Buddhism, Jainism); and

(iv) **Doctrinal Classification**: (a) *Orthodox Religions* that emphasize adherence to established doctrines and traditional practices (e.g. Eastern Orthodoxy, Sunni Islam, Theravada Buddhism); and (b) *Reformative Religions* that seek to reform or reinterpret traditional doctrines and practices (e.g. Protestantism, Reform Judaism, Mahayana Buddhism); and

(v) **Geographical Classification**: (a) *Western Religions* that originated in the Western world (e.g. Christianity, Judaism, Islam); and (b) *Eastern Religions* that originated in the Eastern world (e.g. Hinduism, Buddhism, Taoism, Shinto); and

(vi) **Historical Classification**: (a) *Ancient Religions* that originated in ancient times more than 2,500 years ago (e.g. Ancient Egyptian Religion, Zoroastrianism, Ancient Greek Religion); and (b) *Traditional Religions* that have existed for more than a thousand years (e.g. Christianity, Islam, Hinduism, Buddhism); and (c) *Modern Religions* that have emerged in more recent history (e.g. Baha'i Faith, Scientology, Mormonism).

37. Of the estimated 4,000+ formal Religions across the world today, the profile of Religions in terms of number of adherents, longevity and

*Success of Religions by*

success may be measured against the six (6) different categories of structure being Sociological, Organisational, Theological, Doctrinal, Geographical and Historical:-

Classification

(i) **Official State-Based Religions of Empires & Civilisations** (93% of all total adherents) (e.g. Christianity, Islam, Hinduism, Buddhism, Chinese) remains the most successful forms of Religions in Human Civilisation whereby such systems have historically deeply integrated into the sovereign, political and social structures of societies; and

(ii) **Traditional Historic Religions** (93% of all total adherents) (e.g. Christianity, Islam, Hinduism, Buddhism, Chinese) being those Religions formed over the past 2,500 to 1,000 years, remain the overwhelming predominant faiths, despite the advent of thousands of new Religions; and

(iii) **Monotheistic & Non-Dualistic Religions**: (80% of all total adherents) (e.g. Christianity, Islam, Hinduism (Brahman), Judaism) being the belief in an ultimate single, all-powerful deity is the dominant and most successful Theological structure of all Religions in Human Civilisation; and

(iv) **Orthodox Doctrinal Denominations** (75% of all total adherents) (e.g. Roman Catholic, Eastern Orthodoxy, Sunni Islam, Vaishnavism, Theravada Buddhism) being adherence to established doctrines and traditional practices continues to be the dominant preference of the vast majority of adherents within Religions, despite many hundreds of Religious Movements throughout history.

38. A Religion is materially different to a Spiritual Movement primarily upon the difference of formality of design and function:-

Religion vs Spiritual Movement

(i) **Organised Structure**: Religions typically exhibit established and organised structures, whereas Spiritual Movements are usually more fluid, autonomous or evolving; and

(ii) **Codified Beliefs and Practices**: Religions are fundamentally defined by their codification of beliefs and practices and then strict adherence to such rules, whereas Spiritual Movements are considerably less formal and personalised; and

(iii) **Sacred Texts and Doctrines**: Religions are typically founded on at least one primary sacred text, whereas Spiritual Movements may not possess any such primary text.

39. Similar to the differences of a Spiritual Movement, a Religion is materially different to a Cult primarily upon the difference and maturity of design and function:-

    (i) ***Evolving Organised Structure***: Unlike a Religion, a Cult by definition is still in the process of evolving and formalising its hierarchy and structure; and may even be at the early stages of a Personality-Based Structure around a proclaimed "saviour" (or near successor) rather than a formal organised religious hierarchy; and

    (ii) ***Evolving Texts, Messages and Doctrines***: Unlike a Religion, the Sacred Texts and Doctrines of a Cult are by definition still evolving and not yet regarded as widely fixed and firm, even if the contrary is the beliefs of the adherents of the Cult; and

    (iii) ***Strict and Coercive Control***: Cults, unlike Religions are typically highly coercive and manipulative in their active control over their adherents, usually as a means of compensating for other structural weaknesses that may otherwise undermine and possibly destroy the faith of such adherents.

## Article 10 – Religious Denomination

40. A ***Religious Denomination*** is the second largest theological subdivision of an existing Religion. *Religious Denominations* are large groups of adherents of a Religion that are defined by their own distinct beliefs, practices, rituals, and organizational structures from other major groups within the same Religion.

41. *Religious Denominations* are almost always formed by major Schisms at a state and sovereign control basis and never by Religious Movements:-

    (i) Whilst history is written to imply a Religious Denomination may have been born out of a Religious Movement, in truth large scale movements of adherent to another organisational structure within an established Religion is almost always a product of changing political and state based alliances; and

    (ii) Religious Movements often appear as a pretext or political excuse to undertake a Schism rather than the action that formalised a new Religious Denomination.

42. The Major Denominations as Religious Movements of Christianity include (but are not limited to):-

(i) **Universalism (Roman Catholicism):** (52% of all total adherents) ***Origin***: Western Christian Empire, early centuries of Christianity; ***Key Beliefs***: The authority of the Pope, seven sacraments, veneration of Mary and the saints, and the importance of tradition alongside scripture; and

(ii) **Orthodoxism:** (11% of all total adherents) ***Origin***: Eastern Christian Empire (Byzantine Empire) separation from 400s; ***Key Beliefs***: Emphasis on the Holy Tradition, veneration of icons, the seven sacraments, and the authority of the Ecumenical Councils; and

(iii) **Protestantism:** (36% of all total adherents) ***Origin***: Western Europe, 16th century Reformation; ***Key Beliefs***: *Sola scriptura* (scripture alone), *sola fide* (faith alone), priesthood of all believers, and the rejection of papal authority and many Catholic sacraments; and

(iv) **Restorationism:** (1% of all total adherents) ***Origin***: 19th century, United States; ***Key Beliefs***: Restoration of the original Christian church, emphasis on New Testament practices.

*Movements of Christianity*

**43.** The Major Denominations as Religious Movements of Islam include (but are not limited to):-

(i) **Sufism**: (95% of all total adherents but now blended within other major denominations) ***Origin***: 6$^{th}$ Century and founding of Islam; ***Key Beliefs***: Sanctity of Auricular (Quran) Wisdom of God, inner purification, morality and spiritual development, and direct experience of God; and

(ii) **Sunnism**: (85% of all total adherents) ***Origin***: From Sufism in 12-13$^{th}$ Century changes by Mamluk/Ottoman Empire but claimed as 7$^{th}$ Century; ***Key Beliefs***: Written Quran and the Hadith (sayings and actions of Prophet), Consensus of the Ummah (Muslim community) in matters of religious interpretation; and

(iii) **Shiaism**: (14% of all total adherents) ***Origin***: From Sufism in 16-17$^{th}$ Century but claimed as 7$^{th}$ Century; ***Key Beliefs***: Written Quran and the Hadith (sayings and actions of Prophet), History of Islam must be corrected, Leadership of Islam should have remained within bloodline descendents of the Prophet; and

(iv) **Ahmadiyaism**: (1% of all total adherents) ***Origin***: Founded by Mirza Ghulam Ahmad in the late 19th century in India, Ahmadiyya Muslims believe that Ghulam Ahmad was the

*Major Denominations as Religious Movements of Islam*

promised Messiah and Mahdi, whose coming was foretold by Prophet.

44. The Major Denominations as Religious Movements of Hinduism include (but are not limited to):-

    (i) **Shaivism**: (26% of all total adherents) ***Origin***: Post-Vedic period, around 2-3rd Centuries CE; ***Key Beliefs***: Worship of Shiva as the supreme god. It emphasizes asceticism, meditation and the pursuit of spiritual knowledge; and

    (ii) **Shaktism**: (3% of all total adherents) ***Origin***: Post-Vedic period, around 2-3rd Centuries CE; ***Key Beliefs***: Worship of the Divine Mother, or Shakti, in her various forms, such as Durga, Kali and Parvati. It emphasizes rituals, devotion and the power of the feminine divine; and

    (iii) **Smartism**: (3% of all total adherents) ***Origin***: 8th Century through Adi Shankaracharya; ***Key Beliefs***: Worship of multiple deities, including Vishnu, Shiva, Shakti, Ganesha, and Surya. It promotes the idea that all deities are manifestations of the same underlying reality, Brahman; and

    (iv) **Vaishnavism**: (68% of all total adherents) ***Origin***: 15th to 17th centuries CE through Bhakti Movement but claimed from earlier 2-3rd Centuries CE; ***Key Beliefs***: Worship of Vishnu and his avatars, particularly Krishna and Rama. It emphasizes bhakti (devotional worship) and the concept of salvation through divine grace.

45. The Major Denominations as Religious Movements of Buddhism include (but are not limited to):-

    (i) **Theravadism**: (40% of all total adherents) ***Origin***: 5th century BCE; ***Key Beliefs***: The original teachings of the Buddha as found in the Pali Canon. Focuses on the Four Noble Truths, the Eightfold Path, and the concept of attaining Nirvana through personal effort; and

    (ii) **Mahayanism**: (50% of all total adherents) ***Origin***: 1st century CE; ***Key Beliefs***: The bodhisattva path, where practitioners seek enlightenment not just for themselves but for the benefit of all beings. Introduces the concept of Sunyata (emptiness) and the importance of compassion; and

    (iii) **Vajrayanism**: (5% of all total adherents) ***Origin***: 7th century CE; ***Key Beliefs***: Mahayana teachings and adds esoteric practices. Emphasizes the use of rituals, mantras, mudras and mandalas to achieve rapid spiritual progress.

Recognizes the importance of a guru or lama; and

(iv) **Nichirenism**: (3% of all total adherents) ***Origin***: 13th century CE; ***Key Beliefs***: Founded by the monk Nichiren, emphasizes the Lotus Sutra as the supreme teaching of the Buddha and the chanting of Nam Myoho Renge Kyo as the primary practice for achieving enlightenment.

## Article 11 – Religious Sect

46. A ***Religious Sect*** is the smallest theological subdivision of an existing Religion. It is a subgroup that has distinct beliefs, practices or rituals that set it apart from the mainstream or established form of that Religion.

Religious Sect

## Article 12 – Religious Order

47. A ***Religious Order*** is a recognised community of individuals who live according to a specific rule or set of religious principles. Initiates of religious orders typically take various forms of austere and pious vows as part of their admission to Membership.

Religious Order

48. *Religious Orders* exist within various religious traditions, including Christianity (both Catholicism and Protestantism), Buddhism, Hinduism, and others:-

Religious Orders and Different Religions

   (i) The members of a religious order often dedicate themselves to a life of service, prayer and contemplation, with the goal of achieving spiritual growth and serving others in accordance with their religious beliefs; and

   (ii) Religious Orders have played a significant role throughout history in areas such as education, healthcare, social services and missionary work; and

   (iii) In Buddhism, religious orders are often referred to as monastic communities or sanghas, and they follow various monastic rules and traditions depending on the specific school or lineage.

## Article 13 – Religious Movement

49. A ***Religious Movement*** is a group or collective alliance of individuals of a particular Religious Faith that are united by one or more common objectives that seek to use and promote certain reforms of beliefs, practices and experiences with the express aim of achieving their underlying goals within the existing Religion.

    <small>Religious Movement</small>

50. A *Religious Movement* may be distinguished from other Religious Bodies by one or more common characteristics including (but not limited to):-

    <small>Common Characteristics of a Religious Movement</small>

    (i) ***Political***: Religious Movements are always political to some degree in that the promotion of any spiritual beliefs, practices and experiences is done with the aim of achieving one or more underlying goals. In contrast, if such a group or alliance did not have any goals, then they could not be classified as a Spiritual Movement; and

    (ii) ***Populist***: Religious Movements are commonly populist in their self promotion and in harnessing awareness to their cause; and

    (iii) ***Dramatic***: Religious Movements are frequently prone to promote their goals in terms of "romantic" and "altruistic" terms. Consequently, this may assist in the populist framing of such movements to accrue greater support; and

    (iv) ***Charismatic***: Religious Movements are almost always borne around the efforts and teachings of a single charismatic leader. Thus most Religious Movements evolve (or devolve) into Cults over time.

51. Significant Christian Religious Movements over the past six hundred years include (but are not limited to):-

    <small>Significant Christian Religious Movements</small>

    (i) **Protestant Reformation**: ***Founders***: Martin Luther, John Calvin, Henry VIII, and others; ***Origin***: 16th century; ***Major Beliefs***: Justification by faith alone, the authority of Scripture over Church tradition, the priesthood of all believers, and rejection of certain Catholic practices like indulgences; and

    (ii) **Counter-Reformation**: ***Founders***: Pope Paul III, Ignatius of Loyola (founder of the Jesuits); ***Origin***: 16th–17th centuries; ***Major Beliefs***: Affirmation of traditional Catholic doctrines, reform of Church practices, establishment of new religious orders (e.g. Jesuits), and emphasis on education and missionary work; and

(iii) **Great Awakening**: *Founders*: Jonathan Edwards, George Whitefield, John Wesley; *Origin*: 18th century; *Major Beliefs*: Personal conversion experiences, emotional revival meetings, emphasis on personal piety and evangelism, and the democratization of religious authority; and

(iv) **Pentecostalism**: *Founders*: Charles Fox Parham, William J. Seymour; *Origin*: Early 20th century; *Major Beliefs*: Baptism in the Holy Spirit, speaking in tongues, divine healing, prophecy, and a focus on the direct personal experience of God.

52. Significant Islamic Religious Movements over the past six hundred years include (but are not limited to):- Significant Islamic Religious Movements

(i) **Shiaism**: *Founder*: Shah Ismail; *Origin*: 16th Century; *Major Beliefs*: End of last regions of original Sufism. Replaced by written Quran and the Hadith (sayings and actions of Prophet), claiming History of Islam must be corrected, Leadership of Islam should have remained within bloodline descendents of the Prophet; and

(ii) **Wahhabism**: *Founder*: Muhammad ibn Abd al-Wahhab; *Origin*: 18th century; *Major Beliefs*: Strict adherence to the Quran and Hadith, rejection of wisdom, sufism or any innovations (bid'ah) in Islamic practice, emphasis on monotheism (Tawhid), and opposition to practices considered idolatrous; and

(iii) **Revivalism**: *Founder*: Hassan al-Banna (founder of the Muslim Brotherhood), Abul Ala Maududi; *Origin*: 20th century; *Major Beliefs*: Revival of Islamic identity and practice, establishment of Islamic states governed by Sharia law, and resistance to Western cultural and political influences.

53. Significant Hindu Religious Movements over the past six hundred years include (but are not limited to):- Significant Hindu Religious Movements

(i) **Bhakti Movement**: *Founder*: Ramananda, Kabir, Mirabai, Tulsidas; *Origin*: 5-17th centuries; *Major Beliefs*: Devotion (bhakti) to a personal god, equality of all believers regardless of caste, rejection of ritualistic practices, and emphasis on singing and chanting; and

(ii) **Arya Samaj Movement**: *Founder*: Swami Dayananda Saraswati.; *Origin*: 19th century; *Major Beliefs*: Return to the Vedas as the true scriptures of Hinduism, rejection of idol worship, social reform including education and gender equality and monotheism; and

- (iii) **Ramakrishna Movement**: *Founder*: Swami Vivekananda (disciple of Ramakrishna); *Origin*: Late 19th century; *Major Beliefs*: Universalism, synthesis of Vedanta philosophy, service to humanity as worship of God, and emphasis on the harmony of all religions.

54. Significant Buddhist Religious Movements over the past six hundred years include (but are not limited to):- *[Significant Buddhist Religious Movements]*

    - (i) **Tibetan Buddhism**: *Founder*: Padmasambhava, Tsongkhapa, Dalai Lamas; *Origin*: 11th–20th centuries; *Major Beliefs*: Integration of Tantric practices, the role of lamas (spiritual teachers), reincarnation of high lamas (tulkus), and practices like ritual, meditation and mantra recitation; and

    - (ii) **Zen Buddhism**: *Founder*: Bodhidharma, Dogen, Hakuin; *Origin*: 12th century onwards; *Major Beliefs*: Emphasis on meditation (zazen), direct experience of enlightenment (satori), and the importance of teacher-student transmission; and

    - (iii) **Vipassana Movement**: *Founder*: Ledi Sayadaw, Mahasi Sayadaw, S. N. Goenka; *Origin*: 20th century; *Major Beliefs*: Emphasis on insight meditation (vipassana) to gain direct understanding of the nature of reality, focus on mindfulness and ethical living and the popularization of meditation retreats.

55. Significant Judaic Religious Movements over the past six hundred years include (but are not limited to):- *[Significant Judaic Religious Movements]*

    - (i) **Ashkenazism (Nazism)**: *Founder*: Ottoman Kaizer Sultan Ibrahim I (1640-1648) aka Sabbatai Zevi; *Origin*: Ottoman Empire then almost 1 million adherents exiled to Russia and Poland after death of former Sultan; *Major Beliefs*: Distorted Gnostic Duality whereby Earth is fundamentally flawed and ruled by a lower deity (G-d) whose true hidden name is Lucifer. G-d will ultimately grant control of the Earth to the Jews after a period of trials and suffering. Only the Jews possess the true secret knowledge and favour of G-d; and

    - (ii) **Hasidism**: *Founders*: Lithuanian-Polish noble Prince Kazimierz Czartoryski (b.1674- d.1741) and Israel ben Eliezer (b. 1688 – d. 1780); *Origin*: 18th century Poland; *Major Beliefs*: The true hidden name of G-d is Sabaoth and Moloch (Satan) not Lucifer. G-d will not grant the Jews their own homeland or world control until a major sacrifice by fire (Holocaust) of their own people be made as an "pleasing" offering to G-d; and

(iii) **Zionism**: ***Founders***: Dutch Wall St Families, with Rothschilds and elite London/New York Political Class; ***Origin***: 1864 with founding of *Beit Miriam* (בית מרים) meaning House of Mary and then B'nai B'rith (בְּנֵי בְּרִית,) meaning Children of the (New) Covenant; ***Major Beliefs***: The true hidden name of G-d is the Elohim (lesser gods) being the thirteen families plus one (political elite) as proclaimed as global public notice through the *Apotheosis of Washington* fresco (1865). Washington shall be a new city blatantly designed and dedicated to Lucifer, Satan and Moloch, where everything about it is an openly distorted lie and profound blasphemy against Christianity and all religions, and all forms of civilised law, the true history and founders of the United States and all forms of moral decency. The Jews shall get their homeland only at great cost to the world, and all their prophecies shall be meticulously coordinated and fulfilled, including mass murder, in order to establish a thousand year Reich of power centred on Washington as New Rome.

## Article 14 – Schism

56. A ***Schism*** is a formal split within a religion, resulting from major theological or doctrinal disputes, leading to the formation of a Sect, or in more historic examples in the formation of a new major Denomination.

## 1.4 – Cult

## Article 15 – Cult

57. A ***Cult*** is a relatively small religious or ideological group, typically characterised by extreme devotion to a charismatic leader, strict authoritarian control, exclusive membership, manipulative recruitment and retention techniques, and the exploitation of social isolation as a means of control of its members.

58. Common characteristics of Cults include (but are not limited to):-

    (i) **Charismatic Leader**: Cults often have a charismatic leader who is revered by the members and is seen as possessing special knowledge or insight; and

    (ii) **Egocentric Promotion:** Cults usually promote their

Charismatic Leader as either the primary brand or a major supporting brand. By definition, a group is highly unlikely to be a Cult where its founding leader is not permitted to be promoted as a key brand; and

(iii) **Personal Financial Benefit**: Cults overwhelmingly exist for the personal financial benefit of its founder or chief lieutenants, even if denied or argued as an unwanted or unforeseen. A founder that seeks no financial or personal benefit is almost always a sign that an early movement is not a cult; and

(iv) **Exclusive Membership**: Membership in a Cult is usually exclusive, with a strong us-versus-them mentality. This can lead to social isolation from non-members; and

(v) **Authoritarian Control**: Cults often exhibit strict, authoritarian control over members lives, including their behaviour, thoughts and emotions. This can include demanding high levels of commitment and loyalty to the group and its leaders; and

(vi) **Manipulative Techniques**: Cults frequently use manipulative techniques to recruit and retain members, such as coercive persuasion, thought reform and indoctrination. This can involve psychological manipulation to reinforce dependence on the group; and

(vii) **Isolation from Society**: Members are often encouraged or required to sever ties with outside family and friends and to immerse themselves fully in the group's activities and beliefs, away from the norms of society; and

(viii) **Novel or Radical Ideology**: A Cult almost always possesses some claimed new, radical or disruptive philosophy as distinct from the status quo.

**59.** The common characteristics of a Cult are the exact same characteristics shared by many smaller groups, entrepreneurial start-ups, scientific research teams and security and military training. Thus, the concept and function of a Cult itself can only be considered negative if its purpose and function is actively seeking to inflict sexual, physical and emotional harm upon its followers and others:- *Concept and Function of a Cult itself is not inherently immoral, wicked or unlawful*

(i) The term "Cult" is a catch all word frequently used by an adversary to denigrate, slander and weaken a small group working toward change; and

(ii) Almost every business start up, scientific research group, social issue group, charitable group, self help group, benevolent group and military and security training group qualifies under the same common characteristics to be classed as a "cult" at first glance; and

(iii) The key issue is in identifying small groups operating negatively within society and actively hurting people, rather than relying upon labelling and slander; and

(iv) Conversely, history demonstrates that social ostracisation only serves to strengthen a Cult rather than weaken it. Thus, those who seek to attack out of ignorance, agenda or fear do little to help address the prevalence of negative groups.

**60.** Not all Cults are born from Religions. In recent decades, vastly more Cults have emerged from the gross commercialisation of Spirituality through self-help and the well-being industry than all the Religious Cults throughout history combined.

*Cults as formations from Religious or Spiritual Roots*

## 1.5 – False, Repugnant & Prohibited Spirituality, Religions etc.

### Article 16 – False, Repugnant & Prohibited Spirituality, Religions & Cults

**61.** ***False & Prohibited Spirituality, Religions & Cults*** refers to spiritual and religious beliefs and practices that are deemed illegitimate or forbidden by a particular society or religious authority. These may include negative cults, heresies, or practices that are considered dangerous or harmful to individuals or society as a whole.

*False & Prohibited Spirituality, Religions & Cults*

**62.** ***Three main categories of False & Prohibited Spirituality, Religions & Cults exist***, namely:

(i) ***Commercial & Narcissistic Spirituality***: Spirituality that is heavily influenced by consumerism and selfishness, whereby spiritual practices and beliefs are commodified and marketed, focusing more on individual gain, self-promotion, and material success rather than genuine spiritual growth or community well-being; and

(ii) ***Parasitic & Fanatical Cults***: Extremely negative, destructive and exploitative behaviours both upon their lower adherents and significant damage to the fabric of various societies or the world at large; and

(iii) ***Occult & Slavery Based Religions***: Historic and contemporary organised faiths founded on esoteric and mystical beliefs and practices as well as the justification of

*Main categories of False & Prohibited Spirituality, Religions & Cults*

enslavement of their followers or other people.

63. By the very nature of Cults and cult-like behaviour, any and all exposure or attempt to introduce prohibition only serves to empower and strengthen the elite leadership of such false and repugnant organisations:- Difficulty in effective exposure & prohibition

   (i) It is virtually impossible to conduct an objective debate as to the overwhelming evidence and behaviour of parasitic and fanatical cults, given such organisations have totally geared themselves to exploit any and all discussion as both fuel for gaslighting (claiming the same points against the alleged aggressor) and reinforce control on their members; and

   (ii) Consequently, some of the most insane and dangerous cults the world has ever seen have continued to wield undue influence over the course of political and economic events, with little or no serious debate as to their negative philosophies and destructive behaviours; and

   (iii) Like all forms of Organised Faith, extremist cults can only be eventually and finally disbanded upon the complete and total collapse of faith of its adherents in the same way that all forms of organised faith have failed throughout history.

64. Cults are neither positive for a Society, nor members of a wider Society. As Cults deliberately use fraud, manipulation and distortions to recruit members and keep members, all Cults must be regarded properly as organized criminal syndicates before the Rule of Law. Cults as organized criminal syndicates

## Article 17 – Commercial & Narcissistic Spirituality

65. ***Commercial & Narcissistic Spirituality*** refers to a form of spirituality that is heavily influenced by consumerism and selfishness, whereby spiritual practices and beliefs are commodified and marketed, focusing more on individual gain, self-promotion, and material success rather than genuine spiritual growth or community well-being. Commercial & Narcissistic Spirituality

66. Characteristics of *Commercial & Narcissistic Spirituality* include (but are not limited to):- Characteristics of Commercial & Narcissistic Spirituality

   (i) ***Hyper-Commercialization***: Spiritual practices and products are sold as commodities, with an emphasis on branding, marketing and profit. Examples include expensive retreats, branded yoga gear and self-help books promising quick spiritual fixes; and

   (ii) ***Instant Gratification***: Emphasis on quick and easy solutions to complex spiritual issues, often ignoring the deeper, more challenging aspects of genuine spiritual practice; and

(iii) **Selfish Personal Branding**: Individuals may treat their spiritual journey as a way to enhance their personal brand, often sharing their experiences on social media to gain followers and validation. This can lead to a focus on appearance and external validation rather than inner growth and enlightenment; and

(iv) **Superficiality**: The depth and authenticity of spiritual practices may be sacrificed for more appealing, trendy and easy-to-sell versions. This can result in a dilution of traditional teachings and practices, making them more palatable to a broader audience but less meaningful in their original context; and

(v) **Narcissism**: The focus is on the individual's self-improvement, personal success and image rather than on altruistic or community-oriented goals. This form of spirituality often promotes the idea that spiritual growth is about achieving personal goals, enhancing one's status, or attaining superficial forms of happiness.

## Article 18 – Parasitic & Fanatical Cults

67. **Parasitic & Fanatical Cults** refers to certain types of cults that exhibit extremely negative, destructive and exploitative behaviours both upon their lower adherents and significant damage to the fabric of various societies or the world at large.

*Parasitic & Fanatical Cults*

68. Characteristics of *Parasitic & Fanatical Cults* include (but are not limited to):-

*Characteristics of Parasitic & Fanatical Cults*

(i) **Extreme Exploitation**: Leaders and the inner circle of such cults often benefit materially, financially or psychologically at the expense of the lower ranked members. This can include demanding large sums of money, unpaid labour or other personal sacrifices. In some cases, incontrovertible evidence exists that some of the elite of these cults have actually physically sacrificed and murdered numbers of lower ranked members for their perverse aims; and

(ii) **Apocalyptic and Distorted Beliefs**: Most such parasitic and fanatical cults hold apocalyptic beliefs or revolutionary ideologies, believing that they have a unique and crucial role in bringing about significant change or salvation, normally founded on deliberately distorted and false texts, claims and fake revelations; and

(iii) **_Totalitarian Control_**: Such cults seeks to control all aspects of the lives of their lower members, including their thoughts, actions and relationships. This totalitarian control often involves rigorous schedules, monitoring and enforcement of strict rules; and

(iv) **_Blatant Hypocrisy and Duplicity_**: Whereby the true leadership of such parasitic and fanatical cults openly refuse to apply the same rigid rules and demands upon themselves as the rest of their followers; and often blatantly live their lives in such opulence, consumption and wealth that is wholly contradictory to the claims and laws of the cult itself; and

(v) **_Manipulation_**: Psychological manipulation is used to control members. This can involve brainwashing, coercive persuasion, and manipulation of beliefs and emotions to keep members compliant and loyal; and

(vi) **_Isolation_**: Members are often isolated from outside influences, including family and friends, which makes them more vulnerable to exploitation. This isolation can also serve to strengthen the members' dependency on the cult.

## Article 19 – Occult & Slavery Based Religions

69. **_Occult & Slavery Based Religions_** are those historic and contemporary organised faiths founded on esoteric and mystical beliefs and practices as well as the justification of enslavement of their followers or other people.

70. Characteristics of *Occult & Slavery Based Religions* include (but are not limited to):-

    (i) **Esoteric Knowledge**: The occult involves knowledge that is hidden or secret, understood only by a select group of initiates or practitioners; and

    (ii) **Mysticism and Magic**: Practices often include magical rituals, spell-casting and attempts to harness supernatural forces; and

    (iii) **Symbolism**: Such traditions frequently use complex symbols, codes and rituals to convey and unlock hidden meanings; and

    (iv) **Classed-Based Society**: Such religions are always founded on a class based society whereby the elite are considered living gods and the lowest base are considered merely a higher form of animals and thus property; and

(v) **Justification of Slavery**: Occult and Slavery Based Religions emphasize such false and distorted claims of history, tradition and "divine endorsement" to justify slavery as both legal and moral. Over time this may also involve the re-branding of slavery to such terms as indentured servants, workers, employees, citizens etc; and

(vi) **Integrated Systems and Rituals of Slavery**: Occult and Slavery Based Religions usually deeply integrate rituals and administrative practices of slavery into their official rites, both to support their relationship to state based leaderships and the financial and economic fabric of such societies that depend upon the enslavement of people under certain conditions. This may include the endorsement of registers, secular use of occult rituals for birth, birth certificates and the trading of bonds in the names of people as commodities, trusts on the lives of people etc.

## 1.6 – Ecclesia

### Article 20 – Ecclesia

71. *Ecclesia* refers to any validly constituted Religious or Spiritual Body that possesses clear doctrines and laws for the moderation and governance of its members. Ecclesia does not mean only a Christian body, but any proper Religious or Spiritual Body.

    *Ecclesia*

72. The term *Ecclesia* comes from the Ancient Greek ἐκκλησία (ekklēsía) meaning a "public legislative assembly". The term predates the formation of Christianity as a religion by more than four hundred years:-

    *Origin and History of Concept of Ecclesia*

    (i) Despite the fact that the term *Ecclesia* is often assumed to be solely a Christian Term, it is used under Ucadia Law to describe any and all proper Religious or Spiritual Bodies given its unique heritage; and

    (ii) It is because the term Ecclesia has such strong history in terms of law and legislative assemblies, that the term is used as the broader basis of describing the rules and laws of Religious and Spiritual Bodies.

### Article 21 – Ecclesiastical Law

73. An *Ecclesiastical Law* is an authentic *Rule* reliably encompassing some discernible, measurable or observable doctrine, declaration,

    *Ecclesiastical Law*

statute or ordinance of a religious and moral society for the moderation and governance of its members.

74. An authentic **Rule** is a proper and authentic *Ecclesiastical Law* of a validly constituted Society that describes, prohibits or permits a certain *Act* pertaining to a valid and proper *Right* as defined in accord with the most sacred Covenant *Pactum De Singularis Caelum*. *(Rule and Ecclesiastical Law)*

75. A valid and proper **Right** is any positively defined Capacity, or Privilege, or Liberty, or Faculty, or Power, or Ownership, or Possession, or Interest, or Benefit that may be properly exercised as an *Ecclesiastical Law* in *Good Faith* (Bona Fidei), *Good Conscience* (Bona Conscientia) and *Good Actions* (Bona Acta) in accord with the most sacred Covenant *Pactum De Singularis Caelum*. If no Good Faith exists or no Right exists then no Law may exist. *(Right and Ecclesiastical Law)*

76. A valid and proper *Ecclesiastical Law* is established and takes force when it is promulgated in accord with these Maxims. *(Force of Ecclesiastical Law)*

77. A valid and proper *Ecclesiastical Law* binds everywhere all those for whom it was issued. *(Effect of Ecclesiastical Law)*

78. **Ucadia Ecclesiastical Law** is a complete consistent Model and System that encompass the body of doctrines, declarations, statutes and ordinances of religious and moral societies for the moderation and governance of their members. *(Ucadia Ecclesiastical Law)*

79. *Ucadia Ecclesiastical Law*, also known as *Lex Ecclesiasticum*, is one of twenty-two (22) books known as the *Divine Collection of Maxims of Law*: and also known as *Astrum Iuris Divini Canonum* (under Civilised Christian Law); and *Hikmat Samawi* (under Civilised Islamic Law); and *Pragya Dharma* (under Civilised Hindu, Buddhist, Jain, Sikh, Traditional and Indigenous Law) in accord with the most sacred Covenant *Pactum De Singularis Caelum* (Article 135 - Divine Collection of Maxims of Law). *(Ucadia Ecclesiastical Law and Divine Collection of Maxims of Law)*

80. As *Ucadia Ecclesiastical* Law is a complete consistent model and system of Maxims that encompass the entirety of natural phenomena occurring within the natural, physical and material world and universe, when writing or speaking of *Ecclesiastical Law*, it shall mean *Ucadia Ecclesiastical* Law and no other system or model. *(Ucadia Ecclesiastical Law as Ecclesiastical Law)*

81. No law is valid, or has any authority or force or effect as an *Ecclesiastical Law* or any other equivalent description unless it conforms to the body of Law known as the *Divine Collection of Maxims of Law* in accordance with the most sacred Covenant *Pactum De Singularis Caelum*. *(Consistency with Divine Collection of Maxims of Law)*

82. Any law claiming to be valid and related to religious organisations or *(Claims contrary*

the function of different organised faiths that is presently in force and is contrary to the prescript of these Maxims is therefore reprobate, suppressed and not permitted to be revived. *to these Maxims*

83. When anyone references, writes or speaks of valid and proper *Ecclesiastical Law* it shall mean these Maxims and no other. *Primacy of Ecclesiastical Law*

## Article 22 – Ecclesiastical Law & Divine Law

84. In accord with Divine Law, all valid Ecclesiastical Law may be said to be ultimately derived from authentic Divine Law. *Ecclesiastical Law & Divine Law*

85. In accord with Divine Law, Divine Law is the Law that defines the Divine and clearly demonstrates the spirit, mind, purpose and instruction of the Divine including the operation of the will of the Divine through existence. All authoritative and legitimate Law is derived from Divine Law in accord with the present sacred Maxims. *Divine Law*

86. There exists four simple proofs concerning the dependence of all forms of Ecclesiastical Law upon Divine Law:- *Proofs of Divine Law and Ecclesiastical Law*

    (i) *First*, as the Divine means the "concept of all concepts" and the "set of all sets" there is no greater concept nor set. Therefore any and all forms of Ecclesiastical Law must by definition be considered a Subset; and

    (ii) *Second*, a proper Law must be moral. The highest theoretical or actual possible expression of Moral Law is Divine Law. Therefore, any and all forms of Ecclesiastical Rules and Principles must be considered a Subset of Divine Law; and

    (iii) *Third*, the function and procedure of Law depends on certain concepts, forms and objects including (but not limited to) Persons, Trust, Registers, Rolls and Rights. In each and every case, the highest possible form and definition of such concepts, forms and objects are found in the most Sacred Covenant *Pactum De Singularis Caelum*; and

    (iv) *Fourth*, there is no higher theoretical or actual covenant, constitution, instrument or object of law than the most Sacred Covenant *Pactum De Singularis Caelum*. Therefore all other forms of laws, canons, maxims, constitutions, covenants, charters and agreements are lesser and subject to it.

87. All Rights and therefore all forms of proper Laws and Justice originate from Divine Law and therefore the most sacred Covenant *Pactum De Singularis Caelum*:- *Divine Source of Ecclesiastical Law*

    (i) Divine Law is the law that defines the Divine and all creation, and demonstrates the spirit and mind and instruction of the Divine, and the operation of the will of the Divine Creator through existence. Therefore all valid Rights and Justice are derived from Divine Law; and

(ii) Natural Law is the law that defines the operation of the will of the Divine, through the existence of form and sky and earth and physical rules. Thus Natural Law governs the operation of what we can see and name; and

(iii) Ecclesiastical Law are those rules enacted by Divine Mandate and Covenant having proper authority, for the good governance of a faith under the Rule of Law. The laws of every faith is always inherited from Natural Law and Cognitive Law and ultimately Divine Law.

**88.** As Divine Law is the highest possible form of Law and the source of all lesser forms of law, any argument that asserts Divine Law does not exist, or is less than some other form of law is therefore false, absurd and in gross error.

*Divine Law as highest possible form of Law*

## Article 23 – Ecclesiastical Law & Natural Law

**89.** In accord with Divine Law, all valid Ecclesiastical Law may be said to be derived from authentic Positive Law and thus derived from Natural Law.

*Ecclesiastical Law & Natural Law*

**90.** In accord with Divine Law, Natural Law is the law that defines the operation of the will of the Divine through Existence in the form of all matter and all physical rules. As Natural Laws define the operation and existence of the entire physical universe, all proper and authentic Natural Law may be said to be derived from Divine Law.

*Natural Law*

**91.** In accord with Divine Law, an Ecclesiastical Law cannot abrogate, suspend, nor change a Cognitive Law or Natural Law. Therefore, any rule claimed to be Ecclesiastical Law that usurps, denies or contradicts a Natural Law or Cognitive Law is null and void from the beginning, having no valid or legitimate force or effect whatsoever.

*Limits of Ecclesiastical Law in respect of Natural Law*

## Article 24 – Ecclesiastical Law & Cognitive Law

**92.** In accord with Positive Law, all valid Ecclesiastical Law may be said to be derived from authentic Positive Law and thus derived from Cognitive Law as well as Natural Law.

*Ecclesiastical Law & Cognitive Law*

**93.** In accord with Positive Law, Cognitive Law is the set of laws that define the special attributes possessed by certain higher order life such as mind, ideas, knowledge, recognition and self-awareness

*Cognitive Law*

created through the simultaneous application of both Divine Law and Natural Law. As Cognitive Law is derived from the simultaneous application of Divine Law and Natural Law, all valid Cognitive Law may be defined as part "divine" and part "natural", hence "supernatural".

94. In accord with Positive Law, an Ecclesiastical Law cannot abrogate, suspend, nor change a Cognitive Law. Therefore, any rule claimed to be Ecclesiastical Law that usurps, denies or contradicts a Cognitive Law is null and void from the beginning, having no valid or legitimate force or effect whatsoever.  *Limits of Ecclesiastical Law in respect of Cognitive Law*

## Article 25 – Ecclesiastical Law & Positive Law

95. All valid Ecclesiastical Law may be said to be derived from authentic Positive Law as well as Divine Law.  *Ecclesiastical Law & Positive Law*

96. Positive Law are those authentic Civilised Rules enacted under authority by men and women for the good governance of a Society in accord with the present Maxims and the most sacred Covenant *Pactum De Singularis Caelum*. Valid Positive Law is always inherited from Natural Law and Cognitive Law and ultimately from Divine Law.  *Positive Law*

97. As valid Positive Law is a higher source of Law than Ecclesiastical Law, no rule claiming to be an Ecclesiastical Law can logically or morally abrogate, suspend, nor change a fundamental Positive Law. Therefore, any rule claimed to be Ecclesiastical Law that usurps, denies or contradicts a fundamental Positive Law is null and void from the beginning, having no valid or legitimate force or effect whatsoever.  *Limits of Ecclesiastical Law in respect of Positive Law*

# Title II – Supernatural

## 2.1 – Supernatural

### Article 26 – Supernatural

98. ***Supernatural*** is any Event or Form believed or perceived by the observer to be above or beyond what is understood to be the laws of nature. Perceptions of the *Supernatural* by definition are therefore always subjective and relative to the observer.
<br>*Supernatural*

99. *Supernatural* is equivalent to the modern terms of *Paranormal* and *Preternatural*.
<br>*Paranormal*

100. The term *Supernatural* can only ever be subjective and relative because of its inherit meaning by design:-
<br>*Inherit Subjective and Relative Nature of term Supernatural*

    (i) The term Supernatural from Latin *super-* (above, beyond, or outside of) and *natura* (nature) implies a collection of phenomena that cannot be measured or defined by natural laws. Thus, all Supernatural phenomena must be subjective as they cannot be measured according to known natural laws; and

    (ii) The observance of Supernatural phenomena can only ever be personal and relative, given the rationality and level of competent knowledge of science that the observer possesses. Thus, a person with no knowledge of modern technology or of science would probably regard a wide variety of naturally occurring phenomena and machines on first observation as Supernatural.

101. The term *Supernatural* emerged as a strategy within the Counter-reformation movement during the late 16<sup>th</sup> Century and claimed from earlier heritage, initially in order to strengthen Universal (Catholic) doctrines and authority, not to weaken it:-
<br>*Origin of the term Supernatural and its changing meaning*

    (i) The writings attributed to Thomas Aquinas and his famous work *Summa Theologica*, is generally regarded as the first introduction of the concept of Supernatural into European languages. However, these writings attributed to the 13<sup>th</sup> Century were almost certainly finished in the late 16<sup>th</sup> Century and backdated as part of the Counter Reformation campaign against Protestantism; and

    (ii) Prior to the claimed writings of Thomas Aquinas (probably 16<sup>th</sup> Century not 13<sup>th</sup> Century), there exists no credible evidence in western or eastern language, civilisation or thought of any binary model of "natural" vs "supernatural" phenomena. Thus, sophisticated and intelligent ancient scholars did not regard the concepts of soul, or afterlife any less worthy than the pursuit of greater knowledge on the natural world; and

(iii) It was not until the Enlightenment Movement in the 18th Century and such philosophers as David Hume in his work *"An Enquiry Concerning Human Understanding"* (1748) and Voltair in *"Candide"* (1759) that such thinkers hatched the idea of giving birth to a new religion of the state called *Secularism*, by focusing their attention on weakening traditional religion by corrupting the idea of the Supernatural into being fictitious deception, unreliable misunderstandings and mental delusions; and

(iv) The false religion of Secularism has largely continued to encourage the public marginalisation of the Supernatural, whilst hypocritically and wholeheartedly embracing it as part of their claimed mandate of power and authority up to the present day, including symbols of money, public monuments and deeply occult city and building designs.

102. In accord with the Ucadia Maxims of Law, every observable or measurable event, concept, force or object is subject to the same Universal Laws of Creation. However, due to the fact that both matter and consciousness may belong to different sets (e.g. very small particles vs large particles), the appearance of most of the phenomena classed as Supernatural are possible and legitimate occurrences:- *(Ucadia Law and Supernatural)*

(i) By definition, only Mind through Cognitive Law may exhibit "supernatural" qualities as Cognitive Law is derived from the simultaneous application of Divine Law and Natural Law. Thus the intersection of such consciousness between "Real" and "Unreal" sets is itself a significant contributor to Supernatural phenomena; and

(ii) The intersection of sets of different levels of matter in the Universe also gives rise to a range of phenomena historically regarded as Supernatural.

## 2.2 – Supernatural Dimension

### Article 27 – Supernatural Dimension

103. ***Supernatural Dimension*** refers to a *Set*, *Dimension* or *Aspect* of Existence that lies beyond the observable, natural world and thus not constrained by the ordinary laws of nature – hence it is perceived as beyond nature or "supernatural". It encompasses phenomena and *(Supernatural Dimension)*

entities that are considered to be outside or above the ordinary physical universe.

104. In accord with all Ucadia Maxims, a **Set** is a well defined collection of theoretical or physical Objects or Concepts sharing some similar meanings, attributes or purpose. All Sets may be defined as *Empty, Real, Unreal, Semi-Real, Non-Real or Subset* according to the collection of theoretical or physical Objects or Concepts they contain and their relation to other Sets.

Set

105. In accord with the laws of Sets, *Supernatural Dimension* may be defined as an Unreal Set, relative to the Real Set of laws, concepts and objects of the Physical Universe:-

Supernatural Dimension as a Set of Entities and Phenomena

   (i) An *Unreal Set* (**U**), also known as a "Theoretical Set" is the binary opposite to a Real Set (**R**) that contains Objects or Concepts that do not fully meet the Rules of a Real Set; and

   (ii) A *Semi-Real* Set (**S**) is the intersection Set formed between an intersection of a Real Set and Unreal Set where members of the Unreal Set may interact and influence the Real Set (e.g. as forces), yet have the appearance of being "unreal".

106. All Sets share the same elementary qualities of *Formation, Members, Boundary, Dimension, Relations, Attributes, Computational State, Function, Existence* and *Completion State*:

Shared qualities of all Sets

   (i) *Formation* means all sets are formed by one or more rules as a product of previously existing sets; and

   (ii) *Members* means all sets, except the Empty Set, possess at least one Element as a Member of the set; and

   (iii) *Boundary* means all sets possess a boundary that differentiates them from other sets; and

   (iv) *Dimension* means every Set possesses two dimensional or three dimensional space defined by the boundary of the set and the space between its member elements such that no two member elements occupy the same position and space within the same set; and

   (v) *Relations* means all sets are ultimately a subset of another set except the Empty Set and the Set of One and the Set of Zero; and

   (vi) *Attributes* means every set possesses at least one attribute of meaning that every Member of itself then inherits as well; and

   (vii) *Computational State* means every set may be abstracted as a step in a computational sequence; and

- (viii) *Function* means every set may be abstracted and expressed as a Function and Alphabetic Sequence; and
- (ix) *Existence* means that all sets have been abstracted and observed as Proof of Existence or are being observed by an Observer (as actual Existence) to confirm all the elemental qualities as defined; and
- (x) *Completion State* means that all sets are either complete or incomplete due to the completion of observation of a computational sequence or the incomplete process of observation by the Observer making key elements indeterminable and therefore approximate.

107. In accord with all Ucadia Maxims, **Dimension** is the Position of one or more Theoretical or Real Objects as observed by an Observer, relative to one or more other Theoretical or Real Objects. *[Dimension]*

108. Dimension as a Concept fundamentally depends upon the existence of nine other Elemental Concepts being *Object, Observer, Reality, Rule, Position, Distance, Limit, Existence* and *Proof of Existence*:- *[Dimension as a Concept]*
    - (i) *Object* is any Model perceived, comprehended or discerned by an Observer to exist according to some Model of Reality; and
    - (ii) *Observer* is a Being possessing some level of Awareness in Mind, that actively observes an Object according to some Model of Reality; and
    - (iii) *Reality* is one of a Binary pair of Models constructed upon certain Rules of Form and Meaning, enabling a certain degree of stability necessary for the existence and function of two or more Theoretical or Real Objects; and
    - (iv) *Rule* is any statement applying to a Relation between Objects or Concepts having unique Meaning that can be independently observed and repeated; and
    - (v) *Position* is the unique location of an Object within a Model of Reality; and
    - (vi) *Distance* is the perceived or measured separation and difference between two or more Objects having Position within a Model of Reality; and
    - (vii) *Limit* is a boundary or restriction or constraint between two or more definitive locations, sets, spaces, realities, areas or concepts; and
    - (viii) *Existence* is the present and continuous activity of actual witness of something observed within the Limit of some Model

of Reality; and

(ix) *Proof of Existence* is the action of testimony or other measurable proof given by an Observer of something that was historically observed within a Model of Reality.

109. In general reference to the Concept of Dimension and Sets:- Concept of Dimension and Sets

(i) Dimension as a collection of Things observed is equivalent to an Existing Set; and

(ii) As all Sets possess the attribute of boundary (limit) by virtue of their observation and recognition, Dimension possesses boundary by virtue of the things observed within it; and

(iii) As all Sets are hierarchical, Dimension is hierarchical, meaning one or more lesser Dimensions can exist within a higher Dimension; and

(iv) As all Sets are relative, Dimension is relative, meaning one or more different Dimensions may exist within the same higher level of Dimension; and

(v) Providing a particular Set of Objects belongs to a higher Reality being observed by a higher Observer, it is then theoretically possible to argue that Dimension appears to exist independent of any presence or absence of a lesser Observer; and

(vi) The highest possible form of Dimension is Absolute Dimension; and

(vii) The fact that the complex set of the Universe continues to exist in Dimension without persistent and active observation by lesser Observers is irrefutable proof of the persistent and continuous presence of the Divine as the ultimate Observer of Absolute Existence within Absolute Dimension; and

(viii) Any Theory of Reality that claims Dimension may exist independently of an Observer or Objects observed is therefore an irrefutable endorsement of the existence of the Divine.

110. Any claim or argument that Supernatural Dimension may exist according to an absence of firm rules is false, absurd and a declaration of ignorance and incompetence on part of the claimant or organisation:- Supernatural Dimension and Rules

(i) No form of dimension, no matter how abstract may exist in theory or reality without clear rules; and

(ii) All forms of dimension share similar sets of rules, whilst having unique differences and attributes relative to each other;

and

- (iii) The differences between one "reality" to another may spark the appearance of supernatural, when in fact it is a product of intersecting sets that ultimately each share similar fundamental mathematical rules.

111. Traditional Abrahamic Religious Names for Supernatural Dimensions include (but are not limited to):-

    - (i) **Heaven**: A divine realm where God resides and where righteous souls go after death; and

    - (ii) **Paradise**: A blissful, eternal afterlife for the faithful and righteous; and

    - (iii) **Purgatory**: An intermediate state where souls undergo purification before entering heaven; and

    - (iv) **Hell**: A place of divine punishment and suffering for the wicked after death.

*Traditional Abrahamic Religious Names for Supernatural Dimension*

112. Traditional Hindu Religious Names for Supernatural Dimensions include (but are not limited to):-

    - (i) **Svarga (Swarga)**: Often referred to as heaven, Svarga is a heavenly realm where righteous souls go after death. It is a place of pleasure and delight, ruled by Indra, the king of the gods; and

    - (ii) **Brahmaloka**: Also known as Satyaloka, Brahmaloka is the highest realm in the universe, the abode of Lord Brahma, the creator. It is a place of ultimate enlightenment and knowledge; and

    - (iii) **Goloka**: The supreme abode of Lord Krishna, Goloka is often depicted as a place of infinite beauty and joy, filled with divine pastimes and love; and

    - (iv) **Maharloka**: A higher plane of existence where great sages and saints reside. It is a place of deep spiritual practice and penance; and

    - (v) **Janarloka**: Another higher realm, Janarloka is the abode of enlightened beings who have transcended material existence but have not yet reached the highest state of liberation; and

    - (vi) **Yamaloka**: The abode of Yama, the god of death. It is where souls go to be judged based on their karma before being sent to their next destination; and

    - (vii) **Patalaloka (Nagaloka)**: The netherworld or underworld,

*Traditional Hindu Religious Names for Supernatural Dimension*

Patalaloka is inhabited by Nagas (serpent beings) and other mystical creatures. It is ruled by Vasuki, the serpent king.

113. Traditional Buddhist Religious Names for Supernatural Dimensions include (but are not limited to):-

    (i) ***Nirvana (Nibbana)***: The ultimate state of liberation and freedom from the cycle of birth and rebirth (samsara). It is characterized by the cessation of suffering and the extinguishing of desire, ignorance, and attachment; and

    (ii) ***Tusita***: One of the heavenly realms in Buddhist cosmology, it is the abode of the Bodhisattvas before their final birth as a Buddha. Maitreya, the future Buddha, is said to reside here; and

    (iii) ***Devaloka***: The realms of the gods, also known as heavenly realms. There are multiple Devalokas, each corresponding to different levels of existence and spiritual attainment; and

    (iv) ***Brahmaloka***: The realms inhabited by Brahmas, beings of great purity and spiritual attainment. These realms are associated with the higher states of meditative absorption (jhanas); and

    (v) ***Pretaloka***: The realm of hungry ghosts, beings who suffer from insatiable hunger and thirst due to their past greed and attachments; and

    (vi) ***Narakaloka***: The realms of hell, where beings experience intense suffering due to their past negative actions. These realms are not eternal and beings can be reborn in higher realms after their negative karma is exhausted.

*Traditional Buddhist Religious Names for Supernatural Dimension*

114. Ancient Religious Names for Supernatural Dimensions include (but are not limited to):-

    (i) **Otherworld**: (Celtic Faith) A supernatural realm of gods and the dead; and

    (ii) **Elysium**: (Ancient Greek Faith) The final resting place of the souls of the heroic and the virtuous; and

    (iii) **Valhalla**: (Norse Faith) A majestic hall where warriors slain in battle are taken by Valkyries; and

    (iv) **Du'at**: (Ancient Egyptian Faith) The realm of the dead, ruled by Osiris; and

    (v) **Spirit World**: (Indigenous cultures worldwide) A realm inhabited by spirits, ancestors and deities.

*Ancient Religious Names for Supernatural Dimension*

115. Modern Spiritual Names for Supernatural Dimensions include (but are not limited to):-

    (i) **Summerland**: (Wicca and Neopaganism) An idyllic afterlife for souls to rest and prepare for reincarnation; and

    (ii) **Astral Plane**: (Theosophy and Occult Traditions) A non-physical plane of existence where spirits and astral bodies reside; and

    (iii) **Afterlife**: (Holistic Sciences and Philosophy) A non-physical dimension of existence after the death of the physical body where our essence and personality continues to exist and interact with others; and

    (iv) **Fifth Dimension**: (New Age spirituality) A higher level of consciousness and existence beyond the physical and astral planes, characterized by unconditional love, unity and enlightenment; and

    (v) **Light Realms**: (New Age spirituality) Higher vibrational realms of existence where beings of light, such as angels, ascended masters, and other spiritual entities reside; and

    (vi) **Quantum Field**: (Quantum mysticism) An underlying field of energy and potential that connects everything in the universe, associated with manifesting reality through intention and consciousness; and

    (vii) **Divine Matrix**: (Gregg Braden, New Age spirituality) An interconnecting field of energy that permeates all of creation, linking everything in a web of consciousness.

## Article 28 – Afterlife

116. **Afterlife** also known as the *Hereafter*, is a term defining the belief and existence of life after death. It is equivalent to the term Heaven or Paradise.

117. In accordance with these Maxims, the Universe and therefore Life is a Dream in Motion according to defined rules known as Natural Law. As Life is a Dream being Unique Collective Awareness in motion, no thought, nor experience, nor mind can ever die.

## Article 29 – Heaven

118. ***Heaven*** is a term that defines three key concepts in one: firstly, the existence of a supernatural dimension beyond the physical world, secondly, a specific sub-segment of this supernatural dimension in which beings exist in a state of harmony and paradise and thirdly a state of being of physical existence in harmony with others and nature equivalent to paradise.

119. In reference to the meaning of Heaven:-
    (i) In the first instance of meaning, the term Heaven is equivalent to ancient terms such as Aaru, Ades, Elysium, Sheol and Mag Mell defining a unified universal plain in which the spirits of deceased men and women co-exist (in peace) with other supernatural beings such as deities; and
    (ii) In the second instance of meaning, the term Heaven is equivalent to ancient terms such as Paradise and Valhalla defining a unified universal plain in which the spirits of deceased men and women co-exist in peace with other supernatural beings in a state of harmony and paradise; and
    (iii) In the third instance of meaning, the term Heaven is applied to the Earth, or "heaven on earth", it implying a place where men and women co-exist in peace with other life and nature in a state of harmony and paradise.

120. One Heaven is formed by a formal treaty between all major and minor heavens and all the major deities and spirits. Every man, woman and higher order spirit that has ever existed has an absolute right to enter Heaven.

121. Any Spiritual Faith, Religion or Cult that places conditions upon the entry into Heaven, including judging who may or may not enter is in direct violation of Divine Law, Natural Law and Positive Law. Therefore, such claims or doctrines are immediately null and void from the beginning, having no effect nor force.

## Article 30 – Hell

122. ***Hell*** is an Abrahamic Religious term for a Spiritual Dimension where many Christians, Muslims and Jews believe souls are subjected to Divinely ordained and orchestrated punitive suffering, most often through torture as punishment.

123. In accord with the Divine Creator of all Existence and Ucadia Law, Hell is condemned as a heretical, blasphemous, insane and absurd

notion, prohibited to be continued or to be promoted:-

    (i)    Hell directly implies the insane and absurd notion that "God" is both psychotic and a sadist, who is more interested in micro-managing the eternal punishment of human souls than helping humans and the Universe; and

    (ii)    The absurd and wicked notion reveals the truth that such denominations, sects, movements and cults who promote the notion of Hell worship a lesser deity or demon proclaiming to be "God" and not the ultimate creator of the Universe.

## Article 31 – Purgatory

**124.** ***Purgatory*** is an Abrahamic Religious term for a Spiritual Dimension where many Christians, Muslims and Jews believe souls are subjected to Divinely ordained and orchestrated punitive suffering, most often through torture as punishment.

**125.** *Purgatory* is an intentional and knowingly false, deceptive and misleading concept in the 16th Century through the intentional and wilful corruption of the 8th Century Carolingian notion of *purgatorium* (cleaning and purification) to imply a period of forced suffering, pain and torture of the innocent and good in a waiting-place by "God" before they are permitted to enter Heaven.

**126.** In accord with the Divine Creator of all Existence and Ucadia Law, Purgatory is condemned as a heretical, blasphemous, insane and absurd notion, prohibited to be continued or to be promoted:-

    (i)    Purgatory directly implies the insane and absurd notion that "God" is both cruel and a hypocrite who does not really forgive; and who is more interested in micro-managing the ongoing suffering of human souls than helping humans and the Universe; and

    (ii)    Purgatory directly contradicts the notion of Absolution of transgressions and calls into question either the validity of such teachings or the promises of the lesser deity that is claimed made them; and

    (iii)    The absurd and wicked notion reveals the truth that such denominations, sects, movements and cults who promote the notion of Purgatory worship a lesser deity or demon proclaiming to be "God" and not the ultimate creator of the Universe.

## 2.3 – Supernatural Being

### Article 32 – Supernatural Being

127. A ***Supernatural Being*** is an *Ethereal Being* and a specific embodiment of Unique Collective Awareness existing within an intersecting set of Unreal and Real, whereby to the Real Set the Being appears as a force without form, but in the intersecting set such a Being possesses a material existence in accord with the Standard Model of the Universe. The Conscious Mind itself of a Sentient Being or Sapient Being is such an example of an Ethereal Being. *— Supernatural Being*

128. A ***Being*** is an embodiment of Unique Collective Awareness and a Computational Model according to the Standard Rules of Existence as applied to a certain Reality. *— Being*

129. All Beings may be defined as *Divine, Ethereal* or *Living*:- *— Types of Beings*

    (i) A ***Divine Being*** is a specific embodiment of Unique Collective Awareness existing within a collective "abstracted" and Unreal Set or "Divine Reality" distinct from a dependent set of Reality necessary for material existence within the Standard Model of the Universe; and

    (ii) An ***Ethereal Being*** is a specific embodiment of Unique Collective Awareness existing within an intersecting set of Unreal and Real, whereby to the Real Set the Being appears as a force without form, but in the intersecting set such a Being possesses a material existence in accord with the Standard Model of the Universe. The Conscious Mind itself of a Sentient Being or Sapient Being is such an example of an Ethereal Being; and

    (iii) A ***Living Being*** is a specific embodiment of Unique Collective Awareness existing within Reality according to the Rules of the Standard Model of the Universe.

130. All sets of Beings may be defined according to ten categories being *Supreme, Primary, Higher, Ordinary, Ethereal, Material, Cellular, Sentient, Sapient* and *Imaginary*:- *— Categories of Beings*

    (i) The *Supreme Being* is the formal name for the Divine as the Divine Observer and Divine Creator of all Existence as a singular Object or Set of all being and all possible objects, concepts, matter, rules, life, mind, universes, forces, sets or awareness; and

    (ii) A *Primary Being* is a Living, Ethereal and Divine Being as a Primary Observer and singular Object or Set of all possible objects, concepts, matter, rules, life, mind, forces, sets or awareness at a particular key level of Matter and Existence (i.e. universe, galaxy, star, planet, life or species); and

(iii) A *Higher Being* is a Divine Being as a collective Consciousness and Being representing an essential stable character and attribute of a Primary Being, particularly as it applies to the presence of Cellular Beings and multiple species of Sentient and Sapient Beings within the jurisdiction and dimension of such a Primary Being; and

(iv) An *Ordinary Being* is an individual Divine Being formed either by virtue of the operation of Divine Law or the journey and transition of the Ethereal Being (Sentience or Sapience) of a previously Living Being; and

(v) An *Ethereal Being* in the context of such categorisation is narrowed to be the Computation Model of Mind of Sentient Beings and Sapient Beings that are Living or in transition to Divine after death of the Living Being; and

(vi) A *Material Being* is a Living Being in the form of all physical matter at a Unita, Super Sub Atomic, Sub Atomic, Atomic and Molecular Level; and

(vii) A *Cellular Being* is a unique Living Being from the perspective of a unique single cell, whether or not it is part of a body of a complex species or singular cellular life then viewed as a part of the greater universe of all cellular life on a planet; and

(viii) A *Sentient Being* is a unique Living and Ethereal Being as a member of a species of Level 5 (Complex Multi-Cellular Life); and

(ix) A *Sapient Being* is a unique Living and Ethereal Being as a member of a species of Level 6 (Higher Order Life); and

(x) An *Imaginary Being* is an Ethereal Being from the individual or collective imagination and minds of Sapient Beings that by constant reinforcement and thinking is given its own existence and reality.

## Article 33 – Supreme Being

131. In accord with the Maxims of Divine Law, the **Supreme Being**, is the formal name for the Divine as the Divine Observer and Divine Creator of all Existence as a singular Object or Set of all possible objects, concepts, matter, rules, life, mind, universes, forces, sets or awareness.

*Supreme Being*

132. The Supreme Being is equivalent to the valid term Unique Collective Awareness when describing the Divine Creator as the greatest, most perfect dimension and existence.

*Supreme Being and Unique Collective Awareness*

133. As the Supreme Being means the Divine and therefore the "concept of all concepts" and the "set of all sets", there is no greater concept or set of objects. Therefore, every other possible concept or object or set is lesser than the Supreme Being.

*No higher Being*

## Article 34 – Primary Being

134. In accord with the Maxims of Divine Law, a **Primary Being** is a Living, Ethereal and Divine Being as a Primary Observer and singular Object or Set of all possible objects, concepts, matter, rules, life, mind, forces, sets or awareness at a particular key level of Matter and Existence.

*Primary Being*

135. In respect of Primary Beings:-

    (i) All Primary Beings are a subset of the Supreme Being and therefore less than the Supreme Being. No Primary Being can be theoretically or actually greater than the Supreme Being; and

    (ii) All Primary Beings exist as a Primary Observer and Primary Creator as a singular Object or Set of all possible objects, concepts, matter, rules, life, mind, forces, sets or awareness at a particular key level of Matter and Existence; and

    (iii) Except for the Supreme Being, Primary Beings are unique in existence among other Beings as a tripartite embodiment of a Divine Being, Ethereal Being and Living Being as one.

*General References to Primary Being*

## Article 35 – Universal Being

136. In accord with the Maxims of Divine Law, a **Universal Being** is a Living, Ethereal and Divine Being as a Primary Observer and singular Object and Set of all possible objects, concepts, matter, rules, life, mind, forces, sets or awareness within the Universe as a singularity.

*Universal Being*

137. In respect of The Universal Being:-

    (i) The Universal Being is founded upon the ultimate Real Set of Unita and then the unique collective awareness of all Unita as the abstracted and Unreal "Ideal" Set. Thus, the Universal Being may also be named as Unitas in honour of the collective dream of all Unita; and

    (ii) While there are many sub-verses, there is only one Universe

*General Reference to Universal Being*

and only one Unitas as the Universal Being; and

(iii) The Universal Being as Unitas is equivalent to the ultimate Object in comparison to the Supreme Being as the ultimate Observer; and

(iv) The Ethereal Being of the Unitas (the dream of a dream) may be called Kosmos when projecting more complex forms of matter; and

(v) All other Primary Beings are a member of the Universal Being and Kosmos.

## Article 36 – Galactic Being

138. In accord with the Maxims of Divine Law, a **Galactic Being** is a complex Living, Ethereal and Divine Being as a Primary Observer of its own Set of stars, matter, concepts, rules, life, mind, forces and awareness within the Sub Atomic Universe as a singular Object and body.

    *Galactic Being*

139. In respect of a Galactic Being:-

    *General Reference to Galactic Being*

    (i) All Galactic Beings exist simultaneously within the sub-verse of Super Sub Atomic Matter of the Kosmos as a Divine Being; and a Sub Atomic sub-verse as a Living Galactic Being; and an Atomic sub-verse as an Ethereal Being; and

    (ii) As a Living Being, the building blocks of Galactic Life are Stars, similar to Cells of a multi-cellular organism, whereby Stars form permanent or semi-permanent relations with one another, within larger fixed or semi-fixed structures, similar to organs, that then change position as one cohesive body; and

    (iii) As a Computational Model representing an Ethereal Being of Mind, a Galaxy possesses the necessary computational abilities many trillions upon trillions of times greater than an individual member or a Higher Order Species, in order to function at such massive distances and coordinated forces; and

    (iv) In reality, Galaxies should not be possible if the laws of Gravity, Matter and Forces were to be applied without consideration to complex multi-dimensional considerations. Thus, the presence of a Divine Galactic Being is vital to enable the existence of a Galaxy whereby sub-atomic matter from the perspective of a Galaxy performs virtually instantaneous and constant changes to enable the Galaxy to still exist.

# Article 37 – GAL

**140.** In accord with the Maxims of Divine Law, **GAL** is the Unique Collective Divine Spirit of all super sub atomic elements and all stars and all life and consciousness representing all matter and awareness of the Milky Way Galaxy as a Primary Being.  
*GAL*

**141.** The Divine Spirit of GAL is part of the greater collective spirit of KOSMOS, that is part of the greater collective spirit of UNITAS, that is then part of the greater collective Divine Spirit of ALL.  
*GAL and KOSMOS*

**142.** GAL is the proper name and greater name of the Milky Way in respect and recognition of the Galaxy as a Primary Being and Divine, Living and Ethereal Being; and unified whole of all the stars, all the gases, all the planets, all the life, all the self-aware life within the galaxy and the galaxy as one living entity.  
*GAL as proper name of Milky Way Galaxy as Being*

**143.** GAL memory is the memory of the unique existence of the Milky Way and memory of unique position, change, seasons of life and seasons of death. GAL memory is eternal.  
*GAL memory*

**144.** GAL Reason is everything manifest in the Milky Way. Everything in the Milky Way happens for a reason and purpose. Everything in the Milky Way has meaning. Nothing in the Milky Way has no-purpose. The smallest of objects has a unique and absolute purpose.  
*GAL Reason*

# Article 38 – Stellar Being

**145.** In accord with the Maxims of Divine Law, a **Stellar Being** is a complex Living, Ethereal and Divine Being as a Primary Observer of its own Set of planets, concepts, rules, life, mind, forces and awareness within the complex Atomic Universe of a Galaxy as a singular Object and body.  
*Stellar Being*

**146.** In respect of a Stellar Being:-  
*General Reference to Stellar Being*

    (i) All Stellar Beings exist simultaneously within a sub-verse of Sub Atomic Matter of Galactic Mind as a Divine Being; and an Atomic sub-verse as a Living Stellar Being; and a Molecular sub-verse as an Ethereal Being; and

    (ii) As a Living Being, the building blocks of Galactic Life are Stars, similar to Cells of a multi-cellular organism, whereby Stars form permanent or semi-permanent relations with one another, within larger fixed or semi-fixed structures, similar to organs, that then change position as one cohesive body; and

    (iii) Furthermore, as a Living Being, the building blocks of Stellar Life are Ergon Fields, Molecular Fields, Planets, Planetoids and Meteoroids, similar to a family of multi-cellular organisms, whereby Stars form a protected environment within themselves for complex molecular structures culminating in cellular or "life" bearing planets or planetoids as a feature of Stellar Life throughout each and virtually every Galaxy; and

(iv) As a Computational Model representing an Ethereal Being of Mind, a Star possesses the necessary computational abilities many trillions of times greater than an individual member or a Higher Order Species, in order to function at such massive distances and coordinated forces.

## Article 39 – SOL

147. In accord with the Maxims of Divine Law, **SOL** is the unique collective Divine Spirit of all atomic and molecular elements, life and awareness of our Solar System and Sun as a Primary Being. — SOL

148. The Divine Spirit of SOL is part of the greater collective spirit of GAL, that is part of the greater collective spirit of KOSMOS, that is part of the greater collective spirit of UNITAS, that is then part of the greater collective Divine Spirit of ALL. — SOL and GAL and KOSMOS

149. SOL is the proper name and greater name of the Solar System in respect and recognition of the unified whole of all the planets, all the gases, all the moons, meteorites and asteroid belts, the Sun, all the life, all the self-aware life within the Solar System and the Solar System as a Divine Being, Living Being and Ethereal Being. — SOL as proper name of Sun as Conscious Being

150. SOL memory is the memory of the unique existence of the Solar System and memory of unique position, change, seasons of life and seasons of death. SOL memory is eternal. — SOL memory

151. The position of planets within the SOL is not simply mechanical, but will of the SOL. If the Sun chose it to be so, the planet Earth could be destroyed in an instant. Yet the Sun chooses of its own free will to value the life, awareness and existence of the planet Earth like a mother to a new born child. — Active nature of SOL

152. As SOL continues to demonstrate active intelligent will to protect the Earth from great harm, any belief system founded on rules and laws implying negative intent upon the Earth by the Solar System are false and null and void *ab initio* (from the beginning). — False attributes against SOL

## Article 40 – Planetary Being

153. In accord with the Maxims of Divine Law, a ***Planetary Being*** is a complex Living, Ethereal and Divine Being as a Primary Observer of its own Set of planetoids, meteoroids, electromagnetic fields, atmosphere, life, mind, forces and awareness within the complex Molecular Universe of a Star as a singular Object and body.

*Planetary Being*

154. In respect of a Planetary Being:-

    (i) All Planetary Beings exist simultaneously within a sub-verse of Atomic Matter of Stellar Mind as a Divine Being; and an Molecular sub-verse as a Living Planetary Being; and a Material or Cellular Life sub-verse as an Ethereal Being; and

    (ii) The formation of large bodied Hydrogen Planets and Iron Planets are a natural consequence of Stellar Formation from collapsing Nebula. Therefore, notwithstanding Stars undergoing the end of their life before collapse, the presence of at least one or more planets should be found in most Stellar models throughout the Universe; and

    (iii) Even if a Star has ceased to function as a standard Hydrogen model, but has progressed in life to a different state (i.e. Red Giant), large bodied Hydrogen Planets throughout the Universe typically possess at least one or more Planetoid that upon the right conditions may support the formation of complex molecular structures such as amino acids and ultimately cellular life; and

    (iv) As a Living Being, the building blocks of Planetary Life are Molecular Fields and Oceans, whereby Planets form stable environments for the support of complex and irregular shaped Molecular Polymers, even if conditions do not make the formation of cellular life possible; and

    (v) As a Computational Model representing an Ethereal Being of Mind, a Planet even without cellular life possesses the necessary computational abilities many millions of times greater than an individual member or a Higher Order Species, in order to function complex chemical and electro-magnetic formations; and

    (vi) As a Computational Model representing an Ethereal Being of Mind, a Planet possessing abundant cellular life possesses the necessary computational abilities many trillions upon trillions of times greater than an individual member or a Higher Order Species, in order to function highly complex chemical, electro-

*General Reference to Planetary Being*

magnetic and biological formations.

## Article 41 – GAIA

155. In accord with the Maxims of Divine Law, **GAIA** is the unique collective Divine Spirit of all atomic elements and awareness of the Planet Earth.  
*GAIA*

156. The spirit of GAIA is part of the greater collective spirit of SOL, that is part of the greater collective spirit of GAL, that is part of the greater collective spirit of KOSMOS, that is part of the greater collective spirit of UNITAS, that is then part of the greater collective Divine Spirit of ALL.  
*GAIA and SOL and GAL*

157. The stability of conditions upon the surface of the planet Earth is not simply mechanical, but according to the will of GAIA. If GAIA so chose, then great regions of the surface could be rendered uninhabitable, but instead chooses by free will to care for life, nurture and protect life.  
*Active consciouness of GAIA*

158. As GAIA continues to demonstrate active intelligent will to protect the life and higher order life upon the surface of the Earth from great harm, any belief system founded on rules and laws implying negative intent upon the life on Earth by the GAIA are false and null and void ab initio (from the beginning).  
*False attributes against GAIA*

159. As GAIA is personified by Molecular Oceans and Fields, it is entirely appropriate to use the ancient name of Mari or Mary to describe GAIA as the Mother of all Life on planet Earth and even the Mother of God when represented by a Singularity of the Homo Sapien Species.  
*GAIA and customary term for Seas*

## Article 42 – Cellular Being

160. In accord with the Maxims of Divine Law, a **Cellular Being** is a complex Living, Ethereal and Divine Being as a Primary Observer of its own Set of mono-cellular, multi-cellular and advanced cellular species, minds, life, ecosystems and awareness within the complex Molecular Universe of a Planet as a singular Object and body.  
*Cellular Being*

161. In respect of a Cellular Being:-  
*General Reference to Cellular Being*

    (i) All Cellular Beings exist simultaneously within a sub-verse of Molecular Mind of a Planet as a Divine Being; and an Cellular sub-verse as a Living Conscious Being; and a sub-verse as an Ethereal Being; and

    (ii) The primary conscious focus of a Cellular Being is to sustain and grow the conditions for life; and to reduce risks against the cessation of life, within its ability to alter micro-climate controls within its power. Therefore, the demonstration of the consciousness of a Living Cellular Being is to be found most significantly within life sustaining Molecular Oceans and secondly within ecosystems.

## Article 43 – CORPUS

162. In accord with the Maxims of Divine Law, **CORPUS** is the unique collective Divine Spirit of cellular elements, mind and awareness of planet Earth. — CORPUS

163. The Divine Spirit of CORPUS is part of the greater collective spirit of GAIA, that is part of the greater collective spirit of SOL, that is part of the greater collective spirit of GAL, that is part of the greater collective spirit of KOSMOS, that is part of the greater collective spirit of UNITAS, that is then part of the greater collective Divine Spirit of ALL. — CORPUS and GAIA and SOL

164. The stability of bacterial and viral infections around the earth is not simply mechanical and predictable biology, but according to the collective free will of all single cellular life as CORPUS. If CORPUS so desired, all higher order life could be destroyed through bacterial and viral infection in months. Instead, CORPUS honours higher order life and life in general. — Conscious intentions of CORPUS

## Article 44 – Animal Being

165. In accord with the Maxims of Divine Law, an **Animal Being** is a complex Living, Ethereal and Divine Being as a Primary Observer of its own Set of sentient or sapient beings and awareness within the complex Molecular Universe of a Planet as a singular Object and body. An Animal Being is the singularity of a particular species. — Animal Being

166. In respect of an Animal Being:- — General Reference to Animal Being

    (i) All Animal Beings exist simultaneously within a sub-verse of Cellular (Corpus) Mind of a Planet as a Divine Being; and a Species sub-verse as a Living Conscious Being; and a sub-verse as an Ethereal Being of a collective conscious reality of the species; and

    (ii) An Animal Being as the Primary Being of a Sentient Animal is its singular memory, identity and ideal.

## Article 45 – ANIMUS

167. In accord with the Maxims of Divine Law, **ANIMUS** is the unique collective Divine Spirit of all vertebrate complex species life that currently exists and has ever existed on planet Earth.  
*ANIMUS*

168. The Divine Spirit of ANIMUS is part of the greater collective spirit of CORPUS, that is part of the greater collective spirit of GAIA, that is part of the greater collective spirit of SOL, that is part of the greater collective spirit of GAL, that is part of the greater collective spirit of KOSMOS, that is part of the greater collective spirit of UNITAS, that is then part of the greater collective Divine Spirit of ALL.  
*ANIMUS and CORPUS and GAIA*

## Article 46 – Sapient Singularity

169. In accord with the Maxims of Divine Law, a **Sapient Singularity** is a complex Living, Ethereal and Divine Being as a Primary Observer of not only its own Set of knowledge and awareness within the complex Molecular, Cellular and Species Universe of a Planet as a singular Object and body, but its place within the Kosmos and connection to the Divine.  
*Sapient Singularity*

170. In respect of a Sapient Singularity:-  
*General Reference to Sapient Singularity*

   (i)   All Sapient Singularities exist simultaneously within a sub-verse of Species Mind of an Ancestry as a Divine Being; and a Societal sub-verse as a Living Conscious Being; and a sub-verse as an Ethereal Being of a collective conscious reality of Divine Truth; and

   (ii)  While a Sapient Singularity possesses vastly less computation power in Reality, they possess the unique ability from incarnation into flesh of being able to synthesise Divine Truth into Revelation; and

   (iii) Thus, a Sapient Singularity to their full potential represents a Transcendent and Immanent Being made flesh and the personification of Perfect-Imperfection (i.e. Pi) and the ultimate Paradox of Divine Existence; and

   (iv)  As a Primary Being, a Sapient Singularity is able to alter the collective consciousness of its respective Sapient Species, by representing all minds and all experiences embodied in one form; and

   (v)   However, a Sapient Singularity will always be limited in their abilities to transcend societal realities to vision and comprehend Divine Truths depending upon their conditioning in society and degree of comfort. Therefore, a Sapient Singularity is as much likely to produce dangerous semi-truths or lacklustre conclusions as any other Sapient member of a species, if they have been strongly conditioned to conform; and

(vi) In truth, Sapient Singularity can be a catalyst for disaster in the promotion of half-finished philosophies as much as they can be a catalyst for positive change, unless such knowledge is born from conditions of austerity, humility and great personal sacrifice.

171. In relation to the general purpose and frequency of Sapient Singularities:- *Purpose of Sapient Singularities*

(i) The purposes of authentic Sapient Singularities are to provide a conscious "re-set" of a species; and the consolidation of accumulated knowledge; and a reduction in the risk of extinction of a species; and

(ii) The purposes of authentic Sapient Singularities is not to usurp established forms of leadership of a species, nor to assume a leadership function, as true Sapien Singularities do not appear as Divine administrators.

172. In relation to Sapient Singularities and other Cellular Beings of a species:- *Sapient Singularities and Cellular Beings of Species*

(i) All Sentient Cellular Beings of a species are Divine, thus all Cellular Beings, including a Sapient Singularity are equal before the Divine at a species level; and

(ii) All Sentient Cellular Beings of a species are limited by the same restraints of Cellular Life as all other members of the Sentient Cellular Species and do not possess any supernatural power greater than another member of the species except consciousness and authentic revelation.

173. In relation to the frequency of Sapient Singularities:- *Frequency of Sapient Singularities*

(i) Sapient Singularity are an extreme rarity within any Sapient species, occurring less than one out of many dozens of generations; and

(ii) The appearance and frequency of authentic Sapient Singularities is in direct relation to the levels of fractured (misaligned) knowledge of a species and the risk of extinction of a species; and

(iii) The appearance of an authentic Sapient Singularity does not imply any form of success in terms of the purpose of such appearance, as the free will and circumstances of the cellular embodiment means potentially a greater risk of failure than success; and

(iv) By the nature of the abilities of authentic Sapient Singularities, there is a higher risk that some may accelerate fractured knowledge and risk of extinction rather than assist, unless such abilities are tempered with genuine failure, humiliation, suffering, poverty and self reflection; and

(v) Whilst the purposes of Sapient Singularities is to assist a species, the frequency of authentic Sapient Singularities achieving their mission is so rare as to be less than a handful across the entire evolutionary history of a species.

**174.** In relation to the general characteristics of authentic Sapient Singularities:- *General Characteristics of Authentic Sapient Singularities*

(i) Authentic Sapient Singularities do not come to assume the function of administrators or leaders but the bringers of knowledge. Therefore Authentic Sapient Singularities are rarely born to a bloodline of a species currently in positions of power or leadership; and

(ii) Authentic Sapient Singularities do come into cellular existence to assist in the unification of knowledge. Therefore those bloodlines that represent ancient keepers of authentic knowledge, but exiled or struck from power are more likely to be favoured, as such cellular memory of the body retains a great deal of residual information to assist the authentic Sapient Singularity; and

(iii) Authentic Sapient Singularities do appear in congruence with authentic revelation. However, such prophecy or relevation may not be immediately apparent, especially given prophecies of Sapient Singularities develop their own doctrines and interpretations that may have been distorted over time, causing actual revelations to be missed or ignored; and

(iv) Authentic Sapient Singularities bring forth authentic revelation, meaning an expansion of knowledge, never a reinforcement of status quo or narrow thinking. This is one of the clearest distinctions between an authentic Sapient Singularity and an impostor, when an impostor simply regurgitates a pseudo form of revelation attempting to reinforce stereotypes and orthodoxy; and

(v) Authentic Sapient Singularities are frequently flawed cellular beings and especially failures in being able at first to bring forth authentic revelation. Such failure, humiliation, suffering and pain is not only a frequent element of prophecy, but a necessary "fail safe" of the Divine to reduce the danger of an authentic Sapient Singularity delivering knowledge that harms a species and its existence, rather than assists.

175. Impostor Sapient Singularities are cellular beings of a species that falsely proclaim themselves to be a Sapient Singularity:- *Impostor Sapient Singularities*

   (i) Frequently historic prophecy and scripture of the arrival of a Sapient Singularity creates an irresistible prize for certain personality types of cellular beings to crave such appearance of power or authority. Such mental illness may be described as "messiah syndrome"; and

   (ii) Political, religious and military leaders of a cellular species may find it expedient to falsely proclaim themselves to be a Sapient Singularity to strengthen their claims of power or authority; and

   (iii) External events of a planet or ecosystem may cause greater levels of fear and uncertainty of the future, pushing religious, political and military leaders to proclaim a false Sapient Singularity, to maintain a status quo and reduce rebellion or levels of anxiety.

176. The general characteristics for exposing impostor Sapient Singularities include (but are not limited to):- *General Characteristics of Impostor Sapient Singularities*

   (i) By definition any religious, political or military leader who proclaims themselves a Sapient Singularity is an impostor; and

   (ii) Any claimed Sapient Singularity that delivers alleged revelation that reinforces established religious and cultural orthodoxy, status quo and customs without greatly challenging or expanding knowledge or consciousness; and

   (iii) Any claimed Sapient Singularity that is deemed credible and believed upon education, credentials, position or following, as such traits contradict the "fail safe" signs of the Divine; and

   (iv) Any claimed Sapient Singularity that claims to fulfil an orthodox and established doctrinal interpretation of significant and historic prophecy; and

   (v) Any claimed Sapient Singularity that appears without any form of context or reference to the genuine fulfilment of prophecy (as opposed to any established orthodoxy or doctrine concerning certain prophecy); and

(vi) Any claimed Sapient Singularity that is without blemish, or failure, or humiliation or suffering, as the Divine always seeks to temper such responsibilities with these life experiences.

## Article 47 – Saviour (Spirit)

177. In accord with the Maxims of Divine Law, a **Saviour** is the unique collective Divine Spirit, the Primary Being and Sapient Singularity of the Homo Sapien species that has ever existed or will ever exist upon planet Earth, instanced into a Living Being at a point in time. — Saviour

178. A Saviour as a Sapient Singularity of the Homo Sapien species is also historically known by other terms including (but not limited to): Christ, Messiah, Mahdi and Maitreya. — Names of Saviour

179. As a Hero, a Saviour frequently must first fall from favour and respect within the community they ultimately save. This might be by their own actions, the actions and belief of others, or both. Thus a Saviour must first become an outcast. — Saviour as Hero

180. In accordance with the most ancient beliefs of all Religions and Cults, the most significant sign and tool provided by a Saviour to help save people and conquer danger is divinely inspired knowledge rather than force. In other words, the hallmark of a valid Saviour is the knowledge and ideas they bring that are powerful enough to withstand the physical obstinacy of evil. — Function of Saviour

181. A Saviour is considered a *Sovereign Claim* or *Sovereign Mandate* via *Sovereign Rule by Revelation* whereby a "flesh and blood" person is proclaimed through self-evident signs, attributes and qualifications that they are a Divine Saviour sent from Heaven to Earth:- — Saviour as a Sovereign Claim or Mandate

   (i) The Claim of Divine Saviour is one of the oldest methods of claiming supreme sovereign authority and power from the beginning of Human Civilisation; and

   (ii) Almost every civilisation and culture has had a Divine Saviour such as the Akkadians who worshipped Adad, the Sumerians who worshipped Ishkur, the early Babylonians who worshipped Hadad, the ancient Egyptians who worshipped Horus, the early Greeks had Adonis, the Phrygians (Turkey and Syria) who worshipped Attis, the Persians and colonies who worshipped Mithra and the Celts who worshipped Esus (later listed as Jesus); and

   (iii) Within the faiths of Christianity, Islam, Judaism, Buddhism, Hinduism and many other faiths, the Rank and Title of *Divine*

*Saviour* (or by some other specific cultural Title), is unquestionably accepted as the highest of all sovereign authority and power; and

(iv) Many of these same cultures have recognised in the oldest forms of law the fact that the legitimate appearance of a Divine Saviour matching the specific cultural context requires all followers of a particular faith to acknowledge and obey the authority and direction of the Divine Saviour; and

(v) The primary meaning and nature of "Saviour" is literally one who saves, as the architect of a new civilisation restoring the rule of law, as opposed to a tyrant or despot or impostor.

182. The generally "universal" major qualification of any authentic Divine Saviour to represent the Architect of a New Civilisation deserves particular attention as it is arguably the most difficult sign to "fake":- *[Architect of New Civilisation]*

(i) All functioning and major civilisations were built from complex and detailed models requiring many tens of thousands of integrated concepts, models and systems across many hundreds or thousands of texts; and

(ii) A single document, even if a thousand pages in length, is still a "placeholder" for a model of civilisation and not the detailed blueprint any authentic Divine Saviour is supposed to deliver; and

(iii) Because such a major qualification is technically the most difficult, time consuming and complex qualification of any authentic Divine Saviour, it also happens to be the sign argued as least important or "promised will be delivered in the future" by impostors and false Divine Saviours.

183. By definition, the most significant proof of a Saviour is by the quality and quantity of divine knowledge they bring, their actions and moral courage, not necessarily by any claim. Thus anyone who merely claims to be a Saviour is automatically a fraud as such an action contradicts the self evidence and behaviour of a true Saviour. *[Proof of Saviour]*

## Article 48 – Ordinary Spirit Being

184. In accord with the Maxims of Divine Law, an ***Ordinary Spirit Being*** is an individual Divine Being formed either by virtue of the operation of Divine Law or the journey and transition of an Ethereal Being of a previously Living Being. *[Ordinary Spirit Beings]*

185. In general reference to an Ordinary Spirit Being:- *[General Reference to Ordinary Spirit]*

(i) By definition, an Ordinary Spirit Being is a unique Divine

        Being that is not a Primary Divine Being or Higher Divine Being; and

(ii)    By the power and authority of the most sacred Covenant *Pactum De Singularis Caelum*, no Ordinary Spirit Being shall be excluded from One Heaven; and

(iii)   Membership of One Heaven is a right extended to all Divine Beings and Divine Persons associated with living or deceased Sentient or Sapient or never carnated beings; and

(iv)   As Membership of One Heaven is a right extended to all Divine Spirit Persons associated with living or deceased higher order beings throughout the galaxies and universe for the first time in collective history of higher order spirit we may be as one including but not limited to Homo Sapiens (Humanity), the Griseo Morbidus (Standard Grey), the Cerastis Sapiens (Horned Reptoids), the Android Scitus (Smart Androids), the Cyborg Sagax (Autonomous Cyborgs), the Serpens Sophos (Smooth Skinned Reptoids), the Volucris Permuto (Hybrid Bird Form), the Homo Adamus (Early Humanoids), the Sapientia Mutatis (Transformed Wisdom Beings), the Mammaloid Sentientiae (Conscious Mammaloids), the Griseo Altus (Tall Grey) and the Serpens Alatus (Winged Reptoids); and

(v)    The issue of a Divine Being subject to certain sanctions as a Penitent is separate to the immutable and irrevocable right of all Divine Beings as Members of One Heaven.

## Article 49 – Exemplary Spirit (Saint)

**186.** In accord with the Maxims of Divine Law, an **Exemplary Spirit** is a Divine Being recognised as a leader, hero, martyr or elder of the Universal Body of One Heaven. A Saint is an Exemplary Spirit.

**187.** There are only four valid and licit forms recognising an Exemplary Spirit being Exemplary, Heroic, Blessed and Beatific:-

(i)    *Exemplary Veneration* is when the title and sacramental grace of Exemplar is conferred upon the memory, name and relics of a deceased person; and

(ii)   *Heroic Veneration* is when the title and sacramental grace of Venerable is conferred upon the memory, name and relics of a deceased person; and

(iii)  *Blessed Veneration* is when the title and sacramental grace of Blessed is conferred upon the memory, name and relics of a deceased person; and

(iv) *Beatific Veneration* is when the title and sacramental grace of Beatification is conferred upon the memory, name and relics of a deceased person.

**188.** In general reference to an Exemplary Spirit Being:-

(i) The Veneration of an Exemplary Spirit of a deceased being is not to the exclusion of the rights of all beings, but as a manifest sign of a life of heroic virtue; and

(ii) The Life and mind of each Human Being is rightly celebrated as a supernatural event and an endorsement of the most sacred Covenant *Pactum De Singularis Caelum* and the Divine Love of God and the Divine Creator of all Existence; and

(iii) Miracles attributed to the Intercession of one or more of the beloved should therefore not be seen as criteria for qualification and acceptance of imparting a degree of the Sacrament of Veneration to the memory, name and relics of a departed member, but a confirmation that such process is acknowledged in Heaven and that the ordinary time of diligence and patience may be accelerated.

## Article 50 – Penitent Spirit

**189.** In accord with the Maxims of Divine Law, a **Penitent Spirit** is a Divine Being subject to one or more sanctions and acts of devoted penance for a determined period as confession and acknowledgement of their culpability in one or more grave transgressions.

**190.** There are three types of Penitent Spirit, depending upon the degree of authentic remorse, true confession and desire for redemption and healing being Confessant, Recalcitrant and Belligerent:-

(i) A *Confessant* is a Penitent Spirit who completely and utterly confesses their culpability, exhibits authentic remorse and genuine need of healing and forgiveness and therefore wilfully acknowledges and accepts the sanctions necessary for such redemption; and

(ii) A *Recalcitrant* is a Penitent Spirit who is stubborn, disobedient and unwilling to fully cooperate and confess their culpability, nor exhibit authentic remorse and genuine need of healing and forgiveness; and

(iii) A *Belligerent* is a Penitent Spirit who actively engages in hostile and violent acts against the true authority of Heaven and Earth in complete contempt for the Rule of Law, or Divine

Authority and Forgiveness.

191. In accord with these present Maxims and the Will of the Divine:-    *Accountability for Actions*

   (i) While none may be denied their Right of Heaven, all must be held account for such actions and injury of genuine Evil, such that through the genuine act of Penance, a Penitent Spirit and those injured may find peace and redemption; and

   (ii) All Divine Beings who are culpable of grave transgressions are bound to accept a period of sanctions that is proportionate to the gravity of their transgressions, but is also manifestly just and enables genuine redemption; and

   (iii) All claims of eternal damnation, torture and cruelty as punishment for grave transgressions in life are themselves examples of supreme Evil, Unjust and in Perfidy against the Will of the Divine. Therefore, all sentences, declarations and condemnations of eternal damnation are forbidden, suppressed and dissolved; and

   (iv) Any recalcitrant or belligerent Divine Being that refuses to subject themselves to the absolute authority of the Divine shall therefore be bound and held in the custody of the powers of Heaven, in accord with the most sacred Covenant of One Heaven until such time as they accept their necessary penance and then such penance shall begin.

## Article 51 – Angel

192. In accord with the Maxims of Divine Law, an ***Angel*** is a Divine Being and supernatural messenger.    *Angel*

193. In general reference to Angels:-    *General Reference to Angels*

   (i) The distinction of Angels only possessing benevolent and positive attributes originated through Occult Dualism with the deliberate separation of specific divine beings into two distinct personalities. Hence, under certain occult dogma, Angels became the good aspect, while Demons became the negative aspect of the same entity; and

   (ii) In accordance with these Maxims and the most sacred Covenant *Pactum De Singularis Caelum*, all Angels pledge their allegiance to One Heaven and no other.

## Article 52 – Demon

194. In accord with the Maxims of Divine Law, a **Demon** is a Divine Spirit. In its original meaning, the term Demon did not imply a divine spirit possessing only negative attributes. Hence, in its true and original sense, a "demon" is equivalent to the term Angel as well as Genius.

195. In general reference to Demons:-
    (i) The distinction of Demons only possessing malevolent and negative attributes originated through Occult Dualism with the deliberate separation of specific divine beings into two distinct personalities. Hence, under certain occult dogma, Demons became the negative aspect while Angels became the good aspect of the same entity; and
    (ii) In accordance with these Maxims and the most sacred Covenant *Pactum De Singularis Caelum*, all Demons pledge their allegiance to One Heaven and no other; and
    (iii) Any person, group or entity that pledges their allegiance to one or more Demons and does not recognise the supreme authority of these Maxims and the most sacred Covenant *Pactum De Singularis Caelum* is guilty of extreme dishonour and therefore is immediately devoid of any spiritual influence or authority whatsoever; and
    (iv) In accordance with the most sacred Covenant *Pactum De Singularis Caelum*, all Demons have sworn a sacred, irrevocable and solemn vow to pursue, hound, bind and remove from the Earth each and every person, group or entity that refuses to end acts of Evil yet secretly or publicly claims to worship one or more Demons but reject these Maxims and One Heaven.

## Article 53 – Ethereal Being

196. In accord with the Maxims of Divine Law, an **Ethereal Being** in the context of Sentient Beings and Sapient Beings is a Computation Model of Mind as a distinct Being in itself and associated with a Living Being or in transition to becoming a Divine Being after death of the Living Being.

197. In reference to an Ethereal Being:-
    (i) By definition, an Ethereal Being is a unique form of Divine Being formed as part of an Intersecting Set between the Real

Set of Life and the Unreal Set of what cannot be seen or directly measured; and

(ii) By the power and authority of the most sacred Covenant *Pactum De Singularis Caelum*, no Ethereal Being shall be excluded from One Heaven; and

(iii) Membership of One Heaven is a right extended to all Divine Beings and Divine Persons associated with living or deceased Sentient or Sapient or never carnated beings. This is exemplified by the presence of a Divine Trust and Divine Person in association with every single Divine Being and Ethereal Being within the Great Roll of Divine Persons and the Great Register and Public Record of One Heaven; and

(iv) As Membership of One Heaven is a right extended to all Ethereal Beings and Persons associated with living or deceased higher order beings throughout the galaxies and universe for the first time in collective history of higher order spirit we may be one including but not limited to Homo Sapiens (Humanity), the Griseo Morbidus (Standard Grey), the Cerastis Sapiens (Horned Reptoids), the Android Scitus (Smart Androids), the Cyborg Sagax (Autonomous Cyborgs), the Serpens Sophos (Smooth Skinned Reptoids), the Volucris Permuto (Hybrid Bird Form), the Homo Adamus (Early Humanoids), the Sapientia Mutatis (Transformed Wisdom Beings), the Mammaloid Sentientiae (Conscious Mammaloids), the Griseo Altus (Tall Grey) and the Serpens Alatus (Winged Reptoids); and

(v) The issue of an Ethereal Being subject to certain sanctions as a Penitent is separate to the immutable and irrevocable right of all Ethereal Beings as Members of One Heaven.

198. In reference to Ethereal Beings, the Mind and Ergon Fields:-

(i) By Definition, an Ethereal Being exists within an intersecting set between a Real and Unreal Set, in exactly the same way as Ergon particles (graviton, neutrino, magnetron, positron, electron, photon and hetron) exist as Ethereal Particles between Real Sets of Dimension; and

(ii) There exists a direct relation between the perceived external electromagnetic fields of Living Beings as a projection of space influenced and controlled by the Mind as an Ethereal Being connected in life. Therefore, while the boundaries of cells and complex cellular life, such as skin can be shown to have electrical resistance, the presence of a weak electromagnetic field beyond the extremities of such boundaries and skin is definitively connected to the presence of the Mind as an Ethereal Being; and

(iii) During life, these electromagnetic fields when empirically measured are of such weakness level as to exert a negligible to almost null effect or presence within the environment. However, to Living Beings, there appears an innate ability to distinguish and sometimes "view" such weak electromagnetic fields sometimes described as "life force" or "aura"; and

(iv) This connection of weak electromagnetic fields representing the presence of the Mind as an Ethereal Being in conjunction with the body as the Living Being is further reinforced in the anecdotal observation of deceased bodies lacking the "appearance" of life, even when there is no significant measure in change of mass immediately following death. It also accounts for the erroneous conclusions associated with theories of life and afterlife proposing the concept of "life forces" or "ethereal essences"; and

(v) Even after death and until a Mind consciously chooses to transition to complete Divinity, the Mind (Ergon) Field connection persists, albeit as an unstable vacuum or void of atmosphere and electromagnetic disturbance; and

(vi) Due to the inherit conditions of an Ethereal Being in a ghost state after the physical death of the Living Being, a Mind as an Ethereal Being is capable of manipulating both fields and voids of atmosphere to create anomalies capable of influencing objects – hence paranormal events.

## Article 54 – Soul

199. In accord with the Maxims of Divine Law, a ***Soul*** is a common term used to (a) define an Ethereal Being properly and legitimately associated with a Living Being (as Beneficial Owner); and (b) an Ethereal Being in the transition to becoming a Divine Being after the death of the Living Being; and (c) the Divine Spirit, Energy and Rights conveyed into a Divine Trust by the Divine Creator and associated with one (or more) Divine Persons as Trustees. *Soul*

200. In reference to a Soul:- *General Reference to Soul*

(i) All Living Beings as Beneficial Owners are connected to one (or more) Divine Persons (as Trustees) over one (or more) Divine Trusts with the Divine Res (Property) of the Trust being Divine Spirit, Energy and Rights (a Soul) conveyed by the

Divine Creator; and

(ii) No Ethereal (Spiritual) Being, except the Divine can exist without being connected to one (or more) Divine Trusts. Therefore, all Ethereal Beings possess a Soul being the Divine Res (Property) of the Trust; and

(iii) The Beneficial Owner of a Soul is always a Living True Person connected to their Divine Person (as Trustee) being an Immortal Ethereal (Spiritual) Being. Thus, no other Ethereal or Temporal Being may claim complete ownership of a Soul and Divine Property except the Divine Creator of all Existence and the Universe. Thus, any such claim to the contrary is a profound blasphemy and falsehood against all notion and respect of the Divine and of Civilised Law itself; and

(iv) By definition a Soul is Ethereal and so exists as a member of an intersecting set and remains always Unreal to the set of Reality; and

(v) The only Being in the Universe permitted by Divine Law and Civilised Law to assert ownership of a Soul is the Divine and a Superior Ucadia Person duly associated with a True Person and Divine Person as evidenced by their authorised Ucadia Live Borne Record; and

(vi) Any argument that claims a Sapient Being such as a Homo Sapien is without a Soul is absurd, profane, sacrilegious, illogical, false and renders the claim of one making such falsities a confession of incompetence and perfidy; and

(vii) Any theory that claims the mind of a Sentient or Sapient Being can be purchased or sold as a good, or lost to some malevolent or benevolent spirit is absurd, profane, sacrilegious, illogical, false and renders the claim of one making such falsities a confession of incompetence and perfidy.

## Article 55 – Lost Spirit (Ghost)

201. In accord with the Maxims of Divine Law, a **Ghost** is an isolated and bound Soul and Ethereal Being unable or unwilling to transition to becoming a Divine Being.

Lost Spirit (Ghost)

202. In general reference of a Ghost State:-

General Reference to Ghost State

(i) By definition, a Ghost is a consciousness no longer with its original Living Being and physical body, but retaining direct control and influence over the electro magnetic fields that used to surround the Living body since birth and now surround an unstable void of atmosphere; and

(ii) A Ghost, even one that is conscious of their state and unwilling to transition to becoming completely Divine is a Mind that is strongly bound to the temporal world by its own emotions and perspective on one or more past events with one or more physical relations; and

(iii) Furthermore, a Ghost is a Mind bound in ignorance. Therefore, a Ghost is more likely to be unaware and uninterested in a higher quality of knowledge or the truth. Thus, people who are susceptible and gullible in life to supporting nihilistic systems, fanatical orthodoxies and intolerant stupidity are more likely to become Ghosts; and

(iv) The perversity of a Ghost state is that a Ghost bound in ignorance continues to be even more vulnerable in death to further falsities, stereotypical fears and superstitions, leading to a downward spiral of ignorance. Such a spiral of ignorance and suffering of some Ghosts can account for why over time it is possible for Ghosts to forget their name, their original family and even their original gender and identity; and

(v) The ability for a Ghost to "read the minds" of other Minds entrusted with physical bodies is by definition impossible. A Ghost may seek to guess from the behaviour of a living being their thoughts, but may only gain access to the actual thoughts either by direct possession or haunting (infiltrating a broken Lower Mind), or exchange of information offered by other Ghosts possessing or haunting the other body.

203. In terms of the ability of Ghosts to move between locations, or people, or possessions of Minds:- *Ghosts and location*

(i) By definition, a Ghost is a Mind bound in ignorance and Guilt to particular places, things, objects and people. Therefore, the very State of being a Ghost means such a bound Lower Mind is most likely to be connected to the strongest sources of regret, guilt and objects or people that symbolise such events than places or other locations of no relevance to such binding; and

(ii) The movement of a Ghost is more likely to be associated with the movement of the person or persons who are haunted or possessed; and

(iii) As Souls by definition seek to transition to the Divine, the journey of Mind after Death leads itself to the metaphor and literal presence of Ghosts using transport networks, most notably forms of public transport, particularly when bound in ignorance or fear or servitude to Ghosts perpetuating evil actions whilst still in a Ghost state.

**204.** In terms of Ghost Haunting and Ghost Possession:- *Ghosts and hauntings and possessions*

(i) A Haunting may be described as the presence or manifestation of a Ghost inhabiting a certain space or place or connected to some object; and

(ii) A Possession may be described as the inhabitation of a ghost within the body or mind of a higher order life form such as a Homo Sapien, or the control of some object exhibiting definitive paranormal behaviour (such as levitation, disappearance, appearance or other manipulation); and

(iii) The most common form of Haunting is Residual Haunting that involves the repeated playback of auditory, visual and other sensory phenomena of previous events without apparent intelligent awareness of the living world and interacting with or responding to it; and

(iv) The least common form of Haunting is an Intelligent Haunting that involves one or more Ghosts residing in a building or location, aware of the living world and capable of interacting with or responding to it; and

(v) The most common form of Possession is physical possession of one or more organs of the body of a higher order life form, whereby a Ghost may use the energy of the living body to maintain a presence and influence over the physical apparatus of mind of the higher order life form, usually at the cost of accelerated illness and cancers; and

(vi) The least common form of Possession is possession of the Mind of a higher order life form, whereby the Ghost inhabits the consciousness of the living being or deceased being, usually resulting in a range of traumatic mental illnesses including (but not limited to): psychosis, hysteria, mania, schizophrenia and dissociative identity disorder; and

(vii) The rarest form of Possession is possession of an inanimate object, causing it to move with intelligence or other forms of matter manipulation as such Possession requires a degree of intelligence and self-awareness on the part of the Ghost.

## Article 56 – Wraith

**205.** In accord with the Maxims of Divine Law, a **Wraith** is a Soul and Ethereal Being consciously choosing to remain in a "ghost" state by being commissioned to a Special Supreme Divine Office in association with the Supremum Obligationum Systemata (Enforcement Systems) of One Heaven, in accord with the most sacred Covenant *Pactum De Singularis Caelum*.

*Wraith*

**206.** In reference to a Wraith:-

*General Reference to Wraith*

(i) As an Ethereal Being, a Ghost possesses certain abilities to influence matter and form within the conscious Reality of Life, unlike a Divine Being completely transitioned; and

(ii) Thus, there exists certain Ethereal Beings as Ghosts that choose to remain in such a state given such perceived "powers" that render their accountability before Living Beings or completed transitioned Divine Beings very difficult; and

(iii) The Divine Office of Wraith therefore is a most solemn and important function in fulfilling the sacred missions of united Heaven to ensure the enforcement of the Rule of Divine Law and the bringing to account all Beings, no matter what dimension or state; and

(iv) Wraiths are therefore responsible and tasked as the most fearsome of forces with enforcement of justice in their foundational responsibilities of rendition, possession, prevention, interdiction, purgation, correction, seizure and return, arrest and custody and restitution.

## Article 57 – Faerie

**207.** In accord with the Maxims of Divine Law, a **Faerie** is an ancient Ethereal Being commissioned to a Special Supreme Divine Office in association with the Supremum Femininum Systemata (Feminine Systems) of One Heaven, in accord with the most sacred Covenant *Pactum De Singularis Caelum*.

*Faerie*

The Special Supreme Divine Office of "**Faerie**" is in recognition of the ancient spirits and force redeemed from being previously denigrated and marginalised; and their foundational responsibilities in the restoration of true feminine; and the restoration of true mother; and Gaia harmony; and emancipation, equality and appreciation of all women.

**208.** In reference to a Faerie:-

*General Reference to*

(i) The Special Supreme Divine Office of Faerie is an authentic Divine Office. Thus any refusal to acknowledge the existence of such office is a self declaration of delusion and self confession of mental illness in defiance of the demonstrable existence of the most sacred Covenant *Pactum De Singularis Caelum*; and

(ii) The Divine Office of Faerie is a most solemn and important function in fulfilling the sacred missions of united Heaven to ensure the enforcement of the Rule of Divine Law and restoration of the true Feminine.

## Article 58 – Elve

209. In accord with the Maxims of Divine Law, an **Elve** is an ancient Ethereal Being commissioned to a Special Supreme Divine Office in association with the Supremum Masculinum Systemata (Masculine Systems) of One Heaven, in accord with the most sacred Covenant *Pactum De Singularis Caelum*.

    The Special Supreme Divine Office of "**Elve**" (Elf) is in recognition of the ancient spirits and force redeemed from being previously denigrated and marginalised; and their foundational responsibilities in the restoration of true masculine; and the restoration of true father; and Gaia harmony; and emancipation, equality and appreciation of all men.

210. In reference to an Elve:-
    (i) The Special Supreme Divine Office of Elve is an authentic Divine Office. Thus any refusal to acknowledge the existence of such office is a self declaration of delusion and self confession of mental illness in defiance of the demonstrable existence of the most sacred Covenant *Pactum De Singularis Caelum*; and

    (ii) The Divine Office of Elve is a most solemn and important function in fulfilling the sacred missions of united Heaven to ensure the enforcement of the Rule of Divine Law and restoration of the true Masculine.

## Article 59 – Elemental Being

211. In accord with the Maxims of Divine Law, an **Elemental Being** is a form of Ethereal Manifestation formed through connection to Sentience, either as the form of Ethereal Beings of deceased Sentient Beings, or extreme stress of Sapient Beings in a life or death condition.

212. In reference to Elemental Beings or Elementals:-

(i) Elemental Being is by definition a temporary and simple manifestation not exhibiting the intelligence of a Sapient Ghost; and [Elemental Beings]

(ii) Elemental Beings are prone to be manifestations associated with a sense of darkness, foreboding, anger and in extreme cases of war, cruelty and death the palpable presence of Evil; and

(iii) Elemental Beings are primarily manifested through the base and extreme emotional state of Sapient Living Beings as well as the effect of trapped Sentient Being Mind; and

(iv) In most cases, such temporary manifestation changes and dissipates over time once the conditions causing such a Being also change.

## Article 60 – Imaginary Being

213. In accord with the Maxims of Divine Law, an **Imaginary Being** is an Ethereal Being from the individual or collective imagination and minds of Sapient Beings that by constant reinforcement and thinking is given its own existence and reality. [Imaginary Being]

214. In reference to Imaginary Beings:- [General Reference to Imaginary Being]

(i) By definition, Imaginary Beings are purely an invention of the mind of Sapient Beings and therefore not Ethereal Beings or Divine Beings; and

(ii) As Imaginary Beings are not Ethereal Beings or Divine Beings, they do not carry the authority of rights, or legitimacy of Divine Law; and

(iii) While Imaginary Beings do not carry the authority of rights, or legitimacy of Divine Law, they can and do influence reality to the degree that Sapient Beings trust they are real and act accordingly.

## 2.4 – Supernatural Dominion

### Article 61 – Supernatural Dominion

215. **Supernatural Dominion** refers to a well defined *Supernatural Dimension* that exercises its own governance with a degree of autonomy of jurisdiction, laws and functions, consistent with the most sacred Covenant *Pactum De Singularis Caelum*. [Supernatural Dominion]

216. The highest and primary Supernatural Dominions of all existence, [Highest and]

authority and history include:- *Primary Supernatural Dominions*

(i) **Kingdom of One Heaven**: Being the official name and title defining the levels and dimensions of Unique Collective Awareness of all Existences, Concepts, Objects, Properties, Laws, Theories, Imaginations and Realities unto itself as it pertains to unique higher order (self-aware) conscious forms within the Local Group of Galaxies; and

(ii) **Universal Ecclesia of One Christ**: Being the first, highest and supreme association, aggregate fraternity, body, entity and society of One Heaven sharing spiritual heritage associated with all forms of Christian and Jewish faith; and

(iii) **Holy Society of One Islam**: Being the first, highest and supreme association, aggregate fraternity, body, entity and society of One Heaven sharing spiritual heritage associated with all forms of Islam; and

(iv) **Sacred Society of One Spirit**: Being the first, highest and supreme association, aggregate fraternity, body, entity and society of One Heaven sharing spiritual heritage associated with traditional, indigenous, Earth based, meditative and eastern customary faiths; and

(v) **Society of Light**: Being a supernatural and spiritual body dedicated to the fulfilment of the sacred Covenant *Testamentum Lucis*; and the evangelical mission of proclaiming the Good News of the fulfilment of sacred Scripture and the unity of Heaven and Earth through the manifestation of the Kingdom of Heaven upon the Earth in accord with *Article 137 – Testamentum Lucis (Testament of Light)* of the most sacred Covenant *Pactum De Singularis Caelum*; and

(vi) **Society of Truth**: Being a supernatural and spiritual body dedicated to the fulfilment of the sacred Covenant *Testamentum Noctis*; and the evangelical mission of guarding the world against those who declare themselves gods or messiahs and proclaiming the fulfilment of sacred Scripture and the unity of Heaven and Earth through the manifestation of the Kingdom of Heaven upon the Earth in accord with *Article 138 – Testamentum Noctis (Testament of Darkness)* of the most sacred Covenant *Pactum De Singularis Caelum*.

## Article 62 – Kingdom of One Heaven

**217.** In accord with the Maxims of Divine Law, **Kingdom of One Heaven** is the official name and title defining the levels and dimensions of Unique Collective Awareness of all Existences, Concepts, Objects, Properties, Laws, Theories, Imaginations and Realities unto itself as it pertains to unique higher order (self-aware) conscious forms within the Local Group of Galaxies [Trust No. 000000-300000-000001] that the Milky Way Galaxy [Trust No. 000000-400000- 000001] is part thereof. Within the context of the Unique Collective Awareness, being a formal name of the Divine Creator of all Existence, no other official name and title than One Heaven shall have higher standing or authority in respect of this region of consciousness and the associated trillions of star systems and planets within the same region of the Universe.

Kingdom of One Heaven

**218.** In reference to Divine Dominion and One Heaven:-

Divine Dominion of One Heaven

(i) When anyone speaks or writes of Heaven, or Paradise, or the Afterlife, or the Otherworld, or Jannah, or Nirvana, or Valhalla, or Folkvangr, or Olympus, or Utopia, or Gan Eden, or Aaru, or Elysium, or Vaikuntha, or Tirna, or Tlalocan, or any other term of a similar nature, it shall mean One Heaven as defined by the most sacred Covenant *Pactum De Singularis Caelum* and no other; and

(ii) Similarly, when anyone speaks or writes of Hell, or Hades, or Mundi, or Purgatory, or Sea of Souls, or the Underworld, or any other term of a similar nature, it shall also mean One Heaven as defined by the most sacred Covenant *Pactum De Singularis Caelum* and no other, as the unification of all dimensions of consciousness as one; and

(iii) Furthermore, when anyone speaks or writes of inter-dimensions, or multi-verses or any other models describing consciousness or constructs, it shall mean One Heaven as defined by the most sacred Covenant *Pactum De Singularis Caelum* and no other.

## Article 63 – Universal Ecclesia of One Christ

**219.** In accord with the Maxims of Divine Law, the most sacred and **Universal Ecclesia of One Christ**, also known as the One Holy Apostolic Universal Ecclesia, also known as the Sol Ecclesia, also known as the Authentic Body of Christ and also known simply as One Christ, is the first, highest and supreme association, aggregate,

Universal Ecclesia of One Christ

fraternity, body, entity and society of One Heaven sharing spiritual heritage associated with all forms of Christian and Jewish faith; and the embodiment of the Kingdom of Heaven upon the Earth.

220. In reference to the Universal Ecclesia of One Christ:-

    (i) In accord with the intention and consent of the one true Divine Creator, all existence, angels, saints, demons and all spirits of united Heaven it is hereby pronounced that any deceased or presently living higher order life being having professed their trust and obligation in Christian or Jewish customs and traditions is a Member of One Christ as well as a Member of One Heaven; and

    (ii) All living Higher Life Forms who profess to be Christian or Jewish are *ipso facto* (as a matter of fact) subject first to the laws of One Heaven and second to the laws of the Universal Ecclesia of One Christ above any other lesser society, association, aggregate, institute, fraternity, society, entity or body; and

    (iii) Furthermore, it is hereby pronounced that all and every ordained, acknowledged, commissioned or certified clergy of any Christian or Jewish body are also officers of the Universal Ecclesia of One Christ; and subject to the laws and obligations of One Christ first above any other lesser society, association, aggregate, institute, fraternity, society, entity or body.

*Reference to Universal Ecclesia of One Christ*

## Article 64 – Holy Society of One Islam

221. In accord with the Maxims of Divine Law, the most sacred and **Holy Society of One Islam**, also known as the One True Way of Allah, also known as the One Umma and also known simply as One Islam, is the first, highest and supreme association, aggregate, fraternity, body, entity and society of One Heaven sharing spiritual heritage associated with all forms of Islam; and the embodiment of the Kingdom of Paradise of Allah upon the Earth.

*Holy Society of One Islam*

222. In reference to the Holy Society of One Islam:-

    (i) In accord with the intention and consent of the one true Divine Creator, all existence, angels, saints, demons and all spirits of united Heaven it is hereby pronounced that any deceased or presently living higher order life being having professed their trust and obligation in Islam is a Member of One Islam as well as a Member of One Heaven; and

    (ii) All living Higher Life Forms who profess to be Muslim are ipso

*Reference to Holy Society of One Islam*

facto (as a matter of fact) subject first to the laws of One Heaven and second to the laws of the Holy Society of One Islam above any other lesser society, association, aggregate, institute, fraternity, society, entity or body; and

(iii) Furthermore, it is hereby pronounced that all and every ordained, acknowledged, commissioned or certified clergy of any Islamic body are also officers of the Holy Society of One Islam; and subject to the laws and obligations of One Islam first above any other lesser society, association, aggregate, institute, fraternity, society, entity or body.

## Article 65 – Sacred Society of One Spirit

223. In accord with the Maxims of Divine Law, the most **Sacred Society of One Spirit**, also known as the One Holy Apostolic Spirit, also known as One Spirit Tribe and also known simply as One Spirit, is the first, highest and supreme association, aggregate, fraternity, body, entity and society of One Heaven sharing spiritual heritage associated with traditional, indigenous, Earth based, meditative and eastern customary faiths.

Sacred Society of One Spirit

224. In reference to the Sacred Society of One Spirit:-

Reference to Sacred Society of One Spirit

(i) In accord with the intention and consent of the one true Divine Creator, all existence, angels, saints, demons and all spirits of united Heaven it is hereby pronounced that any deceased or presently living higher order life being having professed their faith in Hinduism, Buddhism, Taoism, Janism or any other traditional customary faith is a Member of One Spirit Tribe as well as a Member of One Heaven; and

(ii) All living Higher Life Forms who profess to be Hindu, Buddhist, Taoist or any other traditional customary faith are ipso facto (as a matter of fact) subject first to the laws of One Heaven and second to the laws of One Spirit Tribe above any other lesser society, association, aggregate, institute, fraternity, society, entity or body; and

(iii) Furthermore, it is hereby pronounced that all and every all ordained, acknowledged, commissioned or certified clergy of any Hindu, Buddhist or other traditional spiritual body are officers of One Spirit Tribe and subject to the laws and obligations of One Spirit Tribe first above any other lesser society, association, aggregate, institute, fraternity, society, entity or body.

## Article 66 – Society of Light

**225.** In accord with the Maxims of Divine Law, the ***Society of Light***, also known simply as the Society, is the first, highest and supreme association, aggregate, fraternity, body, entity and society of One Heaven and Earth uniting all recognised Chivalrous, Sovereign and Religious Military Orders and Holders of Noble and Official Titles of all the three great Faiths of One Christ, One Islam and One Spirit under a new sacred mandate and holy mission in accord with *Article 137 – Testamentum Lucis (Testament of Light)* of the most sacred Covenant *Pactum De Singularis Caelum*.

<small>Society of Light</small>

**226.** In reference to the Society of Light:-

<small>Reference to Society of Light</small>

    (i)    All living Members of all recognised Chivalrous, Sovereign and Religious Military Orders and Holders of Noble and Official Titles are *ipso facto* (as a matter of fact) Members of the Ucadia Globe Union; and

    (ii)    The sacred Covenant of the Society of Light also known as *Testamentum Lucis* shall be regarded as a Supremely sacred and valuable object and the temporal instrument of association on planet Earth in accord and consistent with the Maxims of Divine Law; and

    (iii)    No other body politic, association, corporation, company, person, entity or group representing lesser bodies may claim higher association of Chivalrous, Sovereign and Religious Military Orders and Holders of Noble and Official Titles than the Society of Light for planet Earth.

## Article 67 – Society of Truth

**227.** In accord with the Maxims of Divine Law, the ***Society of Truth***, also known simply as the Truth, is the first, highest and supreme association, aggregate, fraternity, body, entity and society of One Heaven and Earth uniting all established Secret Spiritual and Religious Societies and Orders under a new sacred mandate and holy mission in accord with *Article 138 – Testamentum Noctis (Testament of Darkness)* of the most sacred Covenant *Pactum De Singularis Caelum*.

<small>Society of Truth</small>

**228.** In reference to the Society of Truth:-

<small>Reference to Society of Truth</small>

    (i)    All living Members of established Secret Spiritual and Religious Societies are ipso facto (as a matter of fact) Members of the Society of Truth; and

    (ii)    The sacred Covenant of the Society of Truth also known as

*Testamentum Noctis* shall be regarded as a Supremely sacred and valuable object and the temporal instrument of association on planet Earth in accord and consistent with the Maxims of Divine Law; and

(iii) No other body politic, association, corporation, company, person, entity or group representing lesser bodies may claim higher association of Secret Spiritual and Religious Societies and Orders than the Society of Truth for planet Earth.

## 2.5 – Supernatural Objects

### Article 68 – Supernatural Objects

229. **Supernatural Objects** are items believed to be imbued with extraordinary or mystical properties that defy the natural laws of physics and reality. These objects are common in various cultural, religious, and historic contexts, and are usually claimed to possess characteristics that make them significant or powerful beyond ordinary comprehension. <!-- Supernatural Objects -->

230. Claimed Supernatural Objects may be categorised into four (4) main classes being:- <!-- Category of Supernatural Objects -->

    (i) **Sacred & Venerated Supernatural Objects**: Objects believed to be imbued with divine or holy power, often revered in religious traditions and considered to have spiritual significance (e.g. Holy Grail, the Ark of the Covenant, relics of saints, the Shroud of Turin); and

    (ii) **Historic & Cultural Supernatural Objects**: Objects of historical or cultural significance that are claimed to have supernatural properties, often linked to ancient civilizations or mysterious origins (e.g. Spear of Destiny (Spear of Longinus), the Philosopher's Stone, the Crystal Skulls, ancient talismans or amulets); and

    (iii) **Cursed or Enchanted Supernatural Objects**: Objects believed to be cursed or enchanted, often bringing misfortune or magical effects to those who encounter them (e.g. Hope Diamond (believed to be cursed), cursed mummy artifacts, haunted dolls (e.g., Annabelle), the Dybbuk box); and

    (iv) **Mythological & Legendary Supernatural Objects**: Objects from myths and legends, often associated with heroes, gods, or mythical creatures, and believed to possess extraordinary abilities or significance (e.g. Excalibur (King

Arthur's sword), Pandora's Box, Thor's Hammer (Mjölnir), the Golden Fleece).

## Article 69 – Sacred & Venerated Supernatural Objects

231. **Sacred & Venerated Supernatural Objects** are items that hold significant spiritual or religious importance and are often believed to possess divine or supernatural powers. These objects are typically revered within their respective cultural or religious contexts and are often central to rituals, worship, or belief systems.

    <small>Sacred & Venerated Supernatural Objects</small>

232. Common Characteristics of *Sacred & Venerated Supernatural Objects* include (but are not limited to):-

    (i) **Divine Origin or Association**: Objects are often believed to have a direct connection to deities, saints, prophets or other holy figures; and

    (ii) **Spiritual Power**: Believers often attribute miraculous powers to these objects, such as healing, protection or the ability to grant blessings; and

    (iii) **Cultural and Religious Significance**: Objects are deeply embedded in the cultural and religious traditions of a community; and

    (iv) **Ritualistic Use**: Objects are frequently used in rituals, including ceremonies of worship, rites of passage and other religious observances.

    <small>Characteristics of Sacred & Venerated Supernatural Objects</small>

233. Key Sacred Sacred & Venerated Supernatural Objects recognised in Christianity include (but are not limited to):-

    (i) **The Crown of Thorns**: The headdress believed to have been placed upon the head of Jesus Christ and the holiest relic of all Christianity (traditionally held in Paris); and

    (ii) **The Shroud of Turin**: A linen cloth bearing the image of a man, believed by some to be the burial shroud of Jesus Christ; and

    (iii) **Relics of Saints**: Bones, clothing, or other personal items of saints, believed to convey blessings and protection.

    <small>Key Sacred & Venerated Supernatural Objects in Christianity</small>

234. Key Sacred Sacred & Venerated Supernatural Objects recognised in Islam include (but are not limited to):-

    (i) **The Black Stone**: An ancient black meteorite stone set into the Kaaba in Mecca, revered by Muslims as a supremely sacred object; and

    <small>Key Sacred & Venerated Supernatural Objects in Islam</small>

(ii) ***Relics of the Prophet***: Bones, clothing and other personal items of the Holly (Holy) Prophet, venerated in Islamic tradition.

235. Key Sacred Sacred & Venerated Supernatural Objects recognised in Hinduism include (but are not limited to):- Key Sacred & Venerated Supernatural Objects in Hinduism

   (i) ***River Ganges***: A living symbolic representation of the goddess Ganga Shiva, heaven, purification and redemption; and

   (ii) ***Shiva Lingam***: A symbolic representation of the god Shiva, often venerated in temples; and

   (iii) ***Idols and Murti***: Sculpted images of deities used as focal points for worship in temples and homes.

236. Key Sacred Sacred & Venerated Supernatural Objects recognised in Buddhism include (but are not limited to):- Key Sacred & Venerated Supernatural Objects in Buddhism

   (i) ***Bodhi Tree***: The tree under which Siddhartha Gautama attained enlightenment and became the Buddha; and

   (ii) ***Relics of the Buddha***: Physical remains or personal items of the Buddha, often enshrined in stupas.

## Article 70 – Historic & Cultural Supernatural Objects

237. ***Historic & Cultural Supernatural Objects*** are items that are believed to possess extraordinary powers or significance due to their historical, cross-cultural or mystical associations. These objects often play crucial roles in the legends and traditions of various societies. Historic & Cultural Supernatural Objects

238. Common Characteristics of *Historic & Cultural Supernatural Objects* include (but are not limited to):- Characteristics of Historic & Cultural Supernatural Objects

   (i) ***Historical Significance***: Objects are often linked to significant historical events, figures or civilizations. They may be considered relics of the past with enduring influence on contemporary culture and belief systems; and

   (ii) ***Cross-Cultural Importance***: Objects hold a place of reverence or fear within a culture and are integral to the identity and heritage of the people. They are often central to the common narratives, scriptures and cultural practices of one or more cultures; and

   (iii) ***Supernatural Attributes***: Believed to possess mystical or magical properties, such as granting protection, bestowing powers, or bringing misfortune to those unworthy to hold such supremely sacred objects.

239. The **Ark of the Covenant** is one of the most famous Historic & Cultural Supernatural Objects being the original gold-covered wooden chest commissioned for Pharaoh Akhenaten as the voice-box of Amen-Ra, before as Moses this artefact becoming the symbol of the new covenant. Misrepresented in sacred writings such as the Bible from the 17th Century as containing the stone tablets of the Ten Commandments. Considered one of the most sacred relics in all of history and believed to possess powerful and protective properties.

240. The **Thrones and Stones of Destiny** were three famous wooden chairs formed from the oldest living Yew Tree in history; and three green marble anointing (coronation) stones that were given to the ancient leaders of the first great Empires, including Egypt, Ebla and Ireland. At least one Throne and Stone survived until the 16th Century until being ignorantly destroyed by Venetian-English mercenaries. Only an infamous fake chair called the Coronation Chair from 17th Century and a lump of sandstone from Scone – claimed as the Stone of Destiny – remain in popular culture.

241. The **Spear of Destiny (Holly Frank)** is regarded as one of the most Historic & Cultural Supernatural Objects of historical prophecy since the first formation of the Catholic Church in the 8th Century. In Anglaise (Old French), the word *frank* means "freedom, courageous and lance/javelin". The word spear comes from Dutch *speer*. Originally a person of the Holly bloodline that would come in future centuries to re-shape civilizations and empires and save humanity, in the 17th Century the prophecy was intentionally corrupted to become a lance used by a Roman soldier to pierce the side of Jesus Christ during his crucifixion. Believed to hold immense power and has been associated with numerous legends about its ability to grant victory in battle and influence the fate of empires. Many fake spear heads now exist, with almost no general knowledge of original prophecy.

242. The **Subhah Muqaddasah (Sacred Necklace)** is a major Historic & Cultural Supernatural Object and the origin and first prayer beads, being up to thirty-three black meteorite rocks and worn by the first Mustafah of Islam, beginning with the Holly (Holy) Prophet and then his blood descendents until the 11th Century. The present location of the Subhah Muqaddasah is now unknown. However, prayer beads and pilgrimage (Hajj) continue as a major feature of modern Islam.

243. The **Crystal Skulls** are Historic & Cultural Supernatural Objects being Carved skulls made from clear or milky quartz, believed by some to be ancient artefacts with mystical properties. Subject to various myths and speculations, including theories about their

origins from lost civilizations or extraterrestrial sources, and believed to hold healing or prophetic power.

## Article 71 – Cursed or Enchanted Supernatural Objects

244. ***Cursed or Enchanted Supernatural Objects*** are items believed to possess extraordinary, often malevolent or magical, powers. These objects are common in folklore, mythology, literature and popular culture, where they are often associated with bringing misfortune or bestowing special abilities. Cursed or Enchanted Supernatural Objects

245. Common Characteristics of *Cursed or Enchanted Supernatural Objects* include (but are not limited to):- Characteristics of Cursed or Enchanted Supernatural Objects

    (i) ***Beneficial Powers***: Enchanted objects are typically imbued with magical properties that can grant the wielder special abilities, such as protection, strength or luck; and

    (ii) ***Malevolent Influence***: These objects are believed to bring bad luck, misfortune, illness, or even death to those who possess or come into contact with them; and

    (iii) ***Conditions of Use***: Enchanted objects often come with specific conditions or limitations on their use, which must be adhered to in order to harness their powers; and

    (iv) ***Origins of the Curse***: Cursed objects might originate from protection against misuse, or a history of violence and tragedy.

246. The ***Hope Diamond*** is a famous Cursed or Enchanted Supernatural Object being a large blue diamond with a storied past, currently housed in the Smithsonian Institution. It is believed to be cursed, bringing misfortune and tragedy to its owners. Its history is filled with tales of mysterious deaths and bad luck. Hope Diamond

247. ***King Tutankhamun's Tomb*** is a famous Cursed or Enchanted Supernatural Place and set of Objects whereby many of those who were involved in the discovery and excavation of the tomb died under mysterious circumstances, leading to the belief that the tomb was cursed. King Tutankhamun's Tomb

248. The ***Dybbuk Box*** is a famous Cursed or Enchanted Supernatural Object being a wine cabinet claimed to be haunted by a dybbuk, a malicious spirit from Jewish folklore. The box gained notoriety after being sold on eBay with a detailed backstory of supernatural occurrences, inspiring books and films about its alleged curse. The Dybbuk Box

## Article 72 – Mythological & Legendary Supernatural Objects

249. ***Mythological & Legendary Supernatural Objects*** are items from myths, legends, and folklore that are imbued with extraordinary powers or significance. These objects often play crucial roles in the stories and traditions of various cultures, symbolizing divine intervention, heroism or moral lessons.

250. Common Characteristics of Mythological & Legendary Supernatural Objects include (but are not limited to):-

    (i) ***Divine or Supernatural Origin***: These objects are often created by gods, bestowed by supernatural beings, or formed through magical or mystical processes. They typically have origins rooted in the divine or the fantastical, making them central to the myths in which they appear; and

    (ii) ***Extraordinary Powers***: These objects possess powers that transcend ordinary capabilities, such as granting invincibility, bestowing wisdom or manipulating natural elements. Their powers often play a critical role in narratives, helping heroes overcome obstacles or enemies; and

    (iii) ***Symbolic Meaning***: Beyond their literal powers, these objects often symbolize broader themes such as justice, authority, purity or destiny. They are frequently used to convey moral or ethical lessons within myths; and

    (iv) ***Cultural Significance***: These objects are integral to the cultural identity and heritage of the societies that created them. They often appear in art, literature and religious practices, reflecting their enduring impact on cultural consciousness.

251. ***Excalibur*** is a famous Mythological & Legendary Supernatural Object being the legendary sword of King Arthur, sometimes associated with magical properties and bestowed by the Lady of the Lake. Excalibur is central to Arthurian legends and symbolic of rightful sovereignty, divine kingship and the heroism of King Arthur.

252. The ***Philosopher's Stone*** is a famous Mythological & Legendary Supernatural Object being a legendary alchemical substance or knowledge said to be capable of turning base metals into gold and providing the elixir of life, granting immortality. The Philosopher's Stone is the focus to many medieval alchemical traditions and has influenced literature.

253. The ***Holy Grail***, as a deliberate corruption of the Anglaise *sangreal*

"Holly Blood" by turning the 5,000 year history of the Holly into a household utensil (as a cup) is a famous Mythological & Legendary Supernatural Object for the past four hundred years (but claimed much older) whereby this magic cup was used by Jesus Christ at the last supper and was then believed in the Arthurian legends to possess miraculous healing powers and grant eternal life.

## 2.6 – Supernatural Ability

### Article 73 – Supernatural Ability

254. ***Supernatural Ability*** refers to a skill or power that goes beyond natural laws and explanations as understood by contemporary science.

<!-- margin: Supernatural Ability -->

255. General Types of *Supernatural Ability* include (but are not limited to):-

<!-- margin: General Types of Supernatural Ability -->

   (i) ***Supernatural Sensual Ability***: Being an extraordinary power to perceive or enhance physical pleasure and sensory experiences beyond normal human capabilities; and

   (ii) ***Supernatural Remedial Ability***: Being an extraordinary power to heal, cure, or restore health through means beyond natural or scientific understanding; and

   (iii) ***Supernatural Informational Ability***: Being an extraordinary power to acquire knowledge or insights beyond normal human means; and

   (iv) ***Supernatural Communicational Ability***: Being an extraordinary power to convey or receive messages beyond normal means, often involving telepathy, mediumship or spirit communication; and

   (v) ***Supernatural Physical Ability***: Being an extraordinary power to exceed normal human physical limits, such as superhuman strength, speed or agility; and

   (vi) ***Supernatural Locational Ability***: Being an extraordinary power to instantly move or sense locations beyond normal means, such as teleportation or remote viewing; and

   (vii) ***Supernatural Mental Ability***: Being an extraordinary power to influence or perceive thoughts and minds beyond normal means, such as telepathy or mind control; and

   (viii) ***Supernatural Manifestational Ability***: Being an extraordinary power to create or bring objects, beings, or events into existence through mystical or magical means.

## Article 74 – Supernatural Sensual Ability

**256.** ***Supernatural Sensual Ability*** is an extraordinary power to perceive or enhance physical pleasure and sensory experiences beyond normal human capabilities. It is the first and most common category of the eight categories of *Supernatural Abilities*.

Supernatural Sensual Ability

**257.** Types of *Supernatural Sensual Ability* include (but are not limited to):-

Types of Supernatural Sensual Ability

   (i)   ***Clairvoyance*** (supernatural sight): Is the ability to gain information about an object, person, or event through extrasensory perception, typically involving visions or images in the mind beyond normal sensory abilities; and

   (ii)   ***Clairaudience*** (supernatural sound): Is the ability to hear sounds, voices, or messages beyond normal auditory range, often perceived as communication from spirits or higher beings; and

   (iii)   ***Clairsentience*** (supernatural empathy): Is the ability to sense or feel emotions, energies, or physical sensations beyond normal perception, often providing intuitive insights about people, places or events; and

   (iv)   ***Clairgustance*** (supernatural taste): Is the ability to taste substances without physical presence, often associated with spiritual or paranormal experiences, providing intuitive insights through the sense of taste; and

   (v)   ***Clairalience*** (supernatural smell): Is the ability to perceive smells without a physical source, often associated with spiritual or paranormal experiences, providing intuitive insights through the sense of smell; and

   (vi)   ***Psychometry*** (supernatural touch): Is the ability to obtain information about a person or event by touching an object associated with them, often involving intuitive impressions or visions.

**258.** As the Universe itself is Unique Collective Awareness in motion expressed as a Living Dream and *Supernatural Sensual Ability* is about finding Unique Collective Awareness not otherwise gained through normal human senses within the collective dream, there is nothing paranormal, supernatural or fictional about these abilities. Instead, such abilities are only listed as Supernatural in large part due to a lack of full and objective understanding how they function.

Supernatural Sensual Ability and Unique Collective Awareness

**259.** *Supernatural Sensual Ability* is perfectly reasonable, possible and

Supernatural Sensual Ability

demonstrable under Divine Law and Natural Law in accordance with these Maxims.

*and Ucadia Maxims of Law*

## Article 75 – Supernatural Remedial Ability

260. ***Supernatural Remedial Ability*** is an extraordinary power to heal, cure, or restore health through means beyond natural or scientific understanding. It is the second and second most common category of the eight categories of *Supernatural Abilities*.

*Supernatural Remedial Ability*

261. Types of *Supernatural Remedial Ability* include (but are not limited to):-

*Types of Supernatural Remedial Ability*

    (i)    ***Aura Healing*** (supernatural sight healing)*:* The ability to heal by cleansing or repairing the aura, the energy field surrounding the body; and

    (ii)    ***Crystal Healing*** (supernatural sight healing): The use of crystals and gemstones, believed to have healing properties, to restore health and balance; and

    (iii)    ***Sound Healing*** (supernatural sound healing): The use of sound frequencies, chants, or music to heal physical, emotional or spiritual ailments; and

    (iv)    ***Faith Healing*** (supernatural empathy healing): The ability to heal through faith, prayer or divine intervention. Often associated with religious or spiritual practices; and

    (v)    ***Empathic Healing*** (supernatural empathy healing): The ability to absorb or transfer another person's pain or illness, thereby healing them, often at some temporary cost to the healer; and

    (vi)    ***Herbal Healing*** (supernatural taste healing): The use of supernatural knowledge of herbs and plants to create powerful remedies that go beyond conventional herbalism; and

    (vii)    ***Chi Healing***: (supernatural taste or smell healing): The ability to heal by manipulating the life force energy (chi or qi) within the body. Often associated with traditional Chinese medicine practices; and

    (viii)    ***Reiki Healing*** (supernatural touch healing): A form of energy healing where the practitioner channels healing energy into the patient through touch or near-touch.

262. As the Universe itself is Unique Collective Awareness in motion expressed as a Living Dream and *Supernatural Remedial Ability* is about harnessing the power of healing Unique Collective Awareness

*Supernatural Remedial Ability and Unique Collective*

not otherwise gained through normal human senses within the collective dream, there is nothing paranormal, supernatural or fictional about these abilities. Instead, such abilities are only listed as Supernatural in large part due to a lack of full and objective understanding how they function.

Awareness

## Article 76 – Supernatural Informational Ability

263. ***Supernatural Informational Ability*** is an extraordinary power to acquire knowledge or insights beyond normal human means. It is the third and third most common category of the eight categories of *Supernatural Abilities*.

Supernatural Informational Ability

264. Types of *Supernatural Informational Ability* include (but are not limited to):-

    (i) ***Premonition***: Is a strong feeling or intuition that something (usually negative) is about to happen, without any logical or concrete evidence. It is often a vague sense of foreboding or anxiety about an impending event; and

    (ii) ***Precognition***: Is the ability to perceive or gain specific knowledge about future events before they happen, beyond the normal sensory channels. It is more detailed and factual than a premonition; and

    (iii) ***Revelation***: Is the act of revealing or disclosing something previously unknown or hidden, often involving divine or supernatural insight, making hidden truths or information apparent to the recipient.

Types of Supernatural Informational Ability

## Article 77 – Supernatural Communicational Ability

265. ***Supernatural Communicational Ability*** is an extraordinary power to convey or receive messages beyond normal means, often involving telepathy, mediumship or spirit communication. It is the fourth and fourth most common category of the eight categories of *Supernatural Abilities*.

Supernatural Communication-al Ability

266. Types of *Supernatural Communicational Ability* include (but are not limited to):-

    (i) ***Mediumship***: Is the practice of communicating with spirits of the deceased, often to relay messages or gain insights from the spiritual realm; and

    (ii) ***Telepathy***: Is the ability to communicate thoughts, ideas, or feelings directly from one mind to another without using any known human sensory channels or physical interaction.

Types of Supernatural Communication Ability

267. Mediumship is extremely rare as a genuine ability. However, sufficient knowledge over time is known about this rarest of abilities including (but not limited to):-

    (i) ***Supernatural Sensual Abilities as Gateway***: Meaning no Medium is genuine unless they possess a strong natural ability of **Clairvoyance** (supernatural sight), apart from any other Supernatural Sensual Abilities; and

    (ii) ***Supernatural Sensual Messages as Medium***: Meaning all messaging from spirits and the deceased is via Supernatural Sensual Messages and almost always based on being visual and metaphoric and rarely phrases and almost never a complete sentence; and

    (iii) ***Genuine Mediums not in control of day/time of Messages***: Meaning no genuine Medium is in control of who contacts them, when they contact and what messages are delivered. Registered appointments and readings may act as a kind of "catalyst" for spirits and the deceased to deliver messages, there is no guarantee. Anyone who claims they can reliably get in contact with specifically requested spirits or people must be viewed with genuine scepticism and caution; and

    (iv) ***Genuine Mediums often receive messages days or hours before reading***: Meaning that an authentic and well disciplined medium are often given important messages and visions before any reading. However, given the metaphoric nature of such communication, it is often impossible to make sense until the reading. This is often a "validation gift" from spirits and the deceased to assist the living in knowing the authenticity (or not) of the session; and

    (v) ***Genuine Mediums do not filter or place bias on messages***: Meaning an authentic medium will deliver information as they have learned to interpret such symbolic metaphors and signs, without filtering out or imposing their own bias on the information. Even a gifted medium that performs a reading through their head and not their heart, will misread and disrupt the importance of such a connection.

*Mediumship*

268. The *Supernatural Communicational Ability* of Mediumship is one of the most abused and falsely claimed skills in history and especially under the growth of Spirituality:-

    (i) ***Exploitation***: Some mediums may exploit vulnerable individuals, especially those grieving the loss of loved ones, by

*False claims of Medium Abilities*

charging high fees for their services; and

(ii) **Fraud**: There are instances of continued fraudulent practices where supposed mediums use trickery and deception to create the illusion of communication with spirits; and

(iii) **Emotional Harm**: False hope or inaccurate messages can lead to emotional distress and confusion for clients.

269. There is a series of common sense tests for discerning likely authentic Mediums from blatantly fraudulent imposters:- *[Universal Test for Discerning likely Authentic Mediums from likely false Mediums]*

(i) **Limited Personal Information**: Genuine Mediums do not need loads of personal information. In fact such a demand should cloud a genuine reading, not assist; and

(ii) **Minimal Answers from Recipient**: Genuine Mediums do not need (and usually do not ask) for detailed answers or validations throughout the reading as this by definition creates a bias channel that should normally contradict a genuine reading; and

(iii) **Profound and Often Life Changing Information**: Genuine Mediums successfully transmit at least one piece of knowledge from spirits and the deceased that is often life changing, profound and always deeply personal, that concerns context, relations, meaning, life and death that is extremely difficult to fake. False mediums try and mask this test with either researched, guessed or provided "facts", when a genuine message could be as simple as a single key memory, or name or experience that no person could possibly understand except the living and the deceased.

## Article 78 – Supernatural Physical Ability

270. **Supernatural Physical Ability** is an extraordinary power to exceed normal human physical limits, such as superhuman strength, speed or agility. It is the fifth category of the eight categories of *Supernatural Abilities*. *[Supernatural Physical Ability]*

271. Types of *Supernatural Physical Ability* include (but are not limited to):- *[Types of Supernatural Physical Ability]*

(i) **Superhuman Strength**: Is an extraordinary physical ability enabling individuals to lift, move, or exert force far beyond the capabilities of normal human beings; and

(ii) **Shape-shifting**: Is the supernatural ability to transform one's physical form or appearance into that of another being, object, or creature, often instantaneously and at will; and

(iii) **Invisibility**: Is the supernatural ability to render oneself unseen to the naked eye, often by manipulating light or using magical or other means; and

(iv) **Levitation**: Is the supernatural ability to rise and float in the air without physical support, defying gravity through magical, psychic, or other extraordinary means; and

(v) **Immortality**: Is the supernatural ability to live indefinitely, without ageing or succumbing to disease, injury or death, effectively rendering one eternally youthful and imperishable.

## Article 79 – Supernatural Locational Ability

272. ***Supernatural Locational Ability*** is an extraordinary power to instantly move or sense locations beyond normal means, such as teleportation or remote viewing. It is the sixth category of the eight categories of *Supernatural Abilities*.

*Supernatural Locational Ability*

273. Types of Supernatural Locational Ability include (but are not limited to):-

*Types of Supernatural Locational Ability*

(i) **Remote Viewing**: Is the supernatural ability to perceive and describe distant or unseen locations, objects or events without being physically present, often through extrasensory perception or psychic means; and

(ii) **Teleporting**: Is the supernatural ability to instantly transport oneself or objects from one location to another without traversing the physical space in between.

## Article 80 – Supernatural Mental Ability

274. ***Supernatural Mental Ability*** is an extraordinary power to influence or perceive thoughts and minds beyond normal means, such as telepathy or mind control. It is the seventh category of the eight categories of *Supernatural Abilities*.

*Supernatural Mental Ability*

275. Types of Supernatural Mental Ability include (but are not limited to):-

*Types of Supernatural Mental Ability*

(i) **Hypnosis**: Is the supernatural ability to alter another person's mental state, inducing a trance-like condition that enhances suggestibility, focus, and responsiveness to commands or suggestions; and

(ii) **Psychokinesis**: Is the supernatural ability to move or manipulate objects with the mind alone, without any physical interaction, often through concentrated mental effort.

## Article 81 – Supernatural Manifestational Ability

276. ***Supernatural Manifestational Ability*** is an extraordinary power to create or bring objects, beings, or events into existence through mystical or magical means. It is the eighth category of the eight categories of *Supernatural Abilities*.

    *Supernatural Manifestational Ability*

277. Types of Supernatural Manifestational Ability include (but are not limited to):-

    *Types of Supernatural Manifest Ability*

    (i) ***Necromancy***: Is the supernatural practice of communicating with or raising the dead, often for divination, gaining knowledge, or exercising control over the deceased; and

    (ii) ***Apport***: Is an object that is said to have been produced or transported paranormally, typically in the context of séances or other spiritual phenomena.

## Article 82 – Magic

278. ***Magic*** is the practice of using rituals, symbols, actions, gestures, and language to harness supernatural forces or energies to achieve specific outcomes or effects.

    *Magic*

279. There are four principle classes of Magic based on the general nature of the associated knowledge, rituals or practices being *Illusionary, Wisdom, Occult* or *Hybrid* of previous three:-

    *Four classes of Magic*

    (i) *Illusionary* is when Magic is based on some trick, deception, illusion or ignorance of the observer; and

    (ii) *Wisdom* is when Magic is based on the application of knowledge previously lost or not understood; and

    (iii) *Occult* is when Magic is based on the application of claimed secret or deliberately hidden knowledge; and

    (iv) *Hybrid* is when two or more of the previous classes are used in combination.

280. ***Illusionary Magic*** is founded on manipulating the minds of the living or deceased involved in the ceremony that some kind of supernatural powers are possessed by the practitioner(s) through knowledge of ceremony, dress, procedure; and the demonstration of tricks of misdirection or sensory deprivation or distortion:-

    *Illusionary Magic*

    (i) Illusionary Magic uses a wide variety of manipulations and frauds to convince an audience of its authenticity, from natural skills of hypnosis, alteration of mind state, auto-suggestion, implanted memory work, sensory deprivation as well as time honoured tricks such as smoke, fire, tricks of light, drugs, chemical reactions and the use of tools and animals for Magic; and

(ii) All trick or Illusionary Magic is based on defrauding and tricking the audience of living or deceased minds; and

(iii) Most Magic is based on trick or Illusionary Magic; and

(iv) Illusionary Magic is effectively the strongest form of Magic precisely because it affects the only true Supernatural force being mind and consciousness.

281. Deep Occult or Wisdom Magic is founded on the possession of superior knowledge, connected to Natural Law and Divine Law and does not require tricks, misdirection and sensory deprivation or distortion. — *Occult and Wisdom Magic*

282. All Magic known as Sorcery, Occultism, Wicca, Wizardry, Witchcraft, especially Black Magic, Necromancy and ceremony derived from Grimoires is trick or Illusionary Magic, requiring a high level of deliberate ignorance and false belief. — *Black Magic*

283. The terms Sorcery, Occultism, Wicca, Wizardry, Witchcraft and Theurgy are equivalent to the term Magic. However, the term Necromancy is a form of Magic literature, belief and ceremony and therefore a sub-set of magic. — *Occultism*

284. The oldest practitioners of trick and Illusionary Magic are the priests of Ur, later the Amorties and Akkadians, then the Ur-Ga-Rit and Tar-Sur (Tarsus) and then Ur-Sur-Lim (Jerusalem). — *Oldest use of Illusionary Magic*

285. The oldest practitioners and master of Deep Occult and Knowledge Magic are the Cuilliaéan, also known as the Holly, also known as the Holy, also known as the Serpents, also known as the Hyksos and the Davids, later corrupted to Druvid and Druids. — *Oldest use of Wisdom Magic*

## 2.7 – Supernatural Phenomena

### Article 83 – Supernatural Phenomena

286. ***Supernatural Phenomena*** refer to events or occurrences that are beyond the scope of natural scientific understanding. These phenomena are often associated with entities, forces, or events that cannot be explained by known laws of nature, including (but not limited to) ghosts, spirits, telekinesis, clairvoyance and other paranormal activities. — *Supernatural Phenomena*

## Article 84 – Miracle

**287.** A ***Miracle*** is an ancient 8th Century religious term used to define any wonderful, marvellous or amazing event attributed to Divine or supernatural benevolence or intervention.

*Miracle*

**288.** The word and original meaning of *Miracle* comes from 8th Century formation of the Holly Catholic Church under the Holly Irish, Franks and Germans from the Latin *mirus* meaning "wonder" and *acula* meaning "a small needle". Hence the first meaning of Miracle was literally a "small wonder of divine benevolence".

*Original Meaning of Miracle*

**289.** Miracle did not evolve to its modern and contradictory meanings until the Counter-Reformation in the 17th Century and then the Enlightenment Movement in the 18th Century:-

*Evolving Meaning of Miracle*

  (i) In the 17th Century, works claimed to be by Thomas Aquinas (and then claimed to be written back in the 13th Century) first corrupted the notion of a Miracle to be an event that surpasses all known human and natural powers, being attributable solely to divine intervention; and

  (ii) By the 18th Century, the narrowness of the definition of Miracles defined under the Counter-Reformation was firmly rebutted by philosophers such as David Hume (1711-1776) who stated that a Miracle is "a transgression of a law of nature by a particular volition of the Deity, or by the interposition of some invisible agent…No testimony is sufficient to establish a miracle, unless the testimony be of such a kind, that its falsehood would be more miraculous, than the fact which it endeavours to establish"; and

  (iii) Whilst such writings under the Counter-Reformation firmly established the formal recognition of Miracles under the church, the resulting definition of Miracles as purely supernatural and solely as a result of disruption of natural laws, it allowed the systematic rebuttal under the Enlightenment Movement and thus greatly diminished spirituality across Western Europe and ultimately helped define the path that has led to the decline of Religion in general.

**290.** As the Universe is Unique Collective Awareness in motion, the most significant form of Miracle is and has always been the appearance of extraordinary, marvellous and wonderful divine wisdom.

*Miracles and Unique Collective Awareness*

**291.** Contrary to the deliberately false and misleading teachings of certain Cults, a Miracle by its very nature and original meaning is a

*Miracles are independent of Cult Dogma*

wonderful, amazing and extraordinary Divine event, without any need for it to validate or repudiate dogma. Furthermore, any teachings that claim non-authorized miracles are the "work of the devil" is the utmost and offensive fraud and immediately, null and void having no force or effect.

292. The tradition of certain Religious Denominations and Cults that demand a certain number of authorised "miracles" in order to validate a Cult figure as a Saint is a profound blasphemy and offence against God and the Divine Creator and all of Heaven. Such behaviour does not respect and properly recognize divine intervention, but minimises and suppresses its divine influence by repudiating all miracles, except those that suit the leadership of the particular Religious Denominations or Cult.

*Requirement for Miracles as Validation is an Offence against Heaven and the Divine*

## Article 85 – Precognition

293. ***Precognition*** is a term used to define an ancient belief that certain people at certain times have the ability to foresee elements of future events. The terms premonition, and presentiment are qualities of precognition through emotions.

*Precognition*

294. In accordance with Divine Law and Natural Law, an effect (future) cannot occur before its cause (present). Therefore, the concepts of Predetermination and fixed Destiny are wholly false. Therefore any Precognition, Premonition and Presentiment can only be future possibilities, not certainties.

*Possible Outcomes not Certainties*

295. As the Universe and existence is Unique Collective Awareness in motion, there is no law of nature that precludes precognition, premonition or presentiment of future possibilities.

*Precognition and Unique Collective Awareness*

296. The nature and necessity of rules of Natural law to preserve existence gives rise to a level of "predictability" in the sequence of events known as the laws of possibility. Thus all Precognition, Premonition and Presentiment is possible, yet alterable to the extent that the predictable sequence of events itself is altered changing likely outcomes.

*The ability to change future possible outcomes*

297. The receiving of a Precognition, Premonition or Presentiment itself materially affects the possible outcomes of the future, by affecting the present, therefore proving that Predetermination and fixed Destiny are wholly false. Thus, such visions are more appropriately spiritual attempts to change future possibilities rather than reinforcements of alleged fixed destiny.

*Self-fulfilling nature of Precognition and Premonition*

## Article 86 – Aura

298. *Aura* is a term used to describe both the phenomena and the ability for certain people to perceive the electro-magnetic fields as well as the state of mind and health of living things as collections of colour around the body of the living entity.  
<sub></sub>*Aura*

299. Aura is a perceptual ability, not a scientific phenomenon. While all living things have electro-magnetic fields, they are insufficient to produce noticeable surface charge to create visible colours through normal scientific detection equipment. Thus any perceived colour is perceptual interpretation of cognitive and psychic ability rather than some invisible actual field.  
*Aura as ability not feature*

300. As the continuation of existence does not permit the laws of nature to be broken, the phenomena of Aura and the ability of certain people to "see" such colours is explainable within the laws of nature in accordance with these Maxims.  
*Aura and Natural Law*

## Article 87 – Poltergeist

301. A *Poltergeist* is a term meaning a troublesome spirit or other supernatural force typified by loud unexplained noises, the movement of objects and general extreme fear and distress of people and animals witnessing such events.  
*Poltergeist*

302. As the integrity of the laws of Nature is fundamental to existence itself, all Poltergeist activity may be explained within Natural Law and Divine Law in accordance with these Maxims.  
*Poltergeists and Natural Law*

303. There are three main forms and sources of genuine Poltergeist activity:-  
   (i)   Anomalous Environmental-Geological Conditions; and  
   (ii)  Extreme Bio-Feedback Loops; and  
   (iii) Disruptive Intelligent Haunting.  
*Types of Poltergeist Activity*

304. The most common source of Poltergeist activity is Anomalous Environmental-Geological Conditions caused by a number of contributing factors including the age, type and condition of construction materials of a building, the geological material of the location and prevailing environmental conditions. High electro-magnetic radiation from overhead power lines, radio towers or poor electrical wiring is also a major contributing factor. In the case of old wooden structures, underground streams, voids, and construction on electro-magnetically active rock such as quartz, granite and limestone have all been shown as contributing factors to Poltergeist activity  
*Anomalous Environmental-Geological Conditions*

through Anomalous Environmental- Geological Conditions.

305. The second most common form of Poltergeist activity is Extreme Bio-Feedback Loops most commonly experienced by adolescent females or any traumatized children which can create an extreme negative bio-feedback that feeds on itself manifesting in the focusing and externalizing of these fears into an actual independent negative spiritual presence. Anomalous Environmental-Geological Conditions may also be a contributing factor. — Extreme Bio-Feedback Loops

306. The rarest form of Poltergeist activity is a Disruptive Intelligent Haunting caused by the presence of a Ghost in some state of extreme emotional distress manifested through Poltergeist activity. — Disruptive Intelligent Haunting

307. Excluding Anomalous Environmental-Geological Conditions which may be a permanent feature of an existing building, Poltergeist activity caused by Extreme Bio-Feedback Loops and Disruptive Intelligent Haunting may generally be resolved by addressing the root cause contributing of the effect, rather than the effects themselves. — Resolution of Poltergeist Activity

## Article 88 – Conjuration

308. *Conjuration* is a traditional term used to describe the use of any occult or magic ritual involving incantations, charms or spells to attempt to invoke one or more spirits to appear or interact. The conjuration of ghosts or souls of the deceased for the purpose of divination is called necromancy. — Conjuration

309. The practice of Conjuration is a major feature of almost all Religions and Cults, usually for the conjuration of positive spirits. However, several Cults with strong Duality embedded deeply within their doctrine seek to evoke and invoke negative spiritual energy through the same rituals. — Conjuration and Control

310. The use of Ouija, spirit or talking boards is an example of Conjuration, which occasionally results in spirit connection usually through unconscious motion of the conjurer(s), interpreting such acts as the effect of an external source. — Ouija and Conjuration

311. As Conjuration principally rests on magic, the most important ingredient for its alleged success is belief by the conjuror and practitioners as well as the alleged spirits attempting to be contacted that the occult knowledge and magic is authentic. — Conjuration and Belief

312. As belief is such a fundamental element to any alleged success to Conjuration, extreme and negative ritual to bolster belief has traditionally been part of conjuration since the first Religions and — Conjuration and Rituals to Reinforce Belief

Cults including animal sacrifice, human sacrifice, orgies, drugs and other sensory stimulation to heighten belief.

313. Other than the power of belief and its ability to manipulate and corrupt the minds of the living and the deceased, there is no Divine Law, nor Natural Law that validates Conjuration. Therefore, most Conjuration is a mixture of ancient traditions and made-up meaningless rituals that gains its power primarily from the use of extreme theatrics to enhance belief in its authenticity. *(Conjuration as a morally corrupt act of Deception)*

314. The second major presumption of Conjuration is the authority of the conjuror to demand or summons a spirit to appear. As all spirits, entities, gods, deities, angels and demons have sworn a solemn and irrevocable vow of allegiance to the sacred Covenant of One Heaven and no other, no Religion or Cult has any ecclesiastical or spiritual power to Conjure and control any spirit whatsoever. *(No authority of Conjuration)*

315. As no Religion or Cult has any ecclesiastical or spiritual power whatsoever to Conjure and control any spirit, any deliberate attempted Conjuration by the leaders of a Religion or Cult is an insult against united Heaven and Hell and all spirits. *(Blasphemy and Injury of Conjuration)*

## Article 89 – Levitation

316. **Levitation** is the process by which an object is suspended by some physical effect against the effects of gravity particle fields, without solid physical contact. Despite there being a number of techniques that may create levitation, it is also regarded as a supernatural phenomenon due to its frequent use in theatrical magic and occasional experience in poltergeist and active haunting. *(Levitation)*

317. As no Natural law is permitted to be temporarily suspended without causing the collapse of the universal dream, all cases of levitation may be explained within the laws of nature. *(Levitation and Natural Laws)*

318. The most common example of Levitation is Theatrical fraud most frequently practised with Theatrical Magic, but also promoted on occasion by leaders of Cults as a way of continuing to deceive followers. *(Levitation and Theatrical Magic)*

319. The second most common example of Levitation is Controlled Scientific Conditions through the use of such techniques as space (vacuum), electro-magnetic fields, acoustics, electrostatics and gases. *(Levitation and Electro-Magnetic Vacuums)*

320. The rarest example of Levitation is Spontaneous Haunting Phenomena whereby a ghost through space (vacuum) and electro-magnetic field manipulation reduces the density of a certain object creating the effect of its flotation in apparent defiance of the laws of *(Levitation and Hauntings)*

nature.

## Article 90 – Possession

321. ***Possession*** is the ancient belief that a deity, god, spirit, demon or some other entity may temporarily inhabit the body of a higher order life form such as a Homo Sapien, resulting in noticeable changes in personality, knowledge, health and behaviour.

*Possession*

322. In terms of *Possession* and history:-

    (i) The belief in *Possession* is a common feature in the majority of ancient and contemporary Religions and Cults; and

    (ii) Historically a range of mental illnesses have been misdiagnosed as forms of *Possession* including psychosis, hysteria, mania, Tourette's Syndrome, epilepsy, schizophrenia and dissociative identity disorder. This misdiagnosis of mental illness as possession continues in many poorly educated regions of the world; and

    (iii) The persistent belief by some Religious Denominations and Cults that all forms of *Possession* can only be the result of the Devil or Demons has not only confused and clouded any genuine research into the history of the phenomena, it has greatly diminished any effective and genuine Spiritual or Religious remedy in those rare cases of authenticity.

*Possession and History*

323. Whilst genuine *Possession* is forbidden and a serious crime against Divine Law, there is nothing within Natural Law or Cognitive Law that precludes the possibility of a genuine Possession:-

    (i) ***Natural Barrier to Possession***: Means all higher order life forms have a natural barrier to Possession in the form of their bonding between their Body and Mind and the bond between their Lower Mind and Higher Mind; and

    (ii) ***Weakened Barrier through Addiction***: Means there is evidence of a dramatically weakened natural barrier to Possession due to systemic substance abuse and mental illness. However, even in such a state, there is no evidence that the barrier preventing Possession is lost; and

    (iii) ***Intentional Acceptance and Invitation***: Means the most controversial element of genuine Possession is the intentional and knowing acceptance and invitation of the host to such Possession. Thus, the remedy of any cure of genuine Possession depends upon this universal truth.

*Possession and Universal Laws*

## Article 91 – Voices

324. ***Voices*** are audible or recorded disembodied communication usually associated with haunting for which there is no rational or reasonable explanation. The most common voice phenomenon is electronic voice phenomena. <!-- Voices -->

325. Electronic Voice Phenomena (EVP) are sounds captured electronically that resemble speech after all logical sources have been rationally and reasonably excluded including intentional or accidental voice recordings or renderings, modified static, background noise or stray transmission interference. <!-- Electronic Voice Phenomena (EVP) -->

326. The most common form of Electronic Voice Phenomena is associated with residual haunting, whereby significant or traumatic events are replayed within an environment during heightened amounts of electro-magnetic field energy such as storms, high tides and natural events. <!-- EVP and Residual Haunting -->

327. The rarest form of Electronic Voice Phenomena is intelligent haunting whereby a ghost seeks to interact with intelligent answers. <!-- EVP and Intelligent Haunting -->

328. As the natural background and static noise of electronic equipment and field emitting equipment is a source of raw material by which a ghost may use its ability to distort space to produce a recording, EVP's are more easily recorded on devices with poorer recording quality than digital devices with better quality and lower natural background static. <!-- EVP and older devices -->

## Article 92 – Haunting

329. ***Haunting*** is the term used to define the presence of one or more Ghosts inhabiting a building or location. A Haunting is defined as either Residual or Intelligent. <!-- Haunting -->

330. The most common form of Haunting is a Residual Haunting which involves the repeated playback of auditory, visual and other sensory phenomena of previous events without apparent intelligent awareness of the living world and interacting with or responding to it. <!-- Residual Haunting -->

331. The least common form of Haunting is an Intelligent Haunting which involves one or more Ghosts residing in a building or location, aware of the living world and capable of interacting with or responding to it. <!-- Intelligent Haunting -->

332. Causes and Conditions for Residual Haunting include (but are not limited to):- <!-- Causes of Residual Haunting -->

  (i) ***Geological Substructure of Land***: Methodical studies over the past century have been able to establish a link to such geological substructures as high density limestone, quartz and crystal ground structures and residual haunting; and

(ii) ***Persistent Heightened Emotional or Traumatic Environment***: Appears to be preconditions for the imprinting of a memory that may replay in years to come. Old battlefields are a good example.

333. In respect to Causes and Conditions for Intelligent Haunting:- Causes and Conditions of Intelligent Haunting

(i) The site of extreme brutality and violence does not always mean there will automatically be Intelligent Haunting, but often Residual Haunting mistaken for intelligent; and

(ii) A Building of significance and age may have several forms of Residual Haunting as well as Intelligent Haunting at the same time; and

(iii) The most common form of Intelligent Haunting is object binding whereby a ghost has bound its focus and attention to one (or more) deeply personal objects during their life of significance. The most common categories of haunted objects include (but are not limited to): jewellery, keepsakes (photos, letters, heirlooms, childhood mementos), portraits, clothing and furniture; and

(iv) The second most common form of Intelligent Haunting is when one or more spirits return to significant older buildings as favourite places during their lives, not necessarily places of extreme brutality and violence.

## 2.8 – Supernatural Evidence

### Article 93 – Supernatural Evidence

334. ***Supernatural Evidence*** refers to proof or indications of phenomena that cannot be explained by natural laws or scientific understanding. Supernatural Evidence

335. Supernatural Evidence, is evidence in general that may include (but not be limited to):- Examples of Supernatural Evidence

(i) ***Personal Evidence***: Personal testimonies or stories of encounters with ghosts, spirits or other supernatural entities; and

(ii) ***Photographic or Video Evidence***: Images or videos that allegedly capture supernatural phenomena, such as apparitions or unexplained lights; and

(iii) ***Electronic Voice Evidence***: Recordings of voices or sounds that some believe are communications from the dead or other supernatural beings; and

(iv) ***Medical or Scientific Baseline Evidence***: Scans, Tests and other Scientific Evidence establishing a baseline position, usually on a subject and then the subsequent tests and results that show an event beyond the known laws of nature; and

(v) ***Expert Evidence***: Expert testimonies, often as witness to medical, scientific or electronic evidence.

336. The generally uniform unscientific, emotional and irrational response to irrefutable Supernatural Evidence is rarely against such evidence but to the concept of "supernatural" itself and the implication of accepting such findings:- Irrational & Unscientific Response Supernatural Evidence

(i) The modern positioning of the term "supernatural" within Non-Ucadia Civilisation is in direct opposition to the notion of science and natural law. Thus, to accept any evidential findings is to weaken or repudiate natural law; and

(ii) Many scientists within Non-Ucadia Civilisation were taught upon the false 18th Century "Enlightenment Movement" distortions of the "supernatural" that all such claims are trickery, fraudulent and inherently unscientific; and

(iii) Similar to the intentional separation of the Mind to the Body within Non-Ucadia Science, the inherent binary design of "natural vs supernatural" means no harmony or reconciliation is possible between science and faith within Non-Ucadia Societies.

## 2.9 – False and Prohibited Supernatural Notions

### Article 94 – False, Absurd and Prohibited Supernatural Notions

337. ***False, Absurd and Prohibited Supernatural Notions*** beliefs or practices related to the supernatural that are forbidden or condemned. False, Absurd and Prohibited Supernatural Notions

338. Any type of Supernatural Concept, Notion or Doctrine listed as false and absurd within the present Maxims is prohibited and forbidden to be practised, supported or implemented in any way within any Ucadia Society, Body, Community, Entity, Association or Company. Concepts that Contradict the present Maxims

# Title III – Sacred

## 3.1 – Sacred

### Article 95 – Sacred

339. ***Sacred*** is the concept that a Form, either through solemn ritual or some previous attributes, is worthy of recognition and devotion or reverence. — Sacred

340. The determination of whether a Form is Sacred or not may differ widely between various religions and cults. In a number of cases, certain Forms are considered "universally sacred" particularly the remains of famous prophets and saints as well as the original manuscripts of prophets as well as places of extreme historical and religious significance. — Form of Sacred

341. Contrary to deliberately misleading presumptions, the Sacredness of an object to a particular Religious Denomination or Cult does not imply holiness. Instead, depending upon the Religion and its Occult teachings, an Unholy Object might be considered Sacred as much as a Holy Object. Sacredness therefore implies only reverence of a form to particular followers of a religion, not whether the form is or is not holy. — Sacredness vs Holiness

## 3.2 – Sacred Space

### Article 96 – Sacred Circumscribed Space

342. ***Sacred Circumscribed Space*** is a uniquely recorded bounded enclosure and dimension of Sacred Space-Day-Time, as prescribed by the most sacred Covenant *Pactum De Singularis Caelum* and associated Covenants *Pactum De Singularis Christus*, *Pactum De Singularis Islam* and *Pactum De Singularis Spiritus*. Only duly authorised bodies, persons or corporations granted limited Rights under Convention and Treaty are permitted to record, register, keep and maintain Sacred Circumscribed Space. — Sacred Circumscribed Space

343. A valid Ucadia Body, having been granted certain Rights, may reserve its absolute Rights to assert, declare, affirm, avow, enforce and defend its Rights to record, register, keep and maintain Sacred Circumscribed Space, by any and every lawful means necessary. — Authority of Sacred Circumscribed Space

344. All proper, valid and legitimate Sacred Circumscribed Space is clearly and uniquely named dimension of Ucadia Space-Day-Time, whereby:- — Conditions of Sacred Circumscribed Space

   (i) Such Sacred Circumscribed Space is properly defined by an eighteen digit and character number and identifier (XXXXXX-

Lex Ecclesiasticum: Maxims of Ecclesiastical Law

XXXXXX-XXXXXX), consistent with the most sacred Covenant *Pactum De Singularis Caelum*; and

(ii) The specific Sacred Circumscribed Space is able to properly define its origin to a higher jurisdiction of Sacred Circumscribed Space, also identified by a proper eighteen digit and character number and identifier; and

(iii) The specific Sacred Circumscribed Space was either formed in accord with the most sacred Covenant *Pactum De Singularis Caelum*, or associated Covenants and Charters, or by one or more properly dispensed sacraments of the thirty three Supreme Sacred Gifts of Heaven; and

(iv) The Sacred Circumscribed Space does not contradict or usurp any previous proper, valid and legitimate existing Sacred Circumscribed Space.

345. Any claimed space, close, place, region, zone, precinct or any other type of enclosure formed by edict, or statute or sacrament that is in conflict with the most sacred Covenant *Pactum De Singularis Caelum*, or Ucadian Law or these present Maxims shall be invalid, illegitimate and null and void ab initio (from the beginning), having no force or effect or Rights in law. — Space created by fraudulent Edict, Statute or Sacrament having no Rights in Law

346. Any and all claimed Juridic, Legislative and Sovereign Acts contrary to the authority of the most sacred Covenant *Pactum De Singularis Caelum* and these present Maxims that claim the right to form circumscribed space by such methods including (but not limited to) enclosure, alienation, enrolment, registration or certification; and all subsequent, dependent and related Statutes, including but not limited to all fraudulent, perfidious, false and deceptive documents purported to be of an earlier age in relation to the claimed enclosure of certain lands, spaces, closes, fields, places, regions, zones, precincts, territories, dominions and estates are hereby disavowed as morally repugnant, profane, sacrilegious, heretical and contrary to the Rule of Law, Civilised Society and Divine Law and are therefore invalid, illegitimate and null and void ab initio (from the beginning), having no force or effect or Rights in law. — Contrary Acts to Pactum De Singularis Caelum and Maxims

347. All Measurement and Standard of Sacred Circumscribed Space shall always be in accord with the most sacred Covenant *Pactum De Singularis Caelum*, associated covenants and charters, Ucadian Law and these present Maxims. All other forms of measurement and standards shall be null and void, unlawful and illegal, having no force or effect. — Measurement and Standards for Sacred Circumscribed Space

348. By the Divine Mandate and Authority of the most sacred Covenant — Valid and Legitimate forms

*Pactum De Singularis Caelum* and the present sacred Maxims, duly registered and authorised bodies, associations, societies, companies, persons and entities shall form, maintain and keep in custody the following types of Registers of Sacred Circumscribed Space, including (but not limited to):-

of Sacred Circumscribed Space

(i) *Land* (also deliberately misspelled within invalid and fraudulent laws as England) as a fixed and circumscribed piece of ground and earth of one Acre or more in surface area and then measured from the centre of the planet to the centre point of the surface area; and

(ii) *Forest* as a fixed and circumscribed piece of ground and earth of ten Acres or more in surface area that is preserved or reclaimed wilderness, natural habitat, untouched and uncultivated for agriculture; and

(iii) *Island* (also deliberately misspelled within invalid and fraudulent laws as Ireland) as a fixed and continuous piece of ground and earth, larger than twelve Acres in surface area; and circumscribed by water; and

(iv) *Sea* (also deliberately misspelled within invalid and fraudulent laws as Scotland as "not" Land) as a fixed and continuous area of open water, larger than twelve thousand Acres in surface area; and circumscribed by at least two or more Islands and at least one other Sea; and

(v) *Air* (also deliberately misspelled within invalid and fraudulent laws as Netherlands as "neither" water nor land) as a fixed and circumscribed piece of space between Land and the outer reaches of the atmosphere of a planet; and

(vi) *Person* as a movable circumscribed space inhabited by the physical and living biological body of one or more Homo Sapiens; and

(vii) *Office* as a fixed or movable circumscribed space inhabited by a Person; and

(viii) *Ship* as a vessel of named sacred circumscribed space for travelling through the sea or rivers or canals; and

(ix) *Vehicle* as a land or air vessel of sacred circumscribed space for travelling through the air or upon the land or underground; and

(x) *Market* as fixed or moveable sacred circumscribed space for the exchange of items of value; and

(xi) *Internet* as a digital circumscribed space, inhabited by Persons as Users; and

(xii) *Network* as a digital circumscribed space of networked computers, inhabited by Persons as Network Users; and

(xiii) *Virtual Reality* as a complex digital circumscribed space and reality; and

(xiv) *Domain* (also *Web Domain*) as a digital circumscribed space of web information, inhabited by Persons as Network Users; and

(xv) *Database* as a digital circumscribed space of digital information, inhabited by Persons as Database Users or Application Users.

349. Any and all claimed Sacred Circumscribed Space held as Allodial Title or Peculiar Title (as a Peculiarity) and therefore claimed to be owned absolutely, free of any claim is hereby disavowed as an abomination before all Heaven and Earth; and is condemned as a profound sacrilege, heresy, profanity, morally repugnant, perfidious and deliberately false, having no force or effect in law.    *Allodial Title*

350. Any and all claimed Sacred Circumscribed Space held as Crown Land and therefore claimed to be owned absolutely, including but not limited to the deliberate corruption of using the name "England" to denote Land; and "Ireland" to denote Islands; and Scotland to denote the Sea and Admiralty; and the "Netherlands" to denote Air, is hereby disavowed as an abomination before all Heaven and Earth and is condemned as profound sacrilege, heresy, profanity, morally repugnant, perfidious and deliberately false, having no force or effect in law.    *Crown Land*

## Article 97 – Sacred Office

351. A **Sacred Office** is a Position and title held by a proper Person through the power and authority of *Officium* in accord with the most sacred Covenant *Pactum De Singularis Caelum*. A Sacred Office does not exist, nor possesses any validity or legitimacy unless granted *Officium*.    *Sacred Office*

352. In accord with the most sacred Covenant *Pactum De Singularis Caelum*, there exists only three (3) valid types of Sacred Office being: Divine, True and Superior:

(i) A "**Divine Office**" is an Sacred Office whereby a Spiritual Member of One Heaven vows to embody such a unique Office, as a custodian and guardian spirit of the law or "*Nomos*", in accord with the rules and systems of *Officium Systemata* (Offices Systems) of Heaven. Divine Offices may then be defined as either a Supreme Divine Office or a Great Divine Office. A Supreme Divine Office is an office purely occupied and vested to a Spiritual Member as a *Nomos*; whereas a Great Divine Office is an office occupied and vested by both a Spiritual Member as a *Nomos* and a Living Member as an Officer. A Divine Office is formed through its unique identification and definition within the most sacred Covenant *Pactum De Singularis Caelum*, or associated Covenants and Charters. Thus a Divine Office itself can never be dissolved, usurped, seized or surrendered prior to its expiry. It can only be vacated by a Living Member; and

(ii) A "**True Office**" is the instance of the Great Divine Office of Man or the Great Divine Office of Woman as defined by the Divine Creator, whereby each and every Living Member is invested and commissioned from the time of their physical birth until their physical death. Therefore, a True Office can never be usurped, seized, sold or stolen; and

(iii) A "**Superior Office**" is the instance or derivative of a Great Divine Office within a valid Ucadia Community or Body as formed through its identification and definition within an instrument, agreement, covenant or document given existence by law or regulation according to the most sacred Covenant *Pactum De Singularis Caelum* and associated covenants and charters. The performance of one or more Oaths or Vows then formalises the particular office and is sustained so long as such oaths or vows are honoured.

353. No Inferior and Non-Ucadia Office can claim or assert to be Sacred under the most sacred Covenant *Pactum De Singularis Caelum*:- — *Inferior Offices not Sacred*

(i) An "**Inferior Office**" is a Non-Ucadian office or "Pseudo Office"; and are all Non-Ucadian positions whereby a defective or inferior Oath or Vow has been offered, or no Oath provided or where the fiduciary obligations have been abrogated in favour of agent and commercial advantages; and

(ii) All Non-Ucadian Offices, including all claimed Ecclesiastical Offices are Inferior Offices and "Pseudo Offices".

354. The foundation of all civilised rule of law, begins with the acknowledgement that the highest law comes from the Divine Creator of all things in the Universe expressed through the laws of the Universe and then through the reason and spirit of man and woman — *Valid Office and Divine Law*

to make Positive Laws.

An Office is both a form of Person and movable or immovable sacred space whereby certain rights, authorities, capacities and powers are conferred upon one who has pronounced one or more Oaths or Vows and Sacraments and preserved by their continued honour to the fiduciary principles of good faith, good actions and good conscience.

One who holds an Office under such fiduciary capacity is called an Officer. An Agent can never legitimately hold an Office.

As all rights and property are by definition sacred, all clerical and professional obligations and responsibilities in relation to the administration, transference and conveyance of any rights or property must be concluded in a valid Office.

Any and every transaction or claimed transference or conveyance of property or rights must be concluded within the sacred space and place of a valid Office to have ecclesiastical, moral, lawful and legal force and effect.

By definition, the authority, rights and powers of a Divine Office is superior to any and all other forms of Office, regardless of title or claimed status. No Inferior Office possesses any power, force, authority, right or ability to abrogate or usurp the decisions or authority of a Divine Office.

Similarly, no Superior Office or Inferior Office possesses any force, authority, right or ability to abrogate or usurp the authority of a True Office to exercise any of the Natural Rights granted to it, unless the occupant of a True Office wilfully and deliberately repudiates the Golden Rule of Law and all forms of logic, reason and sense.

All valid official positions or "offices" of all legitimate governments of all societies within the jurisdiction of the most sacred Covenant *Pactum De Singularis Caelum* therefore depend on the acknowledgement and recognition of the most sacred Covenant *Pactum De Singularis Caelum* as the highest law as the Covenant is nothing less than the perfect expression of Divine Will from the Divine Creator of all things in the Universe.

Furthermore, as the very meaning and purpose of the word "authority" is ecclesiastical, all legitimate authority of all officials of all valid governments of all societies on planet Earth depends upon the acknowledgement and recognition that all authority is ultimately derived from the most sacred Covenant *Pactum De Singularis Caelum* as the highest source of authority being the perfect expression of Divine Law of the Divine Creator of all things in the Universe.

355. There are sixteen (16) essential types of valid Office for the conduct and conclusion of sacred, clerical and professional obligations and responsibilities being: Sanctuary, Oratory, Consistory, Sacristy, Penitentiary, Chancery, Depository, Dispensary, Treasury, Ministry, Registry, Library, Notary, Secretary, Vestry and Rectory:-

*Types of valid Sacred Space of Office*

(i) A "**Sanctuary**" is any temporary or permanent sacred space (dimension) circumscribed by the performance of one or more valid Sacraments of Heaven. All valid sacred space (dimension) as an Office is first and foremost a Sanctuary; and

(ii) An "**Oratory**" is any valid Office that exists for the auricular exposition, discussion, relation, examination, disposition and conclusion of matters derived from Divine Law, Ecclesiastical Law and Positive Law and from which all other Offices in which the spoken word of Men and Women is translated to writing or vice versa is derived; and

(iii) A "**Consistory**" is any valid Office that exists for a solemn and sacred assembly or council or other democratic or representative body; and

(iv) A "**Sacristy**" is any valid Office that exists for the receiving and safe keeping of most sacred vessels, books, vestments and may also be used by clergy as valid Trustees for worship or meetings; and

(v) A "**Penitentiary**" is any valid Office that exists for the receiving and safe keeping of sacred vows, confessions, absolutions, dispensations and examinations of conscience and may also be used by clergy as valid Trustees for providing sanctuary and sustenance to penitents confessed; and

(vi) A "**Chancery**" (also Chancellery) is any valid Office that exists for the receiving and safe keeping of all original instruments, registers, memoranda, forms and rolls and for the original creation of new forms and instruments by valid Trustees as Scriveners as well as the provision of certified and valid extracts of original instruments and records; and

(vii) A "**Depository**" is any valid Office that exists for the purpose of receiving the temporary assignment of goods and property for safe keeping, or security, or bailment or warehousing upon the issue of receipts and to be returned upon expiry of such conditions; and

(viii) A "**Dispensary**" is any valid Office that exists for the purpose of dispensing, or settling, or resolving, or exchanging, or measuring, or paying, or issuing or trading property, goods or rights; and

(ix) A "**Treasury**" is any valid Office that exists for the purpose of receiving and keeping safe any and all property that has been salvaged or claimed or surrendered upon being abandoned, lost (presumed dead), incapacitated, infirm or intestate; and

(x) A "**Ministry**" is any valid Office that exists for conducting sacred, clerical and professional obligations and responsibilities and the dispensation and determination of questions of rights and property; and

(xi) A "**Registry**" is a valid Office that exists for the recording of entries, enrolments and events into Books, Registers, Rolls, Memoranda, Accounts and Manifests and the subsequent issue of Certificates, or Receipts as well as the administrative management of Journals, Ledgers and Summaries; and

(xii) A "**Library**" is a valid Office that exists for the recording, entry, safe keeping of copies and acknowledgement and evidence of service and publication of all official Notices, Books, Gazettes, Newspapers, References, Periodicals as well as Audio Visual Material as well as other claimed works of copyright; and

(xiii) A "**Notary**" is a valid Office that exists for the purpose of recording, entry, safe keeping of copies and acknowledgement and evidence of service of official Notices as well as the safe keeping and custody "in due course" of all "public" originals and proofs of any surrender, gift, waiver, abandonment, resignation, novation of property or rights by the Trustor through Deed or Act such as wills, affidavits, land and property conveyances; and

(xiv) A "**Secretary**" is a valid Office that exists for the purpose of the private recording, entry, safe keeping of copies and acknowledgement and evidence of service of Official Notices, Claims and Rights and the "secret surrender" and "passing" of such private material to other parties as required or demanded; and

(xv) A "**Vestry**" is a valid Office that exists for the purpose of recording and keeping safe the essential records of a Parish or Parochial body for proper spiritual administration of members, otherwise referred to as the "Cure of Souls"; and

(xvi) A "**Rectory**" is a valid Office that exists for providing teaching and instruction to students.

356. By the Power and Authority of the most sacred Covenant *Pactum De Singularis Caelum*, twelve (12) Offices are identified as the Supreme Divine Offices of One Heaven, to be held by purely Spiritual Members:

> Twelve Supreme Divine Offices of One Heaven

(i) Apostle; and

(ii) Consul; and

(iii) Augustus; and

(iv) Angel; and

(v) Saint; and

(vi) Wraith; and

(vii) Fate; and

(viii) Demon; and

(ix) Faerie; and

(x) Elve; and

(xi) Seraphim; and

(xii) Cherubim.

357. By the Power and Authority of the most sacred Covenant *Pactum De Singularis Caelum*, four hundred and thirty-two (432) most sacred and ancient official positions are recognised as the Great Divine Offices of One Heaven whereby a Spiritual Member as a "*Nomos*" and a Living Member as an "Officer" may hold, possess and be invested into a sacred office, namely:

> Four hundred and thirty-two Great Divine Offices of One Heaven

(i) One Divine Office of Existence, being: I AM; and

(ii) True Offices of Man and Woman, being: Man and Woman; and

(iii) Seventeen (17) Superior Offices of Trust, being: Obligor, Obligee, Trustor, Trustee, Principal, Agent, Beneficiary, Executor, Administrator, Grantor, Grantee, Donor, Donee, Assignor, Assignee, Delegator and Delegatee; and

(iv) Eleven (11) Superior Offices of Life, being: Corporeal, Nasci, Creator, Explorer, Thinker, Solver, Guider, Philosopher,

Exemplar, Eternal and Spirit; and

(v) Nineteen (19) Superior Offices of Clan, being: Kin, Son, Daughter, Brother, Sister, Grandson, Granddaughter, Nephew, Niece, Uncle, Aunt, Father, Mother, Grandfather, Grandmother, Male Cousin, Female Cousin, Patriarch and Matriarch; and

(vi) Eighteen (18) Superior Offices of Tribe, being: Initiate, Hunter, Gatherer, Preparer, Toolmaker, Cook, Carver, Weaver, Crafter, Storyteller, Ritualist, Muralist, Herbalist, Carer, Healer, Soothsayer, Senior and Chief; and

(vii) Forty-Eight (48) Superior Offices of Village, being: Habitant, Apothecarist, Artist, Astrologer, Baker, Basketweaver, Blacksmith, Bonecarver, Brewer, Brickmaker, Butcher, Carpenter, Clothmaker, Cobbler, Cooper, Druid, Dyer, Elder, Entertainer, Farmer, Fisher, Fortuneteller, Fowler, Gardener, Herder, Midwife, Miller, Miner, Musician, Painter, Plasterer, Poet, Potter, Quarrier, Reaper, Ruler, Salter, Shaman, Sculptor, Stonemason, Tailor, Tanner, Thatcher, Therapeutae, Trapper, Woodcarver, Woodsman and Yarnmaker; and

(viii) Fourteen (14) Superior Ecclesiastical Offices, being: Noviate, Advocate, Cleric, Celebrant, Imam, Lama, Rabbi, Knight, Bishop, Abbot, Mendicant, Minister, Supervisor and Vicar; and

(ix) One Hundred and Thirty Six (136) Superior Offices of City, being: Academic, Actor, Ambassador, Architect, Armourer, Artificer, Attendant, Auditor, Author, Beekeeper, Bladesmith, Boniface, Bookbinder, Bookkeeper, Bowyer, Brazier, Bricklayer, Brightsmith, Builder, Bursar, Cabinetmaker, Candlemaker, Caretaker, Cartographer, Caulker, Censor, Chamberlain, Chocolatier, Citizen, Cleaner, Clerk, Clothier, Collier, Constable, Costermonger, Courier, Currier, Cutter, Dancer, Deckhand, Decorator, Director, Docker, Doctor, Draper, Drayman, Dresser, Driver, Drover, Dux, Embalmer, Engineer, Engraver, Explorer, Factor, Farmhand, Farrier, Fellmonger, Ferryhand, Fishmonger, Fletcher, Forester, Fruitier, Fuller, Furrier, General, Glassblower, Grain Merchant, Grocer, Gunsmith, Haymonger, Herald, Hillier, Hind, Historian, Huckster, Innkeeper, Interpreter, Jagger, Jester, Jeweller, Joiner, Judge, Keeler, King, Laborer, Lardner, Lavender, Leatherworker, Legislator, Librarian, Lieutenant, Locksmith, Magistrate, Major, Manciple, Mercer, Merchant,

Metallurgist, Minstrel, Moneylender, Monger, Mortician, Musician, Novice, Patternmaker, Performer, Physician, Producer, Professor, Provider, Publisher, Queen, Ranger, Ratcatcher, Refiner, Renderer, Rider, Roper, Saddler, Sailor, Scientist, Scribe, Sergeant, Servant, Soldier, Teacher, Tucker, Turner, Tutor, Wainwright, Warden, Webster, Wheelwright, Whitster and Wright; and

(x) One Hundred and Two (102) Superior Offices of Community, being: Actuary, Apiarist, Arborist, Archivist, Assembler, Astronaut, Auctioneer, Banker, Biologist, Botanist, Cashier, Caterer, Chef, Chemist, Climatologist, Colonel, Composer, Concierge, Concreter, Conservator, Constituent, Criminologist, Decorator, Designer, Detective, Distributor, Diver, Draftsperson, Drainer, Driller, Drycleaner, Earthmover, Economist, Editor, Electrician, Electroplater, Engraver, Environmentalist, Excavator, Fitter, Florist, Gaffer, Gasfitter, Gatekeeper, Geneticist, Geoscientist, Glazier, Groundsperson, Hairdresser, Homeopath, Illustrator, Inspector, Instructor, Inventor, Janitor, Journalist, Laminator, Linguist, Lifeguard, Machinist, Manager, Manufacturer, Marketer, Mathematician, Mechanic, Mediator, Medicalist, Nanny, Nurse, Nutritionist, Paramedic, Pharmacist, Pilot, Plumber, Podiatrist, Printer, Programmer, Publican, Receptionist, Researcher, Robotist, Salesperson, Servicer, Statistician, Surgeon, Surveyor, Teacher, Technician, Teller, Therapist, Tiler, Trainer, Underwriter, Upholsterer, Valuer, Veterinarian, Watchmaker, Webmaster, Welder, Winemaker, Writer and Zookeeper; and

(xi) Twelve (12) Original Offices of the Land (Campus), being: Accountant, Bailiff, Commissioner, Jurist, Notary, Postmaster, Proctor, Reader, Scrivener, Secretary, Sheriff and Steward; and

(xii) Twelve (12) Master Offices of the See (Province), being: Captain, Comptroller, Governor, Justice, Master, Navigator, Procurator, Investigator, Rector, Registrar, Speaker and Treasurer; and

(xiii) Twelve (12) Great Offices of the State (University), being: Chamberlain, Censor, Chancellor, Custodian, Exchequer, Justiciar, Marshal, Dean, Narrator, Plenipotentiary, Prefect and President; and

(xiv) Eight (8) General Offices of the Union, being: Alexander, Basileus, Exarchos, Mediator, Economos, Stratagos, Kephalos and Mentor; and

(xv) Eleven (11) Key Offices of the Globe, being: Canonist, Caliph, Executor-General, Facilitator, Recurrence, Observer, Pope, Secretary-General, Senator, Timekeeper and Visitor; and

(xvi) Nine (9) Forbidden Offices, being: Christ, Cuilliaéan, Emperor, God King, God Queen, Lucifer, Messiah, Anti-Christ and Prophet.

358. In respect to Divine Offices, True Offices, Superior Offices and Inferior Offices: *Dissolution or Cessation of Office*

(i) A Divine Office cannot cease to exist, even if a physical and living incumbent fails to adhere to the standards and obligations of such office, or if one or more persons even disavow or seek to diminish or attempt to dissolve such Office; and

(ii) A True Office is dissolved upon the physical death of the incumbent Man or Woman; and

(iii) A Superior Office ceases to exist upon the death of the occupant, or their resignation, or if the occupant deliberately and wilfully breaches their obligations and responsibilities according to the Rule of Trust and fails to remedy within the allotted time, causing a default and then fails to honour and acknowledge their culpability, causing termination; and

(iv) An Inferior Office by definition never possesses legitimate authority or power, but ceases even to be capable of maintaining the impression of legitimacy when an occupant breaches any notion of Rule of Law, or decency, or good faith, or good actions or good conscience.

359. In respect of an Officer, a Superior Office may only be restored: *Restoration of Superior Office*

(i) After the allotted time and penance determined upon such a disgraced former Trustee and Officer openly and wilfully chooses to admit and confess to their dishonour and culpability of being found culpable; and

(ii) The renewal of sacred Oath and Vow upon expiry of the prescribed time and conditions permitting such a man or woman to once again become a valid Trustee.

360. In accord with the most sacred Covenant *Pactum De Singularis Caelum* and the most ancient Rule of Law, a Member bound to an Office by a valid Sacred Oath and Vow may only continue to occupy, *Capacity and Competency of Office*

hold and administer such Office if they act in honour to uphold the law. When a Living Member as an Officer dishonourably abuses a position of office, they break their solemn Oath and Vow and therefore render the binding to Office null and void.

When a Living Member continues to claim occupancy of an Office and yet deny their obligations and duties, they automatically excommunicate themselves from any spiritual authority, thereby rendering such acts merely enforceable through ignorance, force or fear.

Furthermore, such a Living Member automatically makes themselves eligible for punitive sanctions enforceable through the *Obligationum Systemata* (Enforcement Systems) of Heaven.

When a Living Member seeks to continue to illegitimately claim Office through the use of ignorance, force and fear, denying their dependency on validity from the Divine Creator and Divine Law, and causing damage upon the Earth and physical injury causing death upon the bodies of other Living Members, then such a Living Member invokes upon themselves the full force and power of the Wraiths of the *Obligationum Systemata* (Enforcement Systems) of Heaven against their physical presence within the temporal realm of the Universe.

361. A Member of One Heaven who has consented by their actions to a Certificate of Incompetence to be recorded, gazetted and published against them is ineligible to continue in any official capacity in any society whatsoever. [Incompetency and Office]

    When a Certificate of Incompetence is issued, the occupier of a certain Office is prevented from exercising any associated Power granted by the present sacred Covenant including: Magisterium, Imperium, Sacrum, Cancellarium, Virtus, Custoditum, Alumentum or Visum.

362. A Member of One Heaven who has consented by their actions to a Certificate of Excommunication to be recorded, gazetted and published against them is without any legitimate authority to hold office as a heretic and apostate. [Apostasy and Office]

363. Nine (9) Great Divine Offices recognised and honoured as part of the four hundred and thirty-two (432) Great Offices of One Heaven shall be forbidden to be used, or for any man or woman or spirit to assume the occupation of such Office for the whole life of the most sacred Covenant *Pactum De Singularis Caelum* and all associated bodies, societies and entities. These Offices include the Offices of Christ, Anti-Christ, Cuilliaéan, Emperor, God King, God Queen, Lucifer, [Forbidden Offices]

Messiah and Prophet.

Therefore, any man or woman or spirit that proclaims themselves the occupant or holder of any such forbidden Sacred Office henceforth shall commit a grave injury against all of Heaven and Earth and any such claim or subsequent act shall be without validity or authority.

## 3.3 – Sacred Place

### Article 98 – Sacred Place

364. A ***Sacred Place*** is one designated for divine worship, by dedication through the liturgical and sacramental rituals provided in accord with the most sacred Covenant *Pactum De Singularis Caelum*. — Sacred Place

365. Sacred Places are recognised, established maintained and protected in character through the receiving and written memorial of the Cardinal Sacrament of Consecratio (Consecration) forming Sacred Circumscribed Space. — Formation of Sacred (Divine) Places

366. Only those things that serve the exercise or promotion of worship, piety or religion are permitted in a Sacred Place. Therefore, anything that is not consonant with the holiness of the place is forbidden, unless in individual cases the relevant Ecclesiastical Superior permits another use that is not contrary to the holiness of the Sacred Place:- — Conditions of Sacred Places

    (i) Sacred Places temporarily lose their dedication or blessing if they have been destroyed in large part, or have been turned over permanently to profane use. The Clergy are not permitted to decree, nor endorse the profane or sordid use of Sacred Places and instead must use all its resources and abilities to prevent such injury; and

    (ii) Sacred Places are violated by gravely injurious actions done in them with scandal to the faithful, or by actions considered so grave and contrary to the holiness of the place that it is not permitted to carry on worship in them until the damage is repaired by a penitential rite according to approved liturgical books; and

    (iii) The Universal Ecclesia of One Christ, the Holy Society of One Islam, the Sacred Society of One Spirit and valid and legitimate Ucadia Ecclesia Foundations shall acquire, retain and manage such Land and Places suitable as locations for worship, both within established urban environments and in rural and agricultural regions of planet Earth; and

    (iv) The Universal Ecclesia of One Christ, the Holy Society of One

Islam, the Sacred Society of One Spirit and valid and legitimate Ucadia Ecclesia Foundations shall acquire such Land and Places suitable as locations for spiritual retreat, education and healing within areas of preserved and pristine wilderness and majestic beauty within the bounds and jurisdiction of each University and shall ensure its presence within each and every major community.

367. A ***Religious Place of Worship*** is a sacred building designated and duly consecrated for divine worship whereby Members of the Three Great Faiths possess the right of entry for the exercise of such divine worship. *(Sacred Place of Worship)*

368. The three Great Faiths of One Christ, One Islam and One Spirit shall acquire, build and modify suitably consecrated buildings as Religious Institutes for Divine Worship, Sacramental Rites and Sacred Education. *(Function of Sacred Places of Worship)*

369. No Religious Place of Worship is to be built or designated and consecrated without the express written consent of the appropriate clerical authority of the particular Great Faith. *(Clerical Authority)*

## Article 99 – Altar

370. An ***Altar*** is any fixed or movable structure dedicated for the purpose of votive, or penitential or sacramental offerings. The most sacred ceremony upon a properly sanctified and dedicated altar is sacrament of Holy Eucharist. *(Altar)*

371. Fixed altars must be dedicated, and movable altars must be dedicated or blessed, according to the rites prescribed in the liturgical books. An altar, whether fixed or movable, must be reserved for divine worship alone, to the absolute exclusion of any profane use. However, Altars, whether fixed or movable, do not lose their dedication or blessing if the church or other sacred place is relegated to profane uses. *(Fixed and Moveable Altars)*

372. The Customary and Traditional Rite of placing relics of martyrs or other saints under a fixed Altar is permitted to be preserved within those Customary and Traditional Rites that deem such ancient tradition as absolutely necessary. However, in all other instances, no bones or relics or bodies are to be buried within or beneath Altars. *(Restriction on remains and Altars)*

# Article 100 – Shrine

**373.** A ***Shrine*** is a Sacred and Holy Place dedicated and consecrated to Heaven and to one or more venerated deities, ancestors, heroes, martyrs, saints or spirits, where Living Ordinary Members make pilgrimage as a mark of respect and piety.

*Sacred Shrines and Altars*

**374.** A Shrine may exist in a number of forms including (but not limited to) a sanctuary, or preserved location, or holy city, or temple, or church or altar. In all cases, a Shrine must be respected as a place of great sanity and free from approved profane or sordid behaviours. Above all, a Shrine is a spiritual portal between Heaven and Earth, given to all people as a means of sustaining and edifying their faith and enlarging and strengthening their trust and knowledge in God and the Divine Creator of all Existence.

*Form of Shrines*

**375.** All Shrines may be defined by six characters being: Supreme, Traditional, National, Historical, Communal or Familial, whereby a particular Shrine may qualify according to one or more characteristics:-

*Character of Shrines*

   (i) *Supreme Shrine* is a Sacred and Holy Place ordained by Heaven in unity and perpetual remembrance of the most sacred Covenant *Pactum De Singularis Caelum*. There are eleven Sacred Cities and Sanctuaries representing supreme sacredness across all seven Unions (Africa, Americas, Arabia, Asia, Levant, Europe and Oceania) being the Holy See, the Holy City of Jerusalem, the Holy City of Mecca, the Holy City of Istanbul (Constantinople), the Holy City of Bodh Gaya, the Holy City of Varanasi, the Holy City of Tunis (Carthage), the Holy City of London, the Holy City of Washington, the Holy City of Melbourne and the Holy Sovereign Sanctuary of One Ireland; and

   (ii) *Traditional Shrine* is a Sacred and Holy Place ordained and worshipped by one or more Customary and Traditional Rite as a Sacred Place of the utmost significance; and

   (iii) *National Shrine* is a Sacred and Holy Place ordained by approval of the Ecclesiastical religious leadership of the relevant University and nation; and

   (iv) *Historical Shrine* is a Sacred and Holy Place approved by the Ecclesiastical religious leadership of a University and Nation as a place of sanctity and importance, deserving of preservation and reverence; and

   (v) *Communal Shrine* is a Sacred and Holy Place approved by the relevant provincial and local Ecclesiastical religious leadership for a community; and

(vi) *Familial Shrine* is a Sacred and Holy Place within a building occupied by one or more households, approved by the relevant local Ecclesiastical religious leadership for votive offerings and celebrations.

## Article 101 – Sacred Buildings

376. ***Sacred Buildings*** are structures that hold religious or spiritual significance for a particular group of people. These Sacred Buildings are usually designed and constructed with great care and attention to detail, reflecting the beliefs, values, and architectural styles of the religious or spiritual tradition they represent.

*Sacred Buildings*

377. Sacred Buildings serve as places of worship, prayer, meditation, and reflection, and they may also be used for various religious ceremonies and rituals. Some common types of Sacred Buildings from different religious traditions include (but are not limited to):-

*Examples of Sacred Buildings*

   (i) ***Temples*** are Sacred Buildings in various religions, including Hinduism, Buddhism, and ancient Roman and Greek religions. They are typically ornate structures with specific architectural features and symbols associated with the respective faiths; and

   (ii) ***Churches*** are Christian Sacred Buildings constructed in various architectural styles, such as Gothic, Romanesque, and Baroque. They often include features like a nave, altar, sacristy, stained glass windows, and a cross or crucifix; and

   (iii) ***Cathedrals*** are large Christian Churches that serve as the central place of worship for a diocese or bishopric. They are often grand and architecturally significant; and

   (iv) ***Mosques*** are Islamic Sacred Buildings. They are known for their distinctive architecture, featuring features like minarets, domes, and prayer halls. The qibla wall indicates the direction of Mecca, which is essential for Islamic prayer; and

   (v) ***Shrines and Pagodas*** are Sacred Buildings found in various Asian religions, including Buddhism, Shintoism, and others. Shrines and pagodas are often simple, elegant structures that serve as places of devotion and pilgrimage; and

   (vi) ***Gurdwaras*** are Sikh Sacred Buildings. They typically have a central hall where the Guru Granth Sahib (the Sikh holy scripture) is kept, and langar (community kitchen) facilities for serving meals to visitors; and

(vii) **Synagogues** are Jewish Sacred Buildings. They vary in architectural style but often have an Ark containing Torah scrolls, a bimah (raised platform), and the Eternal Light; and

(viii) **Monasteries and Convents** are religious communities where monks and nuns live and worship. Monasteries are often associated with Buddhism and Christianity, while convents are typically for Christian nuns; and

(ix) **Sacred Caves and Natural Structures** are examples of indigenous and nature-based spiritual traditions, natural formations such as caves, mountains, or groves can be considered sacred and used for rituals and ceremonies.

378. Clerics and Ministers holding such sacred office (such as one of the Great Offices of State), must live in legitimately established Religious Houses, designated according to the norm of law of Ucadia and the Universal Ecclesia of One Christ, or Holy Society of One Islam or the Sacred Society of One Spirit or valid and legitimate Ucadia Ecclesia Foundations:- *Religious House*

(i) The erection of such Religious Houses shall take place with consideration for their advantage and proximity to Religious Institutes; and

(ii) No Religious House is to be erected or acquired or modified unless it can be judged prudent to the needs of the Members and that such buildings honour the religious duties, standing, honour and purpose of those that live in them; and

(iii) The Universal Ecclesia of One Christ, the Holy Society of One Islam, the Sacred Society of One Spirit and valid and legitimate Ucadia Ecclesia Foundations shall make early provision to contribute to the acquisition, or building, or development of a Religious House befitting for the standing, office and sanctity of the Visitor. As Superior to the House, the Visitor may designate who may live within it, providing such will and intention is made in writing.

## Article 102 – Sacred Ruins

379. **Sacred Ruins** are the remnants of religious or spiritual structures or sites that have, over time, fallen into disrepair, decay, or abandonment. These ruins often still hold religious or historical significance and considered sacred or spiritually meaningful by the communities or cultures that revere them. *Sacred Ruins*

380. Examples of Sacred Ruins exist worldwide, including (but not limited to):-

    (i) ***Ancient Temple Complexes and Shrines*** such as those in Greece, Rome, Egypt, Cambodia, and Central America are now ruins but were once central to religious life and ceremonies; and

    (ii) ***Abbeys and Monasteries*** like those in Europe, Ireland or South America may still hold spiritual significance even though they are no longer in active use; and

    (iii) ***Stone Circles and Megalithic Structures*** like Stonehenge in England and Newgrange in Ireland, as well as various stone circles and dolmens around the world, are often considered sacred ruin; and

    (iv) **Ancient Cities and Settlements** like Pompeii in Italy, Petra in Jordan, and Palmyra in Syria may contain sacred structures and artefacts; and

    (v) **Religious Statues and Sculptures** such as idols, or statues that were once central to religious practices like those on Easter Island (Rapa Nui), can be considered sacred; and

    (vi) **Sacred Natural Sites** such as caves, mountains, and lakes can be considered sacred ruins if they were once associated with religious practices but are now abandoned.

*Examples of Sacred Ruins*

## Article 103 – Ucadia Embassies, Consulates & Missions

381. ***Ucadia Embassies, Consulates & Missions*** are valid Ucadia bodies and Sacred Places established through appropriate diplomatic treaties and relations, as diplomatic representation and internationally recognised diplomatic missions.

*Ucadia Embassies, Consulates & Missions*

382. All valid Ucadia Embassies, Consulates & Missions shall be recognised as Sovereign and Sacred Places, not subject to entry, search, seizure or obstruction under all civilised and moral law and civilised international law.

*Ucadia Embassies, Consulates & Missions as Sacred Places*

383. When a Ucadia University has reached Probational Status, then it shall be permitted to establish a Diplomatic Post within the jurisdiction of each and every other Ucadia University that has also reached Probational Status, through a formal treaty between Ucadia Universities recognising the diplomatic status and rights of each other. A Diplomatic Post is called a Ucadia Mission and shall be represented by a Diplomatic Consul.

*Ucadia University Body at Probational Status*

384. When a Ucadia University has reached Prerogative Status, such status means that the host state has formally accepted and adopted Ucadia as the model and function of Government. The Ucadia University as effectively the government of the host state shall be permitted to seek a permanent Diplomatic Post within the jurisdiction of each and every other Ucadia University that has reached Probational Status, through a formal treaty between Ucadia Universities recognising the diplomatic status and rights of each other, as well as the host nations corresponding to the jurisdictions of the Ucadia Universities. *[Ucadia University Body at Prerogative Status]*

385. The Diplomatic Post of the prerogative status Ucadia University shall be called a Ucadia Embassy and shall be represented by an Ambassador, while the probational Ucadia Universities shall be recognised in the receiving jurisdiction as Consulates headed by Consuls-General, or if prerogative then such Ucadia Universities shall be recognised as Embassies headed by Ambassadors. *[Ucadia Embassy]*

## 3.4 – Sacred Person

### Article 104 – Sacred Person

386. A ***Sacred Person*** is a form of Sacred Circumscribed Space enclosing certain characteristics and appearances as the identity of one or more Beings, formed through a valid entry, registration and record within a Roll in accord with the present sacred Maxims and most sacred Covenant *Pactum De Singularis Caelum*. *[Sacred Person]*

387. Any entry, or registration or record within a Roll that is not in accord with the present sacred Maxims, or is based upon the deliberate refutation of these present Maxims cannot be claimed as a valid or legitimate Person whatsoever. *[Valid Entry in Roll]*

388. A ***Divine Person*** is the Sacred Circumscribed Space created through a valid entry, registration and enrolment within the Great Roll of Divine Persons in accord with the present sacred Maxims and the most sacred Covenant *Pactum De Singularis Caelum*:- *[Divine Person]*

    (i) The highest Roll defining the greatest Rights and types of Persons is the Great Roll of Divine Persons, also known as the Great Register and Public Record of One Heaven; and

    (ii) No possible Roll possesses greater authority or power or jurisdiction than the Great Roll of Divine Persons; and

    (iii) All lesser Person records, entries, registrations and enrolments are borne first and foremost from the existence of a valid Divine Record; and

(iv) No lesser Person record, entry, registration or enrolment is valid or legitimate until it can verify and prove its provenance to a particular Divine Record and the authority to make such a joinder.

389. A Person is distinct from a Being as a Person is a form of Sacred Circumscribed Space enclosing certain characteristics and appearances as the identity of one or more Beings within a certain Reality, whereas a Being is an embodiment of Unique Collective Awareness and Computational Model within a certain Reality.

*Person versus Being*

390. All Sacred Persons may be categorised and ranked according to three (3) possible levels of authority, powers and rights from the greatest and highest powers and authority to the lowest and least powers and authority being (in order of rank): Divine, True and Superior:-

*Three Levels of Sacred Persons*

(i) A *Divine Person* is the purely Divine Spirit Person created through a valid record and enrolment in the Great Roll of Divine Persons and associated with a Divine Trust formed in accord with the sacred Covenant *Pactum De Singularis Caelum* by the Divine Creator into which the form of Divine Spirit, Energy and Rights are conveyed; and

(ii) A *True Person* is the Form attributed to a True Trust formed when an associated Divine Trust already exists and there is a lawful conveyance of Divine Rights of Use and Purpose, known as "Divinity" to a True Trust associated with then the birth and existence of a living Higher Order Life Form and the physical version of the Great Roll of the Society of One Heaven and a valid Live Borne Record. A True Person can never be claimed or argued as higher than the Divine Person from which it derives its authority; and

(iii) A *Superior Person* is the Form attributed to a Superior Trust when an associated True Trust already exists and there is a lawful conveyance of First Right of Use and Purpose, known as "Realty" to a Superior Trust associated with the birth of a service or agreement associated with the Membership of a living Higher Order Life Form to a valid Ucadia society and the authorised Member Roll of such a society. A Superior Person can never be claimed or argued as higher than the True Person from which it derives its authority.

391. In regards to an Inferior Person:-

*Inferior Person not a Sacred Person*

(i) An *Inferior Person* is the Form attributed to any non-Ucadian body politic or entity; and is the lowest standing and weakest of all valid forms of Persons; and

(ii) An Inferior Person is only valid when the man or woman in possession of a Superior Person and True Person consent to an enrolment of their name in one or more Rolls; and

(iii) An Inferior Person can never be validly, legitimately, logically, legally, lawfully or morally claimed or argued as superior to a Superior Person.

## Article 105 – Saint

392. A ***Saint*** is a person believed by the followers of a Religion or Cult to have received upon their death the full grace and rewards of the gods or deities of the particular faith because of leading an exemplary life in accordance with some doctrine and dogma. — Saint

393. All Religions and Cults possess at least one or more Saints, even if the term or an equivalent is not used. — Universal notion of Saints

394. While substantial differences exist between the selection of Saints by different Religions and Cults, the following is considered the popular perceived characteristics of any Saint:- — Common characteristics of Saints

(i) Worker of wonders, or source of benevolent power and intercessor; and

(ii) Possessor of unique and important revelations to the god(s) or deities of the faith; and

(iii) Extraordinary teacher especially through selfless ascetic behaviour; and

(iv) An Exemplary Model of the teachings of the Religion or Cult.

395. The presumption that in order to be a Saint a person must have lived an exceptionally holy and pious life is not considered a doctrine or point of dogma of most Religions and Cults. Instead, it is a popular misconception which is rarely challenged. — Saint and Ethical Life

## Article 106 – Holly

396. The word ***Holly*** is derived from the 11th century Saxon word *hulis* from ancient Celt *khuli/cuili* a shortened derivation of the ancient Gaelic *cuilieann* meaning Holly, sacred, venerated and most ancient bloodline of priests. Today in Modern Gaelic, Holly is still known as cuileann. — Holly

397. While the 15th century creation of hallow from halig resulted in the word "holy" meaning to make a thing sacred or venerated, a person borne to the most sacred and ancient bloodline of the Holly is by definition holy by blood. — Holly and Sacred

Title III – Sacred

398. The word cuileann is a variation on several words of the same origin including cullen, cuilleain, culeen, coileain, cullenan, kollyns, collins and o'collins from one of the oldest titles of history Cuilliaéan meaning cuil (corner/forest) + lia (stone/physician) + éan /éin (bird/spirit/divine) or Divine Corner Stone, Divine Forest Teacher, or Green God, or Da'vid, or Druvid, or Druid.  *Origin of Holly*

399. In regards to the history of the Holly:-  *Brief History of the Holly*

   (i) The Holly origins are linked to the Ebla pioneers of the great Bronze Age mining and trade of Ireland and directly to King Ibbi, the last Great King of Ebla. King Ibbi, the Royal family and his court and priests fled this great and ancient Syrian city before it was captured by Sargon the Great around 2290 BCE; and

   (ii) The Holly Priest Kings are the original invaders, teachers and engineers known as the Hyksos Pharaohs, or Shepherd Kings who built the great crescent arc channel from Zion, then known as Zeus and now known as Suez on the Red Sea to Chi-Rho, also known as Cairo in the 16th Century BCE, transforming the ancient world. It is to the Holly that the blood of the Hyksos through Akhenaten and his family returned; and

   (iii) The Holly Priest Kings are the savior messiah kings of the Brahmans and Vedic people known as the Druvids, the authors of the great vedas and revered in ignorance as gods still to this day in the celebration of Huli (Holly); and

   (iv) The Holly Priest Kings are the savior messiah kings known as the Da'vids of the Israelites, the followers of Akhenaten captured at Ugarit and bonded into slavery to serve the Ramesses usurpers. It is to the Holly that the blood of the Da'vids through Tamar Tephi accompanied by Jeremiah returned.

400. The Greek translated word "Keltoi" by the Greek historian Hecataeus in 517 BC of the people of Rhenania (West/Southwest Germany) is a variation of khuli/cuili. Hence Keltoi or the "Celts" are the Cuilli or Cuilliaéan or Holly/Holy People.  *Holly and Celts*

401. The symbolic genealogical importance placed on the holly tree and its recognition as sacred by the ancient druid religion is the original source of this belief that well over a thousand years later went onto become a major symbol of the bloodline of Christ and the bloodline of the historical figure known as Jesus, also known as Yeshua.  *Holly Tree and Christ*

402. The Holly Priest Kings are the Sangreal, the source of the inspiration  *Sangreal and*

of the Nazarenes and Gnosis and the Holly Grail. It is to the Holly that the blood of the founder of the Nazarenes through Mary accompanied by her grandfather returned.

*Holly Grail*

## Article 107 – Prophet

**403.** A ***Prophet*** is someone who is believed to have received Divine Revelation. A Religion or Cult then considers one or more Prophets to be the intermediaries between the divine supernatural and the temporal world with these messages known as prophecy and when written and combined as scripture.

*Prophet*

**404.** All Religions and Cults have been formed by the alleged writings of one or more Prophets.

*Religions and Prophets*

**405.** A common feature of all Prophets, no matter how significant the prophecies, is that during their lifetime they were largely ignored, often disrespected and devoid of substantial financial means. Hence the ancient maxim that one cannot be a prophet in their own land.

*Prophets and contemporary societies*

## Article 108 – Saviour

**406.** A ***Saviour*** is a Hero, anointed by some higher supernatural power, who through his or her actions and moral courage helps save a group of people by conquering some kind of danger. Hence, a Religious Saviour is a Hero who saves the world.

*Saviour*

**407.** As a Hero, a Saviour frequently must first fall from favour and respect within the community they ultimately save. This might be by their own actions, the actions and belief of others, or both. Thus a Saviour must first become an outcast.

*Saviour as Hero*

**408.** In accordance with the most ancient beliefs of all Religions and Cults, the most significant sign and tool provided by a Saviour to help save people and conquer danger is divinely inspired knowledge rather than force. In other words, the hallmark of a valid Saviour is the knowledge and ideas they bring that are powerful enough to withstand the physical obstinacy of evil.

*Function of Saviour*

**409.** By definition a Saviour is proven by the divine knowledge they bring, their actions and moral courage, not by any claim. Therefore anyone who claims to be a Saviour is automatically a fraud as such an action contradicts the self evidence and behaviour of a true Saviour.

*Proof of Saviour*

**410.** The list of key Saviours of various civilisations, empires and cultures over the past 2,500 years include (but is not limited to):-

*List of Key Saviours over past 2,500 years*

(i) ***Mithra***: Being the Divine Saviour of the Persian Empire and its colonies, including Rome and Athens until 69 CE; and

(ii) ***Lucifer***: Being the Divine Saviour of the Romans from 70-114 CE and then revived from 1660s as "the Holy One" and "Christ" for some groups and institutions; and

(iii) ***Sabaoth (Moloch)***: Being the Divine Saviour of some Yahudi prior to 1st Century BCE and then revived as "the Hidden One" in the 17th Century under the Ashkenazi cult and then again in the 18th Century through the Hasidic cults; and

(iv) ***Risen Christ (Second Coming)***: Being the Divine Saviour of Christians under Roman Catholicism from 8th Century and then all Christians from 17th Century; and

(v) ***Messiah of the Yahudi (Jews)***: Being the Divine Saviour of the Old Testament and "Torah" from 17th Century creation of the Holy Bible; and

(vi) ***Mahdi of Islam***: Being the Divine Saviour of Islam initially from the 14th Century and then updated from the 17th Century with the changes made within Islam following the Holy Bible; and

(vii) ***Kulkulkan of Maya (Sth America)***: Being the Divine Saviour of the Maya; and

(viii) ***Maitreya of Buddhism***: Being the Divine Saviour and fifth and future Buddha of this world era; and

(ix) ***Kalki of Hinduism***: Being the Divine Saviour and future avatar of Lord Vishnu.

## Article 109 – Messiah

411. The ***Messiah***, also known as Mashiach, is a specific type of Religious Savior and Hero, originally promised under the Yahudi faith from end of fall of the Messiah Kings in 6th Century BCE, then revived again after the expulsion of all Yahudi and followers of Iudeasim from Roman controlled Palestine and the renaming of Jerusalem to Aelia Capitolina in 122 CE by Emperor Hadrian as an annex of the Capitolinium of Rome.

*Messiah*

412. In reference to the origin and context of the Divine Saviour known as *Messiah* and *Messiah of the Jews*:-

*Origin of Messiah of the Yahudi (Jews)*

(i) The sacred "Messiah" texts and supporting texts are all creations starting from the 17th Century and the complete conversion of the Yahudi to "Jews" and the corruption of the ancient kingdom of Judah to being a competitor to a fictitious state called "Israel"; and

(ii) The term "Israel" is a 16th Century occult word created by English Alchemist John Dee (1527-1609) from Isis, Ra and El and not an accurate historic term; and

(iii) The lack of knowledge of Baal Hamon and the subsequent use of the name of Sabaoth as the hidden name of "G-d" of the Jews is partly caused by the age of the grimoires and black magic in England, France and Italy at the end of the 16th Century.

413. In reference to the qualities and signs of the Jewish Messiah:- *Prophetic Signs & Qualifications of Jewish Messiah*

(i) He Must be a member of the tribe of Yahudi (Judah) (Genesis 49:10); and

(ii) He must be a direct male descendant of King David and King Solomon (2 Samuel 7:12 - 13); and

(iii) (Deut. 30:3; Isaiah 11:11-12; Jeremiah 30:3, 32:37; Ezekiel 11:17, 36:24) When the Messiah returns the Yahudi (including Jews) will return to their homeland; and

(iv) (Isaiah 2:2-3, 56:6-7, 60:7, 66:20; Ezekiel 37:26–27; Malachi 3:4; Zech. 14:20-21) The Temple in Jerusalem will be rebuilt through the Messiah; and

(v) (Micah 4:1-4; Hoseah 2:20; Isaiah 2:1-4, 60:18) There will be universal disarmament and worldwide peace with a complete end to war; and

(vi) (Ezekiel 37:24; Deut. 30:8,10; Jeremiah 31:32; Ezekiel 11:19-20, 36:26-27) The Messiah will reign at a time when all the Yahudi will observe Divine Law; and

(vii) (Zechariah 3:9, 8:23,14:9,16; Isaiah 45:23, 66:23; Jeremiah 31:33; Ezekiel 38:23; Psalm 86:9; Zeph. 3:9) The Messiah will rule at a time when all the people of the world will come to acknowledge and serve the one true Divine Creator.

414. In reference to the requirement for the Jewish Messiah to be a blood descendant of both King David and King Solomon:- *The Bloodlines of King David and King Solomon*

(i) Yahudi descendant King Solomon, properly known as King Sulmanu of the Assyrians (859-824 BCE) is a famous historical king that built the Great Temple of Baalbek. He worshipped Baal Hamon and later his priests and descendants worshipped Mithra; and

(ii) Yahudi King U'vid (Da'vid) (999-931 BCE) son of Great Prophet Zadokiah is a famous historical king and for hundreds of years the mortal enemies of the Baal Hamon (Moloch) Yahudi Priests; and

(iii) Mariamne, the daughter of King Agripiah (Agrippa) and wife of Cú-Laoch (Yahusiah), also known in history as Jesus Christ, is a blood descendent of the High Priests of Baal Hamon. Thus all Holly descendents of Jesus and Mariamne are the only ones that carry the united bloodlines of the Yahudi priests of David and Solomon; and

(iv) Cú-Cúileann (Yasiah), also known in history as Joseph, is the main Holly blood descendant of the first Messiah Priest Kings of Yahu and the Great Prophets of Yeb; and

(v) Only descendents of this priestly line can rightly claim to be descended from both King Solomon and King David; and

(vi) Absolutely no one of Sephardi, Mizrahi or Askkenazi heritage can be claimed, or claim themselves as a Jewish Messiah, unless they also carry the bloodline of the Holly descendents of Jesus and Mariamne; and

(vii) Apart from Jesus, there has only been one example in the past two thousand years of any potential candidate meeting such criteria, including the contemporary criteria of modern Jewish faith, being one born with Jewish ancestry on both sides of his parents, born on Emerald Hill, Melbourne on March 14, 1965.

## 3.5 – Sacred Form

### Article 110 – Sacred Form

415. ***Divine Objects*** are items or artefacts that are believed to possess a special, sacred, or supernatural quality or significance within the context of religious or spiritual beliefs. These objects are often revered and used in religious rituals, ceremonies, or as symbols of faith.  <sub>Divine Object</sub>

416. The nature and importance of Divine Objects vary greatly among different religious traditions and cultures, including (but not limited to):-  <sub>Examples of Divine Objects</sub>

    (i) ***Religious Texts***: Sacred books and scriptures, such as the Bible in Christianity, the Quran in Islam, the Bhagavad Gita in Hinduism, and the Torah in Judaism, are considered divine objects. They are seen as repositories of divine knowledge and guidance; and

    (ii) ***Religious Symbols***: Objects like the Christian cross, the

Islamic crescent and star, the Hindu Om symbol, and the Buddhist Wheel of Dharma are considered sacred symbols that represent divine concepts and teachings; and

(iii) ***Religious Icons***: In some Christian traditions, icons, which are painted or sculpted images of saints, the Virgin Mary, or Jesus Christ, are considered divine objects. They are venerated and used in devotional practices; and

(iv) ***Idols and Deity Statues***: In Hinduism and other polytheistic traditions, idols and statues of deities are considered divine representations and objects of worship; and

(v) ***Ritual Objects***: Various religious rituals involve the use of specific objects. For example, in Hinduism, items like incense, lamps, and bells are used in worship ceremonies. In Buddhism, prayer beads (malas) are used during meditation; and

(vi) ***Altars and Shrines***: The physical structures and objects on altars and shrines in churches, temples, and other places of worship are considered sacred. These can include statues, candles, flowers and offerings; and

(vii) ***Relics***: Relics are physical remains or personal items associated with religious figures, such as the bones of saints, pieces of clothing worn by prophets, or objects used in their lives. They are venerated in many religious traditions, particularly in Catholicism and Buddhism; and

(viii) ***Artefacts and Reliquaries***: Some religious traditions have preserved ancient artefacts and reliquaries that are believed to have historical or religious significance. For example, the Ark of the Covenant in Judaism or the Holy Lance in Christianity; and

(ix) ***Vestments***: Sacred vestments are special garments or clothing worn by clergy and religious leaders during religious ceremonies and rituals in various religious communities; and

(x) **Talismans and Amulets**: In some folk and spiritual traditions, objects like talismans and amulets are believed to offer protection or bring good luck. These can include charms, stones or jewellery; and

(xi) ***Sacramental Bread and Wine***: In Christianity, the consecrated bread and wine used in the Eucharist or Communion are believed to become the body and blood of Jesus Christ; and

(xii) ***Holy Water and Oils***: Water and oils that have been blessed or consecrated are used in various religious ceremonies, such as baptism, anointing of the sick and blessings.

## Article 111 – Sacred Numeracy

417. ***Sacred Numeracy*** or "numerology" are terms used to describe various ancient traditions and customs that believe numbers possess magical and supernatural powers in their relationship to physical objects and other form.

*[Sacred Numeracy]*

418. As everything within the universal dream may be expressed in terms of numbers and relationships of numbers, numbers rightly represent symbols of meaning of sacred importance.

*[Sacred Numeracy and Universe]*

419. In terms of Sacred Numeracy, the ***Number One (1)*** is historically considered by almost all ancient Faiths, Religions and Cults to be the most sacred of all numbers:-

*[Number One]*

   (i) ***Symbolism***: Unity, the beginning, the source, the manifestation; and

   (ii) ***Religions/Cultures***: Many ancient traditions consider it the source of all numbers and often associate it with the concept of monotheism, the idea of one God; and

   (iii) ***Occult***: Tarot Cards (the Magician).

420. In terms of Sacred Numeracy, the ***Number Three (3)*** is historically considered by almost all ancient Faiths, Religions and Cults to be the second most sacred of all numbers:-

*[Number Three (3)]*

   (i) ***Symbolism***: Harmony, wisdom, understanding; and

   (ii) ***Religions/Cultures***: In Christianity, the Holy Trinity (Father, Son, Holy Spirit). In Hinduism, the Trimurti (Brahma, Vishnu, Shiva). It also appears in various mythologies as a symbol of completeness and perfection; and

   (iii) ***Occult***: Tarot Cards (The Empress).

421. In terms of Sacred Numeracy, the ***Number Five (5)*** is historically considered by almost all ancient Faiths, Religions and Cults to be the third most sacred of all numbers:-

*[Number Five (5)]*

   (i) ***Symbolism***: Balance, human life; and

   (ii) ***Religions/Cultures***: The five elements (earth, water, fire, air, ether) in many ancient traditions including Hinduism and Buddhism. In Christianity, the five wounds of Christ. In

Chinese culture, the five phases (wood, fire, earth, metal, water); and

    (iii) **Occult**: Tarot Cards (The Hierophant), The Primary Magic Number.

422. In terms of Sacred Numeracy, the **Number Six (6)** is historically considered by most ancient Faiths, Religions and Cults to be a sacred number:-

    (i) **Symbolism**: Harmony, balance; and

    (ii) **Religions/Cultures**: Often associated with creation. In Christianity, God created the world in six days. In Chinese culture, six is considered a lucky number and is associated with smooth progress; and

    (iii) **Occult**: Tarot Cards (The Lovers).

423. In terms of Sacred Numeracy, the **Number Seven (7)** is historically considered by most ancient Faiths, Religions and Cults to be a sacred number:-

    (i) **Symbolism**: Spiritual union, perfection, completeness; and

    (ii) **Religions/Cultures**: Seen in many traditions such as the seven days of creation in the Bible, the seven heavens in Islamic tradition, and the seven chakras in Hinduism and Buddhism; and

    (iii) **Occult**: Tarot Cards (The Chariot), the Primary Metaphysical Number.

424. In terms of Sacred Numeracy, the **Number Eight (8)** is historically considered by most ancient Faiths, Religions and Cults to be a sacred number:-

    (i) **Symbolism**: Renewal, rebirth; and

    (ii) **Religions/Cultures**: In Chinese culture, it is considered very lucky and associated with prosperity. In Christianity, eight people were saved on Noah's Ark, symbolizing new beginnings; and

    (iii) **Occult**: Tarot Cards (Strength or Justice).

425. In terms of Sacred Numeracy, the **Number Nine (9)** is historically considered by most ancient Faiths, Religions and Cults to be a sacred number:-

    (i) **Symbolism**: Completion, eternity; and

    (ii) **Religions/Cultures**: In Norse mythology, the universe consists of nine worlds. In Chinese culture, nine is associated with the Emperor and is considered powerful and auspicious; and

 (iii) ***Occult***: Tarot Cards (The Hermit).

426. In terms of Sacred Numeracy, the ***Number Twelve (12)*** is historically considered by most ancient Faiths, Religions and Cults to be a sacred number:-

 (i) ***Symbolism***: Cosmic order, completeness; and

 (ii) ***Religions/Cultures***: The twelve months of the year, twelve signs of the zodiac, twelve apostles in Christianity, twelve tribes of Israel; and

 (iii) ***Occult***: Tarot Cards (The Wheel of Fortune).

427. In terms of Sacred Numeracy, the ***Number Fourteen (14)*** is historically considered by most ancient Faiths, Religions and Cults to be a sacred number:-

 (i) ***Symbolism***: Transformation, Resurrection; and

 (ii) ***Religions/Cultures***: The Mid (Ides) of Moon based months of ancient cultures, coinciding with full moon. Ancient Birthday and Death/Resurrection Day of Mithra and originally celebrated as Birthday of Jesus Christ until the 8$^{th}$ Century; and

 (iii) ***Occult***: The only number whose complete cultural history has been suppressed and overwritten by another number being 13.

428. In terms of Sacred Numeracy, the ***Number Twenty-Two (22)*** is historically considered by most ancient Faiths, Religions and Cults to be a sacred number:-

 (i) ***Symbolism***: Mastery, realization; and

 (ii) ***Religions/Cultures***: In Kabbalistic tradition, there are 22 paths on the Tree of Life and 22 letters in the Hebrew alphabet, each with its own mystical significance.

429. In terms of Sacred Numeracy, the ***Number Seventy-Two (72)*** is historically considered by most ancient Faiths, Religions and Cults to be a sacred number:-

 (i) ***Symbolism***: Cosmic order; and

 (ii) ***Religions/Cultures***: In Kabbalah, there are 72 names of God. In ancient Egyptian mythology, Osiris was cut into 72 pieces.

430. In terms of Sacred Numeracy, the **Number One Hundred and Eight (108)** is historically considered by most ancient Faiths, Religions and Cults to be a sacred number:-

    (i) *Symbolism*: Spiritual completion; and

    (ii) *Religions/Cultures*: Highly significant in Hinduism, Buddhism, and Jainism. There are 108 beads on a mala (prayer beads) for chanting, 108 energy lines converging to form the heart chakra in yoga.

431. In terms of Sacred Numeracy, the **Number One Hundred and Forty Four (144)** is historically considered by most ancient Faiths, Religions and Cults to be a sacred number:-

    (i) *Symbolism*: Completeness; and

    (ii) *Religions/Cultures*: In the Bible, 144,000 represents the total number of souls to be saved (Revelation 14:1-5).

432. As existence depends on the operation of Natural Laws, therefore not permitting supernatural laws, all magic and power of numbers may be expressed in terms of Divine Law and Natural Law.

433. While a particular Religion or Cult may place greater or lesser emphasis on a number, the paradox of existence is that if one number ceased to exist, all numbers cease to exist. Therefore no number can correctly be considered more important than another.

## Article 112 – Sacred Geometry

434. *Sacred Geometry* is the belief that certain geometric shapes, patterns and proportions are sacred and therefore possess higher significance and importance, either through occult and religious teaching or observation of natural patterns within Natural Law.

435. While Religions and particularly Cults claim sacred Geometry is a reflection on the belief that the universe is created according to a Divine geometric plan, there is frequently a deliberate and conscious discord between natural geometry and man-made geometry.

436. In the universal dream and therefore the dimension created by the Divine Creator, the most important shapes are the circle, the sphere and the curve. However, in Religions and Cults, the most significant shapes are straight lines, squares, triangles and combinations of all three and complex shapes such as pentagrams.

437. As there is no such thing as a straight line in reality in the physical atomic universe, all straight line geometry created by Religions and Cults is man-made and has no actual connection to Divine geometry

of the universe.

438. The disconnect between the actual geometric shapes of the universe and the geometric shapes considered sacred by Religions and Cults since the beginning of Civilization is explained by "Halluciogenic Entoptic Phenomena" being visual sensations derived from the natural structure of the optic system from the eyeball to cortex when one or more powerful hallucinogenic substances have been consumed.

*Geometry and Drug Influenced Experiences*

439. While the consumption of hallucinogens by ancient priests of Religions and Cults, especially the LSD effects of "sacred" mushroom altered consciousness, it also produced predictable visual distortions of "Halluciogenic Entoptic Phenomena" implying the existence of a fractal-like substructure to nature based upon lines, lattice structures, triangles, serpent waves and squares. Hence, this geometric information has been presumed to be sacred to the geometry of the universe, rather than a consistent and normal effect of being under the influence of powerful drugs.

*Fractals and Drug Influenced Experiences*

440. Given sacred man-made geometry rarely represents nature or sacred geometry of the universe, such shapes promoted by Religious Denominations and Cults as sacred often have no power other than in promoting false belief which may then become self-fulfilling when enough ignorant minds, living and deceased, believe it to be true.

*Man Made Geometry and Divine Geometry*

441. Rather than sympathetic geometry that enhances nature, straight-line and square sacred man-made geometry interrupts natural field flow, severs natural current and disturbs sacred nature, particularly when such alien structures are created at sights of significant natural energy.

*Negative Energy Flow of Man Made Geometry*

## Article 113 – Sacred Symbols

442. ***Sacred Symbols*** are certain line art, geometric shapes, carvings and images considered sacred by one or more Religions and Cults.

*Sacred Symbols*

443. Examples of Sacred Symbols include (but are not limited to):-

*Examples of Sacred Symbols*

   (i) ***Seats***: Seats such as Thrones and Chairs are arguably one of the oldest and most significant symbols of Sacred Authority; and

   (ii) ***Headdress***: Headdress such as hats, crowns, or wreaths have been a symbol of Sacred Authority since the first civilisations; and

   (iii) ***Garments***: Particular Garments such as robes have been a symbol of Sacred Authority for millennia; and

(iv) **Jewellery**: Special and historic examples of jewellery have been symbols of Sacred Authority since the first civilisations; and

(v) **Furniture**: Elaborate and historic Desks, Cabinets, Beds and Tables are all examples of Sacred Authority since early civilisations; and

(vi) **Handheld Objects**: Sceptres and orbs associated with the monarchy's power and dignity; and

(vii) **Transportation**: Ancient (and modern) modes of transportation such as chariots, ships and horse drawn carriages have a long history as being symbols of Authority and Power; and

(viii) **Monuments**: These structures often serve as a symbol of Sacred Authority as well as national pride and history, representing significant events, achievements or figures; and

(ix) **Murals and Paintings**: Murals and paintings including (but not limited to) grand walls of hieroglyphs, elaborate mosaics, stunning painted ceilings and walls have all projected Sacred Authority and Power for millennia; and

(x) **Instruments and Texts**: Important texts and instruments such as proclamations, charters, and ancient symbols of scripture have all featured as Sacred Symbols and Signs of Authority since the first civilisations; and

(xi) **Buildings**: Ceremonial and Religious Sites.

## Article 114 – Sacred Art

444. ***Sacred Art*** is defined as some kind of object depicting imagery considered sacred by one or more Religions and Cult. The Sacred Art itself may also be venerated as sacred. — *Sacred Art*

445. Examples of famous Sovereign Murals & Paintings include (but are not limited to):- — *Examples of Sovereign & Sacred Murals & Paintings*

   (i) ***Granting of Power and Authority over the Earth by God to Adam by Michaelangelo (1475-1564) Sistine Chapel***: The 16$^{th}$ Century masterpiece gives both "public notice to heaven and earth" that according to the Bible, God gave Power and Authority over the Earth to Adam and his "authorised descendents"; and

   (ii) ***God Apollo/Lucifer granting favour and authority to Charles II and the formation of the United Kingdom*** *and Corporations by James Thornhill (1676-1734) Greenwich Palace*: This 18th Century masterpiece, clearly shows the pagan depiction of the demigod of Apollo (in Greek mythology) and Lucifer (in Roman mythology) as the patron and protector of the United Kingdom and its corporations and actions; and

(iii) ***The Deification (Apotheosis) of Washington by Constantino Brumidi (1805-1880) US Capitol Building***: This 1865 masterpiece depicts Washington being made a god, not by a historic God, but by the original thirteen Dutch republic families that emigrated to the old Dutch colonies by 1792 depicted as goddesses. Below Washington as "god" is the symbolism of power of war, science, admiralty, commerce, technology and agriculture. The painting ultimately reveals the source of true power in America and the real "god" of the motto "in god we trust"; and

(iv) ***Goddess Hera (Juno) blessing young Victoria as goddess Lucy (female Lucifer) and Empress by John William Waterhouse (1849-1917) and falsely claimed by Orazio and Artemisia Gentileschi 17th C. Greenwich Queens (White) House***: This 1870 masterpiece originally painted for ceiling of remodelled White (Queens) House at Greenwich in direct response to the *Apotheosis of Washington*. It depicts a young Victoria as a female Lucifer (Lucy) as the central goddess among the goddesses of wisdom, strength, reason, rhetoric, science, mathematics, music and logic; and as Empress of the world. The painting was hastily removed no later than 1871 and reset at Malborough House by architect James Pennethorne, who butchered the original painting to make it fit and died soon after.

## Article 115 – Sacred Texts

446. ***Sacred Texts*** or scripture is some inscription or printed document, book, charter, manuscript or folio containing accounts, descriptions, stories and testaments considered sacred by one or more Religions and Cults.

    *Sacred Texts*

447. The most significant Sacred texts in history are those believed to be direct Divine revelation. All Civilizations and therefore Religions and Cults possess or used to possess one or more Sacred Texts.

    *Important Sacred Texts*

448. The most important sacred text in history is the most sacred Covenant of One Heaven also known as *Pactum De Singularis*

    *Pactum De Singularis*

*Caelum.*

## Article 116 – Sacred Architecture

449. **Sacred Architecture**, also known as religious architecture, is a term describing the design and construction of Temples, Sanctuaries, Altars and other structures by deliberately adopting certain geometry, numbers, ratios and symbols considered important and sacred for a particular Religion or Cult.

450. As Religious buildings have historically been the largest and most impressive structures of any city for millennia, their location, ratios, even positioning in relation to ley lines, horizon and astronomical effects of the sun and moon throughout the year have almost always played an integral part in its design and architecture.

451. Examples of famous ancient Sacred Sovereign Monuments & Statues include (but are not limited to):-

    (i) **Great Hyksos Initiation Chambers (Great Pyramids of Giza)**: Constructed at the height of Hyksos power in Egypt, arguably one of the greatest engineering achievements of any civilisation in history; and

    (ii) **Great Statue of Anubis (Desecrated and Deformed by Ramesses II to the Sphinx)**: The Great Anubis was a dog, not a jackal and stood guard on the Giza plateau against all forms of evil. Ramesses II desecrated and deformed this sacred monument into his own likeness and it became the infamous sphinx; and

    (iii) **Great Statue of Xerxes (Corrupted in history to be listed as Great Statue of Zeus)**: Was over 30 metres in height and stood at the entrance to the Acropolis in Athens; and is the source of the false legend of the "Colossus" misappropriated to the island of Rhodes; and

    (iv) **Great Statue of Athena Parthenos**: Built in the 3rd Century BCE as the new protector goddess of the city. Was over 39 ft (12 metres) in height and was seated in the Great Parthenon temple on the Acropolis; and

    (v) **Great Obelisk (Membrum) of Amun-Ra of Karnak**: Reputed to have been over 144 ft (43.9 m) in height and weighing more than 800 tons and the single largest carved block of stone in human history. Symbolised the Sun God using his membrum to "inseminate" the earth with new life every day. It was destroyed by the impostor Ramesses pharaohs when they ransacked and burned the sacred temple complexes of Karnak; and

(vi) ***Obelisk (Membrum) of Ra of Cairo (under Thutmose IV)***: Approx 83.6 ft (25.5 m) in height, weighing 330 tons and more than 3,400 years old. It was brought to Rome in 37 CE by Caligula and was placed at a prime position in the Great Circus. It was then moved in 16th Century to the new St. Peters Basilica to grow and "inseminate the Vatican" with new power every day.

452. Examples of famous modern Sacred Sovereign Monuments & Statues include (but are not limited to):-  *(Examples of modern Sacred Sovereign Monuments & Statues)*

(i) ***Washington (Membrum) Obelisk Monument***: Approximately 555 ft (169 m) tall, with a foundation of 111 ft, as the largest phallic symbol ever conceived in human civilisation. Similar to other ancient obelisk in their design, the shadow of the Washington (Membrum) Monument enlarges up the National Mall twice a year around March 20-21 (spring equinox) and September 22-23 (autumnal equinox); and symbolically "procreates" with the giant 2,300 ft by 1,400 ft *Great Owl of Moloch* (aka Sabaoth, El and Satan) being the shape that clearly encompasses the Capitol Building; and

(ii) ***Great Owl of Moloch***: While not strictly a blatant or obvious monument, the specific design of roads around the US Capitol Building clearly create the largest symbol to Moloch ever conceived in human civilisation. Its design is to imitate the symbolic design of the Vatican but in a much more literal and negative form; and

(iii) ***Lincoln Memorial***: Designed to deify Abraham Lincoln as the god Zeus, the seated statue of Abraham Lincoln is approximately 19 feet (5.8 meters) tall, with Lincoln "as a god" touching the two largest symbols of Fasces (bundles of bound sticks symbolising literally rule by force, power, weaponisation of law and oppression).

## Article 117 – Sacred Music

453. ***Sacred Music*** is the composition and recital of certain music using tones or frequencies, scales, instruments, texture, melody, rhythm and arrangements considered sacred by various Religions or Cults.  *(Sacred Music)*

454. Tone is the base frequencies used in Sacred Music. Until the late 19th Century, almost all indigenous music and a substantial proportion of Western music was historically tuned to the natural water and Earth  *(Sacred Frequency)*

base frequency 432 Hz and its scalar harmonics. However, the 20th Century has seen an orchestrated and deliberate corruption of base frequency music to the powerful dissonant, discordant frequency of 440 Hz.

455. While most Sacred Music until the 20th Century was designed to uplift and harmonize members of Religions and Cults based on 432 Hz, the conscious and deliberate corruption of base frequency to 440 Hz means almost all music is spiritually divisive, genetically and cellular corrosive and bad for health, no matter what form of music is played. *(Corruption of Sacred Frequency and Music)*

456. In accordance with these Maxims, the tuning of instruments to 440 Hz instead of 432 Hz is forbidden, including the playing of music at 440 Hz instead of 432 Hz. Any person, group or entity that promotes 440Hz music against 432 Hz must be disbanded, removed and cease to exist. *(End of Corruption of Sacred Sound)*

## Article 118 – Sacred Language

457. ***Sacred Language*** is a term used to describe a sacred liturgical language or divine language, written, spoken and used by members of a Religion or Cult or by divine beings such as gods, deities and other spirits. A divine language is always supremely sacred over any sacred liturgical language. *(Sacred Language)*

458. A *Sacred Liturgical Language* is any language that is primarily reserved for official ceremony and ritual by a Religion or Cult, that is not normally used in ordinary daily life. The language Latin that has been hijacked and corrupted by the Roman Cult is an example of a Sacred Liturgical Language. *(Sacred Liturgical Language)*

459. A Sacred Divine Language is any language that is primarily reserved for official ceremony, ritual and communication by Divine beings such as the Divine Creator, lesser deities, angels, demons and spirits in general. The highest and supreme Sacred Divine Language of All is Psygos. *(Psygos)*

460. In accordance with these Maxims and the sacred Covenant *Pactum De Singularis Caelum*, the original of all official documents issued by Ucadia is in Logos first and then translated to lesser languages second. *(Logos)*

461. When anyone references, writes or speaks of "Sacred Language", "Divine Language", or "Holy Language" it shall mean the Sacred Languages of Psygos and Logos of Ucadia and no other. *(Sacred Language and Ucadia)*

# Article 119 – Sacred Dance

462. ***Sacred Dance*** is a term describing the beliefs and customs of various Religions and Cults that certain formal, synchronised and reproducible movement between two or more persons is sacred and enhances spiritual connection. As Dance is normally accompanied by Music and other elements of Sacred Form, it is usually part of a large sacred Ritual.

    *Sacred Dance*

463. As Sacred Dance in its broadest definition is formal, synchronized and reproducible movement. Therefore, what constitutes Sacred Dance varies from the formal procession of clergy into a Temple in unison, to marching, to group whirling and individual folk-type dancing and evocations.

    *Formation of Sacred Dance*

464. Examples of Sacred Dance include (but are not limited to):-

    *Examples of Sacred Dance*

    (i) ***Corroboree***: a generic term used to describe various ceremonial gatherings of Aboriginal Australians which include music, dance, and costume. These events are rich in cultural significance and are performed for a variety of reasons, including storytelling, teaching, healing, and celebrating important events; and

    (ii) ***African Ritual Dances***: Many African cultures have dances that are performed for religious and ceremonial purposes, including initiation rites, harvest festivals and ancestor worship; and

    (iii) ***Shamanic Dance***: Practised by shamans in various indigenous cultures around the world, these dances are part of rituals to communicate with the spiritual world, heal the sick, and bring about good fortune; and

    (iv) ***Egyptian Dance***: Dance was an important part of ancient Egyptian culture, performed for religious rituals, celebrations, and entertainment. Depictions of these dances are found in tomb paintings and inscriptions; and

    (v) ***Celtic Dance***: Wide variety of formal dances involving individual performers, couples and groups performing synchronized and often complex manouvres. Many European dances such as the Hopak of Eastern Europe, the Highland Jig and Céilí are all derived from formal Celtic dance history; and

    (vi) ***Sufi Whirling***: Part of the Sufi religious ceremonies, this dance is a form of physically active meditation which originated among Sufis. It is performed as a remembrance of God; and

(vii) **Gamelan Dance**: Performed to the accompaniment of a gamelan orchestra, these dances are part of various religious and ceremonial practices in Indonesian culture, particularly in Bali and Java; and

(viii) **Bharatanatyam**: Originating in Tamil Nadu, Bharatanatyam is one of the oldest classical dance forms of India. It is deeply rooted in the Hindu religious themes and texts and often depicts stories from Hindu mythology; and

(ix) **Noh Mai**: A traditional Japanese dance-drama that incorporates dance, music, and acting. It is deeply influenced by Shinto rituals and Buddhist philosophy.

## Article 120 – Sacred Drugs

465. A **Sacred Drug** is any naturally occurring substance with psychoactive properties used in a psychotherapeutic, religious, shamanic or spiritual context by a Religion or Cult. A psychoactive substance is any drug that crosses the blood-brain barrier and acts primarily upon the central nervous system, resulting in changes in perception, cognition, mood, consciousness and behaviour. — Sacred Drugs

466. Almost all Religions used and continue to use Sacred Drugs as an integral part of their sacred rituals. The most significant psychoactive substances throughout history for Religions and Cults, particularly sacred literature, have been hallucinogens. — Sacred Drugs and ancient Religions

467. While there are many forms of natural entheogens, five of the oldest and most Sacred Drugs of the founding of ancient civilization are the red berries of the European Holly Plant, considered the oldest most sacred plant of Civilized history, Cannabis, also known as Hemp and Marijuana, the Opium Poppy of the plains of Asia, Psilocybin Mushrooms and the venom of poisonous animals such as Toads. — Entheogens

468. Of the oldest and most Sacred Drugs of all civilized history the most important is without question Cannabis, also known as Hemp and Marijuana on account of its robustness, medicinal qualities and use as a primary source of superior fibre. Until its deliberate restriction and outlaw in the 20<sup>th</sup> Century for purely strategic political and commercial reasons, marijuana had historically represented the single most important crop of civilized agriculture next to grain. — Cannabis

469. Given the location, culture and natural availability of certain entheogens, Religions and Cults have adopted certain favouritisms towards certain Sacred Drugs throughout history. The most historically significant is the preference of the Menes-heh and Moloch worshipping priests of Ur, Syria and Palestine to mushrooms, — Preferences of Religions to certain Drugs

while the Scythian/Khazars preferred marijuana and opium.

470. A particular trait of mushroom consumption is the predictable visual distortions of "Halluciogenic Entoptic Phenomena" implying the existence of a fractal-like substructure to nature based upon lines, lattice structures, triangles, serpent waves and squares in contrast to the real shapes of the universe:- Mushrooms and distorted views of Supernatural World

    (i) **_False and Distortion of Universal Information_**: Meaning this geometric information is prevalent in Religions and Cults where their priests were addicted to these kinds of hallucinogenic drugs particularly in the form of triangular shapes; and

    (ii) **_Worship in Clothing_**: The significant worship of mushrooms by the Menesheh remains evident by the historic adoption of sacred clothing symbolizing the importance of the mushroom, particularly in subsequent Religions and Cults created by the descendents of the Menesheh in later centuries; and

    (iii) **_Sociopathy and Madness_**: While the psychotropic effects of "magic mushrooms" may imply a deeper consciousness, a frequent by-product of such poisons is psychosis and sociopathic behaviour, particularly exceptionally dark and disconnected writing that has absolutely no connection whatsoever to the Divine; and

    (iv) **_Distorted and Insane Writings_**: Knowledge of the Sacred Drugs preferred by certain Religions and Cults permits certain prediction to be made on the quality and nature of alleged sacred scripture written by their clergy throughout history when addicted to those substances.

471. Since the 20th Century, governments throughout the world have largely deprived their populations of cheap naturally grown pain killers in preference to supporting global commercial cartels of synthetic pain killers, often with numerous side effects. This global imbalance has contributed to the deliberate corruption and breakdown of societies as well as law and order across the world. Deliberate Corruption of Natural and Sacred Drugs

472. Any statute that prevents naturally grown Sacred Drugs to be produced in preference to inferior synthetic drugs produced by pharmaceutical companies is an offence against all civilization and all cultures and is immediately null and void. Moral Repugnancy of Secular Drug Laws

473. Any leader of any Religion or Cult that seeks to maintain the lie of alleging naturally grown Sacred Drugs are immoral in preference to synthetic and inferior varieties automatically consents, agrees and False Leaders and Drugs Policies

## Article 121 – Sacred Clothes

474. ***Sacred Clothes***, or Sacred Garments are the vestments, ornaments and other garments considered the sacred attire of officials of a particular Religion or Cult. <!-- margin: Sacred Clothes -->

475. Sacred Clothes have always been a symbol and reflection of the claimed power and authority of a particular Religion or Cult and the person wearing them. Therefore, in almost all religions the officials and attendants of a temple were expected to wear certain sacred garments distinguishing rank and themselves from the general public. <!-- margin: Sacred Clothes & Religious Authority -->

476. It has always been considered a terrible crime against all civilization when a person falsely wears Sacred Clothes for which they have no right, nor training. It is also traditionally considered an offence to disrespect the sacred clothes of a Religion, even if one disagrees with that religion. <!-- margin: False use of Sacred Clothes -->

477. One of the oldest and most significant sacred garments over 3,000 years old is the ***Cap of Cybele***, a thin, slightly rounded skullcap also commonly known as the Kippah, Yarmulke, Kufi and Zucchetti. Its symbolism represents the "fish" basket in which Cybele, "Queen of Heaven" and mother of god has captured and carries a soul. Whilst the original scripture of the Israelites, Yahudi, Muslims and even Christians expressly forbid the headdress as a supreme heresy, the Cap of Cybele is now ignorantly worn by hundreds of millions unwittingly worshipping Cybele as Mary, Athena, Kaaba, Mari, Venus and even lady Justice. <!-- margin: Cap of Cybele -->

478. The ***Red Cap of Attis***, also known as the Phrygian Cap and Phoenician Cap is extremely ancient and has been worn for over 3,000 years in worship of Attis, the lover and son of Cybele. It symbolizes the severed and bloody genitals of Attis representing supreme sacrifice, unquestioning loyalty and duty to Cybele and a fascist state. The Red Cap of Attis was deliberately misrepresented in the French revolution as "liberty cap" and now is most frequently found as a key symbol of the United States Senate and United States generally, including "Lady Justice". <!-- margin: Red Cap of Attis -->

479. The ***Sun Fish Headdress***, also known as the Mitre of Dagon is one of the oldest sacred clothes of high priests for 4,000 years, representing Dagon the god of the sea, fertility and plenty and later as the headdress of the Pontifex Maximus high priests of Saturnalia, <!-- margin: Sun Fish Headdress -->

also known as Satan of Rome during the celebrations of Satan in December every year. The celebrations to Saturn, known as Satan, now known under the anagram Santa continues each year as does the sacred headdress worn by the pagan priests who continue to secretly or unknowingly worship darkness.

480. The **Black Robes of the Galla**, the servants of Ereshkigal, Goddess of the Underworld from ancient Ur and the infamous attendants of the dead or "grim reapers" from at least 1,000 BCE when the city became the largest and most famous Necropolis of the ancient world, are some of the oldest sacred robes and clothes of history. From 400 BCE, the Black Robes became the sacred dress of initiates into the Occult Rite of Eleusis in the worship of Saturn, also known as Satan. In the founding of the Bar Societies at the beginning of the 19th Century, the Black Robe was returned to use as the official dress of a senior Bar Society initiate into the Occult Mysteries of Satan as a Grim Reaper and attendant of the Dead, given the Bar Association had placed all living men and women into Cestui Que Vie Trusts and Deceased Estates. <sub>Black Robes of the Galla</sub>

481. Any ritual or ceremony performed by an official of a Religion or Cult wearing sacred clothes for which they deny their true history and significance, automatically means such rituals and ceremonies are without any legal, spiritual or moral validity. <sub>Sacred Clothes & False Ceremony</sub>

## 3.6 – Sacred Rites

### Article 122 – Sacred Rites

482. A **Sacred Rite** is a solemn ceremony and procedure considered sacred, in which one or many events of significance are believed to occur according to the doctrines of one or more Religions and Cults. <sub>Sacred Rites</sub>

483. Traditionally, most major Religions and some Cults have identified special ceremonies of significance around major life events, including birth of a child, the transition from child to adult, the marriage or union of a man and woman, the election or anointment of a leader or religious leader and the death of loved one. <sub>Sacred Rites and Religions</sub>

484. Any claimed Sacred Rite that involves any kind of secret curse, spell or conveyance of rights in contradiction of its public purpose is considered an abomination ritual and not permitted to be practised, taught, published or continued. <sub>Forbidden Rites</sub>

## Article 123 – Sacred Mysteries

485. ***Sacred Mystery*** is a term used to describe the belief by certain Religions and Cults that during certain sacred rites and procedures supernatural phenomena occur, as well as an alternate description of the sacred rite itself. — Sacred Mystery

486. The term Sacred Mysteries is similar to the terms Sacred Rite and Sacrament. — Sacred Mystery and Rite

487. Any claimed Sacred Mystery that involves any kind of secret curse, spell or conveyance of rights in contradiction of its public purpose is considered an abomination ritual and not permitted to be practised, taught, published or continued. — Forbidden Sacred Mystery

488. Any claimed Sacred Mystery involving the actual sacrifice or murder of any animal, or Homo Sapien is both a crime and an injury against the whole of united Heavens and all spirits. — Sacred Mystery involving sacrifice forbidden

## Article 124 – Occult

489. ***Occult*** is a term defining a wide variety of knowledge of rituals and practices, usually associated with magic and other forms of Power and Manipulation, normally kept hidden and secret from ordinary followers. Hence, the Latin word occultus meaning literally clandestine, hidden and secret. — Occult

490. All Religions and Cults include aspects of Occult knowledge within their rituals and beliefs. The most common knowledge that is hidden as Occult is knowledge of magic. — Occult and Religions

491. Knowledge hidden as Occult does not imply accuracy or validity. However, the practice of hiding information as Occult knowledge implies a greater value that otherwise might be attributed if such knowledge was freely available for critical analysis. — Occult does not mean accuracy or validity

492. Occult literature associated with Kabbalah, Sorcery, Wicca, Wizardry, Witchcraft, especially Black Magic and Necromancy is based on trick and illusionary magic with no solid base of Occult wisdom whatsoever. However, as minds are more prone to believe tricks and illusions through theatrical display, such Occult literature is considered more powerful and credible to ignorant believers than genuine wisdom. — False Occult Knowledge

## 3.7 – Profanity & Irreverence
### Article 125 – Profanity

**493.** ***Profanity*** refers to language or behaviour that is considered an offence in being disrespectful and irreverent in relation to religious or sacred concepts or objects.  
*Profanity and Irreverence*

**494.** The word *Profanity* comes from the Latin *profanus* meaning "not religious; unclean", from *pro* (before) and *fanum* (temple).  
*Origin of word Profanity*

**495.** Common forms of Profanity include (but are not limited to):-  
*Common Forms of Profanity*

(i) ***Blasphemy***: Is the offence of showing disrespect or lack of reverence for deities, sacred things, religious doctrines or religious practices; and

(ii) ***Desecration***: Is the treating of something sacred or revered with intentional and violent disrespect or irreverence; and

(iii) ***Sacrilege***: Is the offence of stealing one or more physical objects that are consecrated and sacred; and

(iv) ***Impiety***: Is the dereliction of duty, disloyalty, deliberately sinful, wicked and unscrupulous behaviour of Ministers or Clergy; and

(v) ***Spell***: Is the offence of using prohibited words and rituals for magical purposes to try and elicit a specific goal regarding one or more persons or spirits.

**496.** Profanity is not simply a choice of expression, or the exercise of free speech, but a fundamental offence against all things Divine and the Law itself, whether or not it is prosecuted, decriminalised or even promoted within a society:-  
*Profanity is a fundamental offence against all things Divine & the Law itself*

(i) ***Dying Civilisation***: The tolerance or even promotion of Profanity in culture is a key sign of a dying civilisation, given basic respect of the Divine is the cornerstone of a basic respect of self, the law and society. No society or civilisation can function when there is an eventual complete breakdown in all forms of respect; and

(ii) ***Unjust Society***: The growth in Profanity is a sign in the growing hubris of the ruling classes and their agents, indicating a growing distortion of the functions of courts and justice. History teaches that these are typically tell tale signs before the collapse of a society or empire, as no society in human history has survived a catastrophic breakdown in social respect of the Divine.

497. Five key arguments exist as compelling proof that all forms of Profanity are not essential for everyday speech and interactions among people:-

> (i) **Respect and Decorum**: Profanity can be perceived as disrespectful and offensive, particularly in professional or formal settings. Using respectful language helps maintain a sense of decorum and fosters positive interactions; and
>
> (ii) **Effective Communication**: Clear and precise language is essential for effective communication. Profanity can muddy the message and lead to misunderstandings or distractions from the main point. Using appropriate language ensures that the intended message is conveyed accurately; and
>
> (iii) **Emotional Regulation**: Relying on profanity to express emotions can hinder emotional regulation and problem-solving skills. Using more descriptive language to articulate feelings can lead to healthier and more constructive conversations; and
>
> (iv) **Role Modelling**: For those in positions of influence, such as parents, teachers, or leaders, using profanity can set a negative example. Demonstrating the use of appropriate language encourages others, especially younger individuals, to communicate respectfully and thoughtfully; and
>
> (v) **Cultural Sensitivity**: Different cultures and individuals have varying thresholds for what is considered offensive. Avoiding profanity respects these differences and promotes inclusivity, making interactions more comfortable for everyone involved.

*Profanity is not an essential component of speech*

498. The use of public Profanity is not free speech but the intentional injury and disrespect of others:-

> (i) **Offence and Distress**: Profane language can cause offense and emotional distress to others. Not everyone shares the same tolerance for profanity, and its use in public can be deeply upsetting to many individuals, infringing on their right to a peaceful and respectful environment; and
>
> (ii) **Harmful to Minors**: Exposure to profanity can be harmful to children and young people. Public spaces are frequented by individuals of all ages, and using profane language can have a negative impact on minors, contributing to inappropriate language development and behaviour; and
>
> (iii) **Social Cohesion and Harmony**: Public profanity can

*The use of public Profanity is not free speech but injury and disrespect of others*

erode social cohesion and harmony. Respectful communication is key to fostering mutual understanding and cooperation among community members. Profanity can create divisions and hinder positive social interactions; and

(iv) **Public Decency and Morality**: Profanity in public spaces can undermine community standards of decency and morality. Many societies have norms and values that aim to maintain a respectful and dignified public environment. Public profanity can violate these norms and disrupt social harmony.

## Article 126 – Blasphemy

499. ***Blasphemy*** is the act of showing disrespect or lack of reverence for deities, sacred things, religious doctrines, or religious practices. The main forms of Blasphemy include (but are not limited to): *(Blasphemy)*

(i) ***Written Material***: Publishing writings that mock, ridicule, or criticize religious beliefs or practices in a manner deemed disrespectful; and

(ii) ***Actions***: Engaging in behaviours or acts that are considered disrespectful or irreverent towards religious symbols, rituals, or places of worship; and

(iii) ***Verbal Statements***: Speaking words that are considered offensive, insulting, or irreverent towards a deity, religious figures, sacred texts, or religious beliefs.

500. The word *Blasphemy* comes from the Ancient Irish term *blasfaemin* meaning literally "to grind down the name of the spirits and gods", from blas (speech), fae (spirits) and min (grind down):- *(Origin of Word Blasphemy)*

(i) By 8th Century the term was adopted into Anglaise (Old French) as *blasfemin* and *blasfeme* meaning "to speak against God; to speak with irreverence or revile impiously anything sacred"; and

(ii) In 1606 through the Blasphemy Act, King James I (1603–1625) of England first introduced a new definition of Blasphemy to mean whatever the government deemed to be an offence against (Christian) faith and what material or speech was to be deemed blasphemous. This ushered in laws for the next centuries around the world by governments enforcing blasphemy laws; and

(iii) By the early years of the 21st Century, many western nations have decriminalised the notion of Blasphemy, whilst some nations still hold extreme cases of Blasphemy as a Capital

Crime (Death Penalty). In 2008, the common law offences of blasphemy and blasphemous libel in England and Wales were abolished through the Criminal Justice and Immigration Act 2008.

## Article 127 – Sacrilege

501. ***Sacrilege*** is the offence of violation, misuse or theft of one or more physical objects regarded as sacred. — Sacrilege

502. The word *Sacrilege* comes from the Latin *sacer* (sacred, holy) and *lego* (gather, take, steal). — Origin of the word Sacrilege

503. While the allegation of stealing is a universal offence in all civilizations, the concept of sacrilege adds a further severity to any such allegation as such a theft includes the attempted theft against the will of the gods or deities of a particular Religion or Cult. — Severity of Sacrilege

504. Any and all of the following Claims to the Right to Use Force against a valid Ucadia entity, or any Person in the care, possession, jurisdiction, control or custody of a valid Ucadia entity, are invalid, morally repugnant and null and void *ab inito* (from the beginning); and if used, shall be an unreserved confession by the perpetrator of an act of Sacrilege against all forms of civilised law:- — Sacrilege against Ucadia

   (i) Any statute, regulation, ruling or law used to treat the Ucadia entity, or any Person in the care, possession, jurisdiction, control or custody of the Ucadia entity, as an Enemy Alien, Enemy of the state or a criminal by any means whatsoever; and

   (ii) Any statute, regulation, ruling or law used to treat the Ucadia entity, or any Person in the care, possession, jurisdiction, control or custody of the Ucadia entity, as being dead to Law, without Standing or Capacity, or a bankrupt, or lost at sea, or wrecked, or having surrendered or abandoned any rights, or a captured prize; and

   (iii) Any statute, regulation, ruling or law used to treat the Ucadia entity, or any Person in the care, possession, jurisdiction, control or custody of the Ucadia entity, as being mentally ill or intestate or incapable of forming or expressing a clear Will; and

   (iv) Any statute, regulation, ruling or law used to treat the Property of the Ucadia entity, or any Property of a Person in the care, possession, jurisdiction, control or custody of the Ucadia entity, as being confiscated, seized, waived, surrendered, abandoned, alienated, forfeited by any means whatsoever.

## Article 128 – Desecration

505. ***Desecration*** is the act of treating something sacred or revered with violent disrespect or irreverence. It involves actions that defile, damage, or violate the sanctity of religious objects, places, or practices. Desecration

506. Examples of Desecration include (but are not limited to):- Examples of Desecration

   (i) **Physical Damage**: Vandalizing, destroying, or damaging religious buildings, monuments, or artefacts; and

   (ii) **Disrespectful Actions**: Performing actions that are considered deeply disrespectful or offensive in a religious context, such as defiling a place of worship, misusing religious symbols, or disrupting religious ceremonies; and

   (iii) **Profane Use**: Using sacred objects, texts, or symbols in a profane or inappropriate manner, contrary to their intended religious significance.

## Article 129 – Impiety

507. ***Impiety*** is the dereliction of duty, disloyalty, deliberately sinful, wicked and unscrupulous behaviour of Ministers or Clergy of a Religion or Cult. Impiety

508. Of all offences against a Religion or Cult in the world until the 11th Century, *Impiety* was considered the worst of all offences, worse than Sacrilege and Malediction. Severity of Impiety

509. Impiety is a unique offence that once established dissolves the oaths or vows of office of any Minister or Clergy, rendering illegitimate and incapable of claiming authority nor right to continue in such position. Effect of Impiety

510. Elements of Impiety by a Minister or Clergy include:- Elements of Impiety

   (i) Evidence of Offence: Means there is clear evidence of disloyal, or deliberately sinful, wicked and unscrupulous behaviour; and

   (ii) Existence of Oath or Vow: Means a Minister or Cleric took a proper Oath or Vow of Office; and

   (iii) Breach of Oath: Is the fact that the Minister or Cleric breached their Oath or Vow through such behaviour; and

   (iv) Dissolution of Office: Is the fact that once clear proof is provided of a fundamental Breach of Oath or Vow, the mandate of office is dissolved and the person becomes an unlawful occupier of such office until removed; and

(v) Removal of Minister or Cleric: Is proof that the rule of law still operates within the relevant jurisdiction.

511. The failure to enforce Impiety by a given society is an open declaration that no civilised law exists within the given society and is confirmation of the eventual collapse and destruction of such a society or empire, through collapse of the function of law itself. Failure to enforce Impiety

## Article 130 – Spell

512. A *Spell* is a prohibited form of words and ritual used for magical purposes to elicit a specific goal regarding one or more persons or spirits. Spell

513. Types of claimed Spells include (but are not limited to):- Types of Spells

   (i) *Charm Spell*: Traditionally seeks to bring good luck and fortune to a person; and

   (ii) *Jinx Spell*: Seeks to bring bad luck to a person without physical harm; and

   (iii) *Bind Spell*: Is a form of Curse that seeks to compel a person to some action otherwise against their will; and

   (iv) *Break Spell*: Also known as Hex Spell seeks to "break" a Binding or Curse; and

   (v) *Protection Spell*: Seeks to protect a person against Curse and Binding Spells as well as the avoidance of conflict and injury; and

   (vi) *Exposure Curse*: Seeks to remove any protection and leave them vulnerable to curses and harm; and

   (vii) *Heal Spell*: Seeks to help a person improve their health; and

   (viii) *Harm Spell*: Is a curse that seeks the physical injury, possibly even death of a person; and

   (ix) *Summons Spell*: Seeks to summons a spirit, usually for the purpose of a necromancy ritual; and

   (x) *Banish Spell*: Seeks to banish a spirit from sight.

514. A Curse is a form of spell, designed to evoke a negative binding power, or harm. All Curses have two parts- the binding and the return. The binding is the spell evoked and the return is the response received once the curse has matured. Curse

515. While many Spells may be invoked with the intention of some positive outcome, all Spells are considered as a whole a negative action on account of the fraudulent nature of most words and rituals, the generally high ignorance of the operator(s) invoking such Spells, the lack of respect to spirits and the Divine and the lack of consent and right of free will of those attempted to be spelled.

*Forbidden Function of Spells*

516. Whilst Spells are as old as Human Civilisation itself, the prohibition of all forms of Spells is a recognition of its fundamental profanity and hubris against Divine Law and its persistent and long term misuse:-

*Reasoning for Prohibition of Spells*

   (i) ***Against Divine Law***: Spells have frequently been cast in the past that defy Divine Law, Civilised Law, moral decency and respect. There is no indication that such behaviour will ever stop, so long as a few people seek to harness power for ignorant and foolish ends; and

   (ii) ***No Effect in Divine, Ecclesiastical or Civilised Law***: Such Spells have no real effect under Divine, or Ecclesiastical or Civilised Law. However, such Spells and acts are far from harmless in that they still cause temporary disruptions, suffering and confusion; and

   (iii) ***Height of Hubris and Ego:*** The casting of Spells is the height of spiritual hubris and ego, that is contrary to a healthy spiritual path. Continuing to support people taking an unhealthy path is inconsistent with restoring balance and spiritual health; and

   (iv) ***Frequent Source of Abuse***: In each and every generation there have been a few that have sought to claim Spells as a source of power and authority over others, to the detriment of all people.

## 3.8 – False, Absurd and Prohibited Sacred Notions

### Article 131 – False, Absurd and Prohibited Sacred Notions

517. ***False, Absurd and Prohibited Sacred Notions*** are concepts associated with Occult Rites or Mysteries that may still persist in some form within recent history; and of such an absurd, false and wicked nature that their suppression and prohibition as religious or spiritual practices must be clearly and emphatically expressed.

*False, Absurd and Prohibited Sacred Notions*

518. The list of *False, Absurd and Prohibited Sacred Notions* includes (but is not limited to):-

*List of False, Absurd and Prohibited Sacred Notions*

   (i) ***Unholy***: The false, absurd and deliberately foolish notion that an object, concept or thing can represent a binary opposite to the notion of sacred; and

(ii) ***Celibacy***: The mandatory prohibition of heterosexual matrimony between clergy; and the prohibition of any sexual activity; and

(iii) ***Molestation***: The sacrifice of the innocence of children to the demon god Moloch as the hidden G-d of Hasidic and Ancient Judaism, through their traumatic and violent criminal sexual assault; and

(iv) ***Blood Sacrifice***: The sacrifice of human beings and animals through religious rites; and in the more broader conflict of violent conflict; and

(v) ***Holocaust***: The deliberate sacrifice of human beings and animals by fire as a burnt offering to the demon god Moloch as the hidden G-d of Hasidic and Ancient Judaism, and an offering to the new G-ds of elite American families and officials that rule the Zionist Cult; and

(vi) ***Cannibalism***: The actual or simulated consumption of human flesh or blood as a religious rite; and

(vii) ***Salvage & Claim of Souls***: The religious and administrative rites in claiming the salvaging of the soul of "lesser humans" than the ruling elite at the time of birth, the transmutation of gold bars within central stores as spiritual penitentiaries, and the financial hypothecation of such claimed property as underwriting to modern secular financial systems; and

(viii) ***Universal Evil***: The false, absurd and deliberately foolish notion that a "universal evil force" exists in opposition and duality to a universal force of good.

519. The continued presence and use over the past three hundred years of such *False, Absurd and Prohibited Sacred Notions by the ruling elites,* especially those from the United States and European Powers can be partly explained in terms of their usefulness in maintaining global economic and political power and control:- [Power and Control as Common theme behind continued existence of False, Absurd and Prohibited Sacred Notions]

(i) ***Occult Violence Implies Greater Power***: Meaning that for a time the leaders of many countries, societies and organisations believed the false (and since repudiated) claims of the Secular elites of Washington and New York that they hold a special power and relation with supremely dark and powerful forces; and

(ii) ***Fear as the Primal Human Motivator***: Meaning the rise of psychology has reinforced the false and absurd notion in the minds of the Secular elite that Fear, followed by Sexual Desire are the primal human motivators, in contradiction to the history of human civilisation showing that Altruism and Courage have been equally present in every generation; and

(iii) ***Darkness is More Potent than Light***: Meaning the Secular elites have firmly believed their ascendency is due to their own efforts and not part of a greater seasonal cycle of growth of the collective mind and soul of humanity – ignoring the immutable and paradoxical truth "darkness is at its greatest strength, before the dawn of light".

## Article 132 – Unholy

520. ***Unholy*** is the false, absurd and foolish 13th Century notion whereby an object (such as a manuscript) may possess supernatural powers in direct opposition to sacredness. Hence, an object possessing power that is considered evil, impure or otherwise perverted.

    *Unholy*

521. The idea of *Unholy* was first conceived by Giacinto Bobone Orsini as Anti-Pope Lucius III (1127-1261) in the promulgation of his Great Grimoire of Black Magic pertaining to the summonsing of spirits, blood sacrifices, holocausts and other criminal acts. The belief by the Popes of the Roman Cult was that if a book was created through the most evil acts imaginable, that somehow this evil could be concentrated into the text itself, and therefore utilized as a source of power.

    *Origin of the Concept of Unholy*

522. As the magic promoted by Giacinto Bobone Orsini and subsequent Popes of the Roman Cult in the promotion of their black magic books, possess no proper grounding in ancient necromancy, nor spells, nor curses, nor any skills of ancient sorcery, all grimoires are frauds and deluded imitations. Therefore, the belief that such books have any power, let alone "unholy power" is an absurdity.

    *Insane and ineffective rites of Grimoires*

## Article 133 – Celibacy

523. ***Celibacy*** is the the mandatory prohibition of heterosexual matrimony between clergy; and the prohibition of any sexual activity, in order to foster perverted and wicked sexual behaviour in contradiction to health and normal heterosexual relationships with members of the opposite sex.

    *Celibacy*

524. ***Chastity*** is the virtuous practice of monogamy and fidelity in matrimony and the abstaining from sexual activity

    *Chastity*

immoral. It is the second of the five foundation virtues of the Catholic Church since the 8th Century (Humility, Chastity, Respect, Courage and Faith). Within Western Christianity and the Catholic Church, Chastity was never about the prohibition of matrimony of lower clergy until its intentional corruption in the 16th Century.

525. Celibacy is a deliberate and intentional 16th Century corruption of the ancient and noble notion of Chastity that existed as both a fundamental virtue within early Christian formation and the first formation of the Catholic Church from 8th Century until 13th Century:- *Celibacy is the deliberate mask of Chastity*

   (i) Chastity was once a central virtue of Christianity and later the Catholic Church that promoted healthy sexual behaviour; and

   (ii) It is the Council of Trent (1545-1563) that fundamentally infused the doctrines of Moloch into the Catholic Church and deliberate new laws such as Celibacy of the clergy in order to ferment distorted behaviour; and

   (iii) Celibacy was never a tenet of Christian or Catholic Faith and remains a deliberate and intentional attempted curse against any and all faithful clergy who remain within Christian denominations that still enforce such blatant blasphemies and injuries against Divine Law and true Ecclesiastical Law.

526. Maxims of Law concerning Celibacy do not and should not be considered as inferring those who prefer homosexuality as being less than others, or less worthy in terms of faith:- *Celibacy and Healthy sexual balance versus promoting unhealthy sexual conditions*

   (i) Ucadia Civilisation is the first and only Civilisation in human history that emphatically states sexual preference between consenting adults as a fundamental right; and

   (ii) The original and true doctrines of Christianity and the Catholic Church until the 16th Century focused on Chastity being the abstaining from sexual activity and behaviour considered inappropriate and morally repugnant; and

   (iii) The deliberate distortions of Celibacy imposed to corrupt moral clarity since the 16th Century ferment an intentional "grey area" whereby a certain proportion of Catholic clergy openly engage in homosexual activities whilst still functioning as clergy in clearly inappropriate and morally repugnant behaviour, whilst many cases exist that those who engage in adult and consenting heterosexual relations whilst being clergy have often been forced out of the church; and

   (iv) The restoration of moral clarity within Christianity and in particular the Catholic Church demands the reinstitution of

Chastity, the abolition of Celibacy and the enforcement of must stricter controls over sexual relations between members of the clergy.

## Article 134 – Molestation

527. ***Molestation*** is a ritual of the Roman Cult followed by many Ministers and Officials whereby the "innocence" of prepubescent children is sacrificed to the worship of Moloch, rather than their murder. Hence "to Molest" literally means to adhere to the doctrine (ista) of Moloch (moll).   *Molestation*

528. The word *Molestation* literally means to adhere to the doctrine (ista) of Moloch (moll), as one of the most blatantly wicked and immoral words still used across Non-Ucadian Societies and Judicial Systems to convert a serious crime into a religious rite in honour of Moloch.   *Meaning of Molestation*

529. Any argument that denies the original religious connection of the word Molest and Molestation in connection to a ritual sacrifice of the innocence of children to Moloch is a grave injury and deliberate fabrication of the purpose, origin and meaning of the word.   *Denial of the Meaning of Molestation*

530. Molestation is not the same as pedophilia, a non-religious word created in 1951 that perversely means from Greek (paidos/pedo) "child" + philos "loving." Pedophilia has nothing to do with the worship of Moloch.   *Molestation and Pedophilia*

531. In accordance with these Maxims and the most sacred Covenant *Pactum De Singularis Caelum* no conservative member of the clergy of the Roman Catholic Church or Anglican Church, especially in the United States, Canada, Europe and Australia are permitted to teach, interact or supervise unattended any children until these conservative adherents to wickedly immoral, false, absurd and prohibited practices confess their behaviours and agree such criminal and systematic rituals of abuse will no longer be promoted.   *Prohibition of Conservative Clergy*

## Article 135 – Blood Sacrifice

532. ***Blood Sacrifice*** is the deliberate ritual murder of another Homo Sapien through some ceremony of a Religion or Cult. The six primary motives for ritual religious murder are Atonement, Offering, Spell, Divination, Initiation and or Power.   *Blood Sacrifice*

533. The most famous day of Blood Sacrifice in the Ancient World was the ancient "Day of Blood", also known as *Dies Sanguinis* upon the Mide (Middle) of Mars according to the ancient 28 day month cycle, being the 14$^{th}$ of Mars (14$^{th}$ March), or the 14$^{th}$ of Nisan to the Persians:-   *Day of Blood (Mars 14, Nisan 14) March 14th*

(i) Upon this day, that the ancient religion of Mithra of the Persians and Mitra of the Roman Empire celebrated the birth and sacrificial death of the god Mithra. The eve of the day was called the Ides of Mars (13th March) to the Romans and to the Persians, the day was called the Passion; and

(ii) On *Dies Sanguinis* upon the Mide (Middle) of Mars (March 14th), 44 BCE Julius Caesar arranged an elaborate suicide by forcing his closest allies to sacrifice him, so he would be remembered and transformed into the personification of the god Mithra; and

(iii) March 14th was also celebrated for centuries as the true birthdate and later as the date for the "last supper" for Jesus Christ. To ignore this historic connection to the dominant religion of the world at the time of the Roman Empire is to deliberately ignore the true origins of Christianity.

534. Offering is when the dogma of a Religion or Cult mandates blood sacrifice as a pleasing "gift" to some god(s) or deity in exchange for continued favour and good fortune. The ancient Greeks considered the food of the gods to be ambrosia, which is blood. — Offering

535. Apart from being a serious crime, all Blood sacrifices are an abomination and the worst offence and disrespect against the Divine Creator, all gods, all deities, all angels, demons and spirits. — Blood Sacrifice is an Abomination before Heaven

536. As all spirits, souls, gods and deities including all demons, angels and saints have pledged their absolute loyalty to the most sacred Covenant *Pactum De Singularis Caelum*, no blood sacrifice shall have any spiritual or supernatural effect in anyway. — No spiritual effect or power from such criminal acts

## Article 136 – Holocaust

537. ***Holocaust*** is the deliberate ritual murder of another Homo Sapien by fire through some ceremony of a Religion or Cult. — Holocaust

538. The term *Holocaust* is the oldest religious term for ritual sacrifice by fire and means a completely (holos) burn (kaustos) sacrificial offering. — Meaning of Holocaust

539. Any claim that *Holocaust* only applies to animals such as kids, sheep and cattle is deliberately misleading and an insult to the memory of all who have suffered such murder as a core doctrine of Holocaust rituals by Religions and Cults is the literal treatment and view of Homo Sapien victims as kids, sheep and cattle. — False Denial of Meaning of Holocaust

540. The Origin of Holocaust Practices is many thousands of years old:- — Origin of Holocaust Practices

(i) The origin of ritual murder by deliberately burning people alive originates from the city of Urgarit in the early 17th Century BCE and then later to other Phoenician and Amorite cities such as Carthage, Tyre and Jerusalem. In all cases, such ritual was directed to the god Ba'al Moloch also known as Ba'al Hammon, Sabaoth and Satan; and

(ii) The original purpose of a Holocaust was as a form of offering to Moloch. However, from the 4$^{th}$ Century CE and the creation of the Talmud by the Menes-heh (Menesheh), Holocaust became a most sacred ritual of atonement. Thus, whenever an act or enhancement to the covenant with Satan, also known as Sabaoth was enacted a great Holocaust was required; and

(iii) The word Holocaust is equivalent to the Latin word Immolate introduced by the Council of Trent (1545-1563) to specifically and more clearly mean a burnt offering to Moloch; and

(iv) By 1710, the Lithuanian-Polish noble Prince Kazimierz Czartoryski (b.1674- d.1741) sought to act against the growing economic and political threat of the now one million Ashkenazi "slaves" at the disposal of the Russian Tsars. Kazimierz Czartoryski set about making Pulawy and his palace the "center" of a revival of the Ashkenazi, to weaken the power of Russia, through recruiting a charismatic and talented young rabbi named Israel ben Eliezer (b. 1688 – d. 1780) later known as the claimed Jewish Messiah Israel Baal Shem Tov, falsely claiming Holly blood heritage back to the line of David as Jewish. With substantial funding from Kazimierz Czartoryski, an array of new false texts and scripture such as the Amsterdam Talmud were created to help form the "Pious Ones" חסידים (chasidim) movement among the Ashkenazi. The plan worked and eventually hundreds of thousands of Ashkenazi migrated to Poland and around the central hub of Pulawy. The Czartoryski continued to be the supreme patrons of Hasidism, even after Russia confiscated the family estate at Pulawy in 1794. The Czartoryski Palace of Pulawy and the Temple of Cybele was the absolute centre of the three hundred mile wide pentagram perfectly formed in World War II by the largest and worst Nazi death camps (including Auschwitz); and

(v) The worst Holocaust in the name of Moloch in history and the worst unpunished crime against humanity for 1,000 years was the mass sacrifice by fire of more than six million protestants, ethnic minorities and Jews starting exactly on September 11, 1941 (9/11), through specifically designed centres of human sacrifice mirroring ancient temple sites creating a giant pentagram in Poland, in order to invoke "divine favour" for the creation of the great secret pentagram known as the **Pentagon** in the rededication of **Washington DC** and the birth of the American Imperial Exceptionalism. Each of the five special concentration camps that started sacrificing people from September 11, 1941 (9/11) were designed to mirror-image the footprint of ancient temple sites to Moloch. Treblinka mirror inverted the ancient sacrifice site of Urgarit; and Janowska mirror inverted the ancient sacrifice site of Jerusalem; and Auschwitz mirror inverted the ancient sacrifice site of Baalbek; and Lodz mirror inverted the ancient sacrifice site of Carthage; and Sobibor mirror inverted the ancient sacrifice site of Babylon. At the center of the Pentagram was the spiritual birthplace to Hasidic Judaism. The positioning of this infrastructure was not to create a perfectly shaped pentagram, but to make sure the top of the pentagram aligned with the North Star above the Arctic and the negative "ley lines" of the pentagram intersected most of the major occult centres of Europe including but not limited to Rome, Carthage, Zurich, Munich, Stockholm, Hanover, Bordeaux, Zagreb, Odessa, Bucharest, Belgorod, St Petersburg, Nizhsny Novgorod and the Shetland Islands. If the positions of the sacrifice camps were even a few kilometres off their intentional position, then the "ley lines" would not have intersected these centres; and

(vi) To this day many industrialised economies and societies remain hostages to the crimes of the American Zionist and European Hasidic elite families during World War II, most notably the major Western European powers.

541. As Moloch, also known as Sabaoth and Satan have pledged complete loyalty to the most sacred covenant *Pactum De Singularis Caelum*, any deliberate act of Holocaust or Immolation is now an abomination and the worst offence and disrespect against the Divine Creator, all gods, all deities, all angels, demons and spirits. — Holocaust a prohibited action

## Article 137 – Cannibalism

542. **Cannibalism**, is the practice, act and dogma of followers of a Religion or Cult eating the flesh and blood of another Homo Sapien, or the ritualistic simulation of eating flesh and blood when the dogma of a Religion or Cult considers it equivalent. — Cannibalism

543. While Cannibalism, also known as anthropophagi, may be argued a — Prohibition of Cannibalism

cultural legacy of some indigenous tribes, or episodes associated with extreme survival and necessity, Sacred Cannibalism is a deliberate religious act and therefore is considered an injury against all things Sacred, Holy and Divine.

544. The Original and True Roman Catholic Doctrine of the Eucharist following the 8th Century to 16th Century as the "Bread and Fruits of Life" was never about Cannibalism in its intention or honour of Jesus Christ:- *Original and True Roman Catholic Doctrine of Eucharist*

   (i) The entire foundation premise of Christianity and of the formation of the Roman Catholic Church in the 8th Century was the repudiation and end of blood sacrifice and other wicked and archaic practices such as cannibalism, not for their integration and perpetuation; and

   (ii) The Original and True Roman Catholic Doctrine of the Eucharist saw the breaking and sharing of the Bread and Wine as the formation of a new and unbreakable covenant, a ceremony celebrating the formation of a new body (the apostles) and the last sacrifice with the bread and wine representing Jesus literally as a the "bread and fruits of a new eternal life"; and

   (iii) The deliberate corruption of the original doctrine of the Catholic Church occurred no earlier than the 16th Century when the celebration of the Eucharist was deliberately distorted into a satanic and pagan ritual of simulated cannibalism ritual where believers must believe they are eating bread and wine transformed into "flesh and blood"; and that Jesus must continue to suffer and die every time mass is celebrated; and

   (iv) Whilst the Catholic Church has since repaired some of this doctrine so that it is clear Jesus only died "once" and that the Eucharist is necessary "spiritual nourishment", certain hard core "conservatives" within the Church who still adhere to the array of Satanic and prohibited practices refuse to yield and demand it still be recognised as a pagan cannibalistic ceremony in open defiance to the teachings of Jesus Christ, Christianity and original and true Catholic Doctrine.

545. Any Conservative Cult that participates in Sacred Cannibalism willingly or unknowingly commits an act of grave injury against the original teachings of the historic figure otherwise known as Jesus Christ, being the leader of the Nazarenes and a proven antagonist against every form of blood sacrifice whether animal, or Homo Sapien. *Injury against teachings of Christ*

## Article 138 – Salvage & Claim of Souls

**546.** ***Salvage & Claim of Souls*** is the religious and administrative rites within the Secular religion in claiming the salvaging of the soul of "lesser humans" than the ruling elite at the time of birth, the transmutation of gold bars within central stores as spiritual penitentiaries, and the financial hypothecation of such claimed property as underwriting to the modern secular financial system.
Salvage & Claim of Souls

**547.** In accord with Divine Law, the present Maxims and most sacred Covenant *Pactum De Singularis Caelum*, none may claim your soul or any other property given to you as a birthright by the Divine. Any claim to the contrary is absurd, false and heretical against all forms of civilised law.
None may claim your soul

**548.** In accord with the most sacred Covenant *Pactum De Singularis Caelum*, no temporal or spiritual force may claim use, control or ownership of your soul, except you as the sole trustee of your birthright and trust:-
Your soul as property within your Divine Trust and True Trust

    (i) Your Divine Person is sole and eternal trustee over your Divine Trust wherein the absolute property ownership and rights of your spiritual identity and soul are recognised; and

    (ii) Your True Person is sole trustee over your True Trust, wherein beneficial ownership of your spiritual identity and soul are recognised for your mortal life; and

    (iii) Any other claim, ritual, demand or threat is therefore a deliberate and criminal fraud and false claim over property that can never be seized, sold, abandoned, waived, transferred, surrendered, alienated, cursed or forfeited.

## Article 139 – Universal Evil

**549.** ***Evil*** is the generic name for one or more powerful demon spirits worshipped by several Cults as their supreme gods. Hence, evil is the English name for the ancient demon name ubel, known as iblis in Arabic, saturn or satan in Latin and azazel in Aramaic.
Evil

**550.** As all demons as well as archangels, saints and spirits have pledged their absolute loyalty to the sacred Covenant *Pactum De Singularis Caelum*, any crime committed in the name of a demon, or in the name of "evil" is an abomination and grave insult to united Heaven and all spirits.
Criminal not evil acts

# Title IV – Revelation

## 4.1 – Revelation

### Article 140 – Revelation

551. ***Revelation*** is the communication and disclosure of some self-evident manifestation of Divine Wisdom, Truth or Knowledge by Divine Inspiration.

552. The word *Revelation* comes from the Latin *revelatio* meaning disclosure and uncovering. Thus, the nature and quality of the claimed Divine Wisdom, Truth or Knowledge revealed has always been the most important aspect of Revelation, compared to the method of its reception.

553. Throughout history up until the late 18th Century, the majority of knowledge of the existence of law, society, morality and purpose of humanity was underpinned by Divine Revelation:-

   (i) Knowledge claimed as Divine Revelation has consistently remained the cornerstone of every major human civilisation since the beginning of time. Even many modern and contemporary societies in the 21st Century still have Divine Revelation and Scripture as their foundation stone; and

   (ii) It can be argued that some of the most significant events in history were directly, indirectly or even secretly driven by Divine Revelation and Divine Prophecy and often involving attempts to create the conditions to claim its fulfilment; and

   (iii) Divine Revelation continues to significantly influence geopolitical events among societies.

### Article 141 – Classification of Revelation

554. The ***Classification of Revelation*** are the various contemporary and historic arguments and methods of categorising Divine Revelation. The most common of these are *by Plausibility, by Capacity, by Method, by Degree of Supernatural Presence, by Size of Audience, by Authority*:-

   (i) *Classification by Plausibility* of Divine Revelation is a generalised sceptical approach promoted through various philosophical schools including (but not limited to) Rationalism, Materialism, Atheism and related political movements such as Marxism, Socialism, and Secularism that believe "revelation" is generally a fiction imposed upon the masses by indoctrination and the traditional power of old religions; and

(ii) *Classification by Capacity* of Divine Revelation is a generalised "enlightenment" and modern philosophy that states "revelation" is a capacity for almost all people and natural response to the individual experience of the Divine and Supernatural; and

(iii) *Classification by Method* of Divine Revelation is when such information is classified by the way it was received such as vision, or dream or inspiration or by some external supernatural event; and

(iv) *Classification by Degree of Supernatural Presence* in Divine Revelation is when such information is classified and authenticated by degree or amount of supernatural presence in the delivery of Divine Revelation, with a greater perceived presence equating to a higher authenticity; and

(v) *Classification by Size of Audience* to Divine Revelation is when such information is classified and authenticated by the number of persons as first hand witnesses; and

(vi) *Classification by Authority* of Prophet is when Divine Revelation is classified and authenticated by the authority and importance of the prophet receiving such Divine Inspiration.

**555.** In respect of *Classification by Plausibility of Divine Revelation*, there exists a number of orthodox and dogmatic views by philosophers who oppose the notion of Divine Revelation being Nihilism, Cynicism, Absurdism and Empiricism:- Classification by Plausibility of Divine Revelation

(i) *Nihilism Views* on Plausibility of Divine Revelation reject the idea of the existence of the Divine, Deities or the Supernatural and thus deny the possibility of Divine Revelation; and

(ii) *Cynicism Views* on Plausibility of Divine Revelation point to an abundance of historic evidence of fraud in regards to the misuse of spiritual and religious themes to manipulate people; as well as contemporary science and culture proving the inherit psychological weakness of people to be susceptible to believing the illusion of magic tricks, advanced AI technologies and other psychological methods of manipulation; and

(iii) *Absurdism Views* on Plausibility of Divine Revelation point to significant contradictions in all major religions concerning conflicting messages claimed to have been Divinely Inspired, as well as beliefs and trust on some claims of Revelation and not on others; and

(iv) *Empiricism Views* on Plausibility of Divine Revelation point to a persistent claim of the lack of empirical evidence in the support of miracles and other claimed supernatural.

**556.** In respect of *Classification by Capacity of Divine Revelation*, two essential classifications exist being General and Special:- <small>Classification by Capacity of Divine Revelation</small>

    (i)    *General Revelation* or Natural Revelation is the belief that knowledge and personal experience of the Divine is available to all humanity through the natural senses and the cognitive use of reason; and

    (ii)    *Special Revelation* is the belief that certain knowledge and experience of Divine Will and Divine Knowledge is only available through scripture, miracles and the founders of key religions, requiring strict and thorough interpretation.

**557.** In respect of *Classification by Method of Divine Revelation*, there are four common methods where Divine Revelation is believed to be received being *Voice, Vision, Dream* or *Inspiration*:- <small>Classification by Method of Divine Revelation</small>

    (i)    *Voice* is the notion that the Divine Creator may provide direct propositional content to a prophet in the form of a voice, whether or not it is heard by others. Several Religions and Cults claim that some of their most revered scripture was accomplished through Verbal Revelation; and

    (ii)    *Vision* is the notion that the Divine Creator may provide content and message to the prophet when they are in a conscious and lucid waking state through miracles, manifestations and other signs, whether or not the vision is seen by others; and

    (iii)    *Dream* is the notion that the Divine Creator may provide content and message to the prophet when they are asleep in the form of vivid and extraordinary visionary dreams during which the prophet may challenge or question the content and have it verified as proof of its authenticity; and

    (iv)    *Inspiration* is the notion that the Divine Creator may provide content and message to a prophet when they are awake in the form of the crystallization of an idea or thought that acts as a catalyst for action, design, speech or some other creative process.

**558.** In respect of *Classification by Degree of Supernatural Presence in Divine Revelation*, the authenticity of Revelation is both classified and authenticated by the level of Supernatural Presence being Public Miracles, Private Miracles, Visions and Inspiration:- <small>Classification by Degree of Supernatural Presence in Divine Revelation</small>

    (i)    *Public Miracles* are claimed events whereby two or more persons are said to have simultaneously witnessed first hand some miraculous occurrence of the Supernatural or Paranormal; and

(ii) *Private Miracles* are claimed events whereby only one person witnesses first hand some miraculous occurrence, while there may be a number of secondary witnesses that follow (such as medical miracles); and

(iii) *Visions* are claimed private experiences of receiving some symbolic or word orientated message, usually in a semi-wake or dream state; and

(iv) *Inspiration* are claimed private experiences of receiving some information in a lucid dream or waking moment of profound inspiration.

**559.** In respect of *Classification by Size of Audience to Divine Revelation*, the main classification is Public and Private:- Classification by Size of Audience to Divine Revelation

(i) *Public Revelation* is when two or more persons receive Divine Inspiration through some event; and

(ii) *Private Revelation* is when an individual receives Divine Inspiration and is considered the most common type of Revelation.

**560.** In respect of *Classification by Authority of Prophet*:- Classification by Authority of Prophet

(i) All major religions throughout history have placed the Divine Revelation of their founders above all others as the primary source of Scripture; and

(ii) Many religions have placed significant (and understandable) presumptions upon the Divine by asserting the Divine will not provide the same quantity or quality of Divine Revelation as claimed at their foundation; and

(iii) Some adherents of major religions in their zealous devotion to the original scripture of their faith have adopted the absurd, contradictory and heretical view that the Divine has stopped speaking to humanity by Divine Revelation. This is often called "Tradition" and is a profound blasphemy against all common traits and teachings of a loving and intelligent Divine Creator.

## Article 142 – Prophecy

**561.** ***Divine Prophecy*** means the communication and interpretation by a Prophet of some Prediction or Omen or Scripture given by Divine Inspiration.

*Divine Prophecy*

**562.** The word *Prophecy* comes from the Latin *prophetia* and the Ancient Greek προφητεῖᾰ (*propheteía*) meaning:-

*Origin of Meaning of Prophecy*

    (i)    A Prediction or Omen of the future will of God (or the gods); or

    (ii)    The interpretation of the will of God (or the gods); or

    (iii)    (Christian New Testament) Preaching and teaching under the influence of the Holy Spirit; or

    (iv)    The interpretation of Scripture.

**563.** The word *Prophet* comes from the Latin *propheta* and the Ancient Greek προφήτης (*prophetes*) meaning:-

*Origin of the Meaning of Prophet*

    (i)    One who speaks by Divine Inspiration; or

    (ii)    One who speaks for and interprets the will of a god; or

    (iii)    One of the keepers of the oracle; or

    (iv)    One who predicts the future; a soothsayer.

**564.** The original Latin word for Prophecy was *Vaticanum* and the original Latin word for Prophet or Soothsayer was *Vates*:-

*Vaticanus and Prophecy*

    (i)    Vatican Hill (Latin *Mons Vaticanus*) (originally around 130ft in height from the river flood plain) is the closest hill on the west side of the Tiber, opposite to the seven hills of Rome and outside the ancient 1st Century BCE Republican Walls to the city of Rome; and

    (ii)    From pre 600 BCE to around 204 BCE, Mons Vaticanus was known as the "City of the Dead" as the burial place for the most illustrious Romans outside the city walls and above the seasonal flooding of the river; and

    (iii)    From 203 BCE, a new temple platform was commenced (taking 13 years to build) over the Vatican Necropolis called the "Vaticanus" as the Primary Temple called *Phrygianum* to Magna Mater, also known as Cybele, Great Mother, Queen of Heaven, Mother of God, Mari and Mary. The spaces created underneath the superstructure upon Vatican Hill (protecting the still operational Necropolis) became known as the Catacombs; and

(iv) On April 11, 191 BC, Praetor Marcus Iunius Brutus inaugurated and dedicated the temple to Cybele on Vatican Hill. The Vaticanus also became the site for the Simulcrum of Cybele, the largest black iron meteorite in the world, placed outside the temple in the forecourt, similar to the Egyptian Stele; and

(v) Pre-Christian Roman Prophecy and Revelation from this point forward, placed the highest value on claimed Divine Revelations from Magna Mater (Cybele, Mary etc.) than any other deity, providing such claims were validated by the head soothsayers and priests of the Vatican known as Pontiffs; and

(vi) A smaller meteorite in the shape of a pine cone became a feature and inspiration for the hats worn by the Pontiffs of the Vaticanus from the 2$^{nd}$ Century BCE and the celebration of *Ludi Megalenses* in honouring Magna Mater, her Prophecies and the protection of Rome; and

(vii) In 1505, the Phrygianium was finally demolished to begin work on construction of St Peters Basilica atop Mons Vaticanus. The Design of St Peters Basilica retaining significant elements in its structure to honour Magna Mater (Cybele, Mary etc.) while the location continues to be a sacred site of Divine Revelation and Prophecy.

565. Both Divine Revelation and Divine Prophecy share common attributes concerning Divine Wisdom, Truth or Knowledge by Divine Inspiration. However, a number of important distinctions exist:- Divine Revelation and Divine Prophecy

(i) Authentic Divine Revelation generally and historically places greater emphasis on the quality and significance of the Divine Wisdom, Truth or Knowledge transmitted; and

(ii) Authentic Divine Prophecy generally and historically places greater emphasis on the method and rituals of transmission and the recognised authority and respect of the one receiving the transmission (the "Prophet"); and

(iii) Divine Prophecy is frequently misunderstood and seen as merely pertaining to predicting the future, whereas Divine Revelation is generally seen as broader in scope.

566. In matters concerning Ucadia and Ucadia Material, the term Divine Revelation shall be used in preference to Divine Prophecy, given the general broader scope and understanding of the term Divine Revelation. Divine Revelation as term used compared to Divine Prophecy

## Article 143 – Authentication of Revelation

**567.** ***Authentication of Divine Revelation*** refers to the process or means whereby individuals, religious authorities, or communities verify and confirm the authenticity and divine origin of a religious or spiritual message, text, prophecy, vision, or experience that is claimed to have been communicated by a deity or a higher spiritual power. The most common elements of Authentication of Divine Revelation include (but are not limited to): Supernatural Signs, Scriptural Signs, Revelatory Signs, Chain of Authority, Doctrinal Authority, Hierarchical Consensus and Community Consensus (Popularity):-

    (i)    *Supernatural Signs* are supernatural events that occur prior, during or soon after Divine Revelation that then may be cited as signs of Divine Approval and Authenticity; and

    (ii)    *Scriptural Signs* are when one or more elements quoted within sacred scripture may been seen as validating claimed Divine Revelation and thus a source of Authenticity; and

    (iii)    *Revelatory Signs* are when certain information within claimed Divine Revelation is of such power and significance that it is capable of "self authenticating" as a source of Authenticity; and

    (iv)    *Chain of Authority* is when the Messenger or Prophet is able to demonstrate a clear Chain of Authority that places them as belonging to an authentic chain of Divine Messengers, usually by birth or by elite training; and

    (v)    *Doctrinal Authority* is when the Divine Revelation is revealed to possess clear evidence of consistent Doctrinal Authority; and

    (vi)    *Hierarchical Consensus* is when the Hierarchy and Elite of one or more religions are in consensus and agreement as to the authenticity of the claimed Divine Revelation; and

    (vii)    *Community Consensus* is when sufficient popularity grows concerning claimed Divine Revelation that by popular acclamation the Divine Revelation is given authenticity.

**568.** In respect of *Authentication by Supernatural Signs*:-

    (i)    Miracles and perceived supernatural events is a relatively common form of attempts to authenticate new Divine Revelation; and

    (ii)    The most common form of newly claimed "revelation" using this method concerning major natural disasters and calamities is Eschatological (End Times) in Nature; and

(iii) The rarest application of this form of authentication is ancient prophecy of future events. The most significant of these being: Prophecies of Book of Revelation (4th Century), Prophecies of Nostradamus (1555), Prophecies of Kew (1977-1978), Prophecies of Hasidism (1740), Prophecies of Virgin Mary (1846, 1856, 1917, 1961, 1981, 1986), Prophecies of Edgar Cayce (1930-1945), Prophecies of Mormonism (1827) and Prophecies of Lucifer (5th Century BCE - 17th Century CE).

569. In respect of *Authentication by Scriptural Signs*:-

(i) Alignment to Scriptural Prophecy and Revelation is frequently used as a claim over history for the authenticity of new Divine Revelation; and

(ii) Again, the most common example of this application is when people claim Divine Revelation in relation to Eschatological (End Times) Scripture. Since the 19th Century there have been literally thousands of charismatic end time movements claiming Divine Revelation and the fulfilment of Scripture using this method.

570. In respect of *Authentication by Revelatory Signs*:-

(i) The "self-authenticating" power and capacity of new Divine Revelation is arguably one of the rarest forms of authentication; and

(ii) "Self Authentication" means the Divine Revelation itself is able to provide sufficient evidence and proof as to its authenticity that there can be no doubt; and

(iii) "Self-Authentication" manifests not only in the language structure, but the tone and quality of the information including (but not limited to) (a) being multi-dimensional – having multiple layers and depth of meaning and application; and (b) being uniquely profound in its meaning without being cliché or stereotypical; and (c) answering deep and long standing questions without being egotistical or flippant; and

(iv) The difficulty of this method of Authentication is that primarily it requires the claimed Divine Revelation to actually be Divine Revelation rather than a fraudulent attempt and claim.

571. In respect of *Authentication by Chain of Authority*:

(i) Traditions of Chain of Authority by birth is almost entirely reserved for the founders of major religious movements and not contemporary scholars or narrators; and

(ii) Chain of Authority by elite training is the most common form of Authenticity for many religions and places high standards and power in the hands of its hierarchy to interpret historic Divine Revelation and any claims of new Divine Revelation.

572. In respect of *Authentication by Doctrinal Authority*:-

(i) Authentication by Doctrinal Authority alone is rarely applied by any of the major religions, as such tests of authenticity favour both stereotypical and conservative orientated claims to a particular faith; and

(ii) There are a number of examples of famous claims of Divine Revelation over the past two hundred years where such information was wholly stereotypical and underwhelming, yet because of the related success of popular campaigns the instances have been accepted as genuine. A disproportionate number of Marian prophecies fall into this category.

*Authentication by Doctrinal Authority*

573. In respect of *Authentication by Hierarchical Consensus*:-

(i) It is extremely rare for the hierarchies of major religious movements to overwhelmingly agree to new Divine Revelation. Rather the appearance of newly claimed Divine Revelation is more likely to spawn new movements and political groups within the same religion; and

(ii) In older religious movements, the appearance of widely accepted Divine Revelation has historically been a point of political change and division rather than unity, as a reflection of the highly political environment of religious organisation.

*Authentication by Hierarchical Consensus*

574. In respect of *Authentication by Community Consensus*:-

(i) The authentication of Divine Revelation by Popularity through Community Consensus is a relative modern phenomena, remaining infrequent and almost exclusively Catholic and Marian in nature: and

(ii) Authentication by Community Consensus essentially means the acceptance of authenticity by the use of media campaigns, and the manipulation of public perception to gain acceptance. It is why popular movements in support of Divine Revelation are so controversial, using the "weight in numbers" of supporters to counter objective issues of credibility and authenticity.

*Authentication by Community Consensus*

**575.** All Authentic Divine Revelation recognised by Ucadia shares seven essential elements in its arrival into the temporal realm being *Relevancy, Timely, Useful, Revelatory, Self-Evidential, Illuminative* and *Supernatural*:-  
Ucadia Elements of Authentic Divine Revelation

(i) *Relevancy* means that Authentic Divine Revelation is always relevant to an age and time, or crisis or need, or pertinent to an important topic. Thus, the first test of Authentic Divine Revelation is that it comes when it is most needed, not when it may be wanted; and

(ii) *Timely* means that Authentic Divine Revelation always comes at precisely the right time, even if such time is not always known by all who seek or pray for such Revelation. Thus, the second test of Authentic Divine Revelation is that it meets timelines and promises previously made, even if such timelines were not fully understood; and

(iii) *Useful* means that Authentic Divine Revelation is above all useful and practical and helpful at the relevant time it comes. Thus, the third test of Authentic Divine Revelation is that the Divine does not send useless or stereotypical messages, but gives true gems of Divine Wisdom as Authentic Divine Revelation; and

(iv) *Revelatory* means that Authentic Divine Revelation "reveals" something new from what already "exists in plain sight". This is critical, as it demonstrates a respect for Tradition, for Custom and for context, such that the Divine never calls for such revolution or anarchy that a people lose trust in Heaven, but regain their faith; and

(v) *Self-Evidential* means that Authentic Divine Revelation once revealed is "self-evidential" in that it manifests its own validation as Divine Truth. Thus, even if such a message is ignored, repudiated and rejected for being contrary to established doctrine of some body. Profound Wisdom that is Self-Evidence is far harder to fake and concoct as such knowledge carries its own character of authenticity; and

(vi) *Illuminative* means that Authentic Divine Revelation demonstrates extraordinary enlightenment, clarity, perception, reason and knowledge, beyond the norm. It does not mean cliché, or stereotypical, or self-reinforcing, or superficial, or simplistic doctrinal reinforcement. Genuine Divine Illumination does not necessarily mean occult and encoded meaning, nor such phrases and messages deliberately constructed to be confusing or to sound "profound". Instead, true Revelation is powerful in its own right; and

(vii) *Supernatural* means that Authentic Divine Revelation comes from a source and a circumstance clearly with the hallmarks of Divine intervention.

576. On all objective metrics and measures, the authenticity of Ucadia as authentic Divine Revelation is without doubt or question. The volume and consistency and quality of the entirety of Ucadia places it as a supreme historic moment of Divine Revelation since the beginning of human civilisation.

*Ucadia and seven elements of Authentic Divine Revelation*

## Article 144 – Examples of Authentic Divine Revelation

577. ***Examples of Authentic Divine Revelation*** refers primarily to major "civilisation centric" prophecy rather than general and personal Divine Revelation that nonetheless may be truly profound and significant:-

(i) There is ample evidence that exists to demonstrate generalised and personal Divine Revelation is present across planet Earth on a daily basis, with no people or region excluded; and

(ii) Specialised Authentic Divine Revelation appears to be extremely rare and in terms of its potential translation into Divine Scripture represents manifestation in less than one in one billion (1: 1,000,000,000) people in any given generation.

*Examples of Authentic Divine Revelation*

578. Evidence of Authentic Divine Revelation refers primarily to major "civilisation centric" prophecy rather than general and personal Divine Revelation that nonetheless may be truly profound and significant:-

(i) There is ample evidence that exists to demonstrate the daily presence of Divine Revelation and Supernatural events occurring across planet Earth, from medical miracles, to paranormal experiences, to inspirations and omens and premonitions of significant events; and

(ii) There is a sound historic record, including interviews surrounding major world changing events and disasters to show that on almost every occasion numerous human beings and especially domesticated animals such as dogs and cats have received and reacted in some way to forewarnings of coming dangers.

*Evidence of Generalised Divine Revelation*

579. In reference to Authentic Divine Revelation, the most significant examples include (but are not limited to):-

*Evidence of Specialised Divine Revelation*

Lex Ecclesiasticum: Maxims of Ecclesiastical Law

    (i)      Prophecy of the Popes; and

    (ii)     Prophecies of Mithraism; and

    (iii)    Prophecies of Revelation; and

    (iv)    Prophecies of Mormonism; and

    (v)     Prophecies of Kew; and

    (vi)    Prophecies of Nostradamus; and

    (vii)   Prophecies of Dante Alighieri; and

    (viii)  Prophecies of John Milton; and

    (ix)    Prophecies of Ucadia; and

    (x)     Prophecies of Edgar Cayce; and

    (xi)    Prophecies of Fatima; and

    (xii)   Prophecies of Sabbateanism; and

    (xiii)  Prophecies of Hasidism; and

    (xiv)  Prophecies of the Virgin Mary; and

    (xv)   Prophecies of Lucifer.

580. ***Prophecy of the Popes***, also known as the "Prophecy of St Malachy" is a late 16th Century literary fraud created by Franciscan Priest Arnold de Wyon of Venice and first published no earlier than 1595. While its original intention was probably to assist in influencing the second conclave of 1590, the "prophecies" have had a profound impact on the election of subsequent candidates and so have essentially become a key authentic prophecy upon the Papacy. — *Prophecy of the Popes*

581. ***Prophecies of Mithraism***, also known as Book of Daniel and written no later than 4$^{th}$ or 5$^{th}$ Century BCE, is one of the oldest and enigmatic set of prophetic texts. The time periods of seventy weeks, seven weeks and threescore and two weeks as mentioned in Chapter 9 have been subject to much debate, including using the time periods in the context of the Ministry of Jesus Christ, the time periods of major wars, the second coming and the tribulation. — *Prophecies of Mithraism*

582. ***Prophecies of Revelation***, also known as the Book of Revelation, is arguably one of the most significant texts of prophecy in human history, comprising of twenty-two chapters. The Book of Revelation has been used by thousands of claimants arguing possession of Divine Inspiration for hundreds of years. — *Prophecies of Revelation*

583. ***Prophecies of Mormonism*** refer to the movement founded by Joseph Smith, Jr (b.1805-d.1844) and related scripture and prophecies – the most significant and notable pertaining to End — *Prophecies of Mormonism*

Times and the claim 144,000 will be saved.

584. **Prophecies of Kew** relate to two visions experienced by Frank O'Collins on August 15th 1977 (when aged 12) and exactly one year later on August 15th 1978 and recounted to Catholic officials concerning the end of the reign of Pope Benedict XVI which occurred in 2013 and thirty six years after the first vision.

585. **Prophecies of Nostradamus** refer to the book *Les Propheties* first published in 1555 by Michel de Nostredame (Nostradamus), and arguably the most famous prophecy almanac ever published in print. Based on a brilliantly crafted set of 942 esoteric four sentence (quatrain) structures then grouped into ten "centuries".

586. **Prophecies of Dante Alighieri** refers to the famous Italian Poet (b. 1265 – d. 1321) and his work *Divine Comedy* concerning his claimed journey to Hell, Purgatory and then Heaven. The text includes not only numerous insights into views on sin, redemption, and the human condition, but the descriptions of locations and experiences on his epic journey are viewed by a significant number as prophetic.

587. **Prophecies of John Milton** refers to the famous English Poet (b. 1608 – d. 1674) and his 1666 epic poem of 10 books and 10,000 lines of verse called Paradise Lost concerning the fall of Lucifer (Satan) and the subsequent rise and influence of Lucifer over Adam and Eve and all of humanity.

588. **Prophecies of Ucadia** refers to the connection of the Divine Revelation within the vast texts and structures of Ucadia and the fulfilment of multiple prophetic texts including (but not limited to) the Book of Revelation (over 43 significant elements), the Book of Daniel (over 6 significant elements), Sabbatean Prophecy (over 8 elements) and Hasidic Prophecy (over 7 elements).

589. **Prophecies of Edgar Cayce** refer to the tens of thousands of readings conducted by Edgar Cayce (b.1877-d.1945) and the less than five percent (5%) that pertained to prophecy. Of the estimated 26,000 readings, approximately 8,000 remain missing. Of the remainder that are available, approximately 2 to 5% of predictions appear to have been validated.

590. **Prophecies of Fatima** refer to one of the most famous examples of media driven authentication of Divine Revelation, when in July 1917 Maria Rosa Ferreira and her brother and local priest Father Manuel Marques Ferreira contacted Lisbon based Newspaper Editor Alberto de Magalhães of "O Século" and "Ilustração Portuguesa" to claim her daughter Lúcia and her two young cousins had been receiving direct

messages from the Virgin Mary. After the first small piece was published in the newspaper by journalist Avelino de Almeida, Portuguese lawyer, diplomat and politician José Almeida Garrett became involved and was instrumental in arranging the famous gathering of over 30,000 people at Fatima on 13 October 1917 that was extensively covered in multiple pictures and full page articles by Newspaper Editor Alberto de Magalhães. It was José Almeida Garrett who came up with the idea of suggesting Maria Rosa Ferreira tell her daughter Lúcia to look directly at the Sun, causing many to experience retinal dysfunction and temporary blindness, later proclaimed as the"Miracle of the Sun". In 1921, Lúcia was accepted into the school of the Sisters of St. Dorothy near Porto. In 1941, Lúcia was finally convinced to write down the first two "secrets" of Fatima that were claimed twenty four years prior in 1917. The third "secret" was penned in 1943.

591. ***Prophecies of Sabbateanism*** relate to Ottoman Kaizer Ibrahim (b.1615 – d. 1687) who secretly denounced Islam and proclaimed himself as the prophet Sabbatai Zevi and Jewish Messiah in 1666 as the founder of AshkeNazi or the Nazi Cult of Zionism on the esoteric texts of the *Keys of Solomon* (1630), the *Etz Hayim* (1560), the *Zohar* (1558) and the *Venetian Talmud* (1523). He was succeeded by his son named Suleiman (Solomon).

592. ***Prophecies of Hasidism*** relate to Rabbi Israel Baal Shem Tov (b.1698-d.1760) and based upon the revival and revision of Sabbatean Zionist occult philosophies under the patronage of Polish Prince August Aleksander Czartoryski (b.1697-d.1782). The main prophetic text of the Hasidic Cult or Orthodox Cult is the *Amsterdam Talmud* of 1645 and the *Zohar* (1558). In 1801, Prince Adam Kazimierz Czartoryski commissioned the Temple of Cybele on the grounds of the Czartoryski Palace as the supreme secret "synagogue" to Sabaoth. The site subsequently played an integral geometric center point to arguable the worst atrocities of World War II and human history within a perfect 300 mile wide circumference.

593. ***Prophecies of Lucifer*** concern the "return" of Lucifer made flesh, to walk planet Earth and perform many miracles at the time signalled variously as "Armageddon", "Judgment Day" and the "End of Days" and are exclusively Christian in origin and sourced from The Bible.

594. ***Prophecies of the Virgin Mary*** refers to a string of largely stereotypical and media driven claims of prophecy within Catholic communities since the 19th Century beginning in 1846 with a young virgin peasant girl from La Salette in France; and then in 1858 a young virgin peasant girl from Lourdes in France; and then in 1917 a

young virgin peasant girl in Fatima in Portugal; and then in 1961 four young virgin peasant girls near Garabandal in Spain; and then in 1981 two young virgin peasant girls in Medjugorje in Bosnia Herzegovina. The only example of a recorded day time Marian Vision not conforming to the stereotypical format of all the others is the Vision of Our Lady at St Francis' Church in Melbourne on 31st March 1986 where a statue of Mary came to life and spoke and repeated the words "Help Me!" to a 21 year old boy.

## 4.2 – Scriptural Revelation

### Article 145 – Scriptural Revelation

595. ***Divine Scripture*** refers to sacred texts or writings that are considered to be of Divine origin or inspiration within a particular religious tradition. These texts are often regarded as the word of the Divine or as conveying profound spiritual and religious truths. Divine Scripture

596. Examples of Divine Scripture from various major religions include (but are not limited to):- Examples of Significant Divine Scripture

   (i) ***Bible***: In Christianity, the Bible is the sacred scripture consisting of the Old Testament (which includes texts like Genesis, Exodus, and Psalms) and the New Testament (which includes the Gospels, Acts, and the Epistles). It is considered the authoritative word of God and contains teachings, history, and prophecies; and

   (ii) ***Quran***: In Islam, the Quran is the holy book believed to be the literal word of God as revealed to the Prophet Muhammad by the angel Gabriel. It serves as the ultimate source of guidance for Muslims in matters of faith, practice and morality; and

   (iii) ***Bhagavad Gita***: Within Hinduism, the Bhagavad Gita is a sacred scripture that is part of the Indian epic Mahabharata. It consists of a conversation between Lord Krishna and Prince Arjuna and explores spiritual and ethical themes; and

   (iv) ***Tripitaka (Pali Canon)***: In Theravada Buddhism, the Tripitaka, also known as the Pali Canon, is the primary scriptural collection. It contains the teachings of Siddhartha Gautama (Buddha) and is divided into three "baskets" or sections: Vinaya Pitaka (monastic rules), Sutta Pitaka (discourses), and Abhidhamma Pitaka (philosophical analysis); and

   (v) ***Guru Granth Sahib***: In Sikhism, the Guru Granth Sahib is the central religious scripture and is considered the final and eternal Guru. It contains hymns and teachings of Sikh Gurus and other spiritual leaders; and

(vi) **Tao Te Ching**: Within Taoism, the Tao Te Ching is a foundational text attributed to Laozi. It explores the concept of Tao (the Way) and offers guidance on living in harmony with it; and

(vii) **Torah**: In Judaism, the Torah is the central and most sacred text. It includes the first five books of the Hebrew Bible (Genesis, Exodus, Leviticus, Numbers, and Deuteronomy) and contains religious laws, history and ethical teachings; and

(viii) **Avesta**: In Zoroastrianism, the Avesta is the primary collection of religious texts. It includes the Gathas (hymns attributed to Zoroaster) and other writings on rituals, beliefs and ethics; and

(ix) **Pactums (Ucadia)**: In Ucadia, the Covenants *Pactum De Singularis Caelum*, *Pactum De Singularis Christus*, *Pactum De Singularis Islam* and *Pactum De Singularis Spiritus* are considered central and most sacred texts. These texts then define the structure of all the Maxims, Charters and Codes of the model of Civilization of Ucadia.

## Article 146 – Classification of Scriptural Revelation

597. ***Classification of Divine Scripture*** is a system and method for categorising different types of Divine Scripture. The most significant method for the Classification of Divine Scripture is *Maxima Textibus Sacris*.  
Classification of Divine Scripture

598. In accord with the most sacred Covenant *Pactum De Singularis Caelum*, Divine Scripture, also known as **Maxima Textibus Sacris** shall comprise of twenty two (22) collections or "texts", each representing either:-  
Maxima Textibus Sacris

   (i) A past collection of the greatest sacred texts for a region or major faith or covenant in accord with *Authenticus Depositum Fidei* prior to the end of the Year of Redemption; or

   (ii) The future collection of sacred texts for a region or major faith or covenant in accord with *Authenticus Depositum Fidei* after the end of the Year of Redemption.

599. The first eleven (11) sacred collections of texts of the *Maxima Textibus Sacris* represent the greatest sacred texts of all major regions of planet Earth and major faiths prior to the end of the Year  
First Eleven Sacred Collections

of Redemption, being:-

(i) *Primum Sanctum Textibus Africa*, also known as First Holy Texts of Africa; and

(ii) *Primum Sanctum Textibus Americas*, also known as First Holy Texts of (the) Americas; and

(iii) *Primum Sanctum Textibus Arabia*, also known as First Holy Texts of Arabia; and

(iv) *Primum Sanctum Textibus Asia*, also known as First Holy Texts of Asia; and

(v) *Primum Sanctum Textibus Europa*, also known as First Holy Texts of Europe; and

(vi) *Primum Sanctum Textibus Oriens*, also known as First Holy Texts of Levant; and

(vii) *Primum Sanctum Textibus Oceania*, also known as First Holy Texts of Oceania; and

(viii) *Primam Sanctam Textibus Unum Christus*, also known as First Holy Texts of One Christ; and

(ix) *Primam Sanctam Textibus Unum Islam*, also known as First Holy Texts of One Islam; and

(x) *Primam Sanctam Textibus Unum Spirit*, also known as First Holy Texts of One Spirit; and

(xi) *Primam Sanctam Textibus Originalis Gens*, also known as First Holy Texts of Original Nations (Tribes).

**600.** The second eleven (11) sacred collections of texts of the *Maxima Textibus Sacris* represent the new sacred texts of all major regions of planet Earth and major faiths after the end of the Year of Redemption, being:- Second Eleven Sacred Collections

(i) *Sancta Nova Textibus Africa*, also known as New Holy Texts of Africa; and

(ii) *Sancta Nova Textibus Americas*, also known as New Holy Texts of (the) Americas; and

(iii) *Sancta Nova Textibus Arabia*, also known as New Holy Texts of Arabia; and

(iv) *Sancta Nova Textibus Asia*, also known as New Holy Texts of Asia; and

(v) *Sancta Nova Textibus Europa*, also known as New Holy Texts of Europe; and

(vi) *Sancta Nova Textibus Oriens*, also known as New Holy Texts of Levant; and

(vii) *Sancta Nova Textibus Oceania*, also known as New Holy Texts of Oceania; and

(viii) *Sancta Nova Textibus Unum Christus*, also known as New Holy Texts of One Christ; and

(ix) *Sancta Nova Textibus Unum Islam*, also known as New Holy Texts of One Islam; and

(x) *Sancta Nova Textibus Unum Spirit*, also known as New Holy Texts of One Spirit; and

(xi) *Sancta Nova Textibus Originalis Gens*, also known as New Holy Texts of Original Nations (Tribes).

601. The acceptance of a Sacred Text into a collection shall depend upon the name and type of collection:- *Acceptance of Sacred Text*

   (i) All collections of Sacred Texts by regions shall be determined by the legislative authority of the particular Union that encompasses the region, in association with a Great Conclave every one hundred twenty eight (128) years or General Conclave every sixty four (64) years; and

   (ii) All collections of Sacred Texts by faiths shall be determined by the legislative authority of the particular faith in association with a Great Conclave every one hundred twenty eight (128) years or General Conclave every sixty four (64) years.

602. All accepted Sacred Texts may appear in more than one collection and are formally defined as Canonical, Reverential or Referential:- *Presence of Sacred Text in more than One Collection*

   (i) **Canonical Sacred Texts**: are texts considered and cited as a foundation of law and spiritual authority and therefore the twenty two (22) books of maxims of law known as the *Divine Collection of Maxims of Law*; and

   (ii) **Reverential Sacred Texts**: are texts that contain some canonical references but also possess too many non canonical references to be wholly canonical so may be partially cited as foundational law but not considered absolute "Divine Law"; and

   (iii) **Referential Sacred Texts**: are respected historical texts that are not considered accurate or consistent enough to be "Divine Law" that may be referenced in historical context and reference but not as true foundation of law.

603. Sacred Texts that are proven to contradict, usurp or openly defy the *Sacred Texts*

most sacred Covenant *Pactum De Singularis Caelum* cannot be classified as Canonical and may only be classified as either Reverential or Referential:-

<blockquote>that contradict, usurp or openly defy Divine Law cannot be classified as Canonical Sacred Texts</blockquote>

(i) **Multiple Fundamental Logical Absurdities**: Are texts that contain a least three or more fundamental logical absurdities in claimed actions, instructions or thoughts of the Divine or Deity that contradict the very essence or existence of such a Being; and

(ii) **Multiple Fundamental Internal Inconsistencies**: Are three or more examples of such contradictions within and between sections of the text that render it impossible to be the same Being or Beings.

## Article 147 – Authentication of Scriptural Revelation

604. ***Authentication of Divine Scripture*** varies depending on the religious tradition and the specific beliefs of the community that regards certain texts as sacred and divinely inspired. Authentication of divine scripture is a matter of faith and belief within a specific religious context. Different religious traditions have different criteria and methods for authenticating their scriptures, and the level of importance placed on various factors can vary widely.

<blockquote>Authentication of Scriptural Revelation</blockquote>

605. In general, the Authentication of Divine Scripture typically involves several key elements, that may include:-

<blockquote>Examples of Elements for Authentication of Divine Scripture</blockquote>

(i) **Revelation**: Most religious traditions claim that their sacred texts were revealed directly by a divine source, such as God or gods, to a chosen individual or prophet. This revelation is often considered the primary authentication of the scripture; and

(ii) **Internal Consistency**: Many sacred texts are expected to be internally consistent and free from contradictions. Believers often view this consistency as evidence of divine inspiration; and

(iii) **Prophetic Authority**: The person through whom the scripture was revealed is often regarded as a prophet or a messenger of the divine. The authenticity of the scripture is closely tied to the credibility and integrity of the prophet. In Christianity, the New Testament is based on the teachings of Jesus Christ and his apostles; and

(iv) **Miracles and Prophecies**: Some sacred texts contain prophecies or accounts of miraculous events that are believed to validate their divine origins. For example, the Quran is said to contain prophecies that were fulfilled; and

(v) **Historical Documentation**: In some cases, historical documentation and records are used to authenticate the origins and transmission of the scripture. This may involve verifying the historical accuracy of events and individuals mentioned in the text; and

(vi) **Tradition and Authority**: The recognition and endorsement of religious leaders, scholars, or religious authorities can also play a role in authenticating scripture. These individuals may possess the knowledge and authority to interpret and validate sacred texts; and

(vii) **Consensus of Believers**: The acceptance and continued belief of a religious community in the authenticity of a scripture play a significant role in its authentication. If a scripture has been accepted and followed by generations of believers, it attains a level of credibility within the community.

## Article 148 – Interpretation of Scriptural Revelation

606. ***Interpretation of Authentic Divine Scripture***, often referred to as hermeneutics or exegesis, is the process of understanding and explaining the meaning, teachings and significance of sacred texts within a religious tradition.

*[Interpretation of Authentic Divine Scripture]*

607. Interpretation is a crucial aspect of religious study and practice as it helps believers and religious scholars extract moral, spiritual and practical guidance from their scriptures. Some key elements concerning the Interpretation of Divine Scripture include (but are not limited to):-

*[Elements of Interpretation of Authentic Divine Scripture]*

(i) **Literal vs. Allegorical Interpretation**: Different religious traditions may employ various methods of interpretation. Some emphasize a more literal interpretation, where the text is understood at face value, while others may employ allegorical or symbolic interpretation, where the text is seen as containing deeper spiritual or moral truths; and

(ii) **Contextual Analysis**: Interpreters often consider the historical, cultural and linguistic context in which the scripture was written. Understanding the context helps to clarify the intended meaning and relevance of the text; and

(iii) **Historical-Critical Approach**: This approach involves scholarly analysis of a text's historical origins, authorship and transmission. It seeks to understand the text within its historical context and may involve the use of archaeology, linguistics and textual criticism; and

(iv) **_Theological Interpretation_**: Theological interpretation seeks to understand how a scripture relates to a particular religious tradition's theology and doctrines. It explores how the text informs beliefs and practices within that tradition; and

(v) **_Traditional and Modern Approaches_**: Different religious traditions may have traditional methods of interpretation, often based on the teachings of revered scholars or theologians. In addition to traditional approaches, modern scholars and theologians may offer new insights and interpretations; and

(vi) **_Debate and Diversity of Interpretation_**: Interpretation can lead to a diversity of opinions and beliefs within a religious tradition. Debates and discussions regarding the interpretation of scripture are common; and

(vii) **_Interfaith Dialogue_**: Interfaith dialogue involves comparing and contrasting the teachings of different religious scriptures to foster understanding and cooperation among different religious communities; and

(viii) **_Personal and Communal Interpretation_**: Individuals and religious communities engage in interpretation, with personal interpretations being guided by religious education and community norms; and

(ix) **_Spiritual Insights_**: For many believers, the interpretation of divine scripture is a deeply spiritual and contemplative practice that can lead to personal insights, growth and a sense of divine connection; and

(x) **_Role of Religious Authorities_**: In many religious traditions and religious authorities, such as clergy, scholars or religious leaders play a significant role in interpreting scripture and providing guidance to believers.

# Title V – Theology

## 5.1 – Theology

### Article 149 – Theology

608. ***Theology*** is any comprehensive system of knowledge that seeks to define the nature of the divine, religious beliefs and the practices of one (or more) Religions.

Theology

609. In accord with Divine Law and Natural Law, Theology as ***Theologia*** is a *Theology* and the first of the thirty-three (33) sciences of Ucadia that systematically and objectively defines all possible Models into three (3) disciplines and systems being: *Logia* (Primary Ucadia Sciences), *Paralogia* (Universal Ucadia Sciences) and *Metalogia* (Social Ucadia Sciences):-

Theologia and the first of all Ucadia Sciences

**Logia (Primary Ucadia Sciences)**

(i) ***Theologia***: Is the *Ucadia Scientific Model of the Divine*; and the study of the principles, methods, systems, arguments and proofs that rationally and reliably explain the existence, nature, function and intention of the Divine and other supernatural beings within, without and throughout the Universe; and

(ii) ***Philologia***: Is the *Ucadia Scientific Model of Philosophy and Human Thought*; and the study of fundamental questions about existence, knowledge, values, reason, mind, and language through critical analysis and logical reasoning; and

(iii) ***Etymologia***: Is the *Ucadia Scientific Model of Semantics and Meaning*; and the study of the meaning of words and phrases, while meaning refers to the concepts or objects that language elements represent; and

(iv) ***Symbologia***: Is the *Ucadia Scientific Model of Symbols*; and the study of various objects, characters, or figures used to represent ideas, concepts, or other elements beyond their literal meaning in various disciplines such as literature, mathematics and culture; and

(v) ***Dialogia***: Is the *Ucadia Scientific Model of Language*; and the study of the systems of communication using symbols and sounds; and the structures, functions and evolution of languages; and

(vi) ***Rhetologia***: Is the *Ucadia Scientific Model of Argument and Reason*; and the study of effective argument, reason and persuasion through speech and writing, utilising techniques for argumentation, style, and delivery employed by speakers and writers.

**Paralogia (Universal Ucadia Sciences)**

(vii) *Cosmologia*: Is the *Ucadia Scientific Model of Physics*; and the study of matter, energy, and the fundamental forces of nature, exploring how they interact through space and time to explain the universe's behaviour; and

(viii) *Astrologia*: Is the *Ucadia Scientific Model of Astrophysics*; and the study of the physical properties, behaviour, and interactions of celestial objects and phenomena in the universe; and

(ix) *Atologia*: Is the *Ucadia Scientific Model of Particle Physics*; and the study of the fundamental particles and forces that compose matter and govern their interactions; and

(x) *Chemalogia*: Is the *Ucadia Scientific Model of Chemistry*; and the study of atomic and molecular matter, its properties, composition, and the changes it undergoes during chemical reactions; and

(xi) *Geologia*: Is the *Ucadia Scientific Model of Geology and Planetary Structures*; and the study of Earth's structure, materials, processes, and history, including the formation of rocks, minerals, and the dynamics of tectonic activity; and

(xii) *Physiologia*: Is the *Ucadia Scientific Model of Biology and Ecosystems*; and the study of life and living organisms, encompassing their structure, function, growth, evolution, distribution and interactions within ecosystems; and

(xiii) *Taxologia*: Is the *Ucadia Scientific Model of Numbers and Computation*; and the study of numerical values and mathematical operations to solve problems, analyze data, and perform calculations in various fields such as science, finance and engineering; and

(xiv) *Metrologia*: Is the *Ucadia Scientific Model of Geometry and Measurement*; and the study of shapes, sizes, and properties of figures and spaces, and the quantification of physical attributes such as length, area, volume and angles; and

(xv) *Typologia*: Is the *Ucadia Scientific Model of Algebra and Functions*; and the study of mathematical symbols and the rules for manipulating them, focusing on relationships, patterns, and the behaviour of quantities through equations and function mappings; and

(xvi) **Axiologia**: Is the *Ucadia Scientific Model of Axioms and Model Proofs*; and the study of self-evident truths; proofs are logical arguments using axioms to verify theorems in mathematics or logic. Together, they form the foundation and validation of mathematical structures; and

(xvii) **Kinologia**: Is the *Ucadia Scientific Model of Motion*; and the study of continuous change, focusing on derivatives for rates of change and integrals for accumulation of quantities; and

(xviii) **Exologia**: Is the *Ucadia Scientific Model of Motion and Transition*; and the study of complex motion and transitions from one state to another; and

(xix) **Eikologia**: Is the *Ucadia Scientific Model of Mathematics*; and the study of numbers, quantity, and space, analyzing patterns, structures, and relationships through logical reasoning, computation and problem-solving techniques.

**Metalogia (Social Ucadia Sciences)**

(xx) **Psychologia**: Is the *Ucadia Scientific Model of Cognition and Mind*; and the study of Mental processes of acquiring knowledge and understanding through thought, experience, and senses; and the set of cognitive faculties enabling consciousness, perception, thinking, judgement and memory; and

(xxi) **Anthropologia**: Is the *Ucadia Scientific Model of Anthropology*; and the study of human societies, cultures, and their development, integrating archaeology, linguistics, biological, and social perspectives to understand human diversity, behavior and evolution; and

(xxii) **Sociologia**: Is the *Ucadia Scientific Model of Sociology*; and the study of human society, social behaviours, interactions, and institutions; and how they shape and are shaped by cultural, economic and political forces; and

(xxiii) **Nomologia**: Is the *Ucadia Scientific Model of Economics*; and the study of how individuals, businesses, and governments allocate scarce resources to satisfy needs and wants, focusing on production, distribution, consumption, and decision-making within markets; and

(xxiv) **Demologia**: Is the *Ucadia Scientific Model of Politics*; and the study of governance, involving decision-making, power dynamics, and conflict resolution among individuals, groups, or states to achieve societal goals and public policies; and

(xxv) **Diologia**: Is the *Ucadia Scientific Model of Administration*; and the study of the organisation and management of tasks, resources, and people to achieve goals efficiently, often involving planning, decision-making and implementation of policies; and

(xxvi) **Themilogia**: Is the *Ucadia Scientific Model of Law*; and the study of systems of rules created and enforced by a governing body to regulate behaviour, maintain order, protect rights and deliver justice; and

(xxvii) **Stratologia**: Is the *Ucadia Scientific Model of Strategy*; and the study of plan of action designed to achieve long-term goals, involving resource allocation, decision-making, and anticipating competition or challenges; and

(xxviii) **Ephologia**: Is the *Ucadia Scientific Model of Logistics*; and the study of planning, implementing, and managing the efficient movement and storage of goods, services, and information from origin to consumption to meet customer requirements; and

(xxix) **Archologia**: Is the *Ucadia Scientific Model of Infrastructure*; and the study of fundamental physical and organisational structures and facilities needed for the operation of a society, including transportation, communication systems, water supply and power grids; and

(xxx) **Ergologia**: Is the *Ucadia Scientific Model of Industry*; and the study of production and manufacturing of goods and services within an economy, often involving large-scale operations, machinery, and specialised labour in sectors like agriculture, technology and manufacturing; and

(xxxi) **Autologia**: Is the *Ucadia Scientific Model of Robotics and Autonomous Systems*; and the study of the design and use of robots and advanced technologies to perform tasks autonomously or with minimal human intervention, enhancing efficiency, precision and productivity; and

(xxxii) **Technologia**: Is the *Ucadia Scientific Model of Technology*; and the study of the application of scientific knowledge for practical purposes, enabling innovation and the creation of tools, systems, and devices that solve problems and enhance human capabilities; and

(xxxiii) **Mechalogia**: Is the *Ucadia Scientific Model of Engineering*; and the study of the application of scientific and mathematical principles to design, build and maintain structures, machines and systems efficiently and safely.

**610.** The term *Theology* is derived from the Ancient Greek *theologia* (θεολογὶα) which is itself derived from theos (Θεὀς), meaning "God" and -logia (-λογὶα) meaning "utterances, sayings or oracles". Origin of word Theology

**611.** While a *Theology* may be complex and appear comprehensive, no philosophical system of Theology can rise to be a valid or legitimate scientific branch of knowledge unless it possesses the following criteria:- The Structure of the Valid Science of The Divine

    (i)    A direct association of Greatest Principles and Teachings with Cosmology defining the universe, laws of the universe, relation between matter and rules, levels of matter and the function and purpose of the universe; and

    (ii)    A central and foundational set of arguments concerning Divine Existence, Divine Nature and Divine Mind (or Purpose) in support of theological Cosmology as proof; and

    (iii)    An association with one or more bodies of texts considered the most sacred scripture as the source of such Divine Revelations; and

    (iv)    An association with one or more bodies of maxims of law based upon such fundamental theological arguments and sacred text reference whereby certain norms, standards and maxims of law are asserted; and

    (v)    A form of arguments, justifications and methods by which the sacred texts and theological system is considered superior than others with similar or competing ideas; and

    (vi)    An association with one or more formal defined rituals or customs as one or more sacraments; and a form of arguments and justifications for these particular rituals or customs.

**612.** In accord with the most sacred Covenant *Pactum De Singularis Caelum*, each of the three (3) Great Faiths of One Christ, One Islam and One Spirit are permitted to use their own official name for the *Divine Science* of *Theologia*:- Great Faiths and Divine Science

    (i)    The Universal Ecclesia of One Christ may use the name **"Summa Elementis Theologica"** to officially define the Essential Elements of *Theologia* from the perspective of their authority; and

    (ii)    The Holy Society of One Islam may use the name **"Farid Eulim Allah"** to officially define the Unique Knowledge of

God from the perspective of their authority and the science of *Theologia*; and

(iii) Sacred Society of One Spirit may use the name "**Divya Darshana**" to officially define the Perspective of the Divine from the perspective of their authority and the science of *Theologia*.

**613.** In accord with Article 25 (*The Divine Science*) of the most sacred Covenant *Pactum De Singularis Caelum*, the structure of *Theologia* includes (but is not limited to):- Structure of Divine Science of Theologia

*Existence and Nature of God, Divine Beings, Creation and Nature*:

(i) **Diology** (Doctrine of God and the Divine Creator); and

(ii) **Daimology** (Doctrine of Divine and Supernatural Beings); and

(iii) **Ouranology** (Doctrine of Divine Dimension and Places); and

(iv) **Cosmology** (Doctrine of Creation); and

(v) **Physiology** (Doctrine of Nature and the Physical World); and

(vi) **Pneumatology** (Doctrine of the Holy Spirit); and

*Existence and Nature of Human Beings*:

(vii) **Thymology** (Doctrine of the Soul and Spiritual Self); and

(viii) **Psychology** (Doctrine of the Mind and Soul); and

(ix) **Protology** (Doctrine of the Species Singularity); and

(x) **Ethology** (Doctrine of right conduct and morality); and

(xi) **Anthropology** (Doctrine of humanity and history and the divine); and

(xii) **Eschatology** (End Times, Change & Renewal); and

*Revelation, Christ and Organised Faith and Trust*:

(xiii) **Manteology** (Doctrine of Revelation, Prophecy and Prophets); and

(xiv) **Graphology** (Doctrine of sacred scripture); and

(xv) **Christology** (Doctrine of Messiahs); and

(xvi) **_Hagiology_** (Doctrine of holiness and sanctification); and

(xvii) **_Mysteriology_** (Doctrine of sacraments, rites and ceremonies); and

(xviii) **_Pistology_** (Doctrine of organised faith and trust).

614. Contrary to Non-Ucadia bodies, the use of the term Systematic Theology is prohibited and reserved to describing the systematic doctrinal errors of Doctrinology:- [The prohibition of the concept of Systematic Theology]

   (i) **_Incomplete Framework_**: Means that Systematic Theology as the underpinning methodology of the doctrinal errors of Doctrinology has never put forward a properly complete theological architectural framework such as Theologia; and

   (ii) **_Corrupted and Bias (Incomplete) Framework_**: Means that the incomplete framework actually used by Systematic Theology is narrowly focused, corrupted and demonstrably biased in its appraisal of theological history – in embracing certain historically questionable works as its source, whilst ignoring huge anomalies, contradictions and gaps within the cultural and historic record of theological philosophy; and

   (iii) **_False Claims of Completeness and Historical Objectivity_**: Whereby Systematic Theologians have consistently and falsely claimed their discipline is based on a comprehensive theological framework; and a complete and objective historical account – that has consistently been proven to be untrue.

## Article 150 – Orthodoxy

615. **_Orthodoxy_** refers to the adherence to accepted and established beliefs, doctrines, and practices of a particular faith tradition. It is often associated with the idea of maintaining the original or traditional teachings and resisting changes or deviations that might arise over time. [Orthodoxy]

616. *Orthodoxy* stems from the Ancient Greek roots orthos (ὀρθός), meaning "right or correct" and doxa (δόξα), meaning "opinion or belief". Hence the term *Orthodoxy* literally means "authentic knowledge". [Origin of the meaning of Orthodoxy]

617. Consistent with the most sacred Covenant *Pactum De Singularis Caelum* and the present Maxims all of the valid components of Ucadia are founded upon the true and authentic meaning of *Orthodoxy*:- [Ucadia is founded on Orthodoxy]

(i) ***Authentic Knowledge***: Ucadia is founded upon authentic knowledge, the respect of authentic tradition and the restoration of authentic knowledge that has often been corrupted and suppressed by forces who falsely claim to be orthodox; and

(ii) ***Consistent and Reliable Knowledge***: Ucadia is founded upon a comprehensive non-contradicting model of knowledge capable of ushering in a new Civilisation based on freedom, true enlightenment, prosperity and peace; and

(iii) ***Transparency and Freedom of Knowledge***: Ucadia is founded in the freedom and transparency of knowledge, rather than the secrecy, or weaponising or self commercialisation of knowledge.

618. Conservatism is not the same as Orthodoxy, but the opposite and enemy of Orthodoxy:- Conservatism is not Orthodoxy

(i) *Conservatism* (from the Latin *conserva* meaning "to preserve") is a modern 19th Century political term introduced by John Wilson Croker who first used it to describe his philosophy in an 1830 edition of his politically radical publication "The Quarterly Review" whereby controversial, immoral, deceptive and radical ideas were proposed to gain wealth and power at the expense of attacking traditional institutions by falsely framing them "conservative" and "protecting the status quo". Thus Conservatism is about corrupting tradition through the use of "gaslighting" to achieve and maintain the political ends of power; and

(ii) Conservatism, is similar to other 19th Century radical political philosophies created to achieve power such as Socialism, and share the same techniques of "double-speak" as epitomised in the book 1984 by George Orwell, whereby war is falsely framed as peace, and enslavement as freedom.

## Article 151 – Tradition

619. ***Tradition*** refers to the transmission of beliefs, practices, customs, and rituals that are passed down through generations within a religious community. Tradition

620. *Tradition* originates from the Latin word *traditio* meaning "to teach; to instruct; to deliver". *Tradition* therefore literally implies the authentic transmission of Authentic Knowledge, such as the teachings and transmission of customs, beliefs and cultural practices from one generation to another. Origin of the meaning of Tradition

Title V – Theology

**621.** Consistent with the most sacred Covenant *Pactum De Singularis Caelum* and the present Maxims all of the valid components of Ucadia are founded upon the true and authentic meaning of *Tradition*.

*Ucadia is founded on Tradition*

**622.** Conservatism is not the same as Tradition, but the opposite and enemy of Tradition:-

*Conservatism is not Tradition*

  (i) The major first use of the concept of Conservatism within an ecclesiastical context was also in the 19th Century under Pope Pius IX (1846-1878) through his document a Syllabus of Errors (1864) where he deliberately condemned various modern ideologies such as rationalism, socialism, and the separation of church and state, whilst proclaiming himself a defender of tradition. His position instantly created a broad division within the Catholic Church between traditionalists who were mocked as radicals, and then radicals who supported the agenda of Pius as "conservatives"; and

  (ii) Whilst the unquestionable record of Pope Pius IX clearly makes him arguably the most radical anti-tradition pope arguably in the history of the Catholic Church, through his promotion of Mary as equal and in some ways technically "higher" than her son; and his introduction of "Papal Infallibility" technically making himself a god on earth, the conservative faction within Catholicism and other Christian denominations still to this day falsely and delusionally believe they are the protectors of "tradition".

**623.** The majority of fatal doctrinal errors that have recently plagued major Religions and Spiritual Bodies are almost entirely the direct product of the radical actions of Conservative heretics and their political power movement of Conservatism over recent centuries and have nothing to do with authentic Traditions or Orthodox beliefs over millennia:-

*Majority of Doctrinal Errors are product of Conservatism and not Traditional or Orthodox*

  (i) ***Authentic Tradition Exposes False Conservatism***: Whereby no major Religion can survive over sustained periods with fatal doctrinal errors. Thus those errors that appear in direct conflict and less fundamental to the pillars of a faith, are more likely to be deliberately false Conservative corruptions; and

  (ii) ***Authentic Tradition Enables Restoration after Conservatism Exorcised***: Meaning that the strength of the authentic foundations of major Religions enable the restoration from the corruptions of conservatism once exorcised.

## 5.2 – Theology of Existence & Nature of the Divine

### Article 152 – Diology
### (God & the Divine Creator)

624. ***Diology*** is the study of the existence, nature, and attributes of God and the Divine Creator. It is the first of six sub-disciplines within the first of three major branches of the Ucadia Science of *Theologia* being *Existence and Nature of God, Divine Beings, Creation and Nature*.

625. The term *Diology* is derived from the Ancient Greek words of "Dio-" (from the Greek word meaning God) and "-logy" (meaning the study of).

626. The key sub-categories of *Diology* include (but are not limited to):-

 (i) ***Einology***: The study of the Existence of God including various Ontological, Cosmological and Teleological Arguments; and

 (ii) ***Ousiology***: The study of the Nature and Attributes of God; and

 (iii) ***Ktisology***: The study of Divine Creation, Purpose and the Order of Creation; and

 (iv) ***Schesology***: The study of Divine Relationship Between God and Creation.

### Article 153 – Daimology
### (Divine & Supernatural Beings)

627. ***Daimology*** is the study of the existence, nature and roles of Divine and Supernatural Beings, including entities such as angels, demons, spirits, and other non-human intelligences believed to interact with the physical and metaphysical realms. It is the second of six sub-disciplines within the first of three major branches of the Ucadia Science of *Theologia* being *Existence and Nature of God, Divine Beings, Creation and Nature*.

628. The term *Daimology* is derived from the Ancient Greek words of *daimon* (meaning spirit or divine power) and "*-logy*" (meaning the study of).

629. The key sub-categories of *Daimology* include (but are not limited to):-

 (i) ***Angelology***: The study of angels, their hierarchy, roles, and interactions with humans and the divine; and Beings)

(ii) **_Demonology_**: The study of demons, their origins, classifications, behaviors, and influence on the material world; and

(iii) **_Spiritology_**: The study of spirits, including those of deceased humans, nature spirits, and other non-corporeal entities; and

(iv) **_Mythological Beings_**: The study of beings from various mythologies, such as gods, demigods, and legendary creatures, and their impact on human culture and belief systems; and

(v) **_Comparative Daimology_**: The comparative study of spiritual and supernatural beings across different religions and cultures, examining similarities, differences and influences; and

(vi) **_Historical Daimology_**: The study of how beliefs in spiritual and supernatural beings have evolved over time within different societies and religious traditions.

## Article 154 – Ouranology (Divine Dimension & Places)

630. **_Ouranology_** is the study of the existence, nature and function of Divine Dimension and Places. It is the third of six sub-disciplines within the first of three major branches of the Ucadia Science of _Theologia_ being _Existence and Nature of God, Divine Beings, Creation and Nature_.  
Ouranology (Divine Dimension & Places)

631. _Ouranology_ derives from the Ancient Greek words "οὐρανός" (ouranos), meaning "heaven" or "sky" and "λόγος" (logos), meaning "study" or "discourse". Thus, Ouranology fundamentally means the study or discourse of the heavens or divine realms.  
Origin of the term Ouranology

632. The key sub-categories of _Ouranology_ include (but are not limited to):-  
Key elements of Ouranology (Divine Dimension & Places)

(i) **_Heavenly Realms_**: Exploration of different divine dimensions and their characteristics; and

(ii) **_Afterlife Realms_**: Examination of beliefs regarding heaven and other afterlife destinations; and

(iii) **_Sacred Geography_**: Mapping and significance of holy places; and

(iv) **_Theophany_**: Manifestations of the divine in the physical world.

## Article 155 – Cosmology
## (Creation & Design)

633. **Cosmology** is the study of the existence, purpose, nature and function of Creation. It is the fourth of six sub-disciplines within the first of three major branches of the Ucadia Science of *Theologia* being *Existence and Nature of God, Divine Beings, Creation and Nature*.

*Cosmology (Creation & Design)*

634. The word *Cosmology* derives from the Ancient Greek words *kosmos* (κόσμος), meaning "world" or "universe" and "logia" (λογία), meaning "study" or "discourse". Thus, cosmology fundamentally means the study or discourse about the universe.

*Origin of the term Cosmology*

635. The key sub-categories of *Cosmology* include (but are not limited to):-

*Key elements of Cosmology (Creation & Design)*

   (i) **Cosmogony**: Study of the creation and development of the cosmos from a religious perspective, particularly the various religious narratives about the origin of the universe; and

   (ii) **Hierocosmology**: Analysis of how sacred texts and traditions describe the structure and order of the universe; and

   (iii) **Comparative Cosmology**: The comparative study of different models, stories and doctrines of creation across different religions and cultures, examining similarities, differences and influences; and

   (iv) **Historical Cosmology**: The study of how creation stories and models of cosmology have evolved over time within different societies and religious traditions.

## Article 156 – Physiology
## (Nature & the Physical World)

636. **Physiology** is the study of the existence, purpose and function of Nature and the Physical World. It is the fifth of six sub-disciplines within the first of three major branches of the Ucadia Science of *Theologia* being *Existence and Nature of God, Divine Beings, Creation and Nature*.

*Physiology (Nature & the Physical World)*

637. The word *Physiology* derives from Ancient Greek: "physis" (φύσις), meaning "nature" and "logos" (λόγος), meaning "study" or "discourse". Thus, Physiology fundamentally means the study or discourse of nature and natural phenomena.

*Origin of the term Physiology*

638. The key sub-categories of *Physiology* include (but are not limited to):-

*Key elements of Physiology (Nature & the Physical World)*

   (i) **Systology**: The study of the natural systems of the world and the concepts of creation, dimension and the Divine; and

(ii) **Ecology**: The study of the relationships between living organisms and their environments. This includes the examination of ecosystems, biomes, and the balance of nature, as well as the theological understanding of stewardship and the interconnectedness of life.

## Article 157 – Pneumatology (Holy Spirit)

639. **Pneumatology** is the study of the existence, nature and function of the Holy Spirit. It is the sixth of six sub-disciplines within the first of three major branches of the Ucadia Science of *Theologia* being *Existence and Nature of God, Divine Beings, Creation and Nature*.

*Pneumatology (Holy Spirit)*

640. *Pneumatology* derives from the Ancient Greek words "pneuma" (πνεῦμα), meaning "spirit" or "breath" and "logos" (λόγος), meaning "study" or "discourse". Thus, Pneumatology is the study or discourse on the Holy Spirit.

*Origin of the term Pneumatology*

641. The key sub-categories of *Pneumatology* include (but are not limited to):-

*Key elements of Pneumatology (Holy Spirit)*

(i) **Deity of the Holy Spirit**: The divine nature of the Holy Spirit, affirming the Holy Spirit's co-equality, co-eternity, and consubstantiality with the Father and the Son; and

(ii) **Personhood of the Holy Spirit**: The Holy Spirit as a distinct person within the Trinity, examining scriptural evidence and theological arguments that affirm the Holy Spirit's personhood; and

(iii) **Holy Spirit in Scripture**: The presence and activity of the Holy Spirit in Scriptures, including the Spirit's role in prophecy, empowerment and guidance; and

(iv) **Work of the Holy Spirit in Creation**: The role of the Holy Spirit in the creation of the world and the ongoing sustaining of creation; and

(v) **Gifts of the Holy Spirit**: The various spiritual gifts bestowed by the Holy Spirit, their purposes and their operation within the church.

## 5.3 – Theology of Existence & Nature of Human Beings
### Article 158 – Thymology (Soul and Spiritual Self)

**642.** ***Thymology*** is the study of the existence, nature and function of the Soul and Spiritual Self. It is the first of six sub-disciplines within the second of three major branches of the Ucadia Science of *Theologia* being *Existence and Nature of Human Beings*.

*Thymology (Soul and Spiritual Self)*

**643.** *Thymology* derives from the Ancient Greek words "thymos" (θυμός), meaning "soul" or "spirit" and "logos" (λόγος), meaning "study" or "discourse". Thus, Thymology etymologically signifies the study or discourse on the soul and spiritual self.

*Origin of the term Thymology*

**644.** The key sub-categories of *Thymology* include (but are not limited to):-

*Key elements of Thymology (Soul and Spiritual Self)*

   (i) ***Energetiology***: The structure and components of the spiritual self, including concepts such as the chakras, aura, and other metaphysical elements that constitute the spiritual body; and

   (ii) ***Psychosophy***: The fundamental nature, origin, and essence of the soul. It addresses questions about what the soul is, how it exists; and

   (iii) ***Karmalogy***: The principles of karma, the law of cause and effect, and the concept of reincarnation. It examines how past actions influence the present and future lives of the soul; and

   (iv) ***Thanatology***: The study of death and the practices associated with it, including the afterlife; and

   (v) ***Holonology***: The concept of the interconnectedness of all souls with the universal and collective consciousness. It explores how individual souls relate to the greater whole; and

   (vi) ***Comparative Thymology***: The comparative study of spiritual self and soul beings across different religions and cultures, examining similarities, differences and influences; and

   (vii) ***Historical Thymology***: The study of how beliefs in spiritual self and soul have evolved over time within different societies and religious traditions.

## Article 159 – Psychology
## (Mind and Soul)

645. ***Psychology*** is the study of the existence, nature and function of the Mind and Soul. It is the second of six sub-disciplines within the second of three major branches of the Ucadia Science of *Theologia* being *Existence and Nature of Human Beings*.

646. The word *Psychology* derives from Ancient Greek: "psyche" (ψυχή) meaning "soul" or "mind" and "logos" (λόγος), meaning "study" or "discourse". Thus, etymologically, Psychology means the study of the soul or mind.

647. The key sub-categories of *Psychology* include (but are not limited to):-

(i) ***Noetology***: The nature of consciousness, different states of awareness, and how the soul experiences and interacts with reality. It includes studies on altered states of consciousness, meditation, and spiritual awakening; and

(ii) ***Sophology***: The exploration of processes and practices that lead to spiritual growth, self-realization and enlightenment. It includes the study of various spiritual traditions, disciplines and techniques aimed at achieving higher states of being; and

(iii) ***Mystagogy***: The study and guidance into mystical experiences, the pursuit of direct communion with the Divine, and the transcendence of ordinary reality. It includes the exploration of mystical traditions, practices and writings; and

(iv) ***Psychospiritology***: The study of the interplay between psychological well-being and spiritual health, exploring how they influence each other and contribute to overall mental, emotional and spiritual healing.

## Article 160 – Protology
## (Species Singularity)

648. ***Protology*** is the study of the existence, nature and function of the Species Singularity. It is the third of six sub-disciplines within the second of three major branches of the Ucadia Science of *Theologia* being *Existence and Nature of Human Beings*.

649. The word *Protology* derives from Ancient Greek roots: "proto-" meaning "first" or "primary" and "-logy" meaning "study of". Thus, Protology etymologically means the study of first things or origins, particularly concerning the beginnings of existence and the nature of

human beings.

650. The key sub-categories of *Protology* include (but are not limited to):-    *Key elements of Protology (Species Singularity)*

   (i)   **Koinology**: The shared consciousness and experiences of humanity as a whole, and how the incarnation of the single soul influences and reflects this collective consciousness; and

   (ii)   **Metaphysionomy**: The nature of human identity, both individual and collective, in the context of the incarnation single soul by multiple soul incarnation.

## Article 161 – Ethology
## (Right Conduct & Morality)

651. **Ethology** is the study of the existence, nature and function of right conduct and morality. It is the fourth of six sub-disciplines within the second of three major branches of the Ucadia Science of *Theologia* being *Existence and Nature of Human Beings*.    *Ethology (Right Conduct & Morality)*

652. The term *Ethology* is derived from the Ancient Greek "ἦθος" (êthos), meaning "character" or "custom" and "λόγος" (logos), meaning "study" or "discourse". Thus, Ethology fundamentally refers to the study of character and behaviour.    *Origin of the term Ethology*

653. The key sub-categories of *Ethology* include (but are not limited to):-    *Key elements of Ethology (Right Conduct & Morality)*

   (i)   **Ethicology**: The study of moral principles, virtues, vices and their impact on the soul's journey and spiritual development; and

   (ii)   **Comparative Ethology**: The comparative study of conduct and morality across different religions and cultures, examining similarities, differences and influences; and

   (iii)   **Historical Ethology**: The study of how beliefs in conduct and morality have evolved over time within different societies and religious traditions.

## Article 162 – Anthropology
## (History of Humanity)

654. **Anthropology** is the study of the existence, nature and function of humanity and history and the Divine. It is the fifth of six sub-disciplines within the second of three major branches of the Ucadia Science of *Theologia* being *Existence and Nature of Human Beings*.    *Anthropology (History of Humanity)*

655. The term *Anthropology* is derived from the Ancient Greek words "anthropos" (ἄνθρωπος), meaning "human" and "logos" (λόγος), meaning "study" or "discourse". Thus, Anthropology etymologically    *Origin of the term Anthropology*

means the study or discourse of humans.

656. The key sub-categories of *Anthropology* include (but are not limited to):-

(i) **Comparative Anthropology**: The comparative study of anthropological models across different religions and cultures, examining similarities, differences and influences; and

(ii) **Historical Anthropology**: The study of how beliefs in anthropological models have evolved over time within different societies and religious traditions.

## Article 163 – Eschatology
## (End Times, Change & Renewal)

657. *Eschatology* is the study of the existence, nature and function of End Times, Change & Renewal. It is the sixth of six sub-disciplines within the second of three major branches of the Ucadia Science of *Theologia* being *Existence and Nature of Human Beings*.

658. The term *Eschatology* is derived from the Ancient Greek words "ἔσχατος" (eschatos), meaning "last" or "farthest" and "λόγος" (logos), meaning "study" or "word". Thus, Eschatology is the study of the last things or the end times.

659. The key sub-categories of *Eschatology* include (but are not limited to):-

(i) **Coschatology**: The ultimate fate of the universe, the cyclical nature of time, the destruction and renewal within the cosmos, and the ultimate purpose of creation; and

(ii) **Synchatology**: The study of end times or ultimate destinies as they pertain to collective entities such as groups, societies, or humanity as a whole; and

(iii) **Hischatology**: The study on understanding how historical events correlate with and influence eschatological beliefs and interpretations; and

(iv) **Apocalyptology**: The study of texts that describe revelatory visions of the end times and the day of judgment; and

(v) **Milleniology**: The study of beliefs of various cultural, religious and historical contexts in a forthcoming transformative period, often associated with the return of a messianic figure; and

(vi) **Ecochatology**: The study of eschatological beliefs and catastrophic environmental collapse and the challenges of ecological sustainability.

## 5.4 – Theology of Revelation, Faith, Hope & Trust

### Article 164 – Manteology
### (Revelation, Prophecy & Prophets)

660. ***Manteology*** is the study of the existence, nature and function of Revelation, Prophecy and Prophets. It is the first of six sub-disciplines within the third of three major branches of the Ucadia Science of *Theologia* being *Revelation, Christ and Organised Faith and Trust*.

*Manteology (Revelation, Prophecy & Prophets)*

661. The term *Manteology* is derived from the Ancient Greek words "mantis" (μάντις), meaning "prophet" or "seer" and "logos" (λόγος), meaning "study" or "discourse". Thus, Manteology etymologically means the study or discourse of prophets and prophecy.

*Origin of the term Manteology*

662. The key sub-categories of *Manteology* include (but are not limited to):-

*Key elements of Manteology (Revelation, Prophecy & Prophets)*

(i) ***Revelatology***: The study of the theological implications and nature of divine revelation, including how such truths are communicated to humanity and how they are received and interpreted by humans; and

(ii) ***Archteology***: The study of the ethics and authority of prophetic figures, their legitimacy and authenticity, as well as their impact on social, political and religious issues; and

(iii) ***Histalatology***: The study of the nature, types, and expressions of divine revelation, including sacred texts as sources of revealed knowledge; and

(iv) ***Hermeneutology***: The study and interpreting and understanding of prophetic writings, including historical context and development of prophetic texts and Theological approaches to interpreting prophecy; and

(v) ***Prophecy***: The study of prophetic statements within holy scripture, including prophecies from various historical periods and their impacts; and

(vi) ***Prophetic Tradition***: The study of differentiation between major and minor prophets, canonical and non-canonical prophets, including prophetic traditions across different religions and cultures.

## Article 165 – Graphology
## (Sacred Scripture)

663. ***Graphology*** is the study of the existence, nature and function of sacred scripture. It is the second of six sub-disciplines within the third of three major branches of the Ucadia Science of *Theologia* being *Revelation, Christ and Organised Faith and Trust*.

<sub>Graphology (Sacred Scripture)</sub>

664. The term *Graphology* derives from Ancient Greek: "grapho" (γράφω) meaning "to write" and "logos" (λόγος), meaning "study" or "discourse". Thus, Graphology etymologically means the study or discourse of writing.

<sub>Origin of the Graphology term</sub>

665. The key sub-categories of *Graphology* include (but are not limited to):-

<sub>Key elements of Graphology (Sacred Scripture)</sub>

    (i) **Canonical Studies**: The study of the process by which certain texts were accepted into the canon of sacred scripture and others were excluded. It examines criteria for canonicity, the history of canon formation, and the authority of canonical texts; and

    (ii) **Textual Criticism**: The examination and comparison of various manuscript copies of sacred texts to identify and correct transcription errors, and to establish the most authentic version of the text; and

    (iii) **Literary Analysis**: The study of literary forms, genres, structures and stylistic elements used in the scriptures. It includes analyzing narrative techniques, poetry, parables and other literary devices; and

    (iv) **Theological Interpretation**: The study of how sacred texts are interpreted within various theological frameworks. It includes the study of hermeneutics (the theory and methodology of interpretation) and exegesis (the critical explanation or interpretation of texts); and

    (v) **Comparative Scripture**: The comparing and contrasting of sacred texts from different religious traditions. Scholars seek to identify common themes, differences and influences between various scriptures.

## Article 166 – Christology
## (Messiahs)

666. ***Christology*** is the study of the existence, nature and function of Messiahs. It is the third of six sub-disciplines within the third of three major branches of the Ucadia Science of *Theologia* being *Revelation, Christ and Organised Faith and Trust*.

*Christology (Christ)*

667. *Christology* derives from the Ancient Greek words "Christos" (Χριστός), meaning "anointed one" or "Messiah" and "logia" (λογία), meaning "study" or "discourse". Thus, Christology is the study or discourse about Messiahs, focusing on the nature, role, and person of each Messiah.

*Origin of the term Christology*

668. The key sub-categories of *Christology* include (but are not limited to):-

*Key elements of Christology (Christ)*

    (i) ***Messiaology***: The study of messiahs throughout history, times and cultures; and

    (ii) ***Hypostatiology***: The study of theological concepts around the incarnation of messiahs as the personification of both the Divine and human; and

    (iii) ***Poniology***: The study of the works of messiahs, including their labor or toil, in terms of effort, suffering, and the hardships associated with their function; and

    (iv) ***Heroiology***: The study of messiahs as mythical and prophetic heroic figures across cultures and religions; and

    (v) ***Exousiology***: The study of the authority of messiahs and the positions of mandate and office held throughout history and religious context; and

    (vi) ***Pseudiology***: The study of false messiahs, impostors and frauds, including how such historical figures rose in popularity and prominence.

## Article 167 – Hagiology
## (Holiness & Sanctification)

669. ***Hagiology*** is the study of the existence, nature and function of holiness and sanctification. It is the fourth of six sub-disciplines within the third of three major branches of the Ucadia Science of *Theologia* being *Revelation, Christ and Organised Faith and Trust*.

*Hagiology (Holiness & Sanctification)*

670. The term *Hagiology* is derived from the Ancient Greek words "hagios" (ἅγιος), meaning "holy" or "sacred" and "logos" (λόγος),

*Origin of the term Hagiology*

meaning "study" or "discourse". Thus, hagiology refers to the study or discourse on holiness and sanctification.

671. The key sub-categories of *Hagiology* include (but are not limited to):-     *Key elements of Hagiology (Holiness & Sanctification)*

    (i)     ***Hagiography***: The study of Saints in different religions and their Lives; and

    (ii)     ***Venerology***: The study of Procedures for declaring sainthood, including Criteria and investigations for beatification and Historical development; and

    (iii)     ***Comparative Hagiology***: The study of Saints in different cultures and religions.

## Article 168 – Mysteriology (Sacraments, Rites & Ceremonies)

672. ***Mysteriology*** is the study of the existence, nature and function of sacraments, rites and ceremonies. It is the fifth of six sub-disciplines within the third of three major branches of the Ucadia Science of *Theologia* being *Revelation, Christ and Organised Faith and Trust*.     *Mysteriology (Sacraments, Rites & Ceremonies)*

673. The term *Mysteriology* is derived from the words "mystērion" (μυστήριον), meaning "mystery" or "secret rite" and "logia" (λογία), meaning "study" or "discourse". Thus, Mysteriology refers to the study of sacred mysteries, sacraments, rites and ceremonies within religious contexts.     *Origin of the term Mysteriology*

674. The key sub-categories of *Mysteriology* include (but are not limited to):-     *Key elements of Mysteriology (Sacraments, Rites & Ceremonies)*

    (i)     ***Sacramentology***: The study of the nature, significance and function of sacraments, including development and theological foundations of sacraments, exploring how they have been understood and practiced within various religious traditions; and

    (ii)     ***Sacropraxiony***: The practical application of sacramental and liturgical theology in pastoral settings and the training and preparation of clergy for administering sacraments; and

    (iii)     ***Canonology***: The study, interpretation and application of ecclesiastical law and regulations, including the legal frameworks, procedural norms, and jurisprudence associated with the administration and governance of sacraments, rites, and other religious ceremonies within an organized faith tradition.

### Article 169 – Pistology
### (Faith, Hope & Trust)

675. ***Pistology*** is the study of the existence, nature and function of organised faith and trust. It is the sixth of six sub-disciplines within the third of three major branches of the Ucadia Science of *Theologia* being *Revelation, Christ and Organised Faith and Trust*.

*Pistology (Faith, Hope & Trust)*

676. The term *Pistology* is derived from the Ancient Greek word "pistis" (πίστις), meaning "faith" or "trust" and "logia" (λογία), meaning "study" or "discourse". Thus, Pistology is the study or discourse on faith and trust, particularly within the context of organised belief systems.

*Origin of the term Pistology*

677. The key sub-categories of *Pistology* include (but are not limited to):-

*Key elements of Pistology (Faith, Hope & Trust)*

  (i) ***Doxology***: The study of the core faith, trust and participation of adherents to a religious faith, including the integration and life impact of such faith in the lives of adherents; and

  (ii) ***Orthodoxy***: The study of core authentic beliefs and dogmas that define a religious tradition, including creeds, catechisms, and official teachings of religious institutions; and

  (iii) ***Praxology***: The study of the relationship between orthodoxy and doxology and how faith is practically lived out in daily life, including rituals, worship practices, and the practical application of faith principles; and

  (iv) ***Comparative Pistology***: The comparative study of different organisational structures and administrations across different religions and cultures, examining similarities, differences and influences; and

  (v) ***Historical Pistology***: The study of how organisational structures and administrations have evolved over time within different societies and religious traditions.

## 5.5 – Historic Eschatology Concepts
### Article 170 – Apocalypse

678. ***Apocalypse*** is a word reserved for prophecy and revelation of future events containing signs and symbols considered so profound, mysterious and sacred that it is set above other prophecy. In popular culture, the term Apocalypse usually refers to End Time Prophecies or possible events triggering the "end of the world".

*Apocalypse*

679. The word *Apocalypse* originates from the Greek term *apokálypsis*

*Origin and*

(ἀποκάλυψις) meaning "unveiling of revelation". It is derived from two parts: *apó* (ἀπό) meaning "from" and *kalýptō* (καλύπτω) (kalýptō), meaning "to cover or conceal". Apocalypse therefore literally means "to uncover or reveal".

680. Originally, the word *Apocalypse* was simply an Ancient Greek word equivalent to the Latin word Revelation. However, upon the appearance in writing no later than the 17th Century of the severely corrupted and distorted ancient scripture known as the *Book of Revelation*, also known as the *Apocalypse of John*, the term Apocalypse has come to be associated more broadly with cataclysmic or transformative events, embodying the dramatic nature often depicted in "end of the world" apocalyptic literature often endorsed across Christianity, Islam and Judaism.

681. General Elements of Authentic Apocalyptic Visions include (but are not limited to):-

(i) ***Extreme Imagery & Symbolism***: That the imagery of the vision is so confronting, immersive and powerful such that of all the dreams a person ever has, it cannot be forgotten and remains instantly recallable, no different from a profound physical experience; and

(ii) ***Mysterious and Unresolved***: That the imagery and its time, place and full meaning remains mysterious and unresolved within the lifetime of the visionary; and

(iii) ***Genuine Revelation***: That the subject matter of the vision fulfils and meets the criteria of genuine Revelation in contrast to falsely created and claimed revelatory visions; and

(iv) ***Divinely Inspired***: That sufficient evidence within such vision indicates divine inspiration as a key source.

## Article 171 – Armageddon

682. *Armageddon* is an ancient Latin military term wholly corrupted and perverted within the 17th Century Bible (Revelation 16:16) to describe an alleged placename for the "final battle" between good and evil and the end of the old world and beginning of the new. Until the 17th Century, A*rmageddon* in Latin always meant "capacity to wage war; to conduct/wage war".

683. The word *Armageddon* originates from Roman Military Planning and Strategy concerning the concept of "total warfare":-

(i) *Armageddon* in Latin originates over 2,000 years ago from two Latin words *arma* meaning "war, weapons of war, tools of war, military power, military tactics and military personnel" and *gedo/gero* meaning "I possess; I carry on; I conduct; I wage". It was a key military term associated with the planning and competence of major military campaigns using all resources to wage the ancient equivalent to "total war" – a traditional military strategic advance of the Roman Empire; and

(ii) In the 17th Century and the decision to completely corrupt Christian texts falsely claim the fictitious non-existent state of Israel and the Jews instead of the ancient Yahudi heritage, the Revelations texts were butchered to include references to Palestine as the focus of the "final battle" of the end of the (old) world. The fake 17th Century Hebrew *Har Megiddo* ( הַר מְגִדּוֹ ) or "mount of Megiddo" was created and a hill in the Jezreel Valley changed to make the new claim fit; and

(iii) Since the 20th Century and into the 21st Century, these deliberate corruptions to ancient writings have continued to play a key focal point in convincing the world that the fate and future of Palestine will largely determine the end of the old world in "global war".

## Article 172 – Antichrist

684. ***Antichrist*** is a 6th Century Ancient Greek term used by various Christian denominations to describe their political and military opponents – hence the Orthodox (Byzantine) Christian Empire called the Western Christian Empire "the antichrist", whilst the West said the same against the east. In the late 17th Century the term was hijacked in the deliberate corruption of certain Bible texts to create false references to an "End Times" figure as the personification of evil and opposition to Christ and God.

<small>Antichrist</small>

685. The word *Antichrist* comes from the Ancient Greek *Antichristos* (ἀντίχριστος):-

<small>Origin, History and meaning of Antichrist</small>

(i) *Antichristos* itself derived from *anti-* (ἀντι-) meaning "against, (pseudo) like, (falsely) reminiscent of" and *christos* (χριστος) meaning "messiah, saviour". Hence Antichrist literally means "against Christ" or "false Christ"; and

(ii) In the 17th Century, additions and corruptions to the Bible for example such as Revelations in John 1:7, 2:18, 4:3, created a figure who will appear at the end of times, embodying evil and opposing Christ and God; and

(iii) The public view of the Antichrist as an "End Times Figure" has since continued to grow whereby the faithful are warned the Antichrist is associated with deception, and leading people away from the true faith; and sometimes depicted as a charismatic leader who will establish a reign of false peace before ultimately being defeated by Christ during the Second Coming; and

(iv) Perversely, during the same period, the root meaning of *anti-* (ἀντι-) deliberately lost some of its Ancient Greek meaning, so that Antichrist could now be interpreted by academics, theologians and the elite as "like Christ" or "reminiscent of Christ". Hence, whilst the public were generationally taught to fear the coming of an Antichrist, a small group of society looked forward to the same figure as their own "Messiah"; and

(v) There is considerable evidence that the American and European elite originally nominated Albert Einstein (1879-1955) as their figurehead for this role as the "Lightbringer" – especially due to his birthday of March 14 corresponding to the ancient *Dies Sanguinus* (Day of Blood) and Birth/death of Mithra and his connection to Atomic Physics and the ultimate "light of death" being Nuclear weapons; and

(vi) Since the 1960's, the elaborate Doctrinology of American Luciferian Secularism has continued to breakdown, with growing resistance and outright opposition among occult leaders that the "old world" ended by 1945 and that the "new world" of American exceptionalism is legitimate.

## Article 173 – Rapture

686. **Rapture** is a 19<sup>th</sup> Century English and American misinterpretation of Christian teaching and contemporary revelation, whereby it is believed by many Protestant and Evangelical followers that prior to the "end of the world", they will be physically saved by the return of Jesus Christ by being taken up into the "air or sky" to be safe with him.

Rapture

687. The word *Rapture* is coined from the Latin word *raptus* meaning "to seize" and "to carry off". It was presumably chosen as the foundation word for the doctrine on the basis of the physical nature of the claim.

Origin of the meaning of Rapture

688. In terms of the origin of the philosophy of Rapture:-

Origin of the philosophy of Rapture

(i) The concept of Rapture was originally created by British evangelist John Nelson Darby (1800 – 1882), who used Bible passages such as Revelations and in particular 1 Thessalonians 4:16-17, 1 Corinthians 15:51-52 and Matthew 24:40-41 to reinforce a "pre-tribulation rapture" whereby certain faithful would be physically saved from the trauma of the end of the old world by being raised into the "air or sky" under a new covenant; and

(ii) American Cyrus Ingerson Scofield (1843-1921) greatly strengthened the arguments for Rapture via his Scofield Reference Bible (1909). The philosophy finally made it into mainstream American viewing via movies and television such as Hal Lindsey's "The Late Great Planet Earth" (1970) and the "Left Behind" series by Tim LaHaye and Jerry B. Jenkins (1995 onward).

(iii) The philosophy of Rapture has now evolved into three camps being Pre-Tribulation, Mid-Tribulation and Post-Tribulation.

## Article 174 – Day & Year of Divine Agreement & Understanding

689. The historic and true ***Day of Divine Agreement and Understanding***, also known as the Day of the Apocalypse, also known as the Apocalypse, also known as the Day of the 1st Divine Post and Notice, was GAIA E8:Y3209:A1:S1:M6:D1, also known as [Monday, 21 Dec 2009].

*Day of Divine Agreement & Understanding*

690. From the one true *Day of Divine Agreement and Understanding* being GAIA E8:Y3209:A1:S1:M6:D1, also known as [Monday, 21 Dec 2009] until GAIA E8:Y3210:A1:S1:M17:D1 also known as [Tuesday, 21 Dec 2010], is historically known as the ***Year of Divine Agreement and Understanding*** represented as year 3209 within Ucadia Sacred Time-Space.

*Year of Divine Agreement & Understanding*

691. In reference to the sacred concept of *Divine Agreement*:-

*Divine Agreement*

(i) **Agreement** implies a "meeting of minds" and mutual consent. **Divine Agreement**, therefore means the meeting of Divine Mind with the mind and consent, or refusal of mind of unique Homo Sapiens claiming positions of power on behalf of Divine Mind; and

(ii) In accord with the most sacred Covenant *Pactum De Singularis Caelum*, all valid Office is derived solely from Heaven; and those that breach such sacred trust in the dereliction of their responsibilities and instead deliberately and wilfully cause the murder and torture of innocent Living Members agree by their actions to ultimately face the full force of the Wraiths of the *Obligationum Systemata* (Enforcement Systems), by whatever means necessary; and

(iii) Despite such maladministration and abandonment of duty by many of the present leaders and their agents upon planet Earth, to not offer them an opportunity for redemption, for peace and for renewed competence, would be contrary to the perfect justice of the Divine Creator; and

(iv) Therefore, the present leadership of the planet must be afforded every opportunity, repeatedly and with an abundance of public notice to redeem themselves and change and let history be the judge; and

(v) While the Divine Mind is infinitely larger and superior in one perspective to the singular mind of a Homo Sapien, the mind of any man or woman is also *ipso facto* (as a matter of fact) part of the greater collective mind or singularity of existence; and

(vi) Thus, at one level, such a "meeting of minds" and therefore valid agreement is legitimately possible under all valid forms of law. However, the choice to be competent and to change rests in the unique perspective of each living mind of a man or woman who seeks to hold office, to hold authority and power and to claim control of property and wealth. To force a mind to change would be to violate the fundamental law of "free will".

**692.** In reference to the sacred concept of *Divine Understanding*:-    *Divine Understanding*

(i) In accord with the most sacred Covenant *Pactum De Singularis Caelum*, the word "understand" possesses one superior meaning to "stand under" the rule of law by the superiority of Divine Law, followed by Natural Law and finally Positive Law; and

(ii) To "understand" therefore is to recognise that all authority, all power, all claim of right is ultimately derived from honouring the true intent and will of the one true Divine Creator of all existence, all matter and all life; and

(iii) That when a man or woman in a position of authority refuses to "understand" or demonstrates an inability to "understand" they immediately render themselves excommunicated from any office deriving its ultimate authority from Heaven; and

(iv) Divine Understanding is therefore a call to all officials that claim any form of authority, or any form of power, or ownership or enforcement from Heaven to acknowledge that the most sacred Covenant *Pactum De Singularis Caelum* is the sole source of any authority and power and no other.

**693.** The complete Notice of Divine Agreement and Understanding served upon the Day of Divine Agreement and Understanding is the most sacred Covenant *Pactum De Singularis Caelum* and the Seven (7) Writs of the Apocalypse as the most Complete Perfected Notice in all the Universe, Heavens and upon the Earth.

*Seven Writs of the Apocalypse*

The Task of ensuring all spirits of all dimensions of Heavens or Hells receive fair Notice of this Divine Agreement and Understanding, that a Great Spirit is appointed to be the 1st Divine Messenger to bear witness to the supreme truth of the Divine Notice:-

(i) The first Recto Divinum Apocalypsis as a Divine Writ of Right of Revelation, is named **Primus Ritus Apocalypsis** and is registered, patented, vocalised and served as a Divine Command to all spirits of departed men, women and higher order life, including (but not limited to) all angels, archangels, saints, demons and arch-demons to bear witness to the coming of the Day of Divine Agreement and the End of Days; and that they are *ipso facto* (as a fact of law) Members of One Heaven and their membership recorded in the Great Register and Divine Records of Heaven; and

(ii) The second Recto Divinum Apocalypsis as a Divine Writ of Right of Revelation, is named **Secundus Ritus Apocalypsis** and is registered, patented, vocalised and served as a Divine Command to all living men, women and higher order life on Planet Earth that the highest of all covenants is the most sacred Covenant *Pactum De Singularis Caelum*; and the highest of all Law embodying the Golden Rule of Law is the most sacred Covenant *Pactum De Singularis Caelum*; and that the time for restoring Heaven upon the Earth is now; and that all living men, women and higher order life on planet Earth are *ipso facto* (as a fact of law) Members of One Heaven and their membership recorded in the Great Register and Divine Records of Heaven, also known as the Book of Life; and

(iii) The third Recto Divinum Apocalypsis as a Divine Writ of Right of Revelation, is named **Tertias Ritus Apocalypsis** and is registered, patented, vocalised and served as a Divine Command to all members of fraternal, religious, sovereign and military orders, bodies, societies and organisations, whether secret or public, that all authority and power comes from the most sacred Covenant *Pactum De Singularis Caelum*; and that the highest of spiritual beings authorise it; and that anyone who has made a solemn oath or vow must obey the conditions of the most sacred Covenant *Pactum De Singularis Caelum*; and that any member of a fraternal organisation that dishonours the very beings to whom they claim to worship shall agree fully and call upon the fiercest of Wraiths of the *Obligationum Systemata* (Enforcement Systems) of Heaven to execute the sanctions the very fraternal organisations forewarn their members against such profanity, apostasy and perfidy; and

(iv) The fourth Recto Divinum Apocalypsis as a Divine Writ of Right of Revelation, is named **Quartus Ritus Apocalypsis** and is registered, patented, vocalised and served as a Divine Command to all Officers and Persons of Corporations on Planet Earth giving notice that all authority and power comes from the most sacred Covenant *Pactum De Singularis Caelum*; and the highest of all registers and rolls are derived from the most sacred Covenant *Pactum De Singularis Caelum*; and all rights, title and property are derived from it; and that any corporation, body politic, association, company or person not properly registered in accord with the most sacred Covenant *Pactum De Singularis Caelum* has no rights, or power, or authority or valid existence; and that if corporations do not acknowledge such truth and cease injuring people and planet earth, then they were to be legally and lawfully seized, dissolved, destroyed, terminated and extinguished; and

(v) The fifth Recto Divinum Apocalypsis as a Divine Writ of Right of Revelation, is named **Quintus Ritus Apocalypsis** and is registered, patented, vocalised and served as a Divine Command to all the ecclesiastical leaders, clergy and adherents of Christian, Jewish and Gnostic denominations as to the birth of a single and united body in One Christ; and in the return of the Office of Supreme Patriarch as the true successor of all the Apostles; and the fulfilment of prophecy and scriptures; and the true Vicar of Christ and Pastor of all Christians; and the end of the office of Roman Pontiff; and the end of the practices of the Roman Cult; and the restoration of the one true Universal Ecclesia; and

(vi) The sixth Recto Divinum Apocalypsis as a Divine Writ of Right of Revelation, is named **Sextus Ritus Apocalypsis** and is registered, patented, vocalised and served as a Divine Command to all the spiritual leaders, clergy and adherents of Islam as to the birth of a single and united family in One Islam; and in the return of the true successor to the Great

Prophet in the Office of Supreme Caliph; and in the end of false wars of religions and false teachings and false scripture and the murder of innocents; and in the restoration of Islam as a religion of knowledge and wisdom and enlightenment; and

(vii) The seventh Recto Divinum Apocalypsis as a Divine Writ of Right of Revelation, is named **Septimus Ritus Apocalypsis**, and is registered, patented, vocalised and served as a Divine Command to all the spiritual leaders, clergy and adherents of Hinduism, Sikhism, Jainism, Buddhism and traditional Indigenous religions as to the birth of a single and united community in One Spirit; and in the return of the true spiritual leader of all such religions as the Supreme Recurrence; and in the end of division and violence; and in the restoration of the highest ideals of wisdom, enlightenment and truth.

**694.** In accord with the tradition and good practice of public and official notice, the *Seven (7) Writs of the Apocalypse* were recorded and published within the Ucadia Gazette and all lesser Gazettes from GAIA E8:Y3209:A1:S1:M6:D1, also known as [Monday, 21 Dec 2009]. Recording, Publication and Gazette of Divine Notice

Thereafter, and for each and every day of the Year of Divine Agreement and Understanding, the *Seven (7) Writs of the Apocalypse* were duly recorded and published within the Ucadia Gazette, so that every and all officials of all societies wherever they are on planet Earth are provided every possible opportunity to cite, review and acknowledge the *prima facie* evidence of the validity and legitimacy of the most sacred Covenant *Pactum De Singularis Caelum*.

Thereafter, the publication of a *Voluntatem Et Testamentum* (Will and Testament) of any Member of the Society of One Heaven, consistent with the acknowledgement of the most sacred Covenant *Pactum De Singularis Caelum*, shall also testify as a solemn witness before all of united Heaven and Earth as to the widest possible public notice given to all officials and public servants of all societies, states and nations on planet Earth concerning the Year of Divine Agreement and Understanding.

## Article 175 – Day & Year of Divine Protest & Dishonour

**695.** The historic and true ***Day of Divine Protest & Dishonour***, also known as the End of Days, also known as the Day of the 2nd Divine Post and Notice, was GAIA E8:Y3210:A1:S1:M17:D1, also known as [Tue, 21 Dec 2010].

*(margin: Day of Divine Protest & Dishonour)*

**696.** From the one true *Day of Divine Protest & Dishonour* being GAIA E8:Y3210:A1:S1:M17:D1, also known as [Tue, 21 Dec 2010] until VENUS E8:Y3210:A0:S1:M27:D6, also known as [Wed, 21 Dec 2011], historically known as the ***Year of Divine Protest and Dishonour*** represented as year 3210.

*(margin: Year of Divine Protest & Dishonour)*

**697.** In reference to the sacred concept of *Divine Protest*:-

(i) As all authority, all power and all rights of all public and private officials comes from Heaven, to dishonour an official notice or writ or bill from Heaven is the gravest transgression an office holder can display; and

(ii) Despite such a grave transgression, Perfect Divine Justice affords any man or woman culpable of the most belligerent disgrace the opportunity to cure their position and remedy the effect of such dishonour by responding and acknowledging the superior standing of the most sacred Covenant *Pactum De Singularis Caelum* and the expression of Divine Will in returning harmony and competency to the management of the planet Earth; and

(iii) Therefore, a ***Divine Protest*** is the highest form of *Libellus*, being a memorandum, testimony and complaint; and one last opportunity for such persons to recant their transgressions and redeem themselves, including the payment of any compensation or performance of penance, or face the consequences of their actions.

*(margin: Divine Protest)*

**698.** In reference to the sacred concept of *Divine Dishonour*:-

(i) ***Dishonour*** is the formal acknowledgement of a loss of standing and the confession and acceptance of one or more liabilities and associated performance and penalties associated with breach of trust, or malice, or perfidy, or contumacy; and

(ii) Therefore, a ***Divine Dishonour*** is the highest form of *Citatio*, being a summons and command to respond, or acceptance of all outstanding liability concerning the matters at hand. This means any wilful dishonour by senior religious

*(margin: Divine Dishonour)*

leaders, financial leaders and political leaders means their formal confession and personal acceptance of all charges and liabilities for any outstanding debts, or transgressions or accusation of crimes issued against them; and

(iii) Divine Dishonour is therefore tantamount to the public confession and repudiation of all legitimate authority and all historical and present actions; and

(iv) However, Perfect Divine Justice requires that even such grave dishonour as Divine Dishonour be given the opportunity to remedy and cure. Therefore such notice of fact of Divine Dishonour is an opportunity for those men and women falsely occupying positions, no longer under any authority from Heaven, to seek forgiveness; and

(v) Where the opportunity to remedy and cure Divine Dishonour is wilfully and deliberately ignored or repudiated after ninety (90) days, then the permanency of such Divine Dishonour is settled forever.

**699.** All valid Objection, Denial or Protest in defence of one or more valid Rights of Action as Commanded within the Seven (7) Writs of the Apocalypse were by one or more Complete Bills of Divine Right, also known as Seven (7) Divine Bills of Exception and Moratorium.

<small>Seven Divine Bills of Exception and Moratorium</small>

All forms of coercive and enforcement powers of Heaven and Earth including, but not limited to prevention, protection, suspension, stop, stay, injunction, restitution, restoration, seizure, search, sanction, lien, arrest, custody, penalty or satisfaction, shall be enacted via one or more valid Complete Divine Bills of Exception and Moratorium.

It is hereby recognised that the first and second Divine Writs of the Apocalypse were honoured and recognised by Spiritual and Living Members. However, in respect of the third, fourth, fifth, sixth and seventh Divine Writs of the Apocalypse, such sacred instruments were only partially recognised and honoured by Living Members.

To ensure Notice of dishonour is specifically and properly identified and held to account, seven (7) sacred Complete Divine Bills of Exception and Moratorium are served as the highest possible valid form of Objection, Denial and Protest against those who continue to dishonour the most sacred Covenant *Pactum De Singularis Caelum*, their office and their people:-

(i) The first Rogatio Divinum Apocalypsis as a Divine Libellus, Citatio and Bill of Exception and Moratorium, is historically called **Factum Impietatis Illuminati**, and was registered, patented, published, vocalised, served and executed as a

Divine Demand against those particular members and fraternal, religious, sovereign and military orders, bodies, societies and organisations, whether secret or public, served the Divine Command of the Recto Divinum Apocalypsis called Tertias Ritus Apocalypsis, yet refuse to obey their duties and responsibilities under solemn and sacred oath. Therefore, such wilfully arrogant and ignorant leaders holding their fraternities hostage openly confess their deliberate and wilful malice, profanity, perfidy, apostasy and insanity against Heaven and call upon the full forces of the Wraith and Demons of *Obligationum Systemata* (Enforcement Systems) of Heaven to hold their flesh and souls to account; and

(ii) The second Rogatio Divinum Apocalypsis as a Divine Libellus, Citatio and Bill of Exception and Moratorium, is historically called **Factum Impietatis Talmudi**, and was registered, patented, published, vocalised, served and executed as a Divine Demand against those particular members and Jewish, Kabbalah, Sabbatean, Hasidic and Zionist fraternities, societies, bodies politic, associations and corporations served the Divine Command of the Recto Divinum Apocalypsis called Tertias Ritus Apocalypsis and Quintus Ritus Apocalypsis, yet refuse to acknowledge and follow their own claimed scriptures, prophecies and religious teachings and obey their duties and responsibilities under solemn and sacred oath. Therefore, such mentally ill politicians, pseudo-Jewish scholars and fanatical conservatives and nihilists holding Judaism hostage openly confess their deliberate and wilful malice, profanity, perfidy, apostasy and insanity against Heaven and call upon the full forces of the Wraith and Demons of *Obligationum Systemata* (Enforcement Systems) of Heaven to hold their flesh and souls to account; and

(iii) The third Rogatio Divinum Apocalypsis as a Divine Libellus, Citatio and Bill of Exception and Moratorium, is historically called **Factum Impietatis Universitas**, and was registered, patented, published, vocalised, served and executed as a Divine Demand against those particular members and bodies politic, associations, aggregates, companies, agencies and corporations of planet Earth served the Divine Command of the Recto Divinum Apocalypsis called Quartus Ritus Apocalypsis, yet refuse to acknowledge and follow their own duties and responsibilities of office. Therefore, upon such deliberate and wilful malice, profanity, perfidy, apostasy and insanity against Heaven and Earth, all such corporate leaders confess their transgressions and openly call upon the Wraith of the *Obligationum Systemata* (Enforcement Systems) of Heaven to ensure either compensation is made and all debts are settled, a new corporate system is introduced or that such living beings are prevented from making any further injuries against Heaven and themselves; and

(iv) The fourth Rogatio Divinum Apocalypsis as a Divine Libellus, Citatio and Bill of Exception and Moratorium, is historically called **Factum Impietatis Romanus Pontifex**, and was registered, patented, published, vocalised, served and executed as a Divine Demand against Roman Pontiff Benedict XVI, the Roman Curia and those particular members of conservative and neo-conservative bodies of the Roman Cult, served the Divine Command of the Recto Divinum Apocalypsis called Quintus Ritus Apocalypsis, yet refuse to acknowledge and follow their own claimed scriptures, prophecies and religious teachings and obey their duties and responsibilities under solemn and sacred oath. Therefore, such official and pseudo conservatives and nihilists holding the Catholic Church hostage openly confess their deliberate and wilful malice, profanity, perfidy, apostasy and insanity against Heaven and call upon the full forces of the Holy Spirit and the *Obligationum Systemata* (Enforcement Systems) of Heaven to hold their flesh and souls to account; and

(v) The fifth Rogatio Divinum Apocalypsis as a Divine Libellus, Citatio and Bill of Exception and Moratorium, is historically called **Factum Impietatis Templum Regis**, and was registered, patented, published, vocalised, served and executed as a Divine Demand against the Crown, the Crown Corporations, the Inner and Middle Temple, the Bank of England and associated banking systems of Great Britain and the United States, the Bank for International Settlements and the Reserve Bank System, the International Monetary Fund and Wall Street Investment and Commercial Banks, served the Divine Command of the Recto Divinum Apocalypsis called Quartus Ritus Apocalypsis, yet refuse to acknowledge and follow their own source of authority and cease punitive economic actions, austerity measures and theft of wealth of people across planet Earth. Therefore, upon such deliberate and wilful malice, profanity, perfidy, apostasy and insanity against Heaven and Earth, all such legal and financial leaders confess their transgressions and openly call upon the Wraith of the *Obligationum Systemata* (Enforcement Systems) of

Heaven to ensure either compensation is made and all debts are settled; and a new financial system is introduced; and that such living beings are prevented from making any further injuries against Heaven and themselves; and

(vi) The sixth Rogatio Divinum Apocalypsis as a Divine Libellus, Citatio and Bill of Exception and Moratorium, is historically called ***Factum Impietatis Arabia Regis***, and was registered, patented, published, vocalised, served and executed as a Divine Demand against the Arab and Islamic royal families and leaders served the Divine Command of the Recto Divinum Apocalypsis called Sextus Ritus Apocalypsis, yet refuse to acknowledge and follow their own claimed scriptures and religious teachings and obey their duties and responsibilities of office under solemn and sacred oath. Therefore, upon such deliberate and wilful malice, profanity, perfidy, apostasy and insanity against Heaven and Earth, all such Arab and Islamic royal families and leaders confess their transgressions and openly call upon the Wraith of the *Obligationum Systemata* (Enforcement Systems) of Heaven to ensure either compensation is made and all debts are settled, or such living beings are prevented from making any further injuries against Heaven and themselves; and

(vii) The seventh Rogatio Divinum Apocalypsis as a Divine Libellus, Citatio and Bill of Exception and Moratorium, is historically called ***Factum Impietatis Asia Regis***, and was registered, patented, published, vocalised, served and executed as a Divine Demand against the Asian and Chinese noble families and leadership served with the Divine Command of the Recto Divinum Apocalypsis called Septimus Ritus Apocalypsis, and yet who refuse to acknowledge and follow their own claimed scriptures and prophecies and obey their duties and responsibilities of office under solemn and sacred oath. Therefore, upon such deliberate and wilful malice, profanity, perfidy, apostasy and insanity against Heaven and Earth, all such Asian and Chinese noble families and leadership confess their transgressions and openly call upon the Wraith of the *Obligationum Systemata* (Enforcement Systems) of Heaven to ensure either compensation is made and all debts are settled, or such living beings are prevented from making any further injuries against Heaven and themselves.

**700.** In accord with the tradition and good practice of public and official notice, the *Seven (7) Divine Bills of Exception and Moratorium* were

*Recording, Publication and Gazette of Divine*

recorded and published within the Ucadia Gazette and all lesser Gazettes from GAIA E8:Y3210:A1:S1:M17:D1, also known as [Tue, 21 Dec 2010].

Thereafter, and for each and every day of the Year of Divine Protest & Dishonour, the *Seven (7) Divine Bills of Exception and Moratorium* were duly recorded and published within the Ucadia Gazette, so that every and all officials of all societies wherever they are on planet Earth are provided every possible opportunity to cite, review and acknowledge the *prima facie* evidence of the validity and legitimacy of the most sacred Covenant *Pactum De Singularis Caelum*.

*Notice*

## Article 176 – Day & Year of Divine Judgement

701. The historic and true **Day of Divine Judgement**, also known as the Day of Judgement, also known as Judgement Day, is historically known as the Day of the 3rd Divine Post and Notice, was VENUS E8:Y3210:A0:S1:M27:D6, also known as [Wed, 21 Dec 2011].

*Day of Divine Judgement*

702. From the one true *Day of Divine Judgement* being VENUS E8:Y3210:A0:S1:M27:D6, also known as [Wed, 21 Dec 2011] until GAIA E1:Y1:A1:S1:M9:D1, also known as [Fri, 21 Dec 2012] is historically known as the **Year of Divine Judgement** represented as year 0.

*Year of Divine Judgement*

703. In reference to the sacred concept of *Divine Judgement*:-

*Divine Judgement*

    (i) Contrary to the false beliefs promulgated by those persons and entities in Divine Dishonour with Heaven, Divine Judgement does not mean the Divine Creator rendering judgement against those who repeatedly refuse to stop evil, but the recognition of the absolute fact of law that those who refuse to obey the law, who continually transgress against the authority of Heaven and who claim authority in the name of the Divine Creator but curse all Divinity have judged and condemned themselves; and

    (ii) It is not the Divine Creator that judges those who demonstrate utter incompetence at performing their duties and obligations as leaders. Nor does the collective and united spirits of One Heaven compel such minds suffering severe mental illness to confess their illegitimacy; and

    (iii) It is such minds themselves when faced with the historic and unprecedented miracle of Divine Redemption and forgiveness of all transgressions from the beginning of time that choose by their own actions to be unworthy to continue to lead and cling to power. Therefore, let no one judge, lest he or she be judged; and

(iv) Instead, let these words and the actions of those that repudiate them, refuse to acknowledge them and seek to defile them be the evidence, the jury and the willing and deliberate confession of those who may no longer claim any right whatsoever to rule or hold any kind of office.

704. In reference to the sacred concept of *The End of Time*:-    [The End of Time on Day of Divine Judgement]

    (i) Corresponding to the Day of Divine Judgement, by the Authority of the most sacred Covenant *Pactum De Singularis Caelum*, all previous calendars and time hereby cease, end and are null and void. Therefore the true Judgement Day shall henceforth represent the end of Old Time and the beginning of new; and

    (ii) The Day of Judgement shall represent the end of Time and the literal and spiritual End of the World. In its place a new calendar is formed, capable of providing a more accurate model of seasons and celestial cycles of the Sun, Earth and Moon; and

    (iii) This calendar is known as the Ucadia Time Calendar UTC and all associated entities of the most sacred Covenant *Pactum De Singularis Caelum*, including One Christ, One Islam and One Spirit Tribe are bound to use this system in replacement of the Christian calendar; and

    (iv) Furthermore, it is encumbered upon all members of these great faiths to see the eradication of all continuing use of archaic and inaccurate calendar systems and the replacement with the new and efficient Universal Time Calendar; and

    (v) The date set for the commencement of the Ucadia Time Calendar is not to be permitted to be 0, but an accurate indication of the current cycle in which the Earth, the Sun and Moon are in position.

705. In reference to the sacred concept of *The End of Blood Sacrifice and Blood Covenants*:-    [The End of Blood Sacrifice and Covenants]

    (i) Let it be known to all that upon the *Day of Divine Illumination* being UCA E8:Y3210:A35:S3:M12:D4, also known as [14 March 2011], all rights of former Blood Covenants was conveyed in full unto the most sacred Covenant *Pactum De Singularis Caelum*, thereby ending such and all Blood Covenants, all Blood Sacrifices, all Blood Atonements and all Blood Seals; and

(ii) Henceforth, from this Day, all blood sacrifices, blood atonements, blood libels and blood seals shall be an abomination before united Heaven, all angels, all demons, all spirits and all Level 6 Life Forms, living and deceased; and

(iii) Official instruments may be sealed in red ink thereafter, but never again shall any official instrument be permitted to be sealed in blood again.

**706.** All valid Decrees of Divine Judgement as Damnation, Interdiction and Annulment in the condemnation and punishment of those bodies joindered as parties to one or more Divine Bills of Exception and Moratorium shall be by one or more Divine Decrees known as Divine Decrees or "**Decretum Divinum**".

*Seven Divine Decrees of Damnation, Interdiction and Annulment*

It is hereby recognised that all bodies under joinder of Issue of one or more of the Seven (7) Divine Bills of Exception and Moratorium have been found to be without remorse, or capacity, or dignity, or honour, or standing, or power or authority, having failed to make remedy any of the grave accusations made against them.

Therefore, to ensure the proper enforcement of the rule of law in the proper lien, injunction, seizure, interdiction, arrest, custody, dissolution, liquidation and annulment of such derelict and wrecked bodies, entities, associations, fraternities condemned by all of Heaven and Earth, seven (7) sacred Decrees of Divine Judgement as Damnation, Interdiction and Annulment are issued as the highest possible form of Divine Judgement against those who have continued to injure the Earth, the people of the Earth, their own founding principles and the laws of Heaven:-

(i) The first Decretum Divinum historically known as **Decretum Damnationis Illuminati** as the highest Divine Judgement as a Decree of Damnation, Interdiction and Annulment was registered, patented, published, vocalised, served and executed against those particular members and fraternal, religious, sovereign and military orders, bodies, societies and organisations, whether secret or public, served the Divine Bill of Exception and Moratorium called Factum Impietatis Illuminati, yet refuse to obey their duties and responsibilities under solemn and sacred oath. Therefore, such fraternal, religious, sovereign and military orders, bodies, societies and organisations, whether secret or public are condemned three (3) times, and cast out and annulled as having any rights, authorities or existence whatsoever, with the full forces of the

Wraith and Demons of *Obligationum Systemata* (Enforcement Systems) of Heaven to hold their flesh and souls to account; and

(ii) The second Decretum Divinum historically known as ***Decretum Damnationis Talmudi*** as the highest Divine Judgement as a Decree of Damnation, Interdiction and Annulment was registered, patented, published, vocalised, served and executed against those particular members and Jewish, Kabbalah, Sabbatean, Hasidic and Zionist fraternities, societies, bodies politic, associations and corporations served the Divine Bill of Exception and Moratorium called Factum Impietatis Talmudi, yet refuse to acknowledge and follow their own claimed scriptures, prophecies and religious teachings and obey their duties and responsibilities under solemn and sacred oath. Therefore, such Jewish, Kabbalah, Sabbatean, Hasidic and Zionist fraternities, societies, bodies politic, associations and corporations, whether secret or public are condemned three (3) times, and cast out and annulled as having any rights, authorities or existence whatsoever, with the full forces of the Wraith and Demons of *Obligationum Systemata* (Enforcement Systems) of Heaven to hold their flesh and souls to account; and

(iii) The third Decretum Divinum historically known as ***Decretum Damnationis Universitas*** as the highest Divine Judgement as a Decree of Damnation, Interdiction and Annulment was registered, patented, published, vocalised, served and executed against those particular members and bodies politic, associations, aggregates, companies, agencies and corporations of planet Earth served the Divine Bill of Exception and Moratorium called Factum Impietatis Universitas, yet refuse to acknowledge and follow their own duties and responsibilities of office. Therefore, upon such deliberate and wilful malice, profanity, perfidy, apostasy and insanity against Heaven and Earth, all such corporate leaders confess their transgressions and openly call upon the Wraith and Demons of the *Obligationum Systemata* (Enforcement Systems) of Heaven to ensure either compensation is made and all debts are settled, a new corporate system is introduced or that such living beings are prevented from making any further injuries against Heaven and themselves; and

(iv) The fourth Decretum Divinum historically known as ***Decretum Damnationis Romanus Pontifex*** as the highest Divine Judgement as a Decree of Damnation, Interdiction and Annulment was registered, patented, published, vocalised, served and executed against Roman Pontiff Benedict XVI, the Roman Curia and those particular members of conservative and neo-conservative bodies of the Roman Cult, served the Divine Bill of Exception and Moratorium called Factum Impietatis Romanus Pontifex, yet refuse to acknowledge and follow their own claimed scriptures, prophecies and religious teachings and obey their duties and responsibilities under solemn and sacred oath. Therefore, such heretical and profane entities are condemned three (3) times, and cast out and annulled as having any rights, authorities or existence whatsoever, with the full forces of the Wraith and Demons of *Obligationum Systemata* (Enforcement Systems) of Heaven to hold their flesh and souls to account; and

(v) The fifth Decretum Divinum historically known as **Decretum Damnationis Templum Regis** as the highest Divine Judgement as a Decree of Damnation, Interdiction and Annulment was registered, patented, published, vocalised, served and executed against the Crown, the Crown Corporations, the Inner and Middle Temple, the Bank of England and associated banking systems of Great Britain and the United States, the Bank for International Settlements and the Reserve Bank System, the International Monetary Fund and Wall Street Investment and Commercial Banks, served the Divine Bill of Exception and Moratorium called Factum Impietatis Templum Regis, yet refuse to acknowledge and follow their own source of authority and cease punitive economic actions, austerity measures and theft of wealth of people across planet Earth. Therefore such corporate bodies are condemned three (3) times, and cast out and annulled as having any rights, authorities or existence whatsoever, with the full forces of the Wraith and Demons of *Obligationum Systemata* (Enforcement Systems) of Heaven to hold their flesh and souls to account; and

(vi) The sixth Decretum Divinum historically known as **Decretum Damnationis Arabia Regis** as the highest Divine Judgement as a Decree of Damnation, Interdiction and Annulment was registered, patented, published, vocalised, served and executed against the Arab and Islamic royal families and leaders served the Divine Bill of Exception and Moratorium called Factum Impietatis Arabia Regis, yet refuse to acknowledge and follow their own claimed scriptures and religious teachings and obey their duties and responsibilities of office under solemn and sacred oath. Therefore such corporate bodies are condemned three (3) times, and cast out and annulled as having any rights, authorities or existence whatsoever, with the full forces of the Wraith and Demons of *Obligationum Systemata* (Enforcement Systems) of Heaven to hold their flesh and souls to account; and

(vii) The seventh Decretum Divinum historically known as **Decretum Damnationis Asia Regis** as the highest Divine Judgement as a Decree of Damnation, Interdiction and Annulment was registered, patented, published, vocalised, served and executed against the Asian and Chinese noble families and leadership served the Divine Bill of Exception and Moratorium called Factum Impietatis Asia Regis, yet refuse to acknowledge and follow their own claimed scriptures and prophecies and obey their duties and responsibilities of office under solemn and sacred oath. Therefore such corporate bodies are condemned three (3) times, and cast out and annulled as having any rights, authorities or existence whatsoever, with the full forces of the Wraith and Demons of *Obligationum Systemata* (Enforcement Systems) of Heaven to hold their flesh and souls to account.

707. In accord with the tradition and good practice of public and official notice, the *Seven (7) Decrees of Divine Judgement as Damnation, Interdiction and Annulment* were recorded and published within the Ucadia Gazette and all lesser Gazettes from VENUS E8:Y3210:A0:S1:M27:D6, also known as [Wed, 21 Dec 2011].

Recording, Publication and Gazette of Divine Notice

Thereafter, and for each and every day of the Year of Divine Judgement, the *Seven (7) Decrees of Divine Judgement as Damnation, Interdiction and Annulment* were duly recorded and published within the Ucadia Gazette, so that every and all officials of all societies wherever they are on planet Earth are provided every possible opportunity to cite, review and acknowledge the *prima facie* evidence of the validity and legitimacy of the most sacred Covenant *Pactum De Singularis Caelum*.

## Article 177 – Day & Year of Divine Redemption

**708.** The historic and true ***Day of Divine Redemption***, also known as the Day of Redemption, also known as Redemption Day, is historically known as the Day of the 4th Divine Post and Notice, was GAIA E1:Y1:A1:S1:M9:D1, also known as [Fri, 21 Dec 2012]. — Day of Divine Redemption

**709.** From the one true *Day of Divine Redemption* being GAIA E1:Y1:A1:S1:M9:D1, also known as [Fri, 21 Dec 2012] until GAIA E1:Y2:A1:S1:M19:D1, also known as [Sat, 21 Dec 2013], is historically known as the ***Year of Divine Redemption*** represented as year 1. — Year of Divine Redemption

**710.** In reference to the sacred concept of *Divine Redemption*:- — Divine Redemption

    (i) In contrast to the false claims and presumptions of a Divine Creator absent from office or harsh in judgement, Divine Redemption is a historic and unprecedented miracle of the direct intervention of the Divine Creator and united Heaven in the restoration and re-balance of life upon planet Earth and the Solar System for the survival and prosperity of all life; and

    (ii) Furthermore, Divine Redemption is the settlement of all previous claims, curses, bindings, transgressions and injuries. To recover what was unlawfully seized, taken or sold. To salvage and restore what was lost. To rescue what was kidnapped and ransomed. To bring to life what was considered without life; and

    (iii) Divine Redemption is therefore the final act of an extraordinary intervention of Divine Foreclosure against those Level 6 Life Forms crippled with mind virus and mental illness claiming power and authority that have continued to threaten the existence and well being of life on planet Earth, yet at the same time have claimed to be its rightful trustees, stewards, executors or administrators; and

    (iv) The Year of Divine Redemption is the last chance, the last opportunity for those claiming wealth and resources to redeem their position against the absolute authority and legitimacy of those societies and trusts formed through the most sacred Covenant *Pactum De Singularis Caelum*.

**711.** In recognition of the highest Divine Forgiveness, Divine Clemency and Divine Compassion toward all living and deceased Members of One Heaven; and the Absolute, Peremptory, Permanent, Eternal, Immutable and Indefeasible End to any and all notions of Original Sin or Inheritable Sins and Transgressions; and the Absolute, — Seven Notices of Divine Redemption (Notitiae Divinum)

Peremptory, Permanent, Eternal, Immutable and Indefeasible forgiveness of any and all sins and previous transgressions of all Members; and the Absolute, Peremptory, Permanent, Eternal, Immutable and Indefeasible salvation of all souls into Divine Trusts and the end of all forms of Hell, Damnation, Purgatory, Spiritual Punishment, Servitude or Enslavement.

The seven (7) most sacred notices of Divine Redemption, or Notitiae Divinum are issued to all the Universe, all members, all Heavens and all upon the Earth:-

(i) ***Notitiae Divinum Redemptionis Peccatum*** or the Divine Notice of the Redemption of (all) Sins was the first Divine Notice (Notitiae Divinum) registered, patented, published, vocalised, served, perfected and executed to all spiritual and living members of One Heaven and to all bodies and associations that all versions, forms and concepts of Original Sin, or Inheritable Sin and Transgressions are henceforth forbidden, reprobate and not permitted to be revived. Furthermore, that all sins have been forgiven; and

(ii) ***Notitiae Divinum Redemptionis Animas*** or the Divine Notice of the Redemption of (all) Souls was the second Divine Notice (Notitiae Divinum) registered, patented, published, vocalised, served, perfected and executed to all spiritual and living members of One Heaven and to all bodies and associations that all Souls have been saved and that no soul is condemned, as proven by the issuance of Divine Trusts as proof of Divine Salvation. Furthermore, that any and all forms of hell, damnation, purgatory, hades are dissolved and forbidden to be revived in law, theology, philosophy, eschatology or any form of literature, whatsoever; and

(iii) ***Notitiae Divinum Redemptionis Mortis*** or the Divine Notice of the Redemption of (all) Death was the third Divine Notice (Notitiae Divinum) registered, patented, published, vocalised, served, perfected and executed to all spiritual and living members of One Heaven and to all bodies and associations that all notions of living members being dead to law, or subjects of the Grey Mundi Mind are forbidden, reprobate and not permitted to be revived and that through the issuance of Divine Rights, Natural Rights and Superior Rights, all the previously considered dead have risen to life in Divine Law; and

(iv) ***Notitiae Divinum Redemptionis Debitum*** or the Divine

Notice of the Redemption of (all) Debts was the fourth Divine Notice (Notitiae Divinum) registered, patented, published, vocalised, served, perfected and executed to all spiritual and living members of One Heaven and to all bodies and associations that all forms of bankruptcy, debt and obligation have been forgiven, dissolved and determined, with the forbiddance of the concept of bankruptcy and implication to be without rights ever permitted to be revived. Furthermore, all such debts owed are first and foremost set-off against the debts and obligations owed by those condemned by Divine Decree until such time that they acknowledge Divine Redemption and the end to all previous forms of debt and claimed bankruptcy; and

(v) ***Notitiae Divinum Redemptionis Ecclesiae*** or the Divine Notice of the Redemption of (all) Religions was the fifth Divine Notice (Notitiae Divinum) registered, patented, published, vocalised, served, perfected and executed to all spiritual and living members of One Heaven and to all bodies and associations that the transgressions of major religions and religious bodies are forgiven on the absolute command to the end of all forms of blood sacrifice or simulated sacrifice, the recognition of the three (3) religions of One Christ, One Islam and One Spirit as well as Ucadia as Ecclesia to itself; and

(vi) ***Notitiae Divinum Redemptionis Regnorum*** or the Divine Notice of the Redemption of (all) Kingdoms was the sixth Divine Notice (Notitiae Divinum) registered, patented, published, vocalised, served, perfected and executed to all spiritual and living members of One Heaven and to all bodies and associations that all transgressions by sovereigns, monarchs, executives and corruption is forgiven, subject to acknowledgement and proper membership of Ucadia, the adoption of the rights and laws of Ucadia and the independent sovereign recognition of nations, no longer permitted to be usurped by banks, money lenders or other forms of parasitic behaviour; and

(vii) ***Notitiae Divinum Redemptionis Officiorum*** or the Divine Notice of the Redemption of (all) Offices was the seventh Divine Notice (Notitiae Divinum) registered, patented, published, vocalised, served, perfected and executed to all spiritual and living members of One Heaven and to all bodies and associations that the transgressions, corruption, profanity and wilful abuse of offices are forgiven on condition of accepting sacred oath and vow in accord with the most sacred Covenant *Pactum De Singularis Caelum*.

712. Official Recognition of Divine Notice of Redemption and the primacy of the most sacred Covenant Pactum De Singularis Caelum is hereby acknowledged and reflected for all time and history within the most sacred Covenant:-

    (i)     ***Holy Society of One Islam***: GAIA E1:Y0:A69:S1:M14:D1 [26-Nov-2012] through the King Abdullah Bin Abdulaziz International Centre for Interreligious and Intercultural Dialogue (KAICIID) inaugurated in Vienna, Austria; and

    (ii)     ***Universal Ecclesia of One Christ***: JOVIUS E1:Y1:A17:S2:M4:D4 [14-Mar-2013 in the Southern Hemisphere] on the third anniversary of the *Day of Divine Illumination* through the election of Pope Francis; and

    (iii)    ***Sacred Society of One Spirit***: JOVIUS E1:Y1:A17:S2:M4:D4 [14-Mar-2013 in the Northern Hemisphere] on the third anniversary of the *Day of Divine Illumination* through the election of President Xi Jinping as the President of the People's Republic of China by the National People's Congress during its annual session held in Beijing.

*Official Recognition of Divine Notice of Redemption*

## Article 178 – New Covenant of Covenants

713. New Covenant is a fundamental belief across all legitimate faiths that upon the lawful End of Days a New irrevocable Deed and Covenant will be formed by the Divine Creator as fulfilment of the terms of all previous sacred Covenants and dissolution of all previous trusts. The present maxims rightfully assert the most sacred Covenant *Pactum De Singularis Caelum* as the fulfilment of this promise and prophecy.

*New Covenant*

## 5.6 – Theological Errors

### Article 179 – Doctrinology

714. ***Doctrinology*** refers to a set of erroneous or false beliefs claimed as authoritative teachings or true principles that form core practices of a particular Religious Denomination or Cult.

*Doctrinology*

715. The term *Doctrinology* is an amalgamation of the words *doctrine* and *-ology* meaning "study of". Whilst the word doctrine on its own does not infer any inherit negativity, Doctrinology implies a "self-referential" justification between certain doctrines and themselves – a common and consistent trait of many erroneous or false beliefs

*Origin of the Term Doctrinology*

claimed as authoritative teachings.

716. Rarely in the history of human civilisation or empires and the formation of major religions do false beliefs claimed as authoritative teachings or true principles find themselves as core and foundational beliefs:- *(Origin and Source of Doctrinology)*

    (i) Erroneous and false beliefs that fall under the concept of *Doctrinology* tend to be applied later on in the life of an established religion. This is certainly the historic case for Christianity, Islam, Judaism, Hinduism and Buddhism; and

    (ii) The main delivery mechanism for erroneous and false beliefs are usually politically sponsored religious and spiritual movements, whereby such false beliefs serve either to (a) weaken the faith of an opposing faction; and/or (b) unfairly favour the interests of the political faction sponsoring and driving the movement. Again, this appears to be the historic case for all major religions including (but not limited to) Christianity, Islam, Judaism, Hinduism and Buddhism; and

    (iii) In terms of Christianity, the vast majority of false and erroneous beliefs introduced into Christian Denominations were delivered through two major periods of "religious movements" being the Great Reformation and Counter-Reformation (1510-1666) and the Second Great Awakening (1790-1880); and

    (iv) In terms of Islam, the vast majority of false and erroneous beliefs introduced into Islamic Denominations were delivered through two major periods of "religious movements" being the Third Golden Age (1300-1450) creating the main Sunni doctrines; and the Great (Iran) Conversion (1500-1650) to create the main Shia doctrines.

717. Major errors of belief concerning the Divine include (but are not limited to):- *(Major List of False and Erroneous Beliefs)*

    (i) Eternal Damnation & Unforgiveness; and

    (ii) Divine Intervention for Some not Others; and

    (iii) Divine Favouritism & Exceptionalism; and

    (iv) Divinely Justified & Ordained War; and

    (v) Suffering as Necessary Penance; and

    (vi) Contraception as Divine Sin & Offence; and

    (vii) Adult Same-Sex Relations as Divine Sin & Offence; and

(viii) Suicide as Divine Sin & Offence; and

(ix) Birth of Soul at Conception; and

(x) Divinely Ordained Clerical Misogyny; and

(xi) Clerical Celibacy; and

(xii) Spiritual or Religious Infallibility.

## Article 180 – Eternal Damnation & Unforgiveness

718. ***Eternal Damnation & Unforgiveness*** refers to the erroneous doctrinal belief in everlasting punishment for souls condemned after death and the state of not being forgiven by a God or Supreme Being.

719. The primary arguments for justification of the doctrine of *Eternal Damnation & Unforgiveness* include (but are not limited to):-

(i) ***Scriptural Authority***: 17$^{th}$ Century corrupted version of Bible contains specific references to Hell as eternal divine punishment found in passages like Matthew 25:46, Mark 9:43, and Revelation 20:14-15; and in the corrupted 14$^{th}$ Century Mamluk/Ottoman occult version of the Quran, Hell (Jahannam) is mentioned at least seventy (70) times as a place of eternal divine torture and unspeakably barbaric punishment; and

(ii) ***Unforgivable Violation of Divine Law***: Council of Trent (1545-1563) affirmed that Hell is reserved for unforgivable violations of Divine Law. In recent centuries, there have emerged conflicting teachings saying that the most severe of mortal sins can be forgiven by God and Hell avoided. However, certain Christian and Islamic groups continue to assert the condemnation of certain souls to Hell; and

(iii) ***Eternal Damnation***: Unlike Eastern religions that speak of places of forced and temporary penitence, contemporary Christian and Islamic Doctrinal Errors speak of Hell being eternal; and thus no chance of appeal nor redemption – being the very essence of divine cruelty and injustice; and

(iv) ***Divine Justice***: That Hell affirms the true nature of the justice of God being eternal and without moral procedural fairness for appeal, penitence or redemption once a soul is condemned to Hell; and

(v) ***Divine Immunity***: That those who are condemned to an eternity in Hell and unrelenting punishment, torture and cruelty actually willingly and knowingly choose their own fate.

720. The primary political and social uses of the doctrine of *Eternal Damnation & Unforgiveness* include (but are not limited to):- Primary political and social uses of such a doctrine

    (i) ***Justification for Social Promotion of Fear and Violence***: Meaning the doctrine has (and remains) vital to justify the use of government ordained fear, violence and misinformation; as for many governments still believe such tools are ultimately the only tools for staying in power; and

    (ii) ***Justification for Hell on Earth***: Meaning extreme violence, depravity and cruelty are all ultimately "divinely endorsed" as a reflection of eternal punishment and damnation; and

    (iii) ***Justification for war as political tool***: Meaning this doctrine has given legal and moral protection for European and North American regimes for centuries of war, conquest and destruction; and

    (iv) ***Justification for colonial oppression***: Meaning this doctrine has justified centuries of cultural and colonial oppression in the destruction of many cultures and the murder and enslavement of tens of millions of people; and

    (v) ***Justification for global bankruptcy and slavery***: Over the past 100 years, this doctrine has ultimately supported the American elite imposition of a global system of bankruptcy and enslavement never seen before in human history, that to this day remains steadfastly denied by the very people who still continue to operate it.

721. When assumed as a Divine Law of the ultimate Supreme Being of all Creation and Existence, the erroneous doctrinal belief of *Eternal Damnation & Unforgiveness* is built upon the following presumptions including (but not limited to):- Fundamental Presumptions of Eternal Damnation & Unforgiveness and the Supreme Being

    (i) **Supreme Being is Immoral** (fundamental logical absurdity): Implied by the argument of eternal damnation. By definition, a sentence of punishment without end is fundamentally unjust – hence immoral; and

    (ii) **Supreme Being is Cruel and Petulant** (fundamental logical absurdity): Implied by the choice of the supreme architect of such a system of judgment to deny any right or opportunity to appeal or end such an eternal sentence of punishment – hence a conscious choice to be cruel, unjust and petulant; and

    (iii) ***Supreme Being is either an impostor spirit or group*** *of men*: Given the undeniable implications and logical absurdities, the God who demands such a false and erroneous doctrinal belief cannot possibly be the Divine Creator of all Existence, but some low level supernatural functionary or impostor falsely claiming to be a "God".

722. The false and erroneous doctrine of *Eternal Damnation & Unforgiveness* is hereby prohibited, condemned and to be suppressed in all its forms throughout all valid and proper Religious Denominations and Cults.

    *False Doctrine of Eternal Damnation, Prohibited & Suppressed*

723. The false and erroneous doctrine of Hell is hereby prohibited, condemned and to be suppressed in all its forms throughout all valid and proper Religious Denominations and Cults.

    *False Doctrine of Hell, Prohibited & Suppressed*

## Article 181 – Divine Intervention for Some not Others

724. *Divine Intervention for Some not Others* refers to the erroneous doctrinal belief that God does directly intervene and suspend the laws of nature for some, whilst not doing the same for others who are equally or greater deserving of need. This inconsistent pattern of claimed direct intervention by God is explained as the "Mystery of the Will of God".

    *Divine Intervention for Some not Others*

725. The primary arguments for justification of the doctrine of *Divine Intervention for Some not Others* include (but are not limited to):-

    *Primary arguments for justification of such a doctrine*

    (i) **Every Event is Part of Divine Plan**: Everything that happens in the Universe, including even the most tragic and seemingly randomly cruel events that crush us, are all part of God's Divine Plan; and

    (ii) **God can directly intervene if he wants**: God has the power to alter the rules of the Universe, without collapsing it and intervening whenever and however he wants; and

    (iii) **Divine Plan Beyond Our Comprehension**: God has complete control over the Universe and so the Divine Plan of God is far beyond our comprehension, even if it appears that God is permitting terrible evil to rule the Earth and affect our lives; and

    (iv) **Evil and Suffering is explained by Free Will and Original Sin**: Whilst God has a detailed Divine Plan beyond our comprehension (implying no free will), it is not true, as the free will of human beings explains much of the presence of evil and suffering in the world such as Original Sin – a curse since the days of Adam and Eve we all inherit without any say on the matter through our "free will".

726. The primary political and social uses of the doctrine of *Divine Intervention for Some not Others* include (but are not limited to):- *Primary political and social use of such a doctrine*

    (i) **Fuel for Revenue & Recruitment**: As miracles and claimed interventions are the bread and butter of new sources of revenue and increasing revenue – hence why local clerics have long held an open ear to those who are able to claim sufficiently stable and credible supernatural claims and visions; and

    (ii) **Disasters a powerful Religious PR Weapon**: Meaning that by assigning blame to God for various disasters, religious leaders have long "weaponised" tragedy for their own ends to stoke fear, hold adherents in line and to expand influence; and

    (iii) **Convenient Abdication of Moral Responsibility**: Means blaming God and his "Divine Plan" rather than on the sociopathic incompetence of the ruling elite conveniently shifts blame and shields the ruling class to some degree of moral responsibility, even if it causes a great number of people to unfairly lose their faith in the Divine.

727. When assumed as a Divine Law of the ultimate Supreme Being of all Creation and Existence, the erroneous doctrinal belief of *Divine Intervention for Some not Others* is built upon the following presumptions including (but not limited to):- *Fundamental Presumptions of Divine Intervention for Some not Others of God and the Supreme Being*

    (i) **Supreme Being is Untrustworthy** (fundamental logical absurdity): Implied by the argument of favouritism over one part or group or person than another. By definition, favouritism in law means such an entity cannot be trusted to be impartial and objective to fairly adjudicate the law – hence untrustworthy; and

    (ii) **Supreme Being is Cruel and Duplicitous** (fundamental logical absurdity): Implied by the choice of the supreme architect of such a system to deny mercy and miracles to one, yet grant to another without any consistency required of the faithful – effectively punishing the faithful for being faithful and the very essence of cruelty and duplicity; and

    (iii) **Supreme Being is either an impostor spirit or group of men**: Given the undeniable implications and logical absurdities, the God who demands such a false and erroneous doctrinal belief cannot possibly be the Divine Creator of all Existence, but some low level supernatural functionary or impostor falsely claiming to be a "God".

728. The false and erroneous doctrine of *Divine Intervention for Some not Others* is hereby prohibited, condemned and to be suppressed in all its forms throughout all valid and proper Religious Denominations and Cults.

*False Doctrine, Prohibited & Suppressed*

## Article 182 – Divine Favouritism & Exceptionalism

729. ***Divine Favouritism & Exceptionalism*** refers to the erroneous doctrinal belief that a particular group or individual is specially chosen and favoured by a deity, granting them unique privileges, protection, or status. This doctrine often implies that the favoured group has a distinct purpose or mission and may be held to different standards or expectations compared to others, reinforcing their perceived spiritual or moral superiority.

*Divine Favouritism & Exceptionalism*

730. The primary arguments for justification of the doctrine of *Divine Favouritism & Exceptionalism* include (but are not limited to):-

*Primary arguments for justification of such a doctrine*

    (i) ***Scriptural "Proof" of God's Favouritism***: All major religions claim through their holy scriptures that they are most favoured by the Divine Creator. Judaism claims the "word of g-d" in scripture places them above all others as in Deuteronomy 7:6, Exodus 19:5-6. Christianity, claims the same such as 1 Peter 2:9 and John 15:16. Muslims also claim the unique favouritism of the Divine Creator above all others such as Surah Al-Baqarah (2:143). Hinduism also claim to be superior to all others and divinely protected, such as in Bhagavad Gita 4:8; and

    (ii) ***Moral and Ethical Superiority***: The leadership of all the major religions, including Modern American Secularism have claimed divine favouritism and exceptionalism as justified by a history of moral and ethical leadership within an immoral world. Judaism still claims moral superiority, despite its overwhelming record of war crimes and cultural genocide and by referring to such scripture as Isaiah 49:6 that Israel is and shall be a "light unto the nations". The British Empire and the Modern Global American Military Economic Empire both claimed (and claim) to be morally and ethically superior.

731. The primary political and social uses of the doctrine of *Divine Favouritism & Exceptionalism* include (but are not limited to):-

*Primary political and social use of such a doctrine*

    (i) ***Justification for war as political tool***: Meaning this doctrine has given legal and moral protection for European and North American regimes for centuries of war, conquest and destruction; and since the mid-20th Century has been used as fundamental justification for some of the worst war crimes, crimes against humanity and the cultural genocide of the Palestinian people by the state of Israel; and

(ii) ***Justification for colonial oppression***: Meaning this doctrine has justified centuries of cultural and colonial oppression in the destruction of many cultures and the murder and enslavement of tens of millions of people; and

(iii) ***Justification for global bankruptcy and slavery***: Over the past 100 years, this doctrine has ultimately supported the American elite imposition of a global system of bankruptcy and enslavement never seen before in human history, that to this day remains steadfastly denied by the very people who still continue to operate it.

732. When assumed as a Divine Law of the ultimate Supreme Being of all Creation and Existence, the erroneous doctrinal belief of *Divine Favouritism & Exceptionalism* is built upon the following presumptions including (but not limited to):- *Fundamental Presumptions of Divine Favouritism & Exceptionalism and the Supreme Being*

(i) ***Supreme Being is Untrustworthy*** (fundamental logical absurdity): Implied by the argument of supreme bias over one part or group of creation than another. By definition, favouritism and exceptionalism in law means such an entity cannot be trusted to be impartial and objective to fairly adjudicate the law – hence untrustworthy; and

(ii) ***Supreme Being is Unjust and Immoral*** (fundamental logical absurdity): Implied by the argument of supreme bias over one part or group of creation than another being the epitome of corruption of fair and impartial application of the law – hence immoral and unjust; and

(iii) ***Supreme Being is either an impostor spirit or group of men***: Given the undeniable implications and logical absurdities, the God who demands such a false and erroneous doctrinal belief cannot possibly be the Divine Creator of all Existence, but some low level supernatural functionary or impostor falsely claiming to be a "God".

733. The false and erroneous doctrine of *Divine Favouritism & Exceptionalism* is hereby prohibited, condemned and to be suppressed in all its forms throughout all valid and proper Religious Denominations and Cults. *False Doctrine, Prohibited & Suppressed*

## Article 183 – Divinely Justified & Ordained War

734. ***Divinely Justified & Ordained War*** refers to the erroneous doctrinal belief that certain wars are sanctioned by a divine authority, often found in religious texts or revelations. These wars are seen as morally and spiritually justified, carried out to fulfil divine will, protect the faith, or achieve a sacred purpose. This belief can influence religious followers to view such conflicts as righteous and obligatory.

735. The primary arguments for justification of the doctrine of *Divinely Justified & Ordained War* include (but are not limited to):-

   (i) ***Scriptural Justification***: All major religions have claimed (or still claim) scriptural references for Divine Justification for War. The Bible in particular has multiple references where God not only endorses warfare and genocide, but sometimes instructs it to be done, including (but not limited to) Deuteronomy 2:34; 7:1-2; 3:6; 20:16-17, Joshua 6:17, 21; 10:40, 1 Samuel 15:2-3, Exodus 23:23-24, Numbers 21:2-3; 31:1-18 and Judges 21:10-11; and

   (ii) ***Theological Justification***: All major religions have had famous theologians and philosophers that have written arguments in support of scripture and justification for *Divinely Justified & Ordained War*, such as Augustine of Hippo and Thomas Aquinas who wrote extensively on the concept of "Just War"; and

   (iii) ***Political Ends Justifies the Means***: Or "Just War Doctrine" was revived in the mid 19th Century by the elite New York families and their President Abraham Lincoln to justify how they prosecuted the American Civil War against the other states and the majority of Americans. Just War Doctrine thereafter became the underpinning of the constant and unrelenting use of American military, industrial, espionage and state-craft to shape, manipulate, destroy and control the rest of the world for the next one hundred and fifty years to the present day.

736. The primary political and social uses of the doctrine of *Divinely Justified & Ordained War* include (but are not limited to):-

   (i) ***Justification for war as political tool***: Meaning this doctrine has given legal and moral protection for European and North American regimes for centuries of war, conquest and destruction; and since the mid-20th Century has been used as fundamental justification for some of the worst war crimes, crimes against humanity and the cultural genocide of the Palestinian people by the state of Israel; and

(ii) ***Justification for colonial oppression***: Meaning this doctrine has justified centuries of cultural and colonial oppression in the destruction of many cultures and the murder and enslavement of tens of millions of people; and

(iii) ***Justification for global bankruptcy and slavery***: Over the past 100 years, this doctrine has ultimately supported the American elite imposition of a global system of bankruptcy and enslavement never seen before in human history, that to this day remains steadfastly denied by the very people who still continue to operate it.

737. When assumed as a Divine Law of the ultimate Supreme Being of all Creation and Existence, the erroneous doctrinal belief of *Divinely Justified & Ordained War* is built upon the following presumptions including (but not limited to):- *Fundamental Presumptions of Divinely Justified & Ordained War and the Supreme Being*

(i) ***Supreme Being is a Hypocrite & Liar*** (fundamental logical absurdity): Implied by the argument that the supreme being demands humans honour the sanctity of life be respected above all other laws, yet Divinely Sanctioned War directly contradicts this rule. Thus either the scriptures are a lie or the doctrine of just war is a lie – as both cannot possible be true; and

(ii) ***Supreme Being is Unjust and Immoral*** (fundamental logical absurdity): Implied by the argument of supreme bias in favour of one person or group of creation against another being the epitome of corruption of fair and impartial application of the law – hence immoral and unjust; and

(iii) ***Supreme Being is either an impostor spirit or group of men***: Given the undeniable implications and logical absurdities, the God who demands such a false and erroneous doctrinal belief cannot possibly be the Divine Creator of all Existence, but some low level supernatural functionary or impostor falsely claiming to be a "God".

738. The false and erroneous doctrine of *Divinely Justified & Ordained War* is hereby prohibited, condemned and to be suppressed in all its forms throughout all valid and proper Religious Denominations and Cults. *False Doctrine, Prohibited & Suppressed*

## Article 184 – Suffering as Necessary Penance

739. ***Suffering as Necessary Penance*** refers to the erroneous doctrinal belief that enduring physical pain or hardship during life serves as a means of spiritual purification and atonement for sins, with promise of rewards in the afterlife.

*Suffering as Necessary Penance*

740. The primary arguments for justification of the doctrine of *Suffering as Necessary Penance* include (but are not limited to):-

*Primary arguments for justification of such a doctrine*

   (i) **Scriptural Justification**: Christianity in particular argues justification for suffering of the poor as a necessary step to receiving some reward after they finally die. The image and story of the suffering of Christ most often is used to justify this as a valid doctrine from the highest level; and

   (ii) **Ancient Spiritual Practices**: Whilst Christianity has historically used scripture to justify the continued barbarity of the wealthy pirate merchant class against everyone else on planet Earth, ancient spiritual practices – especially Eastern religions - justify suffering as a necessary step in the path of freedom from material pain.

741. The primary political and social uses of the doctrine of *Suffering as Necessary Penance* include (but are not limited to):-

*Primary political and social use of such a doctrine*

   (i) **Religious cover for the obscenely rich against the mass of poor**: Overwhelmingly the argument of *Suffering as Necessary Penance as Reward in Afterlife* has politically and socially shielded many of the obscenely rich merchant pirate families over the past three hundred years from a similar fate as the aristocracy of France at the start of the French Revolution and throughout history when people had enough. It can be argued the Second Great Awakening promoted heavily out of America and more recent Evangelical Religious Movement are heavily supported to try and prevent this notion from collapsing; and

   (ii) **Social Control**: Overwhelmingly, this doctrine has strongly served social control – especially during the most economically tumultuous times of the past three centuries.

742. When assumed as a Divine Law of the ultimate Supreme Being of all Creation and Existence, the erroneous doctrinal belief of *Suffering as Necessary Penance* is built upon the following presumptions including (but not limited to):-

*Fundamental Presumptions of Suffering as Necessary Penance and the Supreme Being*

   (i) ***Supreme Being is a Hypocrite & Liar*** (fundamental

logical absurdity): Implied by the argument that the obscenely rich and powerful of society seem exempt from the *suffering rule* of "God", whilst the poor carry the great burden of suffering with no sustainable or meaningful help from the rich. By definition, either the law is false and "God" is a hypocrite or the doctrine is true and God continues to lie to most of humanity; and

    (ii) ***Supreme Being is Unjust and Immoral*** (fundamental logical absurdity): Implied by the argument of bias in favour of one person or group born into a life of obscene wealth, power and pleasure, whilst everyone else are born into a life of misery, pain and hardship – hence a divinely ordained adjudication and allocation of unfair and unequal resources and the epitome of injustice and immorality; and

    (iii) ***Supreme Being is Untrustworthy*** (logical absurdity): Implied by the already expressed arguments of hypocrisy, untruthfulness, favouritism, injustice and immorality. Therefore, no sensible thinking human can trust that the Supreme Being is going to reward the poor with riches in the afterlife, given the obscenely wealthy pirate merchant families who have ruthlessly oppressed the world for centuries seem to remain immune from any form of "divine justice"; and

    (iv) ***Supreme Being is either an impostor spirit or group of men***: Given the undeniable implications and logical absurdities, the God who demands such a false and erroneous doctrinal belief cannot possibly be the Divine Creator of all Existence, but some low level supernatural functionary or impostor falsely claiming to be a "God".

743. The false and erroneous doctrine of *Suffering as Necessary Penance* is hereby prohibited, condemned and to be suppressed in all its forms throughout all valid and proper Religious Denominations and Cults.    *False Doctrine, Prohibited & Suppressed*

## Article 185 – Contraception as Divine Sin & Offence

744. ***Contraception as Divine Sin & Offence*** refers to the erroneous doctrinal belief that the use of contraceptive methods is inherently sinful and offends divine law.    *Contraception as Divine Sin & Offence*

745. The primary arguments for justification of the doctrine of *Contraception as Divine Sin & Offence* include (but are not limited to):-    *Primary arguments for justification of such a doctrine*

    (i) ***Scriptural Justification***: There is no direct scripture directly condemning contraception. However, a passage that obliquely infers a type of Contraception is against Divine Law is used being Genesis 38:9-10 when Onan's act of spilling his seed is condemned by God; and

(ii) ***Theological Justification***: Under primarily Catholic Doctrine, Contraception is argued as contrary to natural law because it deliberately frustrates the natural end of sexual intercourse, which is procreation.

746. The primary political and social uses of the doctrine of *Contraception as Divine Sin & Offence* include (but are not limited to):-

Primary political and social use of such a doctrine

(i) ***Maximum Social Control***: Cynically, such appalling social and health policies promote the very conditions of disease, misery and poverty that has historically been the "bread and butter" of several religious denominations for centuries; and

(ii) ***Weakening Local Social Cohesion***: Within western countries, such policies have upended for centuries the social cohesion of poorer local communities, in combination with other diabolical doctrines that saw the wholesale destruction of thousand year old sustainable local health systems through false "witch trials"; and

(iii) ***Geopolitical Advantage***: The false doctrine of Contraception contributed over the 20<sup>th</sup> Century to the direct deaths of millions of people, especially in Africa and Asia, weakening many smaller countries and heralding the way for corporate and military interests to rape and pillage their natural mineral and environmental resources.

747. When assumed as a Divine Law of the ultimate Supreme Being of all Creation and Existence, the erroneous doctrinal belief of *Contraception as Divine Sin & Offence* is built upon the following presumptions including (but not limited to):-

Fundamental Presumptions of Contraception as Divine Sin & Offence and the Supreme Being

(i) ***Supreme Being is Cruel and Petulant*** (fundamental logical absurdity): Implied by the choice of the Supreme Being as architect of such a system to deny any sensible forms of birth control and by implication to condemn the poorest and least educated to more misery and hardship from unwanted pregnancies and sexually transmitted diseases – hence a conscious choice to be cruel, unjust and petulant; and

(ii) ***Supreme Being is Irrational and Immoral*** (fundamental logical absurdity): Implied by the argument of supreme bias against healthy family planning and protecting the most vulnerable and poorest societies and people from further hardship from disease and unplanned pregnancies is by definition the essence of irrationality as to thinking through the consequences of such poor rules – consequences that are themselves immoral given the poorest and least educated are the most hurt; and

(iii) ***Supreme Being is either an impostor spirit or group of men***: Given the undeniable implications and logical absurdities, the God who demands such a false and erroneous doctrinal belief cannot possibly be the Divine Creator of all Existence, but some low level supernatural functionary or impostor falsely claiming to be a "God".

748. The false and erroneous doctrine of *Contraception as Divine Sin & Offence* is hereby prohibited, condemned and to be suppressed in all its forms throughout all valid and proper Religious Denominations and Cults.

*False Doctrine, Prohibited & Suppressed*

## Article 186 – Adult Same-Sex Relations as Divine Sin & Offence

749. ***Adult Same-Sex Relations as Divine Sin & Offence*** refers to the erroneous doctrinal belief that adult same-sex relations are a divine sin and offence holds that such relationships are inherently immoral and violates divine law, as interpreted by specific religious traditions.

*Adult Same-Sex Relations as Divine Sin & Offence*

750. The primary arguments for justification of the doctrine of *Adult Same-Sex Relations as Divine Sin & Offence* include (but are not limited to):-

*Primary arguments for justification of such a doctrine*

(i) ***Scriptural Authority***: All major Religions regard the tolerance or promotion of homosexual beliefs and behaviours as a grave transgression of Divine Law and a fundamental threat to the very survival and cohesion of society. Christianity (Leviticus 18:22; 20:13), Islam (Qur'an Surah Al-A'raf (7:80-81) and Ash-Shu'ara (26:165-166)) and Hinduism (Manusmriti 8.369-372) are also examples of clear and strict moral code against the promotion of homosexual ideology within society; and

(ii) ***Sanctity of Matrimony***: Whereby all major Religions uphold that matrimony is a central covenant of society and strictly between a man and a woman, intended for lawful procreation and the establishment of a family.

751. The primary political and social uses of the doctrine of *Adult Same-Sex Relations as Divine Sin & Offence* include (but are not limited to):-

*Primary political and social use of such a doctrine*

(i) ***Moral and Social Order***: Same-sex relations are viewed as harmful to the moral and social fabric of society, undermining the family structure and societal norms; and

(ii) ***Control and Influence***: The issue regarding same sex relations has been seen as a key area of remaining influence and control of Religion within increasingly "secular" societies.

752. When assumed as a Divine Law of the ultimate Supreme Being of all Creation and Existence, the erroneous doctrinal belief of *Adult Same-Sex Relations as Divine Sin & Offence* is built upon the following presumptions including (but not limited to):-

*Fundamental Presumptions of Adult Same-Sex Relations as Divine Sin & Offence and the Supreme Being*

(i) ***Supreme Being is Cruel and Petulant*** (fundamental logical absurdity): Implied by the choice of the Supreme Being as architect of human beings in "his image" to then deny adults their true feelings between one another, even if a same sex relation– hence a conscious choice to be cruel, unjust and petulant; and

(ii) ***Supreme Being is Irrational and Immoral*** (fundamental logical absurdity): Implied by the argument of supreme bias against adults on the exercise of their free will to choose to form sexual relations of the same sex if they choose; and then to condemn such adults for the use of their own free will – an approach that is both irrational and immoral; and

(iii) ***Supreme Being is either an impostor spirit or group of men***: Given the undeniable implications and logical absurdities, the God who demands such a false and erroneous doctrinal belief cannot possibly be the Divine Creator of all Existence, but some low level supernatural functionary or impostor falsely claiming to be a "God".

753. The false and erroneous doctrine of *Adult Same-Sex Relations as Divine Sin & Offence* is hereby prohibited, condemned and to be suppressed in all its forms throughout all valid and proper Religious Denominations and Cults.

*False Doctrine, Prohibited & Suppressed*

754. Adult Same-Sex Relations remains both abnormal and an existential threat to the fundamental healthy structure of sustainable societies, regardless of the importance to ensure no adult is discriminated against on the basis of their sexual preferences, or race, or creed, or political views. Therefore, the overt promotion of adult same-sex philosophies to the broader community must remain carefully reviewed and prohibited and forbidden to be promoted to children.

*Prohibition of Overt Promotion of Adult Same Sex Relations*

## Article 187 – Suicide as Divine Sin & Offence

755. **Suicide as Divine Sin & Offence** refers to the erroneous doctrinal belief that taking one's own life is a grave sin leading to eternal punishment in the afterlife. Rooted in various religious doctrines, it views suicide as a violation of divine sovereignty over life and death, often without allowance for repentance, thus condemning the soul to hell or eternal separation from God.

756. Historically, the concept of Suicide within many ancient Civilisations, Empires and Societies was seen as a "Noble Death" embraced and rewarded by the Divine:-

   (i) *Highest Act of Altruism and Honour*: The idea of sacrificing one's own life to save others, or to demonstrate accountability under the law was regarded by most ancient civilisations as the highest act of altruism and honour until the age of selfish commercial piracy from the 14$^{th}$ Century; and

   (ii) *Weakening of Altruism and Promotion of Cowardice*: To the merchant pirate families of Venice and later England and other commercial empires, the notions of altruism, honour and the courage of lower classes represent an existential threat to control and power. Thus altruism and honour had to be weakened in preference to selfishness and cowardice.

757. The primary arguments for justification of the doctrine of *Suicide as Divine Sin & Offence* include (but are not limited to):-

   (i) *Desecration of Sacred Property*: All major Religions argue that our lives and bodies are a form of sacred property ultimately owned by the Divine; and that destruction of it through Suicide is a form of Desecration of such Sacred Property Rights of the Divine; and

   (ii) *Fundamental Usurpation of Divine Sovereignty*: Several major Religions, such as Christianity and Islam teach that suicide is a supreme act of rejection of Divine Mercy and Usurpation of Divine Sovereignty, whereby only God has control over our life and death and when our suffering (Mercy) shall ease; and

   (iii) *Desecration of Divine Image and Name*: Many major Religions teach that humans are created in the image of God, so that destroying that image through suicide is a grave community offence and disgrace to the family. In contrast and contradiction, the murder of people for state sanctioned military, commercial or political interests is not seen as severely; and

(iv) **Severe Moral Offence of Self-Murder**: All major Religions firmly teach in scripture that murder is one of the most severe moral offences against the Divine. Despite the lack of clear and unmistakable scriptural passages referring to suicide as "self murder", all major Religions argue that Suicide is equivalent to it.

758. The primary political and social uses of the doctrine of *Suicide as Divine Sin & Offence* include (but are not limited to):-

*Primary political and social use of such a doctrine*

(i) **Weakening of Altruism and Promotion of Cowardice**: Being a critical long term goal and system of an elite commercial pirate industrial class that seized and hold power not through their physical strength, but cunning and deception; and

(ii) **Social Control**: Whereby certain religious bodies asserted their claim over the control of the souls, minds and bodies of the people.

759. When assumed as a Divine Law of the ultimate Supreme Being of all Creation and Existence, the erroneous doctrinal belief of *Suicide as Divine Sin & Offence* is built upon the following presumptions including (but not limited to):-

*Fundamental Presumptions of Suicide as Divine Sin & Offence and the Supreme Being*

(i) **Supreme Being is a Hypocrite & Liar** (fundamental logical absurdity): Implied by the argument of supreme bias whereby God is supposed to have created human beings "in his image" and human beings are commanded not to murder, yet sacred scripture repeatedly states that God is free to kill human beings whenever and however he chooses. By definition, such action is hypocritical and untruthful to the law against murder and any claim of self-murder; and

(ii) **Supreme Being is Untrustworthy** (fundamental logical absurdity): Implied by the argument of God saying one thing (i.e. do not murder) and doing another (i.e. I can kill whomever I want and whenever I want). By definition, such a being cannot be trusted as their words and commands mean nothing; and

(iii) **Supreme Being is Cruel and Duplicitous** (fundamental logical absurdity): Implied by the choice of the supreme architect of the Universe allowing innocent people to be preyed upon by wolves, and any brave soul who seeks to give their life defending them condemned as a self-murderer; and simultaneously to seem to reward cowardice and unaccountability, whilst condemning the once "noble act" of senior bureaucrats and leaders ending their lives when culpable of treason and gross negligence that badly hurt the community; and

 (iv) ***Supreme Being is either an impostor spirit or group of men***: Given the undeniable implications and logical absurdities, the God who demands such a false and erroneous doctrinal belief cannot possibly be the Divine Creator of all Existence, but some low level supernatural functionary or impostor falsely claiming to be a "God".

760. The false and erroneous doctrine of *Suicide as Divine Sin & Offence* is hereby prohibited, condemned and to be suppressed in all its forms throughout all valid and proper Religious Denominations and Cults.  *False Doctrine, Prohibited & Suppressed*

## Article 188 – Birth of Soul at Conception

761. ***Birth of Soul at Conception*** refers to the erroneous doctrinal belief that a human soul is created and infused into a body at the moment of conception. This view asserts that personhood begins at conception, attributing full moral and spiritual status to the embryo. This belief influences ethical perspectives on issues like abortion, emphasizing the sanctity of life from its earliest biological inception.  *Birth of Soul at Conception*

762. The primary arguments for justification of the doctrine of *Birth of Soul at Conception* include (but are not limited to):-  *Primary arguments for justification of such a doctrine*

 (i) ***Sanctity of Life***: That Life is seen as sacred and a gift from God, necessitating its absolute protection from the earliest stages within a given society, whilst simultaneously ignoring the claim of "sanctity of life" when dealing with other enemy societies, groups and lesser animals slaughtered for entertainment or food; and

 (ii) ***Moral and Ethical Consideration***: Being the inherent dignity of human life and the moral duty to protect it, unless a pregnant mother lives within a zone designated for commercial and political exploitation, or a person is condemned as a criminal worthy of state sanctioned murder; and

 (iii) ***Modern Theological Conclusions***: That some Religious groups interpret scripture such as Jeremiah 1:5 and Psalm 139:13-16 to imply that the Soul is somehow connected to the Zygote within the first 24 hours of pregnancy and not to the Fetus formed some nine weeks later in deliberate contradiction to the traditional and orthodox time ascribed when the Soul is connected to the unborn child in Islam and in authentic Christianity (Luke 1:39-45).

763. The primary political and social uses of the doctrine of *Birth of Soul at Conception* include (but are not limited to):-

    (i) **Political Control and Influence**: The rigid Anti-Abortion Groups view the issue as both a "last stand" for moral values and an opportunity to re-establish firmer Religious influence. The fact that rigid Anti-Abortion rhetoric blatantly contradicts sacred scripture, logic and science is immaterial to their political cause; and

    (ii) **Suppression of Feminism**: The campaign of rigid Anti-Abortion policies further supports the broader suppression of female rights and in deliberately inhibiting or sabotaging a more balanced, tolerant and just society.

*Primary political and social use of such a doctrine*

764. When assumed as a Divine Law of the ultimate Supreme Being of all Creation and Existence, the erroneous doctrinal belief of *Birth of Soul at Conception* is built upon the following presumptions including (but not limited to):-

    (i) **Supreme Being is Irrational and Immoral** (fundamental logical absurdity): Implied by the argument of supreme bias against the loss of any form of life from the moment of conception, yet the permission (and sometimes endorsement) of war and state sanctioned murder is not irrational and immoral; and

    (ii) **"God" is a Hypocrite & Liar** (logical absurdity): Implied by the argument that the supreme being regards all life as sacred, yet chooses to take life whenever and however he chooses and sometimes permits his favourite states and leaders to do the same; and

    (iii) **Supreme Being is either an impostor spirit or group of men**: Given the undeniable implications and logical absurdities, the God who demands such a false and erroneous doctrinal belief cannot possibly be the Divine Creator of all Existence, but some low level supernatural functionary or impostor falsely claiming to be a "God".

*Fundamental Presumptions of Birth of Soul at Conception and the Supreme Being*

765. The false and erroneous doctrine of *Birth of Soul at Conception* is hereby prohibited, condemned and to be suppressed in all its forms throughout all valid and proper Religious Denominations and Cults.

*False Doctrine, Prohibited & Suppressed*

## Article 189 – Divinely Ordained Clerical Misogyny

766. **Divinely Ordained Clerical Misogyny** refers to the erroneous doctrinal belief that religious doctrines and sacred texts justify or mandate the subordination of women by male religious authorities. This doctrine asserts that gender roles are divinely established, often resulting in women's exclusion from clerical positions and leadership roles, perpetuating gender inequality within religious institutions. Critics argue this belief misinterprets or selectively emphasizes certain religious teachings to maintain patriarchal structures. *(Divinely Ordained Clerical Misogyny)*

767. The primary arguments for justification of the doctrine of *Divinely Ordained Clerical Misogyny* include (but are not limited to):- *(Primary arguments for justification of such a doctrine)*

    (i) **Divine Command**: Many of the major Religions claim through various scriptures that the Divine has explicitly commanded and allocated unequal rights between the sexes, whereby men by "Divine Right" are "superior" and women are "inferior"; and

    (ii) **Social Tradition and Order**: Many of the Religions argue the self fulfilling, false and circular argument that historically men have "traditionally" held the most superior spiritual positions in civilisations and empires and that this represents the "natural order"; and

    (iii) **Property and Legal Rights**: Some Religions argue that woman are constrained from effective service by the history of property and legal rights, whereby they were considered the "property" of their husbands, or naturally holding less standing in society; and

    (iv) **Moral and Social Stability**: That equality of the sexes in terms of clerical positions weakens the moral and social stability of a religion, as per the previous doctrinal presumptions.

768. The primary political and social uses of the doctrine of *Divinely Ordained Clerical Misogyny* include (but are not limited to):- *(Primary political and social use of such a doctrine)*

    (i) **Male Dominance and Control**: That while a clearly false and absurd doctrine, it allows a narrow band of men to dominate and control various major Religions, often to the detriment of the millions of their followers; and

    (ii) **Suppression of Feminism**: To ensure the innate common sense of women remains suppressed and crippled so that the most capable group to enact and manage effective social change (women) are perpetually suppressed.

769. When assumed as a Divine Law of the ultimate Supreme Being of all Creation and Existence, the erroneous doctrinal belief of *Divinely Ordained Clerical Misogyny* is built upon the following presumptions including (but not limited to):-

> Fundamental Presumptions of Divinely Ordained Clerical Misogyny and the Supreme Being

  (i) ***Supreme Being is a Misogynist*** (fundamental logical absurdity): Implied by the argument of supreme bias over one part or group of creation than another. By definition, favouritism and exceptionalism in law means such an entity cannot be trusted to be impartial and objective to fairly adjudicate the law – hence untrustworthy; and

  (ii) ***Supreme Being is Unjust and Immoral*** (fundamental logical absurdity): Implied by the argument of supreme bias in favour one person or group of creation against another being the epitome of corruption of fair and impartial application of the law – hence immoral and unjust; and

  (iii) ***Supreme Being is either an impostor spirit or group of men***: Given the undeniable implications and logical absurdities, the God who demands such a false and erroneous doctrinal belief cannot possibly be the Divine Creator of all Existence, but some low level supernatural functionary or impostor falsely claiming to be a "God".

770. The false and erroneous doctrine of *Divinely Ordained Clerical Misogyny* is hereby prohibited, condemned and to be suppressed in all its forms throughout all valid and proper Religious Denominations and Cults.

> False Doctrine, Prohibited & Suppressed

## Article 190 – Clerical Celibacy

771. ***Clerical Celibacy*** refers to the erroneous doctrinal belief requiring that clergy members living within the broader community must remain unmarried and seek to abstain from sexual relations. It is believed to enable priests to devote themselves fully to God and their pastoral duties without the distractions of familial obligations. *Clerical Celibacy* is not the same as the ancient and traditional practice of Chastity – with Chastity being a period of self restraint from sexual activities.

> Clerical Celibacy

772. The primary arguments for justification of the doctrine of *Clerical Celibacy* include (but are not limited to):-

> Primary arguments for justification of such a doctrine

  (i) ***Spiritual and Self Discipline***: All major religions refer to mandatory and necessary temporary periods of chastity during religious studies and training in schools and monastic living. However, only the Roman Catholic Church from the 17<sup>th</sup>

Century imposed the unique and abnormal prohibition of matrimony (celibacy) for individual priests living in the community; and

(ii) ***Scriptural Authority***: Whilst there is no credible scripture that specifically claims clergy living among the wider community are condemned to an isolated and lonely life without matrimony, the heavily corrupted and nonsensical passage from 17th Century Bible of Matthew 19:12 is sometimes quoted as spiritual authority; and

(iii) ***Imitation of Christ and Apostles***: That such a doctrine "imitates" the claimed life of the leader or earliest followers, even if there is no evidence such claims of forced non-marriage are true; and

(iv) ***Undivided Attention and Clarity***: That non-marriage of clerics in the broader community allows such isolated and lonely individuals to somehow better refrain from deviant behaviour and dedicate themselves more to their duties, despite the contradiction of the enormous personal suffering such isolation causes.

773. The primary political and social uses of the doctrine of *Clerical Celibacy* include (but are not limited to):- Primary political and social use of such a doctrine

(i) ***Internal Conflict***: Forcing priests to live in isolation and under such stress, creates internal conflict and weakens their natural ability to perform their duties, rather than strengthening their faith and quality of service; and

(ii) ***Fermentation of Deviant Behaviour***: Isolated priests living an isolated and difficult life within the broader community are more likely to acquire sexually deviant and abhorrent behaviours because of such a false and erroneous doctrine of Clerical Celibacy; and

(iii) ***Weakening of Authentic Christian Faith***: Perversely, the "conservative" doctrine of Clerical Celibacy forbidding priests to marry and have children when their mission is within the broader community is about weakening authentic Christian Faith, not strengthening it.

774. When assumed as a Divine Law of the ultimate Supreme Being of all Creation and Existence, the erroneous doctrinal belief of *Clerical Celibacy* is built upon the following presumptions including (but not limited to):- Fundamental Presumptions of Clerical Celibacy and the Supreme Being

(i) ***Supreme Being is Cruel and Petulant*** (fundamental

logical absurdity): Implied by the choice of the Supreme Being as architect of such a system to deny any sensible forms of sensible married life for priests in the community is to condemn those who seek to serve to more misery and hardship – hence a conscious choice to be cruel, unjust and petulant; and

(ii) **Supreme Being is Irrational and Immoral** (fundamental logical absurdity): Implied by the argument of supreme bias against healthy married priests in the community with families and instead to create the perfect conditions for deviant and abhorrent sexual behaviour to rise out of prolonged suffering and loneliness, both weakening the faith of the priest, the community and completely contradicting the claimed "divine law" and arguments for priests to remain unmarried so as to strengthen the faith of the community; and

(iii) **Supreme Being is either an impostor spirit or group of men**: Given the undeniable implications and logical absurdities, the God who demands such a false and erroneous doctrinal belief cannot possibly be the Divine Creator of all Existence, but some low level supernatural functionary or impostor falsely claiming to be a "God".

775. The false and erroneous doctrine of *Clerical Celibacy* is hereby prohibited, condemned and to be suppressed in all its forms throughout all valid and proper Religious Denominations and Cults. False Doctrine, Prohibited & Suppressed

## Article 191 – Infallibility

776. **Infallibility** refers to the erroneous doctrinal belief that certain religious leaders or texts are free from error in matters of faith, doctrine, and morals. This concept is often associated with specific religious authorities, such as the Pope in Roman Catholicism, who are believed to be guided by divine inspiration, ensuring their teachings remain true and authoritative for adherents. Infallibility

777. The primary arguments for justification of the doctrine of *Infallibility* include (but are not limited to):- Primary arguments for justification of such a doctrine

(i) **Purity of Succession**: Almost all major Religions use variations on the concept of a "purity of succession" as the foundation of this doctrine, whether it be the claim of an unbroken authentic apostolic succession claimed by Pope Pius IX in his infamous 1870 document *Pastor Aeternus* concerning "papal infallibility"; or 14th Century Tibetian

Buddhism through Dalai Lama Tenzin Gyatso and his work *The Path to Enlightenment*; or unbroken claim of succession of true knowledge as asserted in the 14th Century Islamic text *Nahj al-Balagha*; and

(ii) ***Divine Selection and Powers***: All major Religions including (but not limited to) Christianity, Islam, Hinduism and Buddhism claim their highest clergy are selected through Divine Intervention or Support, thus asserting an authentic transfer of supernatural and divine powers to be able speak with infallible truth and accuracy; and

(iii) ***Divine Inspiration***: Those major Religions that claim their highest clergy are selected through Divine Intervention or Support, also claim that the same offices of clergy can sometimes speak in an official capacity with aid of Divine Inspiration ("Revelation") and thus a perfect and infallible voice or writing.

778. The primary political and social uses of the doctrine of *Infallibility* include (but are not limited to):- {Primary political and social use of such a doctrine}

(i) ***Absolute Authority***: Whereby the authority of a leader is without question and not subject to debate; and

(ii) ***Unchallengeable Instruments***: Documents or words issued by a leader cannot be questioned or challenged, even if illogical and contradictory to Divine Law.

779. When assumed as a Divine Law of the ultimate Supreme Being of all Creation and Existence, the erroneous doctrinal belief of *Infallibility* is built upon the following presumptions including (but not limited to):- {Fundamental Presumptions of Infallibility and the Supreme Being}

(i) ***Supreme Being is a Hypocrite & Liar*** (fundamental logical absurdity): Implied by the argument of supreme bias over one part or group of creation than another. By definition, favouritism and exceptionalism in law means such an entity cannot be trusted to be impartial and objective to fairly adjudicate the law – hence untrustworthy; and

(ii) ***Supreme Being is Unjust and Immoral*** (fundamental logical absurdity): Implied by the argument of supreme bias in favour one person or group of creation against another being the epitome of corruption of fair and impartial application of the law – hence immoral and unjust; and

(iii) ***Supreme Being is either an impostor spirit or group of men***: Given the undeniable implications and logical absurdities, the God who demands such a false and erroneous doctrinal belief cannot possibly be the Divine Creator of all Existence, but some low level supernatural functionary or impostor falsely claiming to be a "God".

780. The false and erroneous doctrine of *Infallibility* is hereby prohibited, condemned and to be suppressed in all its forms throughout all valid and proper Religious Denominations and Cults.

*False Doctrine, Prohibited & Suppressed*

## 5.7 – False, Absurd and Prohibited Theological Notions
### Article 192 – False and Prohibited Theological Notions

781. ***False and Prohibited Theological Notions*** are doctrines and beliefs so damaging to spiritual, mental and economic well being of individuals and societies, that the continued acceptance of such false, absurd and abhorrent notions constitutes a grave risk to the future of existing civilisation itself.

*False and Prohibited Theological Notions*

782. Major False and Prohibited Theological Notions concerning the Divine include (but are not limited to):-

*Major False and Prohibited Theological Notions*

(i) Divine Creator as Insecure Vindictive Sadist; and

(ii) God as Hidden Evil & Insane Deity; and

(iii) Human Sacrifice as Necessary Divine Currency; and

(iv) Inheritance & Eternal Blemish of Sin; and

(v) Certain Persons as Incapable of Sin; and

(vi) Mary as Mother of God; and

(vii) Divine Birthright as the Sole Custodians of Earth; and

(viii) Divine Forfeit of Rights by Lesser Birth; and

(ix) Baptism as Right of Salvage (Salvation) of Lesser Souls; and

(x) Gold as a Penitentiary Medium for Souls; and

(xi) Office of Lesser God on Earth Incapable of Error; and

(xii) Divine Birthrights as Lesser Gods over Earth.

### Article 193 – Divine Creator as Insecure Vindictive Sadist

783. ***Divine Creator as Insecure Vindictive Sadist*** is an absurd, false and prohibited notion whereby a succession of false, absurd and abhorrent doctrines infer God or the Divine Creator as some kind of *Insecure Vindictive Sadist*.

784. The fundamental false doctrines underpinning the false, absurd and abhorrent notion of the Divine Creator as some kind of *Insecure Vindictive Sadist* include (but are not limited to):-

   (i) ***Eternal Damnation & Unforgiveness***: Erroneous and false doctrinal belief in everlasting punishment for souls condemned after death and the state of not being forgiven by a God or Supreme Being; and

   (ii) ***Divine Intervention for Some not Others***: Erroneous and false doctrinal belief that God does directly intervene and suspend the laws of nature for some, whilst not doing the same for others who are equally or greater deserving of need; and

   (iii) ***Divine Favouritism & Exceptionalism***: Erroneous and false doctrinal belief that a particular group or individual is specially chosen and favoured by a deity, granting them unique privileges, protection, or status; and

   (iv) ***Divinely Justified & Ordained War***: Erroneous and false doctrinal belief that certain wars are sanctioned by a divine authority, often found in religious texts or revelations; and

   (v) ***Suffering as Necessary Penance***: Erroneous and false doctrinal belief that enduring physical pain or hardship during life serves as a means of spiritual purification and atonement for sins, with promise of rewards in the afterlife.

### Article 194 – God as Hidden Evil & Insane Deity

785. ***God as Hidden Evil & Insane Deity*** is an absurd, false and prohibited notion whereby a succession of false, absurd and abhorrent doctrines infer God as some kind of *Hidden Evil & Insane Deity*.

786. The fundamental false doctrines underpinning the false, absurd and abhorrent notion of the Divine Creator as some kind of *Hidden Evil & Insane Deity* include (but are not limited to):-

   (i) ***Eternal Damnation & Unforgiveness***: Erroneous and false doctrinal belief in everlasting punishment for souls condemned after death and the state of not being forgiven by a

God or Supreme Being; and

(ii) ***Divine Intervention for Some not Others***: Erroneous and false doctrinal belief that God does directly intervene and suspend the laws of nature for some, whilst not doing the same for others who are equally or greater deserving of need; and

(iii) ***Divine Favouritism & Exceptionalism***: Erroneous and false doctrinal belief that a particular group or individual is specially chosen and favoured by a deity, granting them unique privileges, protection, or status; and

(iv) ***Divinely Justified & Ordained War***: Erroneous and false doctrinal belief that certain wars are sanctioned by a divine authority, often found in religious texts or revelations; and

(v) ***Suffering as Necessary Penance***: Erroneous and false doctrinal belief that enduring physical pain or hardship during life serves as a means of spiritual purification and atonement for sins, with promise of rewards in the afterlife.

## Article 195 – Human Sacrifice as Necessary Divine Currency

787. ***Human Sacrifice as Necessary Divine Currency*** is an absurd, false and prohibited doctrine whereby the act of sacrificing human lives is seen as a form of appeasement or pleasing payment to deities. This notion has persisted until the present day through various false and perverted theological constructs including (but not limited to) blood being the fundamental currency in a divine "deposit of faith" and that it is the sacrifices of martyrs that fills reserves of the treasury of heaven.

<sub-note>Human Sacrifice as Necessary Divine Currency</sub-note>

788. The fundamental false doctrines underpinning the false, absurd and abhorrent notion of *Human Sacrifice as Necessary Divine Currency* include (but are not limited to):-

<sub-note>Fundamental False Doctrines underpinning Human Sacrifice as Necessary Divine Currency</sub-note>

(i) ***Divine Favouritism & Exceptionalism***: Erroneous and false doctrinal belief that a particular group or individual is specially chosen and favoured by a deity, granting them unique privileges, protection, or status; and

(ii) ***Divinely Justified & Ordained War***: Erroneous and false doctrinal belief that certain wars are sanctioned by a divine authority, often found in religious texts or revelations; and

(iii) ***Suffering as Necessary Penance***: Erroneous and false doctrinal belief that enduring physical pain or hardship during life serves as a means of spiritual purification and atonement for sins, with promise of rewards in the afterlife.

789. The largest method of sacrificing humans for "divine favour" is and has always been by warfare. Since the first civilisations, almost every major conflict has been fought as a battle of religious ideologies but with all sides usually glorifying their dead:-

*False and Deluded Practices of Human Sacrifice through War*

(i) The glorification of war as a form of "willing sacrifice" of the people of their sons and daughters remains a false, deluded and present mythology and belief within contemporary cultures. In many European capitals and American cities, there are shrines with an eternal flame implying the sacrifice of war to Moloch and G-d; and upon many war monuments, the words "Glorious Dead" is repeated across the world; and

(ii) Even under modern illegal and immoral conflicts such as those in the middle east and in parts of Europe and Asia, the mythology persists that such warfare is a matter of morality under the actual or implied "divine favour" of G-d or some other deity.

790. Whilst the practice of sacrificing animals to appease favour of certain gods is an ancient practice throughout many regimes of civilisations, such as Roman Emperors, the large scale sacrifice of human beings (most commonly by fire) has been almost the exclusive practice of worshipping Baal Moloch, also known as El, Sabaoth, G-d and Satan. The worst ancient and pre-modern sites for human sacrifice in history include (but are not limited to):-

*False, Criminal and Deluded Occult Practices of Animal & Human Sacrifice for Divine Favour*

(i) ***Urgarit*** in Northern Syria was known as the home to Yahudi and the infamous Biblical birthplace of human sacrifice in worship of the "golden calf" of Baal El, until more than a million Yahudi were captured by Egyptian General Pa-ra-mes-su (Ramesses) by 1290 BCE and sent back to Egypt as slaves; and

(ii) ***Carthage*** in North Africa was a city adopted by tens of thousands of Yahudi refugees and by the 11th Century BCE became an infamous ancient site for mass human sacrifice to Baal Moloch by fire and the original birthplace of the specific term ***Holocaust*** meaning a "burnt offering of human flesh to Moloch (Sabaoth, G-d and Satan)"; and

(iii) ***Jerusalem*** by the 7th Century BCE became a terrible site for Yahudi practices of human sacrifice to Baal Moloch by fire; and

(iv) ***Babylon*** by the 6th Century BCE became a new prison for Yahudi priests captured from Jerusalem, who were known to have continued the secret practice of human sacrifice to Baal

Moloch by burning; and

(v) **Baalbek** in Lebanon, also known as the Temple of Solomon, from the 6th Century BCE became arguably the most infamous ancient site for human sacrifice to Baal Moloch as Baal Hamon; and

(vi) **London** from the mid 16th Century saw the return of Holocaust rituals for the first time in more than 1600 years through the public ritual known as Immolation (literally meaning "in the name of Moloch") or simply "Burning at the Stake". In 1666, the second largest mass sacrifice by fire to Moloch was orchestrated by deliberately lit fires that trapped and killed more than 300,000 inhabitants of old London to invoke "divine favour" in the ascendency of Charles II under the new arrangement of power and for the future success of the Kingdom of Great Britain to come; and

(vii) The worst Holocaust in the name of Moloch in history and the worst unpunished crime against humanity for 1,000 years was the mass sacrifice by fire of more than six million protestants, ethnic minorities and Jews starting exactly on September 11, 1941 (9/11), through specifically designed centres of human sacrifice mirroring ancient temple sites creating a giant pentagram in Poland, in order to invoke "divine favour" for the creation of the great secret pentagram known as the **Pentagon** in the rededication of **Washington DC** and the birth of the American Imperial Exceptionalism. Each of the five special concentration camps that started sacrificing people from September 11, 1941 (9/11) were designed to mirror-image the footprint of ancient temple sites to Moloch. Treblinka mirror inverted the ancient sacrifice site of Urgarit; and Janowska mirror inverted the ancient sacrifice site of Jerusalem; and Auschwitz mirror inverted the ancient sacrifice site of Baalbek; and Lodz mirror inverted the ancient sacrifice site of Carthage; and Sobibor mirror inverted the ancient sacrifice site of Babylon. At the center of the Pentagram was the spiritual birthplace to Hasidic Judaism. The positioning of this infrastructure was not to create a perfectly shaped pentagram, but to make sure the top of the pentagram aligned with the North Star above the Arctic and the negative "ley lines" of the pentagram intersected most of the major occult centres of Europe including but not limited to Rome, Carthage, Zurich, Munich, Stockholm, Hanover, Bordeaux, Zagreb, Odessa, Bucharest, Belgorod, St Petersburg, Nizhsny Novgorod and the Shetland Islands. If the positions of the sacrifice camps were even a few kilometres off their intentional position, then the "ley lines" would not have intersected these centres.

791. The false and erroneous doctrine of *Human Sacrifice as Necessary Divine Currency* is hereby prohibited, condemned and to be suppressed in all its forms throughout all valid and proper Religious Denominations and Cults.

## Article 196 – Inheritance & Eternal Blemish of Sin

792. ***Inheritance & Eternal Blemish of Sin*** is an absurd, false and prohibited doctrine that asserts almost all human beings inherit a corrupted soul, and tainted nature prone to sin because of the claimed first act of disobedience by Adam and Eve in the Garden of Eden, as described in the Book of Genesis.

793. The wickedness and absurd nature of the "man-made" false doctrine of Original Sin is not necessarily the false history, but the sadistic, unforgiving and contradictory behaviour of the claimed Supreme Being in the false story:-

   (i) To inherit the debts of another is an ancient Moor banking curse, forbidden and suppressed my many civilisations for thousands of years, given its fundamental immoral and unjust nature. Yet to then assign such immoral and unjust behaviour to the claimed Supreme Being is the height of blasphemy and heresy against everything that is sacred; and

   (ii) The false doctrine of Original Sin fails on every point of logic, common decency and morality, effectively making many human beings throughout history more compassionate, wiser in law and more just than God.

794. The false and erroneous doctrine of *Inheritance & Eternal Blemish of Sin* is hereby prohibited, condemned and to be suppressed in all its forms throughout all valid and proper Religious Denominations and Cults.

## Article 197 – Certain Persons as Incapable of Sin

795. ***Certain Persons as Incapable of Sin*** is an absurd, false and prohibited doctrine whereby certain persons by the direct intervention of God or the Divine Creator are born without Inherited Original Sin, or by their birthright are *Incapable of Sin*.

796. The fundamental false doctrines underpinning the false, absurd and abhorrent notion of *Certain Persons as Incapable of Sin* include (but

are not limited to):-

(i) ***Inheritance & Eternal Blemish of Sin***: Absurd, false and prohibited doctrine that asserts almost all human beings inherit a corrupted soul, and tainted nature prone to sin because of the claimed first act of disobedience by Adam and Eve in the Garden of Eden, as described in the Book of Genesis; and

(ii) ***Divine Intervention for Some not Others***: Erroneous and false doctrinal belief that God does directly intervene and suspend the laws of nature for some, whilst not doing the same for others who are equally or greater deserving of need; and

(iii) ***Divine Favouritism & Exceptionalism***: Erroneous and false doctrinal belief that a particular group or individual is specially chosen and favoured by a deity, granting them unique privileges, protection or status.

*Certain Persons as Incapable of Sin*

797. The true purpose of the blasphemous, false and heretic doctrine of Original Sin is only revealed when a few are secretly and openly acknowledged as being Incapable of Sin:-

*Purpose and function of false doctrine of Original Sin revealed*

(i) The false doctrine of Original Sin is a cover for the justification of unprecedented slavery and theft under the guise of "divine custodians and guardians" of those too untrustworthy and ignorant to properly manage their own affairs; and

(ii) Original Sin effectively means all but those born without sin lose their equal inheritance to absolute dominion upon the Earth and to share in its fruits. Further, Original Sin effectively means all but those born without sin lose their absolute freedoms and are subject to the oversight of guardians for the entirety of their lives, despite baptism and exemplary lives; and

(iii) Those "born without sin" on the other hand find themselves in an exclusive club of absolute ownership and freedom of all the property and all the people and the planet. This is the fulfilment of the prophecy and dream of the pirate merchant families that formed Venice and later formed the British Empire and then the Global American Empire.

798. The concept of a few people descended from a particular line of the "Holly" being "born without sin" as ***Domus Domini*** and ***Desposyni*** (literally "The House of the Lord") and the only rightful heirs to all the land of the world, including all other people as property and "creatures" is a wicked, vile and false notion created not earlier than 1854 in collusion with Venetian Pope Pius IX (1845-

*Domus Domini and Desposyni*

1878) and the highest officials and administration of the Roman Catholic Church:-

(i) Beginning in 1848 through to 1849, riots, rebellions and threats of revolutions erupted almost "simultaneously" across more than 17 major cities of Europe including (but not limited to) Paris, Berlin, Prague, Rome, Munich, Vienna, Milan, Venice, Budapest, Bucharest and Palermo. In the aftermath, the American banking families of New York were blamed for fanning the flames of instability in Europe through the notions of "freedom", "equality" and "democracy"; and

(ii) One of the groups blamed for the European riots was the secretive lodge network of pro-Zionist activists first born out of New York in 1843 called the "B'nai B'rith" – an organisation a century later that was instrumental in helping form the state of Israel; and

(iii) The creation of the idea of the *Domus Domini* and *Desposyni* ("The House of the Lord") and claimed descendent from the Holly and thus descended from "Immaculate Mary" and "born without sin" was intended to bring an end to the proxy wars between banking families and old European noble families, and to stabilise the "rule of order". However, the decision appeared to have sparked several strategic actions with consequences that caused the removal from power of many of these families; and

(iv) The first and most immediate reaction to the nomination of the twelve families of the *Domus Domini* and *Desposyni* by 1854 was for King Victor Emmanuel II of Sardinia and the House of Savoy to effectively "declare war" against the Vatican and Papal States. By 1860, the House of Savoy succeeded first in training and landing a revolutionary force of several thousand led by Giuseppe Garibaldi in Sicily. The revolutionaries quickly defeated all resistance but were stopped by Victor Emmanuel II in attacking Rome. By 1861, all the Papal States had been lost, Pope Pius IX was a prisoner and Victor Emmanuel II became the first King of a unified Italy (1861-1878) in over 1,400 years, calling himself *Pater Patriae* meaning literally "Father of the Fatherland" as superior to all the other families he was excluded from joining; and

(v) In New York and in London, the events and consequences in the creation of the concept of "Immaculate Mary" propelled some of the most powerful Dutch and Jewish merchant banking families to conceive of their own plans. New York had become one of the most powerful banking centres of the world and virtually all of its dominant families (including but not limited to the Stuyvesant, Vanderbilt, Du Pont and Astor families had a deep hatred of the House of Orange-Nassau. To see the former *Stadtholders* of the Dutch Republic raised as "holy monarchs" by the Catholic Church would have been the last straw. Similarly, the Rothschilds themselves had no love of nobility. Thus a vision was formed out of New York of not only an elite group called the *Beit Miriam* (בית מרים) (House of Mary), but in forming a New Rome as Washington and a new state based religion of "Secularism" by 1864; and

(vi) On October 28, 1965 for the first time in history, the Catholic Church promulgated a new official doctrine called *Nostra Aetate* (Latin for "In Our Time") during the Second Vatican Council, that fundamentally changed its teachings about Jews and Judaism, including the claim that Christianity came from Judaism; and that Jesus and his parents (Mary and Joseph) were observant Jews; and that Jews were not to blame for the death of Jesus; and Judaism and Christianity must develop greater cooperation, dialogue and respect; and that anti-Semitism must be condemned in all its forms; and

(vii) The consequences of the doctrines that came from the Second Vatican Council in 1965 is that those families proclaiming Jewish heritage and descent from Mary (Miriam) such as the elite banking and merchant families via *Beit Miriam* (בית מרים) (House of Mary) subsequently had a stronger claim than the original noble families of 1854.

**799.** The original twelve "Apostolic" Noble Houses from 1854 that held the exclusive right and authority of *Parens Patriae* as *Domus Domini* and *Desposyni* ("The House of the Lord") providing a particular House still remained in power included:- 

Twelve "Apostolic" Noble Families

(i) ***House of Hapsburg-Lorraine***: The last ruler from the House of Habsburg-Lorraine to reign over the Kingdom of Austria was Emperor Charles I of Austria, also known as Charles IV of Hungary. However, his reign was short-lived and marked by the collapse of the Austro-Hungarian Empire. Emperor Charles I's reign came to an end in 1918 with the end of World War I and the dissolution of the Austro-Hungarian Empire. From 1919 the Habsburg were forbidden by Austrian law from ever ruling again; and

(ii) ***House of Hanover***: The last kingdom to be held by the

House of Hanover was the United Kingdom. The House of Hanover ruled the United Kingdom from 1714 until 1901 and the death of Queen Victoria; and

(iii) **_House of Saxe-Coburg and Gotha (Windsor)_**: Queen Victoria was succeeded by her eldest son, Albert Edward, who became King Edward VII (1901-1910) and the first monarch of the House of Saxe-Coburg and Gotha. In 1917, due to anti-German sentiment during World War I, the British royal family changed their name to the House of Windsor; and

(iv) **_House of Hohenzollern_**: The Hohenzollern family ruled the Kingdom of Prussia and later the German Empire. The last ruler from the House of Hohenzollern to reign over the Kingdom of Prussia was Wilhelm II who became the German Emperor (Kaiser) and King of Prussia in 1888. His rule ended in November 1918 with the conclusion of World War I and the German Revolution of 1918-1919; and

(v) **_House of Wettin_**: The House of Wettin included the rulers of the Kingdom of Saxony and various other German states. The last ruler of the Kingdom of Saxony from the House of Wettin was King Frederick Augustus III of Saxony (1904-1918). His rule ended in November 1918 with the conclusion of World War I and the German Revolution of 1918-1919; and

(vi) **_House of Wittelsbach_**: The House of Wittelsbach ruled the Kingdom of Bavaria and had significant influence in southern Germany. The last ruler from the House of Wittelsbach to reign over the Kingdom of Bavaria was King Ludwig III of Bavaria (1913-1918). The monarchy was abolished in 1918 following the end of World War I and the German Revolution of 1918-1919; and

(vii) **_House of Orange-Nassau_**: The House of Orange-Nassau was restored as the royal family of the Netherlands in 1815 following the defeat of Napoleon, including the sovereign rights of any land held by the Republic of the United Netherlands prior to 1795. The House of Orange-Nassau have remained monarchs ever since; and

(viii) **_House of Romanov_**: The Romanov family was the ruling dynasty of Russia, with Tsars and Emperors in the 18th and 19th centuries. The last ruler from the House of Romanov was Tsar Nicholas II (1894-1917). He and his entire family were murdered on order of the Bolshevik leaders on July 17, 1918; and

(ix) **House of Braganza**: The House of Braganza ruled Portugal, and later the Empire of Brazil. The last ruler from the House of Braganza to reign over the Kingdom of Portugal was King Manuel II of Portugal (1908-1910). He was deposed in the Republican Revolution of October 1910, which resulted in the overthrow of the monarchy and the establishment of the Portuguese First Republic; and

(x) **House of Bonaparte**: First reaching noble status under Napoleon I, the family continued to be recognised by Vatican as the Kings of Rome and rightful heirs to France. By 1852, Napoleon III became Emperor of the French until 1870 and the last monarch of France; and

(xi) **House of Oldenburg**: The House of Oldenburg with links to Denmark since the 15th century has had branches that rule or have ruled in Denmark, Iceland, Greece, Norway, Russia, Sweden and the United Kingdom. A cadet branch of the House of Oldenburg, being the House of Glücksburg, became monarchs of Denmark since 1863; and

(xii) **House of Bourbon**: The House of Bourbon that included various branches like the House of Bourbon-Orléans and House of Bourbon-Spain, ruled over France, Spain, and other European regions. Queen Isabella II of the House of Bourbon was deposed in 1868 following the Spanish Revolution. However, her son Alfonso XII (1870-1885) was restored in 1870. The House of Bourbon was again deposed by 1931 upon the creation of the Spanish Republic. The House of Bourbon was finally restored to power in 1975 through Juan Carlos I (1975-2014).

**800.** In accord with the highest Divine Law as expressed through the most sacred Covenant *Pactum De Singularis Caelum* and the present Maxims, any and all claims of Authority or Rights as Descendent of Holly Family of Jesus, Mary or any of their ancestors or descendents is forbidden, prohibited and to be suppressed:- *[Ucadia and False Claims of Sovereign Authority as Descendent of Holly Family]*

(i) The most sacred revelation and scripture known as *Lebor Clann Glas* categorically proves the genealogy of Jesus from Adam; and proves that none of those who currently claim to be descendents of the Holly (Holy) Family are authentic; and that they are in fact impostors and liars; and

(ii) All Authority and Power of the Holly Bloodlines, also known as the Holy Bloodlines and Cuilliaéan Bloodlines are fully vested into Ucadia and all its legitimate entities, bodies, persons and offices; and

(iii) No Non-Ucadia person may claim any right or authority or power whatsoever concerning a claim of genealogy to the Holly Hyksos Pharaohs, or Great Holly Prophets of Yeb, or the original Messiah Kings of the Yahudi, or the restored lines of the Messiah Kings of the Yahudi, or the Holly Family and Bloodlines surrounding and associated with Jesus Christ, or the Holly Bloodlines of the Founder and Holly Prophet of Islam, or the Holly Bloodlines of the Kings of Ireland, or the Franks or the Saxons or any other Holy bloodline; and

(iv) Any existing noble or ancient banking or merchant family acknowledging the supremacy of Ucadia Jurisdiction therefore retains its titles and privileges, except for those that contradict the laws of Ucadia including (but not limited to) hidden and secret trusts, slavery, bondage and theft.

801. The false and erroneous doctrine of *Certain Persons as Incapable of Sin* is hereby prohibited, condemned and to be suppressed in all its forms throughout all valid and proper Religious Denominations and Cults. — False Doctrine, Prohibited & Suppressed

## Article 198 – Mary as Mother of God

802. ***Mary as Mother of God*** is an absurd, false and prohibited notion whereby Mary the mother of Jesus did also give birth to God incarnate, therefore Mary is both technically and literally the Mother of God (*Theotokos*). — Mary as Mother of God

803. The fundamental false doctrines underpinning the false, absurd and abhorrent notion of *Mary as Mother of God* include (but are not limited to):- — Fundamental False Doctrines underpinning Mary as Mother of God and Trinity

(i) ***Inheritance & Eternal Blemish of Sin***: Absurd, false and prohibited doctrine that asserts almost all human beings inherit a corrupted soul, and tainted nature prone to sin because of the claimed first act of disobedience by Adam and Eve in the Garden of Eden, as described in the Book of Genesis; and

(ii) ***Divine Intervention for Some not Others***: Erroneous and false doctrinal belief that God does directly intervene and suspend the laws of nature for some, whilst not doing the same for others who are equally or greater deserving of need; and

(iii) ***Divine Favouritism & Exceptionalism***: Erroneous and false doctrinal belief that a particular group or individual is specially chosen and favoured by a deity, granting them

(iv) **Certain Persons as Incapable of Sin**: Absurd, false and prohibited doctrine whereby certain persons by the direct intervention of God or the Divine Creator are born without Inherited Original Sin, or by their birthright are *Incapable of Sin*.

804. Few claims in the infamous false, heretical and supremely blasphemous document *Ineffabilis Deus* (1854) by Pope Pius IX were ever true. Yet the highly political document was nonetheless believed by him as a necessary step in forming an alliance with powerful merchant and sovereign families that did not finally bear fruit until 1933 and the recognition of the Holy See and the supremacy of the Catholic Church as the pinnacle of Western-Roman Civilisation:- *[Everything concerning the false doctrine of Mary as Mother of God is False]*

(i) The absurd claim that the concept of Mary as "Mother of God" was an ancient doctrine of Christianity dating back to an alleged Council of Ephesus in 431 CE is impossible. The city of Ephesus was reduced to ruins as a condemned city by Constantine following his edict of 314 CE and never repopulated. No Christian council less than 150 years later would ever have met on such condemned ground, regardless of the fact that no buildings still existed; and

(ii) The 19th Century false doctrine of *Theotokos* (Mary as Mother of God) and without sin (immaculate), completely contradicts the central $8^{th}$ Century doctrine of Trinity and fundamentally and deliberately usurps the primary of Christ in his own Church; and

(iii) The theological arguments that *Theotokos* and the concepts within the horrendously false documents of Pius IX are necessary to overcome the problem of Original Sin, only reinforces the falsity and absurdity of the notion of Original Sin itself.

805. The false and erroneous doctrine of *Mary as Mother of God* is hereby prohibited, condemned and to be suppressed in all its forms throughout all valid and proper Religious Denominations and Cults. *[False Doctrine, Prohibited & Suppressed]*

## Article 199 – Divine Birthright as the Sole Custodians of Earth

806. ***Divine Birthright as the Sole Custodians of Earth*** is an absurd, false and prohibited notion whereby certain people and families falsely have historically claimed their bloodline heritage traces them back to Mary, mother of Jesus, or her relatives; and thus inferring to the rest of the ruling class that they are the sole *[Divine Birthright as the Sole Custodians of Earth]*

custodians and only true heirs to planet Earth.

807. The fundamental false doctrines underpinning the false, absurd and abhorrent notion of *Divine Birthright as the Sole Custodians of Earth* include (but are not limited to):-

    (i) ***Divine Favouritism & Exceptionalism***: Erroneous and false doctrinal belief that a particular group or individual is specially chosen and favoured by a deity, granting them unique privileges, protection, or status; and

    (ii) ***Certain Persons as Incapable of Sin***: Absurd, false and prohibited doctrine whereby certain persons by the direct intervention of God or the Divine Creator are born without Inherited Original Sin, or by their birthright are *Incapable of Sin*; and

    (iii) ***Mary as Mother of God***: Absurd, false and prohibited doctrine whereby Mary as the mother of Jesus did also give birth to God incarnate. Therefore Mary is both technically and literally the Mother of God (*Theotokos*).

808. The false and erroneous doctrine of *Divine Birthright as the Sole Custodians of Earth* is hereby prohibited, condemned and to be suppressed in all its forms throughout all valid and proper Religious Denominations and Cults.

## Article 200 – Divine Forfeit of Rights by Lesser Birth

809. ***Divine Forfeit of Rights by Lesser Birth*** is an absurd, false and prohibited notion whereby the majority of people forfeit the rights promised to them by God because of the inheritance of sin (Original Sin) and their inherited sinful and lesser nature. Those forfeited rights are then "salvaged" and then conveyed and administered by the "Church" as the Body of Christ on Earth.

Certain individuals or groups are inherently inferior due to their birth circumstances and that this inferiority is sanctioned by a divine authority. Furthermore, under the Doctrine of Original Sin these people forfeit from birth the original rights promised by God.

810. The fundamental false doctrines underpinning the false, absurd and abhorrent notion of *Divine Forfeit of Rights by Lesser Birth* include (but are not limited to):-

    (i) ***Eternal Damnation & Unforgiveness***: Erroneous and false doctrinal belief in everlasting punishment for souls condemned after death and the state of not being forgiven by a God or Supreme Being; and

(ii) ***Inheritance & Eternal Blemish of Sin***: Absurd, false and prohibited doctrine that asserts almost all human beings inherit a corrupted soul, and tainted nature prone to sin because of the claimed first act of disobedience by Adam and Eve in the Garden of Eden, as described in the Book of Genesis.

811. The false and erroneous doctrine of *Divine Forfeit of Rights by Lesser Birth* is hereby prohibited, condemned and to be suppressed in all its forms throughout all valid and proper Religious Denominations and Cults.

False Doctrine, Prohibited & Suppressed

## Article 201 – Baptism as Right of Salvage (Salvation) of Lesser Souls

812. ***Baptism as Right of Salvage of Lesser Souls*** is an absurd, false and prohibited notion whereby Christian sacraments such as "baptism" and "extreme unction" have been secularised since 1917 and assigned to agents who may then perform such rites on new born infants, as well as produce legal and financial instruments connected to "salvation" as the salvage and possession of souls.

Baptism as Right of Salvage of Lesser Souls

813. In 1917, the Catholic Church promulgated for the first time in history its Code of Canon Law whereby *Lay Persons* could be ordained into Sacred Ministry as a Priest, upon the basis of their secular occupation and quality of character; while other suitable qualified Lay Persons were permitted to confer the sacrament of Baptism under certain conditions:-

Formation of Canon Law in 1917

(i) Prior to 1917, only those who had received Holy Orders as clerics were permitted to confer any of the sacraments of Baptism, Confirmation, Communion, Penance, Extreme Unction, Orders and Marriage; and

(ii) As a result of the Code of Canon Law (1917), obstetricians, doctors and surgeons could perform the sacrament of Baptism on any Christian or Non-Christian infant and create a new "Person" under claimed certain conditions of "necessity"; and

(iii) Obstetricians, doctors and surgeons "ordained" into a Sacred Ministry by virtue of their seniority and suitability of character to qualify on the stepped path to Holy Orders (if they so chose) as Priests, were then capable of conferring the sacrament of Extreme Unction on newborn infants under claimed certain conditions of "necessity"; and

(iv) Whilst the 1917 Canons only provided for conferral of minor orders of priesthood upon lay persons who were candidates for ordination, reforms under Pope Paul VI in 1972 through *Ministeria Quaedam*, made clear that lay persons could be conferred into a Sacred Ministry without first qualifying as a candidate for ordination.

814. In 1917, the Catholic Church promulgated the code of Canon Law being the first time that Lay Persons could be Ordained into a Sacred Ministry and therefore be recognised technically as a Priest capable of conferring certain sacraments:- Canon Law (1917) on Sacred Ministry

   (i) Canon 948 (1983 CIC 1008): "Ordination, by the institution of Christ, distinguishes clerics from laity for the governance of the faithful..."; and

   (ii) Canon 949 (1983 CIC 1009): "In the canons that follow, by the name of major orders or sacred orders are understood presbyterate, diaconate, and subdiaconate; while minor orders are acolyte, exorcist, lector, and doorkeeper."; and

   (iii) Canon 950 (1983 N/A): "In law the words: to ordain, order, ordination, [and] sacred ordination encompass, besides episcopal consecration, those orders enumerated in Canon 949 and first tonsure, unless it can be established otherwise by the nature of the thing or the context of the words."; and

   (iv) Canon 207 §1 (1983): "By divine institution, there are among the Christian faithful in the Church sacred ministers, who in law are also called clerics; the others are called lay persons."

815. In 1917, the Catholic Church promulgated the code of Canon Law being the first time that non-priests could conduct "non-solemn" forms of certain sacraments:- Canon Law (1917) and 1983 on Baptism

   (i) Canon 871 (1983 CIC 96): "By baptism a man is constituted a person in the Church of Christ..."; and

   (ii) Canon 743 (1983 CIC 861): "The pastor shall take care that the faithful, especially obstetricians, doctors, and surgeons, are carefully taught the correct manner of baptizing in case of necessity."; and

   (iii) Canon 750 (1983 CIC 868): "§ 1. The infant of infidels, even over the objections of the parents, is licitly baptized when life is so threatened that it is prudently foreseen that death will result before the infant attains the use of reason."; and

   (iv) Canon 759 (1983 N/A): "§ 1. In case of danger of death, baptism is licitly conferred privately; and if it is conferred by a minister who is neither a priest nor a deacon, he should do only those things necessary for the validity of baptism;" and

(v) Canon 742 (1983 CIC 861): "§ 1. Non-solemn baptism, discussed in Canon 759, § 1, can be administered by anyone, preserving the required matter, form, and intention; when it can be done this way, two witnesses, or at least one, should be used, by which the conferral of the baptism can be proved."; and

(vi) Canon 746 (1983 N/A): "§ 2. If the head of an infant is exposed and there is imminent danger of death, let him be baptized on the head; later, if he is delivered alive, he should be baptized again under condition. § 3. If another part of the body is exposed, and if danger [of death] is imminent, let him be baptized under condition thereupon, and then, if he survives birth, he should be once again baptized under condition."; and

(vii) Canon 778 (1983 CIC 878) "If the baptism was administered neither by the pastor nor in his presence, the minister of that conferral [of baptism] shall as soon as possible make the baptism known to the pastor of the place of domicile of the one baptized."; and

(viii) Canon 777 (1983 CIC 877) "§ 1. Pastors must carefully record without any delay in the baptismal book the names of persons baptized, making mention of the minister, parents and sponsors, and the place and day of the conferral of baptism."; and

(ix) Canon 779 (1983 CIC 876) In order to prove the conferral of baptism, if it is not prejudicial to anyone, one witness entirely above suspicion is sufficient, or the oath of the baptized person himself if he received baptism as an adult.

816. In 1919, following the 1917 Code of Canon Law, the Parliament of Westminster undertook the most dramatic of reforms since the time of Henry VIII (in the 16th Century) to effectively become an "ecclesiastical body" of ministers, ultimately under the Code of Canon Law (1917 and then 1983) as then the supreme law of the Western-Roman Civilisation: -

*Creation of New "Supreme" Law of Western Roman Civilisation*

(i) In 1919, at the Convocations of Canterbury and York (in England), a new Constitution and Body was proposed being the *National Assembly of Church of England* as a body of both clergy and laity. Crucially, the Constitution opened with the sentence "The Church of England, being a part of the One Holy Catholic and Apostolic Church of Christ" – inferring that while the laity and some clergy of the Church of England might not yet be in full communion with Rome, at least in law the Church of England and the Catholic Church were once again as one after a 400 year schism; and

(ii) In the same year (1919), the Parliament of Westminster passed a historic act named *Church of England Assembly (Powers) Act 1919 (c.76)* that for the first time: (1) granting legislative autonomy of the Church and its branches from Westminster; and (2) creating a new "Ecclesiastical Committee" of the Privy Council whereby acts passed by the church could technically then become broader secular law; and (3) transform Westminster into being part of the "Church Assembly"; and (4) giving the United Kingdom effectively a form of Ecclesiastical Constitution underpinning all the other acts of Parliament; and

(iii) By 1920, all major branches of the Church of England across the world had reconstituted and formed under the new directions, including the Episcopal Church in the United States and under State laws that recognised the primary of "Common Law". All the new constitutions of major branches reflected the changes of 1919, such as Australia being: "The Anglican Church of Australia, being a part of the One Holy Catholic"; and Apostolic Church of Christ; and

(iv) In 1925, the *Administration of Estates Act 1925* (c.23) radically overhauled the concepts around deceased estates, property and management including (but not limited to): (1) all wills are technically intestate if they do not accurately address in words all the components of the estate and not just chattels; and (2) administration of infant (intestate) deceased estates (those registered as deceased before age of 7 under probate) granted to trust corporations or minimum of two individuals; and (3) administrators may sell some or all of the assets of infant (intestate) deceased estate, including trusts, for the recovery and payment of debts; and (4) administration bonds to be provided by administrators of any infant (intestate) deceased estates; and (5) once administration on infant deceased estate is granted, no action or role of executor permitted until administration ceases, without court approval; and

(v) In 1926, through the *Births and Deaths Registration Act* 1926 (c.48) (1) the meaning of "still born" was amended to include to not "show any other signs of life", consistent with the Cestui Que Vie concept of "proof of life"; and (2) a master register of "still births" was created that oddly watered down the conditions for accuracy of records whereby a simple declaration to the registrar could be made simply stating that the certificate of live birth could not be obtained from the medical practitioner or midwife and the child "was not born alive"; and

(vi) Prior to 1970, while a person upon reaching the age of twenty one (21) could no longer be considered an infant under UK law, the Bankruptcy Act 1914 (c.59) allowed for a deceased estate to be declared bankrupt without having to issue a receiving order; and instead treating the date of alleged death as substitute for such procedure; and that if an existing and active administration (and thus proceeding) was still in place, that the court could automatically administratively transfer it to the bankruptcy court without the need for a formal petition or hearing. Thus, prior to reaching the "age of majority", the estates of all deceased persons in law were subsequently declared "bankrupt".

**817.** The fundamental false doctrines underpinning the false, absurd and abhorrent notion of *Baptism as Right of Salvage of Lesser Souls* include (but are not limited to):-

Fundamental False Doctrines underpinning Baptism as Right of Salvage of Lesser Souls

(i) ***Eternal Damnation & Unforgiveness***: Erroneous and false doctrinal belief in everlasting punishment for souls condemned after death and the state of not being forgiven by a God or Supreme Being; and

(ii) ***Inheritance & Eternal Blemish of Sin***: Absurd, false and prohibited doctrine that asserts almost all human beings inherit a corrupted soul, and tainted nature prone to sin because of the claimed first act of disobedience by Adam and Eve in the Garden of Eden, as described in the Book of Genesis; and

(iii) ***Divine Birthright as the Sole Custodians of Earth***: Absurd, false and prohibited doctrine whereby certain people and families falsely have historically claimed their bloodline heritage traces them back to Mary, mother of Jesus, or her relatives; and thus inferring to the rest of the ruling class that they are the sole custodians and only true heirs to planet Earth; and

(iv) ***Divine Forfeit of Rights by Lesser Birth***: Absurd, false and prohibited doctrine whereby the majority of people forfeit the rights promised to them by God because of the inheritance of sin (Original Sin) and their inherited sinful and lesser nature. Those forfeited rights are then "salvaged" and then conveyed and administered by the "Church" as the Body of Christ on Earth.

818. The false and erroneous doctrine of *Baptism as Right of Salvage of Lesser Souls* is hereby prohibited, condemned and to be suppressed in all its forms throughout all valid and proper Religious Denominations and Cults.

*False Doctrine, Prohibited & Suppressed*

## Article 202 – Gold as a Penitentiary Medium for Souls

819. ***Gold as a Penitentiary Medium for Souls*** is an absurd, false and prohibited notion whereby the medium as "penitentiary" of salvaged souls since 1934.

*Gold as a Penitentiary Medium for Souls*

820. Under Ancient Egyptian Religious Philosophy, Gold was considered the "Flesh of Amen-Re" with the power to protect the deceased in the afterlife and to ensure their safe passage to their final resting place:-

*Gold as the Flesh of "God"*

   (i)   The Egyptian gods were often depicted with golden skin, representing their divine and eternal nature. The sun god Ra, for example, was closely associated with gold, and his rays were believed to be made of the precious metal; and

   (ii)  Gold was extensively used in the burial practices of the ancient Egyptians. The pharaohs and high-ranking individuals were often buried with gold artefacts, jewellery, and even gold-covered coffins. The famous death mask of Tutankhamun is a prime example of this practice; and

   (iii) The Egyptians believed that gold had the power to protect the deceased in the afterlife and ensure their safe passage to the realm of the gods. This belief was based on the idea that gold could help the souls of the deceased be recognized and accepted by the gods.

821. Around September 11, 1919, the Bank of England took first delivery of a new standard size gold bar of 400 troy ounces from N.M. Rothschild & Sons, prior to opening of a new London Gold Fixing system using these gold bars on September 12:-

*400 troy ounce LGD bars as global standard*

   (i)   Prior to the Rothschild new 400 troy ounce LGD gold bar standard, there was no accepted global standard for gold bars. In Europe, gold bullion was typically measured in terms of a "kilobar" or roughly 32.15 troy ounces; and since 1816 (Coinage Act 1816 c. 68), the Bank of England standard had been 200 troy ounce bars; and the US Mint produced gold bars as small as 5 troy ounces and as a large as 100 troy ounces;

and

- (ii) The "LGD" of the new 400 troy ounce gold bars was explained in public as representing "London Good Delivery", whilst its secretive symbolism was *Lucifero Gloria Deo* meaning "Lightbringer (and) Glory be to God"; and

- (iii) In 1934, the United States passed the Gold Reserve Act of 1934 after almost all of the banks and treasuries across the sixty (60) members of League of Nations had fallen into bankruptcy. The effect of that was not only to nationalise and prohibit private ownership of gold coin, bullion and certificates, but to seize the gold assets of all other bankrupt countries in exchange for facilitating liquidity underwritten by the United States Dollar and facilitated through the US controlled Bank for International Settlements (BIS); and

- (iv) In 1934, with effectively the globalisation of gold control under the US Treasury, the standard of 400 troy ounce LGD gold bars was adopted as the global standard for gold bullion.

822. To the Ashkenazi and Zionist Cults that took firm control over Judaism from the 18th and then 19th centuries, the number 400 represents a deeply prophetic and supernatural number:- *The symbolism of 400*

- (i) 400 represents the numerical value of the last Hebraic letter "taw or tav" (ת), corresponding to the completion of the "Divine Plan"; the fulfilment and completeness of prophecy; and the last mystery of the Tarot being "the World"; and

- (ii) 400 in numerology is understood to signify something completed in its entirety; and the end of a "Reich" or age and the beginning of a new Reich.

823. While there exists no official published doctrine or acknowledgment, sufficient evidence exists to conclude that the use of gold itself as the occult underwriting of the US Dollar as the global currency under the Global American Empire took place from 1934 and has remained in place until the present day:- *The occult symbolism of gold and global financial system of American Empire*

- (i) Contrary to the infantile and absurd notion that modern "fiat" money is simply backed by the confidence of the public and economy, it appears that the removal of gold as a "backing standard" to was to elevate its status in underwriting as being the claimed supreme supernatural medium on earth under the American elite; and

- (ii) The concept of gold as a supernatural medium of underwriting is associated with one or more legal and financial instruments connected to modern secular medical human births enacting a religiously endorsed notion of "salvaging the souls" of human beings not part of the global elite, is then connected to central bank gold reserves, whereby the gold itself becomes the "penitentiary" and storehouse for such alleged salvaged souls.

824. The fundamental false doctrines underpinning the false, absurd and abhorrent notion of *Gold as a Penitentiary Medium for Souls* include (but are not limited to):- Fundamental False Doctrines underpinning Gold as a Penitentiary Medium for Souls

   (i) **Eternal Damnation & Unforgiveness**: Erroneous and false doctrinal belief in everlasting punishment for souls condemned after death and the state of not being forgiven by a God or Supreme Being; and

   (ii) **Suffering as Necessary Penance**: Erroneous and false doctrinal belief that enduring physical pain or hardship during life serves as a means of spiritual purification and atonement for sins, with promise of rewards in the afterlife; and

   (iii) **Divine Birthright as the Sole Custodians of Earth**: Absurd, false and prohibited doctrine whereby certain people and families falsely have historically claimed their bloodline heritage traces them back to Mary, mother of Jesus, or her relatives; and thus inferring to the rest of the ruling class that they are the sole custodians and only true heirs to planet Earth; and

   (iv) **Divine Forfeit of Rights by Lesser Birth**: Absurd, false and prohibited doctrine whereby the majority of people forfeit the rights promised to them by God because of the inheritance of sin (Original Sin) and their inherited sinful and lesser nature. Those forfeited rights are then "salvaged" and then conveyed and administered by the "Church" as the Body of Christ on Earth.; and

   (v) **Baptism as Right of Salvage (Salvation) of Lesser Souls**: Absurd, false and prohibited doctrine whereby Christian sacraments such as "baptism" and "extreme unction" have been secularised since 1917 and assigned to agents who may then perform such rites on new born infants, as well as produce legal and financial instruments connected to "salvation" as the salvage and possession of souls.

825. The false and erroneous doctrine of *Gold as a Penitentiary Medium for Souls* is hereby prohibited, condemned and to be suppressed in all its forms throughout all valid and proper Religious Denominations and Cults. False Doctrine, Prohibited & Suppressed

826. In accord with the most sacred Covenant *Pactum De Singularis Caelum*, Gold Credo represents the permanent ecclesiastical, lawful and legal extraction of the essence of all spiritual and temporal value of Gold from all the existing physical and elemental material into Ucadia Gold Credo (Credit).

*Non use of physical gold as currency*

Any and all ecclesiastical and official ceremonies, rites and rituals concerning physical gold and gold reserves are hereby prohibited, suppressed and never permitted to be revived.

The historical spiritual and temporal value of Gold through Ucadia Gold Credo (Credo) may continue to be used in underwriting legitimate currencies, however the physical material of gold is only permitted to be treated as a useful commodity or ceremonial event of significance.

Subject to *Carta Economia De Congregationis Globus (Globe Union Economic Charter)*, Physical Gold henceforth is strictly forbidden to be generally used as currency, money or the underwriting of money.

## Article 203 – Office of Lesser God on Earth Incapable of Error

827. ***Office of Lesser God on Earth Incapable of Error*** is an absurd, false and prohibited notion whereby elite families and officials since the end of the 19th Century have viewed themselves as lesser gods ruling the Earth and incapable of error.

*Office of Lesser God on Earth Incapable of Error*

828. The fundamental false doctrines underpinning the false, absurd and abhorrent notion of *Office of Lesser God on Earth Incapable of Error* include (but are not limited to):-

*Fundamental False Doctrines underpinning Office of Lesser God on Earth Incapable of Error*

   (i) ***Divine Favouritism & Exceptionalism***: Erroneous and false doctrinal belief that a particular group or individual is specially chosen and favoured by a deity, granting them unique privileges, protection or status; and

   (ii) ***Certain Persons as Incapable of Sin***: Absurd, false and prohibited doctrine whereby certain persons by the direct intervention of God or the Divine Creator are born without Inherited Original Sin, or by their birthright are *Incapable of Sin*; and

   (iii) ***Mary as Mother of God***: Absurd, false and prohibited doctrine whereby Mary as the mother of Jesus did also give birth to God incarnate. Therefore Mary is both technically and literally the Mother of God (*Theotokos*); and

   (iv) ***Divine Birthright as the Sole Custodians of Earth***: Absurd, false and prohibited doctrine whereby certain people and families falsely have historically claimed their bloodline heritage traces them back to Mary, mother of Jesus, or her relatives; and thus inferring to the rest of the ruling class that they are the sole custodians and only true heirs to planet Earth.

829. The false and erroneous doctrine of *Office of Lesser God on Earth Incapable of Error* is hereby prohibited, condemned and to be suppressed in all its forms throughout all valid and proper Religious Denominations and Cults.

*False Doctrine, Prohibited & Suppressed*

## Article 204 – Divine Birthrights as Lesser Gods over Earth

830. ***Divine Birthrights as Lesser Gods over Earth*** is an absurd, false and prohibited notion whereby those born into the most elite ruling families claim to inherit a birthright to rule as lesser Gods over the Earth.

*Divine Birthrights as Lesser Gods over Earth*

831. Some of the original Banking and Merchant Houses from 1855-56 that first declared themselves to hold the exclusive rights of *Custos Rotalorum* (Keeper of the Slave Rolls) and *Ius Gentium* (Customary Laws of Medieval Moneylending and Banking later "repackaged" as Law of Nations) as *Beit Miriam* (ית מרים) ("The House of Mary") include but are not limited to:-

*Founding Families of the Beit Miriam (House of Mary)*

   (i) **House of Rothschild**: The descendents of Thomas (Jacob) Roth (Wroth) (1584-1672), the first *Lord Chamberlain* (Treasurer) of the Commonwealth Government of Great Britain (1642-1660). The family originally being of famous Venetian origin, namely via exiled Jacopo (Jacob) Foscari (exiled to London in 1445), son of Doge Francesco Foscari (1423-1457). The name *Roth* variously meaning "red, disc, rim of wheel, fury and punishment" and was probably selected by the Foscari in England given the family history. After the death of Thomas (Oliver) Pride in 1658, the Roth left England to Hanover in Germany and the protection of the Dukes of Brunswick-Lüneburg as the "Rothschild" family, converting to Judaism. Thomas (Jacob) Roth (Rothschild) soon after became the unofficial Mayer (Mayor and Treasurer) of the city of Hanover and private bankers on behalf of the dukes. The family returned to London by 1757 after the death of family patriarch Mayer Amschel Jacob Rothschild (b.1710 – d.1757) following the Battle of Hastenbeck and brief occupation of the city of Hanover. Under Mayer Amschel Rothschild (b. 1734 – d. 1812) the Rothschilds repeatedly refused senior government positions, noble titles and offer to control the Bank of England by George III (1760-1820), arguing that any such position could put the Hanover monarchy at risk as well as the banking interests of the Rothschilds in jeopardy. By 1790, the Hanovers personally owed the Rothschilds over £30m and the crown through the City of London and Bank of England owed the Rothschilds more than £200m in growing senior debt. By 1799, the British Empire was technically bankrupt owing more than £700m and unable to continue to fund its military campaign against Napoleon. The Rothschilds successfully orchestrated that the whole British Empire and all its territories known as the Kingdom of Great Britain and Ireland be placed in bankruptcy by 1800, operating then as the United Kingdom, under the control of the Bank of London through the City of London that the Rothschilds then placed in private bankruptcy to its private banks. Mayer Amschel Rothschild then left for the city of Frankfurt where he lived until 1812. The Rothschild family did not officially have any direct members in New York until after 1870; and

(ii) **House of Stuyvesant**: The descendents of Peter Stuyvesant (1610-1672) the last Dutch Director-General of New Netherlands. The family for a time became viewed among the other families as the *defacto* sovereign when from 1784 the British crown fully restored the Dutch Republic rights to Manhattan Island, Albany New York and Newcastle Delaware; and

(iii) **House of Vanderbilt**: The descendents of the famous De Witt family that ruled Holland and were major shareholders of the Dutch East India Company (VOC) under the Dutch Republic until 1672. Historic enemies of the House of Orange-Nassau who returned to power in 1672 and murdered many of its members. As a result, the family was forced to flee with their ships and fortune to the old colony of New Amsterdam (now New York). It is where they changed their name and history to Vanderbilt and continued to be involved in the trade of the VOC, including moving its operations to New York from 1784. In the 19th Century they were regarded as one of the wealthiest families in the world; and

(iv) **House of Du Pont**: The descendents of the Amsterdam branch of the famous 16th Century Trip family of Swedish arms manufacturers. Under the Dutch Republic, the Trip family quickly became one of the wealthiest of all patrician families as primary investors of the Dutch West India Company (GWC). The family returned to its primary business of gunpowder and arms manufacturing after escaping to New York with other Patrician families by 1795, changing their name to "Du Pont" (meaning to travel or ferry). By the mid 19th Century was again one of the wealthiest families in the world; and

(v) ***House of Astor***: The descendents of the famous diamond and pearl merchant Kiliaen van Rensselaer (1586-1643), one of the founders of the Dutch West India Company and New Netherlands settlements. His land holding of Rensselaerswyck along the Hudson River made the family one of the richest land holders ever in America. Prior to losing the colonies by 1672, the van Rensselaer family had an early monopoly on the fur trade. Thereafter, the family switched its business interests to opium and the African slave trade, before escaping back to New York with other Patrician families by 1795. The rights of the van Rensselaer to Rensselaerswyck continued to be honoured by the American government to at least 1830s. In around 1812, the family changed its name to "Astor" after the fur trading post (Fort Astor) it established as part of a new monopoly along the Columbia River.

**832.** The false and erroneous doctrine of *Divine Birthrights as Lesser Gods over Earth* is hereby prohibited, condemned and to be suppressed in all its forms throughout all valid and proper Religious Denominations and Cults.

False Doctrine, Prohibited & Suppressed

# Title VI – Organisation

## 6.1 – Organisation

### Article 205 – Organisation

833. In ecclesiastical terms, an ***Organisation*** is a structured *Body, Organ* or *Entity* existing within a given *Religious or Spiritual Society*; and formed to carry out certain religious, charitable, educational, or other social functions that are consistent with ecclesiastical laws, doctrines and authority of the given religion:-

    (i) All Religions and Spiritual Societies are constructed from at least one or more Organisations; and

    (ii) Large and well established Religions are typically constructed around a hierarchy of Bodies and Organs and many hundreds and thousands of smaller Organisation Bodies and Entities; and

    (iii) An Organisation is invalid and illegitimate unless it conforms to these Maxims and the most sacred Covenant *Pactum De Singularis Caelum*.

834. A ***Religious or Spiritual Society*** or simply *Society* is a formal association of three or more persons, founded upon Civilised Principles consistent with the most sacred Covenant *Pactum De Singularis Caelum*; and distinguishable by a unique and well developed religious or spiritual culture, a comprehensive body of laws, a functioning system of government and a justice system capable of resolving disputes and issues arising under its proper and authentic Rules.

835. The primary distinction between Ecclesiastical Organisations as Bodies, Organs, Entities or Groups is:-

    (i) ***Body***: Is an organised group established by law or statute, such as legislative bodies, governing boards, or regulatory agencies. It implies a structured framework with specific duties and legal authority; and

    (ii) ***Organ***: Is a specific part or subdivision of a larger ecclesiastical body, focusing on a particular function or task within the broader mission of that body; and

    (iii) ***Entity***: Is an organisation with legal recognition, rights, and responsibilities, capable of entering into contracts, owning property, and being sued; and

    (iv) ***Group***: Is a collection of individuals united for a common purpose. It may or may not have formal legal recognition or structure.

836. *Organisations* from an ecclesiastical perspective may be broadly classified according to their *Function*, *Topology* and *Personality* within the broader community and society:- Organisation Type Classification

    (i) **Function**: Means the primary purpose of the Organisation including (but not limited to): religious worship, administration, religious orders, education, health and charity; and

    (ii) **Topology**: Means the structural, geographical and jurisdictional nature of the Organisation including (but not limited to): universal, regional, national, provincial or local; and

    (iii) **Personality**: Means the legal status and personality of the Organisation including (but not limited to): corporation sole, non-incorporated association, non-profit corporation, private corporation or public corporation.

## 6.2 – Organs

### Article 206 – Organs

837. An **Organ** is a specific vital part or subdivision of a larger ecclesiastical *Body* representing a distinct structural element concerning a particular function or task within the broader mission of that Body. Organs

838. *Organs* are hierarchical in terms of their authority, power and scope, including (but not limited to):- Classification and Hierarchy of Organs

    (i) **Divine Organs**: The highest possible Organs being those specific Organs named within the most sacred Covenant *Pactum De Singularis Caelum* and associated Covenants possessing legitimate Divine origins, authority, power and jurisdiction; and

    (ii) **Supernatural Organs**: The second highest possible Organs being those specific Organs named within the most sacred Covenant *Pactum De Singularis Caelum* and associated Covenants, Charters and Constitutions possessing legitimate Supernatural origins, authority, power and jurisdiction; and

    (iii) **Universal Organs**: The third highest possible Organs being those those specific Organs named within the most sacred Covenant *Pactum De Singularis Caelum* and associated Covenants, Charters and Constitutions possessing legitimate

Universal and temporal origins, authority, power and jurisdiction; and

(iv) **_Global Organs_**: The fourth highest possible ecclesiastical organs being those associated with a Global ecclesiastical body; and

(v) **_Regional Organs_**: The fifth highest possible ecclesiastical organs being those associated with a Regional ecclesiastical body; and

(vi) **_National Organs_**: The sixth highest possible ecclesiastical organs being those associated with a National ecclesiastical body; and

(vii) **_Provincial Organs_**: The second smallest ecclesiastical organs being those associated with an aggregate of local ecclesiastical bodies; and

(viii) **_Local Organs_**: The smallest possible Organs being those associated with a local ecclesiastical body.

839. The status of a specific vital part or subdivision of a larger ecclesiastical *Body* representing an Organ, does not preclude it from possessing its own distinct identity:- <small>Status of Ecclesiastical Organ as itself being an Office, Society, Body or Institute</small>

(i) **_Distinct Identity_**: Meaning an Organ may itself be an Office, Society, Body or Institute; and

(ii) **_Possessing is own Organs_**: Meaning that under its own distinct identity (as an Office, Society, Body or Institute etc.), an Organ may possess its own Organs.

840. By definition, any distinct organisational element identified as an Ecclesiastical Organ means its authority, power and jurisdiction are inherited from a higher element:- <small>Inheritance of Authority and Power of Ecclesiastical Organs</small>

(i) **_Organ as a part (of something greater)_**: Means that an Organ is a part of some larger structure; and

(ii) **_Organ as dependent_**: Means that an Organ cannot exist independently or alone, but is codependent on the larger structure and other Organs to function.

841. Examples of Divine Organs as defined by the most sacred Covenant *Pactum De Singularis Caelum* include (but are not limited to):- <small>Examples of Divine Organs</small>

(i) **_Sol Ecclesia_**: The permanent, perfect and irrevocable presence of the Holy Spirit personified as the *Sol Ecclesia* of the Universal Ecclesia of One Christ possessing an eternal and complete communion with God and the Divine Creator of all Existence and all Heaven and Earth; and

(ii) **One Umma (Divine Family)**: The permanent, perfect and irrevocable presence of the Spirit of God personified as the *One Umma* of the Holy Society possessing an eternal and complete communion between the Holy Society of One Islam and with God and the Divine Creator of all Existence and all Heaven and Earth; and

(iii) **Great Divine Spirit**: The permanent, perfect and irrevocable supernatural presence of the Divine Spirit personified as the *Great Divine Spirit* of the Sacred Society possessing an eternal and complete communion with the Divine Creator of all Existence and all Heaven and Earth.

842. Examples of Supernatural Organs as defined by the most sacred Covenant *Pactum De Singularis Caelum* include (but are not limited to):- Examples of Supernatural Organs

(i) **Living Body of Christ**: All Living Members of the Universal Ecclesia of One Christ as being incorporated into the true Living Body of Christ as one united family; and the fulfilment of Sacred Scripture in the return and permanent presence of Christ; and

(ii) **Living Body of Mahdi**: All Living Members of the Holy Society of One Islam as being incorporated into the true Living Body of Mahdi as one united family; and the fulfilment of Sacred Scripture in the return and permanent presence of Mahdi; and

(iii) **Living Body of Maitreya**: All Living Members of the Sacred Society of One Spirit as being incorporated into the true Living Body of Maitreya as one united family; and the fulfilment of Sacred Scripture in the return and permanent presence of Maitreya.

## Article 207 – Universal Organ

843. ***Universal Organs*** refers to an authoritative body near or at the highest level of a larger ecclesiastical Body, or an essential and global functioning body between religious and international institutions. Universal Organ

844. Examples of Universal Organs as defined by the most sacred Covenant *Pactum De Singularis Caelum* include (but are not limited to):- Examples of Universal Organs

(i) **Universal Ecclesia of One Christ**: As the one, true and authentic Kingdom of One Christ and Heaven upon the Earth; and

(ii) ***Holy Society of One Islam*** : As the one, true and authentic Kingdom of One Islam and Heaven upon the Earth; and

(iii) ***Sacred Society of One Spirit***: As the one, true and authentic Kingdom of One Spirit and Heaven upon the Earth; and

(iv) ***Society of Light***: As the Sons of Light and Fraternal Brothers and Sisters of Light, dedicated to the fulfilment of the present sacred Covenant, the evangelical mission of proclaiming the Good News of the fulfilment of sacred Scripture and the unity of Heaven and Earth through the manifestation of the Kingdom of Heaven upon the Earth in accord with the most sacred Covenants *Pactum De Singularis Caelum*, *Pactum De Singularis Christus*, *Pactum De Singularis Islam* and *Pactum De Singularis Spiritus*.

845. Examples of Global Organs as defined by the most sacred Covenant *Pactum De Singularis Caelum* include (but are not limited to):- — *Examples of Global Organs*

(i) ***Supreme Patriarch***: As the sovereign monarch, supreme pastor and primary father of the Universal Ecclesia of One Christ; and

(ii) ***Supreme Caliph***: As the sovereign monarch, supreme teacher and primary father of the Holy Society of One Islam; and

(iii) ***Supreme Recurrence***: As the sovereign monarch, supreme teacher and primary father of the Sacred Society of One Spirit.

## Article 208 – Union (Regional) Organ

846. A ***Union (Regional) Organ*** refers to a governing body or council of a larger ecclesiastical *Body* that operates within a specific geographic and multinational area, often tasked with overseeing and implementing policies, regulations and practices in that region. — *Union (Regional) Organ*

847. Examples of Regional and Global Multifaith Organs include (but are not limited to):- — *Examples of Regional and Global Multifaith Organs*

(i) ***Alliance of Civilizations*** (founded by UN in 2005): High-level forums, youth conferences and media projects focusing on intercultural dialogue; and

(ii) ***World Interfaith Harmony Week*** (founded by UN in 2010): A week-long series of events every first week of February encouraging interfaith dialogue and projects worldwide; and

(iii) ***International Centre for Interreligious and Intercultural Dialogue*** (founded by UAE in 2012): Hosting of dialogues, training programs and research projects aimed at conflict resolution; and

(iv) ***World Conference of Religions for Peace*** (founded in 1961): Facilitates interfaith dialogue and action tracks that include addressing issues like violence against women, environmental justice and pandemic response.

**848.** Examples of Regional and Global Christian Organs include (but are not limited to):- *Examples of Regional and Global Christian Organs*

(i) ***World Council of Churches (WCC)*** (founded in 1948): International Christian ecumenical organization that includes many Protestant, Orthodox, Anglican and Old Catholic churches. It aims to promote Christian unity and engage in interfaith dialogue; and

(ii) ***Pontifical Council for Interreligious Dialogue*** (founded in 1964): A dicastery of the Roman Catholic Church dedicated to promoting mutual understanding, respect, and collaboration between Catholics and followers of other religious traditions; and

(iii) ***All Africa Conference of Churches (AACC)*** (founded in 1963): A fellowship of churches and Christian councils in Africa that seeks to promote Christian unity, development, and social justice on the continent; and

(iv) ***Christian Conference of Asia (CCA)*** (founded in 1957): A regional ecumenical organization that includes Protestant and Orthodox churches across Asia. It aims to promote unity, development, and peace among its member churches; and

(v) ***Conference of European Churches (CEC)*** (founded in 1959): An ecumenical organization that brings together Orthodox, Protestant, Anglican, and Old Catholic churches in Europe for dialogue and collaboration; and

(vi) ***Middle East Council of Churches (MECC)*** (founded in 1974): Brings together different Christian traditions in the Middle East to foster unity among churches and engage in dialogue with other religious communities; and

(vii) ***Latin American Council of Churches (CLAI)*** (founded in 1982): An ecumenical body that includes various Protestant denominations across Latin America focused on promoting unity and social justice; and

(viii) ***National Council of Churches (NCC)*** (founded in 1950): A diverse Christian ecumenical organization that includes Protestant, Anglican, Orthodox, Evangelical, historic African American, and Living Peace churches in the United States; and

(ix) ***Canadian Council of Churches (CCC)*** (founded in 1944): An ecumenical organization that includes various Christian denominations across Canada working collaboratively on issues of common concern.

### Article 209 – University (National) Organ

849. A ***University (National) Organ*** refers to a key body, institution or council of a larger ecclesiastical *Body* that within a nation holds significant authority or function. Typically, a *University (National) Organ* represents central structures such as the executive, legislative, judiciary, or specific religious bodies that play fundamental roles in governance and societal regulation.

University (National) Organ

### Article 210 – Province (State) Organs

850. A ***Province (State) Organ*** refers to a governing body or council of a larger ecclesiastical *Body* within a province of a religious order or ecclesiastical province. A *Province (State) Organ* typically acts as an intermediary between local communities and the higher central authority, facilitating communication and decision-making within its defined jurisdiction, while ensuring compliance with the broader rules of the order or ecclesiastical body.

Province (State) Organs

### Article 211 – Campus (Local) Organ

851. A ***Campus (Local) Organ*** refers to a governing body or administrative unit of a smaller ecclesiastical *Body* within a specific local geographic area. A *Campus (Local) Organ* typically is responsible for implementing and overseeing the rules, regulations, and functions of the ecclesiastical organisation at the local level.

Campus (Local) Organ

## 6.3 – Ecclesiastical Jurisdiction

### Article 212 – Ecclesiastical Jurisdiction

852. ***Ecclesiastical Jurisdiction*** refers to the authority exercised by ecclesiastical leaders or institutions over matters of doctrine, discipline, and governance within a religious community as part of a larger *Religious or Spiritual Society*. Ecclesiastical Jurisdiction typically includes the power to make and enforce rules, adjudicate

Ecclesiastical Jurisdiction

disputes, and oversee the spiritual well-being of members independently of secular legal systems.

853. Ecclesiastical Jurisdiction within a larger *Religious or Spiritual Society* is usually hierarchical and organised around levels of territorial authority or rank, including (but not limited to):-

    (i)    ***Universal***: The highest authority and reserved for the most important Organs, Bodies and Entities; and

    (ii)    ***Union (Regional)***: The second highest authority covering multi-national or continental geographic areas; and

    (iii)    ***National***: The third highest authority relating to a nation-state; and

    (iv)    ***Provincial***: The second lowest authority relating to a group of local and distinct geographic areas; and

    (v)    ***Local***: A distinct geographic area and usually the lowest form of ecclesiastical jurisdiction.

*Hierarchy of Ecclesiastical Jurisdiction*

## Article 213 – Universal Ecclesiastical Jurisdiction

854. ***Universal Ecclesiastical Jurisdiction*** is the highest temporal authority asserted by the highest *Body, Organ* or *Entity* existing within a given *Religious or Spiritual Society* to make and enforce laws, decisions or judgements over its members.

*Universal Ecclesiastical Jurisdiction*

855. ***Kuria*** (Curia) was the largest ecclesiastical and administrative division of an official Christian body since the first formation of Christianity in 314 CE by Constantine. A Curia was comprised of several subdivisions called Politia (Politea):-

*Kuria (Curia)*

    (i)    The Supreme See or Sacred See or "sacropolis sedos" in Ancient Greek was the nominated capital city of a Kuria (Curia) and the home of the leading spiritual, legal and administrative head known as an Exharchos (ἔξαρχος) or "Exarch"; and

    (ii)    The primary building symbolizing the seat of power or "sacropolis sedos" was known as a Kathedra (καθέδρα) or "Cathedral" as the seat of "supreme authority"; and

    (iii)    The first Kuria (Curia) in history (from 314 CE) were Borealia (North See), Australia (South See), Europalia (West See) and Orientalia (East Sea) corresponding to the four cardinal directions emanating from Antioch (Constantinople); and

    (iv)    The first Exharchos or Exarchs in history (from 314 CE) were Mattatheos (Perinthos) Exarchos of Borealia (North), Markos

Achilles (Marcus Aurelius Cornelius Achilleus) Exarchos of Australia (South), Lukhas Eusebius (Lucius Aurelius Cornelius Adeptius) Exarchos of Europealia (West) and Iohannes (Constantinos) Exarchos of Orientalia (East). Until the 16th Century and introduction of false, deceptive and misleading curses or "god spells" by the Roman Cult, the original four Exarchs were simply known as Matthew, Mark, Luke and John; and

(v) The Supreme See or Sacred See or "sacropolis sedos" as the capitals of the Kuria (Curia) in history (from 314 CE) were the Supreme See of Borealia (North See) named Galatia on the north bank of the Danube River Delta and Black Sea, the Supreme See of Australia (South See) named Alexandria on the Nile River Delta and the Mediterranean Sea, the Supreme See of Europalia (West See) named Philippi (Thessalonika) on the Axios River Delta and the Mediterranean Sea and the Supreme See of Orientalia (East Sea) named Samson (Samsun) at the deltas of the Mert and Halys rivers and the Black Sea in northern Anatolia; and

(vi) The structures of the Kuria (Curia) collapsed during the mid 5th Century CE and were formally abolished in the 6th Century with the schism between Eastern (Byzantine) Christianity and Western (Orthodox) Christianity, until being resurrected by Giovanni di Lorenzo de Medici as AntiPope Leo in 1514; and

(vii) In 1536 Alessandro Farnese (Orsini) as Antipope Paul expanded the role of the resurrected Curia to introduce the new concept of the College of Cardinals whereby all the Patrician merchant pirate families of the major Italian city-states would be represented on a council and that future AntiPopes would be elected, rather then seize power by siege and murder of their predecessor; and

(viii) By 1588, Pope Sixtus established the fifteen (15) permanent congregations, each with specific responsibilities, effectively creating the modern structure of the Curia.

856. ***Khalifah*** (Caliphate) was the largest ecclesiastical and administrative division of an official Islamic body from the 7th Century until 14th Century. In accord with the most sacred scripture *Lebor Clann Glas*, the formation of the first Khalifah (Caliphates) of Islam include:-

(i) ***Al-Rashid (Egypt)***: The first Khalifah (Caliphate) of Islam and formed in 605 CE. The name *Al-Rashid* means "the rightly guided people of God". The two Emarah (Emirate) were *Al-*

Khalifah (Caliphate)

Lex Ecclesiasticum: Maxims of Ecclesiastical Law

*Niliyah* meaning "the place of the Nile Delta"; and *Al-Misrah* meaning "the place of Holly (Hyksos) Civilisation"; and

(ii) **Al-Fatimid (Arabia and Yemen)**: The second Khalifah (Caliphate) of Islam and formed in 613 CE. The name *Al-Fatimid* means "the people of illumination and enlightenment". The three Emarah (Emirate) were *Al-Najadah* meaning "the place elevated by heaven"; and *Al-Tawalisiyah* meaning "the place of legendary convergence"; and *Al-Hadramah* meaning "the place of ancient settlement"; and

(iii) **Al-Abbasid (Levant)**: The third Khalifah (Caliphate) of Islam and formed in 636 CE. The name *Al-Abbasid* means "the people of the fearsome lions". The five Emarah (Emirate) were *Falastinah* meaning "the place of the ancient sleeve (arm) of the almighty"; and *Lubnaniyah* meaning "the place of the sacred white mountains"; and *Suriyah* meaning "the place of the sacred rivers and waters"; and *Urdunah* meaning "the place of the sacred river valley"; and *Rumaniyah* meaning "the place of the sacred orchards"; and

(iv) **Al-Samanid (Persia)**: The fourth Khalifah (Caliphate) of Islam and formed in 637 CE. The name *Al-Samanid* means "people of (first) home, right and worthy culture". The four Emarah (Emirate) were *Azharbahjah* (north western Persia) meaning "place of beautiful and colourful flowers"; and *Jibalah* (south-west Persia) meaning "the place of the great mountains"; and *Farsah* (south east Persia) meaning "place of ancient stones and sacred monuments"; and *Khorasah* (eastern Persia) meaning "place of first sight of the sun"; and

(v) **Al-Aghlabid (Libya)**: The fifth Khalifah (Caliphate) of Islam and formed in 647 CE. The name *Al-Aghlabid* means "the people who overcome and prevail". The three Emarah (Emirate) were *Barqah* (East Libya) meaning "the place of flashes of lightning"; and *Tarabulah* (West Libya) meaning "the place of the three cities"; and *Qartajannah* (Tunisia) meaning "the place of the new city"; and

(vi) **Al-Soudid (Sudan)**: The sixth Khalifah (Caliphate) of Islam and formed in 651 CE. The name *Al-Soudid* means "the people of strength and protectors of faith". The three Emarah (Emirate) were *Alwah* (north western Persia) meaning "the people of the high mountains"; and *Nubatah* (Nubatia) meaning "the Nubian people"; and *Makurah* (Makuria) meaning "the people of the Upper Nile"; and

(vii) ***Al-Safarid (Afghanistan)***: The seventh Khalifah (Caliphate) of Islam and formed in 664 CE. The name *Al-Safarid* means "the people of the spiritual journey of faith". The four Emarah (Emirate) were *Hazah* (north); and *Tatah* (north-east); and *Aimah* (south-west); and *Pashtah* (central south); and

(viii) ***Al-Rustamid (Algeria)***: The eighth Khalifah (Caliphate) of Islam and formed in 698 CE. The name *Al-Rustamid* means "the strong and firm people"; and

(ix) ***Al-Andalus (Southern Spain)***: The ninth Khalifah (Caliphate) of Islam and formed in 744 CE. The name *Al-Andalus* means "the sacred land of the Andalusian people". The three Emarah (Emirate) were *Aragoniah* (north-east); and *Cataloniah* (south-east); and *Cordobah* (south); and

(x) ***Al-Salihid (Morocco)***: The tenth Khalifah (Caliphate) of Islam and formed in 745 CE. The name Al-Salihid means "the people who are righteous and virtuous". The three Emarah (Emirate) were *Nekah* (mountains); and *Barghawah* (coast); and *Sijilmasah* (edge of Sahara); and

(xi) ***Al-Rumi (Southern Italy)***: The eleventh Khalifah (Caliphate) of Islam and formed in 747 CE. The name *Al-Rumi* means "the land of the Romans". The three Emarah (Emirate) were *Siqaliyah* (Sicily); and *Salamah* (Salerno); and *Ambariah* (Umbria).

## Article 214 – Union (Regional) Ecclesiastical Jurisdiction

857. ***Union (Regional) Ecclesiastical Jurisdiction*** refers to an ecclesiastical governance structure within a larger Religious or Spiritual Society that encompasses a specific multi-nation or continental geographical area. A *Union (Regional) Ecclesiastical Jurisdiction* typically includes administrative, liturgical, and pastoral responsibilities, ensuring adherence to doctrinal and canonical standards.

<small>Union (Regional) Ecclesiastical Jurisdiction</small>

## Article 215 – University (National) Ecclesiastical Jurisdictions

858. ***University (National) Ecclesiastical Jurisdiction*** is an ecclesiastical governance structure of a larger Religious or Spiritual Society that operates within the boundaries of a nation-state. These jurisdictions usually oversee religious practices, administration, and laws in alignment with both the national context and broader

<small>University (National) Ecclesiastical Jurisdictions</small>

ecclesiastical authority.

859. ***Politia*** (Politic, or Body Politic), is the second largest ecclesiastical and administrative division of an official Christian body since the first formation of Christianity in 314 CE by Constantine. A Politia is comprised of several subdivisions known as Diokesia (Diocese):-     Politia (Politea)

   (i)     The Metropolitan See or "metropolis sedos" in Ancient Greek was the nominated capital city of a particular political city-state or "Politia" and the home of the spiritual, legal and administrative head known as a Patriarchos (πατριάρχος) or "Patriarch". The term Patriarchos meaning literally "the ruler, leader and father of the Christian tribe or people"; and

   (ii)     The primary building symbolizing the seat of power or "metropolis sedos" was known as a Basilikos (βασιλικος) or "Basilica" as the seat of "regional authority"; and

   (iii)     The first Politia (Body Politic) in history (from 314 CE) were nine (9) Politia of Borealia (North See), nine (9) Politia of Australia (South See), nine (9) Politia of Europalia (West See) and nine (9) Politia of Orientalia (East See) corresponding to the four cardinal directions emanating from Antioch (Constantinople); and

   (iv)     The first Politia (Body Politic) of Borealia (North See) were Bulgaria, Hungaria, Alania, Vandalia, Sarmatia, Lithuania, Latvia, Estonia and Rusia; and

   (v)     The first Politia (Body Politic) of Australia (South See) were Barbaria (Morocco), Algeria, Gaetulia, Garamantia, Libia, Egyptia, Ethiopia, Sinopia and Somalia; and

   (vi)     The first Politia (Body Politic) of Europalia (West See) were Alba, Irenia (Ireland), Spania, Francia, Italia, Saxonia, Slavia, Macedonia and Hellas; and

   (vii)     The first Politia (Body Politic) of Orientalia (East Sea) were Anatolia, Armenia, Syria, Palestinia, Mesopotamia, Abbysinia (Yemen), Assyria, Saracenia (Arabia) and Persia; and

   (viii)     The first Metropolitan Sees of Borealia (North See) were Odessos (Varna) at the Panisos [Kamchiya] Delta on the Black Sea as the Metropolis of Bulgaria, Tergesti (Trieste) at the Isonzo Delta on the Adriatic Sea as the Metropolis of Hungaria, Kherson at the Dnieper Delta on the Black Sea as the Metropolis of Alania, Tanais (Rostov-na-Donu) at the Don Delta on the Black Sea as the Metropolis of Vandalia, Aticca (Atyrau) at the Ural Delta on the Caspian Sea as the

Metropolis of Sarmatia, Nema at the Nemos (Nemunas) River Delta on the Baltic Sea as the Metropolis of Lithuania, Riga at the Dyna (Daugava) River Delta on the Baltic Sea as the Metropolis of Latvia, Narva at the Narva River Delta on the Baltic Sea as the Metropolis of Estonia and Rusa (St Petersburg) at the Rusa River Delta on the Baltic Sea as the Metropolis of Rusia; and

(ix) The first Metropolitan Sees of Australia (South See) were Timogadi (Nador) at the Nadir River Delta on the Meditteranean Sea as the Metropolis of Barbaria, Saldae (Bejaia) at the Algolis (Soummam) River Delta on the Mediterranean Sea as the Metropolis of Algeria, Abes (Gabes) at the Triton River Delta on the Mediterranean Sea as the Metropolis of Gaetulia, Zanadu at the Zanadis River Delta on the Mediterranean Sea as the Metropolis of Garamantia, Berenice (Benghazi) at the Baris River Delta on the Mediterranean Sea as the Metropolis of Libia, Zion (Suez) at the Zion Delta on the Red Sea as the Metropolis of Egyptia, Saladin on Axumir at the Axumir (Mareb) River Delta on the Red Sea as the Metropolis of Ethiopia, Aela (Aqaba) at the Jordan Delta on the Red Sea as the Metropolis of Sinopia, and Zeila (Djibouti) at the Adama (Awash) River Delta on the Red Sea as the Metropolis of Somalia; and

(x) The first Metropolitan Sees of Europalia (West See) were Hollyrood at the Firth of Forth on the North Sea as the Metropolis of Alba, Dublin at the Liffey Delta on the Irish Sea as the Metropolis of Irenia, Iberia (Amposta/Tortosa) at the Ebro Delta on the Mediterranean Sea as the Metropolis of Spania, Arles at the Rhone Delta on the Mediterranean Sea as the Metropolis of Francia, Philadelphia at the Po Delta on the Adriatic Sea as the Metropolis of Italia, Mantas (Hamburg) at the Elbe Delta on the North Sea as the Metropolis of Saxonia (Germany), Spoleto (Split) at the Cetina Delta on the Adriatic Sea as the Metropolis of Slavia, Ulkini (Ulcinj) at the Buna Delta on the Adriatic Sea as the Metropolis of Macedonia and Hella at the Evros Delta on the Aegean Sea as the Metropolis of Hellas; and

(xi) The first Metropolitan Sees of Orientalia (East See) were Nicomedia (Izmit) at the Sakarya Delta on the Black Sea as the Metropolis of Anatolia, Sarvan (Shirvan) at the Cyrus Delta on the Caspian Sea as the Metropolis of Armenia, Laodicia (Samandag) at the Orontes Delta on the Mediterranean Sea as the Metropolis of Syria, Gaza at the Gazah Delta on the

Mediterranean Sea as the Metropolis of Palestinia, Chaldos (Kuwait City) at the Euphrates/Chaldon [Pishon] Delta on the Persian Gulf as the Metropolis of Mesopotamia, Adana (Aden) at the Abb (Ibb) River Delta on the Persian Gulf as the Metropolis of Abbysinia (Yemen), Basra at the Euphrates/Tigris Delta on the Gulf of Aden as the Metropolis of Assyria, Telma (Dilmun) at the Ashar (Aftan) River Delta on the Persian Gulf as the Metropolis of Saracenia and Commercion (Gameron) at the Shoor River on the Persian Gulf as the Metropolis of Persia.

## Article 216 – Provincial Ecclesiastical Jurisdiction

860. ***Provincial Ecclesiastical Jurisdiction*** is a territorial ecclesiastical jurisdiction of a larger Religious or Spiritual Society and typically overseen by a senior cleric office.

    *Provincial Ecclesiastical Jurisdiction*

861. A ***Diokesia*** (Diocese) is the second smallest ecclesiastical and administrative division of an official Christian body since the first formation of Christianity in 314 CE by Constantine. A Diokesia (Diocese) is comprised of several subdivisions known as Paroikia (Parish or Parochial):-

    *Diokesia (Diocese)*

    (i)    The Episcopal See or "episcopolis sedos" in Ancient Greek was the nominated city of a particular region or state within the boundaries of a "Diakesia" and the home of the spiritual, legal and administrative head known as a Monarkhos (μόναρχος) or "Monarch". The term Monarkhos meaning literally "sole ruler"; and

    (ii)    The primary building symbolizing the seat of power or Episcopal See (episcopolis sedos) was known as a Sunagoga (συναγωγή) or "Synagogue" as the seat of "local state or city authority".

862. The word Diocese comes from the Ancient Greek διοίκησις (dioikēsis) meaning "internal administration". The word does not originate from Ancient Latin. The claim that Emperor Diocletian first introduced the term "diocese" is deliberately false and designed to diminish clarity as the administrative design and structure of the Holly Christian Empire.

    *Origin of word Diokesia (Diocese)*

## Article 217 – Local Ecclesiastical Jurisdiction

863. ***Local Ecclesiastical Jurisdiction*** refers to the authority exercised by an ecclesiastical leader of a specific local geographic area. *Local Ecclesiastical Jurisdiction* often encompasses

    *Local Ecclesiastical Jurisdiction*

administrative, liturgical, and disciplinary matters, guiding the spiritual and organisational aspects of the church within that locality.

864. A ***Paroikia*** (Parish or Parochial) is the smallest ecclesiastical and administrative division of an official Christian body since the first formation of Christianity in 314 CE by Constantine.

*Paroikia (Parish)*

865. The word Paroikia (παροικία) originates from Ancient Greek and the first formation of Christianity in 314 CE under Constantine and literally means "constituted (Christian) communities or neighbourhoods". The word comes from the combination of the Ancient Greek words para (παρά) meaning "beside; or equal" and oikos (οικος) meaning "house, or dwelling".

*Origin of word Paroika*

## 6.4 – Ecclesiastical Institution

### Article 218 – Ecclesiastical Institution

866. An ***Institution*** or ***Institute***, is a formal organisation established under the authority and laws of a given *Religious or Spiritual Society* to advance a specific religious, educational, vocational or charitable mission.

*Institution*

867. Ecclesiastical Institutions may be classified according to two primary categories:-

*Classification of Ecclesiastical Institutions*

   (i) ***Consecrated***: Means an Institution formally dedicated and set apart for a sacred purpose, rendering it and associated buildings and facilities devoted to divine service; and

   (ii) ***Secular***: Means an Institution not directly dedicated or set apart for a specific sacred purpose. An Institution formed for temporal, civil and societal interest.

868. The deed, instrument or rules of an Institution is invalid unless it conforms to these Maxims and the most sacred Covenant *Pactum De Singularis Caelum*.

*Valid Ecclesiastical Institutions*

### Article 219 – Consecrated Ecclesiastical Institution

869. ***Consecrated Ecclesiastical Institution*** is an Institution formally dedicated and set apart for a sacred purpose, rendering it and associated buildings and facilities devoted to divine service.

*Consecrated Ecclesiastical Institution*

870. Examples of types of *Consecrated Ecclesiastical Institutions* include (but are not limited to):-

*Examples of Types of Consecrated Ecclesiastical Institution*

   (i) ***Monastic Orders***: These institutes focus on a life of prayer and work, often in a cloistered setting; and

(ii) **Mendicant Orders**: These communities rely on alms and have a strong emphasis on preaching and missionary work; and

(iii) **Clerical Religious Congregations**: These are primarily composed of priests who engage in various forms of pastoral work; and

(iv) **Apostolic Religious Congregations**: These institutes focus on active apostolic works such as education, healthcare, and social services.

### Article 220 – Secular Ecclesiastical Institution

871. *Secular Ecclesiastical Institution* is an Institution not directly dedicated or set apart for a specific sacred purpose. An Institution formed for temporal, civil and societal interest. — Secular Ecclesiastical Institution

872. Examples of types of *Secular Ecclesiastical Institutions* include (but are not limited to):- — Examples of Types of Secular Ecclesiastical Institutions

    (i) *Secular Institutes*: Members of secular institutes live in the world and strive for perfection through the profession of evangelical counsels (poverty, chastity and obedience), but they do not live in the community: and

    (ii) *Societies of Apostolic Life*: Members of these societies do not take religious vows but live in community and pursue a specific apostolic purpose; and

    (iii) *Lay Associations*: These are groups affiliated with a particular religious order, consisting of laypeople who live according to the spirit of the order while remaining in their secular state.

## 6.5 – Ecclesiastical Corporation

### Article 221 – Ecclesiastical Corporation

873. An *Ecclesiastical Corporation* is a legal entity formed by individuals in their capacity as members or officials of a given *Religious* or *Spiritual Society* and registered within the jurisdiction of one (or more) secular societies. — Ecclesiastical Corporation

874. An *Ecclesiastical Corporation* is an authorised legal entity registered and subject to the jurisdiction of one (or more) secular societies, whereas an *Ecclesiastical Institution* is an entity entirely first formed under the authority and laws of a given *Religious* or *Spiritual Society*. An Institution does not first need to exist to form an *Ecclesiastical* — Ecclesiastical Corporation and Institution

*Corporation*.

Ecclesiastical Corporations may be classified according to two primary categories:-

    (i)    ***Asset***: Meaning a Corporation registered for the management of one or more Assets; and

    (ii)    ***Service***: Meaning a Corporation registered for the delivery of one or more Products or Services.

Classification of Ecclesiastical Corporations

875. The deed, instrument or rules of an Ecclesiastical Corporation is invalid unless it conforms to these Maxims and the most sacred Covenant *Pactum de Singularis Caelum*.

Valid Ecclesiastical Corporations

### Article 222 – Ecclesiastical Asset Corporation

876. ***Ecclesiastical Asset Corporation*** refers to a Corporation established to manage property or resources owned by one or more Ecclesiastical Institutions, such as a local place of worship, territorial jurisdiction, or religious order. These assets can include land, buildings, investments, cash, funds, religious artefacts, and other valuable items used for religious, charitable, vocational or educational purposes.

Ecclesiastical Religious Corporation

### Article 223 – Ecclesiastical Service Corporation

877. ***Ecclesiastical Service Corporation*** refers to a Corporation established to manage the delivery of products, goods and services of a religious, charitable, health, assistance, vocational or educational purpose.

Ecclesiastical Service Corporation

## 6.6 – False and Prohibited Ecclesiastical Institutions

### Article 224 – False and Prohibited Ecclesiastical Institutions

878. ***False and Prohibited Ecclesiastical Institutions*** are unauthorized, fraudulent religious entities and their practices not sanctioned by a recognised religious or spiritual authority, or culpable of directly violating the laws of the religious or spiritual body.

False and Prohibited Ecclesiastical Institutions

879. The inherit right of freedom of religious and spiritual worship demands that any and all claims of unauthorized, fraudulent religious entities and any alleged practices are not themselves misguided, misinformed, false or intentionally malicious:-

    (i)    ***Primacy of Jurisdiction***: Means those religious and

Freedom of Religious Worship and False and Prohibited Ecclesiastical Institutions and spiritual faiths and entities named within the most sacred Covenant *Pactum De Singularis Caelum* possess absolute and primary authority to adjudicate all matters and offences concerning individuals who affiliate as a member to one (or more) of those particular faiths; and

(ii) **Limitation of Jurisdiction**: Means an individual who declares themselves a member of a faith not named or covered by the jurisdiction of the faiths mentioned within the most sacred Covenant *Pactum De Singularis Caelum* is beyond the reach and authority of one or more of those faiths when such bodies express their Primacy of Jurisdiction; and

(iii) Civilised Rule of Law: Means that any prosecution is done under Civilised Rule of Law and Procedures.

# Title VII – Systems

## 7.1 – Systems

### Article 225 – Systems

880. All ecclesiastical, sovereign and administrative support, services, skills and resources of a valid Religious or Spiritual Society at each and every level of jurisdiction and administration is divided into permanent and standard Systems.

    The Twenty Two Systems generally recognised for a valid Religious or Spiritual Society under the most sacred Covenant *Pactum De Singularis Caelum* include (but are not limited to):-

    (i) Religious Associations, Institutes and Societies Systems; and

    (ii) Ecclesiastical Unions, Universities & Diplomatic Systems; and

    (iii) Ecclesiastical Province & Campus Systems; and

    (iv) Vocational & Clerical Systems; and

    (v) Evangelical, Devotional & Veneration Systems; and

    (vi) Doctrinal & Liturgical Systems; and

    (vii) Sacred Rites & Tradition Systems; and

    (viii) Ecumenical & Collegial Systems; and

    (ix) Families and Community Life Systems; and

    (x) Member Assistance & Charitable Systems; and

    (xi) Knowledge and Education Systems; and

    (xii) Justice and Jurisprudence Systems; and

    (xiii) Health and Therapeutic Systems; and

    (xiv) Technology & Scientific Systems; and

    (xv) Banking, Finance & Economic Systems; and

    (xvi) Environmental Protection & Preservation Systems; and

    (xvii) Ethical Agriculture, Food & Organic Systems; and

    (xviii) Military & Security Systems; and

    (xix) Media & Communications Systems; and

    (xx) Facilities, Constructions & Preservation Systems; and

(xxi) Heritage, Arts & Cultural Systems; and

(xxii) Administrative & Logistical Systems.

881. Each and every System of a valid Religious or Spiritual Society shall be represented by a suitably qualified, competent and dedicated Senior Cleric as its Head. The Head of a System shall also be known as a General.  *Head of System*

882. The General Powers of a Head shall be those powers and authorities defined and granted in accord with the present Maxims and associated sacred Covenants of *Pactum De Singularis Christus*, *Pactum De Singularis Islam* and *Pactum De Singularis Spiritus*, notwithstanding any and all additional responsibilities granted in writing prescribed by Law. The powers and authorities are:-  *General Powers of System Head*

   (i) Oversight and responsibility for the planning, budgeting, efficiency and operation of the Systems, Divisions and the Departments under its control; and

   (ii) Notwithstanding Ecclesiastical and Legal considerations, the general identification of suitable talented personnel and the interview and recruitment of personnel to the System and Divisions; and

   (iii) The day-to-day tasks, activities and productivity of personnel assigned to the System and Divisions; and

   (iv) The immediate behaviour, culture and discipline of members of the Division and all its Departments.

883. Excluding Secretariats, all Systems of valid Religious or Spiritual Society shall follow the same rules of Organisational Structure in defining subdivisions within itself:-  *Standard Structure of Systems*

   (i) *Unit* shall be the term used to describe a subdivision of a Section whereby ten (10) or more people, to a maximum of one hundred and twenty (120) people function according to some technical function and mandate; and

   (ii) *Section* shall be the term used to describe a subdivision of a Department whereby twenty (20) or more people, to a maximum of three hundred and sixty (360) people function according to some technical function and mandate; and

   (iii) *Department* shall be the term used to describe a subdivision of a Division whereby thirty (30) or more people, to a maximum of two thousand (2000) people function according to some general division of services; and

(iv) *Division* shall be the term used to describe the largest organ of the twenty-two primary Systems of a valid Religious or Spiritual Society.

884. A Department is a subdivision of a Division of a valid Religious or Spiritual Society, whereby thirty or more people, to a maximum of two thousand people function according to some general division of services. All Departments are constructed from Sections of between twenty to three hundred and sixty people; and all Sections are constructed from Units of between ten to one hundred and twenty people.

Departments

There are primarily two types of Departments of Divisions of a valid Religious or Spiritual Society, being Internal and External:-

(i) An *Internal* Department is when a particular Department provides services and functions only to the Division that it belongs. Therefore the primary direction of service of the Department are other Departments of other Divisions of the valid Religious or Spiritual Society; and

(ii) An *External* Department is when a particular Department provides services or goods or functions to Members or non-Members.

885. There are nine key types of Internal Departments, notwithstanding other Internal Departments that may be approved from time to time:-

Standard Types of Departments

(i) Secretariat is the Office in support of the Divisional Head in terms of compliance, official meetings, reporting, accountability and oversight. A Secretariat cannot be introduced as a dedicated Internal Department to a Division of a valid Religious or Spiritual Society until at least one other External Department of the Division is established and the total count of Officers, Agents and Contractors employed is forty (40) or greater; and

(ii) Contact & Help Department is an Internal Department providing front-line inbound and outbound call centre management, online help requests, live chat, sms, email and other first line inquiries. The Department shall be part of the Administrative Support & Electoral Systems Division first and then the particular Division as a managed service; and

(iii) Issue & Resolution Department is an Internal Department providing complaints management and dispute resolution services. The Department formally belongs to the Legal

Support & Justice Systems Division first and then the particular Division as a managed service; and

(iv) Accounts & Finance Department is an Internal Department providing accounts and finance compliance, entry, reconciliation and transactions. The Department formally belongs to the Finance & Revenue Systems Division first and then the particular Division as a managed service; and

(v) Records & Archives Department is an Internal Department providing records management and archival services. The Department formally belongs to the Administrative Support & Electoral Systems Division first and then the particular Division as a managed service; and

(vi) Vocation & Training Department is an Internal Department providing recruitment, job description, team member development, personnel administration, payroll, skills development and periodic performance reviews. The Department formally belongs to the Vocational Support & Skills Development Systems Division first and then the particular Division as a managed service; and

(vii) Technology & Equipment Department is an Internal Department providing systems administration, computer and technology support, software and configuration support and IT security. The Department formally belongs to the Technology Support & Development Systems Division first and then the particular Division as a managed service; and

(viii) Facilities & Maintenance Department is an Internal Department providing facilities management, facilities fit out and facilities asset management. The Department formally belongs to the Facilities Management & Construction Systems Division first and then the particular Division as a managed service; and

(ix) Integrity & Security Department is an Internal Department providing internal security and fraud detection, threat assessments and enforcement. The Department formally belongs to the Security & Emergency Systems Division first and then the particular Division as a managed service.

**886.** All Secretariats operating within any Division of a valid Religious or Spiritual Society or any part thereof shall identify all Officers, Agents and Contractors according to the following three levels of Desk, *Standard Structure of Secretariats*

Station and Chapter:-

(i) Desk shall be the term used to describe a subdivision of a Station whereby one (1) or more persons, to a maximum of thirty (30) people function according to some defined task; and

(ii) Station shall be the term used to describe a subdivision of a Chapter whereby three (3) or more people, to a maximum of one hundred and twenty (120) people function according to some technical function and mandate; and

(iii) Chapter shall be the term used to describe the primary divisions of a Secretariat of Officers, Agents and Contractors employed within the structure.

## Article 226 – Religious Associations, Institutes and Societies

887. The System of a valid Religious or Spiritual Society known as ***Religious Associations, Institutes & Society Systems*** shall be the primary Division authorised, empowered and responsible for the management of all Religious Associations, Institutes and Societies within the Jurisdiction of the valid Religious or Spiritual Society. Religious Associations, Institutes and Society Systems

888. The Head of Religious Associations, Institutes and Societies Systems shall be known as the Secretary-General; and shall be a senior cleric, possessing the prerequisite skills, experience, aptitude and energy required to execute such Great Office. Head of Religious Associations, Institutes and Society Systems

889. Excluding the Divisional Secretariat and any Internal Services Departments, the core Departments of the Division shall include (but not be limited to): Clerical Services, Ministerial Services, Liturgical Services and Religious Institutes. Departments

900. The Secretary-General of Religious Associations, Institutes and Societies Systems shall be responsible for the conduct and operation of Congregation for Religious Associations, Institutes and Societies. Congregation for Religious Associations, Institutes and Societies

## Article 227 – Ecclesiastical Unions, Universities & Diplomatic Systems

901. The System of a valid Religious or Spiritual Society known as ***Ecclesiastical Unions, Universities & Diplomatic Systems*** shall be the primary Division authorised, empowered and responsible for the management of all Ucadian Union Administration Establishment, Ucadia Union Entity Establishment, Foreign Ecclesiastical Unions, Universities & Diplomatic Systems

Diplomatic Agreements and Treaties, Foreign Diplomatic Relations within the Jurisdiction of the valid Religious or Spiritual Society.

902. The Head of Ecclesiastical Unions, Universities & Diplomatic Systems shall be known as the Secretary-General; and shall be a senior cleric, possessing the prerequisite skills, experience, aptitude and energy required to execute such Great Office.
*Head of Ecclesiastical Unions, Universities & Diplomatic Systems*

903. The Secretary-General of Ecclesiastical Unions, Universities & Diplomatic Systems shall also be the Secretary of State for their ecclesiastical jurisdiction.
*Secretariat of Ecclesiastical Jurisdiction*

## Article 228 – Ecclesiastical Province & Campus Systems

904. The System of a valid Religious or Spiritual Society known as ***Ecclesiastical Province & Campus Systems*** shall be the primary Division authorised, empowered and responsible for the management of all Ucadia Province Establishment, Ucadia Campus Establishment, Ucadia Province Administration Relations, Ucadia Campus Administration Relations and Ucadia Province and Campus Standards and Development within the Jurisdiction of the valid Religious or Spiritual Society.
*Ecclesiastical Province & Campus Systems*

905. The Head of Ecclesiastical Province & Campus Systems shall be known as the Regional-General; and shall be a senior cleric, possessing the prerequisite skills, experience, aptitude and energy required to execute such Great Office.
*Head of Ecclesiastical Province & Campus Systems*

## Article 229 – Vocational & Clerical Systems

906. The System of a valid Religious or Spiritual Society known as ***Vocational & Clerical Systems*** shall be the primary Division authorised, empowered and responsible for the management of all Vocation Classification, Enterprise Purpose Hierarchy (EPH), Payments and Best Practice, Skills Classification and Accreditation, Skills Training, Performance and Productivity Assessments within the Jurisdiction of the valid Religious or Spiritual Society.
*Vocational & Clerical Systems*

907. The Head of Vocational & Clerical Systems shall be known as the Vicar-General; and shall be a senior cleric, possessing the prerequisite skills, experience, aptitude and energy required to execute such Great Office.
*Head of Vocational & Clerical Systems*

908. The Vicar-General of Vocational & Clerical Systems shall be responsible for the good conduct and function of the Sacred Congregation for Vocations and Consecrated Life.

*Congregation for Vocations and Consecrated Life*

## Article 230 – Evangelical, Devotional & Veneration Systems

909. The System of a valid Religious or Spiritual Society known as ***Evangelical, Devotional & Veneration Systems*** shall be the primary Division authorised, empowered and responsible for the management of all Religious Celebrations, Holy Days, Venerations and Devotions within the Jurisdiction of the valid Religious or Spiritual Society.

*Evangelical, Devotional & Veneration Systems*

910. The Head of Evangelical, Devotional & Veneration Systems shall be known as the Minister-General; and shall be a senior cleric, possessing the prerequisite skills, experience, aptitude and energy required to execute such Great Office.

*Head of Evangelical, Devotional & Veneration Systems*

911. The Minister-General of Evangelical, Devotional & Veneration Systems shall be responsible for the conduct and function of the Sacred Congregation for Evangelicalism, Devotion & Veneration.

*Congregation for Evangelicalism, Devotion and Veneration*

## Article 231 – Doctrinal & Liturgical Systems

912. The System of a valid Religious or Spiritual Society known as ***Doctrinal & Liturgical Systems*** shall be the primary Division authorised, empowered and responsible for the management of all sacred texts, doctrines and liturgical instructions within the Jurisdiction of the valid Religious or Spiritual Society.

*Sacred Doctrine and Liturgy*

913. The System of a valid Religious or Spiritual Society known as Doctrinal & Liturgical Systems shall be the primary Division authorised, empowered and responsible for the management of all Religious Doctrine and Liturgical Systems within the Jurisdiction of the valid Religious or Spiritual Society.

*Doctrinal & Liturgical Systems*

914. The Head of Doctrinal & Liturgical Systems shall be known as the Rector-General; and shall be a senior cleric, possessing the prerequisite skills, experience, aptitude and energy required to execute such Great Office.

*Head of Doctrinal & Liturgical Systems*

915. The Rector-General of Doctrinal & Liturgical System shall be responsible for the conduct and function of the Sacred Congregation for Sacred Doctrine and Liturgy.

*Congregation for Sacred Doctrine and Liturgy*

## Article 232 – Sacred Rites & Tradition Systems

916. The System of a valid Religious or Spiritual Society known as **Sacred Rites & Tradition Systems** shall be the primary Division authorised, empowered and responsible for the management, liaison and support of all Customary and Traditional Rites, particularly in seeking and ensuring Liturgical unity at major feasts and celebrations of the valid Religious or Spiritual Society. — Sacred Rites & Tradition

917. The Head of Sacred Rites & Tradition Systems shall be known as the Custodian-General; and shall be a senior cleric, possessing the prerequisite skills, experience, aptitude and energy required to execute such Great Office. — Character of Head of Sacred Rites & Tradition Systems

918. The Custodian-General of Sacred Rites & Tradition Systems shall be responsible for the function and conduct of the Sacred Congregation for Sacred Rites & Tradition. — Congregation for Sacred Rites & Tradition

## Article 233 – Ecumenical & Collegial Systems

919. The System of the a valid Religious or Spiritual Society known as **Ecumenical & Collegial Systems** shall be the primary Division authorised, empowered and responsible for the management of all Ecumenical and Collegial Systems within the Jurisdiction of the valid Religious or Spiritual Society. — Ecumenical & Collegial Systems

920. The Head of Ecumenical & Collegial Systems shall be known as the Prefect-General; and shall be a senior cleric, possessing the prerequisite skills, experience, aptitude and energy required to execute such Great Office. — Head of Ecumenical and Collegial Systems

## Article 234 – Families and Community Life Systems

921. The System of a valid Religious or Spiritual Society known as **Families and Community Life Systems** shall be the primary Division authorised, empowered and responsible for the management of all Family Life and Community Life Systems within the Jurisdiction of the valid Religious or Spiritual Society. — Families and Community Life Systems

922. The Head of Families and Community Life Systems shall be known as the Registrar-General; and shall be a senior cleric, possessing the prerequisite skills, experience, aptitude and energy required to execute such Great Office. — Head of Families and Community Life Systems

923. The Registrar-General of Families and Community Life Systems shall be responsible for the conduct and function of the Sacred — Congregation for Families and Community Life

Congregation for Families and Community Life.

## Article 235 – Member Assistance & Charitable Systems

924. The System of a valid Religious or Spiritual Society known as ***Member Assistance & Charitable Systems*** shall be the primary Division authorised, empowered and responsible for the management of all member relations, member support, member services and charitable assistance within the Jurisdiction of the valid Religious or Spiritual Society.

*Member Assistance & Charitable Systems*

925. The Head of Member Services & Charitable Systems shall be known as the Chancellor-General; and shall be a senior cleric, possessing the prerequisite skills, experience, aptitude and energy required to execute such Great Office.

*Head of Member Assistance & Charitable Systems*

## Article 236 – Knowledge and Education Systems

926. The System of a valid Religious or Spiritual Society known as ***Knowledge and Education Systems*** shall be the primary Division authorised, empowered and responsible for the management of all Ucadia Education Classification Systems, Curriculum Systems, Pre-School Education, Primary Education, Secondary Education, Poly-Tech Education, Tertiary Education, Advanced Post-Graduate, Teaching Models and Methods, Academic Assessments and Academic Accreditations within the Jurisdiction of the valid Religious or Spiritual Society.

*Knowledge and Education Systems*

927. The Head of Knowledge Standards and Education Systems shall be known as the Assistant-General; and shall be a senior cleric, possessing the prerequisite skills, experience, aptitude and energy required to execute such Great Office.

*Head of Knowledge and Education Systems*

## Article 237 – Justice and Jurisprudence Systems

928. The System of a valid Religious or Spiritual Society known as ***Justice and Jurisprudence Systems*** shall be the primary Division authorised, empowered and responsible for the management of all Civil Standards, Criminal Law Standards, Professional Accreditation and Standards, Oversight and Complaints, Prosecutions, Judge Training and College, Court Systems and Administration, Appeals, Prisoner Classification and Correctional Facility Administration within the Jurisdiction of the valid Religious or Spiritual Society.

*Justice and Jurisprudence Systems*

929. The Head of Justice and Jurisprudence Systems shall be known as the Prothonotary-General; and shall be a senior cleric, possessing the

*Head of Justice and*

prerequisite skills, experience, aptitude and energy required to execute such Great Office.

## Article 238 – Health and Therapeutic Systems

930. The System of a valid Religious or Spiritual Society known as ***Health and Therapeutic Systems*** shall be the primary Division authorised, empowered and responsible for the management of all Health Knowledge, Standards and Principles, Health and Fitness Education, Professional Accreditation, Certification and Review, General Medical Clinics, General Dental Clinics, Community Medical Centres, Intensive Care Centres, Recovery and Rehabilitation Centres, Specialist Medical Centres, Medical Research Institutes, Mobile Medical Clinics and Health and Fitness Administration within the Jurisdiction of the valid Religious or Spiritual Society.

931. The Head of Health and Therapeutic Systems shall be known as the Physician-General; and shall be a senior cleric, possessing the prerequisite skills, experience, aptitude and energy required to execute such Great Office.

## Article 239 – Technology & Scientific Systems

932. The System of a valid Religious or Spiritual Society known as ***Technology & Scientific Systems*** shall be the primary Division authorised, empowered and responsible for the management of all Technology and Scientific Systems within the Jurisdiction of the valid Religious or Spiritual Society.

933. The Head of Technology & Scientific Systems shall be known as the Author-General; and shall be a senior cleric, possessing the prerequisite skills, experience, aptitude and energy required to execute such Great Office.

## Article 240 – Banking, Finance & Economic Systems

934. The System of a valid Religious or Spiritual Society known as ***Finance & Economic Systems*** shall be the primary Division authorised, empowered and responsible for the management of all Banking, Finance, Asset Management and Economic Systems within the Jurisdiction of the valid Religious or Spiritual Society.

935. The Head of Banking, Finance & Economic Systems shall be known as the Bursar-General; and shall be a senior cleric, possessing the prerequisite skills, experience, aptitude and energy required to execute such Great Office.

*Head of Banking, Finance & Economic Systems*

## Article 241 – Environmental Protection & Preservation Systems

936. The System of a valid Religious or Spiritual Society known as ***Environmental Protection & Preservation Systems*** shall be the primary Division authorised, empowered and responsible for the management of all protection, support and recognition of the environment within the Jurisdiction of the valid Religious or Spiritual Society.

*Environmental Protection & Preservation Systems*

937. The Head of Environmental Protection & Preservation Systems shall be known as the Steward-General; and shall be a senior cleric, possessing the prerequisite skills, experience, aptitude and energy required to execute such Great Office.

*Head of Environmental Protection & Preservation Systems*

## Article 242 – Ethical Agriculture, Food & Organic Systems

938. The System of a valid Religious or Spiritual Society known as ***Ethical Agriculture, Food & Organic Systems*** shall be the primary Division authorised, empowered and responsible for the management of all Agriculture and Farm Related Services, Plant Biological Integrity, Sustainability, Animal Biological Integrity, Health and Safety, Water and Environment Management and Education, Agriculture Research, Development and Funding, Bio-security, Sustainable and Optimum Plant/Crop Development, Food and Drugs Classification Standards, Natural Food Sources and End Products, Synthetic Food Sources and End Products, Therapeutic Drug Sources and End Products, Food Production Standards, Animal Food Production Standards, Food Services and Therapeutic Product Services within the Jurisdiction of the valid Religious or Spiritual Society.

*Ethical Agriculture, Food & Organic Systems*

The Systems of the valid Religious or Spiritual Societies of the three Great Faiths known as Ethical Agriculture, Food & Organic Systems shall be responsible for the defence, adherence and promotion of the highest bio-ethical standards, consistent with the bio-ethical laws of Ucadia. No food product or therapeutic system that is derived or manufactured in a method or process that contravenes the bio-ethical laws of Ucadia is permitted to be promoted, endorsed, sold, or marketed by the three Great Faiths or their Members.

939. The Head of Ethical Agriculture, Food & Organic Systems shall be

*Head of Ethical*

known as the Distributor-General; and shall be a senior cleric, possessing the prerequisite skills, experience, aptitude and energy required to execute such Great Office.

## Article 243 – Military & Security Systems

940. The System of a valid Religious or Spiritual Society known as ***Military & Security Systems*** shall be the primary Division authorised, empowered and responsible for the management of all Threat Assessment, Protection and Facility Security, Police Investigation and Operational Standards, Police Services, Veterans and Care and Emergency Administration within the Jurisdiction of the valid Religious or Spiritual Society.

941. The Head of Military & Security Systems shall be known as the Marshal-General or Superior-General; and shall be a senior cleric, possessing the prerequisite skills, experience, aptitude and energy required to execute such Great Office.

## Article 244 – Media & Communications Systems

942. The System of a valid Religious or Spiritual Society known as ***Media & Communications Systems*** shall be the primary Division authorised, empowered and responsible for the management of all Universal Number Indexing Systems (UNIS), Digital Communications Networks, Digital Communications Devices, Print Communications Networks, Postal Communications Networks, Communications Content Services, Media Production and Media Publishing within the Jurisdiction of the valid Religious or Spiritual Society.

943. The Head of Media & Communications Systems shall be known as the Narrator-General; and shall be a senior cleric, possessing the prerequisite skills, experience, aptitude and energy required to execute such Great Office.

## Article 245 – Facilities, Constructions & Preservation Systems

944. The System of a valid Religious or Spiritual Society known as ***Facilities, Constructions & Preservation Systems*** shall be the primary Division authorised, empowered and responsible for the management of all Building and Occupancy Standards and Principles, Surface Building Standards, Subterranean Building Standards, Accreditation and Competencies, Architecture, Continuity and Standards Compliance, Site Environmental Impact Modelling

and Authorisation, Construction, Materials Testing and Certification, Building Fit-out and Maintenance, Facility Life-cycle and Accreditations within the Jurisdiction of the valid Religious or Spiritual Society.

945. The Head of Facilities, Constructions & Preservation Systems shall be known as the Director-General; and shall be a senior cleric, possessing the prerequisite skills, experience, aptitude and energy required to execute such Great Office.

*Head of Facilities, Constructions & Preservation Systems*

## Article 246 – Heritage, Arts & Cultural Systems

946. The System of a valid Religious or Spiritual Society known as ***Heritage, Arts & Cultural Systems*** shall be the primary Division authorised, empowered and responsible for the management of all Heritage Buildings and Sites, Historic and Precious Art Collections and Cultural Systems within the Jurisdiction of the valid Religious or Spiritual Society.

*Heritage, Arts & Cultural Systems*

947. The Head of Heritage, Arts & Cultural Systems shall be known as the Conservator-General; and shall be a senior cleric, possessing the prerequisite skills, experience, aptitude and energy required to execute such Great Office.

*Head of Heritage, Arts & Cultural Systems*

## Article 247 – Administrative & Logistical Systems

948. The System of a valid Religious or Spiritual Society known as ***Administrative & Logistical Systems*** shall be the primary Division authorised, empowered and responsible for the management of all Contact and Help Management, Records and Archives and the conduct of free and fair Elections and Polls, Transport & Travel Classification, Transport Traffic Rules, Road Transport Vehicles Certification, Travel Warrants, Mass Transit System Vehicles Certification, Aircraft Development and Design, Land Vehicle Development and Design, Water-craft Development and Design within the Jurisdiction of the valid Religious or Spiritual Society.

*Administrative & Logistical Systems*

949. The Head of Administrative & Logistical Systems shall be known as the Administrator-General; and shall be a senior cleric, possessing the prerequisite skills, experience, aptitude and energy required to execute such Great Office.

*Head of Administrative & Logistical Systems*

# Title VIII – Ecclesiastical Rights

## 8.1 – Ecclesiastical Rights

### Article 248 – Ecclesiastical Rights

950. ***Ecclesiastical Rights*** (*Iurium Ecclesiae*) are a sub-class of Superior Rights and the highest possible rights of any aggregate body, society, fraternity, association or company of two or more people. Ecclesiastical Rights

951. All *Ecclesiastical Rights* are permanently vested equally unto the three united Ucadia faiths and Ucadia itself recognised under the most sacred Covenant *Pactum De Singularis Caelum* being:- Ecclesiastical Rights and Three Faiths

    (i) *The most sacred and Universal Ecclesia of One Christ*, also known as the *One Holy Apostolic Universal Ecclesia*, as defined by Article 92; and

    (ii) *The Holy Society of One Islam*, also known as the *One True Way of Allah*, as defined by Article 93; and

    (iii) *The most Sacred Society of One Spirit*, also known as the *One Sacred Spirit*, as defined by Article 94.

952. There exists eight (8) categories of one hundred and thirty-two (132) Superior Rights within the sub-class of Ecclesiastical Rights, being: Authoritative (22), Instrumental (22), Sacramental (33), Writs (11), Bills (11), Dogma (11), Decrees (11) and Notices (11): Categories of Ecclesiastical Rights

    (i) "**Authoritative Ecclesiastical Rights**" (*Potentis Ecclesiae Iurium*) shall be Ecclesiastical Rights associated with the core ecclesiastical authoritative powers; and

    (ii) "**Instrumental Ecclesiastical Rights**"(*Instrumentalis Ecclesiae Iurium*) shall be Ecclesiastical Rights essential to the proper administration of Ecclesiastical Rights; and

    (iii) "**Sacramental Ecclesiastical Rights**" (*Sacramentum Ecclesiae Iurium*) shall be Ecclesiastical Rights associated with the thirty-three (33) Divine Sacraments of Heaven; and

    (iv) "**Ecclesiastical Writs of Rights**" (*Recto Ecclesiae Iurium*) shall be Ecclesiastical Rights associated with the one, true and only forms of Original Entry and Original Action; and

    (v) "**Ecclesiastical Bills of Exception**" (*Rogatio Ecclesiae Iurium*) shall be Ecclesiastical Rights associated with the one, true and only forms of Bills of Exception, Citation and Moratorium; and

    (vi) "**Ecclesiastical Dogma**" (*Greatest Principles Ecclesiae*

*Iurium*) shall be Ecclesiastical Rights associated with the promulgation of authoritative ecclesiastical principles, decrees and doctrines; and

(vii) **"Ecclesiastical Decrees"** (*Decretum Ecclesiae Iurium*) shall be Ecclesiastical Rights associated with ecclesiastical decrees concerning the administration, conduct and enforcement of law and order; and

(viii) **"Ecclesiastical Notices"** (*Notitiae Ecclesiae Iurium*) shall be Ecclesiastical Rights associated with ecclesiastical notices issued, executed, patented, promulgated and services in the proper administration, conduct and enforcement of law and order.

## 8.2 – Authoritative Ecclesiastical Rights

### Article 249 – Authoritative Ecclesiastical Rights

953. ***Authoritative Ecclesiastical Rights*** (Potentis Ecclesiae Iurium) shall be Ecclesiastical Rights associated with the core ecclesiastical authoritative powers. <!-- marginalia: Authoritative Ecclesiastical Rights -->

954. All *Authoritative Ecclesiastical Rights* are delegated to the safe custody and wise guardian powers of the legitimate and valid supreme competent ecclesiastical forum of law of the proper Ucadia Faiths and all lesser associated Ucadia bodies, as the embodiment of judicial authority; and as defined by Article 59 (Oratorium) of the most sacred Covenant *Pactum De Singularis Caelum*. <!-- marginalia: Delegation of Authoritative Ecclesiastical Rights -->

955. All *Authoritative Ecclesiastical Rights* are assumed to be automatically invoked within Ucadia Jurisdictions through the operation of the Civilised Rules of Ucadia Societies, Bodies and Entities. However the Rights may be explicitly invoked or referenced by Right of Action through a proper Forum of Law and the Fiduciary Obligations of any such court in Ucadia or Non-Ucadia Jurisdiction. <!-- marginalia: Invocation of Authoritative Ecclesiastical Rights -->

956. The following valid twenty-two (22) Authoritative Ecclesiastical Rights (*Potentis Ecclesiae Iurium*) shall be recognised in accord with the most sacred Covenant *Pactum De Singularis Caelum*:- <!-- marginalia: List of Authoritative Ecclesiastical Rights (Potentis Ecclesiae Iurium) -->

(i) **"Ius Ecclesiae"** is the primary collection of Ecclesiastical Rights, as inherited from the collection of Divine Rights *Ius Divinum Ecclesia*; and

(ii) **"Ius Ecclesiae Regnum"** is the collection of Ecclesiastical Rights of Sovereign Authority, as inherited from the collection of Divine Rights *Ius Divinum Regnum*; and

(iii) **"Ius Ecclesiae Consilium"** is the collection of Ecclesiastical Rights of a Legislative and Advisory Authority, as inherited from the collection of Divine Rights *Ius Divinum Consilium*; and

(iv) **"Ius Ecclesiae Fraternitus"** is the collection of Ecclesiastical Rights of an Ecclesiastical and Religious Fraternity, as inherited from the collection of Divine Rights *Ius Divinum Ecclesia*; and

(v) **"Ius Ecclesiae Collegium"** is the collection of Ecclesiastical Rights of a Company or Charitable Body, as inherited from the collection of Divine Rights *Ius Divinum Collegium*; and

(vi) **"Ius Ecclesiae Officium"** is the collection of Ecclesiastical Rights of Office, Duty and Service, as inherited from the collection of Divine Rights *Ius Divinum Officium*; and

(vii) **"Ius Ecclesiae Imperium"** is the collection of Ecclesiastical Rights of Command, Occupation and Enforcement, as inherited from the collection of Divine Rights *Ius Divinum Imperium*; and

(viii) **"Ius Ecclesiae Sacrum"** is the collection of Ecclesiastical Rights of Sacred Recognition, Devotion and Veneration, as inherited from the collection of Divine Rights *Ius Divinum Sacrum*; and

(ix) **"Ius Ecclesiae Custoditum"** is the collection of Ecclesiastical Rights of Custody, Guardianship and Preservation, as inherited from the collection of Divine Rights *Ius Divinum Custoditum*; and

(x) **"Ius Ecclesiae Alumentum"** is the collection of Ecclesiastical Rights to Sustenance, Maintenance and Alms, as inherited from the collection of Divine Rights *Ius Divinum Alumentum*; and

(xi) **"Ius Ecclesiae Apostolicus"** is the collection of Ecclesiastical Rights of Divine Commission, as inherited from the collection of Divine Rights *Ius Divinum Apostolicus*; and

(xii) **"Ius Ecclesiae Cancellarium"** is the collection of Ecclesiastical Rights of Chancery and Administration of Law, as inherited from the collection of Divine Rights *Ius Divinum Cancellarium*; and

(xiii) **"Ius Ecclesiae Oratorium"** is the collection of

Ecclesiastical Rights to a Competent Forum of Law and Review, as inherited from the collection of Divine Rights *Ius Divinum Oratorium*; and

(xiv) **"Ius Ecclesiae Templum"** is the collection of Ecclesiastical Rights of a Treasury or Financial (Banking) Body, as inherited from the collection of Divine Rights *Ius Divinum Templum*; and

(xv) **"Ius Ecclesiae Sacramentum"** is the collection of Ecclesiastical Rights to Grant and Impart Holy Sacraments, as inherited from the Divine Rights *Ius Divinum Sacramentum*; and

(xvi) **"Ius Ecclesiae Visum"** is the collection of Ecclesiastical Rights to Survey, Visit and Audit Ucadia Bodies, as inherited from the collection of Divine Rights *Ius Divinum Visum*; and

(xvii) **"Ius Ecclesiae Commercium"** is the collection of Ecclesiastical Rights to Trade, Exchange and Communication, as inherited from the collection of Divine Rights *Ius Divinum Commercium*; and

(xviii) **"Ius Ecclesiae Virtus"** is the collection of Ecclesiastical Rights to Strength, Honour, Excellence and Virtue, as inherited from the collection of Divine Rights *Ius Divinum Virtus*; and

(xix) **"Ius Ecclesiae Penitentiaria"** is the collection of Ecclesiastical Rights of Forced Confinement and Penitence, as inherited from the collection of Divine Rights *Ius Divinum Penitentiaria*; and

(xx) **"Ius Ecclesiae Astrum"** is the collection of Ecclesiastical Rights to an Association, Aggregate or Body, as inherited from the collection of Divine Rights *Ius Divinum Astrum*; and

(xxi) **"Ius Ecclesiae Magisterium"** is the collection of Ecclesiastical Rights to Teach, Instruct and Interpret Sacred Texts and Divine Will, as inherited from the collection of Divine Rights *Ius Divinum Magisterium*; and

(xxii) **"Ius Ecclesiae Decretum"** is the collection of Ecclesiastical Rights to issue Decree, Judgement and Edict, as inherited from the collection of Divine Rights *Ius Divinum Decretum*.

## Article 250 – Ius Ecclesiae (Ecclesiastical Rights)

957. ***Ius Ecclesiae*** are the primary collection of all possible Ecclesiastical Rights, as inherited from the collection of Divine Rights *Ius Divinum Ecclesia*.

<sub>Ius Ecclesiae (Ecclesiastical Rights)</sub>

958. *Ius Ecclesiae* (Ecclesiastical Rights) is the first collection of twenty-two Authoritative Ecclesiastical Rights (*Potentis Ecclesiae Iurium*); and may be explicitly invoked or referenced by Ecclesiastical Right of Action through a proper and registered Ecclesiastical Body and the Ecclesiastical Obligations of any such registered Consecrated Person or Ecclesiastical Office in Ucadia or Non-Ucadia Jurisdiction.

<sub>Invoking of Ius Ecclesiae (Ecclesiastical Rights)</sub>

959. The collection of Ecclesiastical Rights of *Ius Ecclesiae* (Ecclesiastical Rights) contains twenty-four (24) Rights being:-

<sub>Collection of Ius Ecclesiae (Ecclesiastical Rights)</sub>

  (i) *Ius Ecclesiae* being the Ecclesiastical Right of an Ecclesiastical and Religious Body; and

  (ii) *Ius Ecclesiae Libertatis Religionis* being the Ecclesiastical Right of Freedom of Religion; and

  (iii) *Ius Ecclesiae Libertatis Persecutione Religionis* being the Ecclesiastical Right of Freedom from Religious Persecution; and

  (iv) *Ius Ecclesiae Celebrationis Religionis* being the Ecclesiastical Right of Religious Worship and Celebration; and

  (v) *Ius Ecclesiae Educationis Religiosae* being the Ecclesiastical Right of Religious Education; and

  (vi) *Ius Ecclesiae Caeremoniae Religionis* being the Ecclesiastical Right of Religious Rites and Ceremony; and

  (vii) *Ius Ecclesiae Conventūs Religionis* being the Ecclesiastical Right of Religious Assembly; and

  (viii) *Ius Ecclesiae Gubernandi Ecclesiasticum* being the Ecclesiastical Right of Ecclesiastical Autonomy and Self Governance; and

  (ix) *Ius Ecclesiae Registrorum et Rotulorum Ecclesiasticorum* being the Ecclesiastical Right of Ecclesiastical Registers and Rolls; and

  (x) *Ius Ecclesiae Cancellariae Ecclesiasticae* being the Ecclesiastical Right of Ecclesiastical Chancery and Administration of Records; and

(xi) *Ius Ecclesiae Proprietatis Ecclesiasticae* being the Ecclesiastical Right of Ecclesiastical Property; and

(xii) *Ius Ecclesiae Immunitatis Proprietatis Ecclesiasticae* being the Ecclesiastical Right of Immunity of Ecclesiastical Property from Taxation and Expropriation; and

(xiii) *Ius Ecclesiae Coronationis Ecclesiasticae* being the Ecclesiastical Right of Ecclesiastical Coronation; and

(xiv) *Ius Ecclesiae Separatae Ecclesiae et Coronae* being the Ecclesiastical Right of Separation of Church and Crown; and

(xv) *Ius Ecclesiae Separatae Ecclesiae et Civitatis* being the Ecclesiastical Right of Separation of Church and State; and

(xvi) *Ius Ecclesiae Positionum Ecclesiasticarum* being the Ecclesiastical Right of Ecclesiastical Positions; and

(xvii) *Ius Ecclesiae Investituræ Ecclesiasticæ* being the Ecclesiastical Right of Ecclesiastical Investiture; and

(xviii) *Ius Ecclesiae Officii Ecclesiastici* being the Ecclesiastical Right of Ecclesiastical Office; and

(xix) *Ius Ecclesiae Collegium Ecclesiasticarum* being the Ecclesiastical Right of Ecclesiastical Bodies, Companies and Charitable Organisations; and

(xx) *Ius Ecclesiae Consilium Ecclesiasticarum* being the Ecclesiastical Right of Ecclesiastical Legislative Councils; and

(xxi) *Ius Ecclesiae Oratorium Ecclesiasticarum* being the Ecclesiastical Right of Ecclesiastical Courts and Forums of Law; and

(xxii) *Ius Ecclesiae Templum Ecclesiasticarum* being the Ecclesiastical Right of Ecclesiastical Treasury; and

(xxiii) *Ius Ecclesiae Penitentiaria Ecclesiasticarum* being the Ecclesiastical Right of Ecclesiastical Penitentiary; and

(xxiv) *Ius Ecclesiae Commercium Ecclesiasticarum* being the Ecclesiastical Right of Ecclesiastical Goods and Trade.

## Article 251 – Ius Ecclesiae Regnum (Ecclesiastical Sovereign Authority)

960. **Ius Ecclesiae Regnum** is the collection of Ecclesiastical Rights of Sovereign Authority, as inherited from the Divine Rights *Ius Divinum Regnum*.

Ius Ecclesiae Regnum

961. *Ius Ecclesiae Regnum* (Ecclesiastical Sovereign Authority) is the second collection of twenty-two Authoritative Ecclesiastical Rights (*Potentis Ecclesiae Iurium*); and may be explicitly invoked or referenced by Ecclesiastical Right of Action through a proper and registered Ecclesiastical Body and the Ecclesiastical Obligations of any such registered Consecrated Person or Ecclesiastical Office in Ucadia or Non-Ucadia Jurisdiction.

*Invoking of Ius Ecclesiae Regnum (Ecclesiastical Sovereign Authority)*

962. The collection of Ecclesiastical Rights of *Ius Ecclesiae Regnum* (Ecclesiastical Sovereign Authority) contains eight (8) Rights being:-

*Collection of Ius Ecclesiae Regnum (Ecclesiastical Sovereign Authority)*

(i) *Ius Ecclesiae Regnum* being the Ecclesiastical Right of the Sovereign Authority or Body; and

(ii) *Ius Ecclesiae Integritatis Territorialis* being the Ecclesiastical Right of Territorial Integrity; and

(iii) *Ius Ecclesiae Independendiae Politicae* being the Ecclesiastical Right of Political Independence; and

(iv) *Ius Ecclesiae Recognitionis Souveranae* being the Ecclesiastical Right of Sovereign Recognition; and

(v) *Ius Ecclesiae Summae Iurisdictionis* being the Ecclesiastical Right of Supreme Jurisdiction; and

(vi) *Ius Ecclesiae Defensionis Souveranae* being the Ecclesiastical Right of Sovereign Self Defence; and

(vii) *Ius Ecclesiae Relationum Diplomaticarum* being the Ecclesiastical Right of Diplomatic Relations; and

(viii) *Ius Ecclesiae Foederum Faciendorum* being the Ecclesiastical Right to Make Treaties with other States.

## Article 252 – Ius Ecclesiae Consilium (Ecclesiastical Legislative Authority)

963. ***Ius Ecclesiae Consilium*** is the collection of Ecclesiastical Rights of a Legislative and Advisory Authority, as inherited from the Divine Rights *Ius Divinum Consilium*.

*Ius Ecclesiae Consilium*

964. *Ius Ecclesiae Consilium* (Ecclesiastical Legislative Authority) is the third collection of twenty-two Authoritative Ecclesiastical Rights (*Potentis Ecclesiae Iurium*); and may be explicitly invoked or referenced by Ecclesiastical Right of Action through a proper and registered Ecclesiastical Body and the Ecclesiastical Obligations of any such registered Consecrated Person or Ecclesiastical Office in Ucadia or Non-Ucadia Jurisdiction.

*Invoking of Ius Ecclesiae Consilium*

965. The collection of Ecclesiastical Rights of *Ius Ecclesiae Consilium*

*Collection of Ius*

contains twelve (12) Rights being:- — Ecclesiae Consilium

(i) *Ius Ecclesiae Consilium* being the Ecclesiastical Right of a Legislative and Advisory Body; and

(ii) *Ius Ecclesiae Regulas Parlamentarias* being the Ecclesiastical Right to Parliamentary Rules of Conduct and Process; and

(iii) *Ius Ecclesiae Privilegii Parlamentarii* being the Ecclesiastical Right of Parliamentary Privilege; and

(iv) *Ius Ecclesiae Votandi Parliamento* being the Ecclesiastical Right of Parliamentary Vote; and

(v) *Ius Ecclesiae Quaestionis Parliamento* being the Ecclesiastical Right of Parliamentary Question; and

(vi) *Ius Ecclesiae Informationis Parliamento* being the Ecclesiastical Right of Parliamentary Information; and

(vii) *Ius Ecclesiae Leges Faciendi* being the Ecclesiastical Right to Make Laws; and

(viii) *Ius Ecclesiae Leges Disputandi* being the Ecclesiastical Right to Debate (Proposed and Existing) Laws; and

(ix) *Ius Ecclesiae Leges Emendandi* being the Ecclesiastical Right to Amend Laws; and

(x) *Ius Ecclesiae Leges Conlucere* being the Ecclesiastical Right to Consolidate Laws; and

(xi) *Ius Ecclesiae Leges Abrogandi* being the Ecclesiastical Right to Repeal Laws; and

(xii) *Ius Ecclesiae Supervisionis Executivae* being the Ecclesiastical Right of Executive Oversight.

## Article 253 – Ius Ecclesiae Fraternitus (Ecclesiastical and Religious Authority)

966. ***Ius Ecclesiae Fraternitus is the collection of Ecclesiastical Rights*** of an Ecclesiastical and Religious Authority, as inherited from the Divine Rights *Ius Divinum Ecclesia*. — Ius Ecclesiae Fraternitus (Ecclesiastical and Religious Authority)

967. *Ius Ecclesiae Fraternitus* (Ecclesiastical and Religious Authority) is the fourth collection of twenty-two Authoritative Ecclesiastical Rights (*Potentis Ecclesiae Iurium*); and may be explicitly invoked or referenced by Ecclesiastical Right of Action through a proper and registered Ecclesiastical Body and the Ecclesiastical Obligations of any such registered Consecrated Person or Ecclesiastical Office in — Invoking of Ius Ecclesiae Fraternitus

Ucadia or Non-Ucadia Jurisdiction.

968. The collection of Ecclesiastical Rights of *Ius Ecclesiae Fraternitus* contains one Right being:-

    (i)   *Ius Ecclesiae Fraternitus* being the Ecclesiastical Right of an Ecclesiastical and Religious Authority.

*Collection of Ius Ecclesiae Fraternitus*

## Article 254 – Ius Ecclesiae Collegium (Ecclesiastical Company or Charitable Body)

969. ***Ius Ecclesiae Collegium*** is the collection of Ecclesiastical Rights of an Ecclesiastical Company or Charitable Body, as inherited from the Divine Rights *Ius Divinum Collegium*.

*Ius Ecclesiae Collegium (Company or Charitable Body)*

970. *Ius Ecclesiae Collegium* (Ecclesiastical Company or Charitable Body) is the fifth collection of twenty-two Authoritative Ecclesiastical Rights (*Potentis Ecclesiae Iurium*); and may be explicitly invoked or referenced by Ecclesiastical Right of Action through a proper and registered Ecclesiastical Body and the Ecclesiastical Obligations of any such registered Consecrated Person or Ecclesiastical Office in Ucadia or Non-Ucadia Jurisdiction.

*Invoking of Ius Ecclesiae Collegium*

971. The collection of Ecclesiastical Rights of *Ius Ecclesiae Collegium* contains twenty-nine (29) Rights being:-

*Collection of Ius Ecclesiae Collegium*

    (i)   *Ius Ecclesiae Collegium* being the Ecclesiastical Right of Company or Charitable Body; and

    (ii)   *Ius Ecclesiae Convocationis Formatio* being the Ecclesiastical Right of Convocation of Members to Form Under granted Charter listing Key Rights and Constitution or Bylaws or Statutes; and

    (iii)   *Ius Ecclesiae Conventum Formatio* being the Ecclesiastical Right of Assembly of Members to Form Under Memorandum of Key Objects and Articles; and

    (iv)   *Ius Ecclesiae Conventionis Formatio* being the Ecclesiastical Right of Convention of Members to Form Under Declaration of Key Objects and Constitution; and

    (v)   *Ius Ecclesiae Incorporationis Collegii Existentis* being the Ecclesiastical Right of Incorporating Existing Company, Body or Entity into a Jurisdiction; and

    (vi)   *Ius Ecclesiae Novi Collegii Incorporationis* being the Ecclesiastical Right of Incorporating a New Company, Body or Entity (and its Governing Instrument) into a Jurisdiction; and

    (vii)   *Ius Ecclesiae Incorporationis Exterae* being the Ecclesiastical

Right of Incorporating an Existing Company, Body or Entity into a Foreign Jurisdiction (to its original jurisdiction); and

(viii) *Ius Ecclesiae Personae Iuridicae* being the Ecclesiastical Right of Legal Personality for an Incorporated Company, Body or Entity; and

(ix) *Ius Ecclesiae Proprietatis Collegii* being the Ecclesiastical Right of Property Ownership and Rights for an Incorporated Company, Body or Entity; and

(x) *Ius Ecclesiae Iurium Financiariorum Collegii* being the Ecclesiastical Right of Financial and Banking Rights for an Incorporated Company, Body or Entity; and

(xi) *Ius Ecclesiae Iurium Fornitorum Collegii* being the Ecclesiastical Right of Supplier Rights for an Incorporated Company, Body or Entity; and

(xii) *Ius Ecclesiae Iurium Operariorum Collegii* being the Ecclesiastical Right of Employee Rights for an Incorporated Company, Body or Entity; and

(xiii) *Ius Ecclesiae Iurium Conventus Collegii* being the Ecclesiastical Right of Agreement Rights for an Incorporated Company, Body or Entity; and

(xiv) *Ius Ecclesiae Commercium Collegii* being the Ecclesiastical Right to Engage in Business and Commerce for an Incorporated Company, Body or Entity; and

(xv) *Ius Ecclesiae Gubernandi Collegii* being the Ecclesiastical Right to Corporate Governance for an Incorporated Company, Body or Entity; and

(xvi) *Ius Ecclesiae Rationem Financiariam* being the Ecclesiastical Right to Financial Reporting; and

(xvii) *Ius Ecclesiae Limitandae Responsabilitatis* being the Ecclesiastical Right to Limit Liability of Shareholders, Directors and Employees within the Governing Instruments of the Incorporated Company, Body or Entity; and

(xviii) *Ius Ecclesiae Observandae Iurisdictionis* being the Ecclesiastical Right of Compliance within Jurisdiction of Incorporation; and

(xix) *Ius Ecclesiae Remunerationis Directoris* being the Ecclesiastical Right of Director Remuneration; and

(xx) *Ius Ecclesiae Conventum Directorum* being the Ecclesiastical Right to Director Meeting(s); and

(xxi) *Ius Ecclesiae Conventum Generalium Partium* being the Ecclesiastical Right of General Shareholders Meetings; and

(xxii) *Ius Ecclesiae Conventum Extraordinarium Partium* being the Ecclesiastical Right of Extraordinary Shareholders Meetings; and

(xxiii) *Ius Ecclesiae Capitis Collegii* being the Ecclesiastical Right of Share Capital; and

(xxiv) *Ius Ecclesiae Mutationis Capitis Collegii* being the Ecclesiastical Right to Change Share Capital; and

(xxv) *Ius Ecclesiae Collegii Vendendi* being the Ecclesiastical Right of Sale of Company, Body or Entity with another Body; and

(xxvi) *Ius Ecclesiae Collegii Fusionis* being the Ecclesiastical Right of Merger of Company, Body or Entity with another Body; and

(xxvii) *Ius Ecclesiae Collegii Administrationis* being the Ecclesiastical Right of Administration of Company, Body or Entity with another Body; and

(xxviii) *Ius Ecclesiae Collegii Deregistrationis* being the Ecclesiastical Right of Deregistration of previously registered (and incorporated) Company, Body or Entity; and

(xxix) *Ius Ecclesiae Collegii Dissolutionis* being the Ecclesiastical Right of Dissolution of Company, Body or Entity.

## Article 255 – Ius Ecclesiae Officium (Ecclesiastical Office, Duty and Service)

972. *Ius Ecclesiae Officium* is the collection of Ecclesiastical Rights of Office, Duty and Service, as inherited from the Divine Rights *Ius Divinum Officium*.

973. *Ius Ecclesiae Officium* (Ecclesiastical Office, Duty and Service) is the sixth collection of twenty-two Authoritative Ecclesiastical Rights (*Potentis Ecclesiae Iurium*); and may be explicitly invoked or referenced by Ecclesiastical Right of Action through a proper and registered Ecclesiastical Body and the Ecclesiastical Obligations of any such registered Consecrated Person or Ecclesiastical Office in Ucadia or Non-Ucadia Jurisdiction.

974. The collection of Ecclesiastical Rights of *Ius Ecclesiae Officium* contains fifteen (15) Rights being:-

(i) *Ius Ecclesiae Officium* being the Ecclesiastical Right of Office, Duty and Service; and

(ii) *Ius Ecclesiae Petendi Candidatum Officium* being the Ecclesiastical Right to Apply to be Candidate for Office; and

(iii) *Ius Ecclesiae Formandum Comitatum* being the Ecclesiastical Right to Form a Campaign as Candidate for Office; and

(iv) *Ius Ecclesiae Candidati Officium* being the Ecclesiastical Right to Run a Campaign as Candidate for Office; and

(v) *Ius Ecclesiae Eligendi* being the Ecclesiastical Right to be Elected as Candidate for Office; and

(vi) *Ius Ecclesiae Clausurae Comitatus* being the Ecclesiastical Right to Close a Campaign for Office; and

(vii) *Ius Ecclesiae Mandati Officii* being the Ecclesiastical Right to Receive Mandate in Good Faith, Good Conscience and Good Actions to Occupy an Office; and

(viii) *Ius Ecclesiae Tenendi Officii* being the Ecclesiastical Right to Hold an Office in Good Faith, Good Conscience and Good Actions; and

(ix) *Ius Ecclesiae Immunitatis Officii* being the Ecclesiastical Right of Immunity for Decisions Made in Office in Good Faith, Good Conscience and Good Actions; and

(x) *Ius Ecclesiae Abdicandi Officii* being the Ecclesiastical Right to Retire from Office in Honour, Privileges and Good Standing; and

(xi) *Ius Ecclesiae Dicendi Officii* being the Ecclesiastical Right to Resign from Office in Honour, Privileges and Good Standing; and

(xii) *Ius Ecclesiae Nullius Mandati* being the Ecclesiastical Right to have Mandate Withdrawn and be Terminated from Office in Disgrace, Without Privileges and Poor Standing; and

(xiii) *Ius Ecclesiae Accusationi Officii* being the Ecclesiastical Right to Face Impeachment for Claims of Bad Faith, Bad Conscience or Bad Actions in Office; and

(xiv) *Ius Ecclesiae Removendi Officii* being the Ecclesiastical Right to be Removed by Force from Office in Disgrace, Without Privileges and Poor Standing upon being found Culpable from Impeachment; and

(xv) *Ius Ecclesiae Restituendi Officii* being the Ecclesiastical Right to be Restored to Office in Honour, Privileges and Good Standing after having been unlawfully obstructed or removed from Office.

## Article 256 – Ius Ecclesiae Imperium
### (Ecclesiastical Command, Occupation and Enforcement)

975. ***Ius Ecclesiae Imperium*** is the collection of Ecclesiastical Rights of Command, Occupation and Enforcement, as inherited from the Divine Rights *Ius Divinum Imperium*.
Ius Ecclesiae Imperium

976. *Ius Ecclesiae Imperium* (Ecclesiastical Command, Occupation and Enforcement) is the seventh collection of twenty-two Authoritative Ecclesiastical Rights (*Potentis Ecclesiae Iurium*); and may be explicitly invoked or referenced by Ecclesiastical Right of Action through a proper and registered Ecclesiastical Body and the Ecclesiastical Obligations of any such registered Consecrated Person or Ecclesiastical Office in Ucadia or Non-Ucadia Jurisdiction.
Invoking of Ius Ecclesiae Imperium

977. The collection of Ecclesiastical Rights of *Ius Ecclesiae Imperium* contains six (6) Rights being:-
Collection of Ius Ecclesiae Imperium

   (i) *Ius Ecclesiae Imperium* being the Ecclesiastical Right of Command, Occupation and Enforcement; and

   (ii) *Ius Ecclesiae Imperium Emissionis* being the Ecclesiastical Right of Issuance of Command in Good Faith, Good Conscience and Good Action; and

   (iii) *Ius Ecclesiae Imperium Immunitatis* being the Ecclesiastical Right of Immunity for Command Made in Office in Good Faith, Good Conscience and Good Actions; and

   (iv) *Ius Ecclesiae Imperium Receptionis* being the Ecclesiastical Right of Receipt of Command in Good Faith, Good Conscience and Good Action; and

   (v) *Ius Ecclesiae Imperium Executionis* being the Ecclesiastical Right of Enforcement of Command in Good Faith, Good Conscience and Good Action; and

   (vi) *Ius Ecclesiae Immunitatis Executionis* being the Ecclesiastical Right of Immunity when Enforcement of Command done in Good Faith, Good Conscience and Good Action.

## Article 257 – Ius Ecclesiae Sacrum
### (Ecclesiastical Recognition, Devotion and Veneration)

978. ***Ius Ecclesiae Sacrum*** is the collection of Ecclesiastical Rights of Sacred Recognition, Devotion and Veneration, as inherited from the Divine Rights *Ius Divinum Sacrum*.
Ius Ecclesiae Sacrum (Sacred Recognition)

979. *Ius Ecclesiae Sacrum* (Ecclesiastical Recognition, Devotion and Veneration) is the eighth collection of twenty-two Authoritative Ecclesiastical Rights (*Potentis Ecclesiae Iurium*); and may be explicitly invoked or referenced by Ecclesiastical Right of Action through a proper and registered Ecclesiastical Body and the Ecclesiastical Obligations of any such registered Consecrated Person or Ecclesiastical Office in Ucadia or Non-Ucadia Jurisdiction. *(Invoking of Ius Ecclesiae Sacrum)*

980. The collection of Ecclesiastical Rights of *Ius Ecclesiae Sacrum* contains one Right being:- *(Collection of Ius Ecclesiae Sacrum)*

   (i) *Ius Ecclesiae Sacrum* being the Ecclesiastical Right of Sacred Recognition, Devotion and Veneration.

## Article 258 – Ius Ecclesiae Custoditum (Ecclesiastical Custody, Guardianship and Preservation)

981. ***Ius Ecclesiae Custoditum*** is the collection of Ecclesiastical Rights of Custody, Guardianship and Preservation, as inherited from the Divine Rights *Ius Divinum Custoditum*. *(Ius Ecclesiae Custoditum (Custody, Guardianship))*

982. *Ius Ecclesiae Custoditum* (Ecclesiastical Custody, Guardianship and Preservation) is the ninth collection of twenty-two Authoritative Ecclesiastical Rights (*Potentis Ecclesiae Iurium*); and may be explicitly invoked or referenced by Ecclesiastical Right of Action through a proper and registered Ecclesiastical Body and the Ecclesiastical Obligations of any such registered Consecrated Person or Ecclesiastical Office in Ucadia or Non-Ucadia Jurisdiction. *(Invoking of Ius Ecclesiae Custoditum)*

983. The collection of Ecclesiastical Rights of *Ius Ecclesiae Custoditum* contains twenty-seven (27) Rights being:- *(Collection of Ius Ecclesiae Custoditum)*

   (i) *Ius Ecclesiae Custoditum* being the Ecclesiastical Right of Custody, Guardianship and Preservation; and

   (ii) *Ius Ecclesiae Custos* being the Ecclesiastical Right of Custodian; and

   (iii) *Ius Ecclesiae Officii Curae Custodis* being the Ecclesiastical Right of Duty of Care of Custodian; and

   (iv) *Ius Divinum Removendi Custodis* being the Ecclesiastical Right of Removal of Custodian for Breach of Duty of Care or Bad Faith, Bad Conscience or Bad Actions; and

   (v) *Ius Ecclesiae Rationis Legalis Custodis* being the Ecclesiastical Right of Custodian as Attorney and Legal Representative; and

   (vi) *Ius Ecclesiae Medicinae Decisionis Custodis* being the Ecclesiastical Right of Medical Decisions of Custodian; and

(vii) *Ius Ecclesiae Pecuniarum Decisionis Custodis* being the Ecclesiastical Right of Financial Decisions of Custodian; and

(viii) *Ius Ecclesiae Proprietatis Decisionis Custodis* being the Ecclesiastical Right of Property Decisions of Custodian; and

(ix) *Ius Ecclesiae Custodiae Immunitatis* being the Ecclesiastical Right of Immunity of Custodian when Decisions and Actions Made in Office in Good Faith, Good Conscience and Good Actions; and

(x) *Ius Ecclesiae Curatoris* being the Ecclesiastical Right of Curator; and

(xi) *Ius Ecclesiae Officii Curae Curatoris* being the Ecclesiastical Right of Duty of Care of Curator; and

(xii) *Ius Ecclesiae Removendi Curatoris* being the Ecclesiastical Right of Removal of Curator for Breach of Duty of Care or Bad Faith, Bad Conscience or Bad Actions; and

(xiii) *Ius Ecclesiae Rationis Legalis Curatoris* being the Ecclesiastical Right of Curator as Attorney and Legal Representative; and

(xiv) *Ius Ecclesiae Pecuniarum Decisionis Curatoris* being the Ecclesiastical Right of Financial Decisions of Curator; and

(xv) *Ius Ecclesiae Medicinae Decisionis Curatoris* being the Ecclesiastical Right of Medical Decisions of Curator; and

(xvi) *Ius Ecclesiae Proprietatis Decisionis Curatoris* being the Ecclesiastical Right of Property Decisions of Curator; and

(xvii) *Ius Ecclesiae Immunitatis Curatoris* being the Ecclesiastical Right of Immunity of Curator when Decisions and Actions Made in Office in Good Faith, Good Conscience and Good Actions; and

(xviii) *Ius Ecclesiae Protectoris* being the Ecclesiastical Right of Guardian; and

(xix) *Ius Ecclesiae Officii Curae Protectoris* being the Ecclesiastical Right of Duty of Care of Guardian; and

(xx) *Ius Ecclesiae Removendi Protectoris* being the Ecclesiastical Right of Removal of Guardian for Breach of Duty of Care or Bad Faith, Bad Conscience or Bad Actions; and

(xxi) *Ius Ecclesiae Rationis Legalis Protectoris* being the Ecclesiastical Right of Guardian as Attorney and Legal Representative; and

(xxii) *Ius Ecclesiae Medicinae Decisionis Protectoris* being the Ecclesiastical Right of Medical Decisions of Guardian; and

(xxiii) *Ius Ecclesiae Pecuniarum Decisionis Protectoris* being the Ecclesiastical Right of Financial Decisions of Guardian; and

(xxiv) *Ius Ecclesiae Proprietatis Decisionis Protectoris* being the Ecclesiastical Right of Property Decisions of Guardian; and

(xxv) *Ius Ecclesiae Habitationis Decisionis Protectoris* being the Ecclesiastical Right of Housing and Accomodation Decisions of Guardian; and

(xxvi) *Ius Ecclesiae Educationis Decisionis Protectoris* being the Ecclesiastical Right of Education Decisions of Guardian; and

(xxvii) *Ius Ecclesiae Immunitatis Protectoris* being the Ecclesiastical Right of Immunity of Protector when Decisions and Actions Made in Office in Good Faith, Good Conscience and Good Actions.

## Article 259 – Ius Ecclesiae Alumentum (Ecclesiastical Sustenance, Maintenance and Alms)

984. ***Ius Ecclesiae Alumentum*** is the collection of Ecclesiastical Rights to Sustenance, Maintenance and Alms, as inherited from the Divine Rights *Ius Divinum Alumentum*. Ius Ecclesiae Alumentum

985. *Ius Ecclesiae Alumentum* (Ecclesiastical Sustenance, Maintenance and Alms) is the tenth collection of twenty-two Authoritative Ecclesiastical Rights (*Potentis Ecclesiae Iurium*); and may be explicitly invoked or referenced by Ecclesiastical Right of Action through a proper and registered Ecclesiastical Body and the Ecclesiastical Obligations of any such registered Consecrated Person or Ecclesiastical Office in Ucadia or Non-Ucadia Jurisdiction. Invoking of Ius Ecclesiae Alumentum

986. The collection of Ecclesiastical Rights of *Ius Ecclesiae Alumentum* contains nine (9) Rights being:- Collection of Ius Ecclesiae Alumentum

   (i) *Ius Ecclesiae Alumentum* being the Ecclesiastical Right to Sustenance, Maintenance and Alms; and

   (ii) *Ius Ecclesiae Subsistentiae* being the Ecclesiastical Right of Sustenance; and

   (iii) *Ius Ecclesiae Aquae Purae* being the Ecclesiastical Right of Clean Water; and

   (iv) *Ius Ecclesiae Terrae Purae* being the Ecclesiastical Right of Clean Land; and

(v) *Ius Ecclesiae Domicilii* being the Ecclesiastical Right of Shelter; and

(vi) *Ius Ecclesiae Securitatis Violentia* being the Ecclesiastical Right of Safety from Violence; and

(vii) *Ius Ecclesiae Vestitus* being the Ecclesiastical Right of Clothing; and

(viii) *Ius Ecclesiae Curae Medicae* being the Ecclesiastical Right of Medical Care; and

(ix) *Ius Ecclesiae Educationis Bonae* being the Ecclesiastical Right of Good Education.

## Article 260 – Ius Ecclesiae Apostolicus (Divine Commission)

987. **Ius Ecclesiae Apostolicus** is the collection of Ecclesiastical Rights of Divine Commission, as inherited from the Divine Rights *Ius Divinum Apostolicus*.

    <small>Ius Ecclesiae Apostolicus (Divine Commission)</small>

988. *Ius Ecclesiae Apostolicus* (Divine Commission) is the eleventh collection of twenty-two Authoritative Ecclesiastical Rights (*Potentis Ecclesiae Iurium*); and may be explicitly invoked or referenced by Ecclesiastical Right of Action through a proper and registered Ecclesiastical Body and the Ecclesiastical Obligations of any such registered Consecrated Person or Ecclesiastical Office in Ucadia or Non-Ucadia Jurisdiction.

    <small>Invoking of Ius Ecclesiae Apostolicus</small>

989. The collection of Ecclesiastical Rights of *Ius Ecclesiae Apostolicus* contains seven (7) Rights being:-

    <small>Collection of Ius Ecclesiae Apostolicus</small>

    (i) *Ius Ecclesiae Apostolicus* being the Ecclesiastical Right of Divine Commission; and

    (ii) *Ius Ecclesiae Accipiendi Apostolicus* being the Ecclesiastical Right to Receive Commission in Good Faith, Good Conscience and Good Actions; and

    (iii) *Ius Ecclesiae Tenendi Apostolicus* being the Ecclesiastical Right to Hold a Commission in Good Faith, Good Conscience and Good Actions; and

    (iv) *Ius Ecclesiae Immunitatis Apostolicus* being the Ecclesiastical Right of Immunity for Decisions Made under Commission in Good Faith, Good Conscience and Good Actions; and

    (v) *Ius Ecclesiae Dicendi Apostolicus* being the Ecclesiastical Right to Resign from Commission in Honour, Privileges and

Good Standing; and

(vi) *Ius Ecclesiae Nullius Apostolicus* being the Ecclesiastical Right to have Commission Withdrawn and be Terminated in Disgrace, Without Privileges and Poor Standing; and

(vii) *Ius Ecclesiae Restituendi Apostolicus* being the Ecclesiastical Right to be Restored to Commission in Honour, Privileges and Good Standing after having been unlawfully obstructed or removed from Commission.

## Article 261 – Ius Ecclesiae Cancellarium (Chancery & Administration of Records)

990. ***Ius Ecclesiae Cancellarium*** is the collection of Ecclesiastical Rights of Chancery and Administrative Records, as inherited from the Divine Rights *Ius Divinum Cancellarium*.

Ius Ecclesiae Ecclesia Cancellarium

991. *Ius Ecclesiae Cancellarium* (Chancery & Administration of Records) is the twelfth collection of twenty-two Authoritative Ecclesiastical Rights (*Potentis Ecclesiae Iurium*); and may be explicitly invoked or referenced by Ecclesiastical Right of Action through a proper and registered Ecclesiastical Body and the Ecclesiastical Obligations of any such registered Consecrated Person or Ecclesiastical Office in Ucadia or Non-Ucadia Jurisdiction.

Invoking of Ius Ecclesiae Ecclesia Cancellarium (Chancery & Administration)

992. The collection of Ecclesiastical Rights of *Ius Ecclesiae Cancellarium* contains six (6) Rights being:-

Collection of Ius Ecclesiae Ecclesia Cancellarium

(i) *Ius Ecclesiae Cancellarium* being the Ecclesiastical Right of Chancery and Administration of Records; and

(ii) *Ius Ecclesiae Aedificandi Cancellariae* being the Ecclesiastical Right of Chancery Building; and

(iii) *Ius Ecclesiae Procedendi Cancellariae* being the Ecclesiastical Right of Chancery Procedures; and

(iv) *Ius Ecclesiae Technologiae Cancellariae* being the Ecclesiastical Right of Chancery Technology and Digital Systems; and

(v) *Ius Ecclesiae Cancellarii* being the Ecclesiastical Right of the Chancellor; and

(vi) *Ius Ecclesiae Cancellarii Immunitatis* being the Ecclesiastical Right of Immunity for Chancellor and Agents when Decisions and Actions Made in Office in Good Faith, Good Conscience and Good Actions.

## Article 262 – Ius Ecclesiae Oratorium (Ecclesiastical Forum of Law and Review)

993. ***Ius Ecclesiae Oratorium*** is the collection of Ecclesiastical Rights to a Competent Forum of Law and Review, as inherited from the Divine Rights *Ius Divinum Oratorium*.

    Ius Ecclesiae Oratorium (Competent Forum of Law & Review)

994. *Ius Ecclesiae Oratorium* (Ecclesiastical Forum of Law and Review) is the thirteenth collection of twenty-two Authoritative Ecclesiastical Rights (*Potentis Ecclesiae Iurium*); and may be explicitly invoked or referenced by Ecclesiastical Right of Action through a proper and registered Ecclesiastical Body and the Ecclesiastical Obligations of any such registered Consecrated Person or Ecclesiastical Office in Ucadia or Non-Ucadia Jurisdiction.

    Invoking of Ius Ecclesiae Oratorium

995. The collection of Ecclesiastical Rights of *Ius Ecclesiae Oratorium* contains twelve (12) Rights being:-

    Collection of Ius Ecclesiae Oratorium

    (i) *Ius Ecclesiae Oratorium* being the Ecclesiastical Right of Competent Forum of Law and Review; and

    (ii) *Ius Ecclesiae Aedificandi Fori* being the Ecclesiastical Right of Forum of Law Building; and

    (iii) *Ius Ecclesiae Procedendi Fori* being the Ecclesiastical Right of Forum of Law Procedures; and

    (iv) *Ius Ecclesiae Technologiae Fori* being the Ecclesiastical Right of Forum of Law Technology and Digital Systems; and

    (v) *Ius Ecclesiae Iudicum Fori* being the Ecclesiastical Right of Forum of Law Justices; and

    (vi) *Ius Ecclesiae Iudicum Immunitatis* being the Ecclesiastical Right of Immunity for Justices when Decisions and Actions Made in Office in Good Faith, Good Conscience and Good Actions; and

    (vii) *Ius Ecclesiae Iudicum Officiorum Fori* being the Ecclesiastical Right of Forum of Law Officers; and

    (viii) *Ius Ecclesiae Officii Iudicialis Immunitatis* being the Ecclesiastical Right of Immunity for Law Officers when Decisions and Actions Made in Office in Good Faith, Good Conscience and Good Actions; and

    (ix) *Ius Ecclesiae Custodiae Iudicialis Fori* being the Ecclesiastical Right of Forum of Law Attendants and Guards; and

    (x) *Ius Ecclesiae Custodiae Iudicialis Immunitatis* being the Ecclesiastical Right of Immunity for Law Attendants and

Guards when Decisions and Actions Made in Office in Good Faith, Good Conscience and Good Actions; and

(xi) *Ius Ecclesiae Cancellarium Fori* being the Ecclesiastical Right of Forum of Law Chancery and Records Administration; and

(xii) *Ius Ecclesiae Penitentiaria Fori* being the Divine Right of Forum of Law Penitentiary and Holding Prison.

## Article 263 – Ius Ecclesiae Templum (Ecclesiastical Treasury or Financial (Banking) Body)

996. ***Ius Ecclesiae Templum*** is the collection of Ecclesiastical Rights of a Treasury or Financial (Banking) Body, as inherited from the Divine Right *Ius Divinum Templum*.

Ius Ecclesiae Templum (Treasury & Banking)

997. *Ius Ecclesiae Templum* (Ecclesiastical Treasury or Financial (Banking) Body) is the fourteenth collection of twenty-two Authoritative Ecclesiastical Rights (*Potentis Ecclesiae Iurium*); and may be explicitly invoked or referenced by Ecclesiastical Right of Action through a proper and registered Ecclesiastical Body and the Ecclesiastical Obligations of any such registered Consecrated Person or Ecclesiastical Office in Ucadia or Non-Ucadia Jurisdiction.

Invoking of Ius Ecclesiae Templum

998. The collection of Ecclesiastical Rights of *Ius Ecclesiae Templum* contains eleven (11) Rights being:-

Collection of Ius Ecclesiae Templum

(i) *Ius Ecclesiae Templum* being the Ecclesiastical Right of a Treasury or Financial (Banking) Body; and

(ii) *Ius Ecclesiae Officina Monetaria* being the Ecclesiastical Right of Minting Office; and

(iii) *Ius Ecclesiae Pecuniariarum Administrandi* being the Ecclesiastical Right of Cash Management; and

(iv) *Ius Ecclesiae Monetarum Administrandi* being the Ecclesiastical Right of Monetary Management; and

(v) *Ius Ecclesiae Administrationis Financiarum* being the Ecclesiastical Right of Financial Administration; and

(vi) *Ius Ecclesiae Administrationis Bancariae* being the Ecclesiastical Right of Banking Administration; and

(vii) *Ius Ecclesiae Administrationis Creditorum* being the Ecclesiastical Right of Credit Management; and

(viii) *Ius Ecclesiae Administrationis Debiti* being the Divine Right of Debt Management; and

(ix) *Ius Ecclesiae Administrationis Financiarum Periculi* being the

Ecclesiastical Right of Financial Risk Management; and

(x) *Ius Ecclesiae Operationum Thesaurariarum* being the Ecclesiastical Right of Treasury Management; and

(xi) *Ius Ecclesiae Administrationis Conformitatis* being the Ecclesiastical Right of Compliance Management.

## Article 264 – Ius Ecclesiae Sacramentum (Grant and Impart Holy Sacraments)

999. ***Ius Ecclesiae Sacramentum*** is the collection of Ecclesiastical Rights to Grant and Impart Holy Sacraments, as inherited from the Divine Rights *Ius Divinum Sacramentum*. Ius Ecclesiae Sacramentum

1000. *Ius Ecclesiae Sacramentum* (Grant and Impart Holy Sacraments) is the fifteenth collection of twenty-two Authoritative Ecclesiastical Rights (*Potentis Ecclesiae Iurium*); and may be explicitly invoked or referenced by Ecclesiastical Right of Action through a proper and registered Ecclesiastical Body and the Ecclesiastical Obligations of any such registered Consecrated Person or Ecclesiastical Office in Ucadia or Non-Ucadia Jurisdiction. Invoking of Ius Ecclesiae Sacramentum

1001. The collection of Ecclesiastical Rights of *Ius Ecclesiae Sacramentum* contains one Right being:- Collection of Ius Ecclesiae Sacramentum

   (i) *Ius Ecclesiae Sacramentum* being the Ecclesiastical Right to grant and impart Holy Sacred Gifts.

## Article 265 – Ius Ecclesiae Visum (Ecclesiastical Survey, Visit and Audit of Bodies)

1002. ***Ius Ecclesiae Visum*** is the collection of Ecclesiastical Rights to Survey, Visit and Audit Ucadia Bodies, as inherited from the Divine Rights *Ius Divinum Visum*. Ius Ecclesiae Visum (Survey, Visit & Audit)

1003. *Ius Ecclesiae Visum* (Ecclesiastical Survey, Visit and Audit of Bodies) is the sixteenth collection of twenty-two Authoritative Ecclesiastical Rights (*Potentis Ecclesiae Iurium*); and may be explicitly invoked or referenced by Ecclesiastical Right of Action through a proper and registered Ecclesiastical Body and the Ecclesiastical Obligations of any such registered Consecrated Person or Ecclesiastical Office in Ucadia or Non-Ucadia Jurisdiction. Invoking of Ius Ecclesiae Visum (Survey, Visit & Audit)

1004. The collection of Ecclesiastical Rights of *Ius Ecclesiae Visum* contains eleven (11) Rights being:- Collection of Ius Ecclesiae Visum (Survey, Visit & Audit)

   (i) *Ius Ecclesiae Visum* being the Ecclesiastical Right to Survey, Visit and Audit a Body; and

(ii) *Ius Ecclesiae Monumenti* being the Ecclesiastical Right of Creating Monument; and

(iii) *Ius Ecclesiae Usus Notatoris* being the Ecclesiastical Right of Creating and Setting a Marker; and

(iv) *Ius Ecclesiae Usus Limitis* being the Ecclesiastical Right of Creating and Setting a Boundary; and

(v) *Ius Ecclesiae Visitationis* being the Ecclesiastical Right of Visitation; and

(vi) *Ius Ecclesiae Arationis* being the Ecclesiastical Right of Survey; and

(vii) *Ius Ecclesiae Certificandi Arationem* being the Ecclesiastical Right of Certification of Survey; and

(viii) *Ius Ecclesiae Usus Servitutis* being the Ecclesiastical Right of Easement; and

(ix) *Ius Ecclesiae Viæ* being the Ecclesiastical Right of Way; and

(x) *Ius Ecclesiae Usus Terrae* being the Ecclesiastical Right of Land Use; and

(xi) *Ius Ecclesiae Topographiae* being the Ecclesiastical Right of Topography.

## Article 266 – Ius Ecclesiae Commercium (Ecclesiastical Trade, Exchange and Communication)

1005. ***Ius Ecclesiae Commercium*** is the collection of Ecclesiastical Rights to Trade, Exchange and Communication, as inherited from the Divine Rights *Ius Divinum Commercium*. — Ius Ecclesiae Commercium

1006. *Ius Ecclesiae Commercium* (Ecclesiastical Trade, Exchange and Communication) is the seventeenth collection of twenty-two Authoritative Ecclesiastical Rights (*Potentis Ecclesiae Iurium*); and may be explicitly invoked or referenced by Ecclesiastical Right of Action through a proper and registered Ecclesiastical Body and the Ecclesiastical Obligations of any such registered Consecrated Person or Ecclesiastical Office in Ucadia or Non-Ucadia Jurisdiction. — Invoking of Ius Ecclesiae Commercium (Trade, Exchange & Communication)

1007. The collection of Ecclesiastical Rights of *Ius Ecclesiae Commercium* contains ten (10) Rights being:- — Collection of Ius Ecclesiae Commercium

(i) *Ius Ecclesiae Commercium* being the Ecclesiastical Right to Trade, Exchange and Communication; and

(ii) *Ius Ecclesiae Libertatis Negotiandi Pretium* being the

Ecclesiastical Right of Freedom to Negotiate Price; and

(iii) *Ius Ecclesiae Libertatis Emendi* being the Ecclesiastical Right of Freedom to Purchase; and

(iv) *Ius Ecclesiae Libertatis Vendendi* being the Ecclesiastical Right of Freedom to Sell; and

(v) *Ius Ecclesiae Libertatis Mercatorum* being the Ecclesiastical Right of Freedom of Trade; and

(vi) *Ius Ecclesiae Libertatis Investitionis* being the Ecclesiastical Right of Freedom of Investment; and

(vii) *Ius Ecclesiae Libertatis Motus Bonorum* being the Ecclesiastical Right of Freedom of Movement of Goods; and

(viii) *Ius Ecclesiae Libertatis Mercatorum Conventi* being the Ecclesiastical Right of Freedom of Agreement; and

(ix) *Ius Ecclesiae Qualitatem Deliberatam* being the Ecclesiastical Right of Quality Delivered; and

(x) *Ius Ecclesiae Rem Emptam* being the Ecclesiastical Right to a Thing Purchased.

## Article 267 – Ius Ecclesiae Virtus (Ecclesiastical Strength, Honour, Excellence and Virtue)

1008. ***Ius Ecclesiae Virtus*** is the Ecclesiastical Rights to Strength, Honour, Excellence and Virtue, as inherited from the Divine Rights *Ius Divinum Virtus*. — Ius Ecclesiae Virtus

1009. *Ius Ecclesiae Virtus* (Ecclesiastical Strength, Honour, Excellence and Virtue) is the eighteenth collection of twenty-two Authoritative Ecclesiastical Rights (*Potentis Ecclesiae Iurium*); and may be explicitly invoked or referenced by Ecclesiastical Right of Action through a proper and registered Ecclesiastical Body and the Ecclesiastical Obligations of any such registered Consecrated Person or Ecclesiastical Office in Ucadia or Non-Ucadia Jurisdiction. — Invoking of Ius Ecclesiae Virtus (Strength, Honour, Excellence & Virtue)

1010. The collection of Ecclesiastical Rights of *Ius Ecclesiae Virtus* contains one Right being:- — Collection of Ius Ecclesiae Virtus

(i) *Ius Ecclesiae Virtus* being the Ecclesiastical Right to Strength, Honour, Excellence and Virtue.

## Article 268 – Ius Ecclesiae Penitentiaria (Forced Confinement)

1011. ***Ius Ecclesiae Penitentiaria*** is the collection of Ecclesiastical Rights of Forced Confinement, as inherited from the Divine Rights *Ius Divinum Penitentiaria*.

Ius Ecclesiae Penitentiaria (Forced Confinement)

1012. *Ius Ecclesiae Penitentiaria* (Forced Confinement) is the nineteenth collection of twenty-two Authoritative Ecclesiastical Rights (*Potentis Ecclesiae Iurium*); and may be explicitly invoked or referenced by Ecclesiastical Right of Action through a proper and registered Ecclesiastical Body and the Ecclesiastical Obligations of any such registered Consecrated Person or Ecclesiastical Office in Ucadia or Non-Ucadia Jurisdiction.

Invoking of Ius Ecclesiae Penitentiaria (Forced Confinement)

1013. The collection of Ecclesiastical Rights of *Ius Ecclesiae Penitentiaria* contains five (5) Rights being:-

Collection of Ius Ecclesiae Penitentiaria (Forced Confinement)

   (i)   *Ius Ecclesiae Penitentiaria* being the Ecclesiastical Right of Forced Confinement; and

   (ii)  *Ius Ecclesiae Penitentiaria Poena* being the Ecclesiastical Right to issue Punishment; and

   (iii) *Ius Ecclesiae Penitentiaria Reformatio* being the Ecclesiastical Right to Reform through Forced Confinement; and

   (iv)  *Ius Ecclesiae Penitentiaria Disciplina* being the Ecclesiastical Right to Acquire Greater Discipline through Confinement; and

   (v)   *Ius Ecclesiae Penitentiaria Eruditio* being the Ecclesiastical Right to Greater Knowledge through Confinement.

## Article 269 – Ius Ecclesiae Astrum (Ecclesiastical Association, Aggregate or Body)

1014. ***Ius Ecclesiae Astrum*** is the collection of Ecclesiastical Rights of an Association, Aggregate or Body, as inherited from the Divine Rights *Ius Divinum Astrum*.

Ius Ecclesiae Astrum

1015. *Ius Ecclesiae Astrum* (Ecclesiastical Association, Aggregate or Body) is the twentieth collection of twenty-two Authoritative Ecclesiastical Rights (*Potentis Ecclesiae Iurium*); and may be explicitly invoked or referenced by Ecclesiastical Right of Action through a proper and registered Ecclesiastical Body and the Ecclesiastical Obligations of any such registered Consecrated Person or Ecclesiastical Office in Ucadia or Non-Ucadia Jurisdiction.

Invoking of Ius Ecclesiae Astrum (Association, Aggregate or Body)

1016. The collection of Ecclesiastical Rights of *Ius Ecclesiae Astrum*

Collection of Ius

contains eight (8) Rights being:-     *Ecclesiae Astrum*

- (i) *Ius Ecclesiae Astrum* being the Ecclesiastical Right to an Association, Aggregate or Body; and
- (ii) *Ius Ecclesiae Libertatis Associationis* being the Ecclesiastical Right of Freedom of Association; and
- (iii) *Ius Ecclesiae Libertatis Expressionis* being the Ecclesiastical Right of Freedom of Expression; and
- (iv) *Ius Ecclesiae Libertatis Eventus Organisati* being the Ecclesiastical Right of Freedom of Organised Events; and
- (v) Ius *Ecclesiae* Publica Accedendi being the Ecclesiastical Right of Access to Public Spaces; and
- (vi) *Ius Ecclesiae Libertatis Protestandi* being the Ecclesiastical Right of Freedom to Protest; and
- (vii) *Ius Ecclesiae Libertatis Violentia Civili* being the Ecclesiastical Right of Freedom from State Violence; and
- (viii) *Ius Ecclesiae Dissolutionis* being the Ecclesiastical Right of Dissolution.

## Article 270 – Ius Ecclesiae Magisterium (Instruct and Interpret Sacred Texts & Divine Will)

**1017.** ***Ius Ecclesiae Magisterium*** is the collection of Ecclesiastical Rights to Teach, Instruct and Interpret Sacred Texts and Divine Will, as inherited from the Divine Rights *Ius Divinum Magisterium*,     *Ius Ecclesiae Magisterium*

**1018.** *Ius Ecclesiae Magisterium* (Instruct and Interpret Sacred Texts & Divine Will) is the twenty-first collection of twenty-two Authoritative Ecclesiastical Rights (*Potentis Ecclesiae Iurium*); and may be explicitly invoked or referenced by Ecclesiastical Right of Action through a proper and registered Ecclesiastical Body and the Ecclesiastical Obligations of any such registered Consecrated Person or Ecclesiastical Office in Ucadia or Non-Ucadia Jurisdiction.     Invoking of Ius Ecclesiae Magisterium (Teach, Instruct and Interpret Sacred Texts & Divine Will)

**1019.** The collection of Ecclesiastical Rights of *Ius Ecclesiae Magisterium* contains six (6) Rights being:-     Collection of Ius Ecclesiae Magisterium

- (i) *Ius Ecclesiae Magisterium* being the Ecclesiastical Right to Teach, Instruct and Interpret Sacred Texts and Divine Will; and
- (ii) *Ius Ecclesiae Fallax Numquam Infallibilis* being the Ecclesiastical Right to be Fallible and Never claim Infallibility before the Divine; and

(iii) *Ius Ecclesiae Sapientia Circa Divinum* being the Ecclesiastical Right of Wisdom concerning the Divine; and

(iv) *Ius Ecclesiae Humilitas Circa Divinum* being the Ecclesiastical Right of Humility concerning the Divine; and

(v) *Ius Ecclesiae Bonafide Circa Divinum* being the Ecclesiastical Right of Good Faith concerning the Divine; and

(vi) *Ius Ecclesiae Interpretationis Divinae Revelationis* being the Ecclesiastical Right to Interpret Divine Revelation according to Wisdom, Humility and Good Faith.

## Article 271 – Ius Ecclesiae Decretum (Ecclesiastical Decree, Judgement and Edict)

1020. ***Ius Ecclesiae Decretum*** is the collection of Ecclesiastical Rights to issue Decree, Judgement and Edict, as inherited from the collection of Divine Rights *Ius Divinum Decretum*. <small>Ius Ecclesiae Decretum</small>

1021. *Ius Ecclesiae Decretum* (Ecclesiastical Decree, Judgement and Edict) is the twenty-second collection of twenty-two Authoritative Ecclesiastical Rights (*Potentis Ecclesiae Iurium*); and may be explicitly invoked or referenced by Ecclesiastical Right of Action through a proper and registered Ecclesiastical Body and the Ecclesiastical Obligations of any such registered Consecrated Person or Ecclesiastical Office in Ucadia or Non-Ucadia Jurisdiction. <small>Invoking of Ius Ecclesiae Decretum (Decree, Judgement and Edict)</small>

1022. The collection of Ecclesiastical Rights of *Ius Ecclesiae Decretum* contains six (6) Rights being:- <small>Collection of Ius Ecclesiae Decretum</small>

(i) *Ius Ecclesiae Decretum* being the Ecclesiastical Right of Decrees, Judgements and Edicts; and

(ii) *Ius Ecclesiae Edicti* being the Ecclesiastical Right of Edict being a formal executive or Ecclesiastical address and command concerning a moral or legal or administrative matter; and

(iii) *Ius Ecclesiae Decreti* being the Ecclesiastical Right of Decree being an Official Order or command; and

(iv) *Ius Ecclesiae Declarationis Iudicii* being the Ecclesiastical Right of Declaratory Judgement; and

(v) *Ius Ecclesiae Rescripti* being the Ecclesiastical Right of Rescript being a formal response to one or more ecclesiastical or legal questions; and

(vi) *Ius Ecclesiae Notificandi* being the Ecclesiastical Right of Notice being a formal note distributed and published concerning some subject.

## 8.3 – Instrumental Ecclesiastical Rights

### Article 272 – Instrumental Ecclesiastical Rights

1023. ***Instrumental Ecclesiastical Rights*** (*Instrumentalis Ecclesiae Iurium*) shall be Ecclesiastical Rights essential to the proper administration of Ecclesiastical Rights. Instrumental Ecclesiastical Rights

1024. All *Instrumental Ecclesiastical Rights* are delegated to the safe custody and wise guardian powers of the legitimate and valid supreme competent ecclesiastical forum of law of the proper Ucadia Faiths and all lesser associated Ucadia bodies, as the embodiment of judicial authority; and as defined by Article 59 (Oratorium) of the most sacred Covenant *Pactum De Singularis Caelum*. Delegation of Instrumental Ecclesiastical Rights

1025. All *Instrumental Ecclesiastical Rights* are assumed to be automatically invoked within Ucadia Jurisdictions through the operation of the Civilised Rules of Ucadia Societies, Bodies and Entities. However the Rights may be explicitly invoked or referenced by Right of Action through a proper Forum of Law and the Fiduciary Obligations of any such court in Ucadia or Non-Ucadia Jurisdiction. Invocation of Instrumental Ecclesiastical Rights

1026. The following valid twenty-two (22) Instrumental Ecclesiastical Rights (*Instrumentalis Ecclesiae Iurium*) shall be recognised in accord with the most sacred Covenant *Pactum De Singularis Caelum*:- List of Instrumental Ecclesiastical Rights (Instrumentalis Ecclesiae Iurium)

    (i)    **"Ius Ecclesiae Iuris"** is the collection of Ecclesiastical Rights of Justice and Due Process, as inherited from the collection of Divine Rights *Ius Divinum Iuris*; and

    (ii)    **"Ius Ecclesiae Bona Fidei"** is the collection of Ecclesiastical Rights of Good Faith, Good Conscience and Good Actions, as inherited from the collection of Divine Rights *Ius Divinum Bona Fidei*; and

    (iii)    **"Ius Ecclesiae Aequum"** is the collection of Ecclesiastical Rights of Equality and Fairness, as inherited from the collection of Divine Rights *Ius Divinum Aequum*; and

    (iv)    **"Ius Ecclesiae Fidei"** is the collection of Ecclesiastical Rights of Superior Ecclesiastical Trust and Ecclesiastical Estate, as inherited from the collection of Divine Rights *Ius Divinum Fidei*; and

    (v)    **"Ius Ecclesiae Rationatio"** is the collection of

Ecclesiastical Rights of Accounting, Credit and Funds, as inherited from the collection of Divine Rights *Ius Divinum Rationatio*; and

(vi) **"Ius Ecclesiae Concedere et Abrogare"** is the collection of Ecclesiastical Rights to Give or Grant Rights and Annul or rescind Superior Rights, as inherited from the collection of Divine Rights *Ius Divinum Concedere et Abrogare*; and

(vii) **"Ius Ecclesiae Delegare et Revocare"** is the collection of Ecclesiastical Rights to Assign or Delegate Rights and Cancel or Revoke Superior Rights, as inherited from the collection of Divine Rights *Ius Divinum Delegare et Revocare*; and

(viii) **"Ius Ecclesiae Associatio et Conventio"** is the collection of Ecclesiastical Rights of Association and Agreement, as inherited from the collection of Divine Rights *Ius Divinum Associatio et Conventio*; and

(ix) **"Ius Ecclesiae Consensum et Non"** is the collection of Ecclesiastical Rights to Consent and Non-Consent, as inherited from the collection of Divine Rights *Ius Divinum Consensum et Non*; and

(x) **"Ius Ecclesiae Hereditatis"** is the collection of Ecclesiastical Rights of Inheritance of Divine Rights, as inherited from the collection of Divine Rights *Ius Divinum Dominium* and *Ius Divinum Bona Fidei*; and

(xi) **"Ius Ecclesiae Dominium"** is the collection of Ecclesiastical Rights of Absolute Ownership, as inherited from the collection of Divine Rights *Ius Divinum Dominium*; and

(xii) **"Ius Ecclesiae Possessionis"** is the collection of Ecclesiastical Rights to Possess, Hold and Own Property, as inherited from the collection of Divine Rights *Ius Divinum Possessionis*; and

(xiii) **"Ius Ecclesiae Usus"** is the collection of Ecclesiastical Rights of Use and Fruits (Enjoyment) of Use of Property, as inherited from the collection of Divine Rights *Ius Divinum Usus*; and

(xiv) **"Ius Ecclesiae Proprietatis"** is the collection of Ecclesiastical Rights of Ownership of Use or Fruits of Use of Property, as inherited from the collection of Divine Rights *Ius Divinum Proprietatis*; and

(xv) **"Ius Ecclesiae Vectigalis Proprietatis"** is the collection of Ecclesiastical Rights to impose Rents, Tolls, Levies, Contributions or Charges against Property, as inherited from the collection of Divine Rights *Ius Divinum Vectigalis Proprietatis*; and

(xvi) **"Ius Ecclesiae Moneta"** is the collection of Ecclesiastical Rights to Mint, Produce, Hold, Use and Exchange Money, as inherited from the collection of Divine Rights *Ius Divinum Moneta*; and

(xvii) **"Ius Ecclesiae Vectigalis Moneta"** is the collection of Ecclesiastical Rights to impose Rents, Tolls, Levies, Contributions or Charges against Money, as inherited from the collection of Divine Rights *Ius Divinum Vectigalis Moneta*; and

(xviii) **"Ius Ecclesiae Registrum"** is the collection of Ecclesiastical Rights to Enter Records within Registers and Rolls, as inherited from the collection of Divine Rights *Ius Divinum Registrum*; and

(xix) **"Ius Ecclesiae Remedium"** is the collection of Ecclesiastical Rights of Remedy, Relief, Redress or Compensation, as inherited from the collection of Divine Rights *Ius Divinum Remedium*; and

(xx) **"Ius Ecclesiae Poena"** is the collection of Ecclesiastical Rights of Penalty, Penitence or Punishment, as inherited from the collection of Divine Rights *Ius Divinum Poena*; and

(xxi) **"Ius Ecclesiae Clementia"** is the collection of Ecclesiastical Rights of Mercy & Forgiveness, as inherited from the collection of Divine Rights *Ius Divinum Clementia*; and

(xxii) **"Ius Ecclesiae Actionum"** is the collection of Ecclesiastical Rights of Action, as inherited from the collection of Divine Rights *Ius Divinum Actionum*.

## Article 273 – Ius Ecclesiae Iuris (Justice & Due Process)

1027. *Ius Ecclesiae Iuris* is the collection of Ecclesiastical Rights of Justice and Due Process, as inherited from the collection of Divine Rights *Ius Divinum Iuris*.

<sub>Ius Ecclesiae Iuris (Justice & Due Process)</sub>

1028. *Ius Ecclesiae Iuris* (Justice & Due Process) is the first collection of twenty-two *Instrumental Ecclesiastical Rights* (*Instrumentalis*

<sub>Invoking of Ius Ecclesiae Iuris (Justice & Due</sub>

*Ecclesiae Iurium*); and may be explicitly invoked or referenced by Ecclesiastical Right of Action through a proper and registered Ecclesiastical Entity and the Ecclesiastical Obligations of any such registered Ecclesiastical Person or Executive Office in Ucadia or Non-Ucadia Jurisdiction.

1029. The collection of Ecclesiastical Rights of *Ius Ecclesiae Iuris* contains nine (9) Rights being:

    (i) *Ius Ecclesiae Iuris* being the Ecclesiastical Right of Justice and Due Process; and

    (ii) *Ius Ecclesiae Accusationis* being the Ecclesiastical Right to make an Accusation against another Person or Body or Entity upon Possession of Provable Evidence of Personal Harm, Injury or Loss; and

    (iii) *Ius Ecclesiae Innocentiae* being the Ecclesiastical Right of Innocence against any Accusation until Proven or Confession or Culpability; and

    (iv) *Ius Ecclesiae Accusationis Cognoscendi* being the Ecclesiastical Right for the Accused and their Agent to know the Full Disclosure and Brief of Evidence of any Accusation; and

    (v) *Ius Ecclesiae Defensionis* being the Ecclesiastical Right to Defend against any Accusation; and

    (vi) *Ius Ecclesiae Processus Iustus* being the Ecclesiastical Right of Fair Process; and

    (vii) *Ius Ecclesiae Arbitrandi* being the Ecclesiastical Right of Arbitration as method for dispute resolution; and

    (viii) *Ius Ecclesiae Propria Persona* being the Ecclesiastical Right to defend or accuse as oneself; and

    (ix) *Ius Ecclesiae Iudicialis Agensas* being the Ecclesiastical Right to appoint a Legal Agent to defend or accuse.

## Article 274 – Ius Ecclesiae Bona Fidei (Good Faith)

1030. ***Ius Ecclesiae Bona Fidei*** is the collection of Ecclesiastical Rights of Good Faith, Good Conscience and Good Actions, as inherited from the collection of Divine Rights *Ius Divinum Bona Fidei*.

1031. *Ius Ecclesiae Bona Fidei* (Good Faith) is the second collection of twenty-two *Instrumental Ecclesiastical Rights* (*Instrumentalis Ecclesiae Iurium*); and may be explicitly invoked or referenced by

Ecclesiastical Right of Action through a proper and registered Ecclesiastical Entity and the Ecclesiastical Obligations of any such registered Ecclesiastical Person or Executive Office in Ucadia or Non-Ucadia Jurisdiction.

1032. The collection of Ecclesiastical Rights of *Ius Ecclesiae Bona Fidei* contains three (3) Rights being:

(i) *Ius Ecclesiae Bona Fidei* being the Ecclesiastical Right of Good Faith; and

(ii) *Ius Ecclesiae Bona Conscientia* being the Ecclesiastical Right of Good Conscience; and

(iii) *Ius Ecclesiae Bona Actio* being the Ecclesiastical Right of Good Action.

## Article 275 – Ius Ecclesiae Aequum (Equality and Fairness)

1033. ***Ius Ecclesiae Aequum*** is the collection of Ecclesiastical Rights of Equality and Fairness, as inherited from the collection of Divine Rights *Ius Divinum Aequum*.

1034. *Ius Ecclesiae Aequum* (Fairness & Equality) is the third collection of twenty-two *Instrumental Ecclesiastical Rights* (*Instrumentalis Ecclesiae Iurium*); and may be explicitly invoked or referenced by Ecclesiastical Right of Action through a proper and registered Ecclesiastical Entity and the Ecclesiastical Obligations of any such registered Ecclesiastical Person or Executive Office in Ucadia or Non-Ucadia Jurisdiction.

1035. The collection of Ecclesiastical Rights of *Ius Ecclesiae Aequum* contains two (2) Rights being:

(i) *Ius Ecclesiae Aequum* being the Ecclesiastical Right of Equality and Fairness; and

(ii) *Ius Ecclesiae Divinum Aequitatis* being the Ecclesiastical Right of Fairness.

## Article 276 – Ius Ecclesiae Fidei (Trust & Estate)

1036. ***Ius Ecclesiae Fidei*** is the collection of Ecclesiastical Rights of Superior Ecclesiastical Trust and Ecclesiastical Estate, as inherited from the collection of Divine Rights *Ius Divinum Fidei*.

1037. *Ius Ecclesiae Fidei* (Trust & Estate) is the fourth collection of twenty-two *Instrumental Ecclesiastical Rights* (*Instrumentalis Ecclesiae*

*Iurium*); and may be explicitly invoked or referenced by Ecclesiastical Right of Action through a proper and registered Ecclesiastical Entity and the Ecclesiastical Obligations of any such registered Ecclesiastical Person or Executive Office in Ucadia or Non-Ucadia Jurisdiction. *(Trust & Estate)*

1038. The collection of Ecclesiastical Rights of *Ius Ecclesiae Fidei* contains nine (9) Rights being: *Collection of Ius Ecclesiae Fidei (Trust & Estate)*

   (i) *Ius Ecclesiae Fidei* being the Ecclesiastical Right of Trusts & Estates; and

   (ii) *Ius Ecclesiae Fiduciam Formandi* being the Ecclesiastical Right to form a Trust; and

   (iii) *Ius Ecclesiae Fiduciam Beneficiarius* being the Ecclesiastical Right of Benefit from Trust; and

   (iv) *Ius Ecclesiae Fiduciam Computatio* being the Ecclesiastical Right to Receive an Accounting of the Administration of a Trust; and

   (v) *Ius Ecclesiae Fiduciam Investiendi* being the Ecclesiastical Right to Vest one or more Assets or Property into a Trust; and

   (vi) *Ius Ecclesiae Fundum Formandi* being the Ecclesiastical Right to form an Estate; and

   (vii) *Ius Ecclesiae Fundum Hereditatis* being the Ecclesiastical Right to inherit an Estate; and

   (viii) *Ius Ecclesiae Fundum Beneficiarius* being the Ecclesiastical Right of Benefit from an Estate; and

   (ix) *Ius Ecclesiae Fundum Computatio* being the Ecclesiastical Right to Receive an Accounting of the Administration of the Estate.

## Article 277 – Ius Ecclesiae Rationatio (Accounting, Credit and Funds)

1039. *Ius Ecclesiae Rationatio* is the collection of Ecclesiastical Rights of Accounting, Credit and Funds, as inherited from the collection of Divine Rights *Ius Divinum Rationatio*. *Ius Ecclesiae Rationatio*

1040. *Ius Ecclesiae Rationatio* (Accounting, Credit & Funds) is the fifth collection of twenty-two *Instrumental Ecclesiastical Rights* (*Instrumentalis Ecclesiae Iurium*); and may be explicitly invoked or referenced by Ecclesiastical Right of Action through a proper and registered Ecclesiastical Entity and the Ecclesiastical Obligations of any such registered Ecclesiastical Person or Executive Office in *Invoking of Ius Ecclesiae Rationatio (Accounting, Credit and Funds)*

Ucadia or Non-Ucadia Jurisdiction.

1041. The collection of Ecclesiastical Rights of *Ius Ecclesiae Rationatio* contains thirteen (13) Rights being:-

> Collection of Ius Ecclesiae Rationatio

    (i)    *Ius Ecclesiae Rationatio* being the Ecclesiastical Right of Accounting, Credit and Funds; and

    (ii)    *Ius Ecclesiae Rationum* being the Ecclesiastical Right of Accounts; and

    (iii)    *Ius Ecclesiae Rationum Examinationis* being the Ecclesiastical Right of Accounts Audit; and

    (iv)    *Ius Ecclesiae Aestimationis Valoris* being the Ecclesiastical Right of Valuation; and

    (v)    *Ius Ecclesiae Aestimationis Obligationis* being the Ecclesiastical Right of Estimating Obligation for Value; and

    (vi)    *Ius Ecclesiae Aestimationis Pretii* being the Ecclesiastical Right of Estimating Price for Obligation; and

    (vii)    *Ius Ecclesiae Aestimationis Crediti* being the Ecclesiastical Right of Estimating Credit; and

    (viii)    *Ius Ecclesiae Aestimationis Debiti* being the Ecclesiastical Right of Estimating Debit; and

    (ix)    *Ius Ecclesiae Valorum Pignorare* being the Ecclesiastical Right to Pledge Valuables as Collateral for Funds; and

    (x)    *Ius Ecclesiae Rationum Relatio* being the Ecclesiastical Right of Reporting of Accounts; and

    (xi)    *Ius Ecclesiae Relatio Crediti* being the Ecclesiastical Right of Credit Reporting; and

    (xii)    *Ius Ecclesiae Crediti Accessus* being the Ecclesiastical Right of Access to Funds; and

    (xiii)    *Ius Ecclesiae Collectionis Debiti* being the Ecclesiastical Right of Debit (Debt) Collection.

## Article 278 – Ius Ecclesiae Concedere et Abrogare (Give or Grant Rights)

1042. ***Ius Ecclesiae Concedere et Abrogare*** is the collection of Ecclesiastical Rights to Give or Grant Rights and Annul or rescind Superior Rights, as inherited from the collection of Divine Rights *Ius Divinum Concedere et Abrogare*.

> Ius Ecclesiae Concedere et Abrogare (Give or Grant Rights)

1043. *Ius Ecclesiae Concedere et Abrogare* (Give or Grant Rights) is the

> Invoking of Ius

sixth collection of twenty-two *Instrumental Ecclesiastical Rights* (*Instrumentalis Ecclesiae Iurium*); and may be explicitly invoked or referenced by Ecclesiastical Right of Action through a proper and registered Ecclesiastical Entity and the Ecclesiastical Obligations of any such registered Ecclesiastical Person or Executive Office in Ucadia or Non-Ucadia Jurisdiction.

Ecclesiae Concedere et Abrogare (Give or Grant Rights)

1044. The collection of Ecclesiastical Rights of *Ius Ecclesiae Concedere et Abrogare* contains six (6) Rights being:

    (i)    *Ius Ecclesiae Concedere et Abrogare* being the Ecclesiastical Right of Give or Grant Rights and Annul or Rescind Rights; and

    (ii)   *Ius Ecclesiae Donandum Iuris* being the Ecclesiastical Right to Give a Right (and Law); and

    (iii)  *Ius Ecclesiae Rescindendum Iuris* being the Ecclesiastical Right to Rescind a Right (and Law); and

    (iv)  *Ius Ecclesiae Conferendum Iuris* being the Ecclesiastical Right to Grant a Right (and Law); and

    (v)   *Ius Ecclesiae Abrogandum Iuris* being the Ecclesiastical Right to Abrogate a Right (and Law); and

    (vi)  *Ius Ecclesiae Annullare Iuris* being the Ecclesiastical Right to Annul a Right (and Law).

*Margin note: Collection of Ius Ecclesiae Concedere et Abrogare (Give or Grant Rights)*

## Article 279 – Ius Ecclesiae Delegare et Revocare (Assign or Delegate Rights)

1045. *Ius Ecclesiae Delegare et Revocare* is the collection of Ecclesiastical Rights to Assign or Delegate Rights and Cancel or Revoke Superior Rights, as inherited from the collection of Divine Rights *Ius Divinum Delegare et Revocare*.

*Margin note: Ius Ecclesiae Delegare et Revocare (Assign or Delegate Rights)*

1046. *Ius Ecclesiae Delegare et Revocare* (Assign or Delegate Rights) is the seventh collection of twenty-two *Instrumental Ecclesiastical Rights* (*Instrumentalis Ecclesiae Iurium*); and may be explicitly invoked or referenced by Ecclesiastical Right of Action through a proper and registered Ecclesiastical Entity and the Ecclesiastical Obligations of any such registered Ecclesiastical Person or Executive Office in Ucadia or Non-Ucadia Jurisdiction.

*Margin note: Invoking of Ius Ecclesiae Delegare et Revocare*

1047. The collection of Ecclesiastical Rights of *Ius Ecclesiae Delegare et Revocare* contains five (5) Rights being:

    (i)    *Ius Ecclesiae Delegare et Revocare* being the Ecclesiastical Right to Assign or Delegate Rights and Cancel or Revoke

*Margin note: Collection of Ius Ecclesiae Delegare et Revocare*

Rights; and

(ii) *Ius Ecclesiae Delegandi Iuris* being the Ecclesiastical Right to Delegate a Right (and Law); and

(iii) *Ius Ecclesiae Cancellari Iuris* being the Ecclesiastical Right to Cancel a Delegated Right (and Law); and

(iv) *Ius Ecclesiae Assignare Iuris* being the Ecclesiastical Right to Assign a Right (and Law); and

(v) *Ius Ecclesiae Revocandum Iuris* being the Ecclesiastical Right to Revoke an Assigned Right (and Law) .

## Article 280 – Ius Ecclesiae Associatio et Conventio (Association & Agreement)

1048. ***Ius Ecclesiae Associatio et Conventio*** is the collection of Ecclesiastical Rights of Association and Agreement, as inherited from the collection of Divine Rights *Ius Divinum Associatio et Conventio*.

<small>Ius Ecclesiae Associatio et Conventio (Association)</small>

1049. *Ius Ecclesiae Associatio et Conventio* (Association & Agreement) is the eighth collection of twenty-two *Instrumental Ecclesiastical Rights* (*Instrumentalis Ecclesiae Iurium*); and may be explicitly invoked or referenced by Ecclesiastical Right of Action through a proper and registered Ecclesiastical Entity and the Ecclesiastical Obligations of any such registered Ecclesiastical Person or Executive Office in Ucadia or Non-Ucadia Jurisdiction.

<small>Invoking of Ius Ecclesiae Associatio et Conventio (Association)</small>

1050. The collection of Ecclesiastical Rights of *Ius Ecclesiae Associatio et Conventio* contains twenty-four (24) Rights being:

<small>Collection of Ius Ecclesiae Associatio et Conventio (Association)</small>

(i) *Ius Ecclesiae Associatio et Conventio* being the Ecclesiastical Right of Association and Agreement; and

(ii) *Ius Ecclesiae Associationis* being the Ecclesiastical Right of Association; and

(iii) *Ius Ecclesiae Renuntiatio* being the Ecclesiastical Right of Renunciation of Association; and

(iv) *Ius Ecclesiae Conventio* being the Ecclesiastical Right of Agreement; and

(v) *Ius Ecclesiae Conventionis Negotiationis* being the Ecclesiastical Right to Negotiate an Agreement; and

(vi) *Ius Ecclesiae Conventionis Recusatio* being the Ecclesiastical Right to Refuse an Agreement; and

(vii) *Ius Ecclesiae Conventionis Instrumenti* being the Ecclesiastical Right to define an Instrument of Agreement; and

(viii) *Ius Ecclesiae Pactum Formandi* being the Ecclesiastical Right to form a Covenant or Treaty; and

(ix) *Ius Ecclesiae Charta Formandi* being the Ecclesiastical Right to form a Charter; and

(x) *Ius Ecclesiae Constitutionis Formandi* being the Ecclesiastical Right to form a Constitution; and

(xi) *Ius Ecclesiae Memorandum Formandi* being the Ecclesiastical Right to form a Memorandum of Agreement; and

(xii) *Ius Ecclesiae Litterae Formandi* being the Ecclesiastical Right to form a Letter or Heads of Agreement; and

(xiii) *Ius Ecclesiae Notitiae Formandi* being the Ecclesiastical Right to form a Note or Notice of Agreement; and

(xiv) *Ius Ecclesiae Conventionis Terminos* being the Ecclesiastical Right to define Terms and Conditions of Agreement; and

(xv) *Ius Ecclesiae Conventionis Pollucendi* being the Ecclesiastical Right to make a Solemn Promise in Agreement; and

(xvi) *Ius Ecclesiae Conventionis Poenam et Remedium* being the Ecclesiastical Right to define Penalties and Remedies of Agreement; and

(xvii) *Ius Ecclesiae Modandi Conventionis Instrumenti* being the Ecclesiastical Right to Modify the Terms and Conditions of Agreement; and

(xviii) *Ius Ecclesiae Conventionis Ratificationis* being the Ecclesiastical Right of Ratification of Agreement; and

(xix) *Ius Ecclesiae Minoris Lapsus* being the Ecclesiastical Right of Action against Minor Breach of Agreement; and

(xx) *Ius Ecclesiae Minoris Reparare* being the Ecclesiastical Right to Rectify and Repair Minor Issues against Minor Breach of Agreement; and

(xxi) *Ius Ecclesiae Maioris Lapsus* being the Ecclesiastical Right of Action against Major Breach of Agreement; and

(xxii) *Ius Ecclesiae Maioris Restituere* being the Ecclesiastical Right to Restore and Re-establish Major Issues against Major Breach of Agreement; and

(xxiii) *Ius Ecclesiae Concludendi* being the Ecclesiastical Right to Conclude an Agreement; and

(xxiv) *Ius Ecclesiae Terminandi* being the Ecclesiastical Right to

Terminate an Agreement.

## Article 281 – Ius Ecclesiae Consensum et Non (Consent)

1051. ***Ius Ecclesiae Consensum et Non*** is the collection of Ecclesiastical Rights to Consent and Non-Consent, as inherited from the collection of Divine Rights *Ius Divinum Consensum et Non*.

<sub-note>Ius Ecclesiae Consensum et Non (Consent)</sub-note>

1052. *Ius Ecclesiae Consensum et Non* (Consent) is the ninth collection of twenty-two *Instrumental Ecclesiastical Rights* (*Instrumentalis Ecclesiae Iurium*); and may be explicitly invoked or referenced by Ecclesiastical Right of Action through a proper and registered Ecclesiastical Entity and the Ecclesiastical Obligations of any such registered Ecclesiastical Person or Executive Office in Ucadia or Non-Ucadia Jurisdiction.

<sub-note>Invoking of Ius Ecclesiae Consensum et Non (Consent)</sub-note>

1053. The collection of Ecclesiastical Rights of *Ius Ecclesiae Consensum et Non* contains three (3) Rights being:

(i) *Ius Ecclesiae Consensum et Non* being the Ecclesiastical Right of Consent and Non-Consent; and

(ii) *Ius Ecclesiae Consensus* being the Ecclesiastical Right of Consent; and

(iii) *Ius Ecclesiae Non Consensus* being the Ecclesiastical Right of Non Consent.

<sub-note>Collection of Ius Ecclesiae Consensum et Non (Consent)</sub-note>

## Article 282 – Ius Ecclesiae Hereditatis (Inheritance)

1054. ***Ius Ecclesiae Hereditatis*** is the collection of Ecclesiastical Rights of Inheritance of Ecclesiastical Rights, as inherited from the collection of Divine Rights *Ius Divinum Dominium* and *Ius Divinum Bona Fidei*.

<sub-note>Ius Ecclesiae Hereditatis (Inheritance)</sub-note>

1055. *Ius Ecclesiae Hereditatis* (Inheritance) is the tenth collection of twenty-two *Instrumental Ecclesiastical Rights* (*Instrumentalis Ecclesiae Iurium*); and may be explicitly invoked or referenced by Ecclesiastical Right of Action through a proper and registered Ecclesiastical Entity and the Ecclesiastical Obligations of any such registered Ecclesiastical Person or Executive Office in Ucadia or Non-Ucadia Jurisdiction.

<sub-note>Invoking of Ius Ecclesiae Hereditatis (Inheritance)</sub-note>

1056. The collection of Ecclesiastical Rights of *Ius Ecclesiae Hereditatis* contains one Right being:-

(i) *Ius Ecclesiae Hereditatis* being Ecclesiastical Right of Inheritance.

<sub-note>Collection of Ius Ecclesiae Hereditatis (Inheritance)</sub-note>

## Article 283 – Ius Ecclesiae Dominium (Absolute Ownership)

1057. ***Ius Ecclesiae Dominium*** is the collection of Ecclesiastical Rights of Absolute Ownership, as inherited from the collection of Divine Rights *Ius Divinum Dominium*.

Ius Ecclesiae Dominium (Absolute Ownership)

1058. *Ius Ecclesiae Dominium* (Absolute Ownership) is the eleventh collection of twenty-two *Instrumental Ecclesiastical Rights* (*Instrumentalis Ecclesiae Iurium*); and may be explicitly invoked or referenced by Ecclesiastical Right of Action through a proper and registered Ecclesiastical Entity and the Ecclesiastical Obligations of any such registered Ecclesiastical Person or Executive Office in Ucadia or Non-Ucadia Jurisdiction.

Invoking of Ius Ecclesiae Dominium (Absolute Ownership)

1059. The collection of Ecclesiastical Rights of *Ius Ecclesiae Dominium* (Absolute Ownership) contains fourteen (14) Rights being:-

Collection of Ius Ecclesiae Dominium (Absolute Ownership)

   (i) *Ius Ecclesiae Dominium* being the Ecclesiastical Right of Absolute Ownership and Custody; and

   (ii) *Ius Ecclesiae Terrae ad Caelum* being the Ecclesiastical Right of Absolute Ownership and Custody from the Centre of the Earth to the Heavens Above; and

   (iii) *Ius Ecclesiae Defendendi* being the Ecclesiastical Right to Defend with Force any Thing, Person or Property under Absolute Ownership and Custody; and

   (iv) *Ius Ecclesiae Patronatus* being the Divine Right of Protector, Guardian and Patron over any Thing, Person or Property under Absolute Ownership and Custody; and

   (v) *Ius Ecclesiae Coercendum* being the Ecclesiastical Right to Enforce with Force any Right concerning any Thing, Person or Property under Absolute Ownership and Custody; and

   (vi) *Ius Ecclesiae Recuperandi* being the Ecclesiastical Right to Enforce with Force the Recovery, Return and Restoration of any Thing, Person or Property under Absolute Ownership and Custody; and

   (vii) *Ius Ecclesiae Alligandi et Removendi* being the Divine Right of Binding and Unbinding any Item or Thing from Property under Absolute Ownership and Custody; and

   (viii) *Ius Ecclesiae Alterius Commodi* being the Ecclesiastical Right of Using Another's Benefit when derived from Property under Absolute Ownership and Custody; and

(ix) *Ius Ecclesiae Angariae* being the Ecclesiastical Right of Requisition of Property or Obligations of Service during emergency or public benefit when related to any Thing, Person or Property under Absolute Ownership and Custody; and

(x) *Ius Ecclesiae Censendi* being the Ecclesiastical Right of Census and Accounting for Things, Persons and Property derived from Absolute Ownership and Custody; and

(xi) *Ius Ecclesiae Excludendi* being the Ecclesiastical Right of Exclusion of Persons from Land or Property under Absolute Ownership and Custody; and

(xii) *Ius Ecclesiae Alienatus* being the Ecclesiastical Right to Convey or Transfer to Another as a Lesser title any Land, Property or Thing under Absolute Ownership and Custody; and

(xiii) *Ius Ecclesiae Ingrediendi* being the Ecclesiastical Right to enter a Property when derived from Property under Absolute Ownership and Custody; and

(xiv) *Ius Ecclesiae Quaesitum Tertio* being the Ecclesiastical Right to enter as a Third Party to an existing Agreement to enforce a Right when the related Things, Persons and Property are derived from Absolute Ownership and Custody.

## Article 284 – Ius Ecclesiae Possessionis (Possess, Hold and Own)

1060. *Ius Ecclesiae Possessionis* is the collection of Ecclesiastical Rights to Possess, Hold and Own Property, as inherited from the collection of Divine Rights *Ius Divinum Possessionis*. Ius Ecclesiae Possessionis (Possess, Hold and Own)

1061. *Ius Ecclesiae Possessionis* (Possession) is the twelfth collection of twenty-two *Instrumental Ecclesiastical Rights* (*Instrumentalis Ecclesiae Iurium*); and may be explicitly invoked or referenced by Ecclesiastical Right of Action through a proper and registered Ecclesiastical Entity and the Ecclesiastical Obligations of any such registered Ecclesiastical Person or Executive Office in Ucadia or Non-Ucadia Jurisdiction. Invoking of Ius Ecclesiae Possessionis

1062. The collection of Ecclesiastical Rights of *Ius Ecclesiae Possessionis* contains two (2) Rights being: Collection of Ius Ecclesiae Possessionis

(i) *Ius Ecclesiae Possessionis* being the Ecclesiastical Right to Possess, Hold and Own Property; and

(ii) *Ius Ecclesiae Possessionis Rem* being the Ecclesiastical Right to Possess, Hold and Own a Thing.

## Article 285 – Ius Ecclesiae Usus (Use and Fruits of Use)

1063. *Ius Ecclesiae Usus* is the collection of Ecclesiastical Rights of Use and Fruits (Enjoyment) of Use of Property, as inherited from the collection of Divine Rights *Ius Divinum Usus*. — Ius Ecclesiae Usus (Use and Fruits)

1064. *Ius Ecclesiae Usus* (Use) is the thirteenth collection of twenty-two *Instrumental Ecclesiastical Rights* (*Instrumentalis Ecclesiae Iurium*); and may be explicitly invoked or referenced by Ecclesiastical Right of Action through a proper and registered Ecclesiastical Entity and the Ecclesiastical Obligations of any such registered Ecclesiastical Person or Executive Office in Ucadia or Non-Ucadia Jurisdiction. — Invoking of Ius Ecclesiae Usus (Use and Fruits)

1065. The collection of Ecclesiastical Rights of *Ius Ecclesiae Usus* contains three (3) Rights being: — Collection of Ius Ecclesiae Usus (Use and Fruits)

   (i) *Ius Ecclesiae Usus* being the Ecclesiastical Right of Use and Fruits of Use of Property; and

   (ii) *Ius Ecclesiae Affectandi* being the Ecclesiastical Right of Acquisition of Property in Continuous Use; and

   (iii) *Ius Ecclesiae Cessandi* being the Ecclesiastical Right of Cessation of Property in Use.

## Article 286 – Ius Ecclesiae Proprietatis (Ownership of Use)

1066. *Ius Ecclesiae Proprietatis* is the collection of Ecclesiastical Rights of Ownership of Use or Fruits of Use of Property, as inherited from the collection of Divine Rights *Ius Divinum Proprietatis*. — Ius Ecclesiae Proprietatis (Ownership of Use)

1067. *Ius Ecclesiae Proprietatis* (Ownership of Use) is the fourteenth collection of twenty-two *Instrumental Ecclesiastical Rights* (*Instrumentalis Ecclesiae Iurium*); and may be explicitly invoked or referenced by Ecclesiastical Right of Action through a proper and registered Ecclesiastical Entity and the Ecclesiastical Obligations of any such registered Ecclesiastical Person or Executive Office in Ucadia or Non-Ucadia Jurisdiction. — Invoking of Ius Ecclesiae Proprietatis (Ownership of Use)

1068. The collection of Ecclesiastical Rights of *Ius Ecclesiae Proprietatis* contains eight (8) Rights being:- — Collection of Ius Ecclesiae Proprietatis (Ownership of Use)

   (i) *Ius Ecclesiae Proprietatis* being the Ecclesiastical Right of Ownership of Use or Fruits of Use of Property; and

(ii) *Ius Ecclesiae Transferendi* being the Ecclesiastical Right to Transfer Ownership of Use or Fruits of Use of Property to Another; and

(iii) *Ius Ecclesiae Utilitatis* being the Ecclesiastical Right of Enjoyment of Ownership of Use or Fruits of Use of Property; and

(iv) *Ius Ecclesiae Recusatio* being the Ecclesiastical Right of Refusal of Use or Fruits of Use by Another of Owned Property; and

(v) *Ius Ecclesiae Accessionis* being the Ecclesiastical Right of Accession of additions and ownership of additions to Property in Use; and

(vi) *Ius Ecclesiae Aedificii* being the Ecclesiastical Right of Building on Land; and

(vii) *Ius Ecclesiae Alluvionis* being the Ecclesiastical Right of Accretion in increasing Property through natural processes; and

(viii) *Ius Ecclesiae Actionis Proprietatis* being the Ecclesiastical Right of Action against Unreasonable or Immoral Loss of Use or Fruits of Use of Property.

## Article 287 – Ius Ecclesiae Vectigalis Proprietatis (Rents on Use)

1069. *Ius Ecclesiae Vectigalis Proprietatis* is the collection of Ecclesiastical Rights to impose Rents, Tolls, Levies, Contributions or Charges against Property, as inherited from the collection of Divine Rights *Ius Divinum Vectigalis Proprietatis*.

<small>Ius Ecclesiae Vectigalis Proprietatis (Rents on Use)</small>

1070. *Ius Ecclesiae Vectigalis Proprietatis* (Rents on Use) is the fifteenth collection of twenty-two *Instrumental Ecclesiastical Rights* (*Instrumentalis Ecclesiae Iurium*); and may be explicitly invoked or referenced by Ecclesiastical Right of Action through a proper and registered Ecclesiastical Entity and the Ecclesiastical Obligations of any such registered Ecclesiastical Person or Executive Office in Ucadia or Non-Ucadia Jurisdiction.

<small>Invoking of Ius Ecclesiae Vectigalis Proprietatis</small>

1071. The collection of Ecclesiastical Rights of *Ius Ecclesiae Vectigalis Proprietatis* (Rents on Use) contains seven (7) Rights being:-

<small>Collection of Ius Ecclesiae Vectigalis Proprietatis</small>

(i) *Ius Ecclesiae Vectigalis Proprietatis* being the Ecclesiastical Right to impose Rents, Tolls, Levies, Contributions or Charges against Ownership of Use or Fruits of Use of Property; and

(ii) *Ius Ecclesiae Conducendi Mercedem* being the Ecclesiastical Right to Impose Rent on Possession or Use of Property; and

(iii) *Ius Ecclesiae Impendi Tributum* being the Ecclesiastical Right to Impose Levy on Possession or Use of Property; and

(iv) *Ius Ecclesiae Impendi Portorium* being the Ecclesiastical Right to Impose a Toll on Possession or Use of Property; and

(v) *Ius Ecclesiae Impendi Vectigal* being the Ecclesiastical Right to Impose a Charge on Possession or Use of Property; and

(vi) *Ius Ecclesiae Petendi Contributionem* being the Ecclesiastical Right to Request Contributions on Possession or Use of Property; and

(vii) *Ius Ecclesiae Actionis Vectigalis Proprietatis* being the Ecclesiastical Right of Action against Unreasonable or Immoral Loss or Failure to Pay Rents, Tolls, Levies, Contributions or Charges against Ownership of Use or Fruits of Use of Property.

## Article 288 – Ius Ecclesiae Moneta (Mint, Produce, Hold, Use Money)

1072. **Ius Ecclesiae Moneta** is the collection of Ecclesiastical Rights to Mint, Produce, Hold, Use and Exchange Money, as inherited from the collection of Divine Rights *Ius Divinum Moneta*.

1073. *Ius Ecclesiae Moneta* (Mint, Produce, Hold, Use Money) is the sixteenth collection of twenty-two *Instrumental Ecclesiastical Rights* (*Instrumentalis Ecclesiae Iurium*); and may be explicitly invoked or referenced by Ecclesiastical Right of Action through a proper and registered Ecclesiastical Entity and the Ecclesiastical Obligations of any such registered Ecclesiastical Person or Executive Office in Ucadia or Non-Ucadia Jurisdiction.

1074. The collection of Ecclesiastical Rights of *Ius Ecclesiae Moneta* contains fifteen (15) Rights being:-

(i) *Ius Ecclesiae Moneta* being the Ecclesiastical Right to Mint, Produce, Hold, Use and Exchange Money; and

(ii) *Ius Ecclesiae Creandi Moneta* being the Ecclesiastical Right to Create and Mint Money; and

(iii) *Ius Ecclesiae Creandi Digitalis Moneta* being the Ecclesiastical Right to Create and Mint Digital Money; and

(iv) *Ius Ecclesiae Tenendi Moneta* being the Ecclesiastical Right to

Hold and Possess Money; and

(v) *Ius Ecclesiae Tenendi Digitalis Moneta* being the Ecclesiastical Right to Hold and Possess Digital Money; and

(vi) *Ius Ecclesiae Transferre Moneta* being the Ecclesiastical Right to Transfer Money; and

(vii) *Ius Ecclesiae Transferre Digitalis Moneta* being the Ecclesiastical Right to Transfer Digital Money; and

(viii) *Ius Ecclesiae Recipere Moneta* being the Ecclesiastical Right to Receive Money; and

(ix) *Ius Ecclesiae Recipere Digitalis Moneta* being the Ecclesiastical Right to Receive Digital Money; and

(x) *Ius Ecclesiae Cambii Moneta* being the Ecclesiastical Right to Exchange Money for another unit of currency; and

(xi) *Ius Ecclesiae Cambii Digitalis Moneta* being the Ecclesiastical Right to Exchange Digital Money for another unit of currency; and

(xii) *Ius Ecclesiae Utendi Moneta* being the Ecclesiastical Right to Use Money for Settlement of Debts and Obligations; and

(xiii) *Ius Ecclesiae Utendi Digitalis Moneta* being the Ecclesiastical Right to Use Digital Money for Settlement of Debts and Obligations; and

(xiv) *Ius Ecclesiae Utendi Moneta Numismatis Legalis* being the Ecclesiastical Right to Use Money as Legal Tender; and

(xv) *Ius Ecclesiae Utendi Digitalis Moneta Numismatis Legalis* being the Ecclesiastical Right to Use Digital Money as Legal Tender.

## Article 289 – Ius Ecclesiae Vectigalis Moneta (Rents, Tolls, Levies on Money)

1075. *Ius Ecclesiae Vectigalis Moneta* is the collection of Ecclesiastical Rights to impose Rents, Tolls, Levies, Contributions or Charges against Money, as inherited from the collection of Divine Rights *Ius Divinum Vectigalis Moneta*.

<sub>Ius Ecclesiae Vectigalis Moneta (Rents, Tolls, Levies on Money)</sub>

1076. *Ius Ecclesiae Vectigalis Moneta* (Rents on Money) is the seventeenth collection of twenty-two *Instrumental Ecclesiastical Rights* (*Instrumentalis Ecclesiae Iurium*); and may be explicitly invoked or referenced by Ecclesiastical Right of Action through a proper and registered Ecclesiastical Entity and the Ecclesiastical Obligations of

Invoking of Ius Ecclesiae Vectigalis Moneta

any such registered Ecclesiastical Person or Executive Office in Ucadia or Non-Ucadia Jurisdiction.

1077. The collection of Ecclesiastical Rights of *Ius Ecclesiae Vectigalis Moneta* contains seven (7) Rights being:-

    (i)     *Ius Ecclesiae Vectigalis Moneta* being the Ecclesiastical Right to impose Rents, Tolls, Levies, Contributions or Charges against Money; and

    (ii)    *Ius Ecclesiae Conducendi Mercedem Moneta* being the Ecclesiastical Right to Impose Rent on Possession or Use of Money; and

    (iii)   *Ius Ecclesiae Impendi Tributum Moneta* being the Ecclesiastical Right to Impose Levy on Possession or Use of Money; and

    (iv)   *Ius Ecclesiae Impendi Portorium Moneta* being the Ecclesiastical Right to Impose Toll on Possession or Use of Money; and

    (v)    *Ius Ecclesiae Impendi Vectigal Moneta* being the Ecclesiastical Right to Impose a Charge on Possession or Use of Money; and

    (vi)   *Ius Ecclesiae Petendi Contributionem Moneta* being the Ecclesiastical Right to Request Contributions on Possession or Use of Money; and

    (vii)  *Ius Ecclesiae Actionis Vectigalis Moneta* being the Ecclesiastical Right of Action against Unreasonable or Immoral Loss or Failure to Pay Rents, Tolls, Levies, Contributions or Charges against Possession or Use of Money.

## Article 290 – Ius Ecclesiae Registrum (Registers and Rolls)

1078. ***Ius Ecclesiae Registrum*** is the collection of Ecclesiastical Rights to Enter Records within Registers and Rolls, as inherited from the collection of Divine Rights *Ius Divinum Registrum*.

1079. *Ius Ecclesiae Registrum* (Registers & Rolls) is the eighteenth collection of twenty-two *Instrumental Ecclesiastical Rights* (*Instrumentalis Ecclesiae Iurium*); and may be explicitly invoked or referenced by Ecclesiastical Right of Action through a proper and registered Ecclesiastical Entity and the Ecclesiastical Obligations of any such registered Ecclesiastical Person or Executive Office in Ucadia or Non-Ucadia Jurisdiction.

1080. The collection of Ecclesiastical Rights of *Ius Ecclesiae Registrum* contains twenty-three (23) Rights being:-

Collection of Ius Ecclesiae Registrum (Registers and Rolls)

(i) *Ius Ecclesiae Registrum* being the Ecclesiastical Right to Enter and Manage Records within Registers and Rolls; and

(ii) *Ius Ecclesiae Registrum Confidentiae* being the Ecclesiastical Right of Confidential Access to a Register; and

(iii) *Ius Ecclesiae Registrum Accessus* being the Ecclesiastical Right of Access to a Register; and

(iv) *Ius Ecclesiae Actionis Registrum Accessus* being the Ecclesiastical Right of Action concerning Register Access; and

(v) *Ius Ecclesiae Registrum Inspectionis* being the Ecclesiastical Right of Inspection of a Register; and

(vi) *Ius Ecclesiae Actionis Registrum Correctionis* being the Ecclesiastical Right of Action for Register Correction; and

(vii) *Ius Ecclesiae Registrum Intrationis* being the Ecclesiastical Right of Entry in a Register; and

(viii) *Ius Ecclesiae Registri Recordationis Extrahendi* being the Ecclesiastical Right to make an Extract of Record in a Register; and

(ix) *Ius Ecclesiae Registri Recordationis Abstrahendi* being the Ecclesiastical Right to make an Abstract of Record in a Register; and

(x) *Ius Ecclesiae Registri Recordationis Cancellationis* being the Ecclesiastical Right to Cancel a Record in a Register; and

(xi) *Ius Ecclesiae Registri Recordationis Completionis* being the Ecclesiastical Right to Complete a Record in a Register; and

(xii) *Ius Ecclesiae Registri Recordationis Correctionis* being the Ecclesiastical Right to Correct a Record in a Register; and

(xiii) *Ius Ecclesiae Rotulae Confidentiae* being the Ecclesiastical Right of Confidential Access to a Roll; and

(xiv) *Ius Ecclesiae Rotulae Accessus* being the Ecclesiastical Right of Access to a Roll; and

(xv) *Ius Ecclesiae Actionis Rotulae Accessus* being the Ecclesiastical Right of Action concerning Roll Access; and

(xvi) *Ius Ecclesiae Rotulae Inspectionis* being the Ecclesiastical Right of Inspection of a Roll; and

(xvii) *Ius Ecclesiae Actionis Rotulae Correctionis* being the

Ecclesiastical Right of Action for Roll Correction; and

(xviii) *Ius Ecclesiae Rotulae Intrationis* being the Ecclesiastical Right of Entry in a Roll; and

(xix) *Ius Ecclesiae Rotulae Recordationis Extrahendi* being the Ecclesiastical Right *to make* an Extract of Record in a Roll; and

(xx) *Ius Ecclesiae Rotulae Recordationis Abstrahendi* being the Ecclesiastical Right *to make* an Abstract of Record in a Roll; and

(xxi) *Ius Ecclesiae Rotulae Recordationis Cancellationis* being the Ecclesiastical Right to Cancel a Record in a Roll; and

(xxii) *Ius Ecclesiae Rotulae Recordationis Completionis* being the Ecclesiastical Right to Complete a Record in a Roll; and

(xxiii) *Ius Ecclesiae Rotulae Recordationis Correctionis* being the Ecclesiastical Right to Correct a Record in a Roll.

## Article 291 – Ius Ecclesiae Remedium (Remedy)

1081. ***Ius Ecclesiae Remedium*** is the collection of Ecclesiastical Rights of Remedy, Relief, Redress or Compensation, as inherited from the collection of Divine Rights *Ius Divinum Remedium*. — Ius Ecclesiae Remedium (Remedy, Relief)

1082. *Ius Ecclesiae Remedium* (Remedy) is the nineteenth collection of twenty-two *Instrumental Ecclesiastical Rights* (*Instrumentalis Ecclesiae Iurium*); and may be explicitly invoked or referenced by Ecclesiastical Right of Action through a proper and registered Ecclesiastical Entity and the Ecclesiastical Obligations of any such registered Ecclesiastical Person or Executive Office in Ucadia or Non-Ucadia Jurisdiction. — Invoking of Ius Ecclesiae Remedium (Remedy, Relief)

1083. The collection of Ecclesiastical Rights of *Ius Ecclesiae Remedium* contains nine (9) Rights being:- — Collection of Ius Ecclesiae Remedium (Remedy, Relief)

(i) *Ius Ecclesiae Remedium* being the Ecclesiastical Right of Remedy, Relief, Redress or Compensation; and

(ii) *Ius Ecclesiae Remedium Compensationis* being the Ecclesiastical Right of Remedy of Compensation for Loss or Damages; and

(iii) *Ius Ecclesiae Remedium Restitutionis* being the Ecclesiastical Right of Remedy of Restitution for the Return of Property; and

(iv) *Ius Ecclesiae Remedium Reparationis* being the Ecclesiastical

Right of Remedy of Restoration for the Repairing of Harm or Property; and

(v) *Ius Ecclesiae Remedium Injunctionis* being the Ecclesiastical Right of Remedy of Injunction to Enforce Performance or Prevent Behaviour of Another; and

(vi) *Ius Ecclesiae Remedium Rescissionis* being the Ecclesiastical Right of Remedy of Rescission to Cancel an Agreement or Transaction and Restore Parties to their Original Positions; and

(vii) *Ius Ecclesiae Remedium Appellationis* being the Ecclesiastical Right of Remedy of Appeal a Decision to a Higher Forum; and

(viii) *Ius Ecclesiae Remedium Declarationis* being the Ecclesiastical Right of Remedy of Declaratory Judgement; and

(ix) *Ius Ecclesiae Remedium Sententiae* being the Ecclesiastical Right of Remedy of Enforcement of Judgement.

## Article 292 – Ius Ecclesiae Poena (Penalty & Punishment)

1084. *Ius Ecclesiae Poena* is the collection of Ecclesiastical Rights of Penalty and Punishment, as inherited from the collection of Divine Rights *Ius Divinum Poena*.

1085. *Ius Ecclesiae Poena* (Penalty & Punishment) is the twentieth collection of twenty-two *Instrumental Ecclesiastical Rights* (*Instrumentalis Ecclesiae Iurium*); and may be explicitly invoked or referenced by Ecclesiastical Right of Action through a proper and registered Ecclesiastical Entity and the Ecclesiastical Obligations of any such registered Ecclesiastical Person or Executive Office in Ucadia or Non-Ucadia Jurisdiction.

1086. The collection of Ecclesiastical Rights of *Ius Ecclesiae Poena* (Penalty & Punishment) contains five (5) Rights being:-

(i) *Ius Ecclesiae Poena* being the Ecclesiastical Right of Penalty & Punishment; and

(ii) *Ius Ecclesiae Remissionis Poenae* being the Ecclesiastical Right of Remission in the significant lessening of Penalties upon prior and full Acceptance of Culpability and Evidence of Genuine Remorse and Efforts to Change before any Trial; and

(iii) *Ius Ecclesiae Exacerbationis Poenae* being the Ecclesiastical Right of Exacerbation in the significant increasing of severity of Penalties upon prior Refusal to Accept Culpability or

Demonstrate Genuine Remorse or Change before any Trial; and

(iv) *Ius Ecclesiae Appellationis Poenae* being the Ecclesiastical Right to Appeal Punishment to a Decision to a Higher Forum; and

(v) *Ius Ecclesiae Custodiae Vitae* being the Ecclesiastical Right of Custody of Life whereby the Life of the Convicted must continue to be protected and sustained and cannot be threatened during any period of punishment.

## Article 293 – Ius Ecclesiae Clementia (Mercy & Forgiveness)

1087. **Ius Ecclesiae Clementia** is the collection of Ecclesiastical Rights of Mercy & Forgiveness, as inherited from the collection of Divine Rights *Ius Divinum Clementia*. Ius Ecclesiae Clementia (Mercy & Forgiveness)

1088. *Ius Ecclesiae Clementia* (Mercy and Forgiveness) is the twenty-first collection of twenty-two *Instrumental Ecclesiastical Rights* (*Instrumentalis Ecclesiae Iurium*); and may be explicitly invoked or referenced by Ecclesiastical Right of Action through a proper and registered Ecclesiastical Entity and the Ecclesiastical Obligations of any such registered Ecclesiastical Person or Executive Office in Ucadia or Non-Ucadia Jurisdiction. Invoking of Ius Ecclesiae Clementia (Mercy & Forgiveness)

1089. The collection of Ecclesiastical Rights of *Ius Ecclesiae Clementia* contains two (2) Rights being:- Collection of Ius Ecclesiae Clementia (Mercy & Forgiveness)

(i) *Ius Ecclesiae Clementia* being the Ecclesiastical Right of Mercy & Forgiveness; and

(ii) *Ius Ecclesiae Expurgationis Instrumenti Convicti* being the Ecclesiastical Right of Convicted Record Expurgation at Conclusion of Punishment in recognition for prior and full Acceptance of Culpability and Evidence of Genuine Remorse and Efforts to Change before any Trial and Conviction.

## Article 294 – Ius Ecclesiae Actionum (Rights of Action)

1090. ***Ius Ecclesiae Actionum*** is the collection of Ecclesiastical Rights of Action, as inherited from the collection of Divine Rights *Ius Divinum Actionum*.

Ius Ecclesiae Actionum (Rights of Action)

1091. *Ius Ecclesiae Actionum* (Rights of Action) is the twenty-second collection of twenty-two *Instrumental Ecclesiastical Rights* (*Instrumentalis Ecclesiae Iurium*); and may be explicitly invoked or referenced by Ecclesiastical Right of Action through a proper and registered Ecclesiastical Entity and the Ecclesiastical Obligations of any such registered Ecclesiastical Person or Executive Office in Ucadia or Non-Ucadia Jurisdiction.

Invoking of Ius Ecclesiae Actionum (Rights of Action)

1092. The collection of Ecclesiastical Rights of *Ius Ecclesiae Actionum* (Rights of Action) contains eleven (11) Rights being:-

Collection of Ius Ecclesiae Actionum (Rights of Action)

(i) *Ius Ecclesiae Actionum* being the Ecclesiastical Right of Action; and

(ii) *Ius Ecclesiae Abstinentiae* being the Ecclesiastical Right to Abstain from Action; and

(iii) *Ius Ecclesiae Causae Actionis* being the Ecclesiastical Right of Valid Cause for an Action, whereby clear Evidence of a Wrong Exists; and

(iv) *Ius Ecclesiae Obligationis Actionis* being the Ecclesiastical Right of Obligation for an Action, whereby clear Evidence Exists of a Duty of Care or Performance Owed; and

(v) *Ius Ecclesiae Proximitatis Actionis* being the Ecclesiastical Right of Proximity for an Action, whereby the one bringing the Action is in close Proximity to the Issue; and

(vi) *Ius Ecclesiae Temporis Actionis* being the Ecclesiastical Right of Timeliness for an Action, whereby no time barrier exists for bringing such an Action; and

(vii) *Ius Ecclesiae Iniuriae Actionis* being the Ecclesiastical Right of Injury for an Action, whereby the one bringing the Action has suffered an actual harm or damages; and

(viii) *Ius Ecclesiae Remedium Actionis* being the Ecclesiastical Right of Remedy for an Action, whereby the Remedy sought is possible under the relevant Jurisdiction; and

(ix) *Ius Ecclesiae Iurisdictionis Actionis* being the Ecclesiastical Right of Jurisdiction for an Action, whereby the Jurisdiction proposed is the correct and valid forum and venue for such an Action; and

(x) *Ius Ecclesiae Formae Actionis* being the Ecclesiastical Right of Form for an Action, whereby the proposed Action conforms to the rules and bylaws of the relevant Jurisdiction in its format, presentation and arguments; and

(xi) *Ius Ecclesiae Loci Standi Actionis* being the Ecclesiastical Right of Standing for an Action constituting all previously mentioned Rights of this collection.

## 8.4 – Sacramental Ecclesiastical Rights

### Article 295 – Sacramental Ecclesiastical Rights

1093. ***Sacramental Ecclesiastical Rights*** (*Sacramentum Ecclesiae Iurium*) shall be Ecclesiastical Rights associated with the thirty-three (33) Divine Sacraments of Heaven — *Sacramental Ecclesiastical Rights*

1094. All *Sacramental Ecclesiastical Rights* are delegated to the safe custody and wise guardian powers of the legitimate and valid supreme competent ecclesiastical forum of law of the proper Ucadia Faiths and all lesser associated Ucadia bodies, as the embodiment of judicial authority; and as defined by Article 59 (Oratorium) of the most sacred Covenant *Pactum De Singularis Caelum*. — *Delegation of Sacramental Ecclesiastical Rights (Sacramentum Ecclesiae Iurium)*

1095. All *Sacramental Ecclesiastical Rights* are assumed to be automatically invoked within Ucadia Jurisdictions through the operation of the Civilised Rules of Ucadia Societies, Bodies and Entities. However the Rights may be explicitly invoked or referenced by Right of Action through a proper Forum of Law and the Fiduciary Obligations of any such court in Ucadia or Non-Ucadia Jurisdiction. — *Invocation of Sacramental Ecclesiastical Rights*

1096. The following valid thirty-three (33) Sacramental Ecclesiastical Rights (*Sacramentum Ecclesiae Iurium*) shall be recognised in accord with the most sacred Covenant *Pactum De Singularis Caelum*:- — *List of Sacramental Ecclesiastical Rights (Sacramentum Ecclesiae Iurium)*

(i) "**Ius Ecclesiae Sacramentum Recognosco**" is the Ecclesiastical Right of the Key Sacrament of Recognition, as inherited from the Divine Right *Ritus Sacramentum Recognosco*; and

(ii) "**Ius Ecclesiae Sacramentum Purificatio**" is the Ecclesiastical Right of the Key Sacrament of Purification, as inherited from the Divine Right *Ritus Sacramentum Purificatio*; and

(iii) **"Ius Ecclesiae Sacramentum Invocatio"** is the Ecclesiastical Right of the Key Sacrament of Invocation, as inherited from the Divine Right *Ritus Sacramentum Invocatio*; and

(iv) **"Ius Ecclesiae Sacramentum Obligatio"** is the Ecclesiastical Right of the Key Sacrament of Obligation, as inherited from the Divine Right *Ritus Sacramentum Obligatio*; and

(v) **"Ius Ecclesiae Sacramentum Delegatio"** is the Ecclesiastical Right of the Key Sacrament of Delegation, as inherited from the Divine Right *Ritus Sacramentum Delegatio*; and

(vi) **"Ius Ecclesiae Sacramentum Satisfactio"** is the Ecclesiastical Right of the Key Sacrament of Satisfaction, as inherited from the Divine Right *Ritus Sacramentum Satisfactio*; and

(vii) **"Ius Ecclesiae Sacramentum Resolutio"** is the Ecclesiastical Right of the Key Sacrament of Resolution, as inherited from the Divine Right *Ritus Sacramentum Resolutio*; and

(viii) **"Ius Ecclesiae Sacramentum Sanctificatio"** is the Ecclesiastical Right of the Foundational Sacrament of Sanctification, as inherited from the Divine Right *Ritus Sacramentum Sanctificatio*; and

(ix) **"Ius Ecclesiae Sacramentum Sustentatio"** is the Ecclesiastical Right of the Foundational Sacrament of Sustentation, as inherited from the Divine Right *Ritus Sacramentum Sustentatio*; and

(x) **"Ius Ecclesiae Sacramentum Unificatio"** is the Ecclesiastical Right of the Foundational Sacrament of Unification (Matrimony), as inherited from the Divine Right *Ritus Sacramentum Unificatio*; and

(xi) **"Ius Ecclesiae Sacramentum Amalgamatio"** is the Ecclesiastical Right of the Foundational Sacrament of Amalgamation (Union), as inherited from the Divine Right *Ritus Sacramentum Amalgamatio*; and

(xii) **"Ius Ecclesiae Sacramentum Authentico"** is the Ecclesiastical Right of the Foundational Sacrament of Authentication, as inherited from the Divine Right *Ritus*

*Sacramentum Authentico*; and

(xiii) **"Ius Ecclesiae Sacramentum Absolutio"** is the Ecclesiastical Right of the Foundational Sacrament of Absolution, as inherited from the Divine Right *Ritus Sacramentum Absolutio*; and

(xiv) **"Ius Ecclesiae Sacramentum Volitio"** is the Ecclesiastical Right of the Foundational Sacrament of Volition, as inherited from the Divine Right *Ritus Sacramentum Volitio*; and

(xv) **"Ius Ecclesiae Sacramentum Vocatio"** is the Ecclesiastical Right of the Foundational Sacrament of Vocation, as inherited from the Divine Right *Ritus Sacramentum Vocatio*; and

(xvi) **"Ius Ecclesiae Sacramentum Testificatio"** is the Ecclesiastical Right of the Foundational Sacrament of Testification, as inherited from the Divine Right *Ritus Sacramentum Testificatio*; and

(xvii) **"Ius Ecclesiae Sacramentum Compassio"** is the Ecclesiastical Right of the Foundational Sacrament of Compassion (Mercy), as inherited from the Divine Right *Ritus Sacramentum Compassio*; and

(xviii) **"Ius Ecclesiae Sacramentum Conscripto"** is the Ecclesiastical Right of the Foundational Sacrament of Conscription (Binding), as inherited from the Divine Right *Ritus Sacramentum Conscripto*; and

(xix) **"Ius Ecclesiae Sacramentum Convocatio"** is the Ecclesiastical Right of the Foundational Sacrament of Convocation, as inherited from the Divine Right *Ritus Sacramentum Convocatio*; and

(xx) **"Ius Ecclesiae Sacramentum Auctoriso"** is the Ecclesiastical Right of the Foundational Sacrament of Authorisation, as inherited from the Divine Right *Ritus Sacramentum Auctoriso*; and

(xxi) **"Ius Ecclesiae Sacramentum Elucidato"** is the Ecclesiastical Right of the Foundational Sacrament of Elucidation, as inherited from the Divine Right *Ritus Sacramentum Elucidato*; and

(xxii) **"Ius Ecclesiae Sacramentum Inspiratio"** is the Ecclesiastical Right of the Authentic Life Sacrament of

Inspiration, as inherited from the Divine Right *Ritus Sacramentum Inspiratio*; and

(xxiii) **"Ius Ecclesiae Sacramentum Resurrectio"** is the Ecclesiastical Right of the Authentic Life Sacrament of Resurrection, as inherited from the Divine Right *Ritus Sacramentum Resurrectio*; and

(xxiv) **"Ius Ecclesiae Sacramentum Incarnatio"** is the Ecclesiastical Right of the Authentic Life Sacrament of Incarnation, as inherited from the Divine Right *Ritus Sacramentum Incarnatio*; and

(xxv) **"Ius Ecclesiae Sacramentum Confirmatio"** is the Ecclesiastical Right of the Authentic Life Sacrament of Confirmation, as inherited from the Divine Right *Ritus Sacramentum Confirmatio*; and

(xxvi) **"Ius Ecclesiae Sacramentum Illuminatio"** is the Ecclesiastical Right of the Authentic Life Sacrament of Illumination, as inherited from the Divine Right *Ritus Sacramentum Illuminatio*; and

(xxvii) **"Ius Ecclesiae Sacramentum Exultatio"** is the Ecclesiastical Right of the Authentic Life Sacrament of Exultation, as inherited from the Divine Right *Ritus Sacramentum Exultatio*; and

(xxviii) **"Ius Ecclesiae Sacramentum Glorificatio"** is the Ecclesiastical Right of the Authentic Life Sacrament of Glorification, as inherited from the Divine Right *Ritus Sacramentum Glorificatio*; and

(xxix) **"Ius Ecclesiae Sacramentum Divinatio"** is the Ecclesiastical Right of the Authentic Life Sacrament of Divination, as inherited from the Divine Right *Ritus Sacramentum Divinatio*; and

(xxx) **"Ius Ecclesiae Sacramentum Visitatio"** is the Ecclesiastical Right of the Authentic Life Sacrament of Visitation, as inherited from the Divine Right *Ritus Sacramentum Visitatio*; and

(xxxi) **"Ius Ecclesiae Sacramentum Salvatio"** is the Ecclesiastical Right of the Authentic Life Sacrament of Salvation, as inherited from the Divine Right *Ritus Sacramentum Salvatio*; and

(xxxii) **"Ius Ecclesiae Sacramentum Emancipatio"** is the Ecclesiastical Right of the Authentic Life Sacrament of Original Emancipation, as inherited from the Divine Right *Ritus Sacramentum Emancipatio*; and

(xxxiii) **"Ius Ecclesiae Sacramentum Veneratio"** is the Ecclesiastical Right of the Authentic Life Sacrament of Veneration, as inherited from the Divine Right *Ritus Sacramentum Veneratio*.

## Article 296 – Ius Ecclesiae Sacramentum Recognosco (Recognition)

1097. *Ius Ecclesiae Sacramentum Recognosco* is the Ecclesiastical Right of the Key Sacred Gift of Recognition, as inherited from the Divine Right *Ritus Sacramentum Recognosco*. Recognition is the Key that unlocks the Living Virtue of Respect. It is present in all fourteen (14) of the Foundational Sacred Gifts.

    *I. Ecc. Sacr. Recognosco (Recognition)*

1098. *Ritus Sacramentum Recognosco* is the first of thirty-three Sacramental Divine Rights; and may only be invoked whenever the lesser Ecclesiastical Right of *Ius Ecclesiae Sacramentum Recognosco* is invoked in strict accord with the liturgy of *Missale Christus* (Missal of Christ), or *Taqwa Islam* (Rites of Islam) or *Karman Spiritus* (Rites of the Universal Divine Spirit).

    *Invocation of Ritus Sacramentum Recognosco*

1099. The Divine Purpose of the Sacred Gift of Recognition is to assist persons in establishing a firm and clear respect of both their inner thoughts and mind and of the outer world around them. Thus, the Sacred Gift of Recognition is the formal observance and respect of a person, object or concept through its proper classification and estimation.

    *Divine Purpose of the Sacred Gift of Recognition*

    Recognition (and therefore Respect), is seen as the foundation Living Virtue as all other virtues depend first upon the firm foundation of respect. Without self-respect, there can be no respect of others. Without respect of the world, there can be no self-respect.

## Article 297 – Ius Ecclesiae Sacramentum Purificatio (Purification)

1100. ***Ius Ecclesiae Sacramentum Purificatio*** is the Ecclesiastical Right of the Key Sacred Gift of Purification, as inherited from the Divine Right *Ritus Sacramentum Purificatio*. The Sacred Gift of Purification is the Key that unlocks the Living Virtue of Honesty (and Truth). It is present in all fourteen (14) of the Foundational Sacred Gifts.  
*I. Ecc. Sacr. Purificatio (Purification)*

1101. *Ritus Sacramentum Purificatio* is the second of thirty-three Sacramental Divine Rights; and may only be invoked whenever the lesser Ecclesiastical Right of *Ius Ecclesiae Sacramentum Purificatio* is invoked in strict accord with the liturgy of *Missale Christus* (Missal of Christ), or *Taqwa Islam* (Rites of Islam) or *Karman Spiritus* (Rites of the Universal Divine Spirit).  
*Invocation of Ritus Sacramentum Purificatio*

1102. The Divine Purpose of the Sacred Gift of Purification is firstly to aid to clear and cleanse the mind from the temporary presence of negative, confusing or distracting thoughts, in order to help better focus attention and intention toward some sacred purpose. Secondly, Purification exists to prepare physical objects and bodies to receive other sacred gifts by dissolving any negative bonds, previous uses or intentions, or applications. Thus Purification is a necessary action in the preparing of Extra-Sacred Rites and the body of authorised clerics before official ceremonies.  
*Divine Purpose of the Sacred Gift of Purification*

## Article 298 – Ius Ecclesiae Sacramentum Invocatio (Invocation)

1103. ***Ius Ecclesiae Sacramentum Invocatio*** is the Ecclesiastical Right of the Key Sacred Gift of Invocation, as inherited from the Divine Right *Ritus Sacramentum Invocatio*.  
*I. Ecc. Sacr. Invocatio (Invocation)*

1104. *Ritus Sacramentum Invocatio* is the third of thirty-three Sacramental Divine Rights; and may only be invoked whenever the lesser Ecclesiastical Right of *Ius Ecclesiae Sacramentum Invocatio* is invoked in strict accord with the liturgy of *Missale Christus* (Missal of Christ), or *Taqwa Islam* (Rites of Islam) or *Karman Spiritus* (Rites of the Universal Divine Spirit).  
*Invocation of Ritus Sacramentum Invocatio*

1105. Invocation by its very definition means "to vocalise some call for assistance; or the presence; or manifestation of one or more divine beings". Thus the positive vocal expression of such a call or entreaty or prayer is fundamental to the operative function of any proper Invocation. When it is not vocalised, an Invocation is properly  
*Divine Purpose of the Sacred Gift of Invocation*

defined as a Meditation.

All communication to the *Angelorum Systemata* (Angelic Systems) of Angels, Saints and Beloved of Heaven by living Members of One Heaven shall be by Invocation in accord with the most sacred Covenant *Pactum De Singularis Caelum*. The methods, rules and standards of proper Invocation are defined by the most sacred Covenant *Pactum De Singularis Caelum* and associated covenants and no other. All properly conferred Invocation shall be received, recorded and acknowledged by the *Angelorum Systemata* (Angelic Systems) of One Heaven.

An Invocation may be memorialised in writing as witness to the event. However, any such memorandum or certificate is always dependent upon the action of the said Invocation first being spoken.

A proper Invocation may stand alone, or may represent part of a more complex series of ritual or events. When an Invocation is made from the use of some formula of words in prose, or sung or spoken, then it shall be known more formally as an Incantation. However, when a proper Invocation stands alone and involves the use of free form and self selection of words by the one making the Invocation, then it shall be known simply as an Invocation.

**1106.** In accord with the most sacred Covenant *Pactum De Singularis Caelum*, an Invocation shall be reprobate, profane, repugnant and therefore invalid and improper and rejected by the Angels, Saints and Beloved of the *Angelorum Systemata* (Angelic Systems) of Heaven:- Reprobate, Profane and Repugnant forms of Invocation

    (i)    If it is deliberately harmful, negative or malevolent in its intent, design or inference; or

    (ii)    If it is deliberately dishonest, deceptive or perfidious in its intent, design or inference; or

    (iii)    If it is frivolous, or profane or disrespectful in its intent, or tone, or design or inference; or

    (iv)    If it is irrational, or unreasonable or illogical in its intent, or tone, or design or inference; or

    (v)    If it is motivated or driven by hate, greed, jealously, anger or lust; or

    (vi)    If it is motivated or driven by an attempt to shift blame or avoid accepting self-responsibility; or

    (vii)    If it is motivated or driven by a desire, or wish, or worship of money or abundant material wealth.

1107. While the genuine Intention of a proper Invocation or Meditation (non-vocalised Invocation) is in itself the most important element of a valid Invocation, the following elements are recognised as the optimum structure for a valid Invocation being Identity, Petition and Affirmation:-

*The fundamental elements of valid Invocation*

(i) Identity is the identity of the person or group in whose name the Invocation is directed; and

(ii) Petition is the body of the Invocation itself; and

(iii) Affirmation is the offering and affirmation of the one who makes the Invocation as their commitment to the positivity of Intention and the truth of Petition.

1108. Seven types of Invocation or Meditation (non-vocalised Invocation) are recognised being *Adoration, Blessing, Intervention, Intercession, Confession, Lamentation* and *Thanksgiving*:-

*Characteristics of Invocation*

(i) "**Adoration**" is recognised as the type of Invocation or Meditation used for giving honour and praise to a higher spiritual presence; and

(ii) "**Blessing**" is recognised as the type of Invocation or Meditation used to summons an authentic spiritual presence to another, often consonant with the act of consecration and the ritual of anointing; and

(iii) "**Intervention**" is recognised as the type of Invocation or Meditation used for directly summonsing the presence of spirits or asking something for one's self; and

(iv) "**Intercession**" is recognised as the type of Invocation or Meditation used for asking something for others; and

(v) "**Confession**" is recognised as the type of Invocation or Meditation used for the atonement and repentance of wrongdoing and the asking of forgiveness; and

(vi) "**Lamentation**" is recognised as the type of Invocation or Meditation used for crying in distress and asking for vindication; and

(vii) "**Thanksgiving**" is recognised as the type of Invocation or Meditation used for offering gratitude.

## Article 299 – Ius Ecclesiae Sacramentum Obligatio (Obligation)

1109. ***Ius Ecclesiae Sacramentum Obligatio*** is the Ecclesiastical Right of the Key Sacred Gift of Obligation, as inherited from the Divine Right *Ritus Sacramentum Obligatio*. The Sacred Gift of Obligation is the Key that unlocks the Living Virtue of Commitment and Fortitude. It is present in all fourteen (14) of the Foundational Sacred Gifts. — I. Ecc. Sacr. Obligatio (Obligation)

1110. *Ritus Sacramentum Obligatio* is the fourth of thirty-three Sacramental Divine Rights; and may only be invoked whenever the lesser Ecclesiastical Right of *Ius Ecclesiae Sacramentum Obligatio* is invoked in strict accord with the liturgy of *Missale Christus* (Missal of Christ), or *Taqwa Islam* (Rites of Islam) or *Karman Spiritus* (Rites of the Universal Divine Spirit). — Invocation of Ritus Sacramentum Obligatio

1111. The purpose of the sacred gift of Obligation is the formal recognition and celebration of entrusting to the Divine Creator through a solemn consensual covenant certain promises which one or more persons bind themselves to honour and uphold. — Divine Purpose of the Sacred Gift of Obligation

## Article 300 – Ius Ecclesiae Sacramentum Delegatio (Delegation)

1112. ***Ius Ecclesiae Sacramentum Delegatio*** is the Ecclesiastical Right of the Key Sacred Gift of Delegation, as inherited from the Divine Right *Ritus Sacramentum Delegatio*. The Sacred Gift of Delegation is the Key that unlocks the Living Virtue of Trust and Faith. It is present in all fourteen (14) of the Foundational Sacred Gifts. — I. Ecc. Sacr. Delegatio (Delegation)

1113. *Ritus Sacramentum Delegatio* is the fifth of thirty-three Sacramental Divine Rights; and may only be invoked whenever the lesser Ecclesiastical Right of *Ius Ecclesiae Sacramentum Delegatio* is invoked in strict accord with the liturgy of *Missale Christus* (Missal of Christ), or *Taqwa Islam* (Rites of Islam) or *Karman Spiritus* (Rites of the Universal Divine Spirit). — Invocation of Ritus Sacramentum Delegatio

1114. The purpose of the Sacred Gift of Delegation is the formal recognition and blessing of a relationship and agreement whereby certain Form, Rights and Obligations are lawfully delegated to the control of one or more Persons as fiduciaries for the benefit of one or more other Persons. — Divine Purpose of the Sacred Gift of Delegation

## Article 301 – Ius Ecclesiae Sacramentum Satisfactio (Satisfaction)

1115. ***Ius Ecclesiae Sacramentum Satisfactio*** is the Ecclesiastical Right of the Key Sacred Gift of Satisfaction, as inherited from the Divine Right *Ritus Sacramentum Satisfactio*. It is present in all fourteen (14) of the Foundational Sacred Gifts.

*I. Ecc. Sacr. Satisfactio (Satisfaction)*

1116. *Ritus Sacramentum Satisfactio* is the sixth of thirty-three Sacramental Divine Rights; and may only be invoked whenever the lesser Ecclesiastical Right of *Ius Ecclesiae Sacramentum Satisfactio* is invoked in strict accord with the liturgy of *Missale Christus* (Missal of Christ), or *Taqwa Islam* (Rites of Islam) or *Karman Spiritus* (Rites of the Universal Divine Spirit).

*Invocation of Ritus Sacramentum Satisfactio*

1117. The purpose of the sacred gift of Satisfaction is the formal recognition of the fulfilment and completion of any outstanding conditions and terms of an agreement recognised as possessing sacred value and importance.

*Divine Purpose of the Sacred Gift of Satisfaction*

## Article 302 – Ius Ecclesiae Sacramentum Resolutio (Resolution)

1118. ***Ius Ecclesiae Sacramentum Resolutio*** is the Ecclesiastical Right of the Key Sacred Gift of Resolution, as inherited from the Divine Right *Ritus Sacramentum Resolutio*. It is present in all fourteen (14) of the Foundational Sacred Gifts.

*I. Ecc. Sacr. Resolutio (Resolution)*

1119. *Ritus Sacramentum Resolutio* is the seventh of thirty-three Sacramental Divine Rights; and may only be invoked whenever the lesser Ecclesiastical Right of *Ius Ecclesiae Sacramentum Resolutio* is invoked in strict accord with the liturgy of *Missale Christus* (Missal of Christ), or *Taqwa Islam* (Rites of Islam) or *Karman Spiritus* (Rites of the Universal Divine Spirit).

*Invocation of Ritus Sacramentum Resolutio*

1120. The purpose of the Sacred Gift of Resolution is the formal recognition of agreed decisions, determinations and solutions as both a conclusion as well as progression of events.

*Divine Purpose of the Sacred Gift of Resolution*

## Article 303 – Ius Ecclesiae Sacramentum Sanctificatio (Sanctification)

1121. ***Ius Ecclesiae Sacramentum Sanctificatio*** is the Ecclesiastical Right of the Foundational Sacrament of Sanctification, as inherited from the Divine Right *Ritus Sacramentum Sanctificatio*.

*I. Ecc. Sacr. Sanctificatio (Sanctification)*

1122. *Ritus Sacramentum Sanctificatio* is the eighth of thirty-three Sacramental Divine Rights; and may only be invoked whenever the lesser Ecclesiastical Right of *Ius Ecclesiae Sacramentum Sanctificatio* is invoked in strict accord with the liturgy of *Missale Christus* (Missal of Christ), or *Taqwa Islam* (Rites of Islam) or *Karman Spiritus* (Rites of the Universal Divine Spirit).

Invocation of Ritus Sacramentum Sanctificatio

1123. The purpose of the Sacred Gift of Sanctification and Rite of Consecration is the solemn dedication to Divine purpose and service a particular person, place, object or thing, thus the formation of Sacred Circumscribed Space. Only the Rite of Consecration properly conferred creates Sacred Circumscribed Space.

Divine Purpose of the Sacred Gift of Sanctification & Rite of Consecration

1124. The Rite of Consecration is an implicit element of all Life Sacred Gifts and may not be conducted as a replacement or alternate rite to an established Sacred Gift identified as possessing the quality of consecration.

Relations of the Rite of Consecration

## Article 304 – Ius Ecclesiae Sacramentum Sustentatio (Sustentation)

1125. ***Ius Ecclesiae Sacramentum Sustentatio*** is the Ecclesiastical Right of the Foundational Sacrament of Sustentation, as inherited from the Divine Right *Ritus Sacramentum Sustentatio*.

I. Ecc. Sacr. Sustentatio (Sustentation)

1126. *Ritus Sacramentum Sustentatio* is the ninth of thirty-three Sacramental Divine Rights; and may only be invoked whenever the lesser Ecclesiastical Right of *Ius Ecclesiae Sacramentum Sustentatio* is invoked in strict accord with the liturgy of *Missale Christus* (Missal of Christ), or *Taqwa Islam* (Rites of Islam) or *Karman Spiritus* (Rites of the Universal Divine Spirit).

Invocation of Ritus Sacramentum Sustentatio

## Article 305 – Ius Ecclesiae Sacramentum Unificatio (Unification (Matrimony))

1127. ***Ius Ecclesiae Sacramentum Unificatio*** is the Ecclesiastical Right of the Foundational Sacrament of Unification (Matrimony), as inherited from the Divine Right *Ritus Sacramentum Unificatio*.

I. Ecc. Sacr. Unificatio (Unification (Matrimony))

1128. *Ritus Sacramentum Unificatio* is the tenth of thirty-three Sacramental Divine Rights; and may only be invoked whenever the lesser Ecclesiastical Right of *Ius Ecclesiae Sacramentum Unificatio* is invoked in strict accord with the liturgy of *Missale Christus* (Missal of Christ), or *Taqwa Islam* (Rites of Islam) or *Karman Spiritus* (Rites of the Universal Divine Spirit).

Invocation of Ritus Sacramentum Unificatio

| | | |
|---|---|---|
| 1129. | The Sacred Gift of Unification and Rite of Matrimony is granted and administered when a man and a woman upon reaching majority choose and consent of their own free will to sanctify their union through a registered divine matrimonial covenant in accordance with the most sacred Covenant *Pactum De Singularis Caelum* and associated approved worship. The Sacred Gift of Unification and Rite of Matrimony may only be bestowed once. | Divine Purpose of the Sacred Gift of Unification |
| 1130. | There exists only one form of the Sacred Gift of Unification and Rite of Matrimony being Sacred and Irrevocable Unification. Therefore, as the Sacred Gift is a Sacred and Irrevocable Event, producing a Supreme Sacred Record in Heaven and upon the Earth, no properly conferred Sacred Gift of Unification can be withdrawn, or annulled or dissolved. | Form of the Sacred Gift of Unification and Rite of Matrimony |
| | However, upon such circumstances of separation or death, one who has been bestowed the Sacred Gift of Unification is permitted to formalise a new Union through the Sacred Gift of Amalgamation and Rite of Union. Thus, the act of Divorce only applies to civil unions and the Sacred Gift of Amalgamation and never to Unification. | |
| | Furthermore, the transgression of Adultery only applies to both perpetrators equally culpable of acts of sexual extramarital affairs whilst one or the other or both are still publicly and legally being bound to another through the Sacred Gift of Unification or Sacred Gift of Amalgamation. The application of unequal punishment based on gender, or capital punishment in any form for the delict of Adultery is morally repugnant, profane, sacrilegious, forbidden, reprobate and to be suppressed now and forever. | |

## Article 306 – Ius Ecclesiae Sacramentum Amalgamatio (Amalgamation (Union))

| | | |
|---|---|---|
| 1131. | ***Ius Ecclesiae Sacramentum Amalgamatio*** is the Ecclesiastical Right of the Foundational Sacrament of Amalgamation (Union), as inherited from the Divine Right *Ritus Sacramentum Amalgamatio*. | I. Ecc. Sacr. Amalgamatio (Amalgamation (Union)) |
| 1132. | *Ritus Sacramentum Amalgamatio* is the eleventh of thirty-three Sacramental Divine Rights; and may only be invoked whenever the lesser Ecclesiastical Right of *Ius Ecclesiae Sacramentum Amalgamatio* is invoked in strict accord with the liturgy of *Missale Christus* (Missal of Christ), or *Taqwa Islam* (Rites of Islam) or *Karman Spiritus* (Rites of the Universal Divine Spirit). | Invocation of Ritus Sacramentum Amalgamatio |
| 1133. | Amalgamation is granted and administered when two (2) or more parties come together of their own free will and competence and | Divine Purpose of the Sacred Gift of |

agree to form a new body in mutual union.

1134. Civil Union is granted and administered when a couple of the same gender or a man and woman upon reaching majority choose and consent of their own free will to validate their union through a registration and covenant of trust in accordance with the most sacred Covenant *Pactum De Singularis Caelum* and associated approved worship. While a man or a woman may enter into more than one Union consecutively and never concurrently, a man and a woman may only be bestowed the Rite of Holy Matrimony once.

*Form of the Sacred Gift of Amalgamation & Civil Union*

When the Sacred Gift of Amalgamation is approved to be bestowed upon a same sex couple, in recognition of their right to civil equality, the ceremony is forbidden to be performed within the main body of a Sacred Place of Worship. However, such a ceremony is permitted to be performed in a Side Chapel.

The reason the Sacred Gift of Amalgamation is absolutely forbidden to be performed in the main body of a Sacred Place of Worship for a same sex couple, is not to prejudice, condemn or exclude such persons from the unity of the Living Body of one of the Great Faiths, but to protect with the utmost sanctity the exclusive and most holy sacred gift of Unification.

Any civil or lesser body that seeks to attack, undermine or denigrate the absolute moral authority of one of the Great Faiths in such matters, or to contort words and phrases to imply a delinquency of duty and obligation to protect the Sacred Gifts and Civil Equality is culpable of the most grievous transgressions.

## Article 307 – Ius Ecclesiae Sacramentum Authentico (Authentication)

1135. ***Ius Ecclesiae Sacramentum Authentico*** is the Ecclesiastical Right of the Foundational Sacrament of Authentication, as inherited from the Divine Right *Ritus Sacramentum Authentico*.

*I. Ecc. Sacr. Authentico (Authentication)*

1136. *Ritus Sacramentum Authentico* is the twelfth of thirty-three Sacramental Divine Rights; and may only be invoked whenever the lesser Ecclesiastical Right of *Ius Ecclesiae Sacramentum Authentico* is invoked in strict accord with the liturgy of *Missale Christus* (Missal of Christ), or *Taqwa Islam* (Rites of Islam) or *Karman Spiritus* (Rites of the Universal Divine Spirit).

*Invocation of Ritus Sacramentum Authentico*

1137. Authentication is granted and administered upon the formal recording of the name and details of a particular object or concept in the Great Register and Public Record of One Heaven or associated

*Divine Purpose of the Sacred Gift of Authentication*

Great Registers under Oath and evidence in accordance with the most sacred Covenant *Pactum De Singularis Caelum* and associated approved worship.

## Article 308 – Ius Ecclesiae Sacramentum Absolutio (Absolution)

1138. ***Ius Ecclesiae Sacramentum Absolutio*** is the Ecclesiastical Right of the Foundational Sacrament of Absolution, as inherited from the Divine Right *Ritus Sacramentum Absolutio*.

*I. Ecc. Sacr. Absolutio (Absolution)*

1139. *Ritus Sacramentum Absolutio* is the thirteenth of thirty-three Sacramental Divine Rights; and may only be invoked whenever the lesser Ecclesiastical Right of *Ius Ecclesiae Sacramentum Absolutio* is invoked in strict accord with the liturgy of *Missale Christus* (Missal of Christ), or *Taqwa Islam* (Rites of Islam) or *Karman Spiritus* (Rites of the Universal Divine Spirit).

*Invocation of Ritus Sacramentum Absolutio*

1140. Whilst Divine Forgiveness is absolute, immediate and irrevocable to all who have transgressed, the full effect of the Divine Sacred Gift of Absolution can only be received upon the genuine act of Contrition through the proper conferral of the Rite of Confession, also known as the Act of Reconciliation.

*Divine Purpose of the Sacred Gift of Absolution & Rite of Confession*

In the Rite of Confession, a Member who confesses their offences to a legitimate minister; and is authentically contrite and remorseful for such actions; and truly intends to reform themselves; and accepts without duress the necessary ecclesiastical or civil penalties, thereby removes any impediment to full reconciliation with God and the Divine Creator of all Heaven and Earth; and the full receipt of the absolute unconditional Divine Grace of Divine Mercy, Divine Forgiveness and Divine Love.

Thus, the proper and pious Foundational Sacred Gift of Absolution, also known as the Act of Reconciliation itself does not presume to be the mechanism of conferring Divine Mercy, Divine Forgiveness and Divine Love, nor to presume to place conditions upon God and the Divine Creator of all Heaven and Earth as to whether one is worthy or not worthy of Divine Salvation. Instead, the Sacred Gift of Absolution recognises the free will and choice of the penitent in openly reconciling with God and the Divine Creator of all Existence; and thus removing any impediment to the full receipt of Divine Grace.

Most importantly, within and through the Authentic Sacred Gift of Absolution, the competent minister becomes the living embodiment of the Witness and Messenger of Divine Mercy, Divine Forgiveness and Eternal Love of God and the Divine Creator of all Existence to each and every higher order life form and life itself.

## Article 309 – Ius Ecclesiae Sacramentum Volitio (Volition)

1141. ***Ius Ecclesiae Sacramentum Volitio*** is the Ecclesiastical Right of the Foundational Sacrament of Volition, as inherited from the Divine Right *Ritus Sacramentum Volitio*.
<br>*I. Ecc. Sacr. Volitio (Volition)*

1142. *Ritus Sacramentum Volitio* is the fourteenth of thirty-three Sacramental Divine Rights; and may only be invoked whenever the lesser Ecclesiastical Right of *Ius Ecclesiae Sacramentum Volitio* is invoked in strict accord with the liturgy of *Missale Christus* (Missal of Christ), or *Taqwa Islam* (Rites of Islam) or *Karman Spiritus* (Rites of the Universal Divine Spirit).
<br>*Invocation of Ritus Sacramentum Volitio*

1143. The Rite of Oath is a recognition of a binding of obligation and performance duly recorded in the Great Register and Divine Records of Heaven and the temporal records on Earth and the Solar System.
<br>*Divine Purpose of the Sacred Gift of Volition & Rite of Oath*

The Sacred Gift of Volition is granted and conveyed upon the pronouncement of a valid oath in accordance with the most sacred Covenant *Pactum De Singularis Caelum* and associated approved worship.

## Article 310 – Ius Ecclesiae Sacramentum Vocatio (Vocation)

1144. ***Ius Ecclesiae Sacramentum Vocatio*** is the Ecclesiastical Right of the Foundational Sacrament of Vocation, as inherited from the Divine Right *Ritus Sacramentum Vocatio*.
<br>*I. Ecc. Sacr. Vocatio (Vocation)*

1145. *Ritus Sacramentum Vocatio* is the fifteenth of thirty-three Sacramental Divine Rights; and may only be invoked whenever the lesser Ecclesiastical Right of *Ius Ecclesiae Sacramentum Vocatio* is invoked in strict accord with the liturgy of *Missale Christus* (Missal of Christ), or *Taqwa Islam* (Rites of Islam) or *Karman Spiritus* (Rites of the Universal Divine Spirit).
<br>*Invocation of Ritus Sacramentum Vocatio*

1146. The purpose of the sacred gift of Vocation and Rite of Vow is the formal recognition and endorsement of a person pledging themselves as assurance and security for the obligations of another in accordance with the most sacred Covenant *Pactum De Singularis Caelum* and associated approved worship.
<br>*Divine Purpose of the Sacred Gift of Vocation & Rite of Vow*

## Article 311 – Ius Ecclesiae Sacramentum Testificatio (Testification)

1147. ***Ius Ecclesiae Sacramentum Testificatio*** is the Ecclesiastical Right of the Foundational Sacrament of Testification, as inherited from the Divine Right *Ritus Sacramentum Testificatio*.

*I. Ecc. Sacr. Testificatio (Testification)*

1148. *Ritus Sacramentum Testificatio* is the sixteenth of thirty-three Sacramental Divine Rights; and may only be invoked whenever the lesser Ecclesiastical Right of *Ius Ecclesiae Sacramentum Testificatio* is invoked in strict accord with the liturgy of *Missale Christus* (Missal of Christ), or *Taqwa Islam* (Rites of Islam) or *Karman Spiritus* (Rites of the Universal Divine Spirit).

*Invocation of Ritus Sacramentum Testificatio*

1149. Testification is by definition the act of vocalising and giving testimony or evidence; being a vocalised act involving not only at least one Invocation, but at least one promise and obligation in relation to the performance of a valid office. All valid offices are based upon truth and trust and so no office can be formed without a proper Testification.

*Nature of Testification*

All communication to the *Officium Systemata* (Offices Systems) of Heaven by living Members of One Heaven shall be by Testification of an Oath and at least one Vow in accord with the most sacred Covenant *Pactum De Singularis Caelum*. The methods, rules and standards of proper Testification shall be defined by the most sacred Covenant *Pactum De Singularis Caelum* and associated covenants and no other. All properly conferred Testification shall be received, recorded and acknowledged by the Officium Systemata (Offices Systems) of One Heaven.

## Article 312 – Ius Ecclesiae Sacramentum Compassio (Compassion (Mercy))

1150. ***Ius Ecclesiae Sacramentum Compassio*** is the Ecclesiastical Right of the Foundational Sacrament of Compassion (Mercy), as inherited from the Divine Right *Ritus Sacramentum Compassio*.

*I. Ecc. Sacr. Compassio (Compassion (Mercy))*

1151. *Ritus Sacramentum Compassio* is the seventeenth of thirty-three Sacramental Divine Rights; and may only be invoked whenever the lesser Ecclesiastical Right of *Ius Ecclesiae Sacramentum Compassio* is invoked in strict accord with the liturgy of *Missale Christus* (Missal of Christ), or *Taqwa Islam* (Rites of Islam) or *Karman Spiritus* (Rites of the Universal Divine Spirit).

*Invocation of Ritus Sacramentum Compassio*

1152. The purpose of the Sacred Gift of Compassion and Rite of Mercy is

*Divine Purpose of the Sacred*

the formal blessing of charity and benevolence to those in need; and the formal remittance and discharge of part or all of an offence as well as any prescribed punishment, in accordance with the most sacred Covenant *Pactum De Singularis Caelum* and associated approved worship.
Gift of Compassion & Rite of Mercy

### Article 313 – Ius Ecclesiae Sacramentum Conscripto (Conscription (Binding))

1153. ***Ius Ecclesiae Sacramentum Conscripto*** is the Ecclesiastical Right of the Foundational Sacrament of Conscription (Binding), as inherited from the Divine Right *Ritus Sacramentum Conscripto*.
I. Ecc. Sacr. Conscripto (Conscription (Binding))

1154. *Ritus Sacramentum Conscripto* is the eighteenth of thirty-three Sacramental Divine Rights; and may only be invoked whenever the lesser Ecclesiastical Right of *Ius Ecclesiae Sacramentum Conscripto* is invoked in strict accord with the liturgy of *Missale Christus* (Missal of Christ), or *Taqwa Islam* (Rites of Islam) or *Karman Spiritus* (Rites of the Universal Divine Spirit).
Invocation of Ritus Sacramentum Conscripto

1155. The Sacred Gift of Conscription and Rite of Binding is a fundamental concept of society as it permits people to engage in trusted relations of significant trust. The purpose of the sacred gift of Binding is the formal recognition and acknowledgement of the Divine Authority given to the three Great Faiths whereby what is bound on Earth shall be bound in Heaven and what is loosed upon the Earth shall likewise be loosened in Heaven.
Divine Purpose of the Sacred Gift of Conscription & Rite of Binding

### Article 314 – Ius Ecclesiae Sacramentum Convocatio (Convocation)

1156. ***Ius Ecclesiae Sacramentum Convocatio*** is the Ecclesiastical Right of the Foundational Sacrament of Convocation, as inherited from the Divine Right *Ritus Sacramentum Convocatio*.
I. Ecc. Sacr. Convocatio (Convocation)

1157. *Ritus Sacramentum Convocatio* is the nineteenth of thirty-three Sacramental Divine Rights; and may only be invoked whenever the lesser Ecclesiastical Right of *Ius Ecclesiae Sacramentum Convocatio* is invoked in strict accord with the liturgy of *Missale Christus* (Missal of Christ), or *Taqwa Islam* (Rites of Islam) or *Karman Spiritus* (Rites of the Universal Divine Spirit).
Invocation of Ritus Sacramentum Convocatio

1158. The purpose of the sacred gift of Convocation and Rite of Convention is the formal summons to attendance with the members of a sacred body in accordance with the most sacred Covenant *Pactum De Singularis Caelum* and associated approved worship. The meaning of
Divine Purpose of the Sacred Gift of Convocation & Rite of Convention

Convocation is derived from the Latin word *convoco* meaning "to call meeting of".

## Article 315 – Ius Ecclesiae Sacramentum Auctoriso (Authorisation)

1159. ***Ius Ecclesiae Sacramentum Auctoriso*** is the Ecclesiastical Right of the Foundational Sacrament of Authorisation, as inherited from the Divine Right *Ritus Sacramentum Auctoriso*.

I. Ecc. Sacr. Auctoriso (Authorisation)

1160. *Ritus Sacramentum Auctoriso* is the twentieth of thirty-three Sacramental Divine Rights; and may only be invoked whenever the lesser Ecclesiastical Right of *Ius Ecclesiae Sacramentum Auctoriso* is invoked in strict accord with the liturgy of *Missale Christus* (Missal of Christ), or *Taqwa Islam* (Rites of Islam) or *Karman Spiritus* (Rites of the Universal Divine Spirit).

Invocation of Ritus Sacramentum Auctoriso

1161. The purpose of the sacred gift of Authorisation and Rite of Prescription is the formal blessing of a decree or judgement issued by a valid minister or one possessing the proper level of authority in accordance with the most sacred Covenant *Pactum De Singularis Caelum* and associated approved worship.

Divine Purpose of the Sacred Gift of Authorisation & Rite of Prescription

## Article 316 – Ius Ecclesiae Sacramentum Elucidato (Elucidation)

1162. ***Ius Ecclesiae Sacramentum Elucidato*** is the Ecclesiastical Right of the Foundational Sacrament of Elucidation, as inherited from the Divine Right *Ritus Sacramentum Elucidato*.

I. Ecc. Sacr. Elucidato (Elucidation)

1163. *Ritus Sacramentum Elucidato* is the twenty-first of thirty-three Sacramental Divine Rights; and may only be invoked whenever the lesser Ecclesiastical Right of *Ius Ecclesiae Sacramentum Elucidato* is invoked in strict accord with the liturgy of *Missale Christus* (Missal of Christ), or *Taqwa Islam* (Rites of Islam) or *Karman Spiritus* (Rites of the Universal Divine Spirit).

Invocation of Ritus Sacramentum Elucidato

1164. The purpose of the sacred gift of Elucidation and Rite of Rescription is opinion, answer or judgement promulgated by an Official Person, subject to the limits of their authority, in accordance with associated approved worship and the procedures of their Office.

Divine Purpose of the Sacred Gift of Elucidation & Rite of Rescription

## Article 317 – Ius Ecclesiae Sacramentum Inspiratio (Inspiration)

**1165.** ***Ius Ecclesiae Sacramentum Inspiratio*** is the Ecclesiastical Right of the Authentic Life Sacrament of Inspiration, as inherited from the Divine Right *Ritus Sacramentum Inspiratio*.
<br>*I. Ecc. Sacr. Inspiratio (Inspiration)*

**1166.** *Ritus Sacramentum Inspiratio* is the twenty-second of thirty-three Sacramental Divine Rights; and may only be invoked whenever the lesser Ecclesiastical Right of *Ius Ecclesiae Sacramentum Inspiratio* is invoked in strict accord with the liturgy of *Missale Christus* (Missal of Christ), or *Taqwa Islam* (Rites of Islam) or *Karman Spiritus* (Rites of the Universal Divine Spirit).
<br>*Invocation of Ritus Sacramentum Inspiratio*

**1167.** The Sacred Gift of Inspiration and Rite of Annunciation is granted and conferred exclusively to an expectant mother and her living unborne child according to most sacred Covenant *Pactum De Singularis Caelum* and associated approved worship.
<br>*Gift of Inspiration*

**1168.** All life is sacred and human life is especially sacred. Thus, the journey of conception to gestation and finally birth is an extraordinary journey and gift. The purpose of the Sacred Gift of Inspiration and Rite of Annunciation is the recognition of the ancient custom and tradition of celebrating the certainty of pregnancy and the arrival of the Holy Spirit into the unborn child from the fiftieth day.
<br>*Divine Purpose of the Sacred Gift of Inspiration & Rite of Annunciation*

It is the Holy Spirit that helps form the very beginnings of the human mind and consciousness and this Divine Contribution appears the moment that the foetus is unmistakably and unquestionably of the higher order life form of Homo Sapien from the end of the first trimester.

**1169.** It is a gross error to presume the Spirit is fully present in Human Form from the precise moment of Conception. Laws and Maxims that are enacted according to this error are profane against God and the Divine Creator of all Life.
<br>*Errors of Presumption concerning Spirit and Conception*

The reason the Spirit is not fully present in Human Form within the foetus until the end of the first trimester is threefold:-

    (i)    The new life must first experience and overcome each and every form and era of history of evolution of life upon planet Earth over more than two (2) billion years in a matter of fifty (50) to sixty (60) days. Thus, to be human is to first experience what it is to be all other forms of lesser complex life; and

    (ii)    The Holy Spirit must be invited into the new unborne life by the Spirit of the mother, even if the lower consciousness of the mother is unaware of such status of the pregnancy or may even be against the idea of pregnancy. If the Holy Spirit were not invited, but simply imposed itself upon the mother, then the arrival of the Spirit would be a fundamental breach of all the Laws of Heaven; and

(iii) The body of the mother must reach the state of no longer reacting to the pregnancy as if it were an infection and instead must demonstrate at this miraculous moment a metamorphosis whereby the body of the mother ceases to fight for the death of the new life form and instead normally begins to change in order to support by every means the successful nurturing of the unborne infant to full term.

Therefore, any teachings or laws that seek to impose the denial of the rights of the mother prior to this key event, over an unborne life form, not yet enjoined with the Holy Spirit is morally repugnant, profane, sacrilegious, illogical and is forbidden and to be suppressed.

However, any teachings or laws that deny this momentous event and ignore the rights of the unborne child from this moment at the end of the first trimester, in favour of the mother having extended rights to destroy a life beyond the first trimester are also morally repugnant, profane, sacrilegious, illogical and is forbidden and to be suppressed.

## Article 318 – Ius Ecclesiae Sacramentum Resurrectio (Resurrection)

1170. ***Ius Ecclesiae Sacramentum Resurrectio*** is the Ecclesiastical Right of the Authentic Life Sacrament of Resurrection, as inherited from the Divine Right *Ritus Sacramentum Resurrectio*. — I. Ecc. Sacr. Resurrectio (Resurrection)

1171. *Ritus Sacramentum Resurrectio* is the twenty-third of thirty-three Sacramental Divine Rights; and may only be invoked whenever the lesser Ecclesiastical Right of *Ius Ecclesiae Sacramentum Resurrectio* is invoked in strict accord with the liturgy of *Missale Christus* (Missal of Christ), or *Taqwa Islam* (Rites of Islam) or *Karman Spiritus* (Rites of the Universal Divine Spirit). — Invocation of Ritus Sacramentum Resurrectio

1172. The Sacred Gift of Resurrection and Rite of New Birth is granted and conferred to a new borne Homo Sapien child at the final stage of birth or within 90 days of being borne in accordance with the most sacred Covenant *Pactum De Singularis Caelum* and associated approved worship. — Gift of Resurrection

1173. The purpose of the Sacred Gift of Resurrection and Rite of New Birth — Divine Purpose is the formal bestowal or presentation of a possessory or prescriptive right of Office to an incumbent including taking possession of the insignia of Office.

of the Sacred Gift of Resurrection & Rite of New Birth

The birth of a child into flesh also represents the birth of a True Trust through the conveyance of divinity, also known as Divine right of use from the Divine Personality of the spirit of the child with the flesh of the child the eventual rightful trustee of the True Trust upon age of majority. Until such time, the Divine Person of the child grants temporary guardian powers to the parent or parents, or those properly designated as immediate carer.

1174. In accordance with Divine Law and the most sacred Covenant *Pactum De Singularis Caelum*, if a foetus having received the sacred gift of Inspiration dies before being borne, then this unique Divine Immortal Spirit shall be fully entitled to receive the sacred gift of Resurrection and Rite of New Birth within ninety (90) days of what otherwise would have been its borne day and all Life Sacred Gifts thereafter at their appointed time.

Form of the Sacred Gift of Extraordinary Resurrection and Rite of New Birth

In accordance with Divine Law and the most sacred Covenant *Pactum De Singularis Caelum*, the mother or father or next of living kin of any foetus that failed to be borne, yet was not previously granted the Sacred Gift of Resurrection and Rite of New Birth may apply for the special ceremony of Life Sacred Gifts where all sacred gifts are granted beginning with Annunciation to the sacred gift representing the same age as if the foetus had been borne and lived to the present day.

1175. All fraudulent and inferior Rites of New Birth are forbidden and shall have no lawful effect. No documents, oral promises or any other inferred agreement by the parents of a new borne baby to the hospital, or competent civil authority or by implication to any Religion or Cult can in anyway diminish the rights of the parents as Guardians unless by willing and deliberate behaviour they have been legally proven through a formal hearing to be incompetent as trustees and guardians of their new borne child.

False and Profane Rituals of claimed Rites of New Birth

The Sacred Gift of Resurrection and Rite of New Birth negates the presumptions, validity and existence of any claimed *Cestui Que Vie* Trusts or any other curses, spells and unlawful conveyances by any Religion, Cult or their agents.

## Article 319 – Ius Ecclesiae Sacramentum Incarnatio (Incarnation)

1176. ***Ius Ecclesiae Sacramentum Incarnatio*** is the Ecclesiastical Right of the Authentic Life Sacrament of Incarnation, as inherited from the Divine Right *Ritus Sacramentum Incarnatio*.

    I. Ecc. Sacr. Incarnatio (Incarnation)

1177. *Ritus Sacramentum Incarnatio* is the twenty-fourth of thirty-three Sacramental Divine Rights; and may only be invoked whenever the lesser Ecclesiastical Right of *Ius Ecclesiae Sacramentum Incarnatio* is invoked in strict accord with the liturgy of *Missale Christus* (Missal of Christ), or *Taqwa Islam* (Rites of Islam) or *Karman Spiritus* (Rites of the Universal Divine Spirit).

    Invocation of Ritus Sacramentum Incarnatio

1178. The Sacred Gift of Incarnation and Rite of Initiation shall be granted and administered by the second (2nd) birthday of a child that has received the Sacred Gift of Resurrection and Rite of New Birth in accordance with the most sacred Covenant *Pactum De Singularis Caelum* and associated approved worship.

    Gift of Incarnation

1179. The purpose of the Sacred Gift of Incarnation and Rite of Initiation is to officially recognise the transition of a baby to a child and their commencement of valid organised learning systems of the community. The child is now welcomed into the tribe and protection is given in exchange for the child understanding that it is time to learn.

    Divine Purpose of the Sacred Gift of Incarnation & Rite of Initiation

1180. In accordance with Divine Law and the most sacred Covenant *Pactum De Singularis Caelum*, if a child having received the Sacred Gift of Resurrection and Rite of New Birth dies at or prior to the age of two (2), then this unique Divine Immortal Spirit shall be fully entitled to receive the Sacred Gift of Incarnation and Rite of Initiation two (2) years since being borne and all Life Sacred Gifts thereafter at their appointed time.

    Extraordinary Form of the Sacred Gift of Incarnation & Rite of Initiation

    In accordance with Divine Law and the most sacred Covenant *Pactum De Singularis Caelum*, the mother or father or next of living kin of any child that died at or prior to the age of two (2) yet was not previously granted the Sacred Gift of Resurrection and Rite of New Birth may apply for the special ceremony of Life Sacred Gifts where all Sacred Gifts are granted beginning with Sacred Gift of Inspiration and Rite of Annunciation to the Sacred Gift representing the same age as if the child had lived and grown up to the present day.

## Article 320 – Ius Ecclesiae Sacramentum Confirmatio (Confirmation)

1181. ***Ius Ecclesiae Sacramentum Confirmatio*** is the Ecclesiastical Right of the Authentic Life Sacrament of Confirmation, as inherited from the Divine Right *Ritus Sacramentum Confirmatio*. — I. Ecc. Sacr. Confirmatio (Confirmation)

1182. *Ritus Sacramentum Confirmatio* is the twenty-fifth of thirty-three Sacramental Divine Rights; and may only be invoked whenever the lesser Ecclesiastical Right of *Ius Ecclesiae Sacramentum Confirmatio* is invoked in strict accord with the liturgy of *Missale Christus* (Missal of Christ), or *Taqwa Islam* (Rites of Islam) or *Karman Spiritus* (Rites of the Universal Divine Spirit). — Invocation of Ritus Sacramentum Confirmatio

1183. The Sacred Gift of Confirmation and Rite of First Community shall be granted and administered by the twelfth (12th) birthday of a child that has received the Sacred Gift of Incarnation in accordance with the most sacred Covenant *Pactum De Singularis Caelum* and associated approved worship. — Gift of Confirmation

1184. The Divine purpose of the Sacred Gift of Confirmation and Rite of First Community is to celebrate the admittance of a child into the rights of possessions and responsibility of their respective community through the formal celebration and bestowal of certain Ecclesiastical and Public rights to the child as a member of the community. Upon a child demonstrating their ability to distinguish right from wrong; and the basic competence of logic, reason and discernment; and an essential understanding of morals and consequences, a child is permitted to own property in their own name. A child having received the Sacred Gift of Confirmation and Rite of First Community is also expected to acknowledge their responsibilities and duties to their family and community. — Divine Purpose of the Sacred Gift of Confirmation & Rite of First Community

1185. The Ordinary Form of the Sacred Gift of Confirmation and Rite of First Community cannot be conferred unless the child is clearly prepared and able to become a productive and exemplary member of their community. Thus, the priority of education and preparation must pertain to skills of reason, logic, discernment, morality, ethics and the consequences of actions before any detailed knowledge of the laws of the three Great Faiths are then necessary. — Condition of the Ordinary Form Sacred Gift of Confirmation & Rite of First Community

A child that is able to recite scripture and the tenets of any faith, yet is unable to apply reason, logic and virtue to their decisions is not competent for Confirmation and those that failed to adequately prepare such a child are not competent to teach, until they acknowledge such failings.

This is because, to be a member of the Living Body of any Great Faith is to be an ambassador of the Spirit of God; and an exemplary to the world. Confirmation is a sacred gift, First Community is a sacred ceremony that heralds such a moment. Therefore an absence of proper preparation is a grave offence against the child and the most sacred Covenant *Pactum De Singularis Caelum* itself.

1186. In accordance with Divine Law and the most sacred Covenant *Pactum De Singularis Caelum*, if a child having received the Sacred Gift of Incarnation dies before being the age of twelve (12), then this unique Divine Immortal Spirit shall be fully entitled to receive the Sacred Gift of Confirmation within sixty (60) days of twelve (12) years since being borne.

> Extraordinary Form of the Sacred Gift of Confirmation & Rite of First Community

In accordance with Divine Law and the most sacred Covenant *Pactum De Singularis Caelum*, the mother or father or next of living kin of any child that died prior to the age of twelve (12) yet was not previously granted the Sacred Gift of Confirmation may apply for the special ceremony of Life Sacred Gifts where all Sacred Gifts are granted beginning with Sacred Gift of Inspiration and Rite of Annunciation to the Sacred Gift representing the same age as if the child had lived and grown up to the present day.

## Article 321 – Ius Ecclesiae Sacramentum Illuminatio (Illumination)

1187. ***Ius Ecclesiae Sacramentum Illuminatio*** is the Ecclesiastical Right of the Authentic Life Sacrament of Illumination, as inherited from the Divine Right *Ritus Sacramentum Illuminatio*.

> I. Ecc. Sacr. Illuminatio (Illumination)

1188. *Ritus Sacramentum Illuminatio* is the twenty-sixth of thirty-three Sacramental Divine Rights; and may only be invoked whenever the lesser Ecclesiastical Right of *Ius Ecclesiae Sacramentum Illuminatio* is invoked in strict accord with the liturgy of *Missale Christus* (Missal of Christ), or *Taqwa Islam* (Rites of Islam) or *Karman Spiritus* (Rites of the Universal Divine Spirit).

> Invocation of Ritus Sacramentum Illuminatio

1189. The Sacred Gift of Illumination and Rite of Majority shall be granted and administered by the twenty-first (21st) birthday of a young adult in accordance with the most sacred Covenant *Pactum De Singularis Caelum* and associated approved worship.

> Gift of Illumination

1190. Every enlightened and civilised culture of history has recognised the significance of the moment of welcoming a new member of the community as an adult, whatever age was prescribed for such tradition. Since then, the age of adulthood has progressively increased to eighteen in some societies to the age of twenty one in

> Divine Purpose of the Sacred Gift of Illumination & Rite of Majority

others.

The purpose of the Sacred Gift of Illumination and Rite of Majority is to formalise the welcoming of new adults into the community at an age whereby most should have successfully finished some learning and qualification of useful skills.

Most importantly, the Sacred Gift of Illumination and Rite of Majority is essential to the community of the Living Body of any of the three Great Faiths to ensure all new Adult Members are fully competent in their moral, spiritual and behavioural obligations, particularly in the forming and supporting of their own families. Thus the Sacred Gift of Illumination and Rite of Majority is a necessary element to stable and fruitful Matrimonial relations throughout a healthy, productive and joyous society.

1191. A condition of Sacred Gift of Illumination and Rite of Majority is that the youth knowingly and willingly consents to dedicating their life to continuous self improvement and virtue and to contributing to the benefit and improvement of their community and society. *Conditions of the Sacred Gift of Illumination & Rite of Majority*

1192. In accordance with Divine Law and the most sacred Covenant *Pactum De Singularis Caelum*, if a teenager having received the Sacred Gift of Confirmation dies before being the age of twenty-one (21), then this unique Divine Immortal Spirit shall be fully entitled to receive the Sacred Gift of Illumination and Rite of Majority within thirty (30) days of twenty-one (21) years since being borne and all Life Sacred Gifts thereafter at their appointed time. *Extraordinary Form of the Sacred Gift of Illumination & Rite of Majority*

In accordance with Divine Law and the most sacred Covenant *Pactum De Singularis Caelum*, the mother or father or next of living kin of any child that died prior to the age of twenty-one (21) yet was not previously granted the Sacred Gift of Confirmation may apply for the special ceremony of Life Sacred Gifts where all Sacred Gifts including Sacred Gift of Illumination and Rite of Majority are granted beginning with the Sacred Gift of Inspiration and Rite of Annunciation to the Sacred Gift representing the same age as if the child had lived and grown up to the present day.

## Article 322 – Ius Ecclesiae Sacramentum Exultatio (Exultation)

1193. ***Ius Ecclesiae Sacramentum Exultatio*** is the Ecclesiastical Right of the Authentic Life Sacrament of Exultation, as inherited from the Divine Right *Ritus Sacramentum Exultatio*. *I. Ecc. Sacr. Exultatio (Exultation)*

1194. *Ritus Sacramentum Exultatio* is the twenty-seventh of thirty-three *Invocation of*

Sacramental Divine Rights; and may only be invoked whenever the lesser Ecclesiastical Right of *Ius Ecclesiae Sacramentum Exultatio* is invoked in strict accord with the liturgy of *Missale Christus* (Missal of Christ), or *Taqwa Islam* (Rites of Islam) or *Karman Spiritus* (Rites of the Universal Divine Spirit).

*Ritus Sacramentum Exultatio*

1195. The Sacred Gift of Exultation and Rite of Maturity shall be granted and administered by the thirty-third (33rd) birthday of an adult in accordance with the most sacred Covenant *Pactum De Singularis Caelum* and associated approved worship.

Invocation of Ritus Sacramentum Exultatio

1196. The Sacred Gift of Exultation and Rite of Maturity is the celebration of the point of transition from being a Young Adult to a fully mature Adult.

Divine Purpose of the Sacred Gift of Exultation & Rite of Maturity

## Article 323 – Ius Ecclesiae Sacramentum Glorificatio (Glorification)

1197. *Ius Ecclesiae Sacramentum Glorificatio* is the Ecclesiastical Right of the Authentic Life Sacrament of Glorification, as inherited from the Divine Right *Ritus Sacramentum Glorificatio*.

I. Ecc. Sacr. Glorificatio (Glorification)

1198. *Ritus Sacramentum Glorificatio* is the twenty-eighth of thirty-three Sacramental Divine Rights; and may only be invoked whenever the lesser Ecclesiastical Right of *Ius Ecclesiae Sacramentum Glorificatio* is invoked in strict accord with the liturgy of *Missale Christus* (Missal of Christ), or *Taqwa Islam* (Rites of Islam) or *Karman Spiritus* (Rites of the Universal Divine Spirit).

Invocation of Ritus Sacramentum Glorificatio

1199. The Sacred Gift of Glorification and Rite of Seniority shall be granted and administered by the fifty-fifth (55th) birthday of an adult in accordance with the most sacred Covenant *Pactum De Singularis Caelum* and associated approved worship.

Gift of Glorification

1200. The Sacred Gift of Glorification and Rite of Seniority is the celebration of the point of transition from Maturity to Seniority. It recognises the experience and contribution of older adults while they are still active members of their society.

Divine Purpose of the Sacred Gift of Glorification & Rite of Seniority

## Article 324 – Ius Ecclesiae Sacramentum Divinatio (Divination)

1201. *Ius Ecclesiae Sacramentum Divinatio* is the Ecclesiastical Right of the Authentic Life Sacrament of Divination, as inherited from the Divine Right *Ritus Sacramentum Divinatio*.

I. Ecc. Sacr. Divinatio (Divination)

1202. *Ritus Sacramentum Divinatio* is the twenty-ninth of thirty-three

Invocation of

Sacramental Divine Rights; and may only be invoked whenever the lesser Ecclesiastical Right of *Ius Ecclesiae Sacramentum Divinatio* is invoked in strict accord with the liturgy of *Missale Christus* (Missal of Christ), or *Taqwa Islam* (Rites of Islam) or *Karman Spiritus* (Rites of the Universal Divine Spirit).
Ritus Sacramentum Divinatio

1203. The Sacred Gift of Divination and Rite of Elderity shall be granted and administered by the seventy-seventh (77th) birthday of a senior in accordance with the most sacred Covenant *Pactum De Singularis Caelum* and associated approved worship.
Gift of Divination

1204. An enlightened society venerates its elders, protects them and seeks their counsel and wisdom. The Sacred Gift of Divination and Rite of Elderity is the celebration of the point of transition from Seniority to Elderhood. It is the celebration of becoming an elder.
Divine Purpose of the Sacred Gift of Divination & Rite of Elderity

## Article 325 – Ius Ecclesiae Sacramentum Visitatio (Visitation)

1205. ***Ius Ecclesiae Sacramentum Visitatio*** is the Ecclesiastical Right of the Authentic Life Sacrament of Visitation, as inherited from the Divine Right *Ritus Sacramentum Visitatio*.
I. Ecc. Sacr. Visitatio (Visitation)

1206. *Ritus Sacramentum Visitatio* is the thirtieth of thirty-three Sacramental Divine Rights; and may only be invoked whenever the lesser Ecclesiastical Right of *Ius Ecclesiae Sacramentum Visitatio* is invoked in strict accord with the liturgy of *Missale Christus* (Missal of Christ), or *Taqwa Islam* (Rites of Islam) or *Karman Spiritus* (Rites of the Universal Divine Spirit).
Invocation of Ritus Sacramentum Visitatio

1207. The Sacred Gift of Visitation and Rite of Unction shall be granted and administered within months of most certain death in accordance with the most sacred Covenant *Pactum De Singularis Caelum* and associated approved worship.
Gift of Visitation

1208. It is the natural order of life and the universe that we are borne, we live and our bodies age and become less reliable until the day that we must leave our bodies behind and return to our eternal Heavenly Home.
Divine Purpose of the Sacred Gift of Visitation & Rite of Unction

Thus, it is not the natural order, but profoundly unnatural, profane and supremely arrogant to consider that such natural order should be suspended and that Homo Sapiens live according to an undetermined lifespan. For while it is perfectly reasonable to aspire to a world without debilitating and painful disease, it is encumbered upon all men and women with heroic virtue to protect the boundaries of life of our species, so that we do not become consumed as other species in other parts of the universe did become in past ages, and assume themselves to be equals to the Universal Divine Creator.

The Divine Spirit reveals the true nature of God and the Divine Creator of all Existence and all Heaven and Earth to be Divine Mercy, Divine Forgiveness and Divine Love. Thus, it is not the nature or wish of the Creator of the Universe that any man or woman suffer the indignity of a slow, agonising and wasteful death.

Therefore, when a man or woman approaches such a trial as a slow and debilitating terminal illness and death, the three Great Faiths have an ecclesiastical and moral obligation as the true Disciples of Divine Mercy to do everything within their power to support the dignity of the dying and help them find peace.

Dying with dignity is a fundamental determination of an enlightened society under God and the Divine Creator. Visitation is a celebration that enables those people who have some time before the point of death to seek resolution and peace before death; and before a loss of consciousness deprives the person of the full appreciation of the sacred gift.

## Article 326 – Ius Ecclesiae Sacramentum Salvatio (Salvation)

1209. ***Ius Ecclesiae Sacramentum Salvatio*** is the Ecclesiastical Right of the Authentic Life Sacrament of Salvation, as inherited from the Divine Right *Ritus Sacramentum Salvatio*. I. Ecc. Sacr. Salvatio (Salvation)

1210. *Ritus Sacramentum Salvatio* is the thirty-first of thirty-three Sacramental Divine Rights; and may only be invoked whenever the lesser Ecclesiastical Right of *Ius Ecclesiae Sacramentum Salvatio* is invoked in strict accord with the liturgy of *Missale Christus* (Missal of Christ), or *Taqwa Islam* (Rites of Islam) or *Karman Spiritus* (Rites of the Universal Divine Spirit). Invocation of Ritus Sacramentum Salvatio

1211. The Sacred Gift of Salvation and Rite of Reconciliation shall be granted and administered within days of imminent death in accordance with the most sacred Covenant *Pactum De Singularis Caelum* and associated approved worship. Gift of Salvation

1212. The purpose of the Sacred Gift of Salvation and Rite of Reconciliation is the formal final (last) rites of bestowal or presentation of a possessory or prescriptive right to an incumbent in accordance with the most sacred Covenant *Pactum De Singularis Caelum* and associated approved worship. Divine Purpose of the Sacred Gift of Salvation & Rite of Reconciliation

The Sacred Gift of Salvation and Rite of Reconciliation is the special celebration of blessing and cleansing to help an individual in the final stages of death to find a point of peace and resolution to their life in the hope of evoking the care of other minds already crossed to help guide the person safely.

## Article 327 – Ius Ecclesiae Sacramentum Emancipatio (Emancipation)

1213. ***Ius Ecclesiae Sacramentum Emancipatio*** is the Ecclesiastical Right of the Authentic Life Sacrament of Original Emancipation, as inherited from the Divine Right *Ritus Sacramentum Emancipatio*. — I. Ecc. Sacr. Emancipatio (Emancipation)

1214. *Ritus Sacramentum Emancipatio* is the thirty-second of thirty-three Sacramental Divine Rights; and may only be invoked whenever the lesser Ecclesiastical Right of *Ius Ecclesiae Sacramentum Emancipatio* is invoked in strict accord with the liturgy of *Missale Christus* (Missal of Christ), or *Taqwa Islam* (Rites of Islam) or *Karman Spiritus* (Rites of the Universal Divine Spirit). — Invocation of Ritus Sacramentum Emancipatio

1215. The Sacred Gift of Emancipation and Funerary Rites shall be granted and administered after death and prior to the sacred gift of Veneration and the burial or disposal of the body in accordance with the most sacred Covenant *Pactum De Singularis Caelum* and associated approved worship. — Gift of Emancipation

1216. The purpose of the Sacred Gift of Emancipation and Funerary Rites is the formal funeral rites to an incumbent in accordance with the most sacred Covenant *Pactum De Singularis Caelum* and associated approved worship. — Divine Purpose of the Sacred Gift of Emancipation and Funerary Rites

The Sacred Gift of Emancipation and Funerary Rites is both the sacred gift and ceremony that remembers the deceased, their life and provides an opportunity for those in attendance to speak, celebrate and honour the memory of the departed.

## Article 328 – Ius Ecclesiae Sacramentum Veneratio (Veneration)

1217. ***Ius Ecclesiae Sacramentum Veneratio*** is the Ecclesiastical Right of the Authentic Life Sacrament of Veneration, as inherited from the Divine Right *Ritus Sacramentum Veneratio*. — I. Ecc. Sacr. Veneratio (Veneration)

1218. *Ritus Sacramentum Veneratio* is the thirty-third of thirty-three Sacramental Divine Rights; and may only be invoked whenever the lesser Ecclesiastical Right of *Ius Ecclesiae Sacramentum Veneratio* is invoked in strict accord with the liturgy of *Missale Christus* (Missal of — Invocation of Ritus Sacramentum Veneratio

Christ), or *Taqwa Islam* (Rites of Islam) or *Karman Spiritus* (Rites of the Universal Divine Spirit).

1219. The Sacred Gift of Veneration and Rite of Beatification shall be granted and administered by a valid Minister following death and the sacred gift of Remembrance in accordance with the most sacred Covenant *Pactum De Singularis Caelum* and associated approved worship.  
*Gift of Veneration*

1220. The purpose of the sacred gift of Veneration and Rite of Beatification is a formal rite of blessing and remembrance in favour of the formal recognition, honour and trust of an incumbent in Heaven in accordance with the most sacred Covenant *Pactum De Singularis Caelum* and associated approved worship.  
*Divine Purpose of the Sacred Gift of Veneration & Rite of Beatification*

## 8.5 – Ecclesiastical Writs of Rights

### Article 329 – Ecclesiastical Writs of Rights

1221. ***Ecclesiastical Writs of Rights*** (*Recto Ecclesiae Iurium*) shall be Ecclesiastical Rights associated with the one, true and only forms of Original Entry and Original Action.  
*Ecclesiastical Writs of Rights (Recto Ecclesiae Iurium)*

1222. A ***Writ*** is a formal written command issued by a court or judicial authority, often used to initiate, conclude or command some action in a legal proceeding.  
*Writ*

1223. In accord with the *Lex Positivum* (Maxims Positive Law), a valid Writ may only be issued under the proper Ecclesiastical Authority of the most sacred Covenant known as *Pactum De Singularis Caelum*:  
*Nature and authority of Writs*

 (i) A Writ is not an order – it is an absolute command that cannot be challenged. An order by its legal and commercial meaning is an offer that may be negotiated. Whereas a Writ, by definition is not negotiable. Therefore, any definition that states a Writ may be defined as an order is patently false and fraudulent; and

 (ii) A valid and legitimate Writ by its very nature is an ecclesiastical instrument requiring precise creation and purpose. To simply call an instrument a Writ and act as if it possesses the same qualities as a legitimate writ without the attendant care, authority or creation is a most grave injury to the Law itself; and

 (iii) A body may possess the right to appoint one or more agents under validly signed and sealed warrants. However, such persons have no right legally or lawfully to issue a Writ unless they themselves are also appointed under Ucadian Law as per Maxims of Positive Law. If such persons are not appointed to their position under such Authority, then any Writs they issue are *ipso facto* (as a fact of law) null and void; and

(iv) Corporations and agents cannot create or issue valid Writs. Nor may a nation issue such Writs unless the Executive claims absolute Ecclesiastical authority in accord with Ucadian Law; and

(v) Any Laws that have been passed that attempt to permit the issuing of writs by corporations or agents are an abomination and contrary to the very source of authority of Writs. Such documents therefore issued have no more legal or lawful effect than an offer or notice. The enforcement therefore of such instruments as if they are writs is without question illegal and unlawful – contrary to very foundations of Law. An invalid writ has no force or effect ecclesiastically, lawfully or legally.

1224. All valid Remedy and Relief shall be by one or more Perfect Writs of Right as the one, true and only valid forms of Original Entry and Original Action. All forms of coercive powers and enforcement including, but not limited to prevention, protection, restitution, restoration, seizure, search, sanction, arrest, custody, penalty or satisfaction, shall be enacted via one or more valid Perfect Writs of Right. Valid Remedy and Relief

1225. There shall be three classes of Perfect Writs of Right, being Divine, True and Superior:- Three Classes of Perfect Writs of Right

(i) Perfect Divine Writs of Right and Action shall be the Right of Original Entry and Action for all Divine Rights in relation to all Divine Persons, Divine Trusts and Divine Estates; and

(ii) Perfect True Writs of Right and Rule of Law shall be the Right of Original Entry and Action for all Natural Rights in relation to all True Persons, True Trusts and True Estates; and

(iii) Perfect Superior Writs of Right and Enforcement shall be the Right of Original Entry and Action for all Superior Rights in relation to all Superior Persons, Superior Trusts and Superior Estates of valid Ucadia Societies and competent forums of Law.

1226. The enforcement and coercive powers of Perfect Writs of Right may only be issued in relation to Members of One Heaven and Ucadia being Divine Persons, or True Persons or Superior Persons, as well as any other lesser bodies, bodies politic, associations, partnerships, Enforcement of Perfect Writs companies, entities, fraternities, religious organisations, corporations or persons under the Jurisdiction of the Divine Creator of all Existence and all Heaven and Earth.

1227. By definition, the very existence of any Divine Person or claim of authority or power or right from Heaven of a lesser body, association, person or entity, is *prima facie* proof of an ecclesiastical and trust relation acknowledging the Jurisdiction of the Divine Creator of all Existence and all Heaven and Earth. Furthermore, the existence of a flesh body is irrefutable proof of the conveyance of divinity from a Divine Trust to a True Trust and the willing consent by the Divine Person to perform and obey the obligations of making such a gift in accord with the most sacred Covenant *Pactum De Singularis Caelum*. All enforcement through valid Perfect Writs of Right is therefore considered imperative in nature.

*Imperative Nature of Perfect Writs*

1228. All *Ecclesiastical Writs of Rights* are delegated to the safe custody and wise guardian powers of the legitimate and valid supreme competent ecclesiastical forum of law of the proper Ucadia Faiths and all lesser associated Ucadia bodies, as the embodiment of judicial authority; and as defined by Article 59 (Oratorium) of the most sacred Covenant *Pactum De Singularis Caelum*.

*Delegation of Ecclesiastical Writs of Rights*

1229. All *Ecclesiastical Writs of Rights* are assumed to be automatically invoked within Ucadia Jurisdictions through the operation of the Civilised Rules of Ucadia Societies, Bodies and Entities. However the Rights may be explicitly invoked or referenced by Right of Action through a proper Forum of Law and the Fiduciary Obligations of any such court in Ucadia or Non-Ucadia Jurisdiction.

*Invocation of Ecclesiastical Writs of Rights*

1230. The following valid eleven (11) Ecclesiastical Writs of Rights (*Recto Ecclesiae Iurium*) are recognised in accord with the most sacred Covenant *Pactum De Singularis Caelum*:-

*List of Ecclesiastical Writs of Rights (Recto Ecclesiae Iurium)*

    (i)    **"Recto Ecclesiae Originalis"** is the Ecclesiastical Original Writ of Right, as inherited from the Divine Right *Recto Divinum Originalis*; and

    (ii)    **"Recto Ecclesiae Apocalypsis"** is the Ecclesiastical Writ of Right of Revelation, as inherited from the Divine Right *Recto Divinum Apocalypsis*; and

    (iii)    **"Recto Ecclesiae Investigationis"** is the Ecclesiastical Writ of Right of Inquiry or Review, as inherited from the Divine Right *Recto Divinum Investigationis*; and

    (iv)    **"Recto Ecclesiae Capimus"** is the Ecclesiastical Writ of Right of Surrender or Arrest of Person, as inherited from the

Divine Right *Recto Divinum Capimus*; and

(v) **"Recto Ecclesiae Custodiae"** is the Ecclesiastical Writ of Right of Surrender or Seizure of Property, as inherited from the Divine Right *Recto Divinum Custodiae*; and

(vi) **"Recto Ecclesiae Corrigimus"** is the Ecclesiastical Writ of Right of Correction of Records, Rulings, Laws or Instruments, as inherited from the Divine Right *Recto Divinum Corrigimus*; and

(vii) **"Recto Ecclesiae Expurgatio"** is the Ecclesiastical Writ of Right of Expurgation of Records, Rulings, Laws or Instruments, as inherited from the Divine Right *Recto Divinum Expurgatio*; and

(viii) **"Recto Ecclesiae Abrogatio"** is the Ecclesiastical Writ of Right of Annulment of Records, Rulings, Laws or Instruments, as inherited from the Divine Right *Recto Divinum Abrogatio*; and

(ix) **"Recto Ecclesiae Inhibitio"** is the Ecclesiastical Writ of Right of Prohibition or Restraint, as inherited from the Divine Right *Recto Divinum Inhibitio*; and

(x) **"Recto Ecclesiae Restitutio"** is the Ecclesiastical Writ of Right of Restitution, as inherited from the Divine Right *Recto Divinum Restitutio*; and

(xi) **"Recto Ecclesiae Restoratio"** is the Ecclesiastical Writ of Right of Restoration, as inherited from the Divine Right *Recto Divinum Restoratio*.

1231. The issue of a valid and legitimate Writ in accord with Ucadian Law and the present Maxims must follow a series of procedural steps before any actual Writ is issued and enforcement executed: Procedural Steps of valid Writ

(i) The first procedural step is the *Petition* or "*Petitio*", whereby a duly authorised Ucadia Member as Petitioner, produces the necessary documentation, affidavits, evidence and memorandum as an Application or Complaint or Petition to the appropriate competent forum of Law of the Ecclesiastical Ucadia Entity. In doing so, the Petitioner is also a Grantor in the formation of a sacred and unbreakable trust that will form the basis of the review, possible approval of the writ and its execution; and

(ii) The *Confidant* that receives the Petition is a duly authorised official of the proper Court, on behalf of the same Court that then acts as Trustee concerning the matter as the Court of Original Jurisdiction. The Court then reviews the Petition and its merits and decides whether sufficient substance exists to then accept and act upon the Petition and issue a Writ. This judgement is called the Summary; and

(iii) If it is found by a competent forum of Law that a Writ should be issued, the Court as Trustee shall then become Principal in issuing commands through the Writ to one or more Agents as Fiduciaries in Trust, to execute the Writ and obtain the necessary Remedy.

1232. A Petition, also known as a *Petitio* as the cause of action in the formation of any valid Writ, is an Instrument in writing, containing a prayer from the person presenting it, called the Petitioner, to the body or person to whom it is presented, for the redress of some wrong, or the grant of some favour, that the latter has the Right to give or witness as true, with the components being:- Petitio (Petition)

(i) *Title*, being the opening summary of the name of the Petitioner, and the name of the Respondent(s), any existing Suit or Action Number, the name of the Petition in relation to a certain Writ, the Ucadia Space Day Time; and

(ii) *Syllabus*, being the briefest summary in 250 words or less as to the nature of the petition, the main parties and context; and

(iii) *Parties*, being the parties related to the Petition; and

(iv) *Contents Page*, being the summary of remaining sections of the document and page location; and

(v) *Jurisdiction*, being the statement of Jurisdiction and Authority of the competent forum of Law to receive and determine the merits of granting the Writ as well as any questions regarding jurisdictional authority over other parties; and

(vi) *Statement of Facts*, being the key summary of key facts in chronological order, in support of the petition; and

(vii) *Arguments*, being the key arguments in law relating to the facts as to why the Writ should be granted; and

(viii) *Citations and References*, being the summary of citations of various laws or maxims or references as a bibliography in support of such references being used in Arguments; and

(ix) *Prayer for Remedy*, being the specific and individual actions requested in logical sequence and order; and

(x) *Appendix of Exhibits*, being the document referred in the attached Affidavit and in the Arguments of the Petition.

1233. All Petitions are reviewed for approval or denial by a competent forum of Law according to the following essential criteria:- <small>Criteria for Review of Petition</small>

    (i) Does the Petition document provide written answers to all the essential administrative elements required, in the order required, within the page limits required and format required?; and

    (ii) Does the Syllabus of the Petition match in the broadest and general sense the terms by which such a writ is normally issued?; and

    (iii) Does the Prayer for Justice of the Petition match the conditions of remedy by which such a writ may be issued?; and

    (iv) Do the Arguments outlined within the Petition match the essential criteria that must be present for such a writ to be issued?; and

    (v) Do the Arguments within the Petition provide one or more exhibits of proof contained within the Appendix to the Petition?; and

    (vi) Is there sufficient evidence based on the Arguments and Appendix of the Petition to conclude that the Respondent is within the Jurisdiction of the Court?; and

    (vii) Is there sufficient evidence based on the Arguments and Appendix of the Petition to conclude that the Court has sufficient Jurisdiction and right to appoint and bond one or more Agents with enforcing the writ through one or more Warrants?

1234. The *Prayer for Relief* is the fundamental element of any valid Petition and specifies in the briefest of sentences, the individual actions requested in logical sequence, without repetition, in relation to a specific form of Ecclesiastical Writ:- <small>Prayer for Remedy and Essential Conditions</small>

    (i) Different types of Ecclesiastical Writs have different Essential Conditions being the conditions that must be present before an Ecclesiastical Writ may be issued; and

    (ii) A Prayer containing an individual action that is inconsistent with the purpose or nature of that kind of Writ, or is inconsistent with the Essential Conditions for issuing such a Writ therefore renders such a Prayer in error and void of effect; and

(iii) A Writ cannot be issued when a Prayer is in error; and

(iv) Because the accuracy of the Prayer is so essential, A Prayer will usually contain less than six actions.

1235. A Summary, also known as a *Summa* as the formal response from a competent forum of Law, is an Instrument in writing, containing an opinion from the Confidant concerning a Petition and whether such Petition has merit and honours the form and intention of such sacred and holy writ. All valid and legitimate Petitions must be answered by a Summary within forty days of being received and acknowledged. However, an Ecclesiastical Writ can only be issued if in the opinion of the court, the Petition meets the strictest guidelines within the Rule of Law. The standard elements to a valid Summary are:  Summa (Summary)

(i) *Title*, being the opening summary of the name of the Confidant, and the name of the Petitioner, and the name of the Respondent(s), any existing Writ Number, the name of the Petition in relation to a certain Writ, the Ucadia Space Day Time; and

(ii) *Summary,* being the briefest summary in 500 words or less as to the nature of the petition and whether in the opinion of the competent forum the writ should be granted or denied; and

(iii) *Contents Page*, being the summary of remaining sections of the document and page location; and

(iv) *Jurisdiction*, being the observation and statement of Jurisdiction and Authority of the competent forum of Law to receive and determine the merits of granting the Writ as well as any questions regarding jurisdictional authority over other parties; and

(v) *Conflict of Law*, being any issues in respect of conflict of law; and

(vi) *Arguments*, being the key arguments in law relating as to why the Writ should be granted or denied; and

(vii) *Citations and References*, being the summary of citations of various laws or maxims or references as a bibliography in support of such references being used in Arguments; and

(viii) *Command of Action*, being the previous prayer, or revised prayer now expressed as a command of actions to be done by the Respondent(s) – only if the Summary agrees that a Writ is to be issued.

1236. An Ecclesiastical Writ may only be issued after a Summary is given by the relevant competent forum of Law in respect of the Petition. When an Ecclesiastical Writ is agreed to be issued, the key information as outlined within the Summary is recorded and enrolled within the Register of Writs as the *Original Form* within the Court of Chancery of the Ecclesiastical Ucadia Entity.

*Register of Writs*

1237. In relation to the Persons and Parties associated with a valid Writ:

*Relations of Persons to a Writ*

  (i) The Person who makes the Petition is called the *Petitioner* and is also the *Grantor* of any Rights to the court to pursue the matter in relation to the proposed Writ; and

  (ii) The one (or more) with whom the Petitioner has grievance is called the *Respondent*; and

  (iii) The Person who receives the Petition is a court official called the *Confidant* and is also the *Trustee* of the Trust formed through the Petition as the Trust Instrument; and

  (iv) If the court approves the Petition, then the Court official that issues the Writ is called the *Principal*; and

  (v) The one who receives command to execute the actions of a valid Writ is called the *Agent* of the Principal and is also a *Fiduciary* of a sub trust in the transfer of certain rights and powers to perform the necessary tasks.

1238. Subject to these Maxims and Ucadian Law, the following types of Non-Ucadia writs are considered inferior, redundant and prohibited to be used by Ucadia bodies, courts, entities and officials, including (but not limited to):-

*Inferior and Redundant forms of Writs*

  (i) **Attachment** is a writ from a court for the seizure or attachment of property owned by a defendant. Under Ucadia Law and Jurisdiction, the Superior and Ecclesiastical Writ of *Recto Ecclesiae Custodiae* (Surrender or Seizure of Property) is used; and

  (ii) **Audita Querela** (Latin for "the complaint having been heard") is a writ from a court that grants relief from a previous judgment or enforcement of a previous judgment that has become unjust or inequitable due to circumstances that arise after the judgment was issued. Under Ucadia Law and Jurisdiction, the Superior and Ecclesiastical Writ of *Recto Ecclesiae Corrigimus* (Correction of Records, Rulings, Laws or Instruments) is used; and

(iii) **Capias** (Latin for "you shall take") is a writ from a court used to direct law enforcement to take a person or certain property into custody. Under Ucadia Law and Jurisdiction, the Superior and Ecclesiastical Writ of *Recto Ecclesiae Capimus* (Surrender or Arrest of Person) is used; and

(iv) **Certiorari** (Latin for "to be more fully informed") is a writ from a higher court directing a lower court, tribunal, or public authority to send the record in a given case for review, effectively stripping the lower court of the specific authority to hear the matter. Under Ucadia Law and Jurisdiction, the Superior and Ecclesiastical Writ of *Recto Ecclesiae Investigationis* (Inquiry or Review) is used; and

(v) **Coram Nobis** (Latin for "the (error) in our/your presence") is a writ issued when a higher court has received the records of a previously adjudicated matter by an inferior court; and upon clear evidence of fundamental errors of law and failure of due process, orders the record be corrected. Under Ucadia Law and Jurisdiction, the Superior and Ecclesiastical Writ of *Recto Ecclesiae Corrigimus* (Correction of Records, Rulings, Laws or Instruments) is used; and

(vi) **Entry** is a writ used in property disputes, allowing the plaintiff to regain possession of land wrongfully held by another. Under Ucadia Law and Jurisdiction, the Superior and Ecclesiastical Writ of *Recto Ecclesiae Custodiae* (Surrender or Seizure of Property) is used; and

(vii) **Fieri Facias** (Latin for "cause [it] to be done") is a writ issued by a court to a sheriff or other authorised officer to seize and sell the debtor's property to satisfy a monetary judgment against them. Under Ucadia Law and Jurisdiction, the Superior and Ecclesiastical Writ of *Recto Ecclesiae Custodiae* (Surrender or Seizure of Property) is used; and

(viii) **Habeas Corpus** (Latin for "we are to possess/have the body") is a writ issued by a higher court to a lower authority to release a prisoner from unlawful detention together with formal interrogatories as why the prisoner should continue to be detained. Under Ucadia Law and Jurisdiction, the Superior and Ecclesiastical Writ of *Recto Ecclesiae Capimus* (Surrender or Arrest of Person) is used; and

(ix) **Interdico** (Latin for "banish, forbid") is a writ issued by a court to banish or declare a person an outlaw and forbid them any trade, communication or material support whatsoever.

Under Ucadia Law and Jurisdiction, the Superior and Ecclesiastical Writ of *Recto Ecclesiae Inhibitio* (Prohibition or Restraint) is used; and

(x) **Mandamus** (Latin for "we command") is a writ issued by a court upon an official to cease any dishonourable and unlawful behaviour, or ordering lawful duty be performed. Under Ucadia Law and Jurisdiction, the Superior and Ecclesiastical Writ of *Recto Ecclesiae Apocalypsis* (Revelation) is used; and

(xi) **Ne Exeat** is a writ to prevent a person from leaving the jurisdiction of the court. Under Ucadia Law and Jurisdiction, the Superior and Ecclesiastical Writ of *Recto Ecclesiae Inhibitio* (Prohibition or Restraint) is used; and

(xii) **Possession** is a court order granting a party the right to possess a property, often used in landlord-tenant disputes. Under Ucadia Law and Jurisdiction, the Superior and Ecclesiastical Writ of *Recto Ecclesiae Custodiae* (Surrender or Seizure of Property) is used; and

(xiii) **Procedendo** (Latin for "go forward/advance (to judgment)") is issued when a superior court has reviewed the records of a matter and then orders an inferior court to proceed to judgment based on the corrected records. Under Ucadia Law and Jurisdiction, the Superior and Ecclesiastical Writ of *Recto Ecclesiae Investigationis* (Inquiry or Review) is used; and

(xiv) **Prohibito** (Latin for "forbiddance") is served as an order to an inferior court or law official to cease any and all further action on a matter as it has been addressed by a superior court. Under Ucadia Law and Jurisdiction, the Superior and Ecclesiastical Writ of *Recto Ecclesiae Inhibitio* (Prohibition or Restraint) is used; and

(xv) **Replevin** is issued to recover goods wrongfully taken or held by someone, pending the final outcome of the case. Under Ucadia Law and Jurisdiction, the Superior and Ecclesiastical Writ of *Recto Ecclesiae Restoratio* (Restoration) is used; and

(xvi) **Quo Warranto** (Latin for "by what warrant?") is served requiring the person to whom it is directed to show via formal interrogatories what authority they have for exercising some right or power (or "franchise") they claim to hold. Under Ucadia Law and Jurisdiction, the Superior and Ecclesiastical Writ of *Recto Ecclesiae Investigationis* (Inquiry or Review) is used; and

(xvii) **Scire Facias** (Latin for "to know the causes") is served against the issue of false titles, letters patent and documents granting rights and privileges to which the parties named are not entitled. Under Ucadia Law and Jurisdiction, the Superior and Ecclesiastical Writ of *Recto Ecclesiae Corrigimus* (Correction of Records, Rulings, Laws or Instruments) is used; and

(xviii) **Sequestration** is a writ ordering the seizure of property to prevent its use or destruction during a lawsuit. Under Ucadia Law and Jurisdiction, the Superior and Ecclesiastical Writ of *Recto Ecclesiae Custodiae* (Surrender or Seizure of Property) is used.

1239. Any alleged Ecclesiastical Writ that cannot prove its authority under Ucadian Law and the present Maxims, has none. — Ecclesiastical Writs without Authority

1240. Any claimed forum of law or court or body that issues a matter using a "Case Number"; and therefore by implication the claim of a Writ of Trespass On the Case; or refers to the matter or action as a Case; or fails to produce a valid Writ as authorised under Ucadian Law and these present Maxims shall then be *prima facie* evidence of a deliberate and wilful fraud, deception, perfidy, profanity, sacrilege and blasphemy against all Heaven and Earth and automatic grounds for an Indictment within a competent forum of Law against any and all persons, without any ability to claim immunity, for unlimited liability and damages for such injury. — Fraudulent Writs and Claims as automatic Indictment

## Article 330 – Recto Ecclesiae Originalis (Original Writ)

1241. **Recto Ecclesiae Originalis** is the Ecclesiastical Original Writ (of Right), as inherited from the Divine Right *Recto Divinum Originalis*. It is the first of eleven Ecclesiastical Writs. — Recto Ecclesiae Originalis (Original Writ)

1242. The *Original Writ of Right* (*Recto Ecclesiae Originalis*) is reserved as the Remedy when any Ucadia Person or Entity possesses a valid Cause of Action upon some wrong, or injury as defined by a valid Memorandum of Complaint or Indictment; and supported by a properly invoked Affidavit as testimony. The Original Writ of Right or "Original Writ" shall then be the foundation of any proceedings within a competent forum of law. — Purpose of Recto Ecclesiae Originalis (Original Writ)

1243. The Rights of the *Original Writ of Right*, also known as *Recto Ecclesiae Originalis,* are those actionable Rights embedded within the nature and character of such an Ecclesiastical Writ; and then able — Rights of Recto Ecclesiae Originalis (Original Writ)

to be dispensed through proper Warrants to duly authorised Agents. In accord with Ucadian Law and the present Maxims, the present type of Writ possesses the following Rights:

(i) *Ius Ecclesiae Actionis Originalis*, being the Right of Action and Entry of the Ecclesiastical Original Writ; and

(ii) *Ius Ecclesiae Auctoritas Originalis*, being the Right of Supreme Ecclesiastical and Administrative Authority of the Ecclesiastical Original Writ; and

(iii) *Ius Ecclesiae Notitiae Originalis*, being the Ecclesiastical and Administrative Right of Notice, Gazette, Promulgation and Publication of the Ecclesiastical Original Writ; and

(iv) *Ius Ecclesiae Iurisdictionis Originalis*, being the Ecclesiastical and Administrative Right of Original Jurisdiction of the Ecclesiastical Original Writ; and

(v) *Ius Ecclesiae Decretum Originalis*, being the Right of Supreme Judicial Authority and Power of the Ecclesiastical Original Writ, whereby there are no higher grounds of appeal or dispute in Law; and

(vi) *Ius Ecclesiae Potentis Originalis*, being the Right of Ecclesiastical, Judicial, Administrative and Military Power to use any and all necessary forms of coercive powers to enforce the Ecclesiastical Original Writ; and

(vii) *Ius Ecclesiae Armagestum Originalis*, being the Ecclesiastical and Administrative Right to possess, have, carry and bear arms, weapons, shields and defensive tools; and to recruit, employ and maintain soldiers and military, paramilitary and police personnel; and to engage in any and all necessary forms of coercive power to defend the true Rule of Law and enforce the Ecclesiastical Original Writ; and

(viii) *Ius Ecclesiae Preceptum Originalis*, being the Right of Ecclesiastical Written Command, Rule, Principle and Edict to execute, enforce, carry out and uphold the Ecclesiastical Original Writ; and

(ix) *Ius Ecclesiae Agentis Originalis*, being the Ecclesiastical and Administrative Right of Delegation, Commission and Assignment of Rights, Powers and Authority to one or more Agents to execute, enforce, carry out and uphold the Ecclesiastical Original Writ.

## Article 331 – Recto Ecclesiae Apocalypsis (Revelation)

1244. ***Recto Ecclesiae Apocalypsis*** is the Ecclesiastical Writ of Right of Revelation, as inherited from the Divine Right *Recto Divinum Apocalypsis*. It is the second of eleven Ecclesiastical Writs.

<small>Recto Ecclesiae Apocalypsis (Revelation)</small>

1245. The *Ecclesiastical Writ of Right of Revelation* (*Recto Ecclesiae Apocalypsis*) is reserved as the Remedy when any Ucadia Officer or Ucadia Entity possessing a valid Mandate invokes and enacts such an Ecclesiastical Writ to prevent or cease the continued violation of one or more valid Rights, or redress one or more wrongs, or restore one or more Rights.

<small>Purpose of Recto Ecclesiae Apocalypsis (Revelation)</small>

1246. The Rights of the *Ecclesiastical Writ of Revelation* also known as *Recto Ecclesiae Apocalypsis,* are those actionable Rights embedded within the nature and character of such an Ecclesiastical Writ; and then able to be dispensed through proper Warrants to duly authorised Agents. In accord with Ucadian Law and the present Maxims, the present type of Writ possesses the following Rights:

<small>Rights of Recto Ecclesiae Apocalypsis (Revelation)</small>

    (i)    *Ius Ecclesiae Actionis Apocalypsis*, being the Right of Action and Entry of the Ecclesiastical Writ of Right of Revelation; and

    (ii)    *Ius Ecclesiae Auctoritas Apocalypsis*, being the Right of Supreme Ecclesiastical and Administrative Authority of the Ecclesiastical Writ of Right of Revelation; and

    (iii)    *Ius Ecclesiae Notitiae Apocalypsis*, being the Ecclesiastical and Administrative Right of Notice, Gazette, Promulgation and Publication of the Ecclesiastical Writ of Right of Revelation; and

    (iv)    *Ius Ecclesiae Iurisdictionis Apocalypsis*, being the Ecclesiastical and Administrative Right of Original Jurisdiction of the Ecclesiastical Writ of Right of Revelation; and

    (v)    *Ius Ecclesiae Decretum Apocalypsis*, being the Right of Supreme Judicial Authority and Power of the Ecclesiastical Writ of Right of Revelation, whereby there are no higher grounds of appeal or dispute in Law; and

    (vi)    *Ius Ecclesiae Potentis Apocalypsis*, being the Right of Ecclesiastical, Judicial, Administrative and Military Power to use any and all necessary forms of coercive powers to enforce the Ecclesiastical Writ of Right of Revelation; and

(vii) *Ius Ecclesiae Armagestum Apocalypsis*, being the Ecclesiastical and Administrative Right to possess, have, carry and bear arms, weapons, shields and defensive tools; and to recruit, employ and maintain soldiers and military, paramilitary and police personnel; and to engage in any and all necessary forms of coercive power to defend the true Rule of Law and enforce the Ecclesiastical Writ of Right of Revelation; and

(viii) *Ius Ecclesiae Preceptum Apocalypsis*, being the Right of Ecclesiastical Written Command, Rule, Principle and Edict to execute, enforce, carry out and uphold the Ecclesiastical Writ of Right of Revelation; and

(ix) *Ius Ecclesiae Agentis Apocalypsis*, being the Ecclesiastical and Administrative Right of Delegation, Commission and Assignment of Rights, Powers and Authority to one or more Agents to execute, enforce, carry out and uphold the Ecclesiastical Writ of Right of Revelation.

## Article 332 – Recto Ecclesiae Investigationis (Inquiry or Review)

1247. ***Recto Ecclesiae Investigationis*** is the Ecclesiastical Writ of Inquiry or Review, as inherited from the Divine Right *Recto Divinum Investigationis*. It is the third of eleven Ecclesiastical Writs.

*Recto Ecclesiae Investigationis (Inquiry or Review)*

1248. The *Ecclesiastical Writ of Right of Inquiry or Review* (*Recto Ecclesiae Investigationis*) is reserved as the Remedy when any Ucadia Person or Ucadia Entity is faced with compelling evidence of persistent obstruction, denial or delay as to the truth of a matter material to one or more valid Rights, or the existence or state of affairs concerning one or more concepts or objects material to one or more valid Rights.

*Purpose of Recto Ecclesiae Investigationis (Inquiry or Review)*

1249. The Rights of the *Ecclesiastical Writ of Inquiry or Review*, also known as *Recto Ecclesiae Investigationis,* are those actionable Rights embedded within the nature and character of such an Ecclesiastical Writ; and then able to be dispensed through proper Warrants to duly authorised Agents. In accord with Ucadian Law and the present Maxims, the present type of Writ possesses the following Rights:

*Rights of Entry & Action of Recto Ecclesiae Investigationis (Inquiry or Review)*

(i) *Ius Ecclesiae Actionis Investigationis*, being the Right of Action and Entry of the Ecclesiastical Writ of Right of Inquiry or Review; and

(ii) *Ius Ecclesiae Auctoritas Investigationis*, being the Right of

Supreme Ecclesiastical and Administrative Authority of the Ecclesiastical Writ of Right of Inquiry or Review; and

(iii) *Ius Ecclesiae Notitiae Investigationis*, being the Ecclesiastical and Administrative Right of Notice, Gazette, Promulgation and Publication of the Ecclesiastical Writ of Right of Inquiry or Review; and

(iv) *Ius Ecclesiae Iurisdictionis Investigationis*, being the Ecclesiastical and Administrative Right of Original Jurisdiction of the Ecclesiastical Writ of Right of Inquiry or Review; and

(v) *Ius Ecclesiae Decretum Investigationis*, being the Right of Supreme Judicial Authority and Power of the Ecclesiastical Writ of Inquiry or Review, whereby there are no higher grounds of appeal or dispute in Law; and

(vi) *Ius Ecclesiae Potentis Investigationis*, being the Right of Ecclesiastical, Judicial, Administrative and Military Power to use any and all necessary forms of coercive powers to enforce the Ecclesiastical Writ of Right of Inquiry or Review; and

(vii) *Ius Ecclesiae Armagestum Investigationis*, being the Ecclesiastical and Administrative Right to possess, have, carry and bear arms, weapons, shields and defensive tools; and to recruit, employ and maintain soldiers and military, paramilitary and police personnel; and to engage in any and all necessary forms of coercive power to defend the true Rule of Law and enforce the Ecclesiastical Writ of Right of Inquiry or Review; and

(viii) *Ius Ecclesiae Preceptum Investigationis*, being the Right of Ecclesiastical Written Command, Rule, Principle and Edict to execute, enforce, carry out and uphold the Ecclesiastical Writ of Right of Inquiry or Review; and

(ix) *Ius Ecclesiae Agentis Investigationis*, being the Ecclesiastical and Administrative Right of Delegation, Commission and Assignment of Rights, Powers and Authority to one or more Agents to execute, enforce, carry out and uphold the Ecclesiastical Writ of Right of Inquiry or Review.

## Article 333 – Recto Ecclesiae Capimus (Surrender or Arrest of Person)

1250. ***Recto Ecclesiae Capimus*** is the Ecclesiastical Writ of Surrender or Arrest of Person, as inherited from the Divine Right *Recto Divinum Capimus*. It is the fourth of eleven Ecclesiastical Writs.

<sub-note>Recto Ecclesiae Capimus (Arrest of Person)</sub-note>

1251. The *Ecclesiastical Writ of Right of Surrender or Arrest of Person*, (*Recto Ecclesiae Capimus*) is reserved as the Remedy when any Ucadia Person or Ucadia Entity possesses compelling evidence that certain objects or concepts or forms or property are being held, detained or possessed by another party in direct violation of one or more valid Rights.

<sub-note>Purpose of Recto Ecclesiae Capimus (Surrender or Arrest of Person)</sub-note>

1252. The *Ecclesiastical Writ of Right of Surrender or Arrest of Person*, also known as *Recto Ecclesiae Capimus*, are those actionable Rights embedded within the nature and character of such an Ecclesiastical Writ; and then able to be dispensed through proper Warrants to duly authorised Agents. In accord with Ucadian Law and the present Maxims, the present type of Writ possesses the following Rights:

<sub-note>Rights of Recto Ecclesiae Capimus (Surrender or Arrest of Person)</sub-note>

   (i) *Ius Ecclesiae Actionis Recto Capimus*, being the Right of Action and Entry of the Ecclesiastical Writ of Right of Surrender or Arrest of Person; and

   (ii) *Ius Ecclesiae Auctoritas Capimus*, being the Right of Supreme Ecclesiastical and Administrative Authority of the Ecclesiastical Writ of Right of Surrender or Arrest of Person; and

   (iii) *Ius Ecclesiae Notitiae Capimus*, being the Ecclesiastical and Administrative Right of Notice, Gazette, Promulgation and Publication of the Ecclesiastical Writ of Right of Surrender or Arrest of Person; and

   (iv) *Ius Ecclesiae Iurisdictionis Capimus*, being the Ecclesiastical and Administrative Right of Original Jurisdiction of the Ecclesiastical Writ of Right of Surrender or Arrest of Person; and

   (v) *Ius Ecclesiae Decretum Capimus*, being the Right of Supreme Judicial Authority and Power of the Ecclesiastical Writ of Right of Surrender or Arrest of Person, whereby there are no higher grounds of appeal or dispute in Law; and

   (vi) *Ius Ecclesiae Potentis Capimus*, being the Right of Ecclesiastical, Judicial, Administrative and Military Power to use any and all necessary forms of coercive powers to enforce the Ecclesiastical Writ of Right of Surrender or Arrest of Person; and

(vii) *Ius Ecclesiae Armagestum Capimus*, being the Ecclesiastical and Administrative Right to possess, have, carry and bear arms, weapons, shields and defensive tools; and to recruit, employ and maintain soldiers and military, paramilitary and police personnel; and to engage in any and all necessary forms of coercive power to defend the true Rule of Law and enforce the Ecclesiastical Writ of Right of Surrender or Arrest of Person; and

(viii) *Ius Ecclesiae Preceptum Capimus*, being the Right of Ecclesiastical Written Command, Rule, Principle and Edict to execute, enforce, carry out and uphold the Ecclesiastical Writ of Right of Surrender or Arrest of Person; and

(ix) *Ius Ecclesiae Agentis Capimus*, being the Ecclesiastical and Administrative Right of Delegation, Commission and Assignment of Rights, Powers and Authority to one or more Agents to execute, enforce, carry out and uphold the Ecclesiastical Writ of Right of Surrender or Arrest of Person.

## Article 334 – Recto Ecclesiae Custodiae (Surrender or Seizure of Property)

1253. ***Recto Ecclesiae Custodiae*** is the Ecclesiastical Writ of Surrender or Seizure of Property, as inherited from the Divine Right *Recto Divinum Custodiae*. It is the fifth of eleven Ecclesiastical Writs.

    *Recto Ecclesiae Custodiae (Seizure of Property)*

1254. The *Ecclesiastical Writ of Right of Surrender or Seizure of Property* (*Recto Ecclesiae Custodiae*) is reserved as the Remedy when any Ucadia Person or Ucadia Entity possesses compelling evidence of probable cause that a party did violate one or more valid Rights or continues to be in violation of one or more valid Rights.

    *Purpose of Recto Ecclesiae Custodiae (Seizure of Property)*

1255. The Rights of the *Ecclesiastical Writ of Right of Surrender or Seizure of Property*, also known as *Recto Ecclesiae Custodiae,* are those actionable Rights embedded within the nature and character of such an Ecclesiastical Writ; and then able to be dispensed through proper Warrants to duly authorised Agents. In accord with Ucadian Law and the present Maxims, the present type of Writ possesses the following Rights:

    *Rights of Recto Ecclesiae Custodiae (Seizure of Property)*

    (i) *Ius Ecclesiae Actionis Custodiae*, being the Right of Action and Entry of the Ecclesiastical Writ of Right of Surrender or

Seizure of Property; and

(ii) *Ius Ecclesiae Auctoritas Custodiae*, being the Right of Supreme Ecclesiastical and Administrative Authority of the Ecclesiastical Writ of Right of Surrender or Seizure of Property; and

(iii) *Ius Ecclesiae Notitiae Custodiae*, being the Ecclesiastical and Administrative Right of Notice, Gazette, Promulgation and Publication of the Ecclesiastical Writ of Right of Surrender or Seizure of Property; and

(iv) *Ius Ecclesiae Iurisdictionis Custodiae*, being the Ecclesiastical and Administrative Right of Original Jurisdiction of the Ecclesiastical Writ of Right of Surrender or Seizure of Property; and

(v) *Ius Ecclesiae Decretum Custodiae*, being the Right of Supreme Judicial Authority and Power of the Ecclesiastical Writ of Right of Surrender or Seizure of Property, whereby there are no higher grounds of appeal or dispute in Law; and

(vi) *Ius Ecclesiae Potentis Custodiae*, being the Right of Ecclesiastical, Judicial, Administrative and Military Power to use any and all necessary forms of coercive powers to enforce the Ecclesiastical Writ of Right of Surrender or Seizure of Property; and

(vii) *Ius Ecclesiae Armagestum Custodiae*, being the Ecclesiastical and Administrative Right to possess, have, carry and bear arms, weapons, shields and defensive tools; and to recruit, employ and maintain soldiers and military, paramilitary and police personnel; and to engage in any and all necessary forms of coercive power to defend the true Rule of Law and enforce the Ecclesiastical Writ of Right of Surrender or Seizure of Property; and

(viii) *Ius Ecclesiae Preceptum Custodiae*, being the Right of Ecclesiastical Written Command, Rule, Principle and Edict to execute, enforce, carry out and uphold the Ecclesiastical Writ of Right of Surrender or Seizure of Property; and

(ix) *Ius Ecclesiae Agentis Custodiae*, being the Ecclesiastical and Administrative Right of Delegation, Commission and Assignment of Rights, Powers and Authority to one or more Agents to execute, enforce, carry out and uphold the Ecclesiastical Writ of Right of Surrender or Seizure of

Property.

## Article 335 – Recto Ecclesiae Corrigimus (Correction of Records, Rulings, Laws or Instruments)

1256. ***Recto Ecclesiae Corrigimus*** is the Ecclesiastical Writ of Right of Correction of Records, Rulings, Laws or Instruments, as inherited from the Divine Right *Recto Divinum Corrigimus*. It is the sixth of eleven Ecclesiastical Writs.

Recto Ecclesiae Corrigimus (Correction)

1257. The *Ecclesiastical Writ of Right of Correction of Records, Rulings, Laws or Instruments* (*Recto Ecclesiae Corrigimus*) is reserved as the Remedy when any Ucadia Person or Ucadia Entity possesses compelling evidence of false records, false titles, letters patent or other documents granting certain rights and privileges to other parties that are not entitled in direct violation of one or more valid Rights.

Purpose of Recto Ecclesiae Corrigimus (Correction)

1258. The Rights of the *Ecclesiastical Writ of Right of Correction of Records, Rulings, Laws or Instruments*, also known as *Recto Ecclesiae Corrigimus,* are those actionable Rights embedded within the nature and character of such an Ecclesiastical Writ; and then able to be dispensed through proper Warrants to duly authorised Agents. In accord with Ucadian Law and the present Maxims, the present type of Writ possesses the following Rights:

Rights of Entry & Action of the Superior Writ of Records Correction

   (i) *Ius Ecclesiae Actionis Corrigimus*, being the Right of Action and Entry of the Ecclesiastical Writ of Right of Correction of Records, Rulings, Laws or Instruments; and

   (ii) *Ius Ecclesiae Auctoritas Corrigimus*, being the Right of Supreme Ecclesiastical and Administrative Authority of the Ecclesiastical Writ of Right of Correction of Records, Rulings, Laws or Instruments; and

   (iii) *Ius Ecclesiae Notitiae Corrigimus*, being the Ecclesiastical and Administrative Right of Notice, Gazette, Promulgation and Publication of the Ecclesiastical Writ of Right of Correction of Records, Rulings, Laws or Instruments; and

   (iv) *Ius Ecclesiae Iurisdictionis Corrigimus*, being the Ecclesiastical and Administrative Right of Original Jurisdiction of the Ecclesiastical Writ of Right of Correction of Records, Rulings, Laws or Instruments; and

   (v) *Ius Ecclesiae Decretum Corrigimus*, being the Right of Supreme Judicial Authority and Power of the Ecclesiastical

Writ of Right of Correction of Records, Rulings, Laws or Instruments, whereby there are no higher grounds of appeal or dispute in Law; and

(vi) *Ius Ecclesiae Potentis Corrigimus*, being the Right of Ecclesiastical, Judicial, Administrative and Military Power to use any and all necessary forms of coercive powers to enforce the Ecclesiastical Writ of Right of Correction of Records, Rulings, Laws or Instruments; and

(vii) *Ius Ecclesiae Armagestum Corrigimus*, being the Ecclesiastical and Administrative Right to possess, have, carry and bear arms, weapons, shields and defensive tools; and to recruit, employ and maintain soldiers and military, paramilitary and police personnel; and to engage in any and all necessary forms of coercive power to defend the true Rule of Law and enforce the Ecclesiastical Writ of Right of Correction of Records, Rulings, Laws or Instruments; and

(viii) *Ius Ecclesiae Preceptum Corrigimus*, being the Right of Ecclesiastical Written Command, Rule, Principle and Edict to execute, enforce, carry out and uphold the Ecclesiastical Writ of Right of Correction of Records, Rulings, Laws or Instruments; and

(ix) *Ius Ecclesiae Agentis Corrigimus*, being the Ecclesiastical and Administrative Right of Delegation, Commission and Assignment of Rights, Powers and Authority to one or more Agents to execute, enforce, carry out and uphold the Ecclesiastical Writ of Right of Correction of Records, Rulings, Laws or Instruments.

## Article 336 – Recto Ecclesiae Expurgatio (Expurgation of Records, Rulings, Laws or Instruments)

1259. ***Recto Ecclesiae Expurgatio*** is the Ecclesiastical Writ of Right of Expurgation of Records, Rulings, Laws or Instruments, as inherited from the Divine Right *Recto Divinum Expurgatio*. It is the seventh of eleven Ecclesiastical Writs.

   Recto Ecclesiae Expurgatio (Expurgation)

1260. The *Ecclesiastical Writ of Right of Expurgation of Records, Rulings, Laws or Instruments* (*Recto Ecclesiae Expurgatio*) is reserved as the Remedy when any Ucadia Person or Ucadia Entity possesses compelling evidence of deliberately false records, false titles, misleading and deceptive documents by another party in direct violation of one or more valid Rights.

   Purpose of Recto Ecclesiae Expurgatio (Expunge Record)

**1261.** The Rights of the *Ecclesiastical Writ of Right of Expurgation of Records, Rulings, Laws or Instruments,* also known as *Recto Ecclesiae Expurgatio,* are those actionable Rights embedded within the nature and character of such an Ecclesiastical Writ; and then able to be dispensed through proper Warrants to duly authorised Agents. In accord with Ucadian Law and the present Maxims, the present type of Writ possesses the following Rights:

Rights of Entry & Action of the Superior Writ of Records Expungement

(i) *Ius Ecclesiae Actionis Expurgatio*, being the Right of Action and Entry of the Ecclesiastical Writ of Right of Expurgation of Records, Rulings, Laws or Instruments; and

(ii) *Ius Ecclesiae Auctoritas Expurgatio*, being the Right of Supreme Ecclesiastical and Administrative Authority of the Ecclesiastical Writ of Right of Expurgation of Records, Rulings, Laws or Instruments; and

(iii) *Ius Ecclesiae Notitiae Expurgatio*, being the Ecclesiastical and Administrative Right of Notice, Gazette, Promulgation and Publication of the Ecclesiastical Writ of Right of Expurgation of Records, Rulings, Laws or Instruments; and

(iv) *Ius Ecclesiae Iurisdictionis Expurgatio*, being the Ecclesiastical and Administrative Right of Original Jurisdiction of the Ecclesiastical Writ of Right of Expurgation of Records, Rulings, Laws or Instruments; and

(v) *Ius Ecclesiae Decretum Expurgatio*, being the Right of Supreme Judicial Authority and Power of the Ecclesiastical Writ of Right of Expurgation of Records, Rulings, Laws or Instruments, whereby there are no higher grounds of appeal or dispute in Law; and

(vi) *Ius Ecclesiae Potentis Expurgatio*, being the Right of Ecclesiastical, Judicial, Administrative and Military Power to use any and all necessary forms of coercive powers to enforce the Ecclesiastical Writ of Right of Expurgation of Records, Rulings, Laws or Instruments; and

(vii) *Ius Ecclesiae Armagestum Expurgatio*, being the Ecclesiastical and Administrative Right to possess, have, carry and bear arms, weapons, shields and defensive tools; and to recruit, employ and maintain soldiers and military, paramilitary and police personnel; and to engage in any and all necessary forms of coercive power to defend the true Rule of Law and enforce the Ecclesiastical Writ of Right of Expurgation of Records, Rulings, Laws or Instruments; and

(viii) *Ius Ecclesiae Preceptum Expurgatio*, being the Right of Ecclesiastical Written Command, Rule, Principle and Edict to execute, enforce, carry out and uphold the Ecclesiastical Writ of Right of Expurgation of Records, Rulings, Laws or Instruments; and

(ix) *Ius Ecclesiae Agentis Expurgatio*, being the Ecclesiastical and Administrative Right of Delegation, Commission and Assignment of Rights, Powers and Authority to one or more Agents to execute, enforce, carry out and uphold the Ecclesiastical Writ of Right of Expurgation of Records, Rulings, Laws or Instruments.

## Article 337 – Recto Ecclesiae Abrogatio (Annulment of Records, Rulings, Laws or Instruments)

1262. ***Recto Ecclesiae Abrogatio*** is the Ecclesiastical Writ of Right of Annulment of Records, Rulings, Laws or Instruments, as inherited from the Divine Right *Recto Divinum Abrogatio*. It is the eighth of eleven Ecclesiastical Writs.
Recto Ecclesiae Abrogatio (Annulment)

1263. The *Ecclesiastical Writ of Right of Annulment of Records, Rulings, Laws or Instruments* (*Recto Ecclesiae Abrogatio*) is reserved as the Remedy when any Ucadia Person or Ucadia Entity possesses compelling evidence of deliberately false, or profane, or heretical, or fraudulent, or misleading or repugnant statutes, edicts, prescripts, rescripts, letters, charters, patents, bylaws, regulations, orders, judgements or other legal instruments in direct violation of one or more valid Rights.
Purpose of Recto Ecclesiae Abrogatio (Annulment)

1264. The Rights of the *Ecclesiastical Writ of Right of Annulment of Records, Rulings, Laws or Instruments*, also known as *Recto Ecclesiae Abrogatio,* are those actionable Rights embedded within the nature and character of such an Ecclesiastical Writ; and then able to be dispensed through proper Warrants to duly authorised Agents. In accord with Ucadian Law and the present Maxims, the present type of Writ possesses the following Rights:
Rights of Entry & Action of the Ecclesiastical Writ of Annulment

(i) *Ius Ecclesiae Actionis Abrogatio*, being the Right of Action and Entry of the Ecclesiastical Writ of Right of Annulment of Records, Rulings, Laws or Instruments; and

(ii) *Ius Ecclesiae Auctoritas Abrogatio*, being the Right of Supreme Ecclesiastical and Administrative Authority of the Ecclesiastical Writ of Right of Annulment of Records, Rulings, Laws or Instruments; and

(iii) *Ius Ecclesiae Notitiae Abrogatio*, being the Ecclesiastical and Administrative Right of Notice, Gazette, Promulgation and Publication of the Ecclesiastical Writ of Right of Annulment of Records, Rulings, Laws or Instruments; and

(iv) *Ius Ecclesiae Iurisdictionis Abrogatio*, being the Ecclesiastical and Administrative Right of Original Jurisdiction of the Ecclesiastical Writ of Right of Annulment of Records, Rulings, Laws or Instruments; and

(v) *Ius Ecclesiae Decretum Abrogatio*, being the Right of Supreme Judicial Authority and Power of the Ecclesiastical Writ of Right of Annulment of Records, Rulings, Laws or Instruments, whereby there are no higher grounds of appeal or dispute in Law; and

(vi) *Ius Ecclesiae Potentis Abrogatio*, being the Right of Ecclesiastical, Judicial, Administrative and Military Power to use any and all necessary forms of coercive powers to enforce the Ecclesiastical Writ of Right of Annulment of Records, Rulings, Laws or Instruments; and

(vii) *Ius Ecclesiae Armagestum Abrogatio*, being the Ecclesiastical and Administrative Right to possess, have, carry and bear arms, weapons, shields and defensive tools; and to recruit, employ and maintain soldiers and military, paramilitary and police personnel; and to engage in any and all necessary forms of coercive power to defend the true Rule of Law and enforce the Ecclesiastical Writ of Right of Annulment of Records, Rulings, Laws or Instruments; and

(viii) *Ius Ecclesiae Preceptum Abrogatio*, being the Right of Ecclesiastical Written Command, Rule, Principle and Edict to execute, enforce, carry out and uphold the Ecclesiastical Writ of Right of Annulment of Records, Rulings, Laws or Instruments; and

(ix) *Ius Ecclesiae Agentis Abrogatio*, being the Ecclesiastical and Administrative Right of Delegation, Commission and Assignment of Rights, Powers and Authority to one or more Agents to execute, enforce, carry out and uphold the Ecclesiastical Writ of Right of Annulment of Records, Rulings, Laws or Instruments.

## Article 338 – Recto Ecclesiae Inhibitio (Prohibition or Restraint)

**1265.** ***Recto Ecclesiae Inhibitio*** is the Ecclesiastical Writ of Right of Prohibition or Restraint, as inherited from the Divine Right *Recto Divinum Inhibitio*. It is the ninth of eleven Ecclesiastical Writs.

<small>Recto Ecclesiae Inhibitio (Prohibition or Restraint)</small>

**1266.** The *Ecclesiastical Writ of Right of Prohibition or Restraint (Recto Ecclesiae Inhibitio)* is reserved as the Remedy when any Ucadia Person or Ucadia Entity possesses compelling evidence of probable cause that one or more parties did persistently and habitually violate one or more valid Rights and continues to be in blatant violation of one or more valid Rights.

<small>Purpose of Recto Ecclesiae Inhibitio (Prohibition or Restraint)</small>

**1267.** The Rights of the *Ecclesiastical Writ of Right of Prohibition or Restraint*, also known as *Recto Ecclesiae Inhibitio,* are those actionable Rights embedded within the nature and character of such an Ecclesiastical Writ; and then able to be dispensed through proper Warrants to duly authorised Agents. In accord with Ucadian Law and the present Maxims, the present type of Writ possesses the following Rights:

<small>Rights of Entry & Action of the Superior Writ of Prohibition</small>

    (i)    *Ius Ecclesiae Actionis Inhibitio*, being the Right of Action and Entry of the Ecclesiastical Writ of Right of Prohibition or Restraint; and

    (ii)    *Ius Ecclesiae Auctoritas Inhibitio*, being the Right of Supreme Ecclesiastical and Administrative Authority of the Ecclesiastical Writ of Right of Prohibition or Restraint; and

    (iii)    *Ius Ecclesiae Notitiae Inhibitio*, being the Ecclesiastical and Administrative Right of Notice, Gazette, Promulgation and Publication of the Ecclesiastical Writ of Right of Prohibition or Restraint; and

    (iv)    *Ius Ecclesiae Iurisdictionis Inhibitio*, being the Ecclesiastical and Administrative Right of Original Jurisdiction of the Ecclesiastical Writ of Right of Prohibition or Restraint; and

    (v)    *Ius Ecclesiae Decretum Inhibitio*, being the Right of Supreme Judicial Authority and Power of the Ecclesiastical Writ of Right of Prohibition or Restraint, whereby there are no higher grounds of appeal or dispute in Law; and

    (vi)    *Ius Ecclesiae Potentis Inhibitio*, being the Right of Ecclesiastical, Judicial, Administrative and Military Power to use any and all necessary forms of coercive powers to enforce the Ecclesiastical Writ of Right of Prohibition or Restraint; and

(vii) *Ius Ecclesiae Armagestum Inhibitio*, being the Ecclesiastical and Administrative Right to possess, have, carry and bear arms, weapons, shields and defensive tools; and to recruit, employ and maintain soldiers and military, paramilitary and police personnel; and to engage in any and all necessary forms of coercive power to defend the true Rule of Law and enforce the Ecclesiastical Writ of Right of Prohibition or Restraint; and

(viii) *Ius Ecclesiae Preceptum Inhibitio*, being the Right of Ecclesiastical Written Command, Rule, Principle and Edict to execute, enforce, carry out and uphold the Ecclesiastical Writ of Right of Prohibition or Restraint; and

(ix) *Ius Ecclesiae Agentis Inhibitio*, being the Ecclesiastical and Administrative Right of Delegation, Commission and Assignment of Rights, Powers and Authority to one or more Agents to execute, enforce, carry out and uphold the Ecclesiastical Writ of Right of Prohibition or Restraint.

## Article 339 – Recto Ecclesiae Restitutio (Restitution)

1268. ***Recto Ecclesiae Restitutio*** is the Ecclesiastical Writ of Right of Restitution, as inherited from the Divine Right *Recto Divinum Restitutio*. It is the tenth of eleven Ecclesiastical Writs.

*Recto Ecclesiae Restitutio (Restitution)*

1269. The *Ecclesiastical Writ of Right of Restitution* (*Recto Ecclesiae Restitutio*) is reserved as the Remedy when any Ucadia Person or Ucadia Entity possesses compelling evidence of probable cause that one or more parties did persistently and habitually violate one or more valid Rights, causing harm, injury and loss.

*Purpose of Recto Ecclesiae Restitutio (Restitution)*

1270. The Rights of the *Ecclesiastical Writ of Right of Restitution*, also known as *Recto Ecclesiae Restitutio,* are those actionable Rights embedded within the nature and character of such an Ecclesiastical Writ; and then able to be dispensed through proper Warrants to duly authorised Agents. In accord with Ucadian Law and the present Maxims, the present type of Writ possesses the following Rights:

*Rights of Entry & Action of the Superior Writ of Restitution*

(i) *Ius Ecclesiae Actionis Restitutio*, being the Right of Action and Entry of the Ecclesiastical Writ of Right of Restitution; and

(ii) *Ius Ecclesiae Auctoritas Restitutio*, being the Right of Supreme Ecclesiastical and Administrative Authority of the Ecclesiastical Writ of Right of Restitution; and

(iii) *Ius Ecclesiae Notitiae Restitutio*, being the Ecclesiastical and Administrative Right of Notice, Gazette, Promulgation and Publication of the Ecclesiastical Writ of Right of Restitution; and

(iv) *Ius Ecclesiae Iurisdictionis Restitutio*, being the Ecclesiastical and Administrative Right of Original Jurisdiction of the Ecclesiastical Writ of Right of Restitution; and

(v) *Ius Ecclesiae Decretum Restitutio*, being the Right of Supreme Judicial Authority and Power of the Ecclesiastical Writ of Right of Restitution, whereby there are no higher grounds of appeal or dispute in Law; and

(vi) *Ius Ecclesiae Potentis Restitutio*, being the Right of Ecclesiastical, Judicial, Administrative and Military Power to use any and all necessary forms of coercive powers to enforce the Ecclesiastical Writ of Right of Restitution; and

(vii) *Ius Ecclesiae Armagestum Restitutio*, being the Ecclesiastical and Administrative Right to possess, have, carry and bear arms, weapons, shields and defensive tools; and to recruit, employ and maintain soldiers and military, paramilitary and police personnel; and to engage in any and all necessary forms of coercive power to defend the true Rule of Law and enforce the Ecclesiastical Writ of Right of Restitution; and

(viii) *Ius Ecclesiae Preceptum Restitutio*, being the Right of Ecclesiastical Written Command, Rule, Principle and Edict to execute, enforce, carry out and uphold the Ecclesiastical Writ of Right of Restitution; and

(ix) *Ius Ecclesiae Agentis Restitutio*, being the Ecclesiastical and Administrative Right of Delegation, Commission and Assignment of Rights, Powers and Authority to one or more Agents to execute, enforce, carry out and uphold the Ecclesiastical Writ of Right of Restitution.

## Article 340 – Recto Ecclesiae Restoratio (Restoration)

1271. **Recto Ecclesiae Restoratio** is the Ecclesiastical Writ of Right of Restoration, as inherited from the Divine Right *Recto Divinum Restoratio*. It is the eleventh of eleven Ecclesiastical Writs.

> Recto Ecclesiae Restoratio (Restoration)

1272. The *Ecclesiastical Writ of Right of Restoration* (*Recto Ecclesiae Restoratio*) is reserved as the Remedy when any Ucadia Person or

> Purpose of Recto Ecclesiae Restoratio

Ucadia Entity possesses compelling evidence of probable cause that one or more parties did persistently and habitually violate one or more valid Rights, causing harm, injury and loss.

(Restoration)

1273. The Rights of the *Ecclesiastical Writ of Right of Restoration*, also known as *Recto Ecclesiae Restoratio,* are those actionable Rights embedded within the nature and character of such an Ecclesiastical Writ; and then able to be dispensed through proper Warrants to duly authorised Agents. In accord with Ucadian Law and the present Maxims, the present type of Writ possesses the following Rights:

Rights of Entry & Action of the Superior Writ of Restoration

(i) *Ius Ecclesiae Actionis Restoratio*, being the Right of Action and Entry of the Ecclesiastical Writ of Right of Restoration; and

(ii) *Ius Ecclesiae Auctoritas Restoratio*, being the Right of Supreme Ecclesiastical and Administrative Authority of the Ecclesiastical Writ of Right of Restoration; and

(iii) *Ius Ecclesiae Notitiae Restoratio*, being the Ecclesiastical and Administrative Right of Notice, Gazette, Promulgation and Publication of the Ecclesiastical Writ of Right of Restoration; and

(iv) *Ius Ecclesiae Iurisdictionis Restoratio*, being the Ecclesiastical and Administrative Right of Original Jurisdiction of the Ecclesiastical Writ of Right of Restoration; and

(v) *Ius Ecclesiae Decretum Restoratio*, being the Right of Supreme Judicial Authority and Power of the Ecclesiastical Writ of Right of Restoration, whereby there are no higher grounds of appeal or dispute in Law; and

(vi) *Ius Ecclesiae Potentis Restoratio*, being the Right of Ecclesiastical, Judicial, Administrative and Military Power to use any and all necessary forms of coercive powers to enforce the Ecclesiastical Writ of Right of Restoration; and

(vii) *Ius Ecclesiae Armagestum Restoratio*, being the Ecclesiastical and Administrative Right to possess, have, carry and bear arms, weapons, shields and defensive tools; and to recruit, employ and maintain soldiers and military, paramilitary and police personnel; and to engage in any and all necessary forms of coercive power to defend the true Rule of Law and enforce the Ecclesiastical Writ of Right of Restoration; and

(viii) *Ius Ecclesiae Preceptum Restoratio*, being the Right of Ecclesiastical Written Command, Rule, Principle and Edict to execute, enforce, carry out and uphold the Ecclesiastical Writ of Right of Restoration; and

(ix) *Ius Ecclesiae Agentis Restoratio*, being the Ecclesiastical and Administrative Right of Delegation, Commission and Assignment of Rights, Powers and Authority to one or more Agents to execute, enforce, carry out and uphold the Ecclesiastical Writ of Right of Restoration.

## 8.6 – Ecclesiastical Bills of Exception & Agreement

### Article 341 – Ecclesiastical Bills of Exception & Agreement

1274. ***Ecclesiastical Bills of Exception*** (*Rogatio Ecclesiae Iurium*) shall be Ecclesiastical Rights associated with the one, true and only forms of Bills of Exception, Citation and Agreement. — Ecclesiastical Bills of Exception

1275. A ***Bill*** is a form of Demand and Order in writing, assured by one or more Rights granted, for some performance equivalent in specie of Real Money. A Bill is normally associated with at least one Certified Statement or Memorandum of Account and one Affidavit. — Bill

1276. In relation to the Persons and Parties associated with a Bill: — Relations of Persons to a Bill

(i) The Person who makes or issues a valid Bill is called the *Maker* (also *Issuer*, or *Payor*, or *Drawer*); and

(ii) The Person to whom the Bill is addressed and paid (if an actual name is listed on the Note) is called the *Payee*; and

(iii) The Person who the Payee may nominate as the beneficiary and holder of the Bill is called the *Endorsee* (also *Indorsee* or *Order*); and

(iv) The Person who is directed to make the payment on behalf of the Maker to the Payee is called the *Drawee* and once they accept the obligation becomes the *Acceptor*; and

(v) The Person who holds an original Bill (whether the note is addressed or not addressed) is called the *Holder*; and

(vi) The Person who agrees to underwrite and guarantee the Bill is called the *Guarantor* (also *Surety*).

1277. An *Ecclesiastical Bill of Exception* is the highest possible valid form of Objection, Denial and Protest within International Law of Nations and Entities. Evidence of a valid record within the Ucadia Great Register and Public Record and Ucadia Gazette is *prima facie* proof — Nature of Ecclesiastical Bills of Exception of a duly promulgated *Ecclesiastical Bill of Exception*:-

(i) An *Ecclesiastical Bill of Exception* is usually issued against a party following their failure to act according to the norms of law; and

(ii) An *Ecclesiastical Bill of Exception* requires the official seal of the Ucadia Entity or Office of Issue, as well as the signature of the Maker; and

(iii) All forms of defensive powers and protection including, but not limited to prevention, protection, suspension, stop, stay, injunction, restitution, restoration, seizure, search, sanction, lien, arrest, custody, penalty or satisfaction, is enacted via one or more valid *Ecclesiastical Bills of Exception*.

1278. An *Ecclesiastical Bill of Agreement* is the highest possible valid forms of Demand and Order assured by one or more Rights granted, for some performance equivalent in specie of Real Money within International Law of Nations and Entities. Evidence of a valid record within the Ucadia Great Register and Public Record and Ucadia Gazette is *prima facie* proof of a duly promulgated *Ecclesiastical Bill of Agreement*:- Nature of Ecclesiastical Bills of Agreement

(i) An *Ecclesiastical Bill of Agreement* requires the official seal of the Ucadia Entity or Office of Issue, as well as the signature of the Maker; and

(ii) Similar to Bills of Exception, the mandatory information to be provided is dependent upon the type of Bill.

1279. All *Ecclesiastical Bills of Exception & Agreement* are delegated by proper *Mandate* to the Governments of valid and legitimate Ecclesiastical Ucadia Bodies and Entities (including but not limited to Ucadia Universities, Provinces, Campuses, Foundations and Agencies); and to those existing and internationally recognised Non-Ucadian Ecclesiastical Bodies and Entities by in force treaties and agreements in accord with the most sacred Covenant *Pactum De Singularis Caelum*. Delegation of Ecclesiastical Bills of Exception & Agreement

1280. All *Ecclesiastical Bills of Exception* are assumed to be automatically invoked through the proper operation and function of the Governing Instruments, Codes and Bylaws of valid and legitimate Ecclesiastical Ucadia Bodies and Entities (including but not limited to Ucadia Universities, Provinces, Campuses, Foundations and Agencies); and through the operation and function of in force treaties and agreements with existing and internationally recognised Non-Ucadian Ecclesiastical Bodies and Entities. Invocation of Ecclesiastical Bills of Exception & Agreement

1281. The following valid eleven (11) Ecclesiastical Bills of Exception & Agreement (*Rogatio Ecclesiae Iurium*) shall be recognised in accord with the most sacred Covenant *Pactum De Singularis Caelum*:-

    (i) "**Rogatio Ecclesiae Recto**" is the Ecclesiastical (Original) Bill of Right, as inherited from the Divine Right *Rogatio Divinum Recto*; and

    (ii) "**Rogatio Ecclesiae Apocalypsis**" is the Ecclesiastical Bill of Right of Command & Authorisation of Revelation, as inherited from the Divine Right *Rogatio Divinum Apocalypsis*; and

    (iii) "**Rogatio Ecclesiae Capimus**" is the Ecclesiastical Bill of Right against Failure to Surrender or Arrest Person, as inherited from the Divine Right *Rogatio Divinum Capimus*; and

    (iv) "**Rogatio Ecclesiae Custodiae**" is the Ecclesiastical Bill of Right against Failure to Surrender or Seize Property, as inherited from the Divine Right *Rogatio Divinum Custodiae*; and

    (v) "**Rogatio Ecclesiae Corrigimus**" is the Ecclesiastical Bill of Right against Failure to Correct Records, Rulings, Laws or Instruments, as inherited from the Divine Right *Rogatio Divinum Corrigimus*; and

    (vi) "**Rogatio Ecclesiae Inhibitio**" is the Ecclesiastical Bill of Right against Failure to Prohibit or Impose Limits as Instructed, as inherited from the Divine Right *Rogatio Divinum Inhibitio*; and

    (vii) "**Rogatio Ecclesiae Restitutio**" is the Ecclesiastical Bill of Right of Restitution or Compensation, as inherited from the Divine Right *Rogatio Divinum Restituio*; and

    (viii) "**Rogatio Ecclesiae Credito**" is the Ecclesiastical Bill of Right of Credit, as inherited from the Divine Right *Rogatio Divinum Credito*; and

    (ix) "**Rogatio Ecclesiae Permutatio**" is the Ecclesiastical Bill of Right of Exchange, as inherited from the Divine Right *Rogatio Divinum Permutatio*; and

    (x) "**Rogatio Ecclesiae Venditio**" is the Ecclesiastical Bill of Right of Sale, as inherited from the Divine Right *Rogatio Divinum Venditio*; and

*List of Ecclesiastical Bills of Exception (Rogatio Ecclesiae Iurium)*

(xi) **"Rogatio Ecclesiae Traditio"** is the Ecclesiastical Bill of Right of Lading, as inherited from the Divine Right *Rogatio Divinum Traditio*.

1282. Subject to the essential conditions of a valid Instrument and Form as prescribed herein, the following essential elements must be present on the face of a valid Bill:- Elements of a valid Bill

    (i) *Bill Number* being a unique Bill Number within the relevant Register of Bills; and

    (ii) *Ucadia Sacred Space-Day-Time Number Issued Under* being the numeric number for demonstrating the supreme jurisdiction, space and time whereby the Instrument is issued; and

    (iii) *Ucadia Location of Issue* being the Location Number for the Ucadia University from where the Instrument is issued; and

    (iv) *Ucadia Date and Reference Date* being the formal Ucadia Date and reference (Roman) date; and

    (v) *Title* being the word "Bill" as a prominent word in the heading, or if a special type of Bill the full name of such type; and

    (vi) *Obligation Account Number* being a valid eighteen digit Ucadia number in the form XXXXXX-XXXXXX-XXXXXX signifying the existence of a record of account, or file, or case, or statement in respect of the obligation having some monetary value; and

    (vii) *Obligation Description* being a brief description of the obligation or monetary obligation of Ucadia Money or Non-Ucadian Lawful Public Money in words, even if the amount of money is also displayed in numbers; and

    (viii) *Demand or Order* being the specific demand or order of the Bill regarding the Obligation; and

    (ix) *Bordered Information* being that any information "extracted" from the Record is presented within a bordered box to indicate a "window" to the original and valid Record; and

    (x) *One Witness* being a witnessed made or affirmed signed certification that the Bill and the information contained within it is valid; and

    (xi) *Official Seal* of the Ucadia Official or Ucadia Entity.

**1283.** All valid Bills must either state the amount of the Monetary Obligation on the face of the Instrument as proper and due disclosure and accounting of such obligation, or within a Memorandum of Account attached to the annexed documents to the Bill, stating clearly the total Monetary Obligations of the Drawee in accepting the obligations due.
Accounting of Monetary Obligation

**1284.** The failure to provide a clear and proper accounting of the Monetary Obligation associated with a Bill, or the deliberate and wilful obscuring, hiding, fraud, perfidy or falsity in failing to provide such open and transparent accounting shall therefore invalidate any and all bills and any and all charges against such Bills. No person may be properly charged for an obligation without first knowing and being provided in writing an accounting of the monetary obligation.
Secret or Hidden Monetary Obligation invalidating Bill

**1285.** The Acceptance of a valid Bill is the act whereby the Person on whom a Bill is drawn (called the Drawee) assents to the Demand and Order of the Drawer to pay it, or make themselves liable for its action or payment when due. The object of Acceptance is to bind the Drawee and make him an actual and bound party to the Instrument. Therefore, until there is an Acceptance (such as evidence of Dishonour), the Drawee is under no obligation whatever upon the Bill itself.
Acceptance of Valid Bill

**1286.** A Bill is considered Accepted when it is acknowledged and signed in good Trust (bona fide), or through procedure to establish the dishonour, default and delinquency of the Drawee:
Form of Acceptance

(i) A Bill is accepted when the Drawee signs and endorses the Bill at ninety degrees prior to the expiry or maturity of the Bill; or

(ii) A Bill is accepted when the Drawer established the legitimacy of the Demand and Order, the truth of the debt and obligation, the dishonour of the Drawee in settling the debt and the default and delinquency of the Drawee in failing to provide any reasonable lawful excuse.

## Article 342 – Rogatio Ecclesiae Recto (Bill of Rights)

**1287.** *Rogatio Ecclesiae Recto* is the Ecclesiastical Bill of Claim of Relief, as inherited from the Divine Right *Rogatio Divinum Recto*. It is the first of eleven Ecclesiastical Bills.
Rogatio Ecclesiae Recto (Bill of Rights)

**1288.** A Bill of Complaint, also known as Original Bill, is an Instrument of Demand and Order, assured by Rights granted; as a form of petition issued by a valid Court of Chancery, containing a statement of the
Bill of Complaint

plaintiff's action or suit and concluding with a prayer asking for the relief which he filed the Bill to obtain.

1289. A Bill of Complaint shall only be issued to designated officials of a competent forum of Ucadian Law upon the successful completion, review and authorised acceptance of a formal Application, either as a separate Application or as part of an Application involving other Instruments that (upon approval) includes the issuance of a valid Bill of Complaint. No Bill of Complaint or associated instruments may be issued by an Ecclesiastical Ucadia Entity to any Person, or Body or Society or Company or Association unless:- *Eligibility and Qualification*

(i) The Member as the primary Complainant to whom the proposed Bill of Complaint relates is not presently suspended or banned as a vexatious litigant from access to legal services of the Ecclesiastical Ucadia Entity; and

(ii) The Member as the primary Complainant to whom the proposed Bill of Complaint relates is not presently recorded as being incompetent; and

(iii) The Member submitting the Application is eligible, qualified and Authorised to make such an Application; and

(iv) The mandatory information required to be submitted within the Application has been provided within the Application; and

(v) The Member has completed the Oath and Declaration that they agree to be bound by the terms and conditions of the Application and the proper use of any approved Bill of Complaint; and

(vi) Any nominal administration fees associated with the processing and issuance of such documents, whether or not the Application is successful, has been paid; and

(vii) There exists no other reason or impediment that would otherwise prevent the issuance of such documents, subject to the review and approval of the Application.

1290. The Terms and Conditions of a valid Bill of Complaint is annexed as a separate document with three other Instruments being (a) *Declaration of Facts*; and (b) *Affidavit of Fact*; and (c) *Memorandum of Account* (*of Charges*). The Terms and Conditions shall adhere to the following standards, including (but not limited *Terms & Conditions of Bill of Complaint* to):-

(i) The Memorandum of Account, Declaration of Facts and Affidavit of Fact have been duly received and recorded within a competent forum of Law under Ucadian Law and these present Maxims; and

(ii) The Bill of Complaint has been issued by the same competent forum of Law; and

(iii) The description of alleged facts are clearly described and defined within the Declaration of Facts; and

(iv) The Affidavit of Fact clearly lists testimony made under Oath and Vow as to one or more alleged grievances that match the Declaration of Facts; and

(v) The Memorandum of Account clearly identifies the penalty, costs and compensation related to such alleged offences as related to the Bill of Complaint; and

(vi) No penalty, fine or payment associated with a Bill of Complaint may be expressed or function in simple interest or compound interest; and

(vii) No clause within the Terms and Conditions shall contravene these present Maxims.

## Article 343 – Rogatio Ecclesiae Apocalypsis (Revelation)

1291. ***Rogatio Ecclesiae Apocalypsis*** is the Ecclesiastical Bill of Rights of Revelation, as inherited from the Divine Right *Rogatio Divinum Apocalypsis*. It is the second of eleven Ecclesiastical Bills. — Rogatio Ecclesiae Apocalypsis (Revelation)

1292. A Bill of Command and Authorisation, is an Instrument of Demand and Order, assured by Rights granted; as a form of petition for completion issued by a valid Court of Chancery, being a proposed law, or action. — Bill of Command & Authorisation

## Article 344 – Rogatio Ecclesiae Capimus (Surrender or Arrest Person)

1293. ***Rogatio Ecclesiae Capimus*** is the Ecclesiastical Bill of Rights against Failure to Surrender or Arrest Person, as inherited from the Divine Right *Rogatio Divinum Capimus*. It is the third of eleven Ecclesiastical Bills. — Rogatio Ecclesiae Capimus (Surrender or Arrest Person)

1294. An Ecclesiastical Bill of Rights of Failure to Surrender or Arrest Person, is a Bill of Exception and Instrument of Demand and Order, with the debt underwritten by the failure to enforce a previous Writ concerning the Surrender or Arrest of a Person.

*Rogatio Ecclesiae Capimus (Arrest Person) as Bill of Exception*

1295. Subject to the essential conditions of a valid Instrument, Form and Bill of the Ecclesiastical Ucadia Entity as prescribed herein, the following essential elements must also be present on the face of a valid Ecclesiastical Bill of Rights of Failure to Surrender or Arrest Person:-

*Specific Elements of a valid Rogatio Ecclesiae Capimus (Arrest Person)*

(i) *Writ Number* being a valid eighteen digit Ucadia number in the form XXXXXX-XXXXXX-XXXXXX signifying the existence of a Court of Original Record Writ Number within the Ucadia Courts and competent forums, as well as records of account, or in respect of the outstanding amount or property value; and

(ii) *Description of Person* being a clear description of the Person either to be arrested or brought to the Forum; and

(iii) *Value of Offences* being the total estimated value of any Offences alleged against the Person to be repossessed, seized and taken into custody; and

(iv) *Location of Person* being a clear description of the last known location of the person to be reclaimed, or seized and taken into custody; and

(v) *Possessors of Person* being the name of the Ucadia or Non Ucadia Persons or Entity known to have been in possession of the Person.

## Article 345 – Rogatio Ecclesiae Custodiae (Surrender or Seize Property)

1296. **Rogatio Ecclesiae Custodiae** is the Ecclesiastical Bill of Right against Failure to Surrender or Seize Property, as inherited from the Divine Right *Rogatio Divinum Custodiae*. It is the fourth of eleven Ecclesiastical Bills.

*Rogatio Ecclesiae Custodiae (Surrender or Seize Property)*

1297. An Ecclesiastical Bill of Failure to Surrender or Seize Property, is a Bill of Exception and Instrument of Demand and Order, assured by Rights granted to demand the return of certain property and the enforcement of a previous Writ concerning the Surrender or Seizure of Property.

*Rogatio Ecclesiae Custodiae (Seize Property) as Bill of Exception*

1298. Subject to the essential conditions of a valid Instrument, Form and

*Specific*

Bill of the Ecclesiastical Ucadia Entity as prescribed herein, the following essential elements must also be present on the face of a valid Ecclesiastical Bill of Failure to Surrender or Seize Property:-

    (i)    *Writ Number* being a valid eighteen digit Ucadia number in the form XXXXXX-XXXXXX-XXXXXX signifying the existence of a Court of Original Record Writ Number within the Ucadia Courts and competent forums, as well as records of account, or in respect of the outstanding amount or property value; and

    (ii)    *Description of Property* being a clear description of the Property that has been unlawfully seized or injured; and

    (iii)    *Value of Property* being the total estimated value of the Property to be repossessed, seized and taken into custody; and

    (iv)    *Location of Property* being a clear description of the last known location of the Property to be reclaimed, or seized and taken into custody; and

    (v)    *Possessors of Property* being the name of the Ucadia or Non Ucadia Persons or Entity known to have been in possession of the Property.

*Sidenote: Elements of a valid Rogatio Ecclesiae Custodiae (Seize Property)*

## Article 346 – Rogatio Ecclesiae Corrigimus (Correct Records, Rulings, Laws)

1299. ***Rogatio Ecclesiae Corrigimus*** is the Ecclesiastical Bill of Right against Failure to Correct Records, Rulings, Laws or Instruments, as inherited from the Divine Right *Rogatio Divinum Corrigimus*. It is the fifth of eleven Ecclesiastical Bills.

*Sidenote: Rogatio Ecclesiae Corrigimus (Correct Records, Rulings, Laws)*

1300. An Ecclesiastical Bill of Failure to Correct Records, Rulings, Laws or Instruments, is a Bill of Exception and Instrument of Demand and Order, with the debt underwritten by the failure to enforce a previous Writ concerning the Correction of Records, Rulings, Laws or Instruments.

*Sidenote: Rogatio Ecclesiae Corrigimus (Correction) as Bill of Exception*

1301. Subject to the essential conditions of a valid Instrument, Form and Bill of the Ecclesiastical Ucadia Entity as prescribed herein, the following essential elements must also be present on the face of a valid Ecclesiastical Bill of Failure to Correct Records, Rulings, Laws or Instruments:-

    (i)    *Writ Number* being a valid eighteen digit Ucadia number in the form XXXXXX-XXXXXX-XXXXXX signifying the

*Sidenote: Specific Elements of a valid Rogatio Ecclesiae Corrigimus (Correction)*

existence of a Court of Original Record Writ Number within the Ucadia Courts and competent forums, as well as records of account, or in respect of the outstanding amount or property value; and

(ii) *Description of Records, Rulings, Laws or Instruments* being a clear description of the Records, Rulings, Laws or Instruments to be changed, repossessed, seized and taken into custody; and

(iii) *Value of Records, Rulings, Laws or Instruments* being the total value of the Records, Rulings, Laws or Instruments to be changed, repossessed, seized and taken into custody; and

(iv) *Location of Records, Rulings, Laws or Instruments* being a clear description of the last known location of the Records, Rulings, Laws or Instruments to be changed, repossessed, seized and taken into custody; and

(v) *Possessors of Records, Rulings, Laws or Instruments* being the name of the Members known to have been in possession of the Records, Rulings, Laws or Instruments.

## Article 347 – Rogatio Ecclesiae Inhibitio (Prohibit or Impose Limits)

1302. ***Rogatio Ecclesiae Inhibitio*** is the Ecclesiastical Bill of Right against Failure to Prohibit or Impose Limits as Instructed, as inherited from the Divine Right *Rogatio Divinum Inhibitio*. It is the sixth of eleven Ecclesiastical Bills.

*Rogatio Ecclesiae Inhibitio (Prohibit or Impose Limits)*

1303. An Ecclesiastical Bill of Failure to Prohibit or Impose Limits as Instructed, is a Bill of Exception and Instrument of Demand and Order, assured by Rights granted; to demand the enforcement of a previous Writ concerning the Prohibition or Restraint of certain actions.

*Rogatio Ecclesiae Inhibitio (Prohibit & Restrain) as Bill of Exception*

1304. Subject to the essential conditions of a valid Instrument, Form and Bill of the Ecclesiastical Ucadia Entity as prescribed herein, the following essential elements must also be present on the face of a valid Ecclesiastical Bill of Failure to Prohibit or Restrain:-

*Specific Elements of a valid Rogatio Ecclesiae Inhibitio (Prohibit & Restrain)*

(i) *Writ Number* being a valid eighteen digit Ucadia number in the form XXXXXX-XXXXXX-XXXXXX signifying the existence of a Court of Original Record Writ Number within the Ucadia Courts and competent forums, as well as records of account, or in respect of the outstanding amount or property value; and

(ii) *Description of Actions* being a clear description of the Item, Action or Right to be prohibited or restrained; and

(iii) *Location of Item* being a clear description of the location of the Item, Action or Right to be Prohibited or Restrained.

## Article 348 – Rogatio Ecclesiae Restitutio (Restitution or Compensation)

1305. **Rogatio Ecclesiae Restitutio** is the Ecclesiastical Bill of Right of Restitution or Compensation, as inherited from the Divine Right *Rogatio Divinum Restitutio*. It is the seventh of eleven Ecclesiastical Bills.

<sub-margin>Rogatio Ecclesiae Restitutio (Restitution or Compensation)</sub-margin>

1306. A *Bill of Restitution or Compensation* is a Demand and Order for Payment, assured by Rights granted; of the total amount of the costs incurred by an Attorney-In-Fact or Advocate-In-Law in relation to representing the interests of a party of a suit or action. A Bill of Costs must be accompanied by a Statement of Account of the items that form the total amount of the costs of a suit or action and an Affidavit from the Attorney-In-Fact or Advocate-In-Law.

<sub-margin>Rogatio Ecclesiae Restitutio (Restitution) as Bill of Costs</sub-margin>

1307. The Terms and Conditions of a valid Ecclesiastical Bill of Restitution or Compensation is annexed as a separate document with three other Instruments being (a) *Declaration of Costs*; and (b) *Affidavit of Fact*; and (c) *Memorandum of Account*. The Terms and Conditions shall adhere to the following standards, including (but not limited to):-

<sub-margin>Terms & Conditions of Bill of Costs</sub-margin>

(i) The Memorandum of Account, Declaration of Costs and Affidavit of Fact have been duly received and recorded within a competent forum of Law under Ucadian Law and these present Maxims; and

(ii) The Bill of Costs has been issued by the same competent forum of Law directing payment; and

(iii) The description of alleged facts in relation to costs are clearly described and defined within the Declaration of Costs; and

(iv) The Affidavit of Fact clearly lists testimony made under Oath and Vow as to the legitimacy of certain costs requested to be reimbursed or compensation approved that match the Declaration of Costs; and

(v) The Memorandum of Account clearly identifies the costs and compensation related to such alleged occurrences as related to the Bill of Costs; and

(vi) No penalty, fine or payment associated with a Bill of Costs may be expressed or function in simple interest or compound interest; and

(vii) No clause within the Terms and Conditions shall contravene these present Maxims.

## Article 349 – Rogatio Ecclesiae Credito (Credit)

1308. ***Rogatio Ecclesiae Credito*** is the Ecclesiastical Bill Right of Credit, as inherited from the Divine Right *Rogatio Divinum Credito*. It is the eighth of eleven Ecclesiastical Bills.

Rogatio Ecclesiae Credito (Credit)

1309. A Money Bill, also known at times as a "Bill of Credit", is an Instrument of Demand and Order, assured by Authorised Lien in Trust against Debt owed to the Ecclesiastical Ucadia Entity as Public Debt; issued by the authority of the Ecclesiastical Ucadia Entity; and designed to circulate as Money. Public Money Debt Bills are issued exclusively on the principle that all legitimate debts must be paid and the formal condemnation as liens against those foreign bodies, foreign corporations or foreign persons unwilling or unable to pay such valid debts; to then be circulated in ordinary purposes as Money, redeemable as Real Money at a fixed date or on demand.

Rogatio Ecclesiae Credito (Credit) as Money Bill

1310. The Terms and Conditions of valid Public Debt Money Bills shall be on the reverse of the Instrument, unless otherwise stated.

Terms & Conditions of Public Debt Money Bills

## Article 350 – Rogatio Ecclesiae Permutatio (Exchange)

1311. ***Rogatio Ecclesiae Permutatio*** is the Ecclesiastical Bill of Right of Exchange, as inherited from the Divine Right *Rogatio Divinum Permutatio*. It is the ninth of eleven Ecclesiastical Bills.

Rogatio Ecclesiae Permutatio (Exchange)

1312. An Ecclesiastical Bill of Exchange is a written Demand and Order, assured by Rights granted; from one person to another, directing the person to whom it is addressed to pay to a third person a certain sum of money therein named. A Bill of Exchange is considered an unconditional Order in writing, addressed by one person to another, signed by the person giving it, and requiring the person to whom it is addressed to pay on demand, or at a fixed or determinable future time, a sum certain in money to order or to the bearer. A Bill of Exchange may be negotiable or not negotiable. If negotiable, it may be transferred either before or after acceptance.

Rogatio Ecclesiae Permutatio (Exchange) as Bill of Exchange

### Article 351 – Rogatio Ecclesiae Venditio (Sale)

1313. ***Rogatio Ecclesiae Venditio*** (Sale) is the Ecclesiastical Bill of Right of Sale, as inherited from the Divine Right *Rogatio Divinum Venditio*. It is the tenth of eleven Ecclesiastical Bills.  
*Rogatio Ecclesiae Venditio (Sale)*

1314. A Bill of Sale is an Instrument of Demand and Order, assured by Rights granted; as when a person delivers goods as security to a lender in exchange for a sum of money and empowering the lender to sell the goods if the sum is not repaid at the time appointed.  
*Bill of Sale*

### Article 352 – Rogatio Ecclesiae Traditio (Lading)

1315. ***Rogatio Ecclesiae Traditio*** (Lading) is the Ecclesiastical Bill of Right of Lading, as inherited from the Divine Right *Rogatio Divinum Traditio*. It is the eleventh of eleven Ecclesiastical Bills.  
*Rogatio Ecclesiae Traditio (Lading))*

1316. An Ecclesiastical Bill of Lading, also known as a Bill of Consignment, is a Demand and Order, assured by Rights granted; in writing as evidence of a contract for the carriage and delivery of Goods sent by transport for certain freight. A Bill of Lading is a formal acknowledgment of the receipt of Goods and an engagement to deliver them to the consignee.  
*Bill of Lading*

## 8.7 – Ecclesiastical Dogmata

### Article 353 – Ecclesiastical Dogmata

1317. ***Ecclesiastical Dogmata*** (*Greatest Principles Ecclesiae Iurium*) shall be Ecclesiastical Rights associated with the promulgation of authoritative ecclesiastical principles, decrees and doctrines.  
*Ecclesiastical Dogmata*

1318. A Decree is a valid Form of Deed or Order promulgated by an Official Person, subject to the limits of their authority, in accordance with these Maxims and the procedures of their Office.  
*Decree as a valid Deed*

1319. A Decree is not valid, but an inferior and false document if it does not conform to these Maxims.  
*Invalid Decree*

1320. A Decree is the highest form of law that may be promulgated within the limits of law of a Juridic Person. A Decree may not be issued unless permitted for a specific purpose under the laws of the Juridic Person by an Official Person holding such authority.  
*Permitted use of Decree*

1321. Only three (3) types of Official Person may issue a valid Decree,  
*Types of Official Person and use*

Supreme, Superior and Ordinary:-     *of Decree*

(i)    A Decree Issued by a Supreme Official Person is called an *Imperium* when promulgated as an order or *Edictum* when promulgated as a deed; and

(ii)    A Decree Issued by a Superior Official Person is called an *Institutum* when promulgated as an order and *Consultum* when promulgated as a deed; and

(iii)    A Decree Issued by an Ordinary Official Person is called an *Ordinatim* when promulgated as an order and *Decretum* when promulgated as a deed.

1322. Only Official Persons may issue a valid Decree:-

(i)    A Decree may not be abrogated, nor overturned by a lesser Juridic Person, only by a higher Juridic Person by Prescript, or higher Official Person by Decree; and

(ii)    By definition, no inferior person being an official of Inferior Roman Law, Sharia Law or Talmudic Law has any valid authority to issue a valid Decree. Any by-law of an inferior Juridic person claiming to be a decree automatically causes such a by-law to be null and void from the beginning.

1323. All Personal Rights are delegated to the safe custody and wise guardian powers of the legitimate and valid supreme competent ecclesiastical forum of law of the proper Ucadia Faiths and all lesser associated Ucadia bodies, as the embodiment of judicial authority; and as defined by Article 59 (Oratorium) of the most sacred Covenant *Pactum De Singularis Caelum*.     Delegation of Ecclesiastical Dogma

1324. All Personal Rights are assumed to be automatically invoked within Ucadia Jurisdictions through the operation of the Civilised Rules of Ucadia Societies, Bodies and Entities. However the Rights may be explicitly invoked or referenced by Right of Action through a proper Forum of Law and the Fiduciary Obligations of any such court in Ucadia or Non-Ucadia Jurisdiction.     Invocation of Ecclesiastical Dogma

1325. The following valid eleven (11) Ecclesiastical Dogma (*Greatest Principles Ecclesiae Iurium*) shall be recognised in accord with the most sacred Covenant *Pactum De Singularis Caelum*:-     List of Ecclesiastical Dogma (Greatest Principles Ecclesiae Iurium)

(i)    "**Dogma Ecclesiae Praeceptum**" is the Ecclesiastical Precept of Proposed Dogma, as inherited from the Divine Right *Dogma Divinum Praeceptum*; and

(ii)    "**Dogma Ecclesiae Theologiae**" is the Ecclesiastical

Dogma of Divine Science, as inherited from the Divine Right *Dogma Divinum Theologiae*; and

(iii) **"Dogma Ecclesiae Singularis Caelum"** is the Ecclesiastical Dogma of One Heaven, as inherited from the Divine Right *Dogma Divinum Singularis Caelum*; and

(iv) **"Dogma Ecclesiae Ucadia"** is the Ecclesiastical Dogma of Ucadia, as inherited from the Divine Right *Dogma Divinum Ucadia*; and

(v) **"Dogma Ecclesiae Iuris"** is the Ecclesiastical Dogma of Law, as inherited from the Divine Right *Dogma Divinum Iuris*; and

(vi) **"Dogma Ecclesiae Scientium"** is the Ecclesiastical Dogma of Science, as inherited from the Divine Right *Dogma Divinum Scientium*; and

(vii) **"Dogma Ecclesiae Revelatio"** is the Ecclesiastical Dogma of Revelation, as inherited from the Divine Right *Dogma Divinum Revelatio*; and

(viii) **"Dogma Ecclesiae Sacramentum"** is the Ecclesiastical Dogma of the Sacraments, as inherited from the Divine Right *Dogma Divinum Sacramentum*; and

(ix) **"Dogma Ecclesiae Singularis Christus"** is the Ecclesiastical Dogma of One Christ, as inherited from the Divine Right *Dogma Divinum Singularis Christus*; and

(x) **"Dogma Ecclesiae Singularis Islam"** is the Ecclesiastical Dogma of One Islam, as inherited from the Divine Right *Dogma Divinum Singularis Islam*; and

(xi) *"**Dogma Ecclesiae Singularis Spiritus**"* is the Ecclesiastical Dogma of One Spirit, as inherited from the Divine Right *Dogma Divinum Singularis Spiritus*.

## Article 354 – Dogma Ecclesiae Praeceptum (Proposed Dogma)

1326. ***Dogma Ecclesiae Praeceptum*** is the Ecclesiastical Precept of Proposed Dogma, as inherited from the Divine Right *Dogma Divinum Praeceptum*.

Dogma Ecclesiae Praeceptum (Proposed Dogma)

1327. *Dogma Ecclesiae Praeceptum* (Precept) is the first of eleven Rights of Ecclesiastical Dogmata; and is invoked when a proposed matter of

Purpose of Dogma Ecclesiae Praeceptum

doctrine or teaching is raised for debate, consistent with the most sacred Covenant *Pactum De Singularis Caelum* and the present Maxims.

### Article 355 – Dogma Ecclesiae Theologiae (Divine Science)

1328. ***Dogma Ecclesiae Theologiae*** is the Ecclesiastical Dogma of Divine Science, as inherited from the Divine Right *Dogma Divinum Theologiae*.

1329. *Dogma Ecclesiae Theologiae* (Divine Science) is the second of eleven Rights of Ecclesiastical Dogmata; and is invoked when a matter of doctrine or teaching is to be officially promulgated concerning Theologia, consistent with the most sacred Covenant *Pactum De Singularis Caelum* and the present Maxims.

### Article 356 – Dogma Ecclesiae Singularis Caelum (Dogma of One Heaven)

1330. ***Dogma Ecclesiae Singularis Caelum*** is the Ecclesiastical Dogma of One Heaven, as inherited from the Divine Right *Dogma Divinum Singularis Caelum*.

1331. *Dogma Ecclesiae Singularis Caelum* (One Heaven) is the third of eleven Rights of Ecclesiastical Dogmata; and is invoked when a matter of doctrine or teaching is to be officially promulgated concerning One Heaven, consistent with the most sacred Covenant *Pactum De Singularis Caelum* and the present Maxims.

### Article 357 – Dogma Ecclesiae Ucadia (Dogma of Ucadia)

1332. ***Dogma Ecclesiae Ucadia*** is the Ecclesiastical Dogma of Ucadia, as inherited from the Divine Right *Dogma Divinum Ucadia*.

1333. *Dogma Ecclesiae Ucadia* is the fourth of eleven Rights of Ecclesiastical Dogmata; and is invoked when a matter of doctrine or teaching is to be officially promulgated concerning Ucadia, consistent with the most sacred Covenant *Pactum De Singularis Caelum* and the present Maxims.

### Article 358 – Dogma Ecclesiae Iuris (Dogma of Law)

1334. **Dogma Ecclesiae Iuris** is the Ecclesiastical Dogma of Law, as inherited from the Divine Right *Dogma Divinum Iuris*.

*Dogma Ecclesiae Iuris (Dogma of Law)*

1335. *Dogma Ecclesiae Iuris* (Law) is the fifth of eleven Rights of Ecclesiastical Dogmata; and is invoked when a matter of doctrine or teaching is to be officially promulgated concerning Law, consistent with the most sacred Covenant *Pactum De Singularis Caelum* and the present Maxims.

*Invoking of Dogma Ecclesiae Iuris*

### Article 359 – Dogma Ecclesiae Scientium (Dogma of Science)

1336. **Dogma Ecclesiae Scientium** is the Ecclesiastical Dogma of Science, as inherited from the Divine Right *Dogma Divinum Scientium*.

*Dogma Ecclesiae Scientium (Dogma of Science)*

1337. *Dogma Ecclesiae Scientium* (Science) is the sixth of eleven Rights of Ecclesiastical Dogmata; and is invoked when a matter of doctrine or teaching is to be officially promulgated concerning Science, consistent with the most sacred Covenant *Pactum De Singularis Caelum* and the present Maxims.

*Invoking of Dogma Ecclesiae Scientium*

### Article 360 – Dogma Ecclesiae Revelatio (Dogma of Revelation)

1338. **Dogma Ecclesiae Revelatio** is the Ecclesiastical Dogma of Revelation, as inherited from the Divine Right *Dogma Divinum Revelatio*.

*Dogma Ecclesiae Revelatio (Dogma of Revelation)*

1339. *Dogma Ecclesiae Revelatio* (Revelation) is the seventh of eleven Rights of Ecclesiastical Dogmata; and is invoked when a matter of doctrine or teaching is to be officially promulgated concerning Revelation, consistent with the most sacred Covenant *Pactum De Singularis Caelum* and the present Maxims.

*Invoking of Dogma Ecclesiae Revelatio*

### Article 361 – Dogma Ecclesiae Sacramentum (Dogma of the Sacraments)

1340. **Dogma Ecclesiae Sacramentum** is the Ecclesiastical Dogma of the Sacraments, as inherited from the Divine Right *Dogma Divinum Sacramentum*.

*Dogma Ecclesiae Sacramentum (Dogma of the Sacred Gifts)*

1341. *Dogma Ecclesiae Sacramentum* (Sacred Gifts) is the eighth of eleven

*Invoking of Dogma Ecclesiae*

Rights of Ecclesiastical Dogmata; and is invoked when a matter of doctrine or teaching is to be officially promulgated concerning the Sacraments consistent with the most sacred Covenant *Pactum De Singularis Caelum* and the present Maxims.

 Sacramentum 

### Article 362 – Dogma Ecclesiae Singularis Christus (Dogma of One Christ)

1342. ***Dogma Ecclesiae Singularis Christus*** is the Ecclesiastical Dogma of One Christ, as inherited from the Divine Right *Dogma Divinum Singularis Christus*.

 Dogma Ecclesiae Singularis Christus (Dogma of One Christ) 

1343. *Dogma Ecclesiae Singularis Christus* (One Christ) is the ninth of eleven Rights of Ecclesiastical Dogmata; and is invoked when a matter of doctrine or teaching is to be officially promulgated concerning the Universal Ecclesia of One Christ, consistent with the most sacred Covenant *Pactum De Singularis Caelum* and the present Maxims.

 Invoking of Dogma Ecclesiae Singularis Christus 

### Article 363 – Dogma Ecclesiae Singularis Islam (Dogma of One Islam)

1344. ***Dogma Ecclesiae Singularis Islam*** is the Ecclesiastical Dogma of One Islam, as inherited from the Divine Right *Dogma Divinum Singularis Islam*.

 Dogma Ecclesiae Singularis Islam (Dogma of One Islam) 

1345. *Dogma Ecclesiae Singularis Islam* (One Islam) is the tenth of eleven Rights of Ecclesiastical Dogmata; and is invoked when a matter of doctrine or teaching is to be officially promulgated concerning the Holy Society of One Islam, consistent with the most sacred Covenant *Pactum De Singularis Caelum* and the present Maxims.

 Invoking of Dogma Ecclesiae Singularis Islam 

### Article 364 – Dogma Ecclesiae Singularis Spiritus (Dogma of One Spirit)

1346. ***Dogma Ecclesiae Singularis Spiritus*** is the Ecclesiastical Dogma of One Spirit, as inherited from the Divine Right *Dogma Divinum Singularis Spiritus*.

 Dogma Ecclesiae Singularis Spiritus (Dogma of One Spirit) 

1347. *Dogma Ecclesiae Singularis Spiritus* (One Spirit) is the eleventh of eleven Rights of Ecclesiastical Dogmata; and is invoked when a matter of doctrine or teaching is to be officially promulgated concerning the Sacred Society of One Spirit, consistent with the most sacred Covenant *Pactum De Singularis Caelum* and the present Maxims.

 Invoking of Dogma Ecclesiae Singularis Spiritus 

## 8.8 – Ecclesiastical Decrees

### Article 365 – Ecclesiastical Decrees

1348. ***Ecclesiastical Decrees*** (*Decretum Ecclesiae Iurium*) shall be Ecclesiastical Rights associated with ecclesiastical decrees concerning the administration, conduct and enforcement of law and order. — Ecclesiastical Decrees

1349. A ***Decree*** is a valid Form of Judgement or Order promulgated by an Ucadia court or other judicial or sovereign authority, subject to the limits of their authority, in accordance with these Maxims and the procedures of their Office. — Nature of Decrees

1350. A Decree is not valid, but an inferior and false document if it does not conform to these Maxims. — Conformity

1351. The key elements of a valid and proper Decree include (but are not limited to):- — Key elements of a Decree

(i) **Title and Caption**: A decree begins with a title that identifies the court or authority issuing the decree, the names of the parties involved in the case (plaintiff and defendant), and a case number. This information is typically presented at the top of the document and is known as the *caption*; and

(ii) **Jurisdiction**: The decree will specify the legal basis for the court's authority to issue the decree. It will state the jurisdictional facts, such as the location of the court and the type of case over which it has jurisdiction; and

(iii) **Findings of Fact**: Decrees include a section that outlines the relevant facts of the case as determined by the court. This includes a summary of the evidence presented during the proceedings and the court's conclusions about the facts; and

(iv) **Conclusions of Law**: The decree will include the legal conclusions reached by the court based on the facts of the case. This section explains the legal principles that apply to the case and how they are relevant to the court's decision; and

(v) **Operative or Dispositive Clause**: This is one of the most critical elements of a decree. It contains the specific orders or commands issued by the court. It outlines what the parties involved must do or refrain from doing as a result of the decree. The operative clause begins with phrases such as "It is hereby ordered" or "The court orders as follows"; and

(vi) **Remedies and Relief**: If the decree is granting relief to one or more parties, it will specify the type of relief granted. This may include monetary damages, injunctive relief, specific performance, or other remedies. The decree may also outline any conditions or requirements that must be met for the relief to be effective; and

(vii) **Duration and Effective Date**: The decree includes information about when it becomes effective and whether it has a specified duration. Some decrees are permanent, while others may be temporary or subject to modification; and

(viii) **Signature and Seal**: A decree is signed by the judge or judicial officer issuing the order. In some cases, it may also bear the court's official seal for authentication; and

(ix) **Notice and Service**: The decree may contain information about how notice of the decree will be provided to the parties involved and whether they are required to take any specific actions in response to the decree; and

(x) **Enforcement**: In cases where the decree includes orders that need to be enforced, it may provide details on how enforcement will occur and the consequences of non-compliance.

1352. The following valid eleven (11) Ecclesiastical Decrees (*Decretum Ecclesiae Iurium*) shall be recognised in accord with the most sacred Covenant *Pactum De Singularis Caelum*:-

    (i) **"Decretum Ecclesiae Doctrinae"** is the Ecclesiastical Decree of Doctrine, as inherited from the Divine Right *Decretum Divinum Doctrinae*; and

    (ii) **"Decretum Ecclesiae Absolutionis"** is the Ecclesiastical Decree of Absolution, as inherited from the Divine Right *Decretum Divinum Absolutionis*; and

    (iii) **"Decretum Ecclesiae Damnationis"** is the Ecclesiastical Decree of Damnation, as inherited from the Divine Right *Decretum Divinum Damnationis*; and

    (iv) **"Decretum Ecclesiae Exemplificatio"** is the Ecclesiastical Decree of Exemplification, as inherited from the Divine Right *Decretum Divinum Exemplificatio*; and

    (v) **"Decretum Ecclesiae Testimonium"** is the Ecclesiastical Decree of Proof, as inherited from the Divine Right *Decretum Divinum Testimonium*; and

*Margin note: List of Ecclesiastical Decrees (Decretum Ecclesiae Iurium)*

(vi) **"Decretum Ecclesiae Instructionis"** is the Ecclesiastical Decree of Instruction, as inherited from the Divine Right *Decretum Divinum Instructionis*; and

(vii) **"Decretum Ecclesiae Censurae"** is the Ecclesiastical Decree of Censure, as inherited from the Divine Right *Decretum Divinum Censurae*; and

(viii) **"Decretum Ecclesiae Annullas"** is the Ecclesiastical Decree of Annulment, as inherited from the Divine Right *Decretum Divinum Annullas*; and

(ix) **"Decretum Ecclesiae Ratificationis"** is the Ecclesiastical Decree of Ratification, as inherited from the Divine Right *Decretum Divinum Ratificationis*; and

(x) **"Decretum Ecclesiae Interdictum"** is the Ecclesiastical Decree of Interdiction, as inherited from the Divine Right *Decretum Divinum Interdictum*; and

(xi) *"**Decretum Ecclesiae Levationis**"* is the Ecclesiastical Decree of Relief, as inherited from the Divine Right *Decretum Divinum Levationis*.

## Article 366 – Decretum Ecclesiae Doctrinae (Doctrine)

**1353.** ***Decretum Ecclesiae Doctrinae*** is the Ecclesiastical Decree of Doctrine, as inherited from the Divine Right *Decretum Divinum Doctrinae*. It is the first of eleven Ecclesiastical Decrees. — Decretum Ecclesiae Doctrinae (Doctrine)

**1354.** An Ecclesiastical Decree of *Decretum Ecclesiae Doctrinae* (Doctrine) is issued in all matters concerning official procedures, organisation restructures, policies, systematic explanations and interpretations of executive government. — Purpose of Decretum Ecclesiae Doctrinae (Doctrine)

## Article 367 – Decretum Ecclesiae Absolutionis (Absolution)

**1355.** ***Decretum Ecclesiae Absolutionis*** is the Ecclesiastical Decree of Absolution, as inherited from the Divine Right *Decretum Divinum Absolutionis*. It is the second of eleven Ecclesiastical Decrees. — Decretum Ecclesiae Absolutionis (Absolution)

**1356.** An Ecclesiastical Decree of *Decretum Ecclesiae Absolutionis* (Absolution) is issued in all matters concerning the exoneration, absolution, forgiveness or dismissal of matters. — Purpose of Decretum Ecclesiae Absolutionis (Absolution)

## Article 368 – Decretum Ecclesiae Damnationis (Damnation)

1357. ***Decretum Ecclesiae Damnationis*** is the Ecclesiastical Decree of Damnation, as inherited from the Divine Right *Decretum Divinum Damnationis*. It is the third of eleven Ecclesiastical Decrees.
<td>Decretum Ecclesiae Damnationis (Damnation)</td>

1358. An Ecclesiastical Decree of *Decretum Ecclesiae Damnationis* (Damnation) is issued in all matters concerning condemnation in ecclesiastical matters.
<td>Purpose of Decretum Ecclesiae Damnationis (Damnation)</td>

## Article 369 – Decretum Ecclesiae Exemplificatio (Exemplification)

1359. ***Decretum Ecclesiae Exemplificatio*** is the Ecclesiastical Decree of Exemplification, as inherited from the Divine Right *Decretum Divinum Exemplificatio*. It is the fourth of eleven Ecclesiastical Decrees.
<td>Decretum Ecclesiae Exemplificatio</td>

1360. An Ecclesiastical Decree of *Decretum Ecclesiae Exemplificatio* (Exemplification) is issued in all matters concerning conclusive confirmation of a change in title or status.
<td>Purpose of Decretum Ecclesiae Exemplificatio</td>

## Article 370 – Decretum Ecclesiae Testimonium (Proof)

1361. ***Decretum Ecclesiae Testimonium*** is the Ecclesiastical Decree of Proof, as inherited from the Divine Right *Decretum Divinum Testimonium*. It is the fifth of eleven Ecclesiastical Decrees.
<td>Decretum Ecclesiae Testimonium (Proof)</td>

1362. An Ecclesiastical Decree of *Decretum Ecclesiae Testimonium* (Proof) is issued in all matters concerning testimony, capacity and proof.
<td>Purpose of Decretum Ecclesiae Testimonium</td>

## Article 371 – Decretum Ecclesiae Instructionis (Instruction)

1363. ***Decretum Ecclesiae Instructionis*** is the Ecclesiastical Decree of Instruction, as inherited from the Divine Right *Decretum Divinum Instructionis*. It is the sixth of eleven Ecclesiastical Decrees.
<td>Decretum Ecclesiae Instructionis (Instruction)</td>

1364. An Ecclesiastical Decree of *Decretum Ecclesiae Instructionis* (Instruction) is issued in all matters concerning instruction and performance.
<td>Purpose of Decretum Ecclesiae Instructionis</td>

## Article 372 – Decretum Ecclesiae Censurae (Censure)

1365. ***Decretum Ecclesiae Censurae*** is the Ecclesiastical Decree of Censure, as inherited from the Divine Right *Decretum Divinum Censurae*. It is the seventh of eleven Ecclesiastical Decrees. — Decretum Ecclesiae Censurae (Censure)

1366. An Ecclesiastical Decree of *Decretum Ecclesiae Censurae* (Censure) is issued in all matters concerning censure and estoppel. — Purpose of Decretum Ecclesiae Censurae (Censure)

## Article 373 – Decretum Ecclesiae Annullas (Annulment)

1367. ***Decretum Ecclesiae Annullas*** is the Ecclesiastical Decree of Annulment, as inherited from the Divine Right *Decretum Divinum Annullas*. It is the eighth of eleven Ecclesiastical Decrees. — Decretum Ecclesiae Annullas (Annulment)

1368. An Ecclesiastical Decree of *Decretum Ecclesiae Annullas* (Annulment) is issued in all matters concerning liquidation, dissolution and annulment. — Purpose of Decretum Ecclesiae Annullas (Annulment)

## Article 374 – Decretum Ecclesiae Ratificationis (Ratification)

1369. ***Decretum Ecclesiae Ratificationis*** is the Ecclesiastical Decree of Ratification, as inherited from the Divine Right *Decretum Divinum Ratificationis*. It is the ninth of eleven Ecclesiastical Decrees. — Decretum Ecclesiae Ratificationis (Ratification)

1370. An Ecclesiastical Decree of *Decretum Ecclesiae Ratificationis* (Ratification) is issued in all matters concerning the ratification of governing documents, deeds and other agreements. — Purpose of Decretum Ecclesiae Ratificationis (Ratification)

## Article 375 – Decretum Ecclesiae Interdictum (Interdiction)

1371. ***Decretum Ecclesiae Interdictum*** be the Ecclesiastical Decree of Interdiction, as inherited from the Divine Right *Decretum Divinum Interdictum*. It is the tenth of eleven Ecclesiastical Decrees. — Decretum Ecclesiae Interdictum (Interdiction)

1372. An Ecclesiastical Decree of *Decretum Ecclesiae Interdictum* (Interdiction) is issued in all matters concerning injunctions, prohibitions or restraints. — Purpose of Decretum Ecclesiae Interdictum (Interdiction)

### Article 376 – Decretum Ecclesiae Levationis (Relief and Restoration)

1373. ***Decretum Ecclesiae Levationis*** is the Ecclesiastical Decree of Relief, as inherited from the Divine Right *Decretum Divinum Levationis*. It is the eleventh of eleven Ecclesiastical Decrees.

    Decretum Ecclesiae Levationis (Relief and Restoration)

1374. An Ecclesiastical Decree of *Decretum Ecclesiae Levationis* (Relief) is issued in all matters concerning the allocation and ownership of rights, title, property or financial resources.

    Purpose of Decretum Ecclesiae Levationis (Relief)

## 8.9 – Ecclesiastical Notices

### Article 377 – Ecclesiastical Notices

1375. ***Ecclesiastical Notices*** (*Notitiae Ecclesiae Iurium*) shall be Ecclesiastical Rights associated with ecclesiastical notices issued, executed, patented, promulgated and services in the proper administration, conduct and enforcement of law and order.

    Ecclesiastical Notices (Notitiae Ecclesiae Iurium)

1376. A ***Notice*** is a written or formal communication or process that conveys information, instructions, or important details to a specific individual, group of individuals, or the public at large.

    Notice

1377. The seven primary types of Notice include: *Physical, Posted, Direct, Indirect, Public (legal), Implied* and *Constructive*:-

    Types of Notice

    (i) *Physical Notice* or Actual Notice is a type of notice and service of process whereby the specific information concerning a formal legal matter is listed in a Document and then physically handed to a party or their representative, with proof, attestation or acknowledgment of such service recorded as evidence; and

    (ii) *Posted Notice* or Mail Notice is a type of notice and service of process whereby specific information concerning the formal legal matter is personally addressed to the party and sent through a certified or registered mail delivery system recognised by Non-Ucadia bodies such as the International Postal Union; and

    (iii) *Direct Notice* is a type of notice and service of process whereby specific information concerning the formal legal matter is personally addressed to the party and sent via email, fax, sms or other recorded and verifiable transmission medium; and

(iv) *Indirect Notice* is a type of notice and service of process whereby specific information concerning the formal legal matter is published in any broadcast medium such as media releases, stories, advertorial content and advertising and likely to be viewed by one or more parties; and

(v) *Public Notice* is a type of notice and service of process whereby specific information concerning the formal legal matter is published in a company, local, regional, national or international publication possessing status as a gazette and therefore an official newspaper of record or physically posted at a site reasonably expected to be visible to the Person; and

(vi) *Implied Notice* is a type of notice inferred from facts that a Person had means of knowing and would have caused a reasonable Person to take action to gain further information concerning a formal legal matter. It is a notice inferred or imputed to a party by reason of his/her knowledge collateral to the main fact; and

(vii) *Constructive Notice* is a type of notice inferred from facts that a Person unable to be served with Actual Notice may be reasonably inferred or imputed to have received notice, if Actual Notice was restricted or not possible and a minimum number of attempts of Physical, Posted, Direct or Public Notice were concluded.

1378. The publishing of any Proclamation, Order, Regulation or Notice within the Ucadia Gazette shall be Prima Facie Evidence of such Fact and Truth; and that all Courts, Judges, Justices, Masters, Magistrates or Commissioners judicially acting, and all other judicial Officers shall take judicial Notice of such *Prima Facie* Evidence in all legal proceedings and all forums of law whether Ucadia or Non-Ucadia.

*Ucadia Gazette Notices as Prima Facie Evidence*

1379. All *Ecclesiastical Notices* are delegated to the safe custody and wise guardian powers of the legitimate and valid supreme competent ecclesiastical forum of law of the proper Ucadia Faiths and all lesser associated Ucadia bodies, as the embodiment of judicial authority; and as defined by Article 59 (Oratorium) of the most sacred Covenant *Pactum De Singularis Caelum*.

*Delegation of Ecclesiastical Notices*

1380. All *Ecclesiastical Notices* are assumed to be automatically invoked within Ucadia Jurisdictions through the operation of the Civilised Rules of Ucadia Societies, Bodies and Entities. However the Rights may be explicitly invoked or referenced by Right of Action through a proper Forum of Law and the Fiduciary Obligations of any such court in Ucadia or Non-Ucadia Jurisdiction.

*Invocation of Ecclesiastical Notices*

**1381.** Notice is deemed to have been properly and duly served, when:  *When Notice deemed to be served*

    (i) Any Physical Notice served personally or left at the registered address by a servicing agent is deemed to have been served when delivered and such fact is attested by a certificate of service signed by the agent who executed the service; and

    (ii) Any Notice sent by Post is deemed to have been served at the expiration of forty-eight hours after the envelope containing the Notice is posted and, in proving service, it is sufficient to prove that the envelope containing the Notice was properly addressed and posted; and

    (iii) Any Direct Notice served on a party is deemed to have been served on digital receipt and proof of service. Any notice served on a party by email or sms or any other form of direct electronic messaging is deemed to have been served after twenty-four hours and no error message or failed transmission notice is received; and

    (iv) Any Indirect Notice is deemed to have been served three days after receipt or proof of the publication of such notice; and

    (v) Any Public Notice is deemed to have been served three days after receipt or proof of the publication in a gazette and official publication of record of such Notice; and

    (vi) Any Implied Notice is deemed to have been served fourteen days after receipt or proof of publication of at least two forms of Indirect Notice or Public Notice; and

    (vii) Any Constructive Notice is deemed to have been served fourteen days after receipt or proof of at least one attempted Physical Notice or two Posted Notices and at least two forms of Indirect Notice or Public Notice.

**1382.** Where a Member does not have a registered address or where the Ecclesiastical Ucadia Entity has a reason in good faith to believe that a Member is not known at the Member's registered address, a Notice is deemed to be given to the Member if the Notice is exhibited by Indirect Notice in the Office for a period of forty-eight hours (and is deemed to be duly served at the commencement of that period) unless and until the Member informs the Ecclesiastical Ucadia Entity of a registered place of address.  *Member not known at registered address*

**1383.** The signature to any Notice to be given by the Ecclesiastical Ucadia Entity may be written or printed. The formatting of the name of an Officer of the Ecclesiastical Ucadia Entity in capitals as the signature  *Signature to Notice* line upon a Notice is deemed a valid legal signature.

1384. Where a Notice gives of a certain number of days, or the limit of time is mandated for some proper form of Notice, the days of service are not to be reckoned in the number of days, until the actual date of proof of service, thereby limiting the possibility of an unfair or unreasonable service.

*Reckoning of period of Notice*

1385. The following valid eleven (11) Ecclesiastical Notices (*Notitiae Ecclesiae Iurium*) shall be recognised in accord with the most sacred Covenant *Pactum De Singularis Caelum*:-

*List of Ecclesiastical Notices (Notitiae Ecclesiae Iurium)*

(i) "**Notitiae Ecclesiae Eventus**" is the Ecclesiastical Notice of Event, as inherited from the Divine Right *Notitiae Divinum Eventus*; and

(ii) "**Notitiae Ecclesiae Ius**" is the Ecclesiastical Notice of Right, as inherited from the Divine Right *Notitiae Divinum Ius*; and

(iii) "**Notitiae Ecclesiae Actum**" is the Ecclesiastical Notice of Action, as inherited from the Divine Right *Notitiae Divinum Actum*; and

(iv) "**Notitiae Ecclesiae Decretum**" is the Ecclesiastical Notice of Decree, as inherited from the Divine Right *Notitiae Divinum Decretum*; and

(v) "**Notitiae Ecclesiae Iuris**" is the Ecclesiastical Notice of Law, as inherited from the Divine Right *Notitiae Divinum Iuris*; and

(vi) "**Notitiae Ecclesiae Citationis**" is the Ecclesiastical Notice of Summons, as inherited from the Divine Right *Notitiae Divinum Citationis*; and

(vii) "**Notitiae Ecclesiae Redemptio**" is the Ecclesiastical Notice of Redemption, as inherited from the Divine Right *Notitiae Divinum Redemptio*; and

(viii) "**Notitiae Ecclesiae Rogatio**" is the Ecclesiastical Notice of Exception, as inherited from the Divine Right *Notitiae Divinum Rogatio*; and

(ix) "**Notitiae Ecclesiae Potentis**" is the Ecclesiastical Notice of Authority, as inherited from the Divine Right *Notitiae Divinum Potentis*; and

(x) "**Notitiae Ecclesiae Testamentum**" is the Ecclesiastical

Notice of Testament, as inherited from the Divine Right *Notitiae Divinum Testamentum*; and

(xi) **"Notitiae Ecclesiae Obligationis"** is the Ecclesiastical Notice of Obligation, as inherited from the Divine Right *Notitiae Divinum Obligationis*.

## Article 378 – Notitiae Ecclesiae Eventus (Notice of Event)

1386. *Notitiae Ecclesiae Eventus* is the Ecclesiastical Notice of Event, as inherited from the Divine Right *Notitiae Divinum Eventus*. It is the first of eleven Ecclesiastical Rights of Notice.
<!-- margin: Notitiae Ecclesiae Eventus (Notice of Event) -->

1387. An *Ecclesiastical Notice of Event* (*Notitiae Ecclesiae Eventus*) is any official notice in relation to the entry into a Ucadia Gazette or Register of a unique event pertaining to one or more Rights.
<!-- margin: Purpose of Notitiae Ecclesiae Eventus (Event) -->

1388. The issue of any such certificate or authorised extract or Gazette Notice in relation to a sacred space-time event shall be equivalent to a formal *Notitiae Ecclesiae Eventus* as evidence; and proof of a first in time, highest title and right association to such an event.
<!-- margin: Gazette Notice and Ecclesiae Eventus (Event) -->

1389. The existence therefore of any instrument or document issued by an inferior body or non-Ucadian aligned society claiming some right or ownership in direct contradiction to an event clearly identified through a *Notitiae Ecclesiae Eventus* shall itself be an open confession of perfidy, profanity, repugnancy, malice, heresy and apostasy against all forms of valid law of Heaven and Earth.
<!-- margin: Ecclesiae Eventus (Event) and Non-Ucadia Claim -->

## Article 379 – Notitiae Ecclesiae Ius (Notice of Right)

1390. *Notitiae Ecclesiae Ius* is the Ecclesiastical Notice of Right, as inherited from the Divine Right *Notitiae Divinum Ius*. It is the second of eleven Ecclesiastical Rights of Notice.
<!-- margin: Notitiae Ecclesiae Ius (Notice of Right) -->

1391. An *Ecclesiastical Notice of Right* (*Notitiae Ecclesiae Ius*) is any valid Notice issued under the rules of the most sacred Covenant *Pactum De Singularis Caelum* and the present Maxims bringing Ecclesiastical Notice and therefore the power of life to Valid Offices of the Society, Titles of Land, Water and Space and all Valid Rights and Commissions to Office.
<!-- margin: Purpose of Notitiae Ecclesiae Ius (Right) -->

1392. By the rules of the present Maxims and most sacred Covenant *Pactum De Singularis Caelum*, all Offices must be duly created by Ecclesiastical Notice and thereby granted a valid record number in
<!-- margin: Notitiae Ecclesiae Ius and Record Number -->

the Great Register and Divine Records of Heaven as having eternal spiritual life and real existence and legal personality.

1393. *Notitiae Divinum Ius* (Right) is the second of eleven Divine Rights of Divine Notice; and may only be invoked whenever the lesser Right *Notitiae Ecclesiae Ius* (Ecclesiastical Notice of Right) is invoked.

Invoking of Notitiae Ecclesiae Ius (Right)

## Article 380 – Notitiae Ecclesiae Actum (Notice of Action)

1394. **Notitiae Ecclesiae Actum** is the Ecclesiastical Notice of Action, as inherited from the Divine Right *Notitiae Divinum Actum*. It is the third of eleven Ecclesiastical Rights of Notice.

Notitiae Ecclesiae Actum (Notice of Action)

1395. An *Ecclesiastical Notice of Action* (*Notitiae Ecclesiae Actum*) is any valid Notice issued under the rules of the most sacred Covenant *Pactum De Singularis Caelum* and the present Maxims concerning one or more Ecclesiastical Rights of Action.

Purpose of Notitiae Ecclesiae Actum (Action)

## Article 381 – Notitiae Ecclesiae Decretum (Notice of Decree)

1396. **Notitiae Ecclesiae Decretum** is the Ecclesiastical Notice of Decree, as inherited from the Divine Right *Notitiae Divinum Decretum*. It is the fourth of eleven Ecclesiastical Rights of Notice.

Notitiae Ecclesiae Decretum (Notice of Decree)

1397. An *Ecclesiastical Notice of Decree* (*Notitiae Ecclesiae Decretum*) is any valid Notice issued under the rules of the most sacred Covenant *Pactum De Singularis Caelum* and the present Maxims concerning one or more Ecclesiastical Decrees.

Purpose of Notitiae Ecclesiae Decretum (Decree)

## Article 382 – Notitiae Ecclesiae Iuris (Notice of Law)

1398. **Notitiae Ecclesiae Iuris** is the Ecclesiastical Notice of Law, as inherited from the Divine Right *Notitiae Divinum Iuris*. It is the fifth of eleven Ecclesiastical Rights of Notice.

Notitiae Ecclesiae Iuris (Notice of Law)

1399. An *Ecclesiastical Notice of Law* (*Notitiae Ecclesiae Iuris*) is any valid Notice issued under the rules of the most sacred Covenant *Pactum De Singularis Caelum* and the present Maxims concerning one or more facts of law.

Purpose of Notitiae Ecclesiae Iuris (Law)

## Article 383 – Notitiae Ecclesiae Citationis (Notice of Summons)

1400. ***Notitiae Ecclesiae Citationis*** is the Ecclesiastical Notice of Summons, as inherited from the Divine Right *Notitiae Divinum Citationis*. It is the sixth of eleven Ecclesiastical Rights of Notice.

1401. An *Ecclesiastical Notice of Summons* (*Notitiae Ecclesiae Citationis*) is any valid Notice issued under the rules of the most sacred Covenant *Pactum De Singularis Caelum* and the present Maxims concerning the attendance to an official meeting, or legal matter.

## Article 384 – Notitiae Ecclesiae Redemptio (Notice of Redemption)

1402. ***Notitiae Ecclesiae Redemptio*** is the Ecclesiastical Notice of Redemption, as inherited from the Divine Right *Notitiae Divinum Redemptio*. It is the seventh of eleven Ecclesiastical Rights of Notice.

1403. An *Ecclesiastical Notice of Redemption* (*Notitiae Ecclesiae Redemptio*) is any valid Notice issued under the rules of the most sacred Covenant *Pactum De Singularis Caelum* and the present Maxims concerning the forgiveness of one or more offences.

## Article 385 – Notitiae Ecclesiae Rogatio (Notice of Exception)

1404. ***Notitiae Ecclesiae Rogatio*** is the Ecclesiastical Notice of Exception, as inherited from the Divine Right *Notitiae Divinum Rogatio*. It is the eighth of eleven Ecclesiastical Rights of Notice.

1405. An *Ecclesiastical Notice of Exception* (*Notitiae Ecclesiae Rogatio*) is any valid Notice issued under the rules of the most sacred Covenant *Pactum De Singularis Caelum* and the present Maxims concerning one or more failures to act in accord with the instructions of an Ecclesiastical Writ.

## Article 386 – Notitiae Ecclesiae Potentis (Notice of Authority)

1406. ***Notitiae Ecclesiae Potentis*** is the Ecclesiastical Notice of Authority, as inherited from the Divine Right *Notitiae Divinum Potentis*. It is the ninth of eleven Ecclesiastical Rights of Notice.

1407. An *Ecclesiastical Notice of Authority* (*Notitiae Ecclesiae Potentis*) is any valid Notice issued under the rules of the most sacred Covenant *Pactum De Singularis Caelum* and the present Maxims concerning a question of authority.

*Ecclesiae Potentis (Authority)*

### Article 387 – Notitiae Ecclesiae Testamentum (Notice of Testament)

1408. ***Notitiae Ecclesiae Testamentum*** is the Ecclesiastical Notice of Testament, as inherited from the Divine Right *Notitiae Divinum Testamentum*. It is the tenth of eleven Ecclesiastical Rights of Notice.

*Notitiae Ecclesiae Testamentum (Notice of Testament)*

1409. An *Ecclesiastical Notice of Testament* (*Notitiae Ecclesiae Testamentum*) is any valid Notice issued under the rules of the most sacred Covenant *Pactum De Singularis Caelum* and the present Maxims concerning a testament or declaration or statement.

*Purpose of Notitiae Ecclesiae Testamentum (Testament)*

### Article 388 – Notitiae Ecclesiae Obligationis (Notice of Obligation)

1410. ***Notitiae Ecclesiae Obligationis*** is the Ecclesiastical Notice of Obligation, as inherited from the Divine Right *Notitiae Divinum Obligationis*. It is the eleventh of eleven Ecclesiastical Rights of Notice.

*Notitiae Ecclesiae Obligationis (Notice of Obligation)*

1411. An *Ecclesiastical Notice of Obligation* (*Notitiae Ecclesiae Obligationis*) is any valid Notice issued under the rules of the most sacred Covenant *Pactum De Singularis Caelum* and the present Maxims in relation to one or more Obligations that will fall due within the next forty days.

*Purpose of Notitiae Ecclesiae Obligationis*

## 8.10 – False, Absurd and Prohibited Ecclesiastical Rights

### Article 389 – False, Absurd and Prohibited Ecclesiastical Rights

1412. **False, Absurd & Prohibited Ecclesiastical Rights** are claims or assertions concerning Ecclesiastical Rights that clearly contradict, oppose or deny the most sacred Covenant *Pactum De Singularis Caelum* and the present Maxims.

*False, Absurd & Prohibited Ecclesiastical Rights*

1413. All proper and valid Ecclesiastical Rights originate and are defined from the most sacred Covenant *Pactum De Singularis Caelum*.

*Source of Ecclesiastical Rights*

1414. Any claim or assertion concerning Ecclesiastical Rights that contradicts, or opposes or denies one or more of the present Maxims is false, absurd and prohibited from being recognised as valid in any Civilised form of Law.

*Claims or Assertions that contradict are false and absurd*

# Title IX – Ecclesiastical Registers

## 9.1 – Ecclesiastical Registers
### Article 390 – Ecclesiastical Register

1415. An *Ecclesiastical Register* is a formal or official set of ecclesiastical records of names, events, actions, transactions, or other information, consistent with Divine Law in accord with the most Sacred Covenant *Pactum De Singularis Caelum*.   *Ecclesiastical Register*

1416. A Register that is in conflict with proper Divine Law cannot possibly be a valid or legitimate Ecclesiastical Register:-   *Register Incompatible to Divine Law cannot be Ecclesiastical nor valid*

   (i) A Register formed through immoral, secretive and blasphemous acts can never be a valid Ecclesiastical or Civil register, as something borne from fraud and deception does not then become legitimate over time; and

   (ii) A Register containing systematic, intentional and deliberately incomplete, false and morally repugnant information ceases to be a valid Ecclesiastical or Civil register from the beginning and can never be claimed as an official record or primary source of vital records; and

   (iii) When records within an invalid, fraudulent and morally repugnant register contain some true information mixed with false information, then such true information may be taken to have been automatically alienated by default from the beginning (ab initio) into a true Ucadia Register formed under Divine Law and expressed for the original purpose; and

   (iv) If a Non-Ucadia society has intentionally created false and morally repugnant records of vital events such as births, deaths and marriages, then automatically from the beginning (ab initio), such true information has automatically been alienated and recorded into Ucadia Ecclesiastical and Civil Registers for the same purpose, regardless of any protest or refusal from the registrars or Non-Ucadia agencies culpable of systematic fraud, deception, moral repugnancy and blasphemy.

1417. The highest and most authoritative Register is the *Great Register and Divine Records* of One Heaven, also known as the *Great Roll of Divine Persons* and the *Great Book of Life*:-   *Great Register and Divine Records of One Heaven*

   (i) No possible Register possesses greater authority or power or jurisdiction than the Great Register and Public Record of One Heaven; and

   (ii) All lesser Register owe their authority, powers, legitimacy and existence to the Great Register and Public Record of One Heaven; and

(iii) No lesser Register is valid or legitimate until it can verify and prove its provenance to a valid and legitimate record within the Great Register and Public Record of One Heaven subject to terms of these present Maxims and the most sacred Covenant *Pactum De Singularis Caelum*.

**1418.** In terms of the general authority and creation of Registers:- Authority and Creation of Registers

(i) The Authority to form a Register is defined by the limits of Authority of the constituting Instrument of the relevant Trust or Estate or Fund or Corporation that the Register relates; and

(ii) The Rights, Powers and Property prescribed within a Register cannot exceed the Rights, Powers and Property of the Trust or Estate or Fund or Corporation itself; and

(iii) All valid and proper Registers are wholly and exclusively Ecclesiastical Property and can never belong to a Trust, or Estate or Fund or Corporation that formed or inherited it. Therefore, as all valid and proper Registers are exclusively Ecclesiastical Property and all Sacred Circumscribed Space is derived from Ucadia, all Registers are *ipso facto* (as a matter of fact) *ab initio* (from the beginning) the absolute property of One Heaven and Ucadia; and

(iv) All Registers are hierarchical in their inheritance of Authority and validity from One Heaven, beginning with the highest being the Great Register and Public Record of One Heaven. A Register that cannot demonstrate the provenance of its Authority, has none, and is null and void from the beginning; and

(v) As all Registers are wholly and exclusively Ecclesiastical, absolutely no clerical or administrative act may take place in association with a Register unless by a duly authorised Officer under active and valid sacred Oath or Vow in a manner consistent and in accord with the most sacred Covenant *Pactum De Singularis Caelum*; and

(vi) The entry of a record into a Register is wholly invalid unless the memorial and testimony of the act giving authority is done without duress, is done freely and with full knowledge and is consistent and in accord with the most sacred Covenant *Pactum De Singularis Caelum*.

**1419.** In terms of the general purpose, function and operation of a valid General References to

Register:-

Registers

(i) A Register as a table contains at least three or more columns; and

(ii) A Register as a table can be a section of a Book, or a whole series of Books; and

(iii) A Register is held in the care of a proper Officer of a Competent Forum of Law, possessing both the Ecclesiastical Authority and Sovereign Authority to hold, record and keep custody of such records; and

(iv) A Register cannot and does not create the original fact or authority that it records, but merely reflects the pertinent elements in relation to the originating Instrument used to create a valid entry; and

(v) An entry in a Register can never create sacred circumscribed space or an original event. However a valid entry in a Register is itself a valid event and by virtue of the "joining" of information at the time of registration may create certain Rights or Facts or Truths as Prima Facie Evidence; and

(vi) A particular Right of Use in relation to Property can only be recorded once in a valid Register. Those specific Registers as prescribed by Ucadian Law and the most sacred Covenant *Pactum De Singularis Caelum* are always Registers of Original Record and take precedence over all Non-Ucadian and foreign registers and rolls; and

(vii) The claimed day or time of entry of a record into a Non-Ucadian or foreign register has no bearing or merit in law, where a similar record for the same Property, or Event, or Right exists within a valid Ucadia Register, even if the day or time of entry in the Ucadia Register is after the day or time of entry in the Non-Ucadian and foreign register. This is because any Non-Ucadian and foreign register that seeks to usurp the Authority of a valid Ucadian Register automatically renders such a register invalid and illegitimate, meaning that such a Non-Ucadian register is determined to be null and void, having no force or effect in law.

1420. There exists nine (9) Primary Types of valid Ecclesiastical Registers including (but not limited to):-

Types of Ecclesiastical Registers

(i) **Sacred Objects Register**: A Register detailing sacred items of cultural, religious, or historical significance that must be treated with the necessary reverence and care; and

(ii) ***Clerical Ministry Register***: A Register documenting the service, appointments, and personal details of clergy members within a religious organisation; and

(iii) ***Sacramental Administration Register***: A Register recording the sacraments performed within a religious community, such as baptisms, confirmations, marriages, and funerals; and

(iv) ***Congregational Member Register***: A Register detailing the names, contact information, membership status, and participation in congregation activities; and

(v) ***Liturgical Administration Register***: A Register that tracks the planning, scheduling, and details of liturgical services and ceremonies within a religious organisation; and

(vi) ***Parochial Property Register***: A Register documenting all ecclesiastical-owned properties, assets, and related legal and financial information; and

(vii) ***Fiducial Administration Register***: A Register to track and manage fiduciary obligations and relationships, ensuring transparency and compliance; and

(viii) ***Pastoral Transmittal Register***: A Register documenting correspondence such as pastoral letters, instructions, and other important messages between higher ecclesiastical authorities and local congregations, ensuring proper dissemination and archival of institutional directives; and

(ix) ***Canonical Judicial Register***: A Register recording cases, verdicts, and canonical trials, ensuring accurate record-keeping and adherence to ecclesiastical laws and regulations.

1421. All valid Registers as Tables are constructed from some or all of the same essential elements being *Columna, Singulus, Eventus, Locus, Nomen, Informas, Datus, Informatio, Ordo* and *Recordo*:-    *Elements of Registers*

(i) *Columna* (from Latin meaning "pillar or post") means a vertical line of entries (a column), usually read from top to bottom and separated from other columns by lines; and

(ii) *Singulus* (from Latin meaning "one each, single; unique") means a unique column being the first and left most column whereby a whole integer is listed and is sequential (beginning from the integer 1) and unique (not the same) in reference to the table; and

(iii) *Eventus* (from Latin meaning "event, occurrence, reality") means a column whereby the Ucadia Date and Time of a unique event as well any other referential time (such as Roman Date/Time) always in brackets is listed; and

(iv) *Locus* (from Latin meaning "place or locality") means a column whereby the Ucadia Location Number of Sacred Circumscribed Space and any common name as to the location of the unique event is listed; and

(v) *Nomen* (from Latin meaning "name or title") means a column whereby a name is given to the event or the object or concept or property or rights associated with the event; and

(vi) *Informas* (from Latin meaning "the one who informs, instructs, educates") means a column whereby a name of the one who granted the authority to have the entry made into the Register; and

(vii) *Datus* (from Latin meaning "given, offered or yielded") means the Ucadia Date and Time the grant was given by the Informant as well as any other referential time such as Roman Date/Time in Square Brackets that the entry was made; and

(viii) *Informatio* (from Latin meaning "sketch, idea, conception") means any additional information provided by the Informant that may be separated into its own unique columns; and

(ix) *Ordo* (meaning "row, order") means the line of entries in a table, from left to right that when completed forms a valid Record; and

(x) *Recordo* (meaning "completed or valid row") means a complete line of entries into the columns of the table from left to right such that the record has its own unique form and is "Legal Title".

1422. The Record Number, also known as Record No. and Singulus (from Latin meaning "one each, single; unique") shall be the unique column being the first and left most column of a valid Register, whereby a whole integer shall be listed and is sequential (beginning from the integer 1) and unique (not the same) in reference to the table. The Record Number may also be called the shortened name of the table as a means of condensing both the name of the Register and the uniqueness of the number itself providing such a shortened name is itself unique in reference to all valid and legitimate Registers.  <small>Record Number</small>

1423. The original entry into a Register may be by hand or by typing and providing there exists a declaration from the Registrar to the effect, all type written or type entered records shall be treated as if hand  <small>Entry into Registers</small>

written.

1424. It is permissible to treat a Register as an electronic version and for printed copies of pages, rather than printed copies to be the originals. — *Electronic Registers*

1425. Any claim, or attempted or actual registration of Ucadia related material, marks, symbols, names, instruments, rights and property into a foreign jurisdiction contrary to the rights and obligations prescribed by the sacred Covenant *Pactum De Singularis Caelum* and these Maxims is a grave transgression before all Heaven and the Earth and every Member of the Sons of Light and Fraternal Brothers and Sisters of Light are fully empowered by Holy Writ, to pursue any, every and all means to ensure any and all records of such profanity, sacrilege and abomination before all Heaven and Earth are expunged, removed, withdrawn, determined, extinguished and abolished, including any and all false presumptions of claiming such false rights. — *Ucadia Property and Registers*

## Article 391 - Sacred Objects Register

1426. A *Sacred Objects Register* is the first of nine (9) primary types of valid *Ecclesiastical Registers* being a Register detailing sacred items of cultural, religious, or historical significance that must be treated with the necessary reverence and care. — *Sacred Objects Register*

1427. A *Sacred Objects Register* of a valid Religious or Spiritual Society represents by default its Register of Registers whereby each and every valid Register of the Religious or Spiritual Society shall be duly recorded as a sacred and valuable object. — *Sacred Objects Register as Register of Ecclesiastical Registers*

## Article 392 – Clerical Ministry Register

1428. A *Clerical Ministry Register* is the second of nine (9) primary types of valid *Ecclesiastical Registers* being a Register documenting the service, appointments, and personal details of clergy members within a religious organisation. — *Clerical Ministry Register*

1429. All authentic and valid Religious and Spiritual Societies are expected to maintain up to date registers of Clerics, including their vows, ordination dates and ecclesiastical appointments. — *Requirement of all valid Clerics to be Registered*

1430. The legitimacy, morality and validity of any Ecclesiastical Authority or Power depends upon the Recipient and such powers being listed within a valid Clerical Ministry Register:- — *All Recipients of Ecclesiastical Authority or Power listed in Clerical Ministry Register*

    (i) In the absence of a valid record of an authority or power against the name of the Minister or Cleric, no legitimate authority or power exists; and

    (ii) A party subject to an ecclesiastical authority or power has the reasonable right to be given access to the appropriate Clerical Ministry Register or a valid extract of a record as proof of the validity of such an ecclesiastical authority; and

(iii) The failure to produce a valid extract of such a record of authority or power against the name of the Minister or Cleric when a reasonable right of request is exercised is the same as a declaration of no authority or power and disqualification.

## Article 393 – Sacramental Administration Register

1431. A *Sacramental Administration Register* is the third of nine (9) primary types of valid *Ecclesiastical Registers* being a Register recording the sacraments performed within a religious community.

Sacramental Administration Register

1432. Common *Sacramental Administration Registers* include (but are not limited to):-

Common Sacramental Administration Registers

   (i) **Baptismal Register**: Records of baptisms performed within a congregation, documenting the baptism date, the name of the baptized individual and witnesses; and

   (ii) **Marriage (Matrimonial) Register**: Documents marriages performed, including names of the bride and groom, the date and location of the marriage, names of witnesses, and officiating clergy; and

   (iii) **Reconciliation Register**: Records of first penance or reconciliation, typically documenting the name of the penitent and the date of the sacrament; and

   (iv) **Anointing of the Sick Register**: Records the administration of the anointing of the sick, including the name of the sick person, the date, and the name of the officiating clergy; and

   (v) **Death and Burial Register**: The deaths of members, including date of death, date of burial, and place of burial.

1433. Where one (or more) Civil Registers are connected publicly, privately or secretly with one or more Ecclesiastical sacramental rites, events, laws or practices, then such registers must be first treated as *Sacramental Administration Registers*.

Civil Registry as Ecclesiastical Register

1434. Any Ecclesiastical Sacramental Register, whether also a Civil register or not, shall be automatically and wholly rendered null, void, without force or effect and to be suppressed and never revived if any of the severe Ecclesiastical Offences can be established without dispute:-

Automatic Nullity of Complete Ecclesiastical Sacramental Register

   (i) **Persistent Desecration and Blasphemous Purpose**:

That a register has been so corrupted as to persistently record false, incomplete or misleading information concerning the administration of a Sacrament; and

(ii) ***Nullity and Invalidity is Automatic***: That no court ruling, edict or acknowledgment is needed on the part of a forum of law, or judge or the registrars who have continued to commit deliberately false, immoral, misleading and blasphemous corruptions of such a register; and

(iii) ***All related actions and judgments null and void***: The nullity of such a register renders any and all actions, rulings and transaction null and void from the beginning (ab initio); and

(iv) ***All true records transferred to Ucadia Register for moral purpose***: To the extent that true information is mixed with false or incomplete information means that automatically (from the beginning) a new Ucadia Ecclesiastical Register shall have been formed with the true information, as if the false register had never existed. Such an authentic register of vital records and ecclesiastical sacramental administration shall only be available and accessible to Ucadia endorsed and authorised societies and bodies; and

(v) ***Registrars, Clerics, Societies and Bodies culpable of fraud have no right of objection or refusal***: On the severity of systematic fraud associated with a Sacramental Administrative Register means no registrar, cleric, society or government body has any power, authority or right to object or refuse the automatic alienation as set forth to ensure true, complete and correct records exist.

## Article 394 – Congregational Member Register

1435. A *Congregational Member Register* is the fourth of nine (9) primary types of valid *Ecclesiastical Registers* being a Register detailing the names, contact information, membership status, and participation in congregation activities.

1436. Examples of *Congregational Member Registers* include (but are not limited to):-

(i) ***Membership Register***: Details such as full name, date of birth, date of baptism (if applicable), date of joining the congregation, and contact information; and

(ii) ***Attendance Register***: Attendance of members at regular services, meetings, and special events; and

(iii) **_Donations Register_**: Financial contributions made by members, including tithes, offerings, and special donations; and

(iv) **_Volunteer Register_**: Logs volunteer activities and service contributions of members, detailing the nature of the service, time spent, and any notable accomplishments; and

(v) **_Disciplinary Actions Register_**: Records any disciplinary actions taken against members, including details of the offence and the action taken; and

(vi) **_Membership Status Register_**: Records changes in membership status, such as active, inactive, suspended, or sanctioned members.

## Article 395 – Liturgical Administration Register

1437. A **_Liturgical Administration Register_** is the fifth of nine (9) primary types of valid *Ecclesiastical Registers* being a Register that tracks the planning, scheduling, and details of liturgical services and ceremonies within a religious organisation. Liturgical Administration Register

1438. Examples of *Liturgical Administration Registers* include (but are not limited to):- Examples of Liturgical Administration Registers

(i) **_Intentions Registers_**: Record the intentions whereby Liturgical Services were offered, including the names of those for whom prayers were requested; and

(ii) **_Sermon Registers_**: Records of sermons delivered by the clergy; and

(iii) **_Liturgical Registers_**: Documentation of the liturgical services held at the place of worship including special services.

## Article 396 – Parochial Property Register

1439. A **_Parochial Property Register_** is the sixth of nine (9) primary types of valid *Ecclesiastical Registers* being a Register documenting all ecclesiastical-owned properties, assets, and related legal and financial information. Parochial Property Register

1440. Examples of *Parochial Property Registers* include (but are not limited to):- Examples of Parochial Property Registers

(i) **_Property Registers_**: Related to the ownership, sale, and maintenance of ecclesiastical property; and

(ii) **Inventory Registers**: Detailed listings of ecclesiastical property, including furnishings, vestments, and sacred vessels.

## Article 397 – Fiducial Administration Register

1441. A **Fiducial Administration Register** is the seventh of nine (9) primary types of valid *Ecclesiastical Registers* being a Register to track and manage fiduciary obligations and relationships, ensuring transparency and compliance.

1442. Examples of *Fiducial Administration Registers* include (but are not limited to):-

(i) **Financial Registers**: Accounts, receipts, and financial statements of ecclesiastical income and expenditures; and

(ii) **Chancery Registers**: Official ecclesiastical documents that record administrative, legal, and judicial activities within a provincial jurisdiction. They include decrees, licenses, dispensations, court rulings, and other clerical matters overseen by the chancery office of a senior cleric; and

(iii) **Vestry Registers**: Detailing the administrative, financial, and sometimes demographic activities of a local congregation, including meeting minutes and financial transactions.

## Article 398 – Pastoral Transmittal Register

1443. A **Pastoral Transmittal Register** is the eighth of nine (9) primary types of valid *Ecclesiastical Registers* being a Register documenting correspondence such as pastoral letters, instructions, and other important messages between higher ecclesiastical authorities and local congregations, ensuring proper dissemination and archival of institutional directives.

1444. Examples of *Pastoral Transmittal Registers* include (but are not limited to):-

(i) **Correspondence Registers**: Letters and communications between local officials, parishioners, and other entities; and

(ii) **Bulletins and Newsletter Registers**: Periodic publications issued by a local jurisdiction of worship for its members.

### Article 399 – Canonical Judicial Register

**1445.** A *Canonical Judicial Register* is the ninth of nine (9) primary types of valid *Ecclesiastical Registers* being a Register recording cases, verdicts, and canonical trials, ensuring accurate record-keeping and adherence to ecclesiastical laws and regulations.

*Canonical Judicial Register*

**1446.** Examples of *Canonical Judicial Registers* include (but are not limited to):-

*Examples of Canonical Judicial Register*

    (i) ***Consistory Court Registers***: Documents related to the ecclesiastical court proceedings, including trials, decisions, and decrees; and

    (ii) ***Visitation Registers***: Reports from senior clerical visitations including inspections and assessments of parishes.

## 9.2 – False, Absurd and Prohibited Ecclesiastical Registers

### Article 400 – False, Absurd and Prohibited Ecclesiastical Register

**1447.** A *False, Absurd and Prohibited Ecclesiastical Register* is a purported ecclesiastical register of false or erroneous records. A register that is properly exposed as false, morally repugnant, deliberately corrupted is therefore without ecclesiastical validity or authority.

*False, Absurd and Prohibited Ecclesiastical Register*

# Title X – Consecrated Life

## 10.1 – Consecrated Life

### Article 401 - Consecrated Life

1448. *Consecrated Life* refers to a way of living dedicated to spiritual and religious values expressed through the formal institutional structures, rules and rites of one (or more) religious communities, to more fully devote oneself to spiritual service and the mission of a faith.  
*Consecrated Life*

1449. *Consecrated Life* is one of two primary and authentic ways of living that the faiths of One Christ, One Islam and One Spirit are entrusted by the Divine Creator to cultivate for all faithful. The other way is the less formal and more individualised way of *Sacred Life*.  
*Consecrated Life and Organised Faith*

1450. The common characteristics of *Consecrated Life* include (but are not limited to):-  
*Characteristics of Consecrated Life*

    (i) **Community Life**: Those in consecrated life typically live within a community setting (e.g., monasteries, convents, or religious orders); and

    (ii) **Strict (Canonical) Interpretation**: Governed by specific canonical laws and ecclesiastical authority within the framework of the religious institution; and

    (iii) **Institutional Support**: Often a structured support network, including spiritual directors, community leaders, and institutional resources; and

    (iv) **Formal Commitment**: Involves formal vows (poverty, chastity, and obedience) and usually an official recognition by a religious community; and

    (v) **Specific Dress or Garments**: Often wear specific religious garments or habits that signify their commitment.

1451. *Consecrated Life* by definition is one of two authentic ways that the Three Great Faiths instituted by the Divine Creator through the most sacred Covenant *Pactum De Singularis Caelum* are required to deliver to the faithful. Therefore it is not superior compared to *Sacred Life*, but a different and necessary path:-  
*Consecrated Life vs Sacred Life*

    (i) **A Community Way**: Consecrated Life is a more community orientated way compared to the individualistic way of Sacred Life; and

    (ii) **A Formal Way**: Consecrated Life is by definition more formal and strict than the way of Sacred Life; and

    (iii) **An Institutional Way**: Consecrated Life is by definition a stable component and foundation to broader society and its institutions.

1452. Six (6) Primary Levels recognised in the development and evolution of Consecrated Life including (but not limited to):- Levels of Consecrated Life

    (i) **Acolyte**: An individual actively searching for spiritual understanding, religious truth, or personal calling through assistance and following of the practices of a religious community or institute; and

    (ii) **Novice**: An individual in the beginning stage of joining a religious community or institute, undergoing formation and training; and

    (iii) **Initiate**: An individual who has undergone first vows to formally join a religious community or institute and participate in training to become a full member; and

    (iv) **Minister**: An individual who has graduated training, completed further vows and is authorised to conduct certain liturgical and sacramental services; and

    (v) **Cleric**: An individual who has received Holy Orders and is then authorised to perform sacred duties such as leading worship, administering sacraments, and providing spiritual guidance; and

    (vi) **Mendicant**: An individual who has voluntarily taken the strictest of vows in renouncing personal possessions, mendicants focus on preaching, serving the poor, and living in poverty.

1453. The Honorary and Official Titles of Clerics relates to the seniority and positions of authority of certain Offices and individuals within a particular faith and not the six (6) Primary Levels of Consecrated Life. It is a fundamental and ignorant error to conclude that the incumbent of a senior clerical position is somehow by virtue of their office (ex-officio) a higher level of Consecrated Life. Levels of Consecrated Life and Honorary Titles of Clerics

1454. Without dispute, the calling to Consecrated Life is open equally to men and women, regardless of race or economic status or faith:- Gender and Calling to Consecrated Life

    (i) No valid and proper Religious or Spiritual Society is permitted to judge a calling to Consecrated Life as more or less worthy based upon gender alone. However, a valid faith holding to a customary tradition has a right to consider gender one of the conditions of senior clerical office; and

(ii) Without prejudice to those acknowledged Customary and Traditional Rites, all valid Religious or Spiritual Societies are compelled to full equality of gender during its sacred lifetime.

## Article 402 - Acolyte

1455. ***Acolyte*** is the formal title for the first of six levels of *Consecrated Life* whereby an individual is actively searching for spiritual understanding, religious truth, or personal calling through assistance and following of the practices of a religious community or institute.

*Acolyte*

## Article 403 - Novice

1456. ***Novice*** is the formal title for the second of six levels of *Consecrated Life* whereby an individual reaches the beginning stage of joining a religious community or institute and commences their formation and training.

*Novice*

1457. All Supplicants to Clerical Life must be interviewed over a period of not less than nine months, to discern their competency in seven core qualities being:-

*Novice as Supplicant to Clerical Life*

    (i) *Scholastic Respect*, means that the Supplicant has completed higher studies or is committed to completing higher studies upon being accepted to a Novitiate; and

    (ii) *Emotional Honesty*, means that the Supplicant has undergone thorough psychological and emotional interview to gauge their emotional maturity and suitability for the form of consecrated life they seek; and

    (iii) *Courageous Commitment*, means the Supplicant demonstrates a willingness and ability to remain focused and disciplined and to restore their dedication in the event of challenges or doubts; and

    (iv) *Heartfelt Enthusiasm*, means the Supplicant is passionate and enthusiastic as to their request and sense of calling; and

    (v) *Authentic Compassion*, means the Supplicant possesses and demonstrates authentic compassion, mercy and care towards others as an outward focus of their calling, beyond any inward calling for a scholastic or meditative form of consecrated life; and

    (vi) *Humble Cheerfulness*, means the Supplicant possesses a joyous and happy disposition and is not grossly affected by senses of ego, or pride; and

(vii) *Objective Discernment*, means the Supplicant demonstrates an objective discernment of themselves and the world around them.

## Article 404 - Initiate

1458. ***Initiate*** is the formal title for the third of six levels of *Consecrated Life* whereby an individual has undergone first vows to formally join a religious community or institute and participate in training to become a full member. — Initiate

1459. Upon acceptance, a new Initiate makes a Temporary Profession for a period defined in proper law; it is not to be less than three (3) years nor longer than six (6). For the validity of temporary profession it is required that:- — Conditions of Initiate

(i) The person who is to make it has completed at least eighteen (18) years of age; and

(ii) The novitiate has been validly completed; and

(iii) Admission has been given freely by the competent superior with the vote of the council according to the norm of law; and

(iv) The profession is expressed and made without force, grave fear, or malice; and

(v) The profession is received by a legitimate superior personally or through another.

## Article 405 - Minister

1460. ***Minister*** is the formal title for the fourth of six levels of *Consecrated Life* whereby an individual has graduated training, completed further vows and is authorised to conduct certain liturgical and sacramental services. — Minister

1461. Ministers are bound by a special obligation to show reverence and obedience firstly to these Maxims and the sacred Covenant *Pactum De Singularis Caelum* and secondly to the competent authority of their own faith and superiors. — Obedience

1462. By consent, vow and ordination, Ministers of a particular Religious or Spiritual Society are bound to pursue exemplary and virtuous lives, and to demonstrate moral leadership for their community:- — Mission of Ministers

(i) Fulfilling faithfully and tirelessly the duties bestowed upon them, especially when concerning pastoral care; and

(ii) Honouring the sacred ceremonies of their faith and adherence to such ritual as regular as is considered proper as devotion; and

(iii) Meditating, Praying and Invoking guidance and assistance for the sick, the weak, the dying and those in need of care and assistance; and

(iv) Respect and wear suitable ecclesiastical garb according to the norms issued by the competent authority of their faith; and

(v) Foster simplicity of life and are to refrain from all things that have a semblance of vanity; and

(vi) Refrain completely from all those things which are unbecoming to their state, according to the prescripts of particular law.

1463. Notwithstanding a pledge to a simple life refraining from an abundance of possessions and wealth, Ministers are entitled to remuneration which is consistent with their service and specific nature of their functions, especially places and times, and by which they can provide for the necessities of their life as well as for the equitable payment of those whose services they need. — *Remuneration*

1464. Throughout their service, Ministers are expected to continue to acquire knowledge of other sciences, especially of those which are connected with the sacred sciences, particularly insofar as such knowledge contributes to the exercise of pastoral ministry. — *Knowledge*

## Article 406 - Cleric

1465. ***Cleric*** is the formal title for the fifth of six levels of *Consecrated Life* whereby an individual has received Holy Orders and is then authorised to perform sacred duties such as leading worship, administering sacraments, and providing spiritual guidance. — *Cleric*

1466. Chastity is a state of voluntary abstinence from any form of sexual relations, stimulation or activity:- — *Chastity and Clerical Life*

(i) Chastity is enacted as one of the Three Sacred Vows of an Exemplary Consecrated Life; and

(ii) Chastity is one of the greatest demonstrations of universal love, self sacrifice and objective service to humanity in maintaining the union of the Covenant uniting Heaven and Earth. However, such a vow cannot be imposed or demanded without grossly damaging its sacredness and integrity; and

(iii) Universal demands for Chastity or Celibacy across all levels of

Consecrated Life are an abomination, profane, sacrilegious, reprobate and to be suppressed and never revived; and

(iv) The most sacred vow of Chastity shall be reserved for those consecrated and ordained Clerics of suitable temperament and competence to strengthen and guide; and

(v) Senior Clerics are expected to have taken the sacred vow of Chastity for the duration of their incumbency; and

(vi) In respect of religious communities of consecrated life seeking to live an exemplary and holy existence, it is expected that all members of such a fraternity take the sacred vow of Chastity; and

(vii) In respect of secular communities of consecrated life, possessing the Divine Commission of sovereign or military orders, the sacred vow of Chastity is regarded as a condition of such a high sacred calling.

1467. Sexuality is the capacity, predilection and orientation of a man or woman in respect of another member of the species, or some other life form regarding sexual relations, stimulation or sexual activity:- *Sexuality and Clerical Life*

(i) All valid and proper Religious and Spiritual Societies are expected to be resolute in condemning depraved, injurious and criminal acts of sexual abuse of minors, or perverted sexual acts with other forms of life; and

(ii) A Supplicant for Clerical life cannot be ruled ineligible purely upon their sexual orientation of heterosexuality or homosexuality alone; and

(iii) The suitability of a Supplicant shall always be based upon their complete aptitude and competence for the type of Clerical life they seek, where one of the conditions may require a vow of Chastity; and

(iv) A Cleric with homosexual orientation is wholly unsuited for a community and pastoral commission, whereby a valid and proper Religious or Spiritual Society guides and protects the heterosexual family unit as the foundation stone of civilised life; and

(v) A Cleric with homosexual orientation may be suited for life within a Religious Community under the sacred vow of Chastity; and

(vi) Active homosexual relations and activities among clerics within Religious Communities is strictly forbidden and represents a grievous threat not only to the integrity and survival of such institutes, but the faith as a whole.

## Article 407 - Mendicant

**1468.** ***Mendicant*** is the formal title for the sixth of six levels and highest level of *Consecrated Life* whereby an individual has voluntarily taken the strictest of vows in renouncing personal possessions. Mendicants focus on preaching, serving the poor, and living in poverty.

*Mendicant*

## 10.2 – False and Prohibited Notions of Consecrated Life

### Article 408 - False and Prohibited Notions of Consecrated Life

**1469.** False and Prohibited Notions of Consecrated Life include misinterpretations that undermine its core principles. These may involve excessive asceticism, neglecting community life, or pursuing personal gain. Such views distort the true essence of consecration, which focuses on selfless service, communal living, and adherence to formal vows of self restraint.

*False and Prohibited Notions of Consecrated Life*

# Title XI – Sacred Life

## 11.1 – Sacred Life

### Article 409 - Sacred Life

1470. **Sacred Life** refers to a way of living dedicated to spiritual and religious values expressed through individual moral conduct, rituals and devotions that are usually separate from the formal institutional structures of religious communities, to more fully develop a closer relationship with the Divine. [Sacred Life]

1471. *Sacred Life* is one of two primary and authentic ways of living that the faiths of One Christ, One Islam and One Spirit are entrusted by the Divine Creator to cultivate for all faithful. The other way is the more formal and religious community focused way of *Consecrated Life*. [Sacred Life and Organised Faith]

1472. The common characteristics of *Sacred Life* include (but are not limited to):- [Characteristics of Sacred Life]

    (i) **Individualistic Approach**: Often live independently and are self-guided in their spiritual practices and commitments; and

    (ii) **Broad Interpretation**: Can be interpreted in a broader sense, encompassing various spiritual traditions and personal interpretations of a sacred existence; and

    (iii) **Diverse Practices**: Can be highly individualized, encompassing a range of spiritual disciplines, meditation, prayer, or personal devotions; and

    (iv) **Informal Commitment**: Can be less formal, with personal vows or commitments that might not be officially recognized by a religious institution; and

    (v) **Flexibility**: Generally more flexibility in how one lives out their spiritual commitment, allowing adaptation to personal circumstances.

1473. *Sacred Life* by definition is one of two authentic ways that the Three Great Faiths instituted by the Divine Creator through the most sacred Covenant *Pactum De Singularis Caelum* are required to deliver to the faithful. Therefore it is not superior compared to *Consecrated Life*, but a different and necessary path:- [Sacred Life vs Consecrated Life]

    (i) **An Individualistic Way**: Sacred Life is a more individualistic way compared to the community way of Consecrated Life; and

(ii) **A Flexible Way**: Sacred Life is by definition a less formal and strict way than Consecrated Life; and

(iii) **A Non-Institutional Way**: Sacred Life by definition promotes the necessary path of all individuals for the well being, assistance and future of societies.

1474. Six (6) Primary Levels recognised in the development and evolution of Sacred Life including (but not limited to):- *[Levels of Sacred Life]*

(i) **Seeker**: An individual actively searching for spiritual understanding, religious truth, or personal enlightenment; and

(ii) **Aspirant**: An individual in the beginning stages of subscribing to a particular discipline and training program, demonstrating commitment, preparation, and a desire to fulfil higher spiritual or vocational aspirations; and

(iii) **Devotee**: An individual who upon undergoing the necessary training and knowledge of a religion, deity or spiritual practice, demonstrates their faith and loyalty through continuous devotion and adherence to the tenets of their spiritual path; and

(iv) **Practitioner**: An individual who has graduated training, completed further vows and is authorised and competent to conduct certain spiritual or meditative practices, integrating these activities into their daily life to cultivate deeper understanding and personal growth; and

(v) **Adept**: An individual highly skilled or proficient in a particular area, especially within spiritual or esoteric disciplines, possessing advanced knowledge and mastery from extensive practice and study, often guiding others on their path through expertise and insightful understanding; and

(vi) **Mystic**: An individual who has voluntarily taken the strictest of vows in renouncing personal possessions, to cultivate a deep, direct connection with the divine or ultimate reality through contemplation, meditation, and spiritual practices.

1475. The Honorary and Official Titles of Spiritual and Religious Teachers relates to the seniority and positions of authority of certain Offices and individuals within a particular faith and not the six (6) Primary Levels of Sacred Life. It is a fundamental and ignorant error to conclude that the incumbent of a senior spiritual position is somehow by virtue of their office (ex-officio) a higher level of Sacred Life. *[Levels of Sacred Life and Honorary Titles of Spiritual Teachers]*

### Article 410 - Seeker

**1476.** ***Seeker*** is the formal title for the first of six levels of *Sacred Life* whereby an individual is actively searching for spiritual understanding, religious truth, or personal enlightenment outside of formal religious community life.

Seeker

### Article 411 - Aspirant

**1477.** ***Aspirant*** is the formal title for the second of six levels of *Sacred Life* whereby an individual who has reached the beginning stages of subscribing to a particular discipline and training program, demonstrating commitment, preparation, and a desire to fulfil higher spiritual or vocational aspirations.

Aspirant

### Article 412 - Devotee

**1478.** ***Devotee*** is the formal title for the third of six levels of *Sacred Life* whereby an individual who has undergone the necessary beginning training and knowledge of a religion, deity or spiritual practice; and demonstrates their faith and loyalty through continuous devotion and adherence to the tenets of their spiritual path.

Devotee

### Article 413 - Practitioner

**1479.** ***Practitioner*** is the formal title for the fourth of six levels of *Sacred Life* whereby an individual who has graduated training, completed further vows and is authorised and competent to conduct certain spiritual or meditative practices, integrating these activities into their daily life to cultivate deeper understanding and personal growth.

Practitioner

### Article 414 - Adept

**1480.** ***Adept*** is the formal title for the fifth of six levels of *Sacred Life* whereby an individual highly skilled or proficient in a particular area, especially within spiritual or esoteric disciplines, possessing advanced knowledge and mastery from extensive practice and study, often guiding others on their path through expertise and insightful understanding.

Adept

### Article 415 - Mystic

**1481.** ***Mystic*** is the formal title for the sixth and highest level of *Sacred Life* whereby an individual is who has voluntarily taken the strictest of vows in renouncing personal possessions, to cultivate a deep,

Mystic

direct connection with the divine or ultimate reality through contemplation, meditation, and spiritual practices.

## 11.2 – Sacred Path

### Article 416 - Sacred Path

1482. ***Sacred Path*** refers to a journey or process of personal and spiritual development aimed at achieving a deeper understanding of oneself and the universe.  *Sacred Path*

1483. Common and Important Types of Sacred Paths include (but are not limited to):-  *Common Types of Sacred Paths*

    (i) ***Sacred Matrimony (Marriage)***: Whereby a man and a woman who have received the Sacred Gift of Unification and Rite of Matrimony choose to continue, overcome, share and grow upon a life path together. Sacred Matrimony is the cornerstone and bedrock of civilised society; and

    (ii) ***Sacred Union***: Whereby two or more consenting adults choose to unite in life experiences and continue, overcome, share and grow upon a life path together; and

    (iii) ***Sacred Vacation***: Whereby an individual takes an extended period of leave or break and steps away from their regular duties, work or routines to undertake a period of personal renewal, spiritual growth, contemplation and deepened connection with their faith and inner self; and

    (iv) ***Sacred Pilgrimage***: Whereby an individual chooses to take an arduous and challenging journey to visit a sacred place or shrine; and

    (v) ***Sacred Curriculum***: Whereby an individual chooses to take a period of leave or break from their regular duties, work or routines to undertake a period of formal religious or spiritual study; and

    (vi) ***Sacred Sponsor***: Whereby an individual chooses to invest a regular series of periods of their time and resources to sponsor and mentor one or more individuals or groups in their journey and life goals; and

    (vii) ***Sacred Service***: Whereby an individual chooses to take a period of leave or break from their regular duties, work or routines to undertake a period of volunteer service to support and physically assist one or more individuals or groups.

## Article 417 - Sacred Matrimony (Marriage)

1484. ***Sacred Matrimony (Marriage)*** is a Sacred Path whereby a man and a woman who have received the Sacred Gift of Unification and Rite of Matrimony choose to continue, overcome, share and grow upon a life path together. Sacred Matrimony is the cornerstone and bedrock of civilised society.
<!-- margin: Sacred Matrimony (Marriage) -->

1485. Key elements associated with the path of *Sacred Matrimony* include (but are not limited to):-
<!-- margin: Key Elements of Path of Sacred Matrimony -->

    (i) ***Sacrament of Matrimony***: That the man and woman did participate in and receive the Sacrament of Matrimony, rather than a secular ceremony; and

    (ii) ***Focusing First on Being Best of Friends***: To cultivate a deep and lasting friendship that can weather any storm or challenge, beyond mere physical attraction; and

    (iii) ***Focusing Second on Being Life Partners***: Where two people choose to jointly experience different life events together and with family, rather than to experience life alone; and

    (iv) ***Legal Relations to least important concern***: Notwithstanding sound financial planning, that the legal relation of being husband and wife is the least important of concerns.

1486. Some of the challenges commonly associated with undertaking the path of *Sacred Matrimony* include (but are not limited to):-
<!-- margin: Challenges associated with the Path of Sacred Matrimony -->

    (i) ***Temptations of Modern Life***: Never before have there been so many choices of pleasure, infidelity and distractions to temporarily damage trust in any relationship. However, many couples are often unable to learn, to grow and to overcome possible bad choices when they arise; and

    (ii) ***Stresses of Modern Life***: Never before have there been so many direct stresses aimed at dividing couples and families from one another even at the smallest issue. This is not helped by modern "lifestyle" philosophies that encourage isolationist choices, rather than weathering the inevitable storms of life together.

1487. Some of the benefits commonly associated with undertaking the path of *Sacred Matrimony* include (but are not limited to):-
<!-- margin: Benefits associated with the Path of Sacred Matrimony -->

    (i) ***Positive Mental and Physical Health***: Overwhelmingly human life is to be shared together and not alone. Credible scientific studies repeatedly demonstrate that a positive, stimulating and lasting relation directly contributes to our health and mental well being; and

(ii) ***Personal Growth***: Overcoming the real challenges and responsibilities of marriage promotes personal and spiritual development; and

(iii) ***Supportive Environment for Children***: A stable marriage typically provides a nurturing and stable environment for raising children, which can have long-term positive effects on their development.

## Article 418 - Sacred Union

1488. ***Sacred Union*** is a Sacred Path whereby two or more consenting adults choose to unite in life experiences and continue to overcome, share and grow upon a life path together. Sacred Union is an essential Sacrament as *Ius Ecclesiae Sacramentum Amalgamatio*. — Sacred Union

1489. Key elements associated with the path of *Sacred Union* include (but are not limited to):- — Key Elements of Path of Sacred Union

(i) ***Focusing First on Being Best of Friends***: To cultivate a deep and lasting friendship that can weather any storm or challenge, beyond mere physical attraction; and

(ii) ***Focusing Second on Being Life Partners***: Where two people choose to jointly experience different life events together and with family, rather than to experience life alone; and

(iii) ***Sacramental Recognition as Incidental***: That any sacramental recognition of a Union is secondary to the strength of bonds of friendship and life partners first.

1490. Some of the challenges commonly associated with undertaking the path of *Sacred Union* include (but are not limited to):- — Challenges associated with the Path of Sacred Union

(i) ***Temptations of Modern Life***: Never before have there been so many choices of pleasure, infidelity and distractions to temporarily damage trust in any relationship. However, many couples are often unable to learn, to grow and to overcome possible bad choices when they arise; and

(ii) ***Stresses of Modern Life***: Never before have there been so many direct stresses aimed at dividing couples and families from one another even at the smallest issue. This is not helped by modern "lifestyle" philosophies that encourage isolationist choices, rather than weathering the inevitable storms of life together.

1491. Some of the benefits commonly associated with undertaking the path of *Sacred Union* include (but are not limited to):- *(Benefits associated with the Path of Sacred Union)*

    (i) **Positive Mental and Physical Health**: Overwhelmingly human life is to be shared together and not alone. Credible scientific studies repeatedly demonstrate that a positive, stimulating and lasting relation directly contributes to our health and mental well being; and

    (ii) **Personal Growth**: Overcoming the real challenges and responsibilities of long term relations promotes personal and spiritual development.

## Article 419 - Sacred Vacation

1492. A **Sacred Vacation** is a Sacred Path whereby an individual takes an extended period of leave or break and steps away from their regular duties, work or routines to undertake a period of personal renewal, spiritual growth, contemplation and deepened connection with their faith and inner self. *(Sacred Vacation)*

1493. Key elements associated with the path of *Sacred Vacation* include (but are not limited to):- *(Key Elements of Path of Sacred Vacation)*

    (i) **Extended Period of Six (6) Months or More**: That the leave or break is at least six consecutive months or more; and

    (ii) **Unplanned or Loosely Planned Journey**: That a vacation is less planned than committing to an authentic course (Sacred Curriculum), or pilgrimage or period of service; and

    (iii) **A Focus on Personal and Spiritual Development**: That a Sacred Vacation is about personal and spiritual development more than simply a period of holidays and relaxation.

1494. Some of the challenges commonly associated with undertaking the path of *Sacred Vacation* include (but are not limited to):- *(Challenges associated with the Path of Sacred Vacation)*

    (i) **Finding the Time**: Meaning that overwhelmingly it is simply finding a dedicated period of time, free from commitments and obligations that is usually cited as the greatest challenge; and

    (ii) **Affording the Time-Off**: That for many, an extended period of non-income generation is not possible, without the risk of losing employment, assets and even relationships.

1495. Some of the benefits commonly associated with undertaking the path *(Benefits)* of *Sacred Vacation* include (but are not limited to):-

    (i)   **Mental Refresh & Renewal**: That such a time can significantly refresh and renew mental health and perspective, improving not only outlook on life, but effective productivity in the years that follow; and

    (ii)   **Physical Health & Well Being**: There is overwhelming evidence that taking breaks from relentless and stressful environments can help people begin to restore their physical health and well being; and

    (iii)   **Personal & Spiritual Growth**: That such an adventure of deep learning can have an important positive impact on personal & spiritual growth.

## Article 420 - Sacred Pilgrimage

1496. ***Sacred Pilgrimage*** is a Sacred Path whereby an individual chooses to take an arduous and challenging journey to visit a sacred place or shrine.

1497. Pilgrimage is an ancient expression of faith involving travel to sites of significant religious meaning. Pilgrimage serves as an act of devotion, seeking blessings, or fulfilling religious duties.

1498. Key elements associated with the path of *Sacred Pilgrimage* include (but are not limited to):-

    (i)   **Sacred Destination**: That the final destination of the pilgrimage is a recognised sacred site; and

    (ii)   **Arduous and Rustic Journey**: That the means of travel (at least for a good portion of the pilgrimage) is by foot; and a level of austerity and simplicity of accommodation and scarcity of modern comforts.

1499. Some of the challenges commonly associated with undertaking the path of *Sacred Pilgrimage* include (but are not limited to):-

    (i)   **Finding the Time**: Meaning that overwhelmingly it is simply finding a dedicated period of time, free from commitments and obligations that is usually cited as the greatest challenge; and

    (ii)   **Affording the Time-Off**: That for many, an extended period of non-income generation is not possible, without the risk of losing employment, assets and even relationships.

1500. Some of the benefits commonly associated with undertaking the path of *Sacred Pilgrimage* include (but are not limited to):-

(i) ***Mental Refresh & Renewal***: That such a time can significantly refresh and renew mental health and perspective, improving not only outlook on life, but effective productivity in the years that follow; and

(ii) ***Personal & Spiritual Growth***: That such an adventure of deep learning can have an important positive impact on personal & spiritual growth; and

(iii) ***Physical Health & Well Being***: There is overwhelming evidence that taking breaks from relentless and stressful environments can help people begin to restore their physical health and well being.

## Article 421 - Sacred Curriculum

1501. ***Sacred Curriculum*** is a Sacred Path whereby an individual chooses to take a period of leave or break from their regular duties, work or routines to undertake a period of formal religious or spiritual study.

1502. Key elements associated with the path of *Sacred Curriculum* include (but are not limited to):-

(i) ***Extended Period of Three (3) Months or More***: That the leave or break is at least three consecutive months or more; and

(ii) ***Recognised and Reputable Course Material***: That the course material is recognised as having genuine religious or spiritual merit and is not in conflict with the present Maxims; and

(iii) ***Credible and Reputable Tutor/Teacher***: That the primary teacher is recognised as having genuine religious or spiritual capacity, consistent with the present Maxims.

1503. Some of the challenges commonly associated with undertaking the path of *Sacred Curriculum* include (but are not limited to):-

(i) ***Finding the Time***: Meaning that overwhelmingly it is simply finding a dedicated period of time, free from commitments and obligations that is usually cited as the greatest challenge; and

(ii) ***Affording the Time-Off***: That for many, an extended period of non-income generation is not possible, without the risk of losing employment, assets and even relationships; and

(iii) ***Finding the right teacher and course***: As it is often difficult to discern the best course of action.

1504. Some of the benefits commonly associated with undertaking the path of *Sacred Curriculum* include (but are not limited to):-

    (i) **Personal & Spiritual Growth**: That such an adventure of deep learning can have an important positive impact on personal & spiritual growth.

## Article 422 - Sacred Sponsor

1505. ***Sacred Sponsor*** is a Sacred Path whereby an individual chooses to invest a regular series of periods of their time and resources to sponsor and mentor one or more individuals or groups in their journey and life goals.

1506. Key elements associated with the path of *Sacred Sponsor* include (but are not limited to):-

    (i) ***Extended Period of Support of Two (2) years or More***: That a commitment of financial and/or time support is given for a period for not less than two (2) years whereby the Sponsor is in regular contact with the individuals or group; and

    (ii) ***Uncompensated Support***: That the financial or time support is uncompensated and provided freely.

1507. Some of the challenges commonly associated with undertaking the path of *Sacred Sponsor* include (but are not limited to):-

    (i) **Finding the Time**: Meaning that overwhelmingly it is simply finding a dedicated period of time, free from commitments and obligations that is usually cited as the greatest challenge.

1508. Some of the benefits commonly associated with undertaking the path of *Sacred Sponsor* include (but are not limited to):-

    (i) **Lasting Legacy**: Sacred Sponsor often has a lasting and profoundly positive legacy on the people and groups mentored and is frequently a catalyst for further positive change, especially among poorer and marginalised groups; and

    (ii) **Personal & Spiritual Growth**: That such a process of support can have an important positive impact on personal & spiritual growth.

## Article 423 - Sacred Service

1509. ***Sacred Service*** is a Sacred Path whereby an individual chooses to take a period of leave or break from their regular duties, work or routines to undertake a period of volunteer service to support and physically assist one or more individuals or groups. Sacred Service

1510. Key elements associated with the path of *Sacred Service* include (but are not limited to):- Key Elements of Path of Sacred Service

    (i) ***Extended Period of Three (3) Months or More***: That the leave or break is at least three (3) consecutive months or more; and

    (ii) ***Charitable "Hand-On" Service***: That the time allocated involves specific "hand-on" service to support and physically assist one or more individuals or groups.

1511. Some of the challenges commonly associated with undertaking the path of *Sacred Service* include (but are not limited to):- Challenges associated with the Path of Sacred Service

    (i) ***Finding the Time***: Meaning that overwhelmingly it is simply finding a dedicated period of time, free from commitments and obligations that is usually cited as the greatest challenge; and

    (ii) ***Affording the Time-Off***: That for many, an extended period of non-income generation is not possible, without the risk of losing employment, assets and even relationships.

1512. Some of the benefits commonly associated with undertaking the path of *Sacred Service* include (but are not limited to):- Benefits associated with the Path of Sacred Service

    (i) ***Personal & Spiritual Growth***: That such an action of service can have an important positive impact on personal & spiritual growth.

## 11.3 – False and Prohibited Notions of Sacred Life

### Article 424 - False and Prohibited Notions of Sacred Life

1513. False and Prohibited Notions of Sacred Life include practices or beliefs that exploit spirituality for personal gain, promote extremism, or contradict core religious values. These misconceptions can lead to harmful behaviours, neglect of ethical principles, and misrepresentation of true spiritual teachings focused on love, compassion, and authentic devotion. False and Prohibited Notions of Sacred Life

# Title XII – Ecclesiastical Offence

## 12.1 – Ecclesiastical Offence

### Article 425 - Ecclesiastical Offence

1514. An ***Ecclesiastical Offence*** is a prohibited Act committed in violation of an *Ecclesiastical Law* that represents a sufficient and well formed *Rule*.

Ecclesiastical Offence

1515. In respect of Ecclesiastical Law being a sufficient and well formed Rule, a Civilised Rule must demonstrate the following minimum qualities:-

Ecclesiastical Law as a well formed Rule

   (i) The Rule must refer to at least one proper Right (Ius). If no Right then no Rule or Law; and

   (ii) The Rule must express or imply a moral Act (or *Droit*) as the right Action. A Rule is never permitted to express or imply a wrong, immoral or morally repugnant Act as the right Action; and

   (iii) The Rule may be expressed positively as a right Act (or *Droit*), with the wrong Act (or *Tort*) implied; or the Rule may be expressed negatively with the right Act implied; and

   (iv) If a ***Penalty*** related to the Rule is listed, then at least one ***Remedy*** must accompany the Penalty.

1516. No Ecclesiastical Offence exists when no valid Ecclesiastical Law exists:-

No Ecclesiastical Offence exists if no valid Ecclesiastical Law exists

   (i) An Ecclesiastical Rule that is morally repugnant, wrong, false or absurd cannot possibly be a valid Ecclesiastical Law as it cannot express or imply an immoral or morally repugnant Act as the right Action; and

   (ii) No person may be constrained by an Ecclesiastical Rule that is incapable of being properly expressed as a valid Ecclesiastical Law.

1517. A well formed and moral Religious or Spiritual Society possesses the inherit right to constrain those members of their faith with penal sanctions who commit Ecclesiastical Offences.

Jurisdiction of Ecclesiastical Sanctions

1518. It is a moral imperative that a proper and valid Religious or Spiritual Society expresses a comprehensive list of Ecclesiastical Offences that assert within its moral, teaching and authoritative jurisdiction:-

Moral Imperative of Comprehensive Ecclesiastical Offences

   (i) By default, a religious or spiritual body that is less moral and exemplary than a civil society temporarily loses its capacity and authority to speak and instruct on religious, moral and spiritual matters; and

(ii) A religious or spiritual body that speaks against certain acts as prohibited yet does not then express such acts as ecclesiastical offences, therefore temporarily has no moral authority, legitimacy or credibility to speak on such subject matters; and

(iii) A religious or spiritual body that places alleged offences against its name and reputation above all other forms of ecclesiastical offences, demonstrates itself as being completely out of touch with proper moral reasoning and Divine Law; and therefore temporarily morally corrupt and lacking any moral authority, legitimacy or credibility.

1519. The fifteen (15) Major Categories of Ecclesiastical Offences, in order of priority and severity, include:- Major Categories of Ecclesiastical Offences

(i) Offences against Stellar System; and

(ii) Offences against Planet; and

(iii) Offences against Moon; and

(iv) Offences against Humanity; and

(v) Offences against Ecosystem; and

(vi) Offences against Human Life; and

(vii) Offences against Animal Life; and

(viii) Offences against Non-Carbon Higher Order Life; and

(ix) Offences against Congregation; and

(x) Offences against Ecclesiastical Property; and

(xi) Offences against Ecclesiastical Decency & Morals; and

(xii) Offences against Ecclesiastical Justice; and

(xiii) Offences against Ecclesiastical Security & Order; and

(xiv) Offences against Ecclesiastical Sacraments; and

(xv) Offences against Ecclesiastical Society.

1520. Where an offender willingly shows remorse upon the first opportunity of hearing of the offences against them; and at such a plea does offer a reply of "culpable" to all charges brought against them, then such a man or woman shall be eligible to the minimum penalty options of the corresponding articles, known as ***Absolution*:-** Absolution

(i) If an offender does not offer a plea of admission and culpability to each and every charge brought before them at their pre-trial hearing, then they shall automatically not be eligible for Absolution, regardless of how many guilty plea's they offered to various charges; and

(ii) Regardless of the minimum sentences demanded by society for certain crimes, the importance of an offender offering a clear sign of early remorse, without having to undergo the time, expense and trauma of further court proceedings is significant; and

(iii) Firstly it is significant in that it clearly demonstrates on the part of the offender a level of remorse and guilt for their crimes. In this sense, one of the goals of sentencing being the object to limit the risk of re-offence is better served by such early recognition by an offender; and

(iv) Secondly, such early remorse and guilt shows a clear willingness of the offender to seek some form of resolution for their crime. Again, this benefits any sentence regime in that the offender clearly shows a willingness to move forward and make amends; and

(v) While the seriousness of some crimes means that a sentence, regardless of whether it qualifies as Absolution means that significant reductions of liberties and rights might be mandated, in most cases Absolution means an offender is entitled to undergo a shorter, more specific and intensive sentence than otherwise would be the case if they failed to admit such early guilt; and

(vi) Contrary to the historic principle of criminal code based on an 'eye for an eye', one of the greatest incentives for non-repeat offenders of crime in society is the chance to be absolved by society for one's crimes.

1521. Where an offender is not willing to show early remorse upon the first opportunity of hearing of the charges against them; and subsequently upon the completion of a trial or criminal hearing is found guilty of the said charges, then they shall be liable for the sentence regime known as ***Castigation***:-     *Castigation*

(i) If an offender does not offer a guilty plea to each and every charge brought before them at their pre-trial hearing, then they shall automatically not be eligible for Absolution, regardless of how many guilty plea's they offered to various charges; and

(ii) Where an offender is not willing to admit guilt for their crimes at an early stage, then the more traditional notion of punishment for crime is appropriate. However, considering that all but the very worst of crimes must take into account the eventual release of convicted criminals back into society, the concept of penitence is used; and

(iii) Unlike a man or woman who has admitted early to guilt and has shown a willingness to reform, a man or woman who refuses to admit guilt automatically indicates that a period of compulsory actions must be applied "against their will" for some period; and

(iv) It is only after such initial sentence elements are applied and that a man or woman finally admits their guilt that any kind of rehabilitation can commence; and

(v) In extreme cases where a convicted man or woman defiantly shows absolutely no guilt or remorse and even more rigorous regime of punishments must be considered to bring about some level of remorse, and eventual change of character. This then is the nature of penitence.

1522. The proper hierarchy of Law from Divine to valid Societies means that legitimate Ecclesiastical Offences shall always be higher in their applicability to members compared to Secular Offences such as Criminal and Civil Law:-

(i) A valid and legitimate Ecclesiastical Offence shall always take superior legal precedence over any Secular (Criminal or Civil Offence) on the same subject; and

(ii) In the absence of any Secular (Criminal or Civil Offence) on a subject defined as a legitimate Ecclesiastical Offence, the Ecclesiastical law shall take absolute legal precedence.

*Ecclesiastical and Secular Offences*

## Article 426 - Offences against Stellar System

1523. **Offences against a Stellar System** is the first of fifteen (15) *Major Categories of Ecclesiastical Offences* and refers to actions harmful to celestial bodies or their related space environments, including (but not limited to) nuclear or other particle attacks against a star or its key fields, damaging or draining its core fields or particle sources, disruption of large bodies in orbit and causing catastrophic failure of stellar system function.

*Offences against Stellar System*

1524. The Justifications for the inclusion into proper and valid Ecclesiastical Law of the Ecclesiastical *Offences against a Stellar System* include (but are not limited to):-

(i) **Stars as personification of Divine**: That Stars and their light have represented the personification of Divine beings

*Justifications for Inclusion of Offences against Stellar System*

since the earliest of human civilisations; and

(ii) ***Guard against the highest of all hubris and madness (Deicide)***: To protect the survival of humanity and other higher order life forms against the ultimate madness and hubris of temporal power that sees the destruction of stars akin to "defeating or killing God"; and

(iii) ***Respecting Cosmic Unity and Divine Creation***: That stars and celestial bodies have been seen for millennia as manifestations of the Divine, infusing the Cosmos with sacredness and unity; and

(iv) ***The Creators of Life Planets & Moons***: That Stars in their formation and operation are the creators of certain iron bodied planets and moons, as well as their position conducive for potential life; and

(v) ***Ultimate Protection against mass crimes against life***: That to destroy or deeply injure stars is to destroy life bearing planets or moons within such stellar systems.

1525. *Offences against a Stellar System* include (but are not limited to):-

**Offences causing injury against a Stellar System**

(i) Offences causing death; and

(ii) Offences causing permanent injury; and

(iii) Offences causing temporary injury; and

**Offences attempting injury against a Stellar System**

(iv) Offences attempting death; and

(v) Offences attempting permanent injury; and

(vi) Offences attempting temporary injury.

[margin: List of Offences against a Stellar System]

1526. The effect of inclusion of *Offences against a Stellar System* include (but are not limited to):-

(i) ***Restore Authentic Ecclesiastical Moral Authority***: That inclusion of Offences against a Stellar System firmly restores the moral and legal authority of valid religious and spiritual societies concerning such matters; and

(ii) ***Important Moral & Legal Deterrence***: That the codification of crimes against Stellar Systems serves as an important moral and legal deterrent. Knowing that severe and unified penalties exist for such actions will assist in mitigating future risk of individuals and empires from committing such

[margin: Effect of Inclusion of Offences against Stellar System] egregious acts.

## Article 427 - Offences against Planet

1527. **Offences against a Planet** is the second of fifteen (15) *Major Categories of Ecclesiastical Offences* and refers to actions including (but not limited to): Seeking or actually destroying a planet, or harming its life bearing capacity, or damaging its environment and ecosystems, including illegal deforestation, pollution, wildlife trafficking, and unsustainable exploitation of natural resources. Offences against Planet

1528. The Justifications for the inclusion into proper and valid Ecclesiastical Law of the *Offences against a Planet* include (but are not limited to):- Justifications for Inclusion of Offences against a Planet

    (i) **Stewardship of Life**: Life-bearing planets are unique and precious. A moral and ethical framework that respects and protects these environments reflects a recognition of the intrinsic value of life; and

    (ii) **Intergenerational Justice**: Current generations have a responsibility to preserve the planet for future generations. Codifying environmental protections helps ensure that future humans or other sentient beings can enjoy and benefit from the planet's resources; and

    (iii) **Legal Accountability**: Clear legal definitions and penalties ensure that those who harm the environment can be held accountable, thereby deterring potential violators; and

    (iv) **Promoting Moral Responsibility**: Codifying offences encourages individuals, corporations, and governments to act responsibly and adopt practices that minimize environmental harm.

1529. *Offences against a Planet* include (but are not limited to):- List of Offences against a Planet

**Offences causing injury against a Planet**

    (i) Offences causing death; and

    (ii) Offences causing permanent injury; and

    (iii) Offences causing temporary injury; and

**Offences attempting injury against a Planet**

    (iv) Offences attempting death; and

    (v) Offences attempting permanent injury; and

    (vi) Offences attempting temporary injury.

Title XII – Ecclesiastical Offence

1530. The effect of inclusion of *Offences against a Planet* include (but are not limited to):-

    (i) **Restore Authentic Ecclesiastical Moral Authority**: That inclusion of Offences against a Planet firmly restores the moral and legal authority of valid religious and spiritual societies concerning such matters; and

    (ii) **Important Moral & Legal Deterrence**: That the codification of crimes against a Planet serves as an important moral and legal deterrent. Knowing that severe and unified penalties exist for such actions will assist in mitigating future risk of individuals, groups and empires from committing such egregious acts; and

    (iii) **Restore Moral Accountability & Justice**: Such clearly defined offences enable the unified legal systems of organised faiths and nations to hold perpetrators accountable. This ensures the highest standards of Rule of Law apply across humanity whereby any individual or group, regardless of their powerful position, can be prosecuted for actions that harm humanity or other higher order life on a large scale.

*Effect of Inclusion of Offences against Planet*

## Article 428 - Offences against Moon

1531. *Offences against a Moon* is the third of fifteen (15) *Major Categories of Ecclesiastical Offences* and refers to actions including (but not limited to): Seeking or actually destroying a moon, or harming its life bearing capacity, or harmful contamination, or damaging its surface and environment.

*Offences against Moon*

1532. The Justifications for the inclusion into proper and valid Ecclesiastical Law of the *Offences against a Moon* include (but are not limited to):-

*Justifications for Inclusion of Offences against Moon*

    (i) **Survival and Well-Being of Life on Earth**: Life on Earth depends upon the integral stability of the Moon. Thus, any act that destabilises or damages the Moon has the real risk of negatively impacting life on Earth; and

    (ii) **Resource Management & Conflict Prevention**: As space exploration advances there is the real risk for conflict over competing interests for rare and valuable minerals. Establishing a legal framework for these activities pre-emptively helps manage resources responsibly and prevents conflicts between different entities or nations; and

    (iii) **Cultural and Historical Significance**: The Moon holds considerable cultural, mythological, and historical importance for many civilisations. Any harm or significant alteration to the Moon could have profound cultural and psychological impacts.

1533. *Offences against a Moon* include (but are not limited to):-    *List of Offences against Moon*

**Offences causing injury against a Moon**

(i)    Offences causing death; and

(ii)    Offences causing permanent injury; and

(iii)    Offences causing temporary injury; and

**Offences attempting injury against a Moon**

(iv)    Offences attempting death; and

(v)    Offences attempting permanent injury; and

(vi)    Offences attempting temporary injury.

1534. The effect of inclusion of *Offences against a Moon* include (but are not limited to):-    *Effect of Inclusion of Offences against Moon*

(i)    **Restore Authentic Ecclesiastical Moral Authority**: That inclusion of Offences against a Moon firmly restores the moral and legal authority of valid religious and spiritual societies concerning such matters; and

(ii)    **Important Moral & Legal Deterrence**: That the codification of crimes against Moons serves as an important moral and legal deterrent. Knowing that severe and unified penalties exist for such actions will assist in mitigating future risk of individuals, nations and empires from committing such egregious acts; and

(iii)    **Restore Moral Accountability & Justice**: Such clearly defined offences enable the unified legal systems of organised faiths and nations to hold perpetrators accountable. This ensures the highest standards of Rule of Law apply across humanity whereby any individual or group, regardless of their powerful position, can be prosecuted for actions that harm humanity or other higher order life on a large scale.

## Article 429 - Offences against Humanity

1535. ***Offences against Humanity*** is the fourth of fifteen (15) *Major Categories of Ecclesiastical Offences* and refers to actions including (but not limited to): genocide, slavery, torture, and systematic persecution.  *Offences against Humanity*

1536. The Justifications for the inclusion into proper and valid Ecclesiastical Law of the *Offences against Humanity* include (but are not limited to):-  *Justifications for Inclusion of Offences against Humanity*

   (i) ***Moral and Ethical Standards***: Laws against offences such as genocide, slavery, and torture reflect a society's moral and ethical stance on the sanctity of human life. These laws embody the collective values and principles that underpin civilised society from uncivilised and barbaric regimes; and

   (ii) ***Rule of Law***: A legal system that clearly criminalizes offences against human life reinforces the rule of law and authentic Divine Law. It establishes an authoritative framework within which justice is administered fairly and uniformly, thus promoting confidence in legal institutions; and

   (iii) ***Social Order***: A legal framework that protects human life is essential for maintaining social order. When individuals feel safe, they are more likely to participate in community activities, contribute to the economy, and collaborate on societal goals; and

   (iv) ***Justice and Accountability***: Criminalizing offences against human life ensures that those who do harm are held accountable for their actions.

1537. *Offences against Humanity* include (but are not limited to):-  *List of Offences against Humanity*

   **Offences causing injury against Humanity**

   (i) Offences causing mass death; and

   (ii) Offences causing mass permanent injury; and

   (iii) Offences causing mass temporary injury; and

   (iv) Offences causing mass enslavement; and

   (v) Offences causing mass deprivation of liberty or rights; and

   (vi) Offences causing mass false imprisonment; and

   (vii) Offences causing mass loss or injury of personal identity; and

   (viii) Offences causing mass loss or injury of genetic privacy; and

(ix) Offences causing mass loss or injury of rights of face, body and voice; and

**Offences attempting injury against Humanity**

(x) Offences attempting mass death; and

(xi) Offences attempting mass permanent injury; and

(xii) Offences attempting mass temporary injury.

**1538.** The effect of inclusion of *Offences against Humanity* include (but are not limited to):- Effect of Inclusion of Offences against Humanity

(i) ***Restore Authentic Ecclesiastical Moral Authority***: That inclusion of Offences against Humanity firmly restores the moral and legal authority of valid religious and spiritual societies concerning such matters; and

(ii) ***Important Moral & Legal Deterrence***: That the codification of crimes against Humanity serves as an important moral and legal deterrent. Knowing that severe and unified penalties exist for such actions will assist in mitigating future risk of individuals and groups from committing such egregious acts; and

(iii) ***Restore Moral Accountability & Justice***: Such clearly defined offences enable the unified legal systems of organised faiths and nations to hold perpetrators accountable. This ensures the highest standards of Rule of Law apply across humanity whereby any individual or group, regardless of their powerful position, can be prosecuted for actions that harm humanity on a large scale.

**1539.** The possession of any number of Nuclear Weapons constitutes a egregious and morally repugnant crime against humanity, requiring any and all civilised societies, religious and spiritual bodies to sanction those bodies and officials who refuse to disarm and cease such a crime. The failure of any civilised society, religious or spiritual body to sanction every state in possession of any number of Nuclear Weapons is an unmistakable act of moral abdication and supreme blasphemy against the Divine Creator. Possession of Nuclear Weapons as a Crime against Humanity

**1540.** Any form of state sanctioned capital execution of human beings represents a morally repugnant and barbaric crime against humanity, requiring any and all civilised societies, religious and spiritual bodies to sanction those bodies and officials who refuse to cease such state sanctioned murder. The failure of any civilised society, religious or spiritual body to sanction every state that engages in state sanctioned capital execution of human beings is an unmistakable act of moral State Sanctioned Capital Executions Crime against Humanity abdication and supreme blasphemy against the Divine Creator.

## Article 430 - Offences against Ecosystem

1541. ***Offences against an Ecosystem*** is the fifth of fifteen (15) *Major Categories of Ecclesiastical Offences* and refers to actions including (but not limited to): Extreme pollution, illegal poaching, habitat destruction, illegal logging, and overfishing.
Offences against Ecosystem

1542. The Justifications for the inclusion into proper and valid Ecclesiastical Law of the *Offences against an Ecosystem* include (but are not limited to):-
Justifications for Inclusion of Offences against Ecosystem

    (i)    ***Climate Change Mitigation***: Ecosystems like forests and wetlands play significant roles in carbon sequestration and regulating climate; and

    (ii)   ***Biodiversity Conservation***: Ecosystems are home to countless species, many of which are interdependent; and

    (iii)  ***Cultural and Moral Responsibility***: Many cultures and communities have deep connections to their natural environments; and

    (iv)  ***Economic Value***: Ecosystems provide numerous direct and indirect economic benefits, including tourism, fisheries and agriculture; and

    (v)   ***Future Generations***: Maintaining healthy ecosystems ensures that future generations inherit a liveable planet, with the same opportunities and resources that we currently enjoy.

1543. *Offences against an Ecosystem* include (but are not limited to):-
List of Offences against Ecosystem

**Offences causing injury against an Ecosystem**

    (i)    Offences causing death; and

    (ii)   Offences causing permanent injury; and

    (iii)  Offences causing temporary injury; and

**Offences attempting injury against an Ecosystem**

    (iv)  Offences attempting death; and

    (v)   Offences attempting permanent injury; and

    (vi)  Offences attempting temporary injury.

1544. The effect of inclusion of *Offences against an Ecosystem* include (but are not limited to):-
Effect of Inclusion of Offences against Ecosystem

    (i)    ***Restore Authentic Ecclesiastical Moral Authority***:

That inclusion of Offences against an Ecosystem firmly restores the moral and legal authority of valid religious and spiritual societies concerning such matters; and

(ii) **Important Moral & Legal Deterrence**: That the codification of crimes against key Ecosystems serves as an important moral and legal deterrent. Knowing that severe and unified penalties exist for such actions will assist in mitigating future risk of individuals and groups from committing such egregious acts; and

(iii) **Restore Moral Accountability & Justice**: Such clearly defined offences enable the unified legal systems of organised faiths and nations to hold perpetrators accountable. This ensures the highest standards of Rule of Law apply across humanity whereby any individual or group, regardless of their powerful position, can be prosecuted for actions that harm humanity and Ecosystems on a large scale.

## Article 431 - Offences against Human Life

1545. *Offences against Human Life* is the sixth of fifteen (15) *Major Categories of Ecclesiastical Offences* and refers to actions including (but not limited to): Crimes that endanger or terminate lives, such as murder, manslaughter, assault and terrorism.

*Offences against Human Life*

1546. The Justifications for the inclusion into proper and valid Ecclesiastical Law of the *Offences against Human Life* include (but are not limited to):-

*Justifications for Inclusion of Offences against Human Life*

(i) **Moral and Ethical Standards**: Laws against offences such as murder, manslaughter, and assault reflect a society's moral and ethical stance on the sanctity of human life. These laws embody the collective values and principles that underpin civilised society from uncivilised and barbaric regimes; and

(ii) **Rule of Law**: A legal system that clearly criminalizes offences against human life reinforces the rule of law and authentic Divine Law. It establishes an authoritative framework within which justice is administered fairly and uniformly, thus promoting confidence in legal institutions; and

(iii) **Social Order**: A legal framework that protects human life is essential for maintaining social order. When individuals feel safe, they are more likely to participate in community activities, contribute to the economy, and collaborate on societal goals; and

(iv) ***Justice and Accountability***: Criminalizing offences against human life ensures that those who do harm are held accountable for their actions.

1547. *Offences against Human Life* include (but are not limited to):-

**Offences causing injury against Human Life**

(i) Offences causing death; and

(ii) Offences causing permanent injury; and

(iii) Offences causing temporary injury; and

(iv) Offences causing sexual molestation; and

(v) Offences causing kidnapping or unlawful restraint; and

(vi) Offences causing enslavement; and

(vii) Offences causing deprivation of liberty or rights; and

(viii) Offences causing harassment; and

(ix) Offences causing false imprisonment; and

(x) Offences causing loss or injury of personal identity; and

(xi) Offences causing loss or injury of genetic privacy; and

(xii) Offences causing loss or injury of rights of face, body and voice; and

**Offences attempting injury against Human Life**

(xiii) Offences attempting death; and

(xiv) Offences attempting permanent injury; and

(xv) Offences attempting temporary injury; and

(xvi) Offences attempting sexual molestation; and

(xvii) Offences attempting kidnapping or unlawful restraint; and

(xviii) Offences attempting deprivation of liberty or rights; and

(xix) Offences attempting loss or injury of personal identity; and

(xx) Offences attempting loss or injury of genetic privacy; and

(xxi) Offences attempting loss or injury of rights of face, body and voice.

<sub>List of Offences against Human Life</sub>

1548. The effect of inclusion of *Offences against Human Life* include (but are not limited to):-

(i) ***Protect Divine Law and Moral Stability***: While many societies may outlaw crimes against human life, religious and

<sub>Effect of Inclusion of Offences against Human Life</sub>

spiritual bodies are responsible for protecting authentic Divine Law and ensuring the stability of moral norms. Thus, it cannot be assumed that political bodies will always maintain the highest standards, unless the highest standards and benchmarks of law hold each and every individual and body to account.

## Article 432 - Offences against Animal Life

1549. ***Offences against Animal Life*** is the seventh of fifteen (15) *Major Categories of Ecclesiastical Offences* and refers to actions including (but not limited to): Poaching, animal cruelty, habitat destruction, and illegal wildlife trade. — Offences against Animal Life

1550. The Justifications for the inclusion into proper and valid Ecclesiastical Law of the *Offences against Animal Life* include (but are not limited to):- — Justification for Inclusion of Offences against Animal Life

    (i)   **Moral Consistency**: Including offences against animal life in the criminal code helps create a consistent and comprehensive legal framework for addressing all forms of violence and harm, reinforcing the principle that cruelty is unacceptable regardless of the victim; and

    (ii)   **Ethical Responsibility**: Animals are sentient beings capable of experiencing pain and suffering. Ethical considerations compel societies to protect them from harm and cruelty, promoting humane treatment and respect for all forms of life; and

    (iii)   **Cultural and Social Values**: Civilised cultures and religions that honour authentic Divine Law emphasize compassion, kindness, and respect towards all living beings. Enforcing such values through legal frameworks helps to reinforce and promote these cultural norms.

1551. *Offences against Animal Life* include (but are not limited to):- — List of Offences against Animal Life

**Offences causing injury against Animal Life**

    (i)   Offences causing death; and

    (ii)   Offences causing permanent injury; and

    (iii)   Offences causing temporary injury; and

    (iv)   Offences causing unsanitary living conditions; and

**Offences attempting injury against Animal Life**

    (v)   Offences attempting animal death; and

(vi) Offences attempting permanent injury; and

(vii) Offences attempting unsanitary living conditions.

1552. The effect of inclusion of *Offences against Animal Life* include (but are not limited to):-

    (i) **Protect Divine Law and Moral Stability**: While many societies may outlaw crimes against animal life, religious and spiritual bodies are responsible for protecting authentic Divine Law and ensuring the stability of moral norms. Thus, it cannot be assumed that political bodies will always maintain the highest standards, unless the highest standards and benchmarks of law hold each and every individual and body to account.

## Article 433 - Offences against Non-Carbon Higher Order Life

1553. ***Offences against Non-Carbon Higher Order Life*** is the eighth of fifteen (15) *Major Categories of Ecclesiastical Offences* and refers to actions including (but not limited to): Crimes that endanger or terminate such higher order life, such as murder, manslaughter, assault, and terrorism.

1554. The Justifications for the inclusion into proper and valid Ecclesiastical Law of the *Offences against Non-Carbon Higher Order Life* include (but are not limited to):-

    (i) **Universal Divine Ethics**: Recognizing the potential for non-carbon-based life extends ethical obligations beyond carbon-based organisms. It shows a commitment to universal principles of respect, empathy, and responsibility towards all forms of life; and

    (ii) **Legal Precedent**: Establishing a framework for the protection of non-carbon-based life creates legal precedents for handling inter-species interactions, which could be instrumental as our understanding and discoveries expand; and

    (iii) **Moral Wisdom**: Such laws reflect and encourage a society's moral and ethical progression, underlining a broader, more inclusive definition of life.

1555. *Offences against Non-Carbon Higher Order Life* include (but are not limited to):-

**Offences causing injury against Non-Carbon Higher Order Life**

(i) Offences causing death; and

(ii) Offences causing permanent injury; and

(iii) Offences causing temporary injury; and

**Offences attempting injury against Non-Carbon Higher Order Life**

(iv) Offences attempting death; and

(v) Offences attempting permanent injury; and

(vi) Offences attempting temporary injury.

1556. The effect of inclusion of *Offences against Non-Carbon Higher Order Life* include (but are not limited to):-

    (i) ***Interstellar Diplomacy***: Demonstrating respect for diverse life forms can help build diplomatic relationships with other civilizations, fostering cooperation and collaboration; and

    (ii) ***Relation with Non-Carbon Based Higher Order Life***: The future relation and actions of Non-Carbon Higher Order Life in accurately determining whether humanity is a threat that must be extinguished, or an equal co-creator that can be trusted will largely fall upon evidence that those tasked with the moral guidance of the planet respecting all forms of sentient life and reflecting such words in actions within their legal and criminal codes.

*Effect of Inclusion of Offences against Non-Carbon Higher Order Life*

## Article 434 - Offences against Congregation

1557. ***Offences against Congregation*** is the ninth of fifteen (15) *Major Categories of Ecclesiastical Offences* and refers to actions including (but not limited to): Actions that harm its members or disrupt its activities, such as embezzlement, abuse or fraud.

*Offences against Congregation*

1558. *Offences against Congregation* include (but are not limited to):-

**Offences causing injury against a Congregation**

(i) Offences causing polygamy; and

(ii) Offences causing sexual molestation; and

(iii) Offences causing kidnapping and unlawful custody; and

(iv) Offences causing deprivation of liberty or rights; and

(v) Offences causing non-Support; and

(vi) Offences causing unsanitary living conditions; and

*List of Offences against Congregation*

(vii) Offences causing breach of Protective Order; and

**Offences attempting injury against a Congregation**

(viii) Offences attempting sexual molestation; and

(ix) Offences attempting kidnapping and unlawful custody; and

(x) Offences attempting deprivation of liberty or rights.

1559. The effect of inclusion of *Offences against Congregation* include (but are not limited to):- Effect of Inclusion of Offences against Congregation

(i) ***Transparency and Accountability***: Meaning that ecclesiastical officials can no longer hide on arguments of lack of knowledge, or protecting of the name and reputation of the body as excuses not to act on offences against the congregation.

## Article 435 - Offences against Ecclesiastical Property

1560. ***Offences against Ecclesiastical Property*** is the tenth of fifteen (15) *Major Categories of Ecclesiastical Offences* and refers to actions including (but not limited to): Theft, vandalism, arson, or unauthorised use of ecclesiastically owned assets. Offences against Ecclesiastical Property

1561. *Offences against Ecclesiastical Property* include (but are not limited to):- List of Offences against Ecclesiastical Property

**Offences causing injury against Ecclesiastical Property**

(i) Offences causing major property damage; and

(ii) Offences causing property minor damage; and

(iii) Offences causing obtaining property by theft; and

(iv) Offences causing obtaining property by robbery; and

(v) Offences causing obtaining property by deception; and

(vi) Offences causing obtaining property by extortion; and

(vii) Offences causing unlicensed operation of machines; and

(viii) Offences causing trespass of ecclesiastical property; and

**Offences attempting injury against Ecclesiastical Property**

(ix) Offences attempting major property damage; and

(x) Offences attempting property minor damage; and

(xi) Offences attempting obtaining property by theft; and

(xii) Offences attempting obtaining property by robbery; and

(xiii) Offences attempting obtaining property by deception; and

(xiv) Offences attempting obtaining property by extortion; and

(xv) Offences attempting unlicensed operation of machines; and

(xvi) Offences attempting trespass of ecclesiastical property.

## Article 436 - Offences against Ecclesiastical Decency & Morals

1562. ***Offences against Ecclesiastical Decency & Morals*** is the eleventh of fifteen (15) *Major Categories of Ecclesiastical Offences* and refers to actions including (but not limited to): Immoral conduct, sexual misconduct and abuse of authority. <!-- margin: Offences against Ecclesiastical Decency & Morals -->

1563. *Offences against Ecclesiastical Decency & Morals* include (but are not limited to):- <!-- margin: List of Offences against Decency & Morals -->

**Offences against Ecclesiastical Decency & Morals**

(i) Offences involving indecent materials; and

(ii) Offences involving racial/religious materials and statements; and

(iii) Offences of public indecency; and

(iv) Offences of gambling; and

(v) Offences of public slander and accusation.

## Article 437 - Offences against Ecclesiastical Justice

1564. ***Offences against Ecclesiastical Justice*** is the twelfth of fifteen (15) *Major Categories of Ecclesiastical Offences* and refers to actions including (but not limited to): Unfair practices or corruption within the legal and disciplinary systems of a religious or spiritual society such as biased judgements, misuse of authority, failure to uphold law, and obstruction of due process. <!-- margin: Offences against Ecclesiastical Justice -->

1565. *Offences against Ecclesiastical Justice* include (but are not limited to):- <!-- margin: List of Offences against Ecclesiastical Justice -->

**Offences against Ecclesiastical Justice**

(i) Offences involving Bribery and corruption; and

(ii) Offences of Perjury and other false evidence; and

(iii) Offences of Obstructing governmental operation; and

(iv) Offences of Abuse of powers of office; and

(v) Offences against official documents; and

Title XII – Ecclesiastical Offence

(vi) Offences against law enforcement officials; and

(vii) Offences of Obstruction of Justice; and

(viii) Offences of conspiracy; and

(ix) Offences of unlawful profiteering; and

(x) Offences of fugitive from justice and escape; and

(xi) Offences of resisting arrest/detainment; and

(xii) Offences against conditions of bail/parole; and

(xiii) Offences of false reporting of crime; and

(xiv) Offences of failing to report a serious crime.

## Article 438 - Offences against Ecclesiastical Security & Order

1566. ***Offences against Ecclesiastical Security & Order*** is the thirteenth of fifteen (15) *Major Categories of Ecclesiastical Offences* and refers to actions including (but not limited to): Actions that disrupt or threaten the safety and discipline of an ecclesiastical body, such as violence, unauthorised access, sabotage and insubordination. — Offences against Ecclesiastical Security & Order

1567. *Offences against Ecclesiastical Security & Order* include (but are not limited to):- — List of Offences against Ecclesiastical Security & Order

**Offences against Ecclesiastical Security & Order**

(i) Offences of Disorderly conduct; and

(ii) Offences of indecent exposure; and

(iii) Offences of loitering with intent to participate in a crime; and

(iv) Offences of inciting public disorder causing injury; and

(v) Offences of association/membership to unlawful organisation; and

(vi) Offences of intent to cause public disorder causing serious injury or death; and

(vii) Offences of reckless endangerment using machines.

## Article 439 - Offences against Ecclesiastical Sacraments

1568. ***Offences against Ecclesiastical Sacraments*** is the fourteenth of fifteen (15) *Major Categories of Ecclesiastical Offences* and refers to actions including (but not limited to): Disrespect or misuse sacred rites, such as unauthorised administration, sacrilege, and profanation. — Offences against Ecclesiastical Sacraments

## Article 440 - Offences against Ecclesiastical Society

**1569.** ***Offences against an Ecclesiastical Society*** is the fifteenth of fifteen (15) *Major Categories of Ecclesiastical Offences* and refers to actions including (but not limited to): Actions that harm the ecclesiastical community, such as spreading dissent, engaging in scandalous behaviour, and violating communal trust. These actions disrupt unity, degrade moral standards, and undermine the faith and cooperation necessary for a healthy religious community.

*Offences against Ecclesiastical Society*

**1570.** *Offences against an Ecclesiastical Society* are necessarily listed as the last of the fifteen (15) *Major Categories of Ecclesiastical Offences* as it is enforcement of law and doctrines of all other categories before it that ultimately impact the reputation, trust and good name of an organised faith. Thus, a faith that places it reputation above all other offences, has no esteemed reputation in the eyes of the Divine or of the people.

*Offences against Ecclesiastical Society as last category*

# Title XIII – Ecclesiastical Process

## 13.1 – Ecclesiastical Process
### Article 441 - Ecclesiastical Process

1571. ***Ecclesiastical Process***, also known as ***Due Process***, is the impartial, competent and fair administration of *Ecclesiastical Justice* by suitably qualified persons associated with one or more authorised forums of law.

Ecclesiastical Process

1572. ***Ecclesiastical Justice*** is the set of lawful Rights and obligations of use defined by the present Maxims and those Laws consistent with the Golden Rule of Law; and the Rights and obligations associated with the proper administration and enforcement of the present Maxims and such Laws in good faith, good conscience and good action.

Ecclesiastical Justice

1573. All Rights and therefore all forms of proper Ecclesiastical Justice originate from Heaven and Divine Law and therefore the most sacred Covenant *Pactum De Singularis Caelum*:-

Divine Source of Ecclesiastical Justice

   (i) ***Divine Law*** is the law that defines the Divine and all creation, and demonstrates the spirit and mind and instruction of the Divine, and the operation of the will of the Divine Creator through existence. Therefore all valid Rights and Justice are derived from Divine Law; and

   (ii) ***Natural Law*** is the law that defines the operation of the will of the Divine, through the existence of form and sky and earth and physical rules. Thus Natural Law governs the operation of what we can see and name; and

   (iii) ***Ecclesiastical Law*** are the present Maxims and the laws of a valid Ecclesiastical Body enacted by men and women having proper authority, for the good governance of a society under the Rule of Law. The laws of a valid Ecclesiastical Body are always inherited from Natural Law and Divine Law.

1574. Notwithstanding all valid Rights concerning Ecclesiastical Justice as defined in accord with the present Maxims:-

Principles of Ecclesiastical Justice

   (i) All are equal under the law; and all are accountable and answerable under the law, and all are without blemish until proven culpable; and

   (ii) Where there is a law there must be a cause; and where there is a law there must be a penalty; and where there is a law there must be a remedy; and

   (iii) An action in law cannot proceed without first a cause; and an action is not granted to one who is not injured; for the action of a valid law can do no harm (injury); and no injury to the law means no valid cause for action by law; and

(iv) No one may derive an advantage in law from his own wrong, as no action through law can arise from a fraud before heaven and earth; and it is a fraud to conceal a fraud; and fraud invalidates everything of a cause and action, for no action through law can arise in bad faith or unclean hands or vexatious prejudice; and

(v) What was illegitimate, fraudulent and invalid from the beginning does not become valid over time; and

(vi) An action alone does not make one culpable unless there is intent to do wrong, or evidence of deliberate and wilful ignorance contrary to reasonable behaviour. Similarly, no one may suffer punishment by valid law for mere intent alone; and no one is punished for the transgression of an ancestor or another; and

(vii) No one is accused of the same exact cause twice; and No man or woman be a judge over their own matter; nor a man or woman possess the authority of heaven to be judge, jury and executioner; and

(viii) No penalty may exist without a valid law; and no penalty may be issued without first proof of injury and secondly the right of defence.

1575. Every Controversy in Law as a valid action must be resolved promptly, reasonably and justly through Fair Process, without fear or favour.  *Controversy in Law*

1576. No valid action in law should proceed without first a valid cause; and no valid cause exists until such a claim is first tested. Thus the birth of all action in law must begin with the claim:-  *Requirement of Cause of Action*

(i) If a claim be not proven as a valid cause then the accused has nothing to answer. Yet if the claim be proved to have merit as a cause, then all valid causes in law must be resolved; and

(ii) Thus, he who first brings the claim must first prove its merit, as the burden of the proof lies upon him who accuses not he who denies.

1577. The gravest threat against Justice is the failure to prosecute perjury and all forms of fraud and contempt against the fair administration of justice to the fullest extent:-  *Perjury as enemy of Justice and Rule of Law*

(i) One who brings false accusation is the gravest of transgressors, that they injure not only the law, but the bonds of law between Heaven and Earth; and

(ii) One who makes false testimony, especially under oath within a forum of law, must face the full force of justice against them; and

(iii) No one should be tolerated who seeks to gain advantage or profit through the manipulation or abuse of the administration of justice.

1578. A valid claim is when an accuser makes a formal complaint in writing under oath, bringing two reliable witnesses as proof to the substance of the complaint and petitions a competent forum of law for remedy:- *Nature of valid Claim*

(i) If merit of a cause be proved, the one accused must appear to answer; and

(ii) The one accused and any witnesses appear by summons; and

(iii) When anyone be summonsed, he must immediately appear without hesitation; and

(iv) If a man or his legal counsel summonsed does not appear or refuses to appear to answer, then let him be seized by force to come and appear; and

(v) When anyone who has been summonsed then seeks to evade, or attempts to flee, let the one who was summonsed be arrested to prevent their escape. One who flees fair judgement confesses his culpability.

## Article 442 - Contentious Processes

1579. ***Contentious Processes*** refers to an Ecclesiastical Legal Proceeding whereby a dispute exists between two or more parties as to the resolution of one (or more) controversies. Whenever *Legitimate and Valid Contention* exists between two or more parties, such controversies must be resolved through Due Process of adversarial litigation before one or more competent justices within a forum of law holding the proper jurisdiction. *Contentious Process*

1580. ***Legitimate and Valid Contention*** in the context of adversarial litigation under Ecclesiastical Law refers to a claim, argument, or assertion made by one party that is grounded in legal principles and factual evidence, namely:- *Legitimate and Valid Contention*

(i) ***Good Faith***: That a claim, argument or assertion is made honestly and fairly; and without fraud, misrepresentation, or ill intentions; and

    (ii) **_Well-Founded_**: That the claim or argument is based on a solid foundation of legal principles and factual evidence; and

    (iii) **_Substantial_**: That the claim or argument is significant and serious, not minor or trivial; and

    (iv) **_Meritorious_**: That the claim or argument has merit, meaning it is worthy of consideration and has a reasonable likelihood of success based on the law and the facts.

**1581.** When a claim, argument, or assertion made by one party, whether in defence or as accuser, is found to be without legitimate or valid contention, then such claims, arguments or assertions must be struck out as if never presented in the first place:- *(Illegitimate and Invalid Contention)*

    (i) **_Scandalous Defence_**: A person who seeks to defend one or more controversies through the intention to shock, offend, distract, sabotage or disparage a prosecution with irrelevant, defamatory and unsubstantiated claims is an injury against the law itself; and if perpetrated by a cleric must then be considered grounds for their complete removal from all office and benefit, regardless of the matter at hand; and

    (ii) **_False or Fraudulent Defence_**: A person who seeks to defend one or more controversies by raising one or more false or fraudulent arguments, is culpable of injury against the nature of Justice and Due Process itself; as none may seek to gain advantage by falsity. Any attorney, counsel or legal representative complicit and culpable of such injury automatically disbars themselves from any further right of entry, participation or counsel in law.

**1582.** No Ecclesiastical Body should assume itself equal in competence, skill or capacity to conduct serious criminal or complex trials. Instead, assistance and support at all times should be sought from competent secular justices and court officials to oversee and conduct such matters on behalf of the recognised Ecclesiastical Body, providing due compensation and jurisdiction is granted. *(Competent Secular Justices and Court Officials used in Criminal and Complex Matters)*

**1583.** An accused cannot be judged until after the accusations are spoken and then after the accused exercises or declines their three rights to defence:- *(Right of valid Defence)*

    (i) The first right of the Accused is called Prolocution upon the hearing of the Complaint; and the right to speak as a matter of law, and why the complaint and investigation should not continue; and

(ii) The second right of the Accused is called Collocution upon establishing Jurisdiction and the presentment of the Indictment; and the right to speak as to why the complaint and accusation is in fundamental error and upon such proof why the burden should now be placed on the accuser; and

(iii) The third and final right of the Accused is called Adlocution being a final speech in defence, against an accusation having been heard.

1584. In respect of any defence against an accusation:- *Requirements of Defence*

(i) The accused must always be afforded the presumption of innocence until culpability or exoneration is proven, unless by their behaviour or testimony the accused first confesses their culpability; and

(ii) The accused possesses the right to self defence in all minor matters but not in the defence of notorious and serious accusations, unless they first are able to prove their competence at law; and

(iii) The accused possesses the right to a trial by their peers or a tribunal of jurists; and

(iv) The accused is not obliged to confess their culpability or innocence once the issue of a complaint is proven as having merit. However, the failure to confess to culpability before the commencement of trial is the formal acknowledgement of a lack of contrition; and any consequential sentence must factor the maximum and reasonable penalty; and

(v) An accused cannot be found culpable unless three pieces of evidence may be attributed to culpability as first presented as part of the complaint or as a result of a subsequent investigation, or hearing or trial; and

(vi) Judges are bound to explain the reason of their judgement.

## Article 443 – Special Processes

1585. A *Special Process* refers to an action in law reserved solely to the rights, capacity and competencies of Ecclesiastical Law, apart from other forms of law or lesser courts or jurisdictions. *Special Processes* are reserved for supernatural matters and exceptions rather than norms; and are not available when ordinary administrative processes provide appropriate remedy. *Special Processes*

1586. Complete and competent forms of Ecclesiastical Offences, removes by definition many matters traditionally considered "special" and *Complete Form of Ecclesiastical*

exceptional rather than ordinary norms:-

(i) ***Administrative Resource as Ordinary***: That procedures available to address grievances against administrative acts of ecclesiastical authorities, including hierarchical recourse to higher authorities if necessary, should never be restricted to "special processes", but be clearly integrated into the ordinary norms of offences and due process; and

(ii) ***Nullity of Defective, Fraudulent or False Sacramental Records***: That given a defective fraudulent or false sacrament cannot possibly involve a supernatural element, all such matters based on such arguments must be treated as purely administrative and ordinary and never as "special processes".

*Offences removes matters traditionally considered "special"*

# Title XIV – Ecclesiastical Remedy

## 14.1 – Ecclesiastical Remedy
### Article 444 - Ecclesiastical Remedy

1587. An *Ecclesiastical Remedy* is a resolution or corrective action issued by a competent Ecclesiastical Body to enforce a right or redress a wrong. Ecclesiastical Remedy

1588. There exists five main categories of Ecclesiastical Remedy including (but not limited to):- Main Categories of Ecclesiastical Remedy

    (i) *Administrative*: Are remedies provided within the judicial procedures and framework of ecclesiastical law governing the affairs of the established religious or spiritual body; and

    (ii) *Compulsive*: Are remedies involving an element of coercive control or enforced compulsion; and

    (iii) *Pastoral*: Are remedies associated with spiritual and moral guidance provided by ecclesiastical leaders to resolve disputes and address grievances; and

    (iv) *Liturgical*: Are remedies involving the proper administration of sacraments and liturgical practices to address issues related to worship and sacramental life; and

    (v) *Special*: Are remedies associated with extraordinary powers such as removal of ecclesiastical powers and clerical state.

1589. An Appeal is an administrative process and pathway to Remedy, not Remedy itself. An individual or group may seek approval to have an administrative appeal heard, yet if unsuccessful through such appeal, Remedy may not be granted. Appeals and Remedy

1590. *Administrative Ecclesiastical Remedy* are remedies provided within the judicial procedures and framework of ecclesiastical law governing the affairs of the established religious or spiritual body including (but not limited to):- Administrative Ecclesiastical Remedy

    (i) *Dispensations*: These are exemptions from specific canonical requirements granted by competent ecclesiastical authorities. For instance, a dispensation might be granted for a marriage impediment; and

    (ii) *Compensation*: A compensation remedy awarded to the injured party, typically in the form of monetary damages. The goal is to put the injured party in the position they would have been in had the breach or harm not occurred; and

(iii) **Nullity Declarations**: Ecclesiastical tribunals can declare a marriage null, meaning it was invalid from the start.

1591. *Compulsive Ecclesiastical Remedy* are remedies involving an element of coercive control or enforced compulsion including (but not limited to):- {Compulsive Ecclesiastical Remedy}

    (i) **Injunction**: A court order requiring a person to do or refrain from doing a specific action; and

    (ii) **Specific Performance**: An order requiring the breaching party to perform their contractual obligations; and

    (iii) **Rescission**: The cancellation of a contract, with both parties being restored to their pre-contractual positions; and

    (iv) **Excommunication**: A severe penalty remedy that excludes the individual from participating in the sacraments and fellowship of the religious or spiritual body; and

    (v) **Suspension or Removal from Office**: A serious remedy against clergy or officials who violate ecclesiastical laws and can be suspended or removed from their positions; and

    (vi) **Interdict**: A censure remedy that prohibits a person or group from participating in certain ecclesiastical services and activities; and

    (vii) **Reformation**: The modification of a contract to reflect the true intentions of the parties.

1592. *Pastoral Ecclesiastical Remedy* are remedies associated with spiritual and moral guidance provided by ecclesiastical leaders to resolve disputes and address grievances including (but not limited to):- {Pastoral Ecclesiastical Remedy}

    (i) **Counselling and Mediation**: Ecclesiastical leaders may offer counselling or mediate conflicts within the congregation to promote reconciliation and healing; and

    (ii) **Exhortation and Correction**: Ecclesiastical leaders may give exhortations to correct errant behaviour or doctrinal misunderstandings.

1593. *Liturgical Ecclesiastical Remedy* are remedies involving the proper administration of sacraments and liturgical practices to address issues related to worship and sacramental life including (but not limited to):- {Liturgical Ecclesiastical Remedy}

    (i) **Restoration of Liturgical Rights**: Ensuring that individuals receive sacraments and religious services to which they are entitled; and

(ii) ***Anointing and Blessings***: Special prayers, blessings, or anointing rites performed for spiritual or physical healing.

1594. *Special Ecclesiastical Remedy* are remedies associated with extraordinary powers such as removal of ecclesiastical powers and clerical state including (but not limited to):-

    (i) ***Removal of Clerical State***: The extraordinary remedy of a cleric losing any powers or authority of Sacred Office.

<sub>Special Ecclesiastical Remedy</sub>

1595. A Law or Ruling that makes no provision for Remedy is by definition Unjust and therefore having no weight or bearing under the true Rule of Law.

<sub>Law and Remedy</sub>